ESSENTIALS OF INVESTING

ESSENTIALS
OF
INVESTING

Keith V. Smith

David K. Eiteman

both of the
Graduate School of Management
University of California, Los Angeles

1974

RICHARD D. IRWIN, INC. Homewood, Illinois 60430
Irwin-Dorsey International London, England WC2H 9NJ
Irwin-Dorsey Limited Georgetown, Ontario L7G 4B3

First Printing, May 1974

ISBN 0-256-01554-6
Library of Congress Catalog Card No. 73–91790
Printed in the United States of America

this book is dedicated
to
Shirley Smith
and
Nobuko Eiteman

Preface

WE WANTED TO WRITE this book on investing. To us, investing is a process undertaken by both individuals and institutions in which information about various investment opportunities is gathered and analyzed for the purpose of making decisions to buy, hold, or sell investment assets for an investment portfolio. We believe that investment decisions should be implemented according to certain prescribed procedures within a complex of financial intermediaries, markets, and governmental regulation. While this description may seem overly complicated, pedantic, and perhaps unnecessary to many potential investors, to us the process is a reality that cannot be avoided, and thus must be confronted. Although there are many textbooks, several readers and casebooks, and countless articles and published papers concerning investment opportunities, investment decision-making, and the investment environment, we felt the need for a basic textbook that would facilitate the teaching of investments and investing to an audience with little if any prior experience.

Essentials of Investing is thus intended for a first course in investments either in an advanced undergraduate course, or in a graduate curriculum. The level of the book assumes some minimal prior coursework or experience in business finance, including at least cursory exposure to financial statements. It would be useful if the reader had some familiarity with the elements of probability and statistics, although this is not a necessary prerequisite. And the enjoyment of reading the book would perhaps be enhanced if the *Wall Street Journal* or the financial pages of a metropolitan newspaper were followed somewhat regularly.

The book is organized into five parts with a total of 21 chapters.

We reverse the traditional sequence of coverage and begin with portfolio construction; then move on to investment valuation, and finally to detailed investment analysis. Part I introduces some perspective for the process of investing and how investment decisions are made on the basis of certain investment attributes. It also includes the rudiments of portfolio choice since the procedure is vital to the process of investing. Part II introduces the basic valuation framework that is reflected throughout the book. The investment value of a particular asset is taken in this book to mean the discounted present value of all future cash benefits that accrue to the owner of that asset. Bonds, stocks, and certain tax-sheltered investments are described, and the valuation framework is applied. Careful development of investment analysis is presented in Part III with particular emphasis on the securities of industrial corporations. Financial statement analysis is followed by a review of important accounting adjustments, and a discussion of various methods that can be used to forecast the future cash benefits of a particular investment. Part IV expands the scope of the book to other than industrial securities. Economic and operating characteristics, financial statement analysis, and special problems of valuation are considered in turn for public utilities, transportation companies, financial institutions, investment companies, and service organizations. Finally, Part V presents discussions of securities markets, procedures needed to implement investment decisions, various sources of information, the nature and importance of timing, and methods of evaluating achieved investment results.

The suggested readings which occur at the end of each chapter include mainly other books, both textual and popular. The *Instructors Manual* includes numerous references to the academic literature of investments—should the instructor decide to use this book in conjunction with outside reading assignments. This book also could be used with one or more of the existing casebooks in investments, although our own teaching style is based on a strong belief that case study should follow a basic understanding of the material being covered. The exercises prepared for each chapter are intended to reinforce the material presented and illustrated in that chapter. We also have long felt that students must do more than just read descriptive text to fully grasp the material presented, and hence we have attempted to incorporate numerous examples and exercises throughout the book.

The completion of *Essentials of Investing* culminates one level of our individual and collective efforts, both in teaching and research, over the past several years at the Graduate School of Management, University of California, Los Angeles. We are grateful to Dean Harold Williams for understanding and respecting our need and desire to write this book while both of us were involved in administrative assignments at the

School. Our colleagues at U.C.L.A., especially J. Fred Weston, John P. Shelton, Alfred E. Hofflander, Burton Zwick, Maxwell Kaufman, and Marvin M. May, continually have constituted an intellectually challenging environment within which we could present our ideas and working papers—many of which ultimately found their way into this book. Appreciation is also expressed to our many talented and highly-motivated students whose penetrating comments and questions frequently caused us to reexamine and reorganize. Robert Bradspies was instrumental in revising the FORTRAN computer programs that are listed and described in the *Instructors Manual*. Special gratitude was earned by Robert W. Johnson of Purdue University whose detailed reviews of the entire manuscript were consistently accurate and helpful. Margaret Eaton cheerfully and competently typed thousands of pages of manuscript and handled all related secretarial matters through several revisions of the manuscript. While we are pleased to acknowledge the foregoing individuals, we take full responsibility for all errors that remain.

Essentials of Investing is dedicated appropriately to our wives, with love, and with appreciation for their encouragement and support during the past two years. We would also like to end this preface with an expression of appreciation to our delightful daughters, who along with our wives somehow tolerated our absence on many evenings, weekends, and during two summers. We look forward to repaying this in the months ahead.

April 1974   KEITH V. SMITH
                                               DAVID K. EITEMAN

Contents

part I

Introduction

PART I provides the reader with an overall perspective of the process of investing and serves as a point of departure for many of the topics covered in this book. In Chapter 1, the setting for investing is explained, alternative opportunities for investing are identified, and investment attributes that provide the basis for choice are discussed. Investing is viewed in Chapter 2 as an ongoing and continuing process that consists of four major activities: investment policy, investment analysis, investment valuation, and portfolio construction. Each of these activities in turn consists of several distinct steps. A portfolio perspective is presented in Chapter 3 suggesting that each investment decision should be made relative to the entire portfolio of assets that is held, rather than just on the relative merits of that single investment opportunity. The theory of portfolio choice is shown to parallel consumer choice by an individual, except that decisions are based on attributes of investment opportunities rather than on services and commodities. Portfolio choice depends on the interaction of investment possibilities and investor preferences, both defined in terms of attributes such as portfolio return and portfolio risk. These in turn are shown to be related to the return and risk attributes of individual assets.

1

The setting for investing

DURING MUCH of their adult lives, individuals in our society are confronted by problems of investing. These problems are complicated by bewildering lists of suggested reasons for investing, alternative investment opportunities, methods for analyzing and deciding among such opportunities, and procedures for implementing the decisions that do result. All this occurs amid contradictory opinions about the health of the economic and market environment including the possibility of change in governmental regulations and taxes. The setting for investing is indeed complex. No single book can hope to deal adequately with all of the complicated and interrelated topics falling within the subject of investing. The goal of this first chapter is to identify that portion of the complex subject that will be treated in this book.

THE NEED FOR INVESTING

The standard economic model of a free enterprise society consists of individuals and families interacting with business firms. Individuals supply both labor and capital resources to firms in exchange for periodic receipts in the form of wages, salaries, interest, and dividends. These payments are used by individuals and households to satisfy basic needs through the process of consumption.

Some consumption needs, such as food and clothing, are satisfied incrementally. That is, the individual or family purchases food and clothing as the need arises. Other consumption needs such as home ownership, automobiles, travel, and education are obtainable only in large or lumpy quantities. In the case of automobiles and travel, the lumpy

3

consumption occurs at intermittent points in time; for home ownership, it typically consists of a substantial down payment followed by periodic payments over time. In any event, individuals and households must "save" their nonconsumed income over time in order to provide for lumpy consumption at future dates, or for building an estate for their heirs. As a result, many individuals and families find themselves with wealth for which they must make certain investment decisions. Specifically, they must decide when to invest, what assets to acquire, how much of their wealth to invest in those assets, and for what future periods to hold those assets. Making and implementing such decisions is here referred to as the *process of investing*.

ALTERNATIVE OPPORTUNITIES FOR INVESTING

Many alternatives exist. These have been categorized in many ways, but for our purpose of briefly reviewing investment alternatives the following categorization scheme is used:

I. Direct investment alternatives.
   A. Fixed-principal investments.
      1. Cash.
      2. Savings accounts.
      3. Marketable savings certificates.
      4. Government bonds.
      5. Corporate bonds.
   B. Variable-principal securities.
      1. Preferred stocks.
      2. Common stocks.
      3. Convertible securities.
      4. Warrants
      5. Options.
   C. Nonsecurity investments.
      1. Real estate.
      2. Mortgages.
      3. Commodities.
      4. Business ventures.
      5. Art, antiques, and other valuables.
II. Indirect investment alternatives.
   A. Pension funds.
   B. Insurance company portfolios.
   C. Investment companies.
   D. Trust funds.

The primary dichotomy in this categorization scheme is between direct and indirect investment alternatives. *Direct investments* are those wherein the individual or the household itself makes the investment decisions. Information and advice may be sought from outside sources, but the final decision is solely the responsibility of the individual or household. *Indirect investments,* on the other hand, are those wherein certain organizations proceed to make investment decisions on behalf of individuals and households. We first consider direct investment alternatives and then indirect investment opportunities.

Fixed-principal investments include those where the contractual terminal value or principal amount of the investment is known with certainty. *Cash,* no matter whether it is a checking account or is kept in a desk drawer or in a safe-deposit box, maintains a constant dollar value into the future; it also does not earn a return of any type over time. Various forms of *savings accounts,* such as at a savings and loan association, differ mainly in the extent of the periodic but fixed return that is earned. The terminal value of savings, however, is just equal to the amount committed to that type of investment, plus any interest that is reinvested. *Marketable savings certificates* have come into vogue in recent years with the advent of higher levels of interest than had prevailed heretofore. Included in this category are such varied items as certificates of deposit (issued by banks), commercial paper (issued by large industrial and financial firms), and treasury bills (issued by the U.S. Treasury). The dominant characteristic of marketable savings certificates, in addition to their immediate marketability, is a comparatively short original maturity. *Government bonds* and *corporate bonds* are sold by governments and corporations, respectively, to raise funds necessary for their many projects. From the standpoint of investing, government bonds and corporate bonds have a fixed maturity value, and they typically provide a fixed rate of income over time.

The category of *variable-principal securities* differs from the foregoing in that the terminal value is not known with certainty. Although *preferred stock* receives a fixed income payment over time, the price of preferred stock is determined by the forces of demand and supply in the marketplace for that stock and there is no maturity date. *Common stock,* on the other hand, represents the residual ownership of a corporation. Neither the periodic dividend (if there is one) nor the market price of common stock is fixed. *Convertible securities,* such as convertible bonds and convertible preferred stock, can be converted into common stock by their owners according to certain prescribed conditions, and thus have features of fixed-principal securities supplemented by the possibility of a variable terminal value. *Warrants* are options to buy the common stock of a corporation at a specified price. They are issued by corporations in conjunction with the sale of other securities, notably corporate bonds.

Bonds, preferred stock, common stock, convertibles, and warrants are all examples of *securities* sold by corporations to investors to raise necessary funds. Investors can also buy or sell *options,* such as puts and calls, on the securities of corporations. Options differ from the other securities mentioned here in that they are not created by corporations, nor are they obligations of corporations. Rather, they are obligations of one investor in corporate stock to another. Such options should not be confused with "stock options" issued by corporations to its chief executives as additional compensation.

Nonsecurity investments include a potpourri of assets that differ from those in the other categories. *Real estate* may include home ownership by a family or investment in a wide spectrum of residential and commercial properties. Real estate may or may not have an associated income. Federal tax laws make real estate ownership an attractive investment opportunity because interest payments may be deducted from taxable income. Depreciation is also deductible in the case of investment real estate. The terminal value of real estate often is highly uncertain, however, and real estate also is relatively illiquid when compared with most corporate securities. *Mortgages,* which represent the financing side of real estate, have characteristics resembling those of corporate bonds. That is, the periodic income is fixed, and the principal is recovered at a stated maturity date.

The remaining nonsecurity investments are generally even more specialized and are outside the scope of most books on investments. *Commodities* are bought or sold in spot markets, while contracts to buy or sell commodities at future dates are traded in future markets. *Business ventures* refer to direct ownership investments in new or growing businesses before the respective firms are able to sell securities on a public basis. Venture capital investments are examples of business ventures, typically in high-technology industries. *Art, antiques, and other valuables,* such as jewelry, sterling silver, and fine china, are yet another type of specialized opportunity for investment that also offers certain aesthetic qualities.

An individual or family also has indirect investment alternatives. Retirement benefits for employed individuals are paid from *pension funds* set aside and managed on behalf of employees. Pension funds typically include investments in corporate securities, government bonds, and mortgages. Certain types of life insurance policies also include an investment component, as a portion of policy premiums is invested on behalf of the policyholder. *Insurance company portfolios* include varying holdings of government bonds, corporate securities, mortgages, and real estate. *Investment companies* are organizations devoted solely to investing collectively the limited wealth of many individuals. Investment companies include mutual funds and certain other specialized portfolios for which diversification and professional management are the two major rationales that attract investors.

Whereas individuals have virtually no control over the selection of investments in pension funds and insurance company portfolios, they can exercise indirect control in their choice of a particular investment company with its unique objectives. Considerably greater control exists for *trust funds*, which often are managed by trust companies and commercial bank trust departments, and which can be tailored to the precise needs of the individual or family. These examples of indirect investment alternatives constitute what is sometimes called the *money management industry*, an important and rapidly growing segment of our economy.

INVESTMENT ATTRIBUTES

Regardless of which of these many investment alternatives are selected by individuals or families, the desired end result is to provide for future consumption, either by the present or by future generations. It must follow, therefore, that it is not the investment assets themselves that are desirable, but rather certain attributes of those assets. An *attribute* is a characteristic of an investment asset that somehow relates to the ability of that asset to provide for future consumption. As we shall see in Chapter 3, attributes are the bases for evaluation of information about investment assets and the feelings and preferences of individuals who must make investment decisions.

Several investment attributes were directly mentioned or at least alluded to in our brief review of alternative investment opportunities. Periodic *income*, whether in the form of interest, dividends, or other cash flow, is certainly a desirable attribute. *Appreciation*, which is an increase in the market value of an asset above its original cost, is a second essential attribute that is realized only when the asset is sold. Income and appreciation are commonly combined into a measure of periodic *return* for the asset in question. Return can be measured as a periodic dollar amount, or as a periodic rate expressed as a percentage of the cost of the investment.

For some assets, such as savings accounts, return is virtually certain. Uninvested cash also provides a certain return, which is zero. For many bonds return is almost certain. But for many corporate securities and other investment assets, return may be very uncertain. *Safety* is an attribute that reflects the degree of certainty in the return of a given investment asset. The opposite of safety is *risk*, an attribute that describes the extent of uncertainty in the return from an investment asset. Return and risk are the two most important attributes to many investors. A generally accepted principle in investments is that higher risk accompanies higher return. Many discussions of investment analysis and portfolio analysis confine their attention to just the two attributes, return and risk. The portfolio perspective in Chapter 3 is presented in terms of return and risk.

But there are other attributes that should be mentioned. *Liquidity* of an investment asset is often of great importance to an individual. Savings accounts for example, are considerably more liquid than real estate. *Manageability* of an investment asset is the extent to which it must be monitored and managed over time. Again, real estate is likely to require more management than a savings account. An investment company, on the other hand, presumably provides management to its shareowners, while direct investment in common stocks leaves all management decisions to the individual investor. *Taxability* of an investment asset has to do with the particular features of the asset that are amenable to special tax treatment. Continuing our example comparison, only the periodic interest payments on a savings account are taxable, while several aspects of a real estate investment may necessitate special tax treatment. Taxability is so important and complex that Chapter 7 will be devoted exclusively to discussion of a series of tax-sheltered investments. Finally, the risk attribute can be further broken down into several components. *Purchasing power risk*, for example, has to do with how an investment asset protects the owner against changes in the value of the dollar. *Interest rate risk* deals with changes in the structure of interest rates in the economy and how that structure affects investment values. *Business risk* is the uncertainty associated with the earning power of the assets of a company, while *financial risk* reflects the capital structure that is used to provide those assets.

INVESTMENT DECISIONS

After considering return, risk, and other investment attributes, individuals or institutions must make decisions to buy, hold, or sell investment assets. They must also decide how many dollars to invest or disinvest in each asset. To reach such decisions, the individual or institution may consider a variety of sources of information (Chapter 19) and weigh them individually. Some of these sources of information are free of charge while others must be purchased commercially. Some sources are purely factual and others are evaluative. Some individuals listen for tips from friends or from their barber, while others may choose to consult with brokers or investment advisors before reaching final investment decisions. Another useful input into the decision-making process is a careful evaluation of past portfolio performance (Chapter 21). Although the literature of investments abounds with institutional information and methods of analysis, specific guidelines to help investors in making final decisions are scarce. In the final analysis, decisions depend on the unique and subjective judgments and preferences of individuals.

To implement investment decisions when they are made, an individual may need to open a savings account or a security account with a brokerage firm (Chapter 18). He may also deal directly with individuals who specialize in handling other types of investment assets such as real estate, options, or commodities. Implementation of security investment decisions may involve organized markets for stocks and bonds, or the over-the-counter market (Chapter 17). Markets for securities as well as other investment assets involve many organizations and people. These markets are typically quite complex because a variety of participants with different functions interact simultaneously. Because of this variety, many customs, rules, and procedures exist in the functioning and regulation of these markets, greatly complicating the implementation of investment decisions.

It should be noted that the setting for investing is not static but instead is continually changing. From time to time, new types of investment alternatives become available. An example would be the dual funds (Chapter 15) that emerged in the mid-1960s. Changing tax laws and changes in brokerage fee schedules affect the transaction costs as investors buy and sell securities. Changing regulations by the stock exchanges and governmental agencies influence reporting practices of corporations, advertising practices of professional money managers, and the overall availability of information about investment opportunities. Finally, recent research findings have changed our understanding of different approaches to investment analysis and of the return-risk relationships that exist in the markets for securities and other investment assets.

SCOPE OF THE BOOK

To reiterate, *investing* is the process of making and implementing decisions regarding various types of investment assets. This process involves the selection of particular assets from among a wide spectrum of available investment opportunities. It also involves the allocation of nonconsumed, investable wealth among the assets that are selected. The investing process occurs within a complex and changing system of markets for securities and other investment assets.

In this book we must necessarily limit our attention to a subset of possible investment assets. Major emphasis will be on securities: bonds and stocks. As for the several investment attributes that were identified, we shall focus primarily on return and risk. Before continuing, however, we will need to develop additional perspective. We proceed, therefore, to a more detailed examination of first the process of investing, and second the nature of portfolios for which investment assets are bought and sold.

SUGGESTED READINGS FOR CHAPTER 1

J. B. Cohen, E. D. Zinbarg, and A. Zeikel. *Investment Analysis and Portfolio Management* (Homewood, Ill.: Richard D. Irwin, Inc., revised edition, 1973), Chapter 1.

H. C. Sauvain. *Investment Management* (Englewood Cliffs, N.J.: Prentice-Hall, Inc., fourth edition, 1973), Part I.

Adam Smith. *The Money Game* (New York: Random House, Inc., 1967).

Adam Smith. *Supermoney* (New York: Random House, Inc., 1972).

D. A. West. *The Investor in a Changing Economy* (Englewood Cliffs, N.J.: Prentice-Hall, Inc., 1968).

2

The process of investing

THE TITLE of our book deliberately includes the gerund "investing." This is in direct contrast with the many books on the same subject that use instead the noun "investments" in their titles. Our choice reflects a strong belief that the subject matter should be more than just a description of how to analyze the many alternatives available to investors. Rather, the subject matter should be thought of as a continuing process of analyzing information about alternatives and reaching investment decisions that are consistent with the objectives of investors. The purpose of this chapter is to present an overview of the process of investing that will prepare the reader for studying the more detailed subject matter that follows.

SUGGESTED OVERVIEW

A schematic diagram of the process of investing is presented as Figure 2–1. Certain reasons for organizing the subject matter in this particular way should be explained. First, the process of investing is divided into four distinct activities: investment policy, investment analysis, investment valuation, and portfolio construction. The last three activities of the process make up the standard approach to investing: first, the analysis of investment assets; second, the valuation of investment assets; and third, the construction of portfolios of investment assets.

In this book, however, we reverse the coverage of these important activities in order to provide better perspective for discussing the individual steps within each activity. Accordingly, Chapter 3 is concerned with portfolios and why ultimate investment decisions should not be made

12

FIGURE 2–1
The process of investing

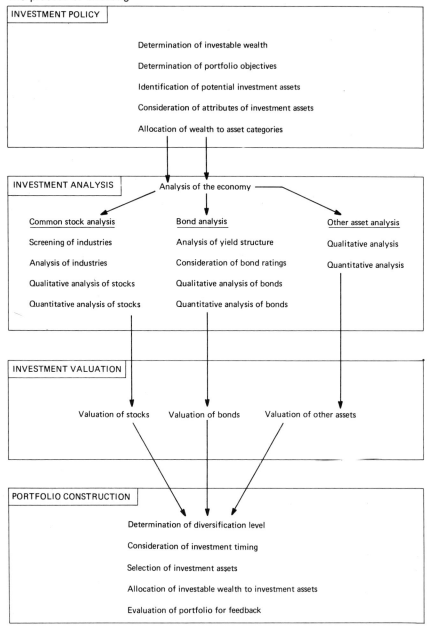

independently. Chapters 4–7 are concerned with valuation, while Chapters 8–11 are concerned with analysis. This logical coverage of the process of investing is followed in Chapters 12–16 by applications to specific types of nonindustrial securities. Chapters 17–21 deal with an assortment of other topics that facilitate the implementation of investment decisions, including the final chapter of the book, which explains how to evaluate an entire portfolio of investment assets.

Second, the arrows in Figure 2–1 indicate a logical progression through the four activities toward the ultimate decisions that must be made and implemented. The schematic diagram is somewhat incomplete, however, in regard to the direction of the arrows. It might be inferred from Figure 2–1 that the process of investing "begins" with investment policy and "ends" with portfolio construction. Instead, managing a portfolio of investment assets should and will be viewed as a continuing or ongoing process in which the activities and detailed steps are executed repeatedly. Furthermore, subsequent activities should logically depend on the results of prior policy, analysis, valuation, and portfolio construction. The importance of feedback will be stressed in our discussion of the process of investing.

Third, the detailed steps in Figure 2–1 should be thought of as how individuals and institutions ought to go about making investment decisions. They are not meant to be descriptive of how investment decisions actually are made in practice. Some investors may well follow an organized set of steps, such as that in Figure 2–1, in reaching their final decisions. Many other investors probably bypass a number of the suggested steps. Some rely heavily on the advice of brokers or investment counselors, others follow the investment tips of friends, while others make intuitive decisions reflecting available information and their current psychological mood.

It is not at all clear which of these practices leads to the most successful investment decisions. No single practice, in fact, is likely to dominate the others. Our contention is that individuals and institutions ought to adopt an organized approach to the process of investing for two reasons. An organized approach is more likely to lead to consistent, above-average results over time. Additionally, investors are more likely to be comfortable with an organized approach to investing. To some, the latter reason may become more important as the sizes of their portfolios increase.

The activities and steps depicted in Figure 2–1 represent one organized approach to the process of investing. We proceed now to examine in more detail the activities and individual steps of that suggested approach. To facilitate our discussion, we will use two investment scenarios as examples. In one example, John and Alice Jones are trying to decide how to invest $2,500. In the other example, the management of Better

Mutual Fund is considering the investment of $2,500,000 acquired when certain of its holdings were liquidated recently.

INVESTMENT POLICY

For the process of investing, a logical starting point is to put the decision that is to be made into perspective. *Investment policy* provides such perspective by focusing on the scope of the decision to be made, why it is to be made, and what attributes are most compatible with the goals of the investor. Five specific steps are needed, as shown in Figure 2–1.

First, the amount of investable wealth must be determined. We have already seen that this amounts to $2,500 for the Jones family and $2,500,000 for Better Mutual Fund. The reason for this first step is that certain investment assets may not be potential candidates if the amount of investable wealth is too small. John and Alice Jones probably do not have enough funds to consider investment in real estate or establishment of a personal trust fund. Better Mutual Fund is less likely to be constrained because of size; it may be constrained for other reasons, such as legal limits imposed on fund investments.

Second, portfolio goals or objectives must be determined, as these will also influence the set of investment opportunities that can be considered. For individuals, objectives can be unique and precise, while for institutional portfolios, objectives may be more general since each institution represents many individuals. Objectives of an institutional portfolio such as that of an investment company are specified in a prospectus, made available to potential investors, so that individuals seeking to invest indirectly via that investment company will have some assurance of the nature and continuity of management policy. We assume, for example, that the objective of the Joneses is to maximize the income from their investment over the next five years while not exposing their capital to an undue amount of risk. The major objective of Better Mutual Fund, according to its prospectus, is long-term appreciation of capital.

Third, potential categories of investment assets that seem to be consistent with these specified objectives should be identified. From among the wide range of assets discussed in Chapter 1, we might select a savings account, government or corporate bonds, certain common stocks, or investment companies as being appropriate to the needs of the Joneses. On the other hand, the prospectus of Better Mutual Fund specifically restricts its investments to common stocks and other securities of major corporations or the government.

Fourth, it is important to decide which attributes of investment assets are to be considered. We recall from Chapter 1 that a systematic listing of attributes is a means of bringing together information about investment assets and the feelings and preferences of individuals. Conversation with John and Alice Jones reveals that they are concerned with income, risk, taxability, and to an extent, liquidity. Investors in Better Mutual Fund selected that fund to pursue appreciation while showing some willingness to take risks.

Specification of objectives, attributes, and categories of assets, such as for our two illustrations, effectively puts a fence around the decision that must be made. Written specification is useful, although mental formulation alone suffices in many instances. Nevertheless, the exercise of writing down general objectives for the overall portfolio and particular objectives for each investment decision is felt to be an important and potentially rewarding step in the process of investing. Such a process provides continuity and retards a drift in objectives caused by emotional responses. An individual whose investment decisions are based on a series of tips received at his golf club should not be surprised if his portfolio holdings and investment performance are erratic over time.

The *fifth* and final step of investment policy is to allocate investable wealth to categories of assets. This is not the final selection of specific investment assets, but rather a preliminary allocation to savings, bonds, stocks, and so forth. Although this step precedes the final selection of specific investment assets, it establishes the long-range posture of the portfolio toward the various markets for investment assets. No matter how well subsequent steps in the process are conducted, overall results will suffer if investable wealth is not properly allocated to asset categories.

Certain constraints may exist, both for individual and institutional portfolios, that limit the extent to which wealth can be switched from category to category. Nevertheless, considerable attention must be given to this final step of investment policy. In the case of our family, the Joneses decide that they should limit their attention to high-grade corporate bonds. For Better Mutual Fund, the managers decide that $200,000 should be placed in 90-day U.S. Treasury Bills as a cash reserve, while the remaining $2,300,000 should be allocated to common stocks, probably in selected high-growth industries.

INVESTMENT ANALYSIS

Central to the process of investing is *investment analysis*. This important activity consists of gathering and processing information about specific assets that are being considered for the portfolio. Certainly more has been discussed and written about this activity than about any of the others shown in Figure 2–1. Just selecting from among the myriad of sources of information is itself a formidable challenge. How best to process that information remains a challenge to anyone confronted with making investment decisions.

We notice in Figure 2-1 that parallel paths exist within investment analysis depending on the particular asset category. Whereas certain steps are common to an analysis of any investment, there are certain attributes and other considerations for certain assets that warrant special attention. All analyses should logically begin, however, with an appraisal of the overall economy. The reason for this first step is to provide additional perspective about the probable markets for different investment assets. Economic analysis is, in fact, a prerequisite to many steps in the process of investing—including the allocation of wealth to asset categories as part of investment policy. It is necessary to understand the changing character of the economy over time, and how varying prospects for segments of the economy affect the markets for bonds, stock, real estate, and other investment assets. This involves both an assessment of the current economy, and forecasts of the economy into the future. Economic forecasting often employs indices of economic activity such as gross national product, industrial production, consumer price index, interest rates, housing starts, and automobile sales.

The traditional approach to analyzing securities focuses first on the economy, then on the industry, and finally on the individual security. Consider common stocks. After assessing current economic conditions and forecasting probable economic developments, the potential investor screens all industries within the economy in order to identify those that would appear to be attractive investments during the next few years. For each industry that seems attractive, more detailed analysis of both demand and supply conditions would be conducted.

Continuing our example, the Jones family decides to concentrate on the purchase of two or three high-grade corporate bonds, while the management of Better Mutual Fund chooses to emphasize the common stocks of industries that are likely to emerge or continue to grow during the next decade. Examples might include computer peripheral equipment, pollution control, low-cost housing, energy-related industries, and leisure time. In particular, they decide to focus on modular housing, which is a small but growing segment of the housing industry. An economic analysis of the modular housing industry might include questions of housing starts both overall and by income and demographic groupings, the interest rate sensitivity of housing demand for this type of home, land costs, and the cost and availability of capital. Also vital would be the changing technology in design and production of modular homes, building codes, stability of firms already in the industry, and the role of governmental agencies in encouraging and regulating further growth of modular housing.

The next step is to analyze individual securities. For common stocks, we see in Figure 2-1 that this analysis involves both qualitative and quantitative aspects. Qualitative factors might include technology, patents, management, competition, and changing consumer tastes. Quantitative factors include some of these plus others that can somehow be measured or described numerically. Although one might be interested in the average age and tenure of the management team, this is only one dimension of company leadership. Not only should the current status of these factors be considered, but also how these factors may change in the future.

To illustrate, suppose that the portfolio manager of Better Mutual Fund is analyzing Happier Construction, one of the leading firms in the modular housing industry. He discovers that the plant area at year-end was 50,000 square feet, and production capacity was about 30 modules per day (three or four modules are used per home). This information may have a bearing on possible growth of company sales and earnings. Probing further, the portfolio manager discovers that the company has opportunities to lease additional space at nominal rates, thus giving the company the capability to increase its capacity and level of production. In addition to production and sales potential, the portfolio manager appraises the working capital position of Happier Construction. This is important because of the high turnover of capital that is characteristic of the construction industry. The portfolio manager is also interested in the capital structure of the firm. During the past year, Happier Construction retired a large portion of its long-term debt, thus improving the company's capacity for acquiring additional long-term financing.

The common thread that interrelates all of the factors in both qualitative and quantitative analyses is that they lead to projections of earnings, dividends, and common stock prices. For corporate bonds, the analogous variables are earnings available to pay interest, interest payments, and bond prices. Earnings are important because they serve as a common denominator in evaluating the progress of the firm over time, and also in making comparisons between firms in the same industry. Earnings are also important because they provide the means for paying interest to creditors and dividends to owners. Perhaps, in our example, earnings per share of Happier Construction have increased 45% in the last two years. An understanding of why this has occurred is important because past earnings form a basis for future earnings projections, particularly if other qualitative and quantitative factors are considered. Several methods of forecasting will be compared in Chapter 11.

INVESTMENT VALUATION

A vital but sometimes overlooked activity in the process of investing is *investment valuation*. Although several concepts of value exist, we shall focus on investment value as the present worth to the owners of future benefits from an investment. In the case of common stock, these future benefits are cash dividends plus realized appreciation in the price of the stock. For bonds, future benefits include interest payments and either the maturity value of the bond or, if the owner decides to sell his bond prior to maturity, the current market price of the bond. For real estate, or other investment assets, future benefits can be identified in a similar manner.

One quickly realizes that future benefits from securities are intimately connected to the earnings generated by the issuing firms. This connection is why qualitative and quantitative investment analysis necessarily precedes a determination of investment value. As we shall see in Part II of this book, there are significant problems in determining the "value" of an investment asset. One immediate problem is in forecasting the future benefits that are expected to accrue to the owner of the investment asset. In the case of Happier Construction, one would need to forecast the earnings per share expected for each year of a chosen horizon. Based on this prediction dividends per share, if any, would be forecast for each year—as well as the terminal price expected at the end of the horizon. In the context of investing, the term *horizon* denotes an interval of time for which the behavior of an asset is being assessed.

A second problem is in determining an appropriate set of weights to apply to the future benefits of the investment. As we shall see in Chapter 4, one logical possibility is to relate such weights to the respective timing of future benefits, and also to the inherent riskiness of the investment asset for which those benefits accrue. Whereas the forecasting of future benefits can be performed in several ways, the establishment of relative weights turns out to be a highly subjective matter. Moreover, the weights are likely to vary considerably across the spectrum of investment assets that might be considered by an investor.

With the use of the forecasted benefits and a set of relative weights the "value" of the investment asset can be estimated. Comparison of this value with the current market price of the asset allows a determination of the relative attractiveness of the asset in question. Attractiveness of an asset can take the form of being undervalued or overvalued in this sense, or it can be appraised directly in terms of its return and risk attributes. Although a common framework can be used for valuation of any asset, particular considerations, unique to each asset category, explain the parallel paths to investment valuation depicted in Figure 2–1.

PORTFOLIO CONSTRUCTION

Comparison of value with price is not sufficient for making final investment decisions. The difficulty is that the asset under consideration, if chosen, becomes but one member of an entire portfolio of investment assets. Corporate bonds chosen by John and Alice Jones become a part of their existing portfolio of investment assets. And if Better Mutual Fund purchases shares of Happier Construction, that common stock will be but one holding among many. Although the management of Better Mutual Fund certainly will be concerned with future developments of Happier Construction or any other of the numerous assets held, they will exhibit greater concern for its entire portfolio of holdings. As shown in Figure 2–1, *portfolio construction*, the final activity in the process of investing, consists of several distinct steps.

To begin portfolio construction, a determination must be made of the proper level of diversification. As we shall see in the next chapter, diversification is the process of combining investment assets having different attributes into a portfolio in order to reduce the total risk of the portfolio. The component of total risk that is unique to individual assets can be reduced by diversification, whereas the second component of total risk, related to the entire market, cannot. Diversification also may be achieved if different industries are represented in the portfolio. This is especially true if the securities in a given industry are highly correlated. Diversification decisions necessarily require, therefore, a specification of how assets are interrelated, particularly with respect to the possible returns they are expected to achieve. There are also legal and institutional constraints with regard to diversification, which must be considered before making investment decisions.

Investment timing can be thought of at two levels. We saw that the final step of investment policy is the allocation of wealth to asset categories. That decision clearly depends on the relative attractiveness of asset categories over time. A second level of timing is influential in implementing the decision of portfolio selection. Suppose that Better Mutual Fund decides to invest a substantial portion of the $2,300,000 allocated to common stocks in the modular housing industry, including an investment in Happier Construction common stock. If the entire position in Happier Construction is acquired in a single block transaction, the price of that common stock may be forced upward significantly. Alternatively, the portfolio manager may choose to build up a position in Happier Construction slowly, over a few months, in order to keep the average acquisition price lower. This is timing in conjunction with implementation. The Joneses do not face such a problem when they purchase a small number of corporate bonds.

Next is portfolio selection. This involves a continual process of deciding which assets are to be added to the portfolio, which assets are to be deleted, and which assets are to remain in the portfolio. It also involves deciding on the dollar size of each transaction to be made. In addition to numbers of shares of stock, numbers of bonds, or number of parcels of real estate, the transaction costs of each transaction must be considered. Transaction costs include brokerage fees, taxes, and possible market effects if the transaction is large. Portfolio selection decisions are based on how the various attributes of investment assets, such as return and risk, are combined into attribute measures for the composite portfolio.

The final step of the process of investing has to do with evaluation for feedback. Earlier in this chapter, the ongoing nature of the investing process was emphasized. In other words, investment policy, investment analysis, investment valuation, and portfolio construction are continuing activities during the investment horizon. Continuing decisions, however, must be based on something specific, and that logically should be the portfolio itself. Evaluation of the portfolio—by asset, by asset category, and by the aggregate portfolio—is needed in order to make continuing decisions. Portfolio evaluation requires appropriate measures of return, risk, and diversification, as well as appropriate comparison standards. Evaluation also depends on the length of the investment horizon that pertains to the investor. The Jones family has a relatively short planning horizon—five years—while Better Mutual Fund has an ongoing portfolio with an indefinite planning horizon.

SUMMARY

The process of investing includes investment policy, investment analysis, investment valuation, and portfolio construction. Each of these major activities in turn consists of several important steps. It was noted that qualitative and quantitative analyses of an investment asset culminate in projections of earnings, interest payments, dividends, and security prices, which, in turn, are determinants of investment value. The continuing nature of investing also suggests a feedback of portfolio results over time as the basis for repeating those steps. Moreover, we have seen in the illustrations of John and Alice Jones and of Better Mutual Fund how the steps and activities differ with the situation. Finally, we have seen that the process of investing culminates with portfolio decisions rather than individual investment decisions. Although the main stress of this book is on investment analysis and investment valuation, the importance of a portfolio perspective must be emphasized.

SUGGESTED READINGS FOR CHAPTER 2

C. D. Ellis. *Institutional Investing* (Homewood, Ill.: Dow Jones-Irwin, Inc., 1971), Chapters 1–2.

D. T. Regan. *A View from the Street* (New York: New American Library, 1972).

Adam Smith. *The Money Game* (New York: Random House, Inc., 1967).

K. V. Smith. *Portfolio Management* (New York: Holt, Rinehart and Winston, 1971), Part I.

3

A portfolio perspective

A WIDOW sells 20 bonds of the American Telephone and Telegraph
Company in order to purchase a new limousine. As part of their investment toward the eventual education of their children, a young married
couple purchases 50 shares of Eastman Kodak common stock. A university professor directs his school to divert $100 of his monthly salary
into a variable annuity plan managed by the trustees of the university,
the proceeds of which will add to his retirement income. Three medical
professionals pool their capital and construct a medical building to house
their individual practices. All of these brief scenarios are characterized
by investment wealth being disallocated from, or allocated to, a single
type of investment asset. In each case, the decision was made toward
either immediate or future consumption by the individual(s) involved.

If each decision were based only on the relative merits of the particular
investment asset, the perspective was incomplete or inadequate. Instead,
each decision should have been made relative to the total wealth of
the individual(s) involved. Total wealth of an individual includes the
portfolio of investment assets that he owns plus the value of future
expected income from his chosen occupation. Although we often will
speak of the "portfolio of investment assets" as if it consisted only of
securities or other owned investments, the potential additions to wealth
arising from an individual's income should never be ignored. Indeed,
for many students and young people, expected future income is the
major component of their wealth.

Thus the young married couple should have evaluated the Eastman
Kodak common stock relative to their other investment holdings as well
as in relationship to their combined salaries. The medical professionals

21

individually should have considered the other components of their wealth. In other words, a portfolio is best defined as the totality of investment assets that are held. It is a distinct entity consisting of one or several component parts—namely, shares of stock, government or corporate bonds, real estate properties, savings, or any of the other investment assets mentioned in Chapter 1. Our contention here is that the process of investing, as described in the previous chapter, results in decisions to buy or sell investment assets, and hence to allocate investable wealth within the framework of an individual's total portfolio. Paralleling any attempt to evaluate the unique characteristics of individual assets should be an attempt to evaluate the aggregate characteristics of the portfolio. The purpose of this chapter is to develop a portfolio perspective within which investment assets can be properly analyzed and evaluated. The portfolio perspective represents a point of departure for subsequent parts of the book.

OVERVIEW OF PORTFOLIO CHOICE

Deciding upon a portfolio of investment assets is similar in many respects to other decisions made by an individual. To show this, consider the standard *theory of consumer choice* among two commodities as illustrated in Figure 3–1. Commodity L represents lobster dinners while commodity C represents philharmonic concerts. The quantities of lobster dinners and philharmonic concerts consumed per month are represented by Q_L and Q_C, respectively, while P_L and P_C are the associated prices. An individual is faced with the decision of how to spend his excess monthly income of W dollars on lobster dinners and philharmonic concerts, both of which he would like to have more. For example, if prices were $P_L = \$7.50$ and $P_C - \$5.00$, and the individual had excess monthly income of $W = \$60$, then he would have the following alternatives each month

Number of lobster dinners, Q_L	Number of philharmonic concerts, Q_C
8	0
6	3
4	6
2	9
0	12

We see in Figure 3–1 that the optimal decision, designated by $(Q_L{}^*, Q_C{}^*)$ is found by combining two distinctly different types of information. First, the locus of consumption possibilities is given by the straight line

$$W = P_L Q_L + P_C Q_C$$

where W, P_L, and P_C are given parameters, and Q_L and Q_C are the choice variables of the individual. The straight possibilities line is com-

FIGURE 3–1
Consumer choice among two commodities

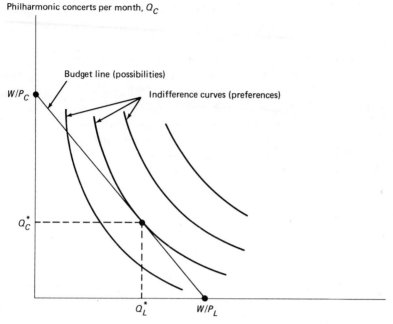

Philharmonic concerts per month, Q_C

Budget line (possibilities)

W/P_C

Indifference curves (preferences)

Q_C^*

Q_L^* W/P_L

Lobster dinners per month, Q_L

monly referred to as the *budget line*. It represents combinations attainable in the markets for lobster dinners and philharmonic concerts. Information on possibilities is obtained by examining those markets.

Second, the locus of investor *preferences* is given by a series of indifference curves, which usually are shaped as shown in the commodity space of Figure 3–1. Each indifference curve represents the locus of monthly quantities of lobster dinners (Q_L) and philharmonic concerts (Q_C) for which the individual consumer is indifferent. The slope of an indifference curve in this example indicates the number of philharmonic concerts that the individual would be willing to give up in order to afford one additional lobster dinner. Such a trade-off is often referred to as the *marginal rate of substitution* between the two consumption choices. As one moves upward or to the right in Figure 3–1, each indifference curve represents a higher level of satisfaction for the consumer. Information on preferences, as represented by indifference curves, is found by talking with individual consumers about their preferences for various combinations of commodities.

Solution of the problem of consumer choice (Q_L^*, Q_C^*) can be seen to occur at the tangency of the budget line and the highest attainable indifference curve. At this solution point, the marginal rate of substitution between the two commodities is just equal to the slope of the budget line. It is important to note that the optimal quantities of monthly lobster dinners and philharmonic concerts, Q_L^* and Q_C^*, are found by combining two types of information: possibilities and preferences. The same is also true when any number of commodities is considered.

One difficulty with this theory is the implicit assumption that individuals base their preferences on quantities of the respective commodities—in our example, lobster dinners and philharmonic concerts. Many economists argue that it is not the commodities themselves that are desired, but rather certain characteristics or attributes of those commodities. Example attributes of lobster dinners would be flavor, temperature, tenderness, or size; example attributes of philharmonic concerts would include artistic ability of the orchestra, choice of program, or the flair of the conductor. Indifference curves might more logically be defined in terms of attributes rather than the commodities which they describe.

The *theory of attribute choice* attacks the same problem of choosing among two (or more) commodities, except that preferences are defined in terms of attributes of the commodities. Since possibilities (the budget line) continue to be defined in terms of commodities, it becomes necessary to specify relationships between attributes and commodities—such as the levels of flavor and tenderness to expect from quantities of lobster dinners. Clearly, there are more formidable problems in trying to quantify certain attributes of services and commodities than in just working with the numbers of units involved. Nevertheless, the theory of attribute choice also involves two types of information, possibilities and preferences, just as does the theory of consumer choice.

The *theory of portfolio choice* is a particular example of attribute choice where both possibilities and preferences can readily be defined in terms of certain attributes of investment assets and portfolios. The reader will recall that several attributes of investment assets, including return and safety, were identified in Chapter 1. Portfolio choice based on just these two attributes is illustrated in Figure 3–2. We assume that both portfolio return (E) and portfolio safety (U) are desirable to the investor, and that he would always prefer more return and greater safety. Accordingly, the indifference curves are of the same general shape as in the consumer choice discussion. The locus of portfolio possibilities, on the other hand, is a curved rather than a straight line. The reason for this curvature is that the investor must give up more and more units of a particular attribute in order to gain one additional unit of the other attribute. In contrast, if lobster dinners cost $7.50 and philharmonic concerts cost $5, the tradeoff is always fixed at three concerts equaling two dinners.

Optimal solution of portfolio choice, designated by (E^*, U^*) is seen

FIGURE 3–2
Portfolio choice based on return and safety

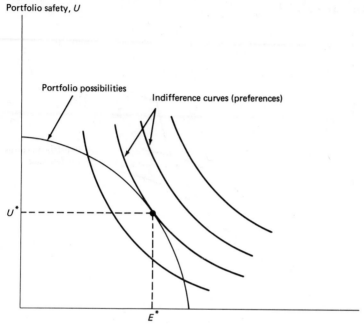

Portfolio return, E

to be at the tangency of the portfolio possibilities curve with the highest attainable indifference curve. As before, the optimal solution point is found by bringing together two types of information: (1) portfolio possibilities based on a study of the relative attributes of investment assets and portfolios of those assets, and (2) investor preferences.

Although the portfolio choice in Figure 3–2 closely parallels the consumer choice in Figure 3–1, most investors and most of the financial literature focus on the riskiness of assets and portfolios rather than their safety. This occurs even though the safety attribute can be viewed as just the mirror image of the risk attribute. Figure 3–3 presents portfolio choice based on portfolio return (E) and portfolio risk (S), which are by far the two most popular attributes used to describe investment assets and portfolios. The optimal solution (E^*, S^*) in Figure 3–3 is exactly analogous to that (E^*, U^*) in Figure 3–2. The only difference is that the respective curves, representing preferences and possibilities, have different shapes in the return-risk diagram than in the return-safety diagram. As we shall see later in this chapter, the possibilities curve is often referred to as the *efficient curve* or the *efficient frontier*.

Many of the properties of efficient portfolios, the assumptions about

FIGURE 3–3
Portfolio choice based on return and risk

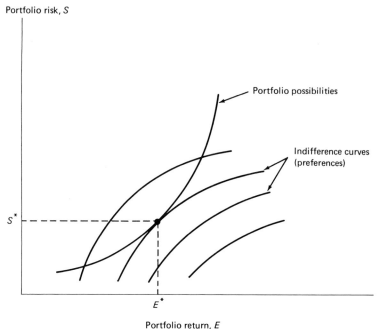

Portfolio return, E

investor behavior, and the implications of portfolio theory are embedded in the types of curves included in Figure 3–3. Before we can fully understand efficient portfolios, the richness of portfolio theory, and the importance of using a portfolio perspective when making investment decisions, we must examine how the attributes of investment assets, particularly return and risk, are combined in order to get the return and risk attributes of entire portfolios.

ASSET RETURN

What is the return on an investment asset? For a savings account, it is the rate paid by the savings institution, while for a government or corporate bond, it is the yield to maturity. In both instances, periodic payments to an investor plus repayment of principal represent legal obligations on the part of the savings institution, the issuing government, or the issuing corporation. Although there is some chance that the investor may not receive either the periodic payments or the principal repayment, the chances are typically quite high that he will receive the full return on his investment.

For the case of common stock and other more risky investment assets such as real estate, neither periodic nor possible terminal payments represent legal obligations on the part of the issuing organization. No calculation can be performed that gives an exact measure of return to the investor. Return may be quite high, or it may be nonexistent. A common procedure in cases where return is subject to uncertainty is to specify the *expected return* of the investment asset. Informally, this may be a "guesstimate" of the return expected by the investor. Formally, expected return is taken as the average value of possible outcomes of return, each weighted by its relative probability. A schedule of possible outcomes and their associated probabilities is referred to as a *probability distribution*, and expected return is a measure of the center of the probability distribution. For example, if there were equal chances of an 8% or a 10% return from a certain investment, the expected return is found to be 9% as follows:

Possible return	Probability	Weighted return
0.08 (8%)	0.50	0.04
0.10 (10%)	0.50	0.05
		Expected return = 0.09 (9%)

If instead the odds were three-to-one in favor of the higher return, expected return would turn out to be 9.5% as follows:

Possible return	Probability	Weighted return
0.08	0.25	0.020
0.10	0.75	0.075
		Expected return = 0.095 (9.5%)

In each case, the procedure is to multiply each possible return by the associated probability of that return and then add the products. Expected return is a convenient measure when there are multiple outcomes that may occur. It does require, however, that the investor, his broker, an investment advisor, or someone must specify the probabilities associated with each possible outcome. Of course, the probabilities so specified must add to unity.

To further illustrate, consider the common shares of RST Corporation which are being analyzed as a potential investment. Three possible outcomes for the per-share return of RST Corporation are projected as shown in Worksheet 3–1. The three possible outcomes for return are 4%, 12%, and 18%. By multiplying each possible return R_k by its associated probability π_k and summing over all $k = 1, 2, 3$ possible outcomes,

28

WORKSHEET 3-1
Calculating expected return for RST Corporation

Possible outcome, k	Return, R_k	Probability, π_k	Weighted return, $\pi_k R_k$
1	0.04 (4%)	0.25	0.010
2	0.12 (12%)	0.50	0.060
3	0.18 (18%)	0.25	0.045
		Expected security return E =	0.115 (11.5%)

we see that the expected return on RST Corporation is 11.5%. We shall not discuss here how the possible outcomes for return are determined since that is a rather complex subject to which Part III of this book is devoted.

PORTFOLIO RETURN

For the young married couple who bought 50 shares of Eastman Kodak, that particular new holding represents only one of the three securities that they own. And the variable annuity of the university professor is but part of a total portfolio since he and his wife also own 400 shares of a growth-oriented mutual fund, and a small trust fund set up at the death of her parents. In addition, they also have a savings account, which they maintain as a cash reserve. Their total portfolio thus contains four different types of investment assets, each of which is really a portfolio itself. The return for their total portfolio, for that of the young married couple, or for that matter any portfolio, is logically measured as a weighted average of the expected returns on all the assets in the portfolio. The weights in such an average usually are based on the relative market values of the individual assets.

To illustrate, we calculate expected return for the portfolio of the university professor and his wife to be 7.16% as follows:

Investment asset	Market value	Relative weight	Expected asset return	Weighted return
Savings account	$ 3,500	0.236	0.050 (5.0%)	0.0118
Mutual fund	4,200	0.284	0.092 (9.2%)	0.0262
Trust fund	6,000	0.406	0.071 (7.1%)	0.0288
Variable annuity	1,100	0.074	0.065 (6.5%)	0.0048
Total	$14,800	1.000		0.0716 (7.16%)

Expected asset returns are based on estimates provided by the manager of each asset. In the calculation, the relative weights are found by dividing the individual market value of each component by $14,800, which is the aggregate market value of the total portfolio at present. Of the component returns, only that of the savings account is known with high certainty. All of the others are expected returns based on the possibilities of return for individual members of the respective portfolios. They range from 9.2% for the mutual fund to 6.5% for the variable annuity. The university professor and his wife could increase their expected portfolio return by shifting dollars out of savings and into any of the other three types of investments. A maximum expected return of 9.2% would be achieved by allocating their entire investment wealth to shares of the mutual fund. But as we shall see, this would result in a more risky portfolio.

ASSET RISK

What is the risk of owning a common share of Eastman Kodak, a corporate bond of American Telephone and Telegraph, a share of a particular mutual fund? Although many possible responses might be made to this question, most would focus on the relative chances that the individual will recover something from his investment. To some, this concept of risk is implemented with a qualitative assignment—such as high-risk, moderate-risk, low-risk, or risk-free. Bond and stock ratings, to be discussed in Chapters 5 and 6, respectively, include qualitative assessment of the risk inherent in such investment assets.

To others, the concept of risk is best expressed with a quantitative measure that somehow expresses the variability of possible returns. For a virtually risk-free asset (such as a U.S. Treasury Bill) whose monetary return is certain, risk is zero; for other investment assets whose return outcome is not certain, a numerical assignment for risk must be made. *Variance* or *standard deviation* of the possible return outcomes is a frequent choice for measuring the risk attribute, because it reflects the extent of spread of the probability distribution. We assume that most investors are *risk-averse,* which means that for a given level of return, they prefer less risk to more risk.

To illustrate how variance and standard deviation are calculated, we expand the calculations for RST Corporation shown in Worksheet 3–2.

WORKSHEET 3–2
Calculating return and risk for RST Corporation

Outcome k	Return R_k	Probability π_k	Weighted $\pi_k R_k$	Deviation $R_k - E_1$	Squared $(R_k - E_1)^2$	Weighted $\pi_k (R_k - E_1)^2$
1	0.04	0.25	0.010	−0.075	0.005625	0.001406
2	0.12	0.50	0.060	0.005	0.000025	0.000013
3	0.18	0.25	0.045	0.065	0.004225	0.001056
		Expected return E_1	= 0.115		Variance $S_1{}^2$	= 0.002475
			(11.5%)		Standard deviation S_1	= 0.049 (4.9%)

The subscripts on R_k and π_k refer to the $k = 1, 2, 3$ outcomes for return. The subscript on E_1 and S_1 indicates that this is the first security to be considered in this illustration. Expected return for RST Corporation, designated by E_1, is calculated as before. Variance of return is seen to be the sum of squared deviations from the expected return ($E_1 = 11.5\%$), each weighted by the probability π_k of that particular outcome. For RST Corporation, variance $S_1{}^2 = 0.002475$. Standard deviation of return is just the square root of variance; hence, $S_1 = 4.9\%$. Since standard deviation of return is in the same units as expected return, we will work with standard deviation rather than variance—even though they are directly related by the square root operation.

Another common stock being considered for inclusion in the portfolio is that of UVW Enterprises. Its probability distribution of return, calculation of expected return, and standard deviation of return are included in Worksheet 3–3.

WORKSHEET 3–3
Calculating return and risk for UVW Enterprises

Outcome k	Return R_k	Probability π_k	Weighted $\pi_k R_k$	Deviation $R_k - E_2$	Squared $(R_k - E_2)^2$	Weighted $\pi_k (R_k - E_2)^2$
1	0.05	0.25	0.0125	−0.040	0.001600	0.000400
2	0.09	0.50	0.0450	0.000	0.000000	0.000000
3	0.13	0.25	0.0325	0.040	0.001600	0.000400
		Expected return E_2	= 0.0900 (9.0%)		Variance $S_2{}^2$	= 0.000800
					Standard deviation S_2	= 0.028 (2.8%)

In comparing the common stocks of RST Corporation and UVW Enterprises, we see that the former has both a higher expected return and a higher level of risk, as measured by the standard deviation of return. These two cases illustrate a feature that usually exists for most investment assets—namely, that higher return is accompanied by higher risk.

The positive relationships between return and risk among investment assets will be reiterated throughout this book. In Figure 3–4, we see a comparison of the probability distributions, the expected returns, and the standard deviations of returns for the common stocks of RST Corporation and UVW Enterprises. We note that the probability distribution for UVW Enterprises is symmetrical about its expected return, while that for RST Corporation is not. This diagram serves to highlight an important property of variance (or standard deviation) as a measure of risk. For as seen in the worksheets for RST Corporation and UVW

FIGURE 3–4
Comparison of return and risk for two common stocks

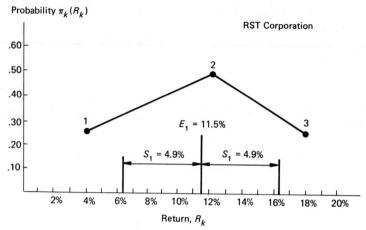

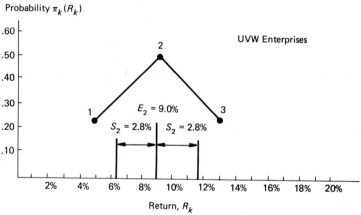

Enterprises, the procedure is to square and add the deviations on *both* sides of expected return. Yet many readers and investors may feel that deviations *above* expected return are desirable rather than undesirable. If feelings about downside variations in return are not comparable to feelings about upside variations, then variance is not a suitable measure of risk. *Semi-variance,* which reflects only downside variations in return, has been suggested as a preferable measure of risk. Other alternatives also exist. Proper measurement of risk remains, however, an unresolved problem in finance and investment, and for now we shall continue to use variance and standard deviation.

PORTFOLIO RISK

In order to explain and illustrate portfolio risk, it is necessary to determine the relative holdings of each asset to be included in the portfolio. We know from our illustrative calculation for the university professor and his wife that portfolio return is simply a weighted average of the expected return of the component members of the portfolio. For different combinations of the common stocks of RST Corporation and UVW Enterprises, we see that portfolio return varies from 9% to 11.5% as follows:

Portfolio holdings	Expected portfolio return
100% RST	(100%)(11.5%) = 11.5%
80% RST and 20% UVW	(80%)(11.5%) + (20%)(9.0%) = 11.0%
60% RST and 40% UVW	(60%)(11.5%) + (40%)(9.0%) = 10.5%
50% RST and 50% UVW	(50%)(11.5%) + (50%)(9.0%) = 10.25%
40% RST and 60% UVW	(40%)(11.5%) + (60%)(9.0%) = 10.0%
20% RST and 80% UVW	(20%)(11.5%) + (80%)(9.0%) = 9.5%
100% UVW	(100%)(9.0%) = 9%

An equal investment in RST Corporation and UVW Enterprises, for example, would give an expected return of 10.25%. For simplicity, we shall assume an equal investment portfolio in order to illustrate portfolio risk.

Unfortunately, calculating a measure of portfolio risk is not as straightforward as that for return. The reason is that we must somehow determine how the uncertainty of RST common stock is related, if at all, to the uncertainty of UVW common stock. In other words, we again measure risk as the uncertainty associated with possible outcomes—except that now we are interested in possible returns to the entire portfolio. One way of interrelating the returns of two different assets is to relate their possible outcomes to states of the world—or of the economic environment in which asset returns materialize. We will consider three extreme cases that span the range of possibilities.

In Case 1, we assume that there are three possible states of the economy during the period over which asset returns are defined. The three states are *optimistic, neutral,* and *pessimistic.* Outcomes for securities are related to these states of the economy. Furthermore, we assume in Case 1 that the returns of RST and UVW common stocks are directly related. That is, both stocks experience their highest returns (18% and 13%, respectively) when economic prospects are optimistic, and their lowest return (4% and 5%, respectively) when economic prospects are pessimistic.

Expanded Worksheet 3–4 is used to calculate expected portfolio return and standard deviation of portfolio return for an equal investment mix of RST Corporation and UVW Enterprises. Notice in that worksheet that probabilities π_k are associated with states of the economy. Portfolio outcomes R_k are equal mixes of the respective returns on RST Corporation and UVW Enterprises. From there, the calculation procedure follows exactly that used for individual assets. We see that expected portfolio return $E = 10.25\%$ is accompanied by standard deviation $S = 3.9\%$.

In Case 2, we assume that the returns of RST and UVW common stocks move in opposite directions to each other relative to the three states of the economy. As seen in the Worksheet 3–5 for Case 2, the expected portfolio return $E = 10.25\%$ remains the same, but standard deviation of portfolio return is only $S = 1.1\%$. The reason for this reduction in risk is that the highest return for RST Corporation occurs with the lowest return for UVW Enterprises, and conversely. This causes the range of portfolio outcomes (8.5% to 11.5%) for Case 2 to be much smaller than the range (4.5% to 15.5%) for Case 1, where the two returns move together. This is the essence of why *diversification* leads to reduced risk, and why the tenets of portfolio theory are of great importance to all investors.

Between the extremes of Case 1 and Case 2 are those situations where the returns of two assets do not move together perfectly. Case 3, in fact, deals with the situation where the return of RST Corporation is completely independent of the return of UVW Enterprises. In Case 3, there are no longer only three states of the economy with which possible outcomes are associated. If each asset has three outcomes, then there are nine (three times three) possible outcomes for portfolios consisting of RST and UVW common stocks. For each of these nine possible outcomes, the joint probability of that outcome π_{k}' is just the product of the probability π_k (RST) of RST common stock return times the probability π_k (UVW) of UVW common stock return. Once the portfolio outcomes R_k (again an equal investment mix) and their associated probabilities π_{k}' are determined, the calculation of return and risk for the portfolio proceeds as before. As seen in Worksheet 3–6 for Case 3, expected portfolio return ($E = 10.25\%$) is the same, while standard deviation ($S = 2.9\%$) is between the extremes of Cases 1 and 2.

Results of combining RST common stock with UVW common stock in a portfolio can now be summarized. Expected portfolio return ranges between 9% and 11.5%. And for an equal investment in RST Corporation and UVW Enterprises, standard deviation ranges between 1.1% and 3.9% depending on how the respective returns are interrelated. In Figure 3–5, we plot expected portfolio return and standard deviation of portfolio return for the three cases which have been discussed. The dotted lines in Figure 3–5 indicate for each case the respective portfolio return and risk values for all possible mixes of the two common stocks. For the

WORKSHEET 3-4
Calculating portfolio return and risk, Case 1

State of economy	Probability π_k	Outcome of RST	Outcome of UVW	Portfolio outcome, R_k	Weighted $\pi_k R_k$	Deviation $R_k - E$	Squared $(R_k - E)^2$	Weighted $\pi_k(R_k - E)^2$
Optimistic	0.25	0.18	0.13	0.155	0.03875	0.0525	0.002756	0.000689
Neutral	0.50	0.12	0.09	0.105	0.05250	0.0025	0.000001	0.000000
Pessimistic	0.25	0.04	0.05	0.045	0.01125	-0.0575	0.003306	0.000827
							Variance, S^2 = 0.001516	
				Expected portfolio return, E = 0.10250 (10.25%)			Standard deviation, S = 0.039 (3.9%)	

WORKSHEET 3-5
Calculating portfolio return and risk, Case 2

State of economy	Probability π_k	Outcome of RST	Outcome of UVW	Portfolio outcome, R_k	Weighted $\pi_k R_k$	Deviation $R_k - E$	Squared $(R_k - E)^2$	Weighted $\pi_k(R_k - E)^2$
Optimistic	0.25	0.18	0.05	0.115	0.02878	0.0125	0.000156	0.000039
Neutral	0.50	0.12	0.09	0.105	0.05250	0.0025	0.000001	0.000000
Pessimistic	0.25	0.04	0.13	0.085	0.02125	-0.0175	0.000306	0.000077
							Variance, S^2 = 0.000116	
				Expected portfolio return, E = 0.10250 (10.25%)			Standard deviation, S = 0.011 (1.1%)	

WORKSHEET 3–6
Calculating portfolio return and risk, Case 3

Possibility	Outcome R_k(RST)	Probability π_k(RST)	Outcome R_k(UVW)	Probability π_k(UVW)	Portfolio outcome R_k	Joint probability π_k'	Weighted $\pi_k'R_k$	Deviation $R_k - E$	Squared $(R_k - E)^2$	Weighted $\pi_k'(R_k - E)^2$
1	0.18	0.25	0.13	0.25	0.155	0.0625	0.00968	−0.0525	0.002756	0.000168
2	0.18	0.25	0.09	0.50	0.135	0.1250	0.01688	−0.0325	0.001056	0.000132
3	0.18	0.25	0.05	0.25	0.115	0.0675	0.00718	−0.0125	0.000156	0.000010
4	0.12	0.50	0.13	0.25	0.125	0.1250	0.01563	−0.0225	0.000506	0.000063
5	0.12	0.50	0.09	0.50	0.105	0.2500	0.02625	−0.0025	0.000001	0.000000
6	0.12	0.50	0.05	0.25	0.085	0.1250	0.01063	0.0175	0.000306	0.000038
7	0.04	0.25	0.13	0.25	0.085	0.0625	0.00531	0.0175	0.000306	0.000019
8	0.04	0.25	0.09	0.50	0.065	0.1250	0.00813	0.0375	0.001406	0.000176
9	0.04	0.25	0.05	0.25	0.045	0.0625	0.00281	0.0575	0.003306	0.000207

Expected portfolio return, $E = 0.10250$
(10.25%)

Variance, $S^2 = 0.000813$
Standard deviation, $S = 0.029$ (2.9%)

FIGURE 3–5

Portfolios of two investment assets equally held

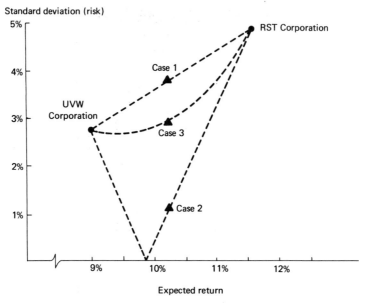

two securities equally held in a portfolio, we see that expected portfolio return is equal to 10.25%, which is just halfway between the respective returns of RST Corporation and UVW Enterprises. The level of risk, as measured by standard deviation, depends on the degree of interrelation between those two returns. Case 1, in which the two security returns move together exactly, is referred to as the case of *perfect positive correlation*. For Case 1, we see in Figure 3–5 that the level of portfolio risk is also just halfway between the respective risk levels of RST Corporation and UVW Enterprises. Case 2, in which the two returns move exactly in opposite directions, is referred to as the case of *perfect negative correlation*. The result of finding two securities so related is a portfolio risk level considerably below that of either individual asset. It is even possible, as seen in Case 2, to obtain a *riskless return* by properly combining two assets whose returns have perfectly negative correlation.[1] When the portfolio is composed of 36.4% RST and 63.6% UVW, the expected portfolio return is 9.9% and standard deviation zero. For the intermediate Case 3 with independent returns, we see a modest reduction in portfolio risk.

---

[1] It can be shown that this occurs when the relative proportions of RST and UVW are $S_2/(S_1 + S_2)$ and $S_1/(S_1 + S_2)$, respectively. For details, see Keith V. Smith, *Portfolio Management* (Holt, Rinehart and Winston, Inc., 1971), Chapter 6.

EFFICIENT PORTFOLIOS

For portfolios consisting of only two securities, we can write specific equations for portfolio return

$$E = X_1E_1 + X_2E_2 \tag{3-1}$$

and portfolio risk

$$S^2 = X_1{}^2S_1{}^2 + X_2{}^2S_2{}^2 + 2X_1X_2S_1S_2C_{12} \tag{3-2}$$

where X_1 and X_2 are the respective percentages of investment wealth allocated to the two assets, and C_{12} is the correlation coefficient, which measures the degree of association between the returns of the two assets. The product $S_1S_2C_{12}$ equals the *covariance* between the return on the two securities. We know that correlation coefficients vary between minus one as in Case 2 (perfect negative correlation) and plus one as in Case 1 (perfect positive correlation). For independent returns, the correlation coefficient is zero and the last term of expression (3–2) disappears. We also see from expression (3–2) that as C_{12} decreases, portfolio risk as measured by variance of portfolio return also decreases. This helps us to understand why diversification is better accomplished if one can find pairs of investment assets whose returns are independent or tend *not* to move together in response to changes in the economic environment.

For portfolios consisting of three securities, portfolio return is given by

$$E = X_1E_1 + X_2E_2 + X_3E_3 \tag{3-3}$$

while portfolio risk would be expressed as

$$S^2 = X_1{}^2S_1{}^2 + X_2{}^2S_2{}^2 + X_3{}^2S_3{}^2 + 2X_1X_2S_1S_2C_{12} \\ + 2X_1X_3S_1S_3C_{13} + 2X_2X_3S_2S_3C_{23} \tag{3-4}$$

Here we note that there are three terms involving variances and three terms involving covariances. These expressions for the return and risk of the portfolio also can be extended for a universe of any size. For a universe of four asssets, there would be six covariance terms—one for each pair of assets among the universe. Hence, as the number of assets in the portfolio increases, the number of covariance terms in the expression for portfolio risk increases even faster.

The problem of portfolio selection is based upon expressions such as (3–1) to (3–4), plus the additional requirements that the relative percentages X_j are nonnegative and must sum to unity. Given estimates of expected return (E_j) and variance $(S_j{}^2)$ for each asset, plus a correlation coefficient (C_{ij}) for each pair of assets, the problem is to determine the percentage holding of each asset (X_j) that maximizes expected portfolio return for a given level of portfolio risk—or that minimizes portfolio risk for a given level of expected portfolio return. An illustrative solution of portfolio selection for a universe of five assets is presented as Figure 3–6. The large dots indicate expected asset return and standard

FIGURE 3–6
Efficient frontier for universe of five assets

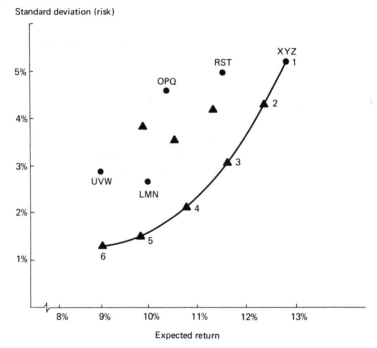

deviation for each of the five investment assets. Along with RST Corporation and UVW Enterprises, the common stocks of companies LMN, OPQ, and XYZ also are represented. The triangles represent a few of the countless number of portfolio combinations that can be constructed from this small population of investment assets. The portfolios along the curve constitute the *efficient frontier;* that is, the curve represents possible portfolios having the highest return for a given risk level, or the lowest risk for a given level of return. In other words, the efficient frontier represents the solution to the problem of portfolio selection. Each efficient portfolio is defined by its value of expected return (E) and standard deviation (S), plus the relative percentages of each asset. Values of expected return and standard deviation can be read directly from the return-risk space in Figure 3–6.

Percentage composition of the six efficient portfolios in Figure 3–6 might be as follows:

Efficient portfolio	Assets represented in portfolio					Total
	LMN	OPQ	RST	UVW	XYZ	
1	–	–	–	–	100%	100%
2	–	20%		–	80%	100%
3	–	28%	26%	–	46%	100%
4	18%	32%	29%	–	21%	100%
5	10%	40%	36%	11%	3%	100%
6	9%	33%	31%	27%		100%

The only asset that itself lies on the efficient frontier is XYZ Company, because it has the highest expected return among the five individual assets in the universe. The second efficient portfolio consists of 80% investment in XYZ Company and 20% investment in OPQ Company. Continuing to move down the efficient frontier, more assets appear in efficient portfolios for purposes of diversification. All five assets appear in the fifth efficient frontier. The sixth and final efficient portfolio has the lowest possible risk level, as measured by standard deviation of portfolio return. It has four members with percentages ranging from 9% (LMN Company) to 33% (OPQ Company).

An efficient frontier thus summarizes the optimal portfolio possibilities that are available from a given population of investment assets. We can now better understand the shape and meaning of the possibilities curve that appeared in Figure 3–3 and our introductory discussion of portfolio choice. The choice of a specific portfolio along the efficient frontier necessitates preference information from an investor. Both investor preferences and portfolio possibilities are defined in terms of expected (or mean) return and standard deviation (or variance), which is used as a measure of risk. The underlying model for portfolio selection, therefore, is based on only two attributes, and it is sometimes referred to as the *mean-variance* model.

VOLATILITY

We thus far have used standard deviation of return as a measure of risk both for individual assets and for portfolios. Standard deviation measures the total variation of return about expected return. An alternative measure of risk that has become popular in recent years is *volatility*. It is also referred to as *beta* (β) since that particular Greek letter is sometimes used to represent volatility in mathematical expressions. Volatility is defined as the slope of a *characteristic line*, which relates the return on an investment asset (such as a common stock) or portfolio to the return on the entire market (such as the New York Stock Exchange). From statistics, we know that the slope is also equal to the covariance between asset return and market return divided by the variance of market return.

A characteristic line can be specified subjectively, or it can be estimated from past observations of asset and market returns—either freehand or using the technique of least squares. In any case, it is intended to indicate the responsiveness of a change in asset or portfolio return to a change in market return. The higher the volatility, the greater that responsiveness. A second component of variability in asset or portfolio return is that component not explained by the characteristic line. Although the second component can be reduced by proper diversification, volatility continues to exist. Because of this, volatility can be used as the sole measure of portfolio risk.

To illustrate the concept of volatility, we shall initially focus on a portfolio consisting of the common stocks of two companies—Growth Industries (G) and Handy Electronics (H). Moreover, we shall base expectations for future returns on the historical returns of Growth Industries and Handy Electronics. The annual returns on the two stocks and the return on a leading stock price index over a recent ten-year period were as follows:

Year	Return on Growth Industries R_G	Return on Handy Electronics R_H	Return on market R_M
1	7%	1%	4%
2	9%	5%	9%
3	-2%	-12%	-3%
4	5%	14%	7%
5	10%	24%	13%
6	1%	8%	2%
7	8%	8%	10%
8	2%	2%	-2%
9	16%	20%	18%
10	13%	18%	12%
Average	6.9%	8.8%	7.0%

The relationship between security return and market return, for each of the two companies, is plotted in Figure 3–7. For each company, the ten pairs of returns have been plotted, and a "freehand fit" characteristic line has been drawn through the set of ten points.

Letting R_G and R_H represent the respective returns for Growth Industries and Handy Electronics, with R_M representing market return, the characteristic line for Growth Industries is given by

$$R_G = A_G + \beta_G R_M + e_G \qquad (3\text{–}5)$$

FIGURE 3–7
Characteristic lines for two common stocks

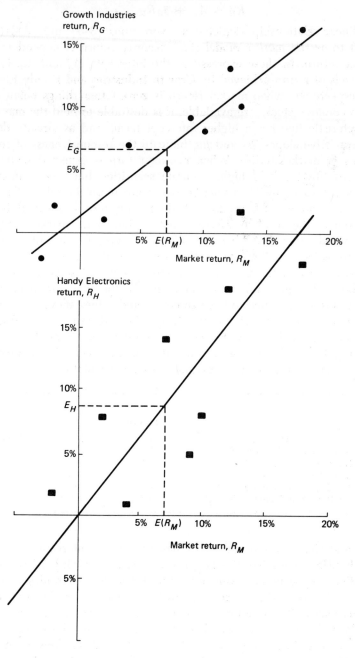

while for Handy Electronics it is given by

$$R_H = A_H + \beta_H R_M + e_H \qquad (3\text{--}6)$$

The linear relationship, depicted in expressions (3–5) and (3–6), is referred to as the *market model* since security return is dependent upon market return. In these expressions, the intercepts, A_G and A_H, indicate the levels of return achieved by Growth Industries and Handy Electronics, respectively, when market return is zero. Other things being equal, if two common stocks are available, it is desirable to hold the one whose characteristic line has a higher intercept term. And as already defined, the respective slopes, β_G and β_H, indicate the responsiveness of security returns to market return. When market return is expected to be high, it is desirable to hold highly volatile securities, but when anticipated market return is low, less volatile issues are more desirable. The other terms, e_G and e_H, are random residual error terms, so-called because they reflect the residual variation not explained by market return. In other words, they arise because all points typically do not lie on the characteristic line. Because of the way in which a characteristic line is drawn through the points, we would expect that some points would be above the line and some points below the line. On balance, the error terms are assumed to have zero expected values and finite variances designated by $Q_G{}^2$ and $Q_H{}^2$, respectively. The better the fit of a characteristic line, the smaller the variance of the residual error term.

Using the ten years of return data for Company G, Company H, and the market, the following parameters were calculated:

	Growth Industries	Handy Electronics	Market
Average asset return E_j	6.9%	8.8%	7.0%
Asset standard deviation, S_j	5.3%	11.4%	6.4%
Intercept term, A_j	1 4%	−0.5%	−
Slope term, β_j	,0.773	1.334	1.000
Residual standard deviation, Q_j	1.8%	7.6%	−
Coefficient of determination, $r_j{}^2$	0.882	0.713	−

We note that Growth Industries has the larger intercept term, while Handy Electronics has the larger slope term. Volatility of the market is defined to be unity. Average return of Handy Electronics was somewhat higher than the return of Growth Industries over the past decade, but its variability of return was over twice as large. As to the residual standard deviations, we see that $Q_H > Q_G$ as would be expected from the two plots in Figure 3–7. Finally, we see that goodness-of-fit of the characteristic line, as measured by the coefficient of determination ($r_j{}^2$), is higher for Growth Industries than for Handy Electronics.

The next step is to combine the common stocks of Growth Industries and Handy Electronics into a portfolio. To do this, we need estimates of expected return and risk for each asset to be included. There is some evidence that historical returns as summarized by characteristic lines are likely to be experienced in the future for many assets. That being the case, expressions (3–5) and (3–6) can be used to estimate future returns of the two common stocks given different levels of market return. Consider Growth Industries for instance. The return on that common stock is viewed, as before, as a random variable subject to some underlying (but unspecified) probability distribution. Similarly, market return is itself a random variable. Expected asset return for the next period is given by

$$E_G = A_G + \beta_G E(R_M) \qquad (3\text{–}7)$$

where $E(R_M)$ is the expected return on the market. The only difference between expressions (3–5) and (3–7) is that the former involves random variables, while the latter involves the expected values of those variables. The variance of asset return for Growth Industries is given by

$$S_G{}^2 = \beta_G{}^2 S^2(R_M) + Q_G{}^2 \qquad (3\text{–}8)$$

where $S^2(R_M)$ is the variance of market return and, again, $Q_G{}^2$ is the variance of the error term for Growth Industries. The corresponding expressions for Handy Electronics are

$$E_H = A_H + \beta_H E(R_M) \qquad (3\text{–}9)$$

and

$$S_H{}^2 = \beta_H{}^2 S^2(R_M) + Q_H{}^2 \qquad (3\text{–}10)$$

Expressions (3–8) and (3–10) are very important relationships in that total asset risk is seen to consist of two components. The first component is termed *systematic risk* since it depends on market risk $S^2(R_M)$ and the responsiveness of asset returns to market return as measured by the respective volatilities β_G and β_H. The second component is termed *non-systematic risk* since it is unique to individual assets and does not depend on the market.

Breakdown of total asset risk into the systematic and nonsystematic components permits a better understanding of the role of diversification in portfolio decision-making. As individual assets are combined into portfolios, nonsystematic risk can be reduced, but the systematic risk inherent in the market remains. To see this, we substitute expressions (3–7) and (3–9) into expression (3–1) and obtain expected portfolio return:

$$E = X_G A_G + X_H A_H + [X_G \beta_G + X_H \beta_H] E(R_M) \qquad (3\text{–}11)$$

Under the market model assumption, portfolio variance can be shown to be

$$S^2 = X_G{}^2 Q_G{}^2 + X_H{}^2 Q_H{}^2 + [X_G \beta_G + X_H \beta_H]^2 S^2(R_M) \qquad (3\text{-}12)$$

The bracketed quantity in each expression is seen to be a weighted average of asset volatilities, and hence is often referred to as *portfolio volatility*. It may be thought of as a weighted average response to the market by the assets held in the portfolio. The first two terms in expressions (3–11) and (3–12) are unique to Growth Industries and Handy Electronics while the third term depends on the weighted average response to the market.

In order to illustrate how individual assets contribute to the total portfolio, we need estimates of market return and risk, as well as the proportional holdings of the assets in the portfolio. The average return of the market and the variance of market return over a past period can be used as estimates of market return and risk, respectively. From the prior calculations, we would have market return $E(R_M) = 7.0\%$ and market risk $S(R_M) = 6.4\%$. And under the assumption of an equal investment portfolio, we would have $X_G = X_H = 0.5$.

Portfolio volatility under these assumptions becomes

$$X_G \beta_G + X_H \beta_H = (0.5)(0.773) + (0.5)(1.334) = 1.054.$$

Expected portfolio return using expression (3–11) becomes

$$E = (0.5)(1.4\%) + (0.5)(-0.5\%) + (1.054)(7.0\%) = 7.8\%,$$

and portfolio variance using expression (3–12) becomes

$$S^2 = (0.5)^2(1.8\%)^2 + (0.5)^2(7.6\%)^2 + (1.054)^2(6.4\%)^2 = 60.75.$$

Standard deviation is just the square root of this variance, or 7.80%. An equal investment portfolio of Growth Industries common stock and Handy Electronics common stock would thus have an expected return of 7.83% and an associated risk level of 7.80%.

Using expression (3–12), it is also possible to decompose total portfolio risk into the systematic risk and nonsystematic risk components of variance as follows

Risk component	Variation	Percentage of total
Nonsystematic, Growth Industries	0.81	1.4%
Nonsystematic, Handy Electronics	14.44	23.7%
Systematic	45.50	74.9%
Total	60.75	100.0%

We see that non-systematic risk accounts for $1.4\% + 23.7\% = 25.1\%$ of the total variation in portfolio return. The remaining 74.9% of total variation is due to systematic risk. This serves to underscore the importance of volatility as an alternative measure of risk. Of course, for other mixes of Growth Industries and Handy Electronics, the relative size of non-systematic risk and systematic risk would be different.

PRACTICAL LEVELS OF DIVERSIFICATION

It is interesting to see what happens to the two components of risk when additional assets are added to the portfolio. To demonstrate this, suppose that the common stock of Ideal Markets (I) is added to the portfolio, and that equal proportions $X_G = X_H = X_I = 0.33$ are established. The parameters of the characteristic line for Ideal Markets are intercept $A_I = 0.13\%$, slope $\beta_I = 1.100$, and residual variance $Q_I = 5.0\%$. The expected return for Company I common stock is

$$E_I = A_I + \beta_I E(R_M) = 0.13\% + (1.100)(7.0\%) = 7.83\%,$$

which is just the value of portfolio return for an equal investment in Growth Industries and Handy Electronics.

Expected portfolio return and portfolio variance for a portfolio of these three securities would be given by

$$E = X_G A_G + X_H A_H + X_I A_I + [X_G \beta_G + X_H \beta_H + X_I \beta_I] E(R_M) \quad (3\text{--}13)$$

and

$$S^2 = X_G{}^2 Q_G{}^2 + X_H{}^2 Q_H{}^2 + X_I{}^2 Q_I{}^2$$
$$+ [X_G \beta_G + X_H \beta_H + X_I \beta_I]^2 S^2(R_M) \quad (3\text{--}14)$$

respectively, where the bracketed quantity in expressions (3–13) and (3–14) is just the portfolio volatility (or beta) for the three-asset case. Substituting appropriate values gives a portfolio volatility of

$$(0.33)(0.773) + (0.33)(1.334) + (0.33)(1.100) = 1.069,$$

which is slightly higher than before. In Figure 3–8, characteristic lines for the three assets are plotted, together with the characteristic line for an equal-investment portfolio. Assets or portfolios are said to be *aggressive* when volatility is greater than unity, but *defensive* when volatility is less than unity. According to these definitions, Handy Electronics and Ideal Markets are aggressive stocks, while Growth Industries is a defensive issue. An equal-investment portfolio of these three common stocks is slightly aggressive since portfolio volatility is 1.069.

FIGURE 3–8
Illustrative characteristic lines

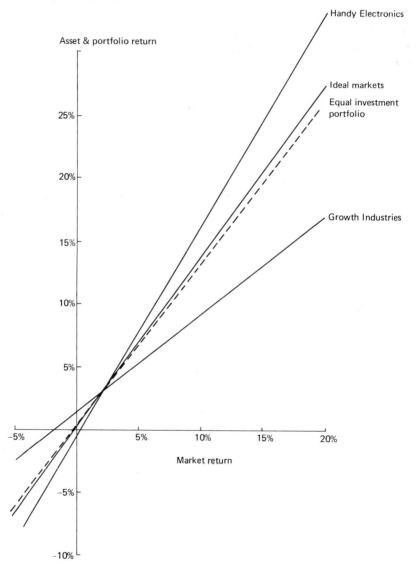

Not surprisingly, expected portfolio return for the equal investment example remains at the same level,

$$E = (0.33)(1.4\%) + (0.33)(-0.5\%) + (0.33)(0.13\%)$$
$$+ (1.069)(7.0\%) = 7.83\%.$$

On the other hand, the breakdown of portfolio variance using expression (3–14) can be summarized as follows:

Risk component	Variation	Percentage of total
Nonsystematic, Growth Industries	0.35	0.75%
Nonsystematic, Handy Electronics	6.30	11.2%
Nonsystematic, Ideal Markets	2.72	4.7%
Systematic	46.81	83.4%
Total	56.18	100.0%

The standard deviation of return for this portfolio is just the square root of the total variation (56.18), or 7.5%, compared with 7.8% for the two-asset portfolio. Thus in this case, portfolio risk is reduced by diversification while keeping expected return at the same level. The percentage of total risk attributed to Growth Industries and Handy Electronics is reduced when Ideal Markets is added. Moreover, non-systematic risk for the portfolio is only 0.7% + 11.2% + 4.7% = 17.6% in this three-asset, equal-investment example, as opposed to 25.1% in the previous two-asset example.

We can generalize this result. As additional assets are added to the portfolio, total risk tends to decrease, as does the ratio of nonsystematic risk to total risk. The absolute level of systematic risk may increase or decrease depending on whether portfolio volatility increases or decreases, but the relative amount of systematic risk will increase. This is why systematic risk is viewed as the critical component of risk for a well diversified portfolio.

For a large mutual fund with numerous holdings, virtually all risk would be systematic risk. It is sometimes stated that systematic risk cannot be avoided. This is not necessarily true, for it can be reduced, by lowering the value of portfolio volatility. If one or more assets with zero volatility were to constitute a portfolio, then systematic risk itself would disappear. Zero portfolio volatility is represented by a perfectly horizontal characteristic line; in other words, there would be no responsiveness of portfolio return to market return.

Very few assets have zero or negative volatilities, and thus zero-volatility portfolios are rarely achieved. Instead, as more and more assets are added to a portfolio, the value of portfolio volatility tends to unity, which is just the volatility of the market itself. Thus in the limiting case, the systematic risk of the portfolio approaches overall market risk.

Individuals and institution exhibit quite different patterns of diversification in their portfolio holdings. On the average, individuals hold four five securities, while at least one type of institutional investor, investment companies, often holds somewhat over fifty securities. It has of interest to researchers to try to determine that level of diversification beyond which addition of securities does little to reduce total risk.

The finding of that research seems to be that a portfolio of ten or fifteen securities is apt to provide sufficient diversification. This is seen in Figure 3–9 by an illustrative curve that plots total portfolio risk as a function of the number of equal-investment securities in the portfolio. The impor-

FIGURE 3–9
Effective limits of diversification

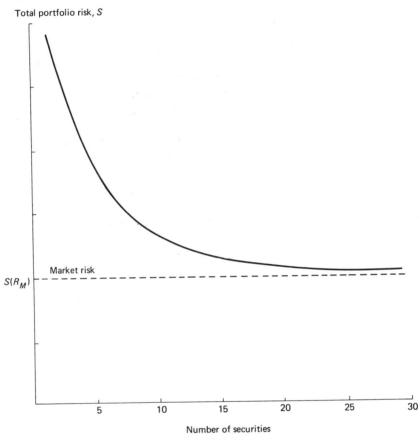

tant bend in the curve occurs between ten and fifteen securities, sug̶ ing that range as a practical level of diversification. While this is where between the average holdings of individuals and the ̶ holdings of institutions, there are, of course, other factors and at̶ that influence portfolio holdings.

SUMMARY

We have seen that investment decisions ultimately involve th̶ holdings of a portfolio. In order to make such decisions prop̶ is necessary to have an adequate portfolio perspective before beginning a study of asset analysis and valuation. Although several attributes of investment assets may be defined, we have limited our attention to measures of return and risk. Portfolio choice, based on return and risk, was seen to follow consumer choice closely in that two important types of information are needed. Preferences represent the feelings of investors toward return, risk, or other attributes. Possibilities describe the alternative assets available to investors for their portfolios.

If one can specify a probability distribution for the return on a particular asset, specific measures of return (expected return) and risk (standard deviation) can be developed for that asset. If correlation coefficients can be specified that reveal the degree of association between pairs of assets, measures of return and risk can be developed for portfolios of investment assets. We have seen how assets are combined into portfolios, and how the efficient frontier is the optimal set of portfolios from among a universe of assets. The final choice of a portfolio by an investor depends on his preferences for portfolio return and portfolio risk.

Further, if that asset's returns are linearly related to market returns, with volatility describing the extent of that relationship, we have seen how diversification reduces the overall risk of a portfolio. Ten to fifteen assets was suggested as a practical level of diversification in a risk-reducing sense.

Application of the portfolio concepts introduced in this chapter is not a simple matter. It requires numerous estimates of return, risk, and interrelationships, as well as consideration of probabilities and the quantification of many variables and attributes. It necessitates lengthy calculations, even for the simplest case of combining but two assets into a portfolio. And if we pursued the analysis further, or attempted to apply the concepts to other types of assets, we would be confronted by an assortment of formidable problems.

Nevertheless, it is our contention in this book that a portfolio perspective is both useful and necessary in properly studying the essentials of investing. Although various discussions and examples throughout the book may seem to be focusing on only a single investment opportunity, must remember that a particular investment asset likely will not held alone, but only as a component member of a total portfolio limets.
ma

In FSTED READINGS FOR CHAPTER 3

ficatio Brealey. *An Introduction to Risk and Return from Common Stocks* four nbridge, Mass.: M.I.T. Press, 1969).
invest Francis and S. H. Archer. *Portfolio Analysis* (Englewood Cliffs, N.J.: been entice-Hall, Inc., 1971), Sections I and II.
tion

H. M. Markowitz. *Portfolio Selection: Efficient Diversification of Investment* (New York: John Wiley & Sons, Inc., 1959), Parts I–III.

W. F. Sharpe. *Portfolio Theory and Capital Markets* (New York: McGraw-Hill Book Company, Inc., 1970), Part I.

K. V. Smith. *Portfolio Management* (New York: Holt, Rinehart and Winston, 1971), Part II.

part II

Valuation of investments

IN PART II we shall introduce and illustrate a method of determining the value of any investment opportunity. Several concepts of value are compared in Chapter 4, and a discounted present value framework is suggested in which each future cash benefit is discounted at a rate that reflects both the timing and riskiness of that benefit. This valuation framework is applied both to holdings of cash and to investment in savings accounts. In Chapter 5, we deal with the valuation of bonds. Investment characteristics of bonds are explained, and various factors in appraising bonds are considered. The risk associated with bonds is related to bond ratings as well as to the choice of an appropriate discount rate. The valuation framework is applied both to straight bonds and callable bonds. Valuation of common and preferred stocks is dealt with in Chapter 6. Characteristics of these equity investments are identified and illustrated. Variables that contribute to corporate earnings and dividends are emphasized, since dividends are received directly by investors and earnings affect stock prices. Dividends and stock price appreciation are the two components of return earned on stock investments. A series of stock valuation models, using different horizons and growth assumptions, are developed and illustrated. In Chapter 7, we consider a number of tax-sheltered investment opportunities that have received attention in recent years. Their unique tax characteristics are discussed together with their implications for other portfolio holdings. Real estate, cattle feeding, and oil and gas exploration are discussed in more detail and the valuation framework is applied.

4

Framework for valuation

INVESTING ultimately requires decisions to buy, hold, or sell particular assets such as stocks, bonds, and real estate properties. After deciding upon the appropriate investment objectives, the investor proceeds to examine individual assets for possible inclusion in his portfolio. The final decision on each asset examined depends in large part on the current price of the asset. But the decision also depends on the *value* of the asset as perceived by the investor. If price exceeds value, the asset is said to be *overvalued* and presumably is regarded as less attractive as a potential purchase or holding. If value exceeds price, the asset is said to be *undervalued* and presumably is regarded as more attractive. The purpose of this chapter is to develop a framework for valuation that the investor can use to determine whether assets are overvalued or undervalued. The framework is applied here to investing in both cash and savings accounts, and in later chapters to other types of investment assets.

CONCEPTS OF VALUE

Many dissimilar concepts of value have been suggested. Value is often quite different to accountants, to owners of firms, and to potential investors. Consider the balance sheet of Able Manufacturing Company, which successfully produces a line of specialized industrial products as shown at the top of page 54. While the original cost of the fixed assets of Able Manufacturing several years ago was $20,000, today the cost would be approximately $22,500. This latter amount can be thought of as the *replacement value* of the assets. On the other hand, the *depreciated value*

ABLE MANUFACTURING COMPANY
Balance Sheet
May 31, 1973

Assets			*Liabilities and Equity*	
Cash.		$ 4,300	Accounts payable.	$ 4,700
Accounts receivable.		12,800	Bank loan payable	12,000
Inventory.		7,300	Common stock ($1 par)	5,000
Fixed assets	$20,000		Retained earnings.	9,300
Less depreciation. . .	13,400	6,600		
Total		$31,000	Total	$31,000

of the fixed assets is seen to be only $6,600 at the date of this balance sheet.

The owners of Able Manufacturing recently were offered $35,000 for its assets by Cautious Conglomerate Enterprises. If the offer were accepted, and after the accounts payable and bank loans payable of Able Manufacturing were paid in full, the owners of Able Manufacturing would have $18,300 left ($35,000 — $4,700 — $12,000 = $18,300). This amount represents the *liquidation value* of Able Manufacturing to its existing ownership. It also is $4,000 greater than the $14,300 *book value* of the owner's equity ($5,000 + $9,300 = $14,300) as shown on the balance sheet of Able Manufacturing.

From the common stock account, we see that there are $5,000/$1 = 5,000 outstanding shares of common stock. These shares of Able Manufacturing are traded in the over-the-counter market; the current price is $4.50 per share. The aggregate *market value* of the common stock is thus (5,000)($4.50) = $22,500. Because market value exceeds the liquidation value in this instance, the owners of Able Manufacturing have decided to decline the takeover offer from Cautious Conglomerate Enterprises.

Suppose that you are considering the purchase of a few shares of Able Manufacturing as a long-term investment. What is the investment value of each share of Able Manufacturing to you? It certainly is not related to the liquidation value, since Able is an on-going concern. Is it the $2.86 book value per share ($14,300/5,000 shares), or is it the $4.50 market value per share as reflected in the current price? Most investors would answer that market value is much more meaningful than either book value or liquidation value as a measure of investment value.

An astute investor, however, may have yet another concept of value—namely, the ability of Able Manufacturing to continue to operate successfully. Although such success will be reflected in their subsequent balance sheets, it is perhaps more easily seen in the after-tax earnings shown on future income statements of the firm. If such earnings continue to grow, the investor can look forward with reasonable expectation to growing dividend payments, to an increased market price per share as other investors recognize this successful industrial firm, or possibly to both increased dividends and increased market price. Whereas various kinds of benefits may accrue to an investor for holding a given asset, we restrict our attention to only those benefits to which a dollar measure can be assigned. In other words, it is the *future dollar benefits* associated with an investment that give rise to *investment value*. This concept is certainly not restricted to common stock. It holds, in fact, for all types of investment opportunities mentioned in Chapter 1.

This concept of investment value reflecting future dollar benefits becomes a major building block for much of what follows in this book. Although the term *intrinsic value* is often used by other authors to mean the same thing, we shall continue to use the term *investment value* in our discussion.

In examining individual assets, the investor focuses directly on a comparison of investment value with current market price. Both of these quantities can change over time. Investment value is likely to change whenever new information about the future benefits associated with the asset becomes available. As far as publicly available information, this is likely to occur rather infrequently. A typical interval between announcements might be quarterly since most firms report earnings and declare dividends on a quarterly basis. Market price, on the other hand, changes more frequently (i.e., day to day and hour to hour) as suppliers and demanders interact in the market for that asset. The market interaction for a particular asset reflects how many investors believe that changes in interest rates, changes in international exchange rates (if applicable), or other economic developments will ultimately affect the future benefits associated with that asset.

We shall make a convergence assumption; namely that, over time, market price will tend to move toward investment value faster than investment value itself will change. Such an assumed pattern is illustrated in Figure 4–1 for Able Manufacturing. During the year, per-share investment value rose from $5.50 to $6.00, then to $7.00, and finally dropped to $5.00. Until the middle of the third quarter, the common stock of Able Manufacturing was *undervalued* since market price was less than investment value. For the rest of the year, market price exceeded investment value, and the stock was said to be *overvalued*.

INVESTMENT VALUE AS A WEIGHTED AVERAGE

We have not been very specific other than to associate investment value with the future benefits of a particular asset. Since several future benefits typically would be considered, it is necessary to aggregate those

FIGURE 4–1
Investment value and market price per share of Able Manufacturing Company during a year

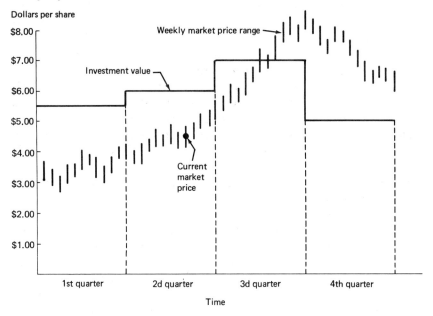

benefits somehow into a single measure of investment value. A weighted average turns out to be a useful measure of aggregation. We define

$$V = \sum_{t=1}^{T} \alpha_t B_t \qquad (4\text{–}1)$$

where V represents investment value, t is an index used to identify each of the T number of benefits being considered, B_t is the dollar measure associated with each benefit t, and α_t is the relative weight assigned to benefit t.[1] If there were only $T = 3$ benefits identified, for example, expression (4–1) could be written simply as

$$V = \alpha_1 B_1 + \alpha_2 B_2 + \alpha_3 B_3.$$

Expression (4–1) is a generalized representation of investment value that can be applied to any type of asset to be considered in this book. The next task is to show how expression (4–1) can be modified to take account of the unique characteristics of different assets. A beginning step in this direction is to adopt the useful convention of aligning future benefits with particular points in time. In other words, B_1 will represent

---

[1] For readers not familiar with the summation sign Σ, it is simply a rule that says to add the weighted dollar measure $\alpha_t B_t$ over all $t = 1, 2, \ldots, T$ benefits.

the dollar benefit accruing to the investor during (or at the end of) period 1, B_2 the benefit during period 2, and so forth.

To illustrate, suppose an individual is considering the purchase of 100 shares of common stock of Able Manufacturing Company at the current market price of $4.50 per share. Suppose further that the investor is considering an investment horizon of three years. He expects a cash dividend per share of $0.30 during all three years. Moreover, he expects to be able to sell each share for $6.00 at the end of the three year horizon. The three cash benefits to the investor thus become:

$$B_1 = \$0.30; \ B_2 = \$0.30; \text{ and } B_3 = \$0.30 + \$6.00 = \$6.30.^2$$

The investment value per share, according to expression (4–1), is given by

$$V = \$0.30\alpha_1 + \$0.30\alpha_2 + \$6.30\alpha_3.$$

To obtain a single measure of investment value it remains to specify the individual relative weights.

RELATIVE WEIGHTS AS DISCOUNT FACTORS

If the three benefits were equally weighted, then $\alpha_1 = \alpha_2 = \alpha_3 = 1$ and investment value would be

$$V = (0.30)(1) + (0.30)(1) + (6.30)(1) = \$6.90.$$

There is reason to believe, however, that an investor might not assign equal weights to the three benefits since they are expected to occur at distinctly different points in time. Since the dollar benefits, when received, can be used by the individual to purchase a lobster dinner, to pay rent, to attend a philharmonic concert, or to engage in any type of immediate consumption, he is likely to prefer the first year benefit to second and third year benefits which he must wait to experience. Even if he decided to reinvest in some other asset, rather than to engage in consumption, the individual surely should prefer earlier benefits to later benefits so that he can begin to earn on that reinvestment.

What we are saying, of course, is that the individual has a *time preference* for dollar benefits—and that his assignment of the relative weights α_t in expression (4–1) should reflect this time preference. The process of assigning relative weights in such a manner typically is referred to as *discounted present value*. Before proceeding with the development and illustration of investment value, we pause to review the mathematics of time discounting and the calculation of discounted present value.

---

[2] For now, we assume that these benefits are known with certainty. In following chapters, we consider the more realistic cases where future benefits associated with common stock and other investments are not known with certainty.

DISCOUNTED PRESENT VALUE

Suppose that you have an amount of money $M = \$100$, which you have decided to place in a savings account that pays interest at the rate $i = 6\%$ annually. At the end of one year, your account will have grown to

$$\$100 + (\$100)(6\%) = \$100(1 + 0.06) = \$106;$$

at the end of the second year, the $106 will have grown to

$$\$106 + (106)(6\%) = \$106(1 + 0.06) = \$112.36.$$

Alternatively, we could have calculated the two year result as follows:

$$\$100(1.06)(1.06) = \$100(1.06)^2 = \$112.36.$$

At the end of five years, your account will have grown to

$$\$100(1.06)^5 = \$133.82.$$

Growth of your account in this way is called *compounding*.

The general expression for showing how an amount M is compounded at the annual rate $i\%$ for N years is $M\,(1+i)^N$. If the interest is paid m times per year rather than once annually, the compounded amount becomes $M\,(1+i/m)^{Nm}$, which means that the compounding rate is reduced, but the number of compounding periods increases correspondingly. For example, if interest is paid quarterly ($m = 4$) in our five year example, the individual would have

$$\$100(1.015)^{20} = \$134.68,$$

and hence he would gain

$$\$134.68 - \$133.82 = \$0.86$$

because of the quarterly compounding.

Discounting is the opposite of compounding. Suppose that the individual wanted to know what amount X he would need now in order for it to compound forward at the annual rate 6% to be equal to $250 in five years. This could be written as $X(1.06)^5 = \$250$. Solving for X, we obtain

$$X = \frac{\$250}{(1.06)^5} = \frac{\$250}{1.3382} = \$186.82,$$

the amount that would be needed to produce $250 at the end of the fifth year. Put another way, $250 received five years from now is worth $186.82 at the present moment in time—because of the time value of money as reflected in the 6% interest rate.

The importance of this example is that it reveals how we can use a modification of the compounding formula to perform a discounting operation. The general expression for determining the discounted present value v_t of a future benefit B_t received at the end of year t, given an interest rate i, is given by

$$v_t = B_t/(1 + i)^t = [1/(1 + i)^t]B_t \qquad (4\text{-}2)$$

The bracketed quantity in expression (4-2) is the discount factor that must be multiplied times the benefit B_t in order to obtain its present value. What we are doing effectively is to penalize at the annual rate i for time delay in experiencing benefits. The rate i, which reflects the time value of money or the price of time, is referred to as the *discount rate*. The bracketed quantity in expression (4-2) is just the relative weight α_t that would be used in determining investment value.[3] Total investment value, according to expression (4-1), is then just equal to the sum of the v_t terms for all future benefits. That is,

$$V_t = \sum_{t=1}^{T} v_t.$$

Values of the discount factors, $1/(1 + i)^t$, for different i and t are included as Appendix A at the end of the book under the column "discounted sum." Interest rates range from 1% through 25%, and time horizons from one year through fifty years. Selected values from Appendix A are shown here.

Present value of $1 received at end of time horizon

Time horizon (years)	Discount rate (percent)					
	2	4	6	8	10	12
1.	$0.980	$0.962	$0.943	$0.926	$0.909	$0.893
2.	0.961	0.925	0.890	0.857	0.826	0.797
3.	0.942	0.889	0.840	0.794	0.751	0.712
4.	0.924	0.855	0.792	0.735	0.683	0.636
5.	0.906	0.822	0.747	0.681	0.621	0.567
6.	0.888	0.790	0.705	0.630	0.564	0.507

Looking across any row or down any column, we see that the discount factors decrease for both larger t and larger i. The present value (at 12%) of $1 to be received six years from today is only $0.507, or just over 50% of the value of $1 today. These weighting or discount factors for use in discounted present value calculations will be used extensively through-

---

[3] If the future benefit is uncertain, a higher discount rate, which reflects both risk and the time value of money, may be appropriate. This issue will be explained further in following chapters.

out the text and examples presented in this book. They also will be needed for many of the exercises at the end of chapters.

To further illustrate the use of discount factors and also the valuation method, we consider again a three-year investment in Able Manufacturing Company. Again, we assume that the future benefits of this situation are known with certainty. Letting the interest rate $i = 6\%$ represent the price of time, we can perform the valuation calculation using appropriate values of α_t from Appendix A as follows

Period	Benefit, B_t	Weight, α_t	Weighted benefit, $\alpha_t B_t$
1	$0.30	0.943	$0.283
2	0.30	0.890	0.267
3	6.30	0.840	5.292
Total	$V = \sum_{t=1}^{3} \alpha_t B_t$		$5.842

The discounted present value of the three-year benefit is seen to be $5.84. This may be taken as a measure of per-share investment value to the individual who is considering the purchase of Able Manufacturing common shares. Since each share is currently selling at a market price of $4.50, we would conclude that the proposed stock is undervalued at present.

Another way of stating the discounted present value procedure is to rewrite our expression for investment value

$$V = \sum_{t=1}^{T} \frac{B_t}{(1 + i)^t} \qquad (4\text{–}3)$$

with the relative weight α_t being replaced by the exact discount factor for each year. Variations of expression (4–3) will be used frequently in this and subsequent chapters.

The discounted present value procedure just described involves a unique discount factor for each future benefit B_t that accrues to the asset in question. If the size of the benefit is constant for all future periods, however, the procedure for calculation can be simplified somewhat. In a three-period horizon, investment value can be rewritten as

$$V = \alpha_1 B + \alpha_2 B + \alpha_3 B = B(\alpha_1 + \alpha_2 + \alpha_3),$$

where B is the benefit in each period. This means that the appropriate discount factors can first be added together, and then multiplied by the equal-sized benefit.

An investment that offers a constant benefit for each period during the lifetime of the investment is referred to as an *annuity*. Retirement benefits and the proceeds of insurance policies are often paid in the form of annuities; it is also possible to purchase an annuity from an insurance company. The general expression for the investment value of an annuity that pays the benefit B for each year t over a total horizon of T years is given by

$$V = B \sum_{t=1}^{T} \alpha_t = B \sum_{t=1}^{T} \left(\frac{1}{1+i}\right)^t \tag{4-4}$$

Expression (4–4) is a special case of expression (4–3) when applied to annuities.

Values of the weighting factors,

$$\sum_{t=1}^{T} \left(\frac{1}{1+i}\right)^t,$$

for different i and t are included in Appendix A under the column "discounted annuity." A selection of such values is shown here

Present value of $1 received annually until end of time horizon

Time horizon (years)	Discount rate (percent)					
	2	4	6	8	10	12
1.......	$0.980	$0.962	$0.943	$0.926	$0.909	$0.893
2.......	1.942	1.886	1.883	1.783	1.736	1.690
3.......	2.884	2.775	2.673	2.577	2.487	2.402
4.......	3.808	3.630	3.465	3.312	3.170	3.037
5.......	4.713	3.452	4.212	3.993	3.791	3.605
6.......	5.601	5.242	4.917	4.623	4.355	4.111

Comparing these with the prior sample of discounted sums, the reader will notice that each weighting factor here is cumulative over the discount factors of individual years up to that point in time. For the case of $i = 8\%$, we see that the $T = 3$ discounted annuity value (2.577) is just the sum of the three discounted sums (0.926 + 0.857 + 0.794). Whereas most of the problems to be encountered will require the use of discounted sums, annuity calculations can be facilitated by using discounted annuities.

Suppose an individual considers the purchase of an annuity that pays $1,000 at the end of each of the next four years. If we continue to let $i = 6\%$ represent the price of time, the investment value of the annuity using expression (4–3) and discounted sums from Appendix A is found to be $3,465 as follows.

Period	Benefit, B_t	Weight, α_t	Weighted benefit, $\alpha_t B_t$
1	$1,000	0.943	$ 943
2	1,000	0.890	890
3	1,000	0.840	840
4	1,000	0.792	792
Total	$V = \displaystyle\sum_{t=1}^{4} \alpha_t B_t$		$3,465

But using one discounted annuity value (for $i = 6\%$, and $T = 4$) from Appendix A, we can calculate directly $V = \$1,000(3.465) = \$3,465$. This again illustrates that each discounted annuity in Appendix A is the sum of all discounted sums up to and including that point in the column.

Appendix B at the end of the book presents compounded sums, discounted sums, and discounted annuities, for 8% and 12% interest rates and time horizons of one through fifty years, for intervals of a year, six months, quarterly, monthly, and continuous. The latter is the limiting case where the interval becomes very short with the number of intervals increasing accordingly.

VALUATION OF CASH

Your eccentric grandfather, reflecting his unfortunate investment experiences during the depression, recently placed his entire wealth of $15,000 in a safe-deposit box at the local bank. Because he can easily live on his retirement income, your grandfather has decided not to touch this amount for a period of six years when he anticipates moving to Florida. What is the value of such an investment in cash? No interest or dividends will be earned by your grandfather, but he is confident that his principal will remain intact. The present value of $15,000 cash six years from now is less than $15,000 because of the time value of money as has been discussed. If the going rate on a risk-free investment is $i = 6\%$, the present value would be only ($15,000)(0.705) = $10,575.

The general expression for investment value of M held in cash for T years can be written as

$$V(\text{CASH}) = M/(1 + i)^T \qquad (4\text{–}5)$$

which is obviously less than M. In other words, we see immediately the loss of value over time when wealth is placed in a non-earning asset such as cash. Your grandfather should be advised, therefore, not to continue to keep his $15,000 in a safe-deposit box.

VALUATION OF SAVINGS

After much talking, you finally persuade your grandfather not to place his $15,000 in a safe-deposit box, but rather to invest in some type of earning asset. Because of his depression experience, however, you decide that he probably should limit his investment to some sort of savings. Possibilities would include a savings account at a commercial bank, a mutual savings bank, a savings and loan association, or the credit union of the firm where he was formerly employed.

All of these possibilities have certain common features. First, the savings earn interest at a stated annual rate. If the interest is paid semi-annually or quarterly, the periodic compounding of both interest and principal causes the effective rate to be slightly higher than the stated rate. Second, the individual may withdraw his total savings, including accumulated interest, at any time. Third, the amount in the savings account is extremely safe—so much so, in fact, that the interest rate on savings is sometimes treated by economists as a risk-free rate.

One disadvantage of savings, however, is that no protection is provided against a decline in the purchasing power of the dollar, which historically has eroded because of inflation. A second disadvantage is that the interest rate sometimes may be changed by the savings institution to reflect current supply and demand conditions in the money market. Although the interest rate may be increased as well as decreased, an element of uncertainty remains for the investor.

After considering these features of savings, you decide to try to persuade your grandfather to place his $15,000 in a savings account at the same savings and loan association where he had his safe-deposit box. The savings account earns at the annual interest rate i. After six years, your grandfather's wealth will grow to $15,000(1 + i)^6$. The present value today of this compounded amount is just $15,000(1 + i)^6/(1 + k)^6$, where k represents an appropriate discount rate.

The general expression for investment value of an investment M in savings for a period of T years is given by

$$V(\text{SAVINGS}) = M(1 + i)^T/(1 + k)^T \qquad (4\text{–}6)$$

Because the future benefits associated with savings are considered to be virtually certain, the discount rate k frequently is taken to be equivalent to the interest rate i. If $k = i$, then expression (4–6) reduces to

$V(\text{SAVINGS}) = M$. The present value of an investment in savings thus is just equal to the original investment provided the compounding rate paid by the savings institution is identical to the discounting rate used by an individual in assessing investment value. Clearly, your grandfather would be better advised to place his $15,000 in some type of savings account at the bank or in another savings institution, rather than leaving the principal in a safe-deposit box.

SOME EXTENSIONS

Certain other factors should be mentioned in connection with our valuation framework. First, it should be understood that inflation, though not explicitly reflected in the valuation model of expression (4–1) or (4–3), can play a critical role in determining the true value of an investment asset. While insurance companies and other institutions that must meet fixed dollar claims are much less concerned about inflation, individual investors are quite concerned because inflation may reduce their future levels of consumption. It is not the dollar benefits themselves that lead to satisfaction by individual investors, but rather the enjoyment of products and services that are consumed, the enrichment of education, the adventure of travel, or the fulfillment of building an estate for one's heirs. All of this is dependent on what can be obtained or purchased with dollars. For many decades, we have witnessed an increase in price levels and hence a decrease in the purchasing power of a dollar. This trend likely will continue. An essential attribute, which should be considered for any investment asset being contemplated, is the ability of that asset to protect against future inflation. Your grandfather will most certainly lose purchasing power in addition to the loss previously identified if he leaves his wealth of $15,000 in a safe-deposit box. The fixed interest earned on his wealth, if placed in a savings account, will provide him a measure of protection against inflation, although his real return will likely be reduced as a result of inflation. Unfortunately, those assets such as common stock and real estate, which historically have provided the best protection against inflation, tend to be more risky assets than those that provide less inflation protection.

Second, taxes thus far have not been explicitly reflected in the valuation model, even though taxability was identified as an investment attribute in Chapter 1. Certainly, decisions made in the process of investing should reflect the taxes associated with all future cash benefits. If future cash benefits to an individual take the form of interest or dividend income, they are taxed at the individual's regular income rate. One exception to this is that the first $100 of dividend income (or $200 for a married couple) is tax-exempt. The final cash benefit may also include a capital gain in many instances. Capital gains to an individual are taxed at half the regular income rate, but not to exceed the maximum rate of 35%.

Because of the complexities of the tax laws, and because taxes affect individuals differently depending on their income and family situations, it is a common practice not to include taxes in discussions of valuation models. However, if future cash benefits are adjusted for taxes, then the discount rate to be used in the valuation must also be adjusted. For example, the interest rate paid on a savings account, if taken as the time value of money, would have to be reduced because interest payments on savings are taxed as regular income. In other words, an *after-tax* discount rate will always be less than the corresponding *before-tax discount* rate for a given investment opportunity. When adjustments for taxes are made both to future cash benefits and to the discount rate that appears in our valuation framework the resulting effect on investment value will not be very large, particularly for security investments. For these reasons, we shall continue our discussion of investment valuation on a before-tax basis. For certain types of tax-sheltered investments, however, the influence of taxes is so significant that it cannot be ignored. Our discussion of tax-sheltered investments in Chapter 7 is necessarily on an after-tax basis.

Third, it is important to provide a link between the valuation framework developed here and the portfolio perspective introduced in Chapter 3. Our convergence assumption is that market price will move toward investment value over time. The return on an investment asset should reflect this adjustment toward investment value as well as changes in investment value. In order to obtain a precise measure of the return expected from an investment asset, it is necessary to specify the length of the adjustment period. To illustrate, we recall the three-year calculation for Able Manufacturing, which resulted in an investment value of $5.84 per share. Because this exceeded the current market price of $4.50, we judged that common stock to be undervalued.

Assuming that market price adjusts to the level of investment in one year, then the percentage price appreciation would be

$$(\$5.84 - \$4.50)/\$4.50 = 29.8\%.$$

A two-year adjustment would give an approximate percentage appreciation of $29.8\%/2 = 14.9\%$. The general expression for annual percentage price appreciation is $(V - P)/nP$ where V is investment value, P is current price, and n is the length of the adjustment period in years. Expected percentage dividend yield would have to be added to percentage price appreciation in order to obtain a measure of total expected return to the investor.

An alternative method of measuring expected return from an investment asset can be obtained from our valuation framework. We substitute current market price in expression (4–3) as follows:

$$P = \sum_{t=1}^{T} \frac{B_t}{(1 + k)^t} \tag{4-7}$$

and solve for that annual discount rate (k) that makes the discounted present value of the future benefits just equal to the current market price. The discount rate k can be used as an estimate of return R_j for an investment asset. By repeating the calculation of k for a range of estimates of future cash benefits, one obtains a range of outcomes. This leads directly to estimates of expected return E_j and standard deviation of return S_j.

Calculating k requires a trial-and-error technique. Because that technique will be illustrated in the next chapter, we simply indicate here that $k = 16\%$ for the three-year horizon of Able Manufacturing. This can be shown as follows

Period	Benefit, B_t	Weight, α_t	Weighted benefit, $\alpha_t B_t$
1	$0.30	0.862	$0.259
2	0.30	0.743	0.223
3	6.30	0.641	4.038
Total	$V = \sum_{t=1}^{3} \alpha_t B_t$		$4.520

CAPITAL MARKET THEORY

We end our discussion of a framework for valuation with brief mention of *capital market theory*, a concept that has received considerable attention in the last few years. Capital market theory indicates the relationship that should exist in equilibrium between the expected return and risk of every investment asset and portfolio, under a number of assumptions such as perfect capital markets, agreement on possible returns for each asset, and the ability to borrow and lend at a single risk-free rate. Perfect capital markets are an idealized situation wherein all investors have full information at no cost on all investment assets, and there are no brokerage fees, taxes, or other transaction costs. The theory can be summarized in the following equation.

$$E_j = i + \beta_j[E(R_M) - i] \tag{4-8}$$

where E_j is the expected return on asset j, β_j is the volatility of asset j, $E(R_M)$ is the expected return on the market, and i is the return on a riskless investment. For example, i might be taken as the yield on U.S. Treasury bills or as the interest rate on a savings account. The linear relationship of expression (4–8) between expected return and risk is plotted in Figure 4–2.

Expression (4–8) states that, in equilibrium, the expected return on a risky asset or portfolio is equal to the riskless return plus an additional

FIGURE 4–2
Valuation under capital market theory

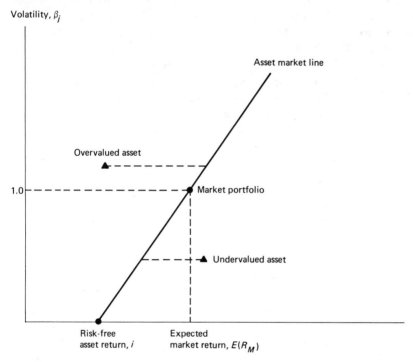

Volatility, β_j

Asset market line

Overvalued asset

1.0 — — — — — — — — — — — Market portfolio

— — — ▲ Undervalued asset

Risk-free asset return, i

Expected market return, $E(R_M)$

Expected return, E_j

return component to compensate the investor for the risk that he faces. The additional return component is the risk of asset or portfolio, as measured by its volatility, multiplied by the excess of expected market return over the riskless return. Volatility that reflects systematic risk is used as the appropriate risk measure because investors are assumed to reduce or eliminate nonsystematic risk by proper diversification as explained in Chapter 3. In other words, expression (4–8) properly reflects a portfolio perspective even though each asset is considered individually.

According to capital market theory, the prices of investment assets adjust to an equilibrium condition wherein all assets lie along an *asset market line* such as in Figure 4–2. The straight line is defined by two points in return-risk space—representing the riskless asset and the market portfolio. The slope of the asset market line is just equal to the excess market return, $E(R_M) - i$, and thus the slope will vary as expectations for market return are changed by various economic developments.

Economic equilibrium cannot exist at all times and thus disequilibria occur. If the expected return and volatility of a particular asset place it to the left of the asset market line, it is said to be overvalued since, at its particular risk level, expected return is less than that predicted by capital market theory for that level of systematic risk. Undervalued assets would appear to the right of the asset market line by similar reasoning. Extent of the disequilibrium in each case is indicated by the horizontal distance from the point to the asset market line.

To illustrate the construction of an asset market line and the valuation of securities within the context of such a relationship, we recall the diversification example of Chapter 3. The relevant parameters for the three common stocks and the market were as follows

	Expected return	Volatility
Growth Industries.	6.9%	0.773
Handy Electronics	8.8%	1.334
Ideal Markets	7.8%	1.100
Market	7.0%	1.000

Assume also that the riskless return is observed to be 4%. With this information, the asset market line is defined in Figure 4–3 by the riskless asset and the market portfolio. The three common stocks are plotted appropriately, and we see that Handy Electronics is slightly overvalued, while Ideal Markets is slightly undervalued. Growth Industries, on the other hand, has an expected return almost 3% greater than the expected return that the asset market line predicts for a risk level of 0.773 and is thus considerably undervalued. In order to reduce its expected return by 3% and thus reach equilibrium, the market price of Growth Industries would have to increase significantly.

The capital market concept of valuation is consistent with the discounted present value framework presented in this chapter, even though capital market theory is in essence a one-period model and even though it is based on a macro-view of market equilibrium. The asset market line can be used to compare a series of assets being considered for inclusion in a portfolio. It can also be used as a means of better understanding the relative risk of those assets. The concept of capital markets is indeed a powerful theory that leads to useful propositions about the process of investing. However, because it is an advanced topic and

FIGURE 4–3
Illustration of valuation under capital market theory

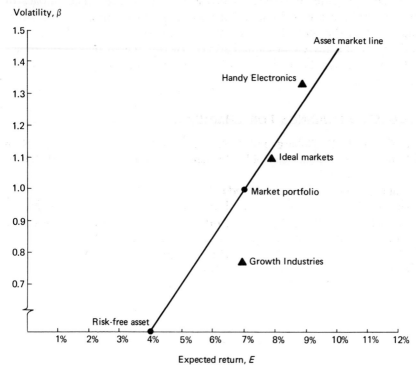

Volatility, β

also because it awaits further empirical justification, we shall continue in subsequent chapters to focus on valuation using the discounted present value framework, which has been discussed here in considerably greater detail.

SUMMARY

We have compared several concepts of value including liquidation value, replacement value, book value, investment value, and market value. Investment decisions involve comparisons of investment value with market price to see if the asset in question is overvalued or undervalued. Investment value of an asset is related to the future dollar benefits associated with that asset. Within the framework of a weighted average definition of investment value, the relative weights are the appropriate discount rates, which reflect the time value of money. When future benefits are known with certainty, the discount rate is just equal to the interest rate. Present value techniques both for single sums and annuities were reviewed and illustrated so that the valuation framework could be implemented. The valuation framework was applied first to investment in cash and then to investment in savings. The impact of inflation and taxes was discussed as was the relationship of the valuation framework to the portfolio perspective presented in the previous chapter. This involved a review of capital market theory, which relates the return and risk of assets and portfolios under conditions of economic equilibrium.

SUGGESTED READINGS FOR CHAPTER 4

J. B. Cohen, E. D. Zinbarg, and A. Ziekel. *Investment Analysis and Portfolio Management* (Homewood, Ill.: Richard D. Irwin, Inc., revised edition, 1973), Chapter 5.

F. Amling. *Investments: An Introduction to Analysis and Management* (Englewood Cliffs, N.J.: Prentice-Hall, Inc., second edition, 1970), Chapter 7.

H. A. Latane and D. L. Tuttle. *Security Analysis and Portfolio Management* (New York: Ronald Press Company, 1970), Chapters 10–13.

W. F. Sharpe. *Portfolio Theory and Capital Markets* (New York: McGraw-Hill Book Company, Inc., 1970), Part II.

5

Characteristics and valuation of bonds

ORGANIZATIONS within the private and public sectors arrange long-term financing by selling their securities to both individual and institutional investors. Depending on the nature of the securities which they purchase, these individual and institutional investors, in turn, become either creditors or owners. The percentage holdings of bonds and stocks in three types of institutional portfolios are as follows:

Investment Asset	Commercial bank trust departments	Life insurance companies	Investment companies
Cash & equivalents	2.1%	–	7.9%
Government bonds	11.7	5.4%	–
Corporate bonds	13.4	35.3	7.5
Common & preferred stock	66.6	7.4	84.6
Other	6.2	51.9	–
Totals	100.0%	100.0%	100.0%

Preferred and common stock, which represent the financing provided by owners and which are more popular in the portfolios of individuals and also investment companies, are discussed in the next chapter. Of interest here are government and corporate bonds, which represent the financing provided by creditors. The investment characteristics of bonds are identified, relevant factors in appraising bonds are discussed, and the valuation framework of the preceding chapter is applied to different types of bonds.

71

CHARACTERISTICS OF GOVERNMENT BONDS

One possible classification of bonds is according to the nature of the issuing organization. Government bonds are issued by the federal government, by various federal agencies, by states, and by state-created municipal organizations. Investors in the United States also may select from bonds issued by international organizations, foreign governments, and foreign municipalities.

United States government bonds

The Treasury of the United States and certain agencies of the U.S. Government issue bonds to raise funds from the public for a variety of purposes. The securities differ in maturity, method of paying interest, and yield. Income on all United States Treasury obligations is subject to federal income taxes but is exempt from state income taxes. Issues of the United States Treasury are grouped into two general categories: marketable and nonmarketable debt.

The *marketable debt* includes treasury bills, treasury certificates, treasury notes, and treasury bonds. *Treasury bills* are sold by auction at a discount from face amount. Each week, the Treasury auctions three-month and six-month bills, and once a month it auctions nine-month and one-year bills. Treasury bills have no coupon rate or "promised" interest payment. Rather a rate of return is earned on the difference between the purchase price, say $985, and the full $1,000 that is recovered by the investor at maturity. *Treasury certificates* are issued with maturities of one year and with a single interest coupon attached, while *treasury notes* are issued with maturities up to five years and have interest coupons attached. *Treasury bonds* are issued with longer maturities and also have interest coupon attached.

The most important *nonmarketable debt* issues of the U.S. Treasury are Series E and Series H savings bonds. Bonds in both series are issued in registered form and are nontransferable. A bondholder may liquidate his investment prior to maturity by turning the bond in for a sum of money preestablished by the terms of the bond. Liquidation prior to maturity necessitates accepting a lower rate of interest during the period of investment. Series E bonds are offered at 75 percent of par and mature in seven years, while Series H bonds are offered at par and mature in ten years.

United States agency bonds

Bonds are also issued by various agencies of the United States Government in order to finance public programs. Bonds of the Federal National

Mortgage Association provide funds for large-scale rental projects. Proceeds from the sale of Federal Home Loan Bank bonds ultimately become mortgage loans to individuals. Bonds of the Federal Intermediate Credit Bank provide a source of intermediate credit to farmers, while bonds of the Federal Land Bank become long-term loans to farmers. U.S. Agency bonds are ranked almost as highly as direct U.S. Treasury issues.

International bonds

At the international level, bonds of the International Bank for Reconstruction and Development (World Bank) generate funds for use in development projects in the emerging countries of the world. Because the United States has a pledge to guarantee World Bank bonds up to a limit determined as a multiple of the United States' paid-in capital to the Bank, and because the total bonded indebtedness of the World Bank does not exceed the amount of this guarantee, World Bank bonds are regarded as equivalent in quality to bonds of other agencies enjoying a U.S. government guarantee. In addition, World Bank bonds are similarly guaranteed by all other member countries. World Bank bonds are available in a variety of currency denominations, permitting investors to hold not only dollar obligations, but others, such as German marks and Swiss francs, which preserve their purchasing power at such times as the U.S. dollar is devalued against stronger world currencies. Also at the international level are bonds issued by foreign governments. For example, the governments of Australia, Japan, Mexico, Norway, and other countries have sold dollar-denominated bonds in the United States. Bonds are also sold by foreign municipalities such as the city of Tokyo.

State and municipal bonds

State and municipal governments sell bonds to finance the roads, utilities, schools, sewers, libraries, and police and fire stations needed by a growing and more service-seeking population. State bonds are, of course, issued by the governments of the fifty states. Municipal securities are issued by regularly constituted subdivisions of states, such as cities and townships, or by bodies created for specific purposes, such as school districts, flood control districts, or public authorities such as the Port of New York Authority or the Ohio Turnpike Commission.

State and municipal bonds are of three general types. *General obligation bonds* are full faith and credit obligations of the taxpayers of the issuing authority, and that authority is obligated to levy sufficient taxes to service (pay interest and repay principal on) the issue. *Revenue bonds* are used to finance revenue-producing projects, such as municipal toll roads and bridges and airports. Service on revenue bonds depends upon the revenue-generating potential of the project, and the bonds may go into default unless the project in fact generates sufficient revenue. In rare instances, revenue bonds may also be guaranteed by a general obligation to levy taxes. *Assessment bonds* are issued to finance improvements related to specific properties such as storm sewers along a specific road, or parking lots within a specific business community. Funds to service these bonds are derived from assessments against the benefited property owners, and a failure to pay the assessment may be grounds for the public authority to legally attach (take title to) and sell the property at a public tax-delinquency sale. Assessment bonds are not normally backed by a general taxing obligation.

Because revenue for servicing municipal bonds tends to be received annually from taxes, assessments, or operating revenues of a project, such bonds are most frequently sold in serial form. With *serial bonds,* a portion of the issue matures at stated intervals during the life of the issue, so that the entire issue is retired in equal annual or semiannual installments over the life of the issue.

Interest payments received on municipal bonds are exempt from federal income tax and may be exempt from state income taxes in certain circumstances. For this reason, municipal bonds are desired investments for individuals in high tax brackets and for corporations (such as fire and casualty insurance companies) that are fully exposed to corporate income taxes. If, for example, a taxpayer in a 60% tax bracket is choosing between a corporate bond yielding 8% and a equally risky municipal bond yielding 6%, he should logically select the municipal bond. After taxes, he would retain only $(8.0\%)(1 - 0.60) = 3.2\%$ on the corporate bond, but he would keep the full 6% earned on the municipal bond.

One might presume that equally risky municipal and nonmunicipal bonds would have the same yield; in the above example one might think that the municipal bond should also sell to yield 8%. This is not true, however, because the tax-free nature of interest received on municipal bonds enhances their value and so causes the market yield to be less than the yield on comparable corporate issues. This lowers the costs of the municipal debt to the taxpayers of the community that issued it. For this reason, institutions that do not pay taxes, such as pension funds, should never buy municipal bonds. Such institutions can earn more at no increase in risk by purchasing equally risky corporate bonds. A clear example of poor financial logic would be a situation where the pension fund of a municipality "loyally" bought bonds of its own municipality, thus sacrificing a degree of financial well-being for the employees whose well-being it should be serving.

As will be further explained later, the yield on any bond (except treasury bills) consists not only of the interest received but also of any difference between purchase price and principal repayment at maturity. To the extent that yield to maturity on a municipal bond includes appreciation between purchase price and principal repayment, that portion of the yield is fully taxable, usually at capital gains tax rates.

CHARACTERISTICS OF CORPORATE BONDS

Corporations within the private sector differ from governmental units in that they offer both bonds and stocks to prospective investors. As compared to governmental bonds, *corporate bonds* are available in a wider spectrum of possibilities of expected return, risk, and other terms of the agreement. A major reason for this is that corporations differ greatly in their ability to generate adequate cash flow to cover both interest payments and the obligation to repay principal on their bonds.

Because debt financing represents a legal obligation on the part of the corporation issuing the bonds, all relevant investment characteristics of the issue are clearly specified in a lending agreement called a *bond indenture*. A corporate trustee, which is typically a commercial bank trust department, represents the collective well-being of all bondholders of the corporation. The indenture covers several important topics. First, the borrowing corporation promises to repay the principal at maturity— which is a specified date in the future. In some instances, principal is repaid over time through a series of *sinking fund* payments. Sinking fund retirement differs from the serial maturity of municipal bonds in that bonds called for retirement via the sinking fund are chosen randomly; thus the investor is uncertain about maturity at the time of purchase. And while serial retirement of municipal bonds is mandatory, sinking fund payments on corporate bonds may be strictly mandatory, or may be mandatory only if adequate funds are earned by the issuing corporation.

Second, the rate and timing of interest payments is indicated in the bond indenture. Third, any particular property that is pledged by the issuer of the bonds as security for the debt is identified. Fourth, a callability feature is explained if one exists. *Callability* is an option on the part of the issuer to retire the bonds prior to maturity, typically at some premium above the maturity amount of the principal. Such premiums gradually decline over the life of the bond. A fifth feature, which pertains to only a small number of bond issues, is *convertibility,* which gives the investor the option to convert each bond that he holds into a specified number of shares of common stock of the same corporation. Convertibility is thus an attribute that allows an investor to switch from being a creditor to being an owner of the issuing corporation. A *straight bond* is one that is not convertible, although it may be callable.

Corporate bonds possess a number of other features that may be of interest to specific investors. Virtually all corporate bonds are issued with a face amount or *par value* of $1,000, which is the amount that must be returned to the bondholder at maturity. The bond will also have a *coupon rate* indicating the interest that must be paid to the bondholder annually. The coupon rate, also sometimes called the *nominal yield*, is multiplied by the par value of the bond to determine the actual dollar interest payment. Although the coupon rate is expressed as an annual rate, most interest payments are made every six months. Thus a 6% coupon rate on a $1,000 par value bond provides in fact for the payment of 3% or $30 every six months.

Corporate bonds may be issued in either bearer or registered form. *Bearer bonds*, which are most common, have no name on the certificate. Anyone holding the certificate can sell it or redeem it when due. Bearer bonds tend to be preferred because delivery following a sale is simple; the seller simply hands the bond over to the buyer. Bearer bonds also make excellent collateral against loans because in the event of default the lending institutions find it easy to sell the collateral immediately with no question as to title. Bearer bonds have coupons attached, which are in effect predated checks for each semiannual interest payment obligation. To receive interest, the holder clips the coupon from the certificate and presents it at his bank for collection. Since bearer bonds are generally issued in $1,000 denominations, an individual or institution purchasing $100,000 worth of a particular issue will in fact receive one hundred certificates.

Registered bonds are sometimes issued to alleviate the physical problem of handling large numbers of certificates when large sums are invested. The owner's name is recorded on the face of the registered bond, which may be issued in any denomination multiple of $1,000. The issuing corporation maintains record books of bondholders, and checks for interest payments are mailed to each bondholder. If the registered bondholder sells the bond, the certificate must be returned to a transfer agent, who will cancel it and issue a new certificate in the name of the new owner. The delay in this process lessens the attractiveness of registered bonds when immediate sale or loan collateral is needed.

Corporate bonds are issued in a variety of other types. *Debentures* are debt obligations backed solely by the general credit of the issuing corporation, unsecured by any pledge of real property. *Mortgage bonds*, by comparison, are backed by a mortgage or lien on real property. *Collateral trust bonds* are backed by the deposit of collateral, usually in the form of securities in other corporations, with a trustee. *Equipment trust certificates* are backed by a lien or claim on equipment or machinery, with legal title to the equipment held by the trustee until the debt is paid in full. Equipment trust certificates are commonly used by railroads to finance their rolling stock (i.e., railroad cars). *Guaranteed bonds* are backed by the promise of a company other than the issuer to make principal or interest payments in case the issuing corporation defaults. Frequently a parent corporation provides a guarantee for bonds issued by its incorporated subsidiaries. A *subordinated bond* is one wherein the bond holders' claim to principal recovery in the event of bankruptcy of the issuer is subordinated to the claims of all other creditors. Only if liquidation proceeds are sufficient first to repay all general creditors in full will the subordinated bondholder receive any funds. Subordinated bonds are frequently issued as *subordinated income debentures,* which means that bondholders also possess weakened claims to interest payments. Interest on such bonds is paid only if earned by the corporation, and failure to pay interest when not earned is not considered an act of default.

BOND QUOTATIONS

Bond prices are usually quoted in points, with one point equal to $10. This is the same as saying that bond prices are expressed as a percentage of par, but without use of the percent mark. Fractions typically indicate eighths of a point. Thus, a bond selling at 105⅜ is in fact selling at $1,053.75 per bond. The expression "Wabash 4s 81 @ 70½" indicates that Wabash Railroad bonds with a 4% coupon and maturing in 1981 are currently selling at $705 each.

Bonds are usually priced "plus accrued interest" or "with interest." The buyer pays the indicated bond price plus a sum of money equal to the accrued interest from the last interest date to the date of trade. The buyer is reimbursed at the next interest date, when he collects on the coupon for the entire period, part of which collection is to reimburse him for his payment to the bond seller and part of which is the interest he has earned during the portion of the interest period that he actually invested in the bond. Income bonds, adjustment bonds, or bonds that are in default are traded "flat." Because there is no assurance that interest will be paid, they are traded at the indicated price, but without accrued interest. Bonds traded flat often bear the notation "f" in price quotations in newspapers.

The extent of published bond quotations depends on the newspaper or source in which the quotations appear. Quotations for corporation bonds listed on the New York Stock Exchange typically include the daily high, daily low, and daily closing prices, as well as the price range for the year to date. Also included is the daily volume of bonds traded. Quotations of government and agency bonds usually include bid and asked prices. The *bid* price is that at which dealers are currently offering to buy bonds. The *asked* price is that at which dealers are currently offering to sell bonds. For example, a certain U.S. Treasury note is quoted at 100.2 bid and 100.6 asking. The numbers following the decimal point indicate thirty-seconds of a full point. Hence, a note can be purchased for $1,001.87½ or sold for $1,000.62½. The spread between the bid and asked quotations represents the profit or markup received by the bond dealer for buying and reselling the bond.

FACTORS IN APPRAISING BONDS

Unlike the case of common stock, where there is no upper limit on the return that may be realized, the maximum return from an investment in bonds if held to maturity is fixed at the time of purchase. This is because both interest and principal for bonds are fixed-amount legal obligations with a specified schedule for payment. Although the probability that interest and principal payments will be made on schedule are quite high for governments and also for many firms, there is no guarantee. This means that the "expected" return (or yield) on a bond will always be somewhat less than the maximum return, which reflects the purchase price and all interest and principal payments to be received by the investor. In appraising bonds for possible inclusion in a portfolio, therefore, the investor should consider a variety of different factors in determining the ability of an issuing firm or government to make all interest and principal payments. We now review certain factors pertaining to investing in corporate bonds. More detailed analyses of securities are presented in Part III of this book.

First, potential investors should become familiar with the nature of the issuing firm, its products, and the markets for these products. Second, there should be an awareness of both current and projected economic conditions, and how various monetary and fiscal policies are likely to influence, if at all, the earnings capability of the firm. Such analyses should provide the basis for projecting the future earnings of the firm as well as the degree of uncertainty inherent in such projections. This degree of uncertainty may be viewed as a measure of the *business risk* associated with the issuing firm.

Third, the investor should ascertain how the capital structure of the firm is likely to affect the relative chances that the creditors and owners of the firm will receive returns on their respective investments. As the amount of debt financing (bonds) increases relative to the amount of equity financing (stocks) within a firm, the level of fixed-income interest (and possibly principal) payments on the bonds necessarily increases. *Financial risk* pertains to the uncertainty of both creditors and owners receiving a return on their investment in the firm. The investor can measure the influence of capital structure by calculating certain debt-equity and coverage ratios. Debt-equity ratios measure the capital structure of the firm. Coverage ratios reveal how many times the interest payments—or alternatively, all fixed obligations, including interest, sinking fund, and lease payments—are earned by the firm. And in addition to calculating coverage ratios based on current financial statements, it is also useful to calculate them based on assumptions of business recession. In other words, how many times would a firm earn its fixed obligations in the event of a serious business downturn?

To illustrate the calculation of such ratios, consider the balance sheet and income statement of Goody Restaurants Corporation, which is a growing chain of family restaurants located in the western United States. The 6% debentures of Goody Restaurants pay interest semiannually and mature in eight years.

GOODY RESTAURANTS CORPORATION
Balance Sheet
December 31, 1973

Assets		*Liabilities and equity*	
Cash	$ 5,400,000	Accounts payable	$ 7,900,000
Accounts receivable	5,900,000	Bank loans payable	1,400,000
Inventory	2,100,000	Other accruals	6,500,000
Net fixed assets	56,700,000	Bonds (6% Debenture)	15,000,000
Total	$70,100,000	Common stock ($1 par)	6,200,000
		Paid-in capital	9,300,000
		Retained earnings	23,800,000
		Total	$70,100,000

GOODY RESTAURANTS CORPORATION
Income Statement
Year ended December 31, 1973

Net sales		$79,300,000
Cost of sales		44,300,000
Gross profit		$35,000,000
Operating expenses:		
Administrative expenses	$14,100,000	
Interest	1,000,000	
Depreciation	2,100,000	
Rent & lease payments	5,000,000	22,200,000
Net profit before taxes		$12,800,000
Federal income taxes		4,300,000
Net profit after taxes		$ 8,500,000

The safety of Goody Restaurants Corporation bonds can be measured in several ways. For example, the capital structure of Goody Restaurants can be measured by the ratio of long-term debt to equity, or

$$\frac{\text{bond liability}}{\text{common stock + paid-in capital + retained earnings}};$$

from the balance sheet, the value of this ratio is

$$\frac{\$15,000,000}{\$6,200,000 + \$9,300,000 + \$23,800,000} = 38\%.$$

Alternatively, capital structure can be measured by the ratio of long-term debt to long-term financing, or

$$\frac{\text{bond liability}}{\text{bond liability} + \text{common stock} + \text{paid-in capital} + \text{retained ernings}};$$

For Goody Restaurants, this ratio is

$$\frac{\$15,000,000}{\$15,000,000 + \$6,200,000 + \$9,300,000 + \$23,800,000} = 28\%.$$

This means that 28% of the long-term financing of Goody Restaurants is accounted for by their debentures.

To calculate coverage ratios, we use before-tax values from the income statement. We see that the ratio of earnings to interest payments, a ratio called "times interest earned" and calculated as follows:

$$\frac{\text{before-tax profit} + \text{interest}}{\text{interest}},$$

was

$$\frac{\$12,800,000 + \$1,000,000}{\$1,000,000} = 13.8.$$

Note that the $1,000,000 interest expense was added to before-tax net profit before dividing. On the other hand, the ratio of earnings to fixed charges ("times fixed charges earned") is

$$\frac{\text{before-tax profit} + \text{interest} + \text{rent \& lease payments}}{\text{interest} + \text{rent \& lease payments}};$$

or

$$\frac{\$12,800,000 + \$1,000,000 + \$5,000,000}{\$1,000,000 + \$5,000,000} = 3.13.$$

Here, we add rent and lease obligations as well as interest payments, since they are fixed annual obligations. As a result, the coverage of 3.13 times is not nearly as high as the 13.8 times when only interest was included. As such, it represents a more comprehensive measure of financial risk.

Suppose in the event of a serious business downturn, it is anticipated that sales would decrease considerably and net profit before taxes would be approximately $4,100,000. As a result, the fixed charge coverage would drop to

$$\frac{\$4,100,000 + \$1,000,000 + \$5,000,000}{\$1,000,000 + \$5,000,000} = 1.68 \text{ times.}$$

Although this coverage value might be considered rather low, it is here calculated under adverse conditions. For even under the worst conceivable circumstances, Goody Restaurants appears likely to earn enough so that bondholders will be paid on schedule. The coverage ratio thus gives the potential investor a quantitative measure of the risk associated with a corporate bond. We turn now to a closer look at the risk attributes of government and corporate bonds.

RISK AND BOND RATINGS

Our discussion of coverage ratios implies that investing in bonds should not be considered as safe as investing in either cash or savings. In the case of Goody Restaurants, for example, we saw that a serious business downturn could substantially increase the chances of the bondholder not receiving his semiannual interest payments, or of receiving the $1,000 maturity value per bond in eight years. This, of course, is risk. And because the financial capability of corporations and governments to meet their interest and principal obligations differs considerably, there is reason to believe that not all bonds should be considered to have the same level of risk.

To guide individuals and institutions in evaluating potential investments in bonds, various methods for systematically assessing the risk characteristics of bonds have been developed. The two most popular rating systems for bonds are those developed by Moody's Investors Service and Standard & Poor's Corporation. Each system consists of general classes and specific grades within each class. The ratings and meanings of the two systems are as follows:

Moody's Investors Service		Standard & Poor's Corporation	
Rating	*Meaning*	*Rating*	*Meaning*
Aaa	Best quality	AAA	Highest grade
Aa	High quality	AA	High grade
A	Higher medium quality	A	Upper medium quality
Baa	Lower medium quality	BBB	Medium grade
Ba	Possess speculative elements	BB	Lower medium grade
B	Lack characteristics of desirable investment	B	Speculative
Caa	Poor standing	CCC CC	Outright speculations
Ca	Speculative in a high degree		
C	Extremely poor prospects	C	Income bonds on which no interest is being paid
		DDD DD D	In default, with rating indicating relative salvage value

We see that A-ratings pertain to bonds considered to be of highest investment quality; B-ratings to bonds judged to be of lower investment quality; C-ratings to bonds felt to be speculative. Standard & Poor's also uses D-ratings for those bonds that are in default.

Bond ratings are based on statistical tests of various financial data followed by a comprehensive interpretation of these tests as they pertain to a particular company and industry. Included among the financial data considered are depreciation and depletion policies, operating and selling costs, research expenditures, asset valuation methods, and so forth. The statistical test results are compared with those of bonds in the same industry or in the same general risk class. Characteristics of the bond such as sinking fund provisions, clauses pertaining to further asset acquisitions, restrictions on further debt, constraints on dividend payments, and restrictions on management compensation also are given meticulous attention. Finally, subjective factors such as management capability, technological progress in the industry, and overall economic projections are considered. From all of this comes a rating for each bond that is based on all available information. The rating expresses the informed judgment of the rating agency of the relative risks of loss to the prospective bondholder and is intended to be of use to both individual and institutional investors.

If the risk of bonds is not uniform, then we would not expect investors to pay the same price for all bonds. Rather, we would expect them to pay higher prices for bonds with higher ratings since the associated risks are less. Put another way, we would expect the yields (expected returns) to be lower for bonds with higher ratings. We can confirm this positive relationship between return and risk by observing the yields and ratings of selected bonds. Using the rating system of Moody's for bonds purchased in June, 1973, the relevant yields were as follows:

Bond and rating	Yield to maturity
U.S. government bonds	6.31%
State & local government (Aaa)	5.00%
State & local government (Baa)	5.50%
Corporate bonds (Aaa)	7.35%
Corporate bonds (Baa)	8.12%

We note that government bonds overall are less risky than corporate bonds and thus are priced to have a lower yield to maturity. Likewise, Baa rated bonds are riskier than Aaa bonds and reflect a higher yield to maturity. State and local government bonds have a lower yield than U.S. government bonds because their interest is free from federal income taxation, rather than because they would be considered less risky.

RISK AND THE DISCOUNT RATE

In Chapter 4, we developed a framework for valuation of investment assets. The relative weights assigned to future benefits, assumed to be known with certainty, were made to reflect the price of time. In extending this framework to bonds and stocks and other assets, it is appropriate to adjust the relative weights (i.e., discount rates) to reflect the lack of certainty over the returns to investors. A useful means of expressing the investment value of a risky asset is as follows:

$$V = \sum_{t=1}^{T} \frac{B_t}{(1 + k)^t} \tag{5-1}$$

where, as before, B_t represents the future benefits in period t. But now the discount rate k is intended to reflect *both* the price of time i and a premium for risk r. In other words, the discount rate for risky assets, k, becomes

$$k = i + r \tag{5-2}$$

As the risk of a future benefit increases, we increase r, which automatically increases the value of k used in present value calculations. And we saw in Chapter 4 that increasing the discount rate to reflect greater risk reduces the investment value of the investment asset in question. In applying our present value framework to various corporate or government bonds, we would thus use a higher discount rate for bonds with lower bond ratings, and conversely. Unfortunately, we cannot provide a formula for helping the investor to select an appropriate discount rate for use in calculating the investment value of a bond, or any other asset for that matter. Neither is it comforting to tell him that such capability comes with experience. The truth is simply that selecting a discount rate is a necessary but subjective step in the process of investing. Useful clues come from bond ratings, which we have seen to reflect the risk of the debt issues in question. Useful clues also come from capital market theory, which explicitly relates expected return and risk for investment assets under conditions of equilibrium.

An alternative approach to handling risk is to multiply forecasted cash benefits, B_t, in the numerator of expression (5–1) by a *certainty equivalent* factor, and to use only the risk-free rate i in the denominator for discounting. This serves to separate the price of time from the price of risk. It still requires, however, a subjective estimation of the certainty equivalent factor. To avoid confusion, we shall confine our treatment of risk in valuation to the denominator adjustment in expressions (5–1) and (5–2).

VALUATION OF STRAIGHT BONDS

Straight bonds have already been defined as those that have no convertibility feature. Since the future benefits accruing to a straight bond are a legal obligation, there is no problem in determining the values of B_t for use in the valuation framework. Selecting an appropriate value for the discount rate k is more subjective, but presumably can be done, possibly by looking at bond yields for other debt issues having the same rating. The next step is to show how the investment value of a bond can be determined using expression (5–1). Suppose, for example, that you were considering the purchase of a debenture of Goody Restaurants Corporation, and that you have decided to use 8% as your discount rate. The $1000 maturity value in eight years presents no problem and should be discounted at 8%. The $30 interest payments cannot be discounted at 8%, however, because they are paid semi-annually. The proper procedure is to use a 4% discount rate (one half of 8%), and to double the effective horizon to sixteen periods. That is, we treat the interest payments as a sixteen-period annuity. The total calculation becomes

Period	Benefit, B_t	Weight, α_t	Weighted benefit, $\alpha_t B_t$
1–16 (semiannually)	$ 30	11.652 (4%)	$349.56
8 (annually)	1000	0.540 (8%)	540.00
Total			$889.56

and thus the investment value of the Goody Restaurants debenture is $889.56. The current market price of the debenture is $P = \$926$, and thus the bond must be considered overvalued.

To value an investment asset such as a corporate bond it is always a good idea to test the sensitivity of the resulting investment value to changes in the parameters used in the valuation process. In our illustration of a debenture of Goody Restaurants, the only parameter that is not certain is the discount rate. The following table shows the investment value of that bond, for differing annual discount rates.

Discount rate	Investment value
5%	$1,068.65
6%	1,003.83
7%	944.82
–	926.00 (market price)
8%	889.56
9%	839.02
10%	792.14

From this we see that the Goody Restaurant debenture is undervalued for discount rates of 7% or smaller, and it is overvalued for discount rates of 8% or higher. The wide range for investment value in this illustration again serves to emphasize the importance of selecting the proper discount rate. Normally, the range of possibilities would not be as large as that reflected in our illustration.

BOND YIELDS

The term "yield" is frequently used in connection with investment assets. A popular connotation of yield in connection with common stock is that it has something to do with the dividend income received by the investor. A similar connotation also applies to other types of investment assets. With respect to bonds, yield has a more precise definition—namely, the yield to maturity. Specifically, *yield to maturity* is that particular discount rate for which the present value of all future benefits to the bondholder is just equal to the current market price of the bond. Letting y represent yield to maturity, we can express

$$P = \sum_{t=1}^{T} \frac{B_t}{(1 + y)^t} \tag{5-3}$$

as a definition of yield to maturity for a bond. For a bond that matures in only three years, expression (5–3) can be written as

$$P = B_1/(1 + y) + B_2/(1 + y)^2 + B_3/(1 + y)^3.$$

Notice in this example that B_3 includes the final interest payment and the repayment of principal to the bondholder.

Solving this expression for yield y is not an easy matter. First, we eliminate the fractions as follows

$$P(1 + y)^3 = B_1(1 + y)^2 + B_2(1 + y) + B_3$$

and upon expanding and rearranging, we obtain

$$Py^3 + (3P - B_1)y^2 + (3P - 2B_1 - B_2)y = B_1 + B_2 + B_3 - P$$

which is seen to be a cubic equation in yield y. Unfortunately, there is no straightforward solution of a cubic equation, or of any higher-order equation. In order to solve for yield, therefore, one must resort to a trial-and-error procedure.

To illustrate, suppose a $1,000 maturity bond that pays $70 interest annually sells currently for $850. The equation to be solved for yield y is

$$\$850 = \$70/(1 + y) + \$70/(1 + y)^2 + \$1070/(1 + y)^3$$

where the third-year benefit consists of $70 interest plus the $1,000 principal repayment. First, we try 10% as a discount rate and obtain

Period	Benefit, B_t	Weight, α_t (10%)	Weighted benefit, $\alpha_t B_t$
1.	$ 70	0.909	$ 63.63
2.	70	0.826	57.82
3.	1,070	0.751	803.57
Total.			$925.02

Since the discounted present value $925.02 exceeds the current price of $850, we did not penalize future benefits at a high enough rate. In other words, yield to maturity is greater than 10% for the example bond. Using 20% as a discount rate, we calculate in a similar manner

Period	Benefit, B_t	Weight, α_t (20%)	Weighted benefit, $\alpha_t B_t$
1	$ 70	0.833	$ 58.31
2	70	0.694	48.58
3	1,070	0.579	619.53
Total.			$726.42

This time, the discounted present value is less than the current price of $850 and so the yield must be less than 20%. We must continue to try in an iterative manner as shown in the following summary of our trial-and-error calculations

Discount rate	Discounted present value	Comment
10%	$925.02	Rate too low
20%	726.42	Rate too high
14%	837.47	Rate too high
12%	880.14	Rate too low
13%	858.27	Approximate solution

Although 13% is slightly high, it is close enough to conclude that the yield to maturity for the 3-year bond is approximately 13%. Because this is quite high relative to the typical yields of most bonds, we conclude that the market, in establishing the market price $P = \$850$ for the bond, is judging that particular bond to be risky as a potential investment.

To reiterate, a trial-and-error procedure is usually necessary to find the appropriate discount rate that equates the discounted present value of future benefits to the bondholder with the current market price of the bond. The result is sometimes referred to as the *internal rate of return*. In the case of the Goody Restaurants debenture, we saw that it was undervalued for discount rates of 7% or smaller, but it was overvalued for discount rates of 8% or greater. The yield to maturity for the Goody Restaurant debenture thus must be between 7% and 8%.

We have already seen that yield is directly related to risk; that is, the greater the risk, the greater the yield that is required by investors. Another dimension is seen in the following tabulation, which reflects existing yields for U.S. government securities of different maturity at four points during the past ten years.

Nature of obligation	Sept., 1962	Sept., 1967	Sept., 1972	June, 1973
Three-month Bills.	2.78%	4.42%	4.60%	6.91%
Six-month Bills	2.93	4.96	5.22	6.99
Three- to five-year Notes	3.56	5.40	6.13	6.79
Long-term Bonds	3.94	4.99	5.75	6.31

At any point in time, the pattern of existing yields as related to maturity is referred to as the *term structure of interest rates*. First, we note the considerable change in yields over time. We see further that yields for six-month bills were always greater than those for three-month bills. But for longer maturities, there was no consistent pattern between yield and maturity. A graph of yield versus maturity is known as a *yield curve*. In September, 1972, the yield curve was upward-sloping, but nine months later, in June, 1973, the yield curve was downward-sloping. Such changes in bond yield over time represent an important component of uncertainty to an investor who buys and sells bonds in anticipation of changing yields. If bonds are held to maturity, however, yields are quite certain.

APPROXIMATE YIELD FORMULA

Calculating yield to maturity for a bond is cumbersome because it involves a trial-and-error procedure. Fortunately, it is possible to estimate the approximate yield y' of a bond using the formula

$$y' = \frac{iM + (M - P)/T}{(M + P)/2} \tag{5–4}$$

where for the bond,

$$M = \text{maturity or par value in dollars}$$
$$P = \text{current market price in dollars}$$
$$T = \text{number of years to maturity}$$
$$i = \text{interest rate per year in percentage}$$

In the numerator of expression (5–4), the first component is the dollar interest payment per year, while the second component is the average per-year amortization of the bond discount (if M is greater than P) or bond premium (if P is greater than M). The denominator in expression (5–4) is the average book value of the bond from now until maturity.

To illustrate the use of the approximation technique, consider again the three-year bond of the preceding example. Substituting $M = \$1,000$, $P = \$850$, $i = 7\%$, and $T = 3$ years into expression (5–4) gives

$$y' = \frac{(0.07)(\$1,000) + (\$1,000 - \$850)/3}{(\$1,000 + \$850)/2} = \frac{\$70 + \$50}{\$925} = 12.97\%$$

In this "averaging" procedure, $50 of bond discount gained per year is added to the annual $70 interest receipt, and the $120 sum is divided by $925, the average investment in the bond. The resulting 12.97% is close to the 13% yield obtained by trial-and-error.

Doing a similar calculation for the corporate bond of Goody Restaurants, we let $M = \$1,000$, $P = \$926$, $i = 6\%$, $T = 8$ and thus obtain

$$y' = \frac{(0.06)(\$1,000) + (\$1,000 - \$926)/8}{(\$1,000 + \$926)/2} = 7.19\%$$

as the approximate yield for that particular bond.

BOND TABLES

Although the approximate yield formula is adequate for rough calculation, it would never suffice for calculating the prices at which actual trades must occur. For this purpose, bond traders use "bond value tables," which include market price P for a large number of combinations of coupon rates i, time to maturity T, and yield to maturity y. A maturity value of $M = \$1,000$ is assumed, interest is assumed to be paid semiannually, and market price is expressed as a percentage of par value. Bond tables are based on a computerized trial-and-error solution of the appropriate equation, such as that in expression (5–3).

The particular page of one bond value table that pertains to the debenture of Goody Restaurants is presented as Figure 5–1. As a percentage of maturity value, the current price of the debenture is 92.6. For a coupon rate $i = 6\%$, and $T = 8$ years to maturity, we see from the left column that yield to maturity is between 7.2% and 7.3%. Since 92.6 is about one third of the way between 92.80 (for 7.2%) and 92.23 (for 7.3%), we can interpolate the yield of the Goody Restaurant debenture to be 7.23%. This more precise result is slightly higher than that obtained using the approximate yield formula.

Glancing across the rows and up and down the columns of bond tables, one can rapidly obtain a feeling of sensitivity as to how the different variables involved in bond valuation are interrelated. For example, if the time to maturity for the Goody Restaurant debenture were only six years and three months, the same price of $P = \$926$ would reflect a yield to maturity of 7.5%. The higher yield results from the fact that the gain for $926 to the $1,000 maturity value would be received almost two years earlier.

Familiarity with bond tables and experience with their use allows one more easily to understand the relationship between yields and bond prices. It also allows a better understanding of three different terms that are sometimes confused in discussions of bond investing: nominal yield, yield to maturity, and current yield. *Nominal yield* was defined earlier as simply the annual coupon rate of interest for the particular bond in question. *Yield to maturity* was also defined earlier as that discount rate which relates future benefits to the bondholder to current market price of the bond. *Current yield* is the dollar annual interest

FIGURE 5-1 Sample page of *Expanded Bond Values Tables*

6% YEARS and MONTHS

Yield	6-3	6-6	6-9	7-0	7-3	7-6	7-9	8-0
4.00	110.96	111.35	111.72	112.11	112.47	112.85	113.21	113.58
4.20	109.80	110.15	110.48	110.82	111.14	111.48	111.79	112.12
4.40	108.65	108.96	109.25	109.55	109.83	110.13	110.40	110.69
4.60	107.52	107.79	108.04	108.30	108.54	108.80	109.03	109.28
4.80	106.40	106.63	106.84	107.06	107.27	107.48	107.68	107.89
5.00	105.30	105.49	105.66	105.85	106.01	106.19	106.35	106.53
5.20	104.21	104.36	104.50	104.64	104.77	104.92	105.04	105.18
5.40	103.14	103.25	103.35	103.46	103.55	103.66	103.75	103.86
5.60	102.07	102.15	102.21	102.29	102.35	102.42	102.48	102.55
5.80	101.03	101.07	101.09	101.14	101.16	101.20	101.22	101.27
6.00	99.99	100.00	99.99	100.00	99.99	100.00	99.99	100.00
6.10	99.48	99.47	99.44	99.44	99.41	99.41	99.38	99.37
6.20	98.97	98.94	98.90	98.88	98.83	98.81	98.77	98.75
6.30	98.46	98.42	98.36	98.32	98.26	98.23	98.17	98.14
6.40	97.95	97.90	97.82	97.77	97.70	97.65	97.57	97.53
6.50	97.45	97.38	97.29	97.22	97.13	97.07	96.98	96.92
6.60	96.96	96.87	96.76	96.68	96.57	96.50	96.39	96.32
6.70	96.46	96.36	96.24	96.14	96.02	95.93	95.81	95.72
6.80	95.97	95.85	95.71	95.60	95.47	95.36	95.23	95.13
6.90	95.48	95.35	95.20	95.07	94.92	94.80	94.65	94.54
7.00	94.99	94.85	94.68	94.54	94.38	94.24	94.08	93.95
7.10	94.51	94.35	94.17	94.01	93.84	93.69	93.52	93.37
7.20	94.03	93.86	93.66	93.49	93.30	93.14	92.95	92.80
7.30	93.55	93.37	93.15	92.97	92.77	92.59	92.39	92.23
7.40	93.08	92.88	92.65	92.46	92.24	92.05	91.84	91.66
7.50	92.61	92.39	92.15	91.95	91.71	91.51	91.29	91.10
7.60	92.14	91.91	91.66	91.44	91.19	90.98	90.74	90.54
7.70	91.68	91.43	91.17	90.93	90.67	90.45	90.20	89.99
7.80	91.21	90.96	90.68	90.43	90.16	89.92	89.66	89.44
7.90	90.75	90.48	90.19	89.93	89.65	89.40	89.13	88.89
8.00	90.30	90.01	89.71	89.44	89.14	88.88	88.60	88.35
8.10	89.84	89.55	89.23	88.95	88.64	88.37	88.07	87.81
8.20	89.39	89.08	88.75	88.46	88.14	87.85	87.55	87.28
8.30	88.94	88.62	88.28	87.97	87.64	87.35	87.03	86.75
8.40	88.50	88.16	87.81	87.49	87.15	86.84	86.51	86.22
8.50	88.05	87.71	87.34	87.01	86.66	86.34	86.00	85.70
8.60	87.61	87.26	86.88	86.54	86.17	85.84	85.49	85.18
8.70	87.18	86.81	86.42	86.06	85.69	85.35	84.99	84.67
8.80	86.74	86.36	85.96	85.59	85.21	84.86	84.49	84.16
8.90	86.31	85.92	85.50	85.13	84.73	84.37	83.99	83.65
9.00	85.88	85.48	85.05	84.67	84.26	83.89	83.50	83.15
9.10	85.45	85.04	84.60	84.21	83.79	83.41	83.01	82.65
9.20	85.03	84.60	84.15	83.75	83.32	82.93	82.52	82.16
9.30	84.60	84.17	83.71	83.30	82.86	82.46	82.04	81.66
9.40	84.18	83.74	83.27	82.84	82.40	81.99	81.56	81.18
9.50	83.77	83.31	82.83	82.40	81.94	81.52	81.09	80.69
9.60	83.35	82.89	82.40	81.95	81.48	81.06	80.61	80.21
9.70	82.94	82.46	81.96	81.51	81.03	80.60	80.14	79.73
9.80	82.53	82.04	81.53	81.07	80.58	80.14	79.68	79.26
9.90	82.12	81.63	81.11	80.64	80.14	79.69	79.22	78.79
10.00	81.72	81.21	80.68	80.20	79.70	79.24	78.76	78.32
10.20	80.92	80.33	79.84	79.35	78.82	78.35	77.85	77.40
10.40	80.12	79.58	79.01	78.50	77.96	77.47	76.96	76.49
10.60	79.34	78.78	78.20	77.66	77.11	76.60	76.07	75.60
10.80	78.57	77.99	77.39	76.84	76.27	75.75	75.21	74.71
11.00	77.80	77.21	76.59	76.03	75.44	74.91	74.35	73.84
11.20	77.05	76.44	75.80	75.22	74.62	74.07	73.50	72.99
11.40	76.30	75.67	75.02	74.43	73.81	73.26	72.67	72.14
11.60	75.56	74.92	74.25	73.65	73.02	72.45	71.85	71.31
11.80	74.83	74.18	73.50	72.88	72.23	71.65	71.04	70.49
12.00	74.11	73.44	72.75	72.12	71.46	70.86	70.24	69.68

Source: Financial Publishing Company, 1970

paid to the bondholder divided by current market price. These three different concepts of yield are identical only when the particular bond is selling at par value.

This is illustrated in Figure 5–2 for a 6% coupon bond maturing in

FIGURE 5–2
Yield response to changing bond prices (6% coupon bond maturing in 25 years)

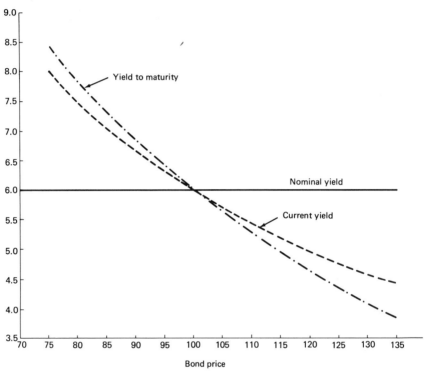

25 years. We thus can see that for bond prices above 100, yield to maturity is less than current yield. But for bond prices below 100, yield to maturity is greater than current yield. Investors concerned with immediate cash benefits from an investment should be well aware of current yield, while investors concerned with total return over an extended time should focus on yield to maturity.

VALUATION AND CALLABILITY

Callability is an attribute of bonds that complicates their valuation. As mentioned before, callability is an option on the part of the issuing firm to terminate the legal contract of the bond obligation prior to the scheduled maturity. If callability exists, management of the firm may exercise this option in order to satisfy sinking fund requirements or to change the capital structure of the firm. More frequently, callability is used for refunding purposes—namely, the firm replaces an existing bond issue with a new issue bearing a lower interest rate. Because the investor must then reinvest his funds at a lower rate than he had been receiving, called bonds usually are redeemed at a premium above their maturity value. In some cases, the callability feature does not exist for some time—say, several years—after issue. This is referred to as *deferred callability*.

From the viewpoint of the issuing firm, callability would be used in refunding only if the discounted present value of annual savings in interest payments to bondholders would exceed the call premium on the old bond plus the issuing costs of the new issue. While a firm would logically always want to have the callability option, the investor should view that feature as another element of uncertainty associated with his investment, and may thus insist upon a higher coupon rate.

Valuation of bonds that might be called necessarily adds a complication to the yield-to-maturity calculation, since the yield to maturity may not be received because the bond is called prior to maturity. One useful procedure is to calculate the *yield to call*, in which the higher call price and the shorter maturity are reflected. The yield-to-call calculation can be used two ways. One way is simply to regard it as the lowest assured yield to be earned by the investor. This is appropriate when purchase of a single bond is considered outside of a portfolio context. Another way is to use relative probabilities that the bond will be called as appropriate weights. We can then calculate a weighted average yield expected by the investor. This procedure is appropriate in a portfolio context wherein bonds of many corporations are being purchased, for it is of course impossible for a single bond to yield the weighted average of the yield to maturity and the yield to call.

To illustrate within a portfolio context, suppose that the debentures of Goody Restaurants are callable after four years at a premium of 5%. Suppose further that we believe there is a 75% chance that interest rates will have dropped to 4% by then and the firm will exercise its option to refund with a 4% debenture. There is thus a 25% chance that the 5% debentures will not be called and the 7.23% yield (as calculated above) will pertain. If the 6% debentures are called, however, we assume that the investor receives $1,050 for each bond, which he in turn reinvests in the new issue of 4% debentures of Goody Restaurants. The semiannual interest on the new issue (for each bond initially owned) would be $(\frac{1}{2})(4\%)(\$1,050) = \$21$, and the market value after four more years is assumed to be $1,050. An investment in a Goody Restaurants debenture would thus pay $30 semiannually for the first four years, $21 semi-annually for the next four years, and have an estimated market value of $1,050 at the end of the eight-year horizon. At the current price of $926, we calculate by trial and error a yield to maturity of 7.00%. This yield, which assumes refunding, is lower than the original yield because the call premium does not fully compensate the bondholder for the lower interest rate that he must accept with the new bond.

The final step is to calculate a weighted average yield as follows

Assumption	Probability	Yield	Weighted yield
Not called	25%	7.23%	1.81%
Called	75%	7.00%	5.25%
Weighted average yield			7.06%

If a higher probability were assigned to the bond's not being called, the weighted average yield would increase, and so forth. The weighted average yield of 7.06% is a summary measure reflecting the two possibilities and their associated probabilities. It is not an "expected yield" since either 7.00% or 7.23% will actually materialize. On the other hand, it is better to use 7.06% as a summary value of yield or to use 7.00% as the minimum yield to be achieved, than simply to ignore the possibility that the Goody Restaurants debentures will be called.

VALUATION AND CONVERTIBILITY

Convertibility is another attribute of bonds that complicates their valuation. In contrast with callability, where the issuing firm has an option to retire debt, the convertible feature is an option given to the bondholder to change his status from bondholder to stockholder— or from creditor to owner. In particular, the bondholder is given the option to convert each bond into a prescribed number of shares of common stock prior to the maturity date of the bond. In some instances, this is a constant number, while in others, it may be a decreasing number of shares over time. The number of shares of common stock is obtained by dividing the $1,000 maturity value of the convertible bond by the conversion price. If the conversion price in a particular instance is $25 per share, then each bond is convertible into $1,000/$25 = 40 shares of common stock.

The purchase price of the bond is also important to the investor in determining his "break-even" common stock price. If he paid $1,100 for the convertible bond mentioned above, for example, then the price of the common stock would have to reach $1,100/40 = $27.50 in order to justify conversion on strictly dollar terms. And if prior to conversion, the stock price grew to $35 per share, the common stock value of the convertible bond would be (40)($35) = $1,400. The convertible bond would not sell below $1,400 in this case, because otherwise investors could purchase the convertible bond, for say $1,200, convert to common shares worth $1,400, and realize an immediate profit of $200.

Purchasing convertible bonds is a popular strategy for many investors. On the one hand, they have the relative safety of initially being a creditor of the firm and receiving fixed interest payments. But because of the convertible feature, they also have a chance to share in the prosperity of the firm via the price appreciation of the common shares. The decision of when to convert from bondholder to stockholder depends on several factors, including the purchase price of the bond, the conversion price, and the value of expected dividends compared to the interest on the bonds. Moreover, most convertible bonds are also callable, and thus in many instances the issuing corporation can force conversion by calling the bonds.

The market price of the convertible bond must necessarily reflect those several features. This is illustrated in Figure 5–3. A convertible bond is purchased for $1,100 at time zero. The value of the bond as a straight debt issue is indicated by the line abc, which moves steadily toward the maturity value of $1,000. Meanwhile, the common stock value of the bond moves along the curve dbef, thus reflecting a steady rate of growth. The investor achieves a break-even position at point e when the common stock value reached his initial investment of $1,100. The combination of straight bond value and common stock value reflected in the heavy kinked curve abef is the minimum market value of the convertible bond, reflecting its dual features of straight debt and common stock.

Because of the flexibility of owning a convertible bond, together with the expectations for common stock growth, the convertible bond would be expected to sell at a premium above this minimum value. This premium is shown as the varying distance between the jagged curve gf and the minimum value, abef. At point f, the firm calls the bonds, thus forcing bondholders to convert to the common shares. From that point on, fh and so forth, the investor is strictly a common stockholder.

Valuation of convertible bonds is more complicated than valuation of straight bonds—even though the basic valuation framework embodied in expression (5–1) still applies. Depending on the length of the investment horizon that is used, the future benefits to an investor include interest payments up to the point of conversion, followed by dividend payments (if there are any), and finally the terminal value of the common shares. In other words, the valuation of convertible bonds is a hybrid process involving both the valuation of bonds and the valuation

94

FIGURE 5–3
Hypothetical price behavior of convertible bond

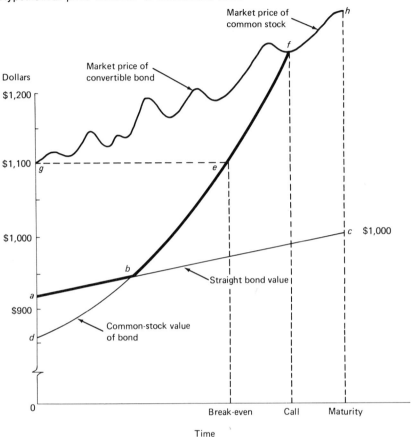

of common stocks. We shall not proceed here since common stock valuation is the subject of the following chapter.

INVESTING IN BONDS

We have seen that there are many characteristics and attributes of government and corporate bonds that should be considered in selecting particular issues for inclusion in the investor's portfolio. While regular income for a particular bond is always an important attribute, the extent of appreciation depends on whether the bond is held to maturity or sold prior to maturity. And because the interest received from municipal bonds is tax-exempt in certain instances, taxability is also an important attribute to many investors. On the negative side, bonds do not protect investors against the loss in purchasing power of the dollar that results from inflation.

Bonds constitute a substantial portion of the total portfolio of many institutional investors. Banks, insurance companies, and pension funds can hold appropriate numbers of bonds that mature at future points in time when funds will be needed. That is, bonds constitute a useful investment asset for portfolios having liquidity requirements that can be forecasted with accuracy. Some institutional investors restrict their bond holdings to issues of only the highest ratings, while other institutional investors prefer to hold bonds with lower ratings in order to receive higher yields. Still other institutions with large bond holdings attempt to diversify over different maturities as well as over different levels of quality.

For individuals and institutional investors that do not have definite liquidity needs in the future, there is still a propensity to hold bonds in many instances. Undoubtedly, two major arguments for doing so include the regularity of interest income and the attempt to reduce overall portfolio risk. Many writers have contended, however, that bonds are at a distinct disadvantage vis-à-vis high quality common stocks, in the presence of continuing inflation. These writers further have argued that, over time, income from high-quality common stocks has exceeded that of bonds. For example, a 7% coupon corporate bond pays more interest in the current year than a public utility common stock yielding a dividend of only 6%. But over the next decade, the dollar payout to common stockholders should increase if the utility grows and prospers, while the dollar payout to bondholders remains constant.

This is not intended as an exhaustive discussion of bonds versus stocks, but rather a reminder that decisions on individual investment assets should always be made within the perspective of the total portfolio. Moreover, it is necessary before proceeding in such a discussion to examine carefully the characteristics, attributes, and valuation of preferred and common stocks. This is the subject of the next chapter.

SUMMARY

Different types of government and corporate bonds have been discussed in terms of their investment characteristics. We also have considered certain factors that influence the ability of an organization to make scheduled interest and principal payments to investors. The degree of risk to an owner of bonds revealed by bond ratings was examined and also the choice of appropriate discount rates for use in bond valuation. It was suggested that the discount rate for any risky asset should reflect both the price of time and the price of risk. The valuation framework was applied to straight bonds, and the sensitivity to choice of discount rate was explored. Calculations of yield to maturity for a bond using bond tables, a trial-and-error procedure, and an approximation formula were explained and illustrated. Extensions of the valuation procedure in the presence of callability and convertibility also were discussed and illustrated. The chapter was concluded with a reminder that investing in bonds should always be considered within the perspective of the total portfolio of investment assets.

SUGGESTED READINGS FOR CHAPTER 5

F. Amling. *Investments: An Introduction to Analysis and Management* (Englewood Cliffs, N.J.: Prentice-Hall, Inc., 1970), Chapters 3–4.

C. D. Ellis. *Institutional Investing* (Homewood, Ill.: Dow Jones-Irwin, Inc., 1971), Chapter 3.

J. C. Francis. *Investments: Analysis and Management* (New York: McGraw-Hill Book Company, Inc., 1972), Chapter 8.

B. Graham, D. L. Dodd, and S. Cottle. *Security Analysis: Principles and Technique*. 4th ed. (New York: McGraw-Hill Book Company, Inc., 1962), Part Three.

H. Levy and M. Sarnat. *Investment and Portfolio Analysis* (New York: John Wiley & Sons, Inc., 1972), Chapter IV.

H. C. Sauvain. *Investment Management*. 4th ed. (Englewood Cliffs, N.J.: Prentice-Hall, Inc., 1973), Chapter 9.

6

Characteristics and valuation of stocks

STOCKS REPRESENT perhaps the most exciting yet perplexing investment asset among those identified in Chapter 1. The basic structure of our free enterprise society rests upon the concept of private ownership of the business organizations that produce and distribute the many commodities and services demanded by individuals, households, other business organizations, and governments. Because the amount of capital needed to finance business organizations is usually in excess of the investable wealth of a single investor, corporations are formed by many investors who pool their investment capital in varying proportions. Corporations issue shares of common and preferred stock, evidenced by engraved certificates as tangible indication of the fractional ownership of each stockholder. The proportions of stocks held by certain institutional investors, relative to those of government and corporate bonds, were indicated at the outset of the previous chapter. The purpose of this chapter is to identify the investment characteristics of preferred and common stock, to discuss the relevant factors in appraising stocks, and to apply once again our valuation framework.

CHARACTERISTICS OF PREFERRED STOCK

We have already seen that the liabilities and owners' equity side of the balance sheet can be divided into two major categories. Liabilities represent debt claims of creditors of the corporation, while owners' equity represents the aggregate investment by those who own the firm. It is possible to categorize total owners' equity further into the ownership of preferred shareholders and the ownership of common shareholders.

An investor should clearly understand both the similarities and the differences between preferred and common stock, even though our valuation framework will be seen to be applicable to both.

Preferred stockholders are a group of owners who have assumed a conservative or cautious position in their ownership relationship with their company. Most preferred stock is issued with a stated par value, often $100, and with a fixed dividend policy expressed as a percentage of this par. The *par value* of a share of stock represents the minimum purchase price an investor must have paid to the corporation at the time the share was first sold. Par value has no relationship to the price of subsequent transactions in those shares. Although the investor cannot purchase a new share from a corporation for less than par, he can pay more. In this case the excess of purchase price over par is recorded in the *paid-in capital* account of the balance sheet. For example, the Columbus and Southern Ohio Electric Company sold cumulative preferred stock during February, 1972, at a price of $102.31 per share. Par value was $100 per share and the dividend rate was 7.52%, or $7.52 per year per share. For every preferred share sold, $100 appeared in the balance sheet as preferred stock, while $2.31 was added to paid-in capital.

In any given year, the $7.52 dividend must be paid on each share of preferred stock before any dividends can be distributed to the common shareholders of Columbus and Southern Ohio Electric Company. It is this priority to dividend payments that gives rise to the "preferred" title. The *cumulative* feature of the preferred issue means that if preferred (and hence common) dividends are not paid in any given year, those omitted or "passed" preferred dividends plus any currently due preferred dividends must be paid in full before any payment of common stock dividends. Although preferred dividends are not a legal obligation in the sense of interest payments for debt, the cumulative feature of preferred stock becomes a constraint causing management to keep paying preferred dividends under all but the most adverse circumstances. Most preferred stock is cumulative, but there are some issues of *noncumulative* preferred stock; if the preferred dividend is not paid on these issues in a given year, that dividend will never be paid.

Some preferred stock has a *participating* feature, granting preferred stockholders the right to share with common shareholders in dividend distributions after a stated rate on the preferred issue has been paid. Most preferred issues are *nonparticipating*, however, meaning that only common shareholders receive a dividend distribution after the stated preferred dividend has been paid. Regardless of the nature of these various features, maintenance of preferred dividend payments is important to management, and preferred stockholders can usually depend upon receiving their stated dividend rate. Another important feature is whether the preferred shares are convertible into common shares at some specified rate of exchange. *Convertibility*, as in the case of corporate bonds, allows the investor to switch from being a preferred type of owner to being a residual common stockholder of the corporation.

Although most preferred stock issues provide the corporation with the option of retiring its preferred stock by calling it in for mandatory retirement at a preestablished price, preferred stock does not have a fixed maturity date as such. This means that preferred stock represents a more or less permanent source of long-term financing, and that the preferred stockholder must rely upon selling his shares in the market to recapture his principal. In the event of either voluntary or involuntary liquidation of the affairs of the corporation, preferred shareholders are legally entitled to the return of the full par value (or some other stated liquidating value) of their shares before common shareholders may receive any liquidating dividend. We see then that preferred stock evidences ownership having preferential treatment over that of common stock both in terms of prior claim to a fixed (but limited) dividend payment and to prior receipt of assets in liquidation. Preferred shareholders also typically are not entitled to vote, although in some instances voting power accrues to the preferred shareholder if preferred dividends are not paid.

On balance, the disadvantages of preferred stock—both to the issuing corporation and the investor—would seem clearly to outweigh the advantages. From the corporate viewpoint, preferred dividends are not deductible before income taxes are calculated, yet they represent a potential constraint to paying dividends to common shareholders. And from the investment viewpoint, preferred stock represents an earlier claim on the earnings and assets of the corporation, but its owners do not participate in the total prosperity of the corporation beyond a fixed level of return. For these reasons, many corporations tend to regard preferred stock as more closely resembling long-term debt, even though preferred stock appears on their balance sheets as part of owners' equity. And even though preferred shares are listed and traded on the various exchanges along with common stock, their prices tend to reflect the pattern of interest rates prevailing in the capital markets at the time, rather than the perceived earnings potential of the corporation. An exception to this occurs for convertible preferred stock, the price of which is often closely related to the price of the corresponding shares.

Why then do we observe so many examples of preferred stock, given that preferred ownership appears to be disadvantageous both to the corporation and to investors? First, many preferred issues date back to the earlier part of this century, when the corporate tax rate was considerably lower than it is today and there was not as great a corporate tax disadvantage to financing via preferred stock. As might be expected, fewer preferred issues appeared as the corporate tax rate increased. As many corporations have become involved in mergers and acquisitions in recent years, however, preferred stock has again become popular, not because of its usual characteristics, but rather because of its use with a convertibility feature. By offering convertible preferred stock with a healthy dividend rate in exchange for the outstanding common stock of another company, an acquiring corporation is able to make the proposed merger more attractive to the shareholder of the company being acquired. These shareholders can be assured of an attractive dividend payment as well as the prospects of benefitting from the merger and future growth of the corporation.

Preferred stock possesses one additional attribute that makes it an attractive holding for an incorporated investor paying U.S. corporate income taxes. United States tax laws provide that only 15% of dividends received by a U.S. corporation from another domestic corporation are taxable as income. If, for example, an insurance company that pays a 48% rate of corporate income tax purchased the preferred share of Columbus and Southern Ohio Electric Company, income taxes would amount to ($7.52)(0.15)(0.48) = $0.54. After taxes, therefore, the insurance company would retain $7.52 − $0.54 = $6.98 of each preferred share dividend. This $6.98 would represent an after-tax return of 6.82% on the $102.31 cost of the share of preferred stock. The insurance company would have to purchase a bond yielding 14.2% in order to retain, after paying a 48% income tax, as much as could be retained from the preferred stock. Quality bonds with yields of this magnitude do not exist at present.

CHARACTERISTICS OF COMMON STOCK

A corporation may or may not choose to issue corporate bonds or preferred stock as part of its total capital structure. No choice exists in the case of common stock, however, for common stock represents the true residual ownership of the corporation. Initial formation of any corporation is necessarily evidenced by common shares, and for many corporations common stock represents the largest single source of long-term financing throughout the life of the firm.

Although *common stock* always appears on the right side of the balance sheet of the corporation, it is only one component of the total investment by the owners of the firm. The other two components are paid-in capital and retained earnings. *Paid-in capital* is the amount paid by investors to the company over and above the par value of the common stock. As in the case of preferred stock, *par value* is the minimum amount that must be paid for each share of common stock purchased. In those instances where the common stock consists of *no-par* shares, a *stated value* is used in place of par value to determine how much of the sales proceeds to include in common stock and paid-in capital, respectively. The sum of common stock and paid-in capital thus represents the aggregate initial contribution of the owners to the corporation.

Retained earnings represent the continuing investment by owners of all earnings generated by the corporation and not distributed as cash dividends. An investor should not make the mistake of believing that investment in common stock is a one-time commitment; instead, it is a continuing investment in the corporation over time. The dollar sum of common stock, paid-in capital, and retained earnings represents, therefore, the total investment of the residual owners of the corporation. That sum is often referred to as the total common stockholders' *equity* or *net worth* in the corporation. *Book value per share* is this dollar equity divided by the number of common shares outstanding. Preferred stock is not considered part of the equity of the common stockholders.

To illustrate these concepts, consider the following balance sheet of Jetway Aviation Corporation, a growing firm within the aerospace industry.

JETWAY AVIATION CORPORATION
Balance Sheet
November 30, 1973

Assets		*Liabilities and equity*	
Cash.	$ 70,000,000	Accounts payable	$185,000,000
Accounts receivable.	120,000,000	Other current liabilities.	230,000,000
Inventory.	400,000,000	Long term debt (6%)	100,000,000
Net fixed assets	380,000,000	Preferred stock (7%)	50,000,000
Total.	$970,000,000	Common stock ($25 par)	250,000,000
		Paid-in capital	30,000,000
		Retained earnings	125,000,000
		Total.	$970,000,000

Observing that the par value per share is $25, we calculate immediately the number of outstanding common shares to be

$$\frac{\$250,000,000}{\$25} = 10,000,000.$$

Assuming for simplicity that common stock has been sold only once during the lifetime of the corporation, we note that the selling price must have been:

$$\frac{\text{common stock} + \text{paid-in capital}}{\text{number of shares outstanding}},$$

or

$$\frac{\$250,000,000 + \$30,000,000}{10,000,000} = \$28 \text{ per share.}$$

The total common equity in the firm is the sum of common stock, paid-in capital, and retained earnings, or

$$\$250,000,000 + \$30,000,000 + \$125,000,000 = \$405,000,000,$$

and thus the book value per share must be

$$\frac{\text{common equity}}{\text{shares outstanding}} = \frac{\$405,000,000}{10,000,000} = \$40.50 \text{ per share.}$$

In pursuing now our discussion of common stock, we are really referring to the total common stockholders' equity in dollars, rather than just the common stock component.

Because we wish to measure some corporate results, such as earnings, on a per-share basis, we are also concerned with several different expressions for the number of shares of stock. Number of shares may be expressed in terms of *authorized stock*, which refers to the maximum number of shares authorized in the corporate charter. A company need not issue all of its authorized shares, but it cannot issue more than have been authorized. *Issued stock* refers to authorized shares that have actually been issued to stockholders in return for invested capital. Sometimes corporations buy back shares of their own stock in the market, which they then hold as *treasury stock*. Treasury stock may be sold for cash, reissued for assets as in the case of a merger, or it may be cancelled, in which case it ceases to be regarded as issued stock. Treasury stock does not possess a vote and does not receive dividends. Issued stock less any treasury stock constitutes *outstanding stock*. Outstanding stock votes and receives dividends, and is therefore the number of shares used for calculating all significant per-share figures for a corporation.

One vital characteristic of each share of common stock is that the owner is entitled to a vote in the management of the corporation. The few votes of small investors in huge corporations may often seem virtually insignificant; investors in small or family-owned corporations may have enough votes to be the major source of influence and power. In either case, the voting privilege of a common shareholder is central to the private ownership of companies within our economic system. The common shareholder is entitled to vote in electing the board of directors of the corporation, and in other matters involving the charter or bylaws of the corporation such as sale of a major portion of the assets, mergers, or dissolution.

The ability of stockholders to vote in such a manner as to influence the affairs of their corporation depends in part on which of two methods of vote counting is used: statutory or cumulative. Under *statutory* (or noncumulative) *voting*, each share of stock is allowed one vote for each vacancy on the board of directors. If a company has a six-man board of directors, a stockholder owning 101 shares out of a total of 700 shares outstanding can cast 101 votes for each of the six openings. Although he casts a total of (101)(6) = 606 votes, no more than 101 can be cast for any single directorship vacancy. A group of stockholders controlling the remaining 700 — 101 = 599 shares can cast their votes for each vacancy and so elect all six directors. In general, any stockholder or group of stockholders owning more than 50% of the outstanding shares can select the entire board of directors. Because existing directors tend to control at least half of all votes through their solicitation of proxies, most boards of directors are self-perpetuating under statutory voting.

Under *cumulative voting*, each share of stock is allowed a number of votes equal to the number of directors to be chosen. However, these votes may be combined into a bloc voted for a single directorship or they may be divided in any way desired. In the above example, the minority stockholder would have 606 votes, which he could cast for a single directorship. The majority stockholders, who have (599)(6) = 3,594 total votes, cannot combine their votes in such a way that they cast over 606 votes for each of the six vacancies. If they should cast exactly 606 votes for five of the vacancies, they would have only 3,594 — (5)(606) = 564 votes remaining for the last vacancy, which would thus go to the minority. The minority, with 606 votes, could elect one representative to the board of directors. In general, cumulative voting allows minority stockholders an opportunity to obtain minority representation on a board of directors.

Another characteristic of common stock ownership, indirectly related to voting rights, is known as the *preemptive right*. If the corporation decides to issue additional common stock, the legal doctrine of preemptive rights requires the corporation to give stock-purchase rights to each existing owner enabling him to purchase enough new common shares to maintain his proportional ownership of the firm. Rights thus are short-term options to purchase shares of common stock at a specified price. They are traded on the organized stock exchanges just as regular common shares. If an investor decides not to exercise his preemptive rights, that investor should sell the rights because they have a market value. Allowing the rights to expire is comparable to losing cash.

Unlike corporate bonds but similar to preferred stock, common stock has no maturity. Morover, there is neither a legal nor an implied obligation on the part of the corporation to pay cash dividends each year. Although the vast majority of large corporations pay dividends, some nevertheless choose to retain all earnings in the corporation. Other corporations vary their dividend payments from year to year depending on the investment opportunities available within the firm.

Apart from dividends, which he may or may not receive, the common shareholder achieves a gain on his investment in the corporation only if the market value of his common stock at the time of sale exceeds the purchase price. For publicly held companies, market value is readily observed in the quoted price of that common stock as it is traded on one of the organized security exchanges or in the over-the-counter markets. For privately held companies, however, the market value of common stock is not so readily observed, and the owner must somehow impute a market value based on the projected earnings of the corporation. In either case, the varying market value of the common shares causes the owner's degree of unrealized appreciation or loss to vary from date to date. This potential variability in price appreciation, coupled with the variability in dividend payments, causes the total return to the common stockholders to be subject to considerable uncertainty. This uncertainty is the reason that common stock is considered to be one of the riskiest and hence most perplexing types of investment assets.

FACTORS IN APPRAISING PREFERRED STOCK

Appraising the preferred stock of a corporation closely parallels an appraisal of corporate bonds. That is, we attempt to determine the extent to which the corporation is able to generate the necessary earnings to provide dividend payments to preferred shareholders. Note, however, that even if there are sufficient earnings to pay the preferred dividends, the corporation is not legally required to pay the dividends. The major distinction is simply that the interest payments on debt, plus any associated sinking fund payment to retire debt, must first be subtracted from available earnings since corporate debt has a higher claim than preferred stock.

To illustrate, we must examine the income statement of Jetway Aviation together with its balance sheet presented earlier in the chapter.

JETWAY AVIATION CORPORATION
Income Statement
Year Ended November 30, 1973

Net sales and other income		$750,000,000
Cost of sales		693,223,000
Gross profit		56,777,000
Operating expenses:		
Administrative expenses.	$3,200,000	
Interest	6,500,000	
Depreciation	4,000,000	13,700,000
Net profit before taxes		43,077,000
Federal income taxes (48%).		20,677,000
Net profit after taxes		$ 22,400,000

As in Chapter 5, interest coverage for debt is calculated as follows:

$$\text{times interest earned} = \frac{\$43,077,000 + \$6,500,000}{\$6,500,000} = 7.63 \text{ times.}$$

The analogous measure for preferred stock is the number of times preferred dividends plus interest (and other prior charges) are earned. By definition, preferred dividends are paid only after interest has been paid. In addition, preferred dividends are paid only out of after-tax income. Preferred dividends at 7% amount to $(7\%)(\$50,000,000) = \$3,500,000$ for Jetway Aviation. The before-tax profit necessary to cover these preferred dividends would be $\$3,500,000/(1 - 0.48) = \$6,730,800$. Preferred dividend and interest (or "overall") coverage for Jetway Aviation may be calculated as follows:

$$\text{overall coverage} = \frac{\text{before-tax profits} + \text{interest expense}}{\text{interest expense} + \text{before-tax preferred dividends}}$$

$$= \frac{\$43,077,000 + \$6,500,000}{\$6,500,000 + \$6,730,800} = 3.75 \text{ times.}$$

Preferred dividends coverage is calculated in conjunction with interest and other prior charges, such as lease payments, because all liabilities must be satisfied before dividends can be paid. Hence, the interest coverage (7.63 times for Jetway) for debt will always be higher than the coverage (3.75 times for Jetway) for preferred stock. Finally, it should be noted that dividends paid to preferred shareholders must be subtracted from net profit after taxes in order to obtain the earnings available to the common shareholders. In our example, the earnings per share for Jetway Aviation would thus become

$$\frac{\text{after-tax profits} - \text{preferred dividends}}{\text{outstanding shares}} = \frac{\$22,400,000 - \$3,500,000}{10,000,000}$$

$$= \$1.89 \text{ per share.}$$

This result will be used later in the chapter.

FACTORS IN APPRAISING COMMON STOCKS

Common stocks may be judged either by published rating systems, similar to the bond rating systems explained in Chapter 5, or by an absolute valuation approach intended to determine the present value of expected future benefits. The latter approach is similar to the method used to derive bond valuation tables, also explained in Chapter 5. Application of this concept to common stocks is more difficult, however, because of the greater variety of inputs that must be specified.

We saw in Chapter 5 that bond ratings were based on statistical tests of various financial data of the issuing corporations. Furthermore, the resulting bond ratings reflect the relative risk to the bondholder of not receiving the full fixed return on investment to which he is legally entitled.

Numerous rating systems also are used to portray the relative risks of being a common or preferred shareholder. Risk to a shareholder is different from the risk to a bondholder because the shareholder is not legally assured of a return on his investment. A preferred shareholder certainly expects to receive a fixed dividend payment, but there is uncertainty as to the terminal value of the investment as measured by the market price of the preferred stock. Uncertainty, and hence risk, to the common shareholder is even greater because neither dividends nor share price is fixed. If the issuing company is prosperous, the common shareholder stands to share in that prosperity through increased dividends or increased share price or both. Since dividends are paid from earnings, and since share price presumably reflects current earnings and the potential for future earnings, it is not surprising that stock ratings are often based on company earnings.

The following rating systems are used by Standard & Poor's Corporation for preferred and common stocks

Common stocks		Preferred stocks	
Rating	*Quality*	*Rating*	*Quality*
A+	Excellent	AAA	Prime
A	Good	AA	High grade
A−	Above average	A	Sound
B+	Average	BBB	Medium grade
B	Below average	BB	Lower grade
B−	Low	B	Speculative
C	Lowest	C	Submarginal

The meanings associated with these ratings reflect the overall investment quality of the issue, rather than just a forecast of probable market behavior. The ratings are based on the historical and projected growth of earnings and dividends, and also the stability of earnings and dividends over time. The rating systems of other agencies and brokerage firms reflect similar approaches to judging common stocks. It should be noted, however, that rating systems for common stocks are probably not used as extensively as are bond ratings.

The Value Line Investment Survey includes evaluation of common stocks on four distinct attributes: (1) expected market performance over the next twelve months, (2) expected market performance over the next three to five years, (3) dividend income, and (4) safety. A total of 1,400 common stocks are evaluated, ranked according to each of the four attributes, divided into five categories (of size 100, 300, 600, 300, and 100) along each attribute dimension, and assigned a score ranging from 1 (highest category) to 5 (lowest category). Assigned scores for each common stock are based on a comprehensive examination of past earnings and dividend performance, as compared to the entire universe of 1,400 common stocks. The Value Line system of scoring and a procedure for combining the four scores into a summary measure for each stock will be explained and illustrated in Chapter 19.

INFINITE HORIZON VALUATION OF COMMON STOCKS

In Chapter 5, it was suggested that the investment value of a risky asset can be expressed as

$$V = \sum_{t=1}^{T} \frac{B_t}{(1 + k)^t} \tag{6-1}$$

where B_t is a future dollar benefit to the investor in period t, and k is an appropriate discount rate that reflects the relative risk of the asset. Our discussion of stock valuation can conveniently begin here also. In this section, we consider situations where the length of the horizon is taken to be infinite. In other words, $T = \infty$ in expression (6-1). Would any individual truly be concerned with an infinite investment horizon? Probably not, but still such a case warrants our attention as a point of departure.

If the investment horizon is infinite, then the sole component of return to a common shareholder is the stream of dividends he receives over time. Part III of this book will be devoted to careful analysis of the prospects for a firm so that reasonable estimates can be made of dividends. In terms of our valuation model

$$V = \sum_{t=1}^{\infty} \frac{D_t}{(1 + k)^t} \tag{6-2}$$

where D_t is the amount of dollar dividends received by the investor during year t. Investment value of a common share has been defined by several writers as the present value of all future dividends. Perhaps the most colorful such definition came from Professor John Burr Williams, an early proponent of discounted future benefits, who in 1938 wrote:

> In short, a stock is worth only *what you can get out of it*. Even so spoke the old farmer to his son:

108

A cow for her milk,
A hen for her eggs,
And a stock, by heck,
For her dividends.
An orchard for fruit,
Bees for their honey,
And stocks, besides,
For her dividends.

Whatever weaknesses may have been apparent in the rhyming did not extend to the logic of obtaining tangible benefits. Professor Williams noted that the farmer did not recommend buying a cow for her cud or bees for their buzz, and that similarly it was dividends rather than earnings that were the ultimate goal of the investment process.

Expression (6–2) gives the essence of such an observation. To use the valuation model in such a form is obviously an impossible task, since a unique dividend would have to be specified for each future period. The model can be made usable, however, by making certain simplifying assumptions about the dividend stream over time. First, we can assume that dividends grow at a constant rate indefinitely. Following the method of compounding explained in Chapter 4, we can express each dividend of such a stream as

$$D_t = D_0(1 + g)^t$$

where D_0 is the current dividend per share, and g is the constant growth rate that is assumed for the dividend stream to be received by the investor. Substituting this compounded growth into expression (6–2) gives

$$V = \sum_{t=1}^{\infty} \frac{D_0(1 + g)^t}{(1 + k)^t} \tag{6–3}$$

If the growth rate g is greater than the discount rate k, expression (6–3) gets larger and larger, and approaches infinity as the number of future periods increases. In other words, a common stock whose dividend stream is expected to grow at a rate greater than the discount rate would have a very large investment value, and would be undervalued at any price. Unfortunately, we do not find such investments.

But if the growth rate g is less than the discount rate k, one can show that investment value reduces to the simpler form

$$V = \sum_{t=1}^{\infty} \frac{D_0(1 + g)^t}{(1 + k)^t} = \frac{D_0(1 + g)}{k - g} \tag{6–4}$$

[1] John Burr Williams, *The Theory of Investment Value* (Harvard University Press, 1938), p. 57.

This first case will be referred to as the *constant growth model*. Expression (6–4) or some equivalent is often used in discussing the cost of equity capital of the firm. Notice that only three variables are needed in expression (6–4) to calculate investment value. Current dividends D_0 are known, and only estimates of g and k are required. For example, if the current dividend of Jetway Aviation is $D_0 = \$1.25$ per share, and we estimate dividend growth to be $g = 8\%$ per year and an appropriate discount rate to be $k = 10\%$, we would have

$$\text{Case (1): } V = \frac{(\$1.25)(1 + 0.08)}{(0.10 - 0.08)} = \$67.50$$

Using a higher discount rate of 12% for a riskier stock would lead to a lower investment value of only $33.75. This serves to illustrate the sensitivity of investment value to one's choice of a discount rate for effectively penalizing future dividend payments.

At the opposite extreme, suppose that there were no prospects for growth within the firm, and that the dividend stream to investors were expected to remain constant forever. We can write for this second case simply $D_t = D_0$ which means that all future dividends are just equal to current dividends. The second case will be referred to as the *zero growth model*. Substituting again in expression (6–2), we obtain a simplified form

$$V = \sum_{t=1}^{\infty} \frac{D_0}{(1 + k)^t} = \frac{D_0}{k} \tag{6–5}$$

Now defining a dividend multiplier m_D as the reciprocal of the discount rate ($m_D = 1/k$), investment value becomes

$$V = D_0 m_D \tag{6–6}$$

This version is sometimes referred to as the *dividend capitalization model*, since current dividends are merely multiplied by a constant factor. For Jetway Aviation and $k = 10\%$, we have

$$\text{Case (2): } V = \frac{\$1.25}{0.10} = (\$1.25)(10) = \$12.50$$

For $k = 12\%$, investment value would be only $10.42. That these values are lower than before is not surprising, since here no growth is assumed in the benefits to be received by the investor.

Another version of the dividend capitalization model can be developed if we specify that the firm will follow a policy of paying out a constant fraction Q of earnings each year. In other words, $D_t = Q e_t$ where e_t

represents earnings per share in year t. For the same case of no growth, $D_t = D_0 = Qe_0$, and using expression (6–5), we see that $V = Qe_0/k$. Defining $m_e = Q/k$ as an effective multiplier for earnings, we have

$$V = e_0 m_e \qquad (6\text{--}7)$$

This version is sometimes referred to as the *earnings capitalization model*, since current earnings are multiplied by a constant factor. The multiplier in this version (m_e) is analogous to the commonly used "price-earnings ratio" reported in newspaper quotations.

Both the dividend capitalization model and the earnings capitalization model are used frequently in practice because of the ease in computation. Only two variables need to be specified in each case, and one of them is currently observable. But as we have shown, both are versions of the infinite horizon situation, and both assume no growth in earnings and hence dividends over time. Some analysts prefer to use "normalized" estimates of dividends and earnings that are expected for the firm during some future period. If normalized earnings or dividends are used instead of current earnings or dividends in stock valuation, then the appropriate earnings or dividend multipliers must be defined accordingly. Normalized earnings will be discussed further and illustrated in Part III of this book.

Thus far, we have considered two extreme cases for infinite horizon valuation: Case (1), which was constant growth, and Case (2), which was zero growth. These are illustrated in Figure 6–1. Neither case is particularly representative of actual investment situations and are included here mainly as benchmarks for comparison. Two additional cases can be identified in connection with certain common stocks that might be classified as growth stocks. A *growth stock* is one that during certain stages of the life-cycle of the firm (say N years) is expected to grow at an above-average rate g. Because that growth rate is high, it is not expected that that rate will continue beyond N years. Case (3) will refer to the situation where the firm grows at rate g for N years and then there is no further growth. This third case will be referred to as the *growth/no growth model*. Valuation of Case (3) would be described as follows

$$V = \sum_{t=1}^{N} \frac{D_0(1+g)^t}{(1+k)^t} + \sum_{t=N+1}^{\infty} \frac{D_0(1+g)^N}{(1+k)^t} \qquad (6\text{--}8)$$

It can be shown that this also reduces to a closed expression, provided g is less than k, namely

$$V = D_0 \left[\frac{k(1+g)(1+k)^N - g(1+k)(1+g)^N}{k(k-g)(1+k)^N} \right] \qquad (6\text{--}9)$$

FIGURE 6–1
Infinite horizon valuation models

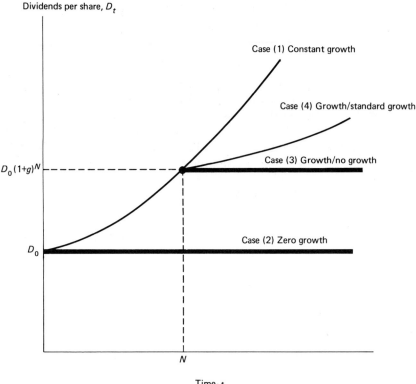

While this appears quite complicated, one can readily substitute estimates of the variables to get investment value. If the current dividend
$D_0 = \$1.25$ for Jetway Aviation is expected to grow for $N = 5$ years
at the above-average rate $g = 8\%$, followed by zero growth, then using
expression (6–9) and again $k = 10\%$ as the discount rate

Case (3):

$$V = (\$1.25) \left[\frac{(0.10)(1.08)(1.10)^5 - (0.08)(1.10)(1.08)^5}{(0.10)(0.02)(1.10)^5} \right] = \$17.32$$

As would be expected, this value of $17.32 per common share is between
the extreme values of Case (1) and Case (2).

Case (4) is even more realistic, in that we assume the firm grows
at the above-average rate g for N years and then assumes an average
or standard growth rate $g_s < g$. This fourth case will be referred to
as the *growth/standard growth model*. The growth stock thus has an
above-average growth for a finite period, and then it becomes an average
company as far as its subsequent growth is concerned.

In terms of our valuation model, we can write

$$V = \sum_{t=1}^{N} \frac{D_0(1 + g)^t}{(1 + k)^t} + \sum_{t=N+1}^{\infty} \frac{D_0(1 + g)^N(1 + g_s)^{t-N}}{(1 + k)^t} \qquad (6\text{--}10)$$

which reduces somewhat to

$$V = D_0 \left[\sum_{t=1}^{N} \left(\frac{1 + g}{1 + k}\right)^t + \left(\frac{1 + g}{1 + k}\right)^N \left(\frac{1 + g_s}{k - g_s}\right) \right] \qquad (6\text{--}11)$$

an expression that still includes one summation sign but only for the N years of above-average growth. To illustrate for Jetway Aviation, suppose that growth $g = 8\%$ occurs for $N = 5$ years, as before, but then standard growth $g_s = 5\%$ is expected from that point on into the future. Using expression (6–11) and again $k = 10\%$, we calculate

$$\text{Case (4): } V = (\$1.25) \left[\sum_{t=1}^{5} \left(\frac{1.08}{1.10}\right)^t + \left(\frac{1.08}{1.10}\right)^5 \left(\frac{1.05}{0.05}\right) \right] = \$29.87$$

Comparing this result with that of Case (3), we conclude that the added assumption of standard growth beyond year N adds $\$29.87 - \$17.32 = \$12.55$ to investment value of the common stock.

Investment values of Jetway Aviation common stock for the four cases that are plotted in Figure 6–1 and have been discussed can now be compared. The current dividend was specified to be $\$1.25$ per share, and a discount rate of 10% was used in each instance.

Growth model	Investment value
Case (1): Constant growth	$67.50
Case (2): Zero growth	$12.50
Case (3): Growth/No growth	$17.32
Case (4): Growth/Standard growth	$29.87

The wide range of values that results serves to underscore the importance of the growth assumptions that must be made.

FINITE HORIZON VALUATION OF COMMON STOCKS

In order to obtain a workable expression for infinite horizon valuation, it was necessary to make certain assumptions about the growth of the dividend stream forever. Unfortunately, none of the assumptions we made is particularly indicative of what one is likely to experience from common stock investments. Moreover, the infinite horizon is hardly representative of how investors perceive investment alternatives. Instead, most investors are likely to employ a finite horizon in considering common stocks and other investment assets for their portfolios.

In this context, the return on a share of common stock arises from two sources—the cash dividends and the change in share price. Although the extent of dividend yield and price appreciation may vary considerably from stock to stock, both are important components of total return on both preferred and common stocks. The valuation model for the finite horizon case already has been used in Chapter 4 for illustrating the concept of discounted present value. It can be written for the case of common stock valuation as

$$V = \sum_{t=1}^{T} \frac{D_t}{(1 + k)^t} + \frac{P_T}{(1 + k)^T} \tag{6-12}$$

where the first term is discounted dividends for T years and the second term is the discounted value of the terminal market value of the common stock at the end of T years. This is the most general expression for finite horizon valuation. It requires an estimate of dividends for each year in the horizon plus an estimate of the terminal market price. Since terminal price P_T can be viewed as the discounted present value of dividends from period T to infinity, the finite horizon valuation model of expression (6–2) is consistent with the infinite horizon valuation model of expression (6–2). Nevertheless, the finite horizon model is more easy to use in practice.

We illustrate the use of expression (6–12) for Jetway Aviation in a worksheet that was used in earlier chapters. A horizon of $T = 4$ years is used. We see that dividends are expected to stay at $1.25 for two years and then increase to $1.35 and $1.40 respectively during the next two years. The expected terminal price of $35 is added to the cash dividend received during the fourth and final year of the investment horizon. The relative weights are based on a discount rate of 10%. According to this calculation, Jetway Aviation common stock would be considered to be slightly overvalued at this point, since investment value $V = 28.04 is less than the current market price $P_0 = 28.50.

Year	Benefit, B_t	Weight, α_t (10%)	Weighted benefit, $\alpha_t B_t$
1	$ 1.25	0.909	$ 1.136
2	1.25	0.826	1.033
3	1.35	0.751	1.014
4	36.40	0.683	24.861
Total			$28.044

Because many analysts and investors are used to thinking in terms of company earnings, we can rewrite our valuation equation as follows

$$V = \sum_{t=1}^{T} \frac{Q_t e_t}{(1 + k)^t} + \frac{e_T m_e}{(1 + k)^T} \tag{6-13}$$

where e_t is earnings per share in year t, Q_t is the dividend payout ratio in that year, and m_e is the market multiplier (price-earnings ratio) expected at the end of the horizon. Notice that in expression (6–13), the components of return are still annual dividends and terminal price. In order to focus on earnings, therefore, it is necessary to specify payout rates and the terminal market multiplier. Again, Part III of this book will be devoted to financial analyses that provide a basis for estimating these parameters.

The number of estimates needed for valuation can be reduced by making two assumptions. First, the dividend payout ratio Q can be assumed to be the same for each year. Second, earnings can be assumed to grow during the finite horizon at a constant rate g in the familiar form $e_t = e_0(1 + g)^t$. Substituting these into the valuation model gives

$$V = \sum_{t=1}^{T} \frac{e_0(1 + g)^t Q}{(1 + k)^t} + \frac{e_0(1 + g)^T m_e}{(1 + k)^T} \qquad (6\text{--}14)$$

where e_0 is current (observable) earnings per share. To use expression (6–14), estimates must be made of growth rate g, payout ratio Q, terminal multiplier m_e, discount rate k, and horizon length T. Of the several valuation models developed in this chapter, this final version is perhaps the most useful for a large sample of common stocks. One of the reasons for this is that the number of required estimates is not great.

To illustrate, let us again consider Jetway Aviation, whose current per-share earnings were shown earlier to be $e_0 = \$1.89$. Earnings are expected to grow at 8% over the next four years of the investment horizon. The existing dividend payout rate is $\$1.25/\$1.89 = 66.1\%$; we expect the payout rate to be increased to $Q = 70\%$ over the investment horizon. The existing price-earnings ratio is $\$28.50/\$1.89 = 15.1$; we expect it to be $m_e = 15$ at the end of the horizon. Terminal market price at the end of four years thus is forecasted to be $(\$2.57)(15) = \$38.55$. Under these assumptions, we would obtain an investment value $V = \$31.40$ as shown in the worksheet. The resulting investment value

Year	Earnings, e_t	Dividends, D_t	Price, P_t	Benefit, B_t	Weight, α_t	Weighted benefit, $\alpha_t B_t$
1	$2.04	$1.43	–	$ 1.43	0.909	$ 1.30
2	2.20	1.54	–	1.54	0.826	1.28
3	2.38	1.67	–	1.67	0.751	1.25
4	2.57	1.80	$38.55	40.35	0.683	27.57
Total						$31.40

is greater than in the previous example, because both terminal price and annual dividends are higher under the assumption of 8% growth.

SENSITIVITY ANALYSIS

A second reason for the usefulness of expression (6–14) is that it is highly amenable to sensitivity analysis. That is, we can vary some or all of the five estimates, g, Q, k, m_e, and T in order to see their effect on common stock value. Again using the common stock of Jetway Aviation, we illustrate the sensitivity of these parameters in Figure 6–2. In the first panel, we see the effect of varying horizon length T and growth rate g with the other parameters fixed at $Q = 70\%$, $m_e = 15$, and $k = 10\%$. For each set of parameters, the resulting investment value V is shown in the body of Figure 6–2. The original case of $T = 4$ and $g = 8\%$ resulting in $V = \$31.40$ is encircled. We see that investment value ranges from \$20.86 to \$57.74 for different values of estimated growth and horizon length.

The only change in the second panel is to increase the terminal multiplier to $m_e = 19$. We see that for the original case of $T = 4$ years and $g = 8\%$, investment value increases to \$38.42. The range of investment value for the case of a higher terminal multiplier is \$23.48 to \$67.47. In the third panel, we go back to $m_e = 15$, but now payout ratio is decreased to $Q = 50\%$. The effect of this is to reduce each investment value from its corresponding level in the first panel. The reason for this is that the reduced dividend payments to owners of Jetway Aviation common stock are not offset by a higher terminal stock price resulting from increased retained earnings. In the fourth panel, payout ratio is set at the original level of $Q = 70\%$, but here the effective discount rate is increased to $k = 14\%$. All future benefits to the owner of Jetway Aviation are penalized at a higher rate, and investment values drop accordingly. The overall range for investment value in Figure 6–2 is from a low of \$14.85 (Panel IV) to a high of \$67.47 (Panel II).

For each set of parameters treated in Figure 6–2, investment value depends also on the level of current earnings, in this instance $e_0 = \$1.89$. If current earnings were to double, then all values in Table 6–1 would double correspondingly. And if we had set $e_0 = \$1.00$, the values in the resulting sensitivity analysis could be viewed as investment value per dollar of current earnings. Either way, we see that sensitivity analysis is a useful way of observing the importance of different parameters on the investment value of common stocks.

INVESTING IN STOCKS

Just as was seen to be the case for government and corporate bonds, preferred and common stocks are an important class of investment assets in the portfolios of individuals and institutional investors. One reason is inflation. It has long been acknowledged that stocks overall represent a means of guarding against the loss of purchasing power that results from inflation. But it has become painfully apparent to many investors

FIGURE 6–2
Sensitivity analysis of investment value: Jetway Aviation Corporation

Panel I. $Q = 70\%; m_e = 15; k = 10\%$.

Growth period (years)	Growth rate (percent)					
	2	4	6	8	10	12
2	26.74	27.78	28.83	29.90	31.00	32.11
4	25.36	27.26	29.27	(31.40)	33.64	36.01
6	24.17	26.80	29.69	32.84	36.29	40.05
8	23.14	26.39	30.07	34.23	38.93	44.23
10	22.26	26.02	30.43	35.57	41.58	48.58
12	21.51	25.70	30.76	36.87	44.23	53.08
14	20.86	25.40	31.06	38.11	46.87	57.74

Panel II. $Q = 70\%; m_e = 19; k = 10\%$.

Growth period (years)	Growth rate (percent)					
	2	4	6	8	10	12
2	33.24	34.53	35.85	37.19	38.56	39.95
4	30.95	33.30	35.79	(38.42)	41.20	44.13
6	28.97	32.20	35.74	39.61	43.85	48.47
8	27.28	31.22	35.69	40.76	46.49	52.97
10	25.82	30.34	35.65	41.87	49.14	57.63
12	24.56	29.55	35.60	42.93	51.79	62.46
14	23.48	28.85	35.57	43.96	54.43	67.47

Panel III. $Q = 50\%; m_e = 15; k = 10\%$.

Growth period (years)	Growth rate (percent)					
	2	4	6	8	10	12
2	26.07	27.08	28.11	29.17	30.24	31.33
4	24.10	25.94	27.89	(29.96)	32.13	34.42
6	22.41	24.93	27.69	30.71	34.02	37.63
8	20.96	24.02	27.50	31.45	35.91	40.95
10	19.71	23.21	27.33	32.15	37.80	44.40
12	18.64	22.49	27.16	32.83	39.69	47.97
14	17.71	21.84	27.01	33.49	41.58	51.67

Panel IV. $Q = 70\%; m_e = 15; k = 14\%$.

Growth period (years)	Growth rate (percent)					
	2	4	6	8	10	12
2	24.94	25.90	26.88	27.89	28.90	29.94
4	22.21	23.87	25.62	(27.47)	29.42	31.48
6	20.02	22.17	24.52	27.09	29.90	32.96
8	18.27	20.76	23.58	26.76	30.35	34.39
10	16.87	19.59	22.76	26.46	30.76	35.77
12	15.75	18.61	22.05	26.18	31.15	37.10
14	14.85	17.79	21.44	25.94	31.51	38.39

Figure 6–2 was prepared using a computer program described in David K. Eiteman, "A Computer Program for Common Stock Valuation," *Financial Analysts Journal*, July–August 1968, pages 107–11

in recent years that such a maxim does not hold for all stocks during all periods of time.

Another well received maxim is that stocks achieve a return for their owners of about 10%. That result appears to have been an optimistic "rounding up" of the 9.2% median return achieved by all common stocks listed on the New York Stock Exchange over the extended period 1926–1960. That result is also based on the return to a tax-exempt institution. The corresponding return to an investor with $10,000 taxable income would have been 8.7%, while a wealthier investor with $50,000 taxable income would have received only 6.8%. There have been many years and horizons during the past few decades when investors would have received considerably more than 9–10% from common stock investments, but there are other years and horizons when achieved returns would have been lower than this or even negative.

A conclusion can be reached that common stocks do offer investors the potential of a 9–10% return or even higher, but only if investors are willing to assume higher risk. Our discussion of return and risk in Chapters 3 and 4 focused on the important relationship between return and risk for investment assets and portfolios of assets. Of the several types of investment assets identified in Chapter 1, common stock has received more attention by researchers, practitioners, and investors—in terms of trying to understand the elusive relationship between return and risk. One reason for this attention is that considerably more data exist in various forms for the hundreds of corporations whose common stocks are listed on the New York Stock Exchange and other organized exchanges.

Another reason for the popularity of common stocks with investors is that common stocks are an extremely liquid investment; a telephone call causes shares to be sold and proceeds to be received by the investor in about one week. In contrast, it may take months or even years for an investor to receive the proceeds from real estate or other business ventures. High liquidity of common stocks also applies to all but the very largest institutional investors.

A final reason for the popularity of common stocks is that they represent an opportunity for individuals, and institutions for that matter, to make a truly large return on their investable wealth in a relatively short period of time. Fortunes have been made in this manner, but opportunities to do so are as improbable as the chances of winning a large-scale lottery. Even if they truly understood the improbability of unusually large gains, some investors would still try. For the vast majority of investors, however, common stocks simply represent higher expected returns accompanied by higher risks—as compared to most of the other investment assets that they might choose to hold in their portfolios.

SUMMARY

Preferred stock and common stock have been described, and their characteristics have been compared with those of alternative investment assets. The return to a share of common stock consists of periodic dividend payments and a terminal stock price, both of which are dependent on the earnings of the issuing corporation. Particular attention was paid to the higher levels of risk associated with common stocks, since payments to stockholders are not legal obligations, and since the market price of common stock at the end of any given investment horizon is subject to considerable uncertainty. Systems for rating common stocks, both overall and according to certain attributes, were reviewed. The valuation framework was applied first to common stocks under the rather unrealistic assumption of an infinite horizon. It was seen that investment value depends heavily on the growth assumptions made for the firm in question. The valuation framework was then applied to common stocks under the assumption of a finite horizon. This requires an estimate of the terminal price-earnings ratio, in addition to growth rates, payout ratios, and an appropriate discount rate. The sensitivity of investment value to changes in those parameters was illustrated. The advantages and disadvantages of investing in common stocks were compared in the final section.

SUGGESTED READINGS FOR CHAPTER 6

F. Amling. *Investments: An Introduction to Analysis and Management* (Englewood Cliffs, N.J.: Prentice-Hall, Inc., 1970), Chapters 5–6.

C. D. Ellis. *Institutional Investing* (Homewood, Ill.: Dow Jones-Irwin, Inc., 1971), Chapter 4.

D. K. Eiteman. "A Computer Program for Common Stock Valuation," *Financial Analysts Journal,* July–August, 1968, pages 107–11.

J. C. Francis. *Investments: Analysis and Management* (New York: McGraw-Hill Book Company, Inc., 1972), Chapter 9.

B. Graham, D. L. Dodd, and S. Cottle. *Security Analysis: Principles and Technique.* 4th ed. (New York: McGraw-Hill Book Company, Inc., 1962), Part Four.

H. Levy and M. Sarnat. *Investment and Portfolio Analysis* (New York: John Wiley & Sons, Inc., 1972), Chapter V.

H. C. Sauvain. *Investment Management.* 4th ed. (Englewood Cliffs, N.J.: Prentice-Hall, Inc., 1973), Chapter 10.

P. A. Shade. *Common Stocks: A Plan For Intelligent Investing* (Homewood, Ill.: Richard D. Irwin, Inc., 1971).

J. B. Williams. *The Theory of Investment Value* (Cambridge, Mass.: Harvard University Press, 1938).

7

Characteristics and valuation of tax-sheltered investments

OUR SUGGESTED FRAMEWORK for valuation has been applied to both bonds and stocks, two of the major categories represented in the total spectrum of investment assets identified in Chapter 1. While it is not within the scope of this book to discuss extensively all types of investment assets, it is useful at least to consider certain opportunities other than stocks and bonds. Tax-sheltered investments are a class of opportunities that have received increased attention in recent years. Included in this class are investments in oil and gas exploration, cattle feeding, citrus farming, equipment leasing, and real estate. Municipal bonds are also a popular type of tax shelter; they have already been discussed in Chapter 5. The purpose of this chapter is to describe the investment characteristics of tax-sheltered investments, and to illustrate the applicability and versatility of the valuation framework to this interesting range of opportunities.

CHARACTERISTICS OF TAX-SHELTERED INVESTMENTS

Tax-sheltered investments are opportunities in which possibilities for economic gain are enhanced by certain tax advantages associated with those opportunities. An understanding of these dual features is important because often only the tax advantages are mentioned in discussions and advertisements of particular tax shelters. Fortunately, both features can be readily handled within our valuation framework. Before showing this, however, we will find it useful to examine in more detail the tax advantages, which may take any of several forms.

One familiar form of tax shelter is in the nature of lower tax rates that may be applied to certain types of income. Two examples are the interest received on state and municipal bonds, which is not taxed at all by the federal government, and capital gains incurred when an investment asset is sold at a profit after having been held a minimum of six months. Capital gains are generally taxed at half the rate applicable to regular income, but at a rate no greater than 35%.

A second form of tax shelter is the provision of noncash tax losses that can be offset immediately against other taxable income of the investor, thus serving to reduce total tax charges on total income. Such a situation typically arises when the investment asset is some type of business activity wherein the investor may deduct certain noncash business expenses (such as depreciation) from income received from other sources.

A third form of tax shelter is created when cash received from an investment asset is deemed to be a "recovery" of the original outlay, rather than a profit earned on that outlay. Under some circumstances, particularly investments in oil and minerals, such "recoveries" may exceed the original outlay. Even if "recoveries" can only equal the original outlay, however, they may return cash—which is not taxed—to the investor at a higher rate or at an earlier time than is possible in fully taxed investment opportunities.

A fourth form of tax shelter is created when the payment of accrued tax liabilities is deferred. Such a deferral is tantamount to an interest-free loan from the government, with the proceeds of such a loan automatically invested in the principal of the investment. The investor, in such situations, effectively is able to use a larger investment base for compounding the future profitability of the particular investment asset. That is, the pool of invested wealth increases more rapidly than it would if portions of that pool were periodically being remitted to the government.

A fifth form of tax shelter arises when returns on certain tax-sheltered investments are enhanced as a result of additional borrowing arranged for a group of owners (typically limited partners) of the tax-sheltered investment. In other words, the owners benefit from *leverage*, which is the use of borrowed funds to increase the return to the owners of an investment project. The partnership format also allows the investor to absorb business expenses personally, thus reducing his personal tax liability, while the limited nature of the partnership agreement frees the same individual investor from the total risk of the particular investment. Borrowing for such ventures is typically arranged on a "nonrecourse" basis so that each investor (limited partner) assumes no risk for loan repayment if the venture itself fails.

Yet a sixth form of tax shelter arises because the original capital outlay may itself possess a tax implication. In "normal" investments, the process of purchasing the investment asset involves the exchange of one form of wealth (usually cash) for another (the investment asset). Such an investment has no unique tax implications in the year of purchase. In certain tax-sheltered investments, on the contrary, the surrender of one form of wealth for another at the time of purchase carries unique tax significance because it is possible to treat the wealth surrendered (the purchase price) as an expense that can be deducted from other taxable income in the year of purchase.

Tax-sheltered investment opportunities are often criticized as being gimmicks or unfair techniques by which wealthy individuals avoid paying their "fair" share of taxes. Their presence is also sometimes attributed to loopholes in the federal tax statutes. A nonpolitical view of the matter is that Congress deliberately established legislation that would motivate wealthier individuals to invest in such high-risk projects as mineral exploration, low-income housing, or purchase and leasing of new equipment. In other words, tax shelters have been deliberately created as a means of inducing investment in projects that are deemed to serve a public need. In this context, a tax shelter is an incentive created by public policy, and is thus differentiated from a loophole, which is an incentive discovered by a defect in a law that permits circumvention of that law in a manner that is legal but is nevertheless contrary to the intent of public policy.

VALUATION OF TAX-SHELTERED INVESTMENTS

In order to understand how the tax advantages of tax shelters are interrelated with the possibilities for economic gain, it is useful to focus once again on our model of investment value as the discounted present value of dollarized future benefits to the investor. Thus far, this took the form of

$$V = \sum_{t=1}^{T} \frac{B_t}{(1 + k)^t} \tag{7-1}$$

where B_t represents the cash benefits to be received by the investor in period t of the T-period horizon, and where k is the appropriate discount rate reflecting the relative risk of the asset being valued. Except for brief mention in Chapter 4, taxes have been conspicuously absent from all discussions of valuation thus far. One assumption that might justify such an oversight is that investors select from among alternative investment opportunities on a tax-free basis because the applicable taxes are relatively constant across all such opportunities. Alternatively, one might assume that each cash benefit in expression (7-1) is specified after taxes. If it were desirable not to confuse tax considerations with periodic benefits, then the valuation framework might instead be written

$$V = \sum_{t=1}^{T} \frac{B_t(1 - q_t)}{(1 + k)^t} \qquad (7\text{--}2)$$

where q_t is the applicable tax rate to be applied to benefit B_t received in period t.

Within the context of tax-sheltered investments, however, it is appropriate to rewrite the valuation model as follows

$$V = \sum_{t=0}^{T} \frac{F_t - H_t}{(1 + k)^t} \qquad (7\text{--}3)$$

where F_t is the net pre-tax cash inflow received in period t and H_t is the dollar amount of taxes (or cash outflow) payable on that income. The latter may include regular income taxes, capital gains taxes, or both, depending on the nature and timing of the particular benefit. It should be noted that cash flow in the initial period, $F_0 - H_0$, may at times reflect the tax deductibility of the original outlay, and that cash flow in the last period, $F_T - H_T$, may also include the after-tax residual value of the investment asset.

Prior to discussion of specific tax-sheltered investments, one danger inherent in the use of expression (7–3), alluded to in the previous paragraph, must be noted explicitly. An important aspect of a tax-sheltered investment is the provision of tax losses that can be used to offset other taxable income. The financial implication of this deductibility characteristic is that a tax-sheltered investment cannot be considered separately from other investments and sources of income of the individual. In other words, valuation must be done relative to the total portfolio. The suggestion in Chapter 3 that all investment decisions should be made relative to the aggregate portfolio, rather than in isolation, is especially relevant to the case of tax-sheltered investments because of the way in which applicable tax rates are altered. For now, however, we continue to use expression (7–3) as a vehicle for examining different types of tax-sheltered investments.

VALUATION OF REAL ESTATE

Among various investment opportunities that might be classified as tax shelters, the most popular and widely used is *real estate*. Probably a large majority of the fortunes amassed during the first two centuries of United States history have included real estate as a major component.

In addition, millions of American families have allocated a major portion of their investable wealth to home ownership. In addition to enjoying the many advantages of home ownership, these families have generally experienced a suitable return on their equity investment—a result both of our tax laws designed to encourage home ownership and of the gradual increase in real estate values over time.

Between these extremes are numerous real estate investment opportunities that can be categorized in different ways. One popular method of categorization is by the particular use of the property, such as residential and nonresidential. Residential real estate includes homes and also condominiums and apartment houses. Nonresidential real estate includes commercial buildings, shopping centers, and land. Each of these categories can be further divided by use, type, or number of units.

Most types of real estate offer the owner an opportunity for appreciation. With expanding population, land values have generally increased over time, thus providing investors with a hedge against inflation. Appreciation of land and property values, of course, is taxed when realized as capital gain at a lower rate than is regular income. With the exception of land and home ownership, most real estate investments also provide a cash flow to the investor during each period of the holding horizon. This feature, of course, prompted the use of net cash flow F_t and applicable taxes H_t in expression (7–3). Even in the case of home ownership, it would be possible to compute a cash flow by measuring what the homeowner would have to pay out for comparable housing. Because of the difficulty of deciding whether he would in fact rent comparable housing for cash, this aspect will not be pursued here.

There are two major determinants of cash flow in each period, one economic and the other a result of our tax laws. The economic determinant is simply a comparison of the cash revenue and cash expenses associated with the real estate property. Cash revenues include rent and lease receipts, while cash expenses include maintenance, property taxes, and management fees. The second determinant is the ability to depreciate all improvements on the property, and thereby to reduce taxable income and taxes payable. Because depreciation does not represent a cash outflow but is a tax-deductible expense, it essentially contributes to the cash flow associated with a real estate investment by reducing cash tax payments.

An example will be used to illustrate these determinants and the valuation of real estate. A group of six professionals is considering the purchase of a 15-unit luxury apartment building in an attractive suburb of a major metropolitan area. The total purchase price is $270,000, which amounts to $18,000 for each of the 15 units. Of the total purchase price, the building itself is appraised at $200,000, while the land is valued at $70,000. The group decides upon a ten-year holding horizon for evaluating this investment. It is estimated that the building will have a negligible value at the end of ten years, but that the land can be sold for $100,000. All six investors are assumed to be in the 50% tax bracket.

Each apartment can be rented for $300 per month, and an average occupancy rate of 95% is expected during the next decade. Annual gross revenue is thus projected at a constant rate equal to

$$g_t = (\$300)(12)(15)(0.95) = \$51,300.$$

Annual cash operating expenses e_t are expected to be $10,500 during the first year, increase by $500 in each subsequent year, and reach a maximum of $15,000 during the tenth year. For tax purposes, the building is to depreciate from its appraised value of $200,000 to zero using the sum-of-the-digits method of accelerated depreciation. Depreciation for each year is denoted by d_t.

Given these data, the suggested method of analysis is to calculate the net cash benefit, $F_t - H_t$, to the investment group for each year of the horizon. An additional benefit must be added to the tenth year as a result of selling the property. Then, as indicated in expression (7–3), these net cash benefits are discounted back to the present time at the rate k to yield the investment value of the apartment project. The discount rate should reflect the relative risk and illiquidity of the project, and the group decides to use the after-tax value $k = 10\%$ in determining investment value. As an alternative method of analysis suggested in Chapter 5, we can calculate that internal rate of return that discounts the net cash benefits back to just equal the purchase price of the investment.

Two cases will be presented. In Case I, each of the six professionals contributes $45,000 and the group purchases the apartment building without the use of additional financing. Determination of investment value for Case I is shown in Figure 7–1. Annual taxable profits on the investment arc given by

$$p_t = g_t - e_t - d_t,$$

which is taxed at the regular income rate $q = 50\%$. In terms of expression (7–3), annual net cash inflow is

$$F_t = g_t - e_t,$$

while taxes are

$$H_t = p_t q;$$

hence the net cash benefit to the investor group is given by

$$F_t - H_t = g_t - e_t - q(g_t - e_t - d_t).$$

We see that over the ten-year horizon F_t, H_t, and the difference $(F_t - H_t)$ all decrease. For the final year $T = 10$, it is necessary to

FIGURE 7-1
Illustrative apartment project, Case I

(1)	(2)	(3)	(4)	(5)	(6)	(7)	(8)	(9)
	Gross	Operating	Depre-	Taxable profit	Taxes	Cash	Weight	Weighted
Year	revenue	expenses	ciation	(loss)	(credit)	benefit	α_t	benefit
t	g_t	e_t	d_t	p_t	$p_t q$	$F_t - H_t$	(10%)	$\alpha_t (F_t - H_t)$
1	$51,300	$10,500	$36,364	$ 4,436	$ 2,218	$38,582	0.909	$35,072
2	51,300	11,000	32,727	7,573	3,787	36,513	0.826	30,160
3	51,300	11,500	29,091	10,709	5,355	34,445	0.751	25,868
4	51,300	12,000	25,455	13,845	6,923	32,377	0.683	22,113
5	51,300	12,500	21,818	16,982	8,491	30,309	0.621	18,822
6	51,300	13,000	18,182	20,118	10,059	28,241	0.564	15,928
7	51,300	13,500	14,545	23,255	11,628	26,172	0.513	13,426
8	51,300	14,000	10,909	26,391	13,196	24,104	0.467	11,257
9	51,300	14,500	7,273	29,527	14,764	22,036	0.424	9,343
10	51,300	15,000	3,636	32,664	16,332	19,968	0.386	7,708
Residual value = $100,000 – ($100,000 – 70,000)(25%)=						92,500	0.386	35,705
Total								$225,402

Note: Column (5) = (2) − (3) − (4)
Column (7) = (2) − (3) − (6)

add the effect of selling the property. We let $P_0 = \$270,000$ and $P_T = \$100,000$ represent the purchase price and the sales price of the property, respectively. Accumulated depreciation is

$$\sum_{t=1}^{10} d_t = \$200,000,$$

final book value of the property is

$$P_0 - \sum_{t=1}^{10} d_t = \$270,000 - \$200,000 = \$70,000,$$

capital gain is

$$P_T - \left(P_0 - \sum_{t=1}^{10} d_t\right) = \$100,000 - \$70,000 = \$30,000,$$

and at the capital gains rate of 25%, the taxes payable are ($30,000)(25%) = $7,500. The residual cash flow at the end of the investment horizon is the $100,000 sales price minus the $7,500 tax payment, or $92,500. The aggregate cash flow in the tenth year, as shown in Figure 7-1, is thus $19,968 + $92,500 = $112,468.

As also seen in Figure 7-1, the discounted cash benefits also decrease over time, and their sum is $225,402. As before, the relative weights for use in calculating discounted cash benefits are obtained from an appropriate column in Appendix A. Since the cost of the property is $270,000, we conclude that the apartment project of Case I is overvalued and hence is not a good investment. Alternatively, the internal rate of return for the project turns out (following an interative procedure) to be 6.5%; this is less than the required rate of return of 10.0%, and the project should be rejected.

Case II allows for leverage, in which each of the six professionals contributes only $15,000 (for a total investment of $90,000), and the group borrows the additional $180,000 needed to purchase the apartment building. The borrowing, which constitutes two thirds of the $270,000 purchase price, is in the form of a ten-year term loan. A *term loan* is one wherein the borrowers pay both interest and principal repayment in equal annual amounts. In this instance, the total annual payment for the term loan is $24,456 per year. Calculations of investment value for Case II are shown in Figure 7–2. Value of gross revenue g_t, operating

FIGURE 7–2
Illustrative apartment project, Case II

(1) Year t	(2) Loan payment $i_t + r_t$	(3) Interest i_t	(4) Remaining loan balance	(5) Taxable profit (loss) p_t'	(6) Taxes (credit) $p_t' q$	(7) Cash benefit $F_t - H_t$	(8) Weight α_t (10%)	(9) Weighted benefit $\alpha_t (F_t - H_t)$
1	$24,456	$10,800	$166,435	($6,364)	($3,182)	$19,526	0.909	$17,749
2	24,456	9,986	151,965	(2,413)	(1,207)	17,051	0.826	14,084
3	24,456	9,118	136,627	1,591	796	14,548	0.751	10,926
4	24,456	8,198	120,369	5,647	2,824	12,020	0.683	8,210
5	24,456	7,222	103,135	9,760	4,880	9,464	0.621	5,877
6	24,456	6,188	84,867	13,930	6,965	6,879	0.564	3,880
7	24,455	5,092	65,503	18,163	9,082	4,262	0.513	2,186
8	24,456	3,930	44,977	22,461	11,231	1,613	0.467	753
9	24,456	2,699	23,220	26,828	13,414	(1,070)	0.424	(454)
10	24,456	1,393	–	31,271	15,636	(3,792)	0.386	(1,464)
Residual value=$100,000–($100,000–$70,000)(25%)=						92,500	0.386	35,705
Total								$97,452

Note: Column (5) = [Figure 7–1(5)] − (3)
      Column (7) = [Figure 7–1(2)] − [Figure 7–1(3)] − (2) − (6)

expense e_t, and depreciation d_t are omitted from Table 7–2, but are the same as in Figure 7–1 for Case I. The residual value of $92,500 also is the same as before. The $24,456 loan payment in each year consists of interest i_t, which decreases over time, and principal repayment r_t, which eliminates the term loan at the end of ten years. Taxable profit for each year is given by

$$p_t' = g_t - e_t - d_t - i_t = P_t - i_t,$$

and taxes payable thus become $p_t'q$. The net cash benefit for this case is given by

$$F_t - H_t = g_t - e_t - \$24,456 - q(g_t - e_t - d_t - i_t).$$

We see in Figure 7–2 that because both interest and depreciation actually cause a taxable loss in the first two years of the horizon, a tax credit results. A tax credit is actually treated as a benefit in the valuation model because the tax loss can be used to offset other taxable income in the current year and/or in subsequent years. As before, cash benefits, $F_t - H_t$, decrease over time and even become negative in the ninth and tenth years of the horizon—because interest and depreciation are not sufficient to keep taxes $H_t = p_t'q$ below the net cash inflow

$$F_t = g_t - e_t - \$24,456.$$

Again using the after-tax discount rate $k = 10\%$, we see that investment value becomes $97,452. Since this amount is greater than the total group investment of $90,000, we conclude that the apartment project of Case II is undervalued and hence is a good investment—provided, of course, that the necessary borrowing can be obtained. Internal rate of return for Case II turns out to be approximately 11.5%, which is greater than the required rate of return of 10%.

This example highlights the importance of borrowing as part of real estate investment. Depreciation of the property and interest on the borrowing used to purchase the property comprise the "tax shield" of a real estate investment opportunity. Although Case I was not a desirable investment, Case II did turn out to be an attractive opportunity at the 10% discount rate. The allowable depreciation and interest payments reduced income taxed at the regular income rate, while the appreciation in land value is taxed only at the lower capital gain rate. It should be noted that both depreciation and interest can be determined prior to making the final investment decision. In contrast, gross revenue and cash operating expenses for the real estate investment can only be estimated before making the final decision. The greatest uncertainty in most real estate investments, however, is the expected sales price of the property several years in the future.

VALUATION OF CATTLE FEEDING

Farming is another interesting type of tax shelter wherein land is used to produce some commercial asset. Included in this category are citrus groves, vineyards, fruit orchards, timber, and cattle. In addition to the possible appreciation of land values, the investor generally can deduct certain expenses associated with farming the land and thereby partially shelter ordinary income from federal income taxes. To illustrate the use of our valuation framework, we shall focus here on a single example of farming—cattle feeding. It is chosen because its characteristics are considerably different from the other types of investment assets that have been considered.

Cattle feeding is the process of purchasing a herd of feeder cattle, feeding the cattle in a feeder yard for several months, and then selling the herd when the steers reach their commercial weight. The herd typically is purchased in the summer or fall and sold sometime during the next year. As opposed to cattle breeding which normally has a cycle of at least five years, the cycle for cattle feeding is less than a full year. A *cattle feeding program* is the repeated investment in cattle feeding projects over an extended period of time.

Apart from the increase in value of the herd, which is realized at the end of the feeding cycle, the investor may deduct the expenses of the feeding operation in the prior year and thus shelter income in that earlier year. Expenses include the cost of grain consumed by the herd, rent paid for using the feeder yard, interest on borrowed funds used to purchase the herd, and a management fee paid to the feeding operation. Apart from the overall health of the herd, the major uncertainty associated with cattle feeding is changing prices per pound for cattle.

To illustrate, suppose an investor buys at midyear a herd of 100 cattle, each weighing 600 pounds, at a cost of 30 cents per pound. His total investment in the cost of the herd would be

$$(100 \text{ head})(600 \text{ pounds per head})(\$0.30 \text{ per pound}) = \$18,000.$$

Suppose, furthermore, that the investor borrows at the bank to finance two thirds of the cost ($12,000) and invests his own funds to pay for the remaining third ($6,000).

Each steer requires two tons of grain, enabling it to grow to 1,100 pounds six months later, and grain costs $50 per ton on the average. Management fees, interest, rent, medical costs, and all other expenses total $20 per head, and all expenses are paid for in cash and in advance to the feed lot operator at the time of the initial purchase of the herd. Expenses of the feed operation would be $12,000, calculated as follows:

$$\text{Grain: } (100 \text{ head})(2 \text{ tons per head})(\$50 \text{ per ton}) = \$10,000$$
$$\text{Operating expenses at \$20 per head: } (100 \text{ head})(\$20 \text{ per head}) = \underline{2,000}$$
$$\$12,000$$

Feed and operating expenses also are financed two-thirds by bank borrowing ($8,000) and one-third by equity ($4,000).

At this point, the investor has supplied a total of $10,000 of his own money and incurred a total bank debt for $20,000. Assume that the investor is in a 50% personal income tax bracket. During the year in which the investment is made, the investor pays for and thus deducts against his other personal income the total feed lot expenses of $12,000. Because the investment produces no associated income, these expenses create a loss that can be used to offset taxable income. As a consequence, the investor has a positive cash flow of $6,000, derived from reducing other taxes and calculated as shown on the left in Figure 7–3.

FIGURE 7–3
Two-year analysis of cattle feeding investment

	Year 0 (purchase herd)	Year 1 (sell herd)
Revenue	$ 0	$33,000
Expenses	−12,000	0
Cost of cattle	0	−18,000
Taxable income (loss)	($12,000)	$15,000
Taxes paid (credit)	(6,000)	7,500
Net income (loss)	($ 6,000)	7,500
Loan repayment	0	20,000
Cash flow	$ 6,000	$ 5,500

Assuming that cattle prices remain constant at 30 cents per pound, the herd can be sold the next year at a price of $33,000, calculated as follows:

(100 head)(1100 pounds per head)($0.30 per pound) = $33,000.

Deducting the $18,000 cost of the herd would leave income of $15,000, which is taxed at the regular income rate of 50%. This would leave an after-tax income of $7,500 as shown on the right in Figure 7–3.

Out of the $33,000 sale proceeds, the investor pays $7,500 in taxes plus $20,000 repayment of the loan, leaving a net cash flow of $5,500 in the year of the sale.

The next step is to calculate the investment value of the cattle feeding investment. Because it is judged to be a riskier type of investment, a discount rate of $k = 12\%$ is chosen. Applying the usual valuation model gives $10,912 as follows

Year	Cash benefit $F_t - H_t$	Weight α_t (12%)	Weighted benefit $(F_t - H_t) \alpha_t$
0	$6,000	1.000	$ 6,000
1	5,500	0.893	4,912
Total			$10,912

Notice that the cash benefit in the current year is not discounted. Since investment value of $10,912 is greater than the needed equity investment of $10,000, the project would be considered as undervalued.

If the cattle prices were to vary, then so would investment value. The current year's benefit would remain the same in each instance, but the gain on sale of the herd would change as would the net cash flow as shown in the following:

Sale price per pound	Sales price of herd	Taxes payable	Cash benefit	Investment value (at 12%)
$0.24	$26,400	$4,200	$2,200	$ 7,965
0.27	29,700	5,850	3,850	9,438
0.30	33,000	7,500	5,500	10,912
0.33	36,300	9,150	7,150	12,385
0.36	39,600	10,800	8,800	13,858

We see that if cattle prices do not fall below $0.30 per pound, the investor will earn his required rate of 12% on his $10,000 investment in cattle feeding.

VALUATION OF OIL AND GAS EXPLORATION

Among the different types of tax-sheltered investments, certainly the most risky would be oil and gas exploration. Although chances of successful drilling are not great, the rate of return can be considerable if drilling is successful. Furthermore, investments in oil and gas exploration present two unique characteristics that contribute significantly to the investment value of a particular exploration project.

First, the tax laws allow the deduction of intangible drilling costs, which can constitute as much as 80–90% of the total cost of an exploratory well. Included in intangible drilling costs are wages, fuel, repairs, transportation of supplies, geological surveys, ground clearing, and construction of physical structures that cannot be salvaged. Tangible drilling costs, on the other hand, include pumps, tubing, and casing, all of which have a salvage value and therefore are not deductible. They may, however, be depreciated. The tax savings from deducting intangible drilling costs effectively reduce the initial investment in the exploration project. In this manner, oil and gas exploration is somewhat similar to cattle feeding.

Second, oil and gas are mineral resources that will be consumed over the lifetime of a production well. Therefore, a portion of the resulting cash flow may be considered as recovery of the original investment in the project and hence a depletion allowance is permitted. Rather than basing depletion on the cost of the project, the investor may deduct 22% of the gross income from the well to compensate for the gradual depletion of the mineral resources. The depletion deduction may not exceed 50% of the net income from the well. Apart from a different basis of asset depreciation, oil and gas exploration is somewhat similar to real estate in this respect.

The success or failure of the drilling obviously becomes a critical variable in determining the investment value of an oil or gas exploration project. If the well is dry, then the remaining costs can be written off against other taxable income. The net result for the project will be a loss despite the fact that some tax shelter was provided. But if the well becomes productive, cash benefits can accrue to the investor for many years, and the project can be highly successful. For a single investment in oil or gas exploration, the result typically is either a loss or a large profit.

If one participates in a program of repeated investments in drilling projects, then a weighted average procedure may be used to calculate the expected return of the drilling program. In this procedure, the investment values of the two extremes (success or failure) are weighted by the relative probabilities of success and failure. These probabilities, in turn, are subjective estimates that should reflect prior experience of the drilling company or other similar investments in that geographic area.

An example can be used to illustrate the two important characteristics of oil and gas exploration, and also the weighted average approach to investment valuation. Suppose that an individual invests $25,000 in an oil drilling project. Of this, 80% can be deducted as intangible drilling expenses. Assuming his income tax rate is 50%, the individual can reduce his taxes by $(\$25,000)(80\%)(50\%) = \$10,000$ during the current year. Since there is no other income or expenses during the current year, then the current cash benefit is $F_0 - H_0 = \$10,000$.

If oil is not found, then the remaining $(20\%)(\$25,000) = \$5,000$ can be written off during the following (first) year, and the cash benefit $F_1 - H_1 = \$2,500$ is due solely to tax savings. Calculation of investment value using a discount rate $k = 12\%$ is as follows:

Failure to find oil

Year	Cash benefit $F_t - H_t$	Weight α_t (12%)	Weighted benefit $(F_t - H_t)\alpha_t$
0	$10,000	1.000	$10,000
1	2,500	0.893	2,233
Total			$12,233

The total, $12,233, is seen to be less than half of the original investment of $25,000 if the drilling project is a failure. That is, failure to find oil produces a loss that is approximately half of the original outlay.

If oil is found, however, income and associated expenses will be created for the lifetime of the well. For purposes of illustration, we assume a ten-year lifetime and the following calculation of net cash benefit for each year.

Gross income	$60,000
– Operating expenses	18,000
Net cash income	$42,000
– Depreciation of tangible drilling costs	500
– Depletion (22%)	13,200
Net taxable income	$28,300
– Taxes (50%)	14,150
After tax income	$14,150
+ Depreciation	500
+ Depletion	13,200
Net cash benefit	$27,850

In each year, net cash income of $42,000 must be reduced by depreciation of $500 (straight line, ten years, $5,000 tangible drilling costs) and depletion of $13,200 (22% of $60,000 gross income) in order to get net taxable income. Both depreciation and depletion are added back to after-tax income to get annual cash flow of $F_t - H_t = \$27,850$. Alternatively, one can subtract taxes of $14,150 from net cash income of $42,000 to get the same result. Investment value is found to be $167,353 as follows.

Success in finding oil

Year t	Cash benefit $F_t - H_t$	Weight α_t (12%)	Weighted benefit $(F_t - H_t)\alpha_t$
0	$10,000	1.000	$ 10,000
1-10	27,850	5.650	157,353
Total			$167,353

Notice that the applicable weight for years 1 to 10 is a discounted annuity from Appendix A. The resulting investment value of $167,353 is considerably greater than the $25,000 investment by the individual.

As suggested above, the final step is to estimate the probabilities of successful or unsuccessful drilling in order to calculate the expected investment value. Suppose they are 5% and 95%, respectively. The overall or average investment value for the uncertain drilling project becomes $19,989 as follows:

Outcome	Probability	Investment value	Weighted value
Failure	95%	$ 12,233	$11,621
Success	5%	167,353	8,368
Total			$19,989

Hence, a program of repeated drilling projects of this type would be considered overvalued in view of the $25,000 cost of the exploration project.

As we have seen before, investment value can vary with a change in the discount rate. In this particular example, it can also vary with different probability assessments. For example, if the probability of success were increased from 5% to 10%, the calculation of investment value would become

Outcome	Probability	Investment value	Weighted value
Failure	90%	$ 12,233	$11,010
Success	10%	167,353	16,735
Total			$27,745

and hence the drilling program would be undervalued. Other variables that could readily affect the determination of investment value include gross income, operating expenses, and estimated project lifetime.

INVESTING IN TAX-SHELTERED INVESTMENTS

This chapter has deliberately avoided many of the detailed characteristics of individual tax shelters in order to focus overall on the essentials of investing in tax-sheltered investments. The major theme of the chapter is that the economic consequences of a tax-sheltered investment must be considered along with the unique tax features of that investment. We have seen that our valuation framework can be used on an after-tax basis to incorporate both the economic and tax implications of a proposed investment.

An important characteristic of tax-sheltered investments that has an impact both on the tax situation and the economic consequences is leverage. Leverage is the use of borrowed funds by an investor to try to increase the rate of return that he will earn on his own invested funds. For example, the borrowing usually associated with a real estate investment or other tax-sheltered opportunity serves to magnify the potential benefits to be received from that opportunity by the investor. Unfortunately, leverage also magnifies the potential losses if the opportunity does not materialize as planned. By widening the range of possible outcomes, leverage thus increases the risk of tax-sheltered investments.

A secondary theme that has not been emphasized in this chapter is that each tax-sheltered opportunity should be evaluated relative to the investor's tax situation and his entire portfolio of investment assets. The importance of a portfolio perspective is particularly critical when tax shelters are included, since, for example, a real estate investment or cattle feeding program can effectively shelter the income expected from securities or other assets in the portfolio.

Whereas voluminous information is available on bonds and stocks, only limited information is available on tax-sheltered investments. Whether it be real estate, cattle farming, oil and gas exploration, or any of the other investment opportunities that have special tax features, there is little in the way of historical experience that can be used to compare them with other investment assets. There are no organized markets or price quotations for tax shelters. We thus see that limited information, uncertainty of future outcomes, the impact of leverage, lack of liquidity, and the possibility of changing tax legislation all contribute to the high degree of risk usually associated with tax-sheltered investment.

For many individuals with modest sums of investable wealth, tax shelters are likely not to be appropriate assets for consideration. At the other extreme, many institutional investors are prohibited from investing in various forms of tax shelters. For other individuals and institutional investors, however, tax-sheltered opportunities may well prove to be useful members of investment portfolios. Because of the high degree of risk involved, it is recommended that individual investors seek advice from tax specialists, estate planners, and other sources before committing funds to tax-sheltered investments.

SUMMARY

Tax sheltered investments have received increased attention in recent years because of the opportunities they provide for reducing taxable income. Within the framework of valuation that has been used in this book, it is necessary to consider the economic characteristics of any investment opportunity along with its tax features. By adjusting the valuation framework to an after-tax basis, we can focus on the cash inflows and cash outflows in each year of the horizon including the current year. Real estate, cattle feeding, and oil and gas exploration were selected as being representative examples of tax shelter. For each of the three, investment characteristics were discussed and application of the valuation framework was illustrated. The chapter ended with a review of the reasons why tax-sheltered investments are considered to be highly risky, and with a word of caution to potential investors.

SUGGESTED READINGS FOR CHAPTER 7

R. Brosterman. *The Complete Estate Planning Guide* (New York: McGraw-Hill Book Company, Inc., 1964).

J. C. Francis. *Investments: Analysis and Management* (New York: McGraw-Hill Book Company, Inc., 1972), Chapter 6.

M. Seldin and R. H. Swesnik. *Real Estate Investment Strategy* (New York: John Wiley & Sons, Inc., 1970).

Tax Sheltered Investments (Chicago: Arthur Andersen & Co., May, 1970).

P. F. Wendt and A. R. Cerf. *Real Estate Investment Analysis and Taxation* (New York: McGraw-Hill Book Company, Inc., 1969).

"The Big Drive for Tax Reform in 1973," *Business Week*, August 12, 1972.

part III

Security analysis

PART III is concerned with identification and evaluation of information potentially useful in forming opinions about future attributes of corporate securities. In other words, this part of our book shows how one should proceed to obtain the inputs necessary for applying the valuation techniques of Part II to specific investment opportunities. In Chapter 8, we introduce the important topic of security analysis and discuss those attributes of an investment asset that tend to be qualitative in nature. Included is analysis of the level of the stock market, of the economic conditions that lead particular industries to thrive during certain periods of time, and of various nonstatistical factors that should be examined in a thorough study of a particular company. Chapter 9 illustrates the method for making a careful assessment of the present and past financial statements of a company. Chapter 10 continues this theme by questioning the extent to which changes in reported financial status might have been caused by changes in "generally accepted" accounting techniques—rather than by changes in actual economic events. In Chapter 11, we review various forecasting techniques whereby a thorough evaluation of the present and past operations of a company may be linked into rational expectations for the future.

8

Introduction to security analysis

SECURITY ANALYSIS is the process of locating, studying, and interpreting information so as to form opinions about future attributes of specific securities. Security analysis thus provides the necessary inputs first for determining the investment value of the security and second for establishing the relative attractiveness of that security within the portfolio of the investor. The purpose of this chapter is to examine in detail the nature of this important process—including the analysis of market conditions, the analysis of particular industries, the proper role of financial statement analysis, and the evaluation of certain qualitative factors about a particular company whose securities are being considered.

NATURE OF SECURITY ANALYSIS

Security analysis is only partially independent of the personal needs of a specific investor. Both investment value of a security (Chapter 4) and design of an optimal portfolio (Chapter 3) depend upon an interaction of facts and opinons about each security with the personal needs, risk bearing ability, and individual idiosyncrasies of each investor. It is the task of the security analyst clearly and logically to investigate and describe these facts and opinions as they relate to the goals of each investor. For convenience, the word "investors" is used in this chapter to mean both individuals and investing institutions.

The information that the security analyst strives to obtain and interpret is of several types. Initial concern usually focuses upon the nature of the economy, for this determines both the wisdom of investing at all and the initial choice between bonds, corporate stocks, or other types of investment assets. Closely related to the strength of the economy in the near future are anticipated conditions in the nation's money and capital markets, including anticipated trends in interest rates and stock prices. Analysis of an industry follows in importance because of the impact overall industrial vitality has upon the success or failure of individual companies within their respective industry. Analysis of individual companies is, of course, the ultimate and major portion of any analytical effort by a security analyst. One facet of such analysis is careful scrutiny of that company's financial and operating conditions over a period of time or in relation to other companies of similar characteristics. Factors about the future of the company which cannot be reduced to quantitative form must also be considered. The analyst must therefore search out every fact that might be relevant in assessing the future of the firm.

The end focus of the process of security analysis, extending from analysis of the economy down through detailed study of the characteristics of a single company, is to identify expected future earnings and dividends, expected growth rates, probable future share prices, and the degree of confidence associated with all these forecasts. For many (though not all) companies, estimating probable future earnings, dividends, and possible share prices will consist of a quantitative analysis of past relationships as modified by perceptible qualitative factors. Notwithstanding the portfolio perspective of Chapter 3, assessment of risk is more frequently a matter of subjective judgment dependent, to a large extent, upon beliefs held about the future of the company, the industry, and the overall economy.

It must be emphasized that the relative attention given to the various facets of security analysis will vary from company to company, and one key task of the security analyst is to determine, *for the particular company at hand,* which factors he deems relevant. For example, an analyst looking at a well-diversified, long-established company such as General Electric might logically place greater weight upon careful interpretation of recent financial statements. The same analyst, trying to assess the future of a company such as McDonnell Douglas or Lockheed Aircraft might conclude early in his examination that corporate history is largely irrelevant, and that the critical variable for this company is product acceptance and market size. For example, would an airline prefer the service characteristics of an "air bus," or would it prefer the Anglo-French supersonic Concorde? It is important, therefore, in considering the multitude of factors that might influence an analyst's perception of the future of a company, to recognize that not all factors are relevant for all companies, and that success often will depend upon accurately perceiving which of several factors is most important rather than upon touching base with every conceivable piece of information.

What we are suggesting, then, is that there is no uniform blueprint for security analysis. Rather, each analysis of a given security must be tailored to the particular conditions that exist at the time of analysis—for the economy, for the industry, and for the individual company. We proceed now to a closer look at how an analyst might investigate those conditions.

ANALYSIS OF MARKET CONDITIONS

Investment decisions are seldom made without reference to general market conditions existing at the time a purchase or sale is intended. This is true both for traditional approaches to security analysis and more recent approaches based on capital market relationshps. If the general outlook is for rising stock prices in the near to intermediate future, investors can reasonably and safely proceed with decisions to include common stocks within their investment portfolio. If, however, the market outlook is less than favorable, restraint may be called for, perhaps in the form of committing a lesser portion of one's investable wealth to common stocks, or in the form of delaying the implementation of purchase decisions already made.

Anyone with experience in the security markets will recognize that prediction of the level of stock prices for the near term or even the intermediate term is, at best, a very inexact science. In occasional types of market conditions, the extremes of clear restraint or aggressive purchases may be appropriate. However, in the great majority of other market conditions, no such clear pattern of behavior may be warranted. In other words, every analysis of the level of the stock market does not lead to specific operational conclusions. Nevertheless, it is worthwhile to pay some attention to market conditions, if for no other reason than to avoid purchasing or selling securities at clearly inappropriate times.

The level of the stock market is normally viewed in terms of one or more of the following popular indexes or averages of stock prices: the Dow Jones Averages, the Standard & Poor's Indexes, and the New York Stock Exchange Index.[1] By far the most popular indicators of stock prices are the Dow Jones Averages. Included are a series of three separate averages for 30 industrial stocks, 20 transportation stocks, and 15 utility stocks, as well as a composite average of all 65 stock prices.

A Dow Jones Average was first published in 1884 by Charles Dow who, in 1889, founded the *Wall Street Journal,* in which the series was continued. Originally, the industrial average was the arithmetic mean

---

[1] See W. J. Eiteman, C. A. Dice, and D. K. Eiteman, *The Stock Market* (McGraw-Hill Book Company, 4th edition, 1966) Chapter 9, for more detailed evaluation of various stock price indexes.

of the closing prices of 11 active representative stocks. Thirty issues are included today, and one might expect that today the Dow Jones Industrial Average (DJIA) would consist of the sum of the 30 stock prices divided by 30. Adherence to such a procedure would have led, over the years, to discontinuities in measuring market levels every time one of the thirty component stocks experienced a stock split or stock dividend. Additional discontinuities would have arisen every time one of the component stocks was replaced to make the average more representative of industrial activity or to compensate for stocks lost through mergers.

To adjust for the cumulative effect of stock splits, stock dividends, and replacements, the arithmetic sum of the 30 stock prices is divided by an appropriate *divisor*, which is adjusted from time to time to provide the desirable continuity. For example, in Figure 8–1, we calculate the

FIGURE 8–1
Calculation of the Dow Jones Industrial Average, July 6, 1973

Stock	Closing price	Stock	Closing price
1. Allied Chemical	$ 32.875	15. General Motors	$ 65.500
2. Aluminum Company		16. Goodyear	21.500
of America	57.000	17. International Harvester	27.875
3. American Brands	38.500	18. International Nickel	28.000
4. American Can	31.875	19. International Paper	33.250
5. American Telephone		20. Johns-Manville	20.625
& Telegraph	51.000	21. Owens-Illinois	28.000
6. Anaconda	18.875	22. Procter & Gamble	99.000
7. Bethlehem Steel	26.375	23. Sears Roebuck	93.500
8. Chrysler	23.500	24. Standard Oil of Calif.	77.250
9. DuPont	162.750	25. Texaco	33.875
10. Eastman Kodak	128.500	26. Union Carbide	33.625
11. Esmark	21.125	27. United Aircraft	27.500
12. Exxon	96.750	28. United States Steel	29.500
13. General Electric	56.500	29. Westinghouse Electric	33.750
14. General Foods	24.875	30. Woolworth	22.000
		Sum of stock prices	$1,445.250

Note:
Divisor for the Dow Jones Industrial Average: 1.661

Calculation of Dow Jones Industrial Average: $\dfrac{\$1,445.250}{1.661} = \$870.11$

Sum of earnings for 30 stocks, 12 months ended March 30, 1973: $85.01

"Earnings per share" calculation: $\dfrac{\$85.01}{1.661} = \$51.18$

Price-earnings ratio for Dow Jones Industrial Average: $\dfrac{\$870.11}{\$51.18} = 17.0$ times

Dow Jones Industrial Average as of July 6, 1973, by summing the prices of the 30 component stocks and dividing the total by the divisor 1.661.

Using earnings per share of the DJIA, $51.18, we see that the Dow Jones Industrial Average represented a price-earnings ratio of 17.0 at that point in time. Dividends per share and book value per share are calculated in a similar manner. Notice that each of the thirty stocks has a relative weight in the Dow Jones Industrial Average equal to its price level. Thus DuPont is over seven times more important than Goodyear as an influence on movements of the DJIA. The effect of a 2-for-1 stock split is to reduce the relative weight of that particular stock in the overall average by half.

Standard & Poor's Corporation also calculates stock price indexes that appear in many financial sources. The Standard & Poor Composite Stock Price Index is based on 500 stocks that collectively represent 85 to 90 percent of the market value of all common stocks listed on the New York Stock Exchange. The Composite Index also is subdivided into indexes for 425 industrials, 25 railroads, and 50 utilities. These price indexes are published daily, as are indexes for a large number of individual industries. The Standard & Poor's method for calculating their various indexes is based on the formula:

$$\text{Index} = \frac{\Sigma P_1 Q_0}{\Sigma P_0 Q_0} \times 10 \qquad (8\text{--}1)$$

where P_1 represents current market price, P_0 the average price in the 1941–1943 base period, and Q_0 the number of shares outstanding in the base period. Summations are over all issues that comprise the particular index, and the level of the index is then adjusted to the value 10 in the 1941–1943 base period.

In contrast to the weighting scheme reflected in a Dow Jones average, each company in a Standard & Poor's index is weighted according to the total market value of its outstanding common stock. As such, a Standard & Poor's index is more representative of the aggregate market value of stocks than is a Dow Jones average. On the other hand, to the extent that any market index is used as a criterion against which to measure individual portfolio performance, there is no reason to assume that the aggregate market value weighting of a Standard & Poor's index is more typical than the price-per-share weighting implicit in a Dow Jones average.

The New York Stock Exchange publishes a common stock index based upon the price of each of the more than 1,250 stocks listed on that largest exchange, with separate indexes also appearing for 75 financial institutions, 76 transportation companies, 136 utilities, and nearly 1,000 industrial stocks not included in the first three groups. The New York Stock Exchange indexes also are calculated with a formula such as expression (8–1), except that the base level is 50 and the base period is the end of 1965. They thus reflect a weighting scheme similar to that of the Standard & Poor's indexes.

Absolute measures of market level

One approach to determining the level of the stock market is the absolute level reached by one of the three major market indexes, relative to levels reached in earlier time periods. Figure 8–2 shows monthly index

FIGURE 8–2
Standard & Poor's Industrial Index, Dow Jones Industrial Average, and New York Stock Exchange Industrial Stock Price Index, monthly averages, 1964–73

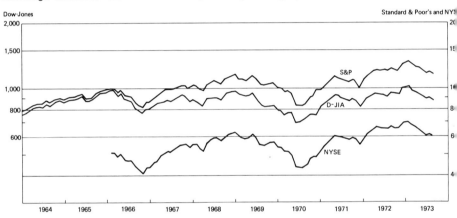

Source: U.S. Department of Commerce, *Survey of Current Business*

levels attained by the industrial stock component of the three averages and indexes explained above. From this graphic portrayal, it is apparent that all three generally move in a parallel fashion. The most opportune time to buy stocks in recent years would have been in mid-1970. It will be noted that this was a period of great pessimism about stocks because of the decline in stock prices that had occurred since early 1969. A generally poor time to buy stocks was in late 1968 or early 1969, when optimistic attitudes toward the stock market were prevalent.

Thus is indicated the major dilemma in basing decisions on the absolute level of the market. One must invariably go against prevailing popular sentiment at major turns in the market—a difficult policy to follow in practice, because it necessitates the investor's rejecting the consensus of investment opinion. Adhering to one's own views in the face of general belief to the contrary requires both a degree of self-confidence lacking in most investors and a reasonable method of determining a normal or appropriate level of the market.

Relative levels of stock prices

A better measure of the reasonableness of stock prices is the relationship between the basic stock price and the underlying economic data that justify a value for stock prices. For example, stock prices may be examined via three ratios: price-earnings, dividend yield (dollar dividend ÷ price), and price divided by book value.

These three ratios for Standard & Poor's Industrial Index are shown in Figure 8–3. The Standard & Poor's Industrial Stock Price Index is

FIGURE 8–3
Relative measures of the level of the stock market and Standard & Poor's Industrial Stock Price Index.

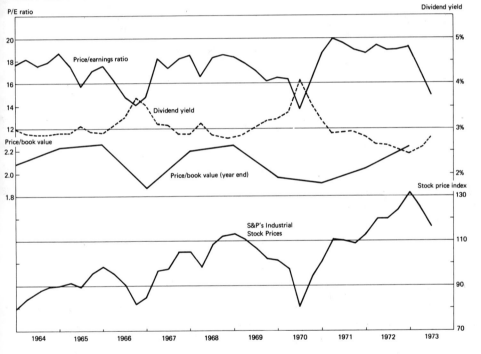

also shown for reference. Bearing in mind the conclusions of Figure 8–2 on absolute levels of the stock market, Figure 8–3 shows that when stocks were a relatively good buy, in late 1966 and mid-1970, the price-earnings ratio dipped below 16 and the dividend yield rose above 3½%. Conversely, when stocks were relatively high and therefore less attractive, as in late 1968 and early 1969, the price-earnings ratio tended to be 18 or more and dividend yield dropped below 3%. The price to book value ratio, available only on an annual basis, tends to support the idea that stocks are perhaps overvalued when their prices approach 2.25 times book value, and are good buys when they are less than twice book value. From this, we might conclude that at extremes of these ranges, which are easily measured, stocks either are exceptionally good purchases or should be generally avoided. Within the ranges, however no clear-cut decisions are indicated.

A stock price level may also be judged in relationship to other variables in the economy. One such approach is suggested by Barron's Confidence Index, which is shown in Figure 8–4. It is the ratio of Barron's

FIGURE 8–4
Barron's Confidence Index and Standard & Poor's Industrial Stock Price Index

Data for last week of each month.

average of the yield on ten high-grade corporate bonds to the yield on the Dow Jones average of 40 bonds. Although this ratio as such does not utilize stock prices, it is commonly interpreted as an indicator of professional investor confidence in the economy and is thus used as a quantitative measure of expected future economic strength. On December 27, 1971, for example, the Dow Jones 40 bond yield was 7.76% and Barron's 10 high-grade bond yield was 7.17%. The ratio of these yields was 92.4%, as compared to 86.8% a year earlier.

The logic of the series consists of the belief that the bond market is dominated by institutional investors, and that when these professional investors are confident about the near future of the economy, they will tend to shift to medium-quality, higher-yielding bonds. The ratio will thus rise. When these professional investors are pessimistic, however, they will become more defensive and shift to higher-quality bonds, causing the yields on these bonds to fall more rapidly than the yield on medium-quality bonds. The Confidence Index then declines. Use of the index implicitly assumes that professional investors are in fact correct in their assessment of the near future of the economy and that they are consistent in adjusting their bond portfolios to this assessment.

Barron's Confidence Index and Standard & Poor's Industrial Stock Price Index are plotted in Figure 8–4. Implicit in use of the index is an often stated (but seldom proved) assumption of the stock market: "Professionals" are correct because they know what they are doing. Following this logic, the Confidence Index suggested a dropping of confidence in the first half of 1966. Had investors sold at that time, they would have avoided the bottom of the market in the last half of 1966. The generally high level of confidence throughout 1967 presaged the market rise of 1968, while the generally lower levels of confidence in 1968 were a prelude to the market drop of 1969 and 1970. However, the major drop in the Confidence Index in the last half of 1970 could be interpreted two ways: one could say that it correctly anticipated the market drop from April, 1971, through November, 1971, or one could say that it gave a false signal for the general rise from mid-1970 through 1972.

Normative level of stock prices

A normative approach to stock prices using the common stock valuation model of Chapter 6 implies first a need to formulate long-run expectations about prices, earnings, and dividend policy. Assume, for example, that on July 6, 1973, one had the following facts and expectations about the Dow Jones Industrial Average:

Actual earnings per share for the most recent twelve
   month period $67.00
Expected growth rate of earnings per share . . . . . 8% per annum
Expected dividend payout ratio. 60%
Growth horizon (time period the investor was
   willing to discount). . . . . 10 years
Probable price-earnings ratio at the end of growth
   period (at growth horizon, in 10 years) . . . . . . 16 times earnings
Rate of return desired . . . . 12% per annum

Solving expression (6–14) in Chapter 6, one obtains a discounted present value of expected future benefits of 1076.08.[2] On July 6, 1973, the actual level of the Dow Jones Industrial Average was 870.11, some 20% below the level judged appropriate by this method. The stock market should be judged a good buy at that time.

---

[2] Details of this calculation are left to the reader as an exercise.

Central value method of evaluating market level

One leading source suggested that a reasonably sound central value for the Dow Jones Industrial Average could be determined by capitalizing the average earnings of the past ten years by a rate equivalent to 1.33 times the current yield on high-grade bonds.[3] *Capitalizing* in this context is the process of imputing a value for an investment asset based on certain benefits that accrue to the owner of the asset. The ratio of 1.33 was arbitrarily chosen to reflect Professor Graham's opinion that stocks should yield in earnings 33% more than bonds yield in interest. Application of this central-value method to the Dow Jones Industrial Average in July 1973, based upon average earnings for the decade 1963–1972, leads to the following result:

Earnings per share
(Dow Jones Industrial Average)

1963	$ 41.21
1964	46.43
1965	53.67
1966	57.68
1967	53.87
1968	57.89
1969	57.02
1970	51.02
1971	55.09
1972	67.11
Total.	$540.99

Note:
Average earnings of ten years,
1963–1972: $54.10
Yields of Moody's Corporate
Aaa Bonds, July 6, 1973:
7.26 %
Central Value:
$54.10/(7.26 %)(1.33)
= 558.88

Average earnings per share on the Dow Jones Average ($54.10) would be exactly 9.68% of the Dow Jones price of 558.88, thus yielding an earnings return about one-third greater than the 7.26% available on high-grade corporate bonds.

The fact that the Dow Jones Industrial Average in July, 1973, was 958, when the central-value method suggested it should be 559, leads to several possible conclusions:

1. The market in 1973 was too high by historical perspective and should be expected to drop during subsequent months.

---

[3] Benjamin Graham, David Dodd, and Sidney Cottle, *Security Analysis: Principles and Techniques* (McGraw-Hill Book Company, fourth edition, 1962), page 422.

2. Investors no longer insist on an earnings yield greater (by one third) than the interest yield on high quality bonds. Such a conclusion might arise from the hypothesis that investors in stocks now anticipate a greater proportion of their gain will be derived from stock price appreciation.
3. The method is simply fallacious, possibly because it ascribes too much weight to the earnings of a decade earlier.

The central-value method does indicate very clearly one aspect of the difficulty of determining a reasonable level for the market. When a developed procedure is established for validating the reasonableness of current stock prices, and when that method then indicates that the stock market is too high, it is extremely difficult to determine if the method is in fact correct, or if the market is in fact correct and the method in error. Human nature will generally cause the question to be resolved in the direction of the market being correct and the method being wrong.

INDUSTRY ANALYSIS

Any company, no matter how well managed, can thrive only with great difficulty if it operates in an industry that is economically weak. Conversely, even a mediocre management may do quite well, at least for a number of years, if operating in a buoyant, rapidly growing, and profitable industry. Industry analysis may thus be viewed from two perspectives. At one level, proper identification of industries expected to thrive in the near future can be a beginning step in identifying individual companies whose future will be tied to the growth of that industry. During the early 1960s, many small companies manufacturing peripheral computer equipment, such as disc files or line printers, prospered simply because of the fact that computer sales were growing rapidly. By the late 1960s, the emphasis had shifted to companies providing computer software facilities such as ready-made programs for solving business or engineering problems.

At a second and perhaps less publicized area, a strong and buoyant industry can help cover, at least for a period of time, errors made in the assessment of a particular company. The choice of the weaker, rather than the stronger, company in a strong industry frequently results in excellent profits simply because the weaknesses of the particular company are overcome by the strength of the industry. This is not to suggest that this lesser company will not eventually find itself in difficulty, or even that the better company would not, over the same time interval, have proved itself an even better investment. When industry strength diminishes, the weaker company frequently declines even more rapidly.

Nevertheless, industry strength provides a cushion against the risk of errors in individual company analyses.

No simple checklist exists of those variables which, if collected and analyzed, will establish the probable future of an industry. True success in industry analysis often resides with that individual most able to ferret out a unique piece of knowledge not yet perceived as important by other observers. Lacking a complete list of variables to be studied, however, some general factors can be identified and discussed. These tend to group themselves into those factors that will influence future demand for products of an industry and those factors that relate to the ability of the industry to supply products at a quality and price level that is competitive.

Industry demand factors

One factor to consider in assessing the future of an industry is expected demand for the products of that industry. A logical starting point is to search for a key economic statistic with which future industry sales might reasonably be correlated. One such statistic is population projections; the Bureau of the Census publishes periodic projections of population size and distribution for the United States. A simple and logical use of such data would be the obvious correlation between sale of primary school teaching material and the birth rate in the country six to nine years previously. The birth rate, in turn, might be correlated with the marriage rate of several prior years, although changes in attitude toward family size and availability of birth-control devices may alter historical patterns. All of this would have an ultimate bearing on the demand for baby food from a particular firm.

A second variable to consider in estimating future industry demand is changes in consumer tastes. The demand for wine as a table beverage in the United States has risen much more rapidly than the adult population. Early identification of this change in taste, when considered against the fact that the lead time in adding to the wine producing capacity of the country is several years, would have led to the conclusion that ownership of vineyards or vineyard-owning corporations would in all likelihood be very profitable. One might hypothesize that increased wine consumption per person has resulted from a higher level of discretionary personal income or has been the consequence of the interaction of more Americans' traveling abroad (exposing U.S. residents to alternate styles of dining) plus the very rapid rise in the dining-out habits of the growing urban portion of the U.S. population.

Yet another approach to estimating the future of an industry is to estimate what portion of industry sales will replace existing products and what portion will be truly new market penetrations. The growth of the automobile industry within the United States for many decades was sustained by the fact that an increasing proportion of the population was acquiring an automobile and, in later years, by the trend to multiple-auto families. Yet a practical limit exists to expansion induced by such trends, especially after most family units acquire their first car and many own two or more. As the ratio of new car sales to total registered automobiles in use declines, it becomes apparent that sales within the United States are increasingly limited to replacement of old automobiles and to growth caused by population expansion—a rate of growth significantly less than the rate of growth experienced by the industry from 1920 or even from 1945 to the 1960s. One might interject other hypotheses into this projection, based upon changes in patterns of urban living, upon expected traffic congestion, upon the long-run effects of the ecology movement, upon changes in the prestige once associated with owning a larger and more luxuriously appointed vehicle, or upon major changes in fuel availability and cost.

Industry demand is also a function of the degree of competition between industries. Thus the aluminum industry competes with the tin-plate industry in supplying the metal for beer and soft-drink cans, while the plastics industry in turn competes with the aluminum industry in supplying certain parts for automobiles. Indeed, the international airline industry competes with the camping equipment industry for a share of the consumer's recreation dollar, and the television industry competes with both the movie industry and the amusement park industry for a portion of the consumer's entertainment dollar.

Cost and supply factors

The second major category of factors to be identified in assessing the future of an industry consists of those events that influence the ability of an industry to deliver its product to the consumer at a price that is competitive and yet allows a reasonable degree of profit. One such factor is the degree of competition *within* the industry (as distinct from competition between industries as mentioned earlier). A healthy, balanced degree of competition with minimum government regulation generally creates the best investment climate. Excessive competition can be destructive for all members of an industry until such time as competition weeds out the less-efficient firms. During an excessively competitive period, profits of even the strongest companies tend to suffer. Too little competition, especially if accompanied by unduly high profits, may attract new firms into the industry and thus create a future surplus of competitive pressures. Examples would be manufacture and sale of television sets in the late 1950s or pocket electronic calculators in the early 1970s. Government regulation, although necessary in some categories, may prevent the flexibility need for healthy survival.

A second factor is foreign competition. If U.S. costs have risen above the cost of equivalent foreign imports for such reasons as higher labor costs not matched by higher productivity (the automobile industry), greater product innovation (miniaturized tape recorders from Japan) or style (shoes from Italy or Brazil), the U.S. industry is at an inherent disadvantage. If as a consequence of foreign competition, the domestic industry successfully turns to the government for import protection (cotton textiles), such an industry will very likely remain forever dependent upon political whims for its financial success. Government protection also tends to encourage continued inefficiency in many instances. United States industries that cannot maintain an unprotected competitive stance on a world-wide basis are not likely to be the viable industries of the remainder of the 20th century.

A third factor, at times related to foreign competition and at times related only to domestic performance, is labor relations. Healthy survival of American corporate enterprise has not been a significant policy goal of organized American labor. Thus in industries where the bargaining position of organized labor is strong relative to the bargaining position of the employer, possibilities for long-run health of the industry may be severely limited. Perhaps the classic case of such pressures is the gradual erosion of the strength of the railroad industry relative to the competitive strength of the trucking industry, although admittedly factors in addition to labor productivity played a part.

Industry diversification

A popular recommendation for investors with limited investable wealth is to diversify their portfolio holdings according to industries. In other words, by selecting a single security from each of a few industries, the small investor is likely to attain a reasonably well diversified portfolio. The underlying premise for such a recommendation is that securities within the same industry are apt to have rather similar characteristics. Clearly there are exceptions to this, but still a portfolio diversified by industries is likely to have securities with characteristics different enough to protect the total portfolio against adverse economic developments affecting single companies and industries.

In the spirit of such a portfolio perspective, therefore, it is of interest to examine those industries that would have contributed to well-diversified portfolios during recent years. To do this, the mean-variance approach to portfolio selection (of Chapter 3) can be applied to the universe of industries identified by Standard & Poor's Corporation. With expectations for future returns of each industry based on ten prior quarters of experience within that industry, efficient portfolios of industries were calculated as of the end of each year in the period 1966–1971. The industry holdings for each of the six years are identified in Figure 8–5. Several observations should be made of these holdings. First, only 28 of the 83 industries, as defined by Standard & Poor's, appeared in one or more of the efficient portfolios. Second, the number of industries in efficient portfolios ranged from three in 1970 to eleven in 1968. This suggests that it did not take a large number of industries for efficient diversification, provided the proper industries were selected. Third, there was considerable turnover in holdings from year to year as expectations changed for various industries. The industry holdings reported in Figure 8–5 are intended to illustrate the concept of portfolio diversification, and not that expectations for the future can be based solely on the

FIGURE 8–5
Industry holdings in efficient portfolios, 1966–71

Industry	Holdings at the end of year					
	1966	*1967*	*1968*	*1969*	*1970*	*1971*
New York City banks			X			
Banks outside New York City			X			
Beverages–brewers				X		X
Beverages–soft drinks						X
Building materials–Heating & Plumbing			X			
Coal–Bituminous					X	
Containers–Metal & Glass	X					
Containers–Paper			X			
Cosmetics		X		X		
Electronics	X	X				
Gold mining		X		X		
Home furnishings			X			
Hotel/Motel			X			
Lead & Zinc				X		
Mobile home builders			X	X		X
Motion pictures	X	X				
Office & building equipment			X			
Oil–Integrated international				X		
Pollution control	X			X	X	
Radio broadcasters	X					
Real estate			X			
Retail stores–Food chains			X			
Retail stores–Variety chains				X		
Savings & Loan			X	X		
Soap						X
Tobacco–Cigarettes					X	X
Truckers						X
Toy manufacturers		X				

past. Rather, a careful investor should use the demand and cost factors existing in each industry to augment the historical trends observed. Nonetheless, the holdings reported in Figure 8–5 suggest that a careful industry analysis can be used as a prerequisite step for more detailed analyses of individual securities within the chosen industries.

FINANCIAL STATEMENT ANALYSIS

Financial statement analysis is the process of forming judgments about the present and past financial health of a company from evidence available in its balance sheets, income statements, or other financial statements. It is also the process of identifying corporate characteristics that warrant further, often direct, investigation. In other words, careful analysis of financial statements may lead to specific conclusions about the past and present financial condition of a company that will cause an investor to reach a decision, or the analysis may serve rather to identify characteristics needing further verification before they can be relied upon as the base for an investment decision.

As seen in Part II, security valuation and portfolio construction is essentially forward-looking; a potential investor must formulate and act upon opinions about the future. Financial statement analysis, on the other hand, is essentially backward-looking; a potential investor seeks to identify and clarify trends in the past or to compare current characteristics of one company with those of another or with a tabulation of industry averages.

Therefore, an investor reviewing financial statements must always ask himself the crucial question: *What relevance does the past have in trying to determine what the future will hold?* For many types of companies, such as those dominated by new products (electronic desk calculators) or those whose sales are tied to political decisions (defense and aerospace industries), the appropriate answer may be "not at all" or "very little." In such instances, the analyst will reasonably spend little time scrutinizing financial statements.

However, for the great majority of companies, economic and financial relationships of the past do have relevance in estimating the future. Barring a specific reason to expect the contrary, recent trends for these companies are more likely to continue than to reverse, perhaps because the same management is producing the same product with the same plant and equipment and selling it against the same competition. Relative levels of past efficiency, both in terms of the amount and types of investment required to generate activity and in terms of the costs associated with likely levels of revenue are a starting point for making assumptions about probable future efficiency. The reader should thus understand that analysis of financial statements seldom leads to absolute conclusions. Rather the process reveals additional evidence about a company that must be considered and evaluated along with all other known facts.

Financial statements may also be analyzed as a preliminary screening process to sort potential investments into sets for further immediate consideration, for continued casual watching if circumstances change, and for exclusion from the group of stocks for which detailed evaluations will be made. Given that thousands of securities are potentially available for purchase, it is important to avoid expanding time and energy looking at issues not worthy of immediate purchase. Rather, one's analytical effort must be quickly focused on those issues having potential at the present time.

One system of screening might be to have a computer sort from a universe of securities for which data are available a set that satisfy certain basic financial conditions. For example, all common stocks listed on the New York Stock Exchange might be screened for those that possess the following arbitrary characteristics:

1. A pre-tax rate of return on operating assets greater than 25 percent.
2. Growth of earnings per share at an average rate in excess of 12 percent per year.
3. A present price-earnings ratio no greater than the present price-earnings ratio of the Dow Jones Industrial Average.

Actual parameters to be used as cut-off points in such a procedure could be adjusted upwards or downwards as needed to allow a certain number of stocks through the screen. An alternate formulation would be to pick screening parameters that would allow through the screen any stock in the top, say 20% of all stocks, when measured by that test.

Another approach to preliminary screening is to plot key financial characteristics on sheets of semilogarithmic paper. The use of semilogarithmic paper causes constant rates of change to appear as straight lines. Thus the characteristic with the greatest rising slope has been increasing at the highest rate. Consider Figure 8–6, in which sales, net income, and market price for three companies in the paper industry are compared. Sales of all three have been rising during the decade, but sales of Union Camp, the smallest company, have in recent years increased more rapidly than sales of either Crown Zellerbach or Scott Paper Company. This is apparent from the greater slope of Union Camp sales as plotted on the semilogarithmic paper. Sales of Scott Paper, it might be noted, actually dropped in 1971. In 1970 and 1971, earnings per share of all three paper companies fell sharply. However, the drop for Union Camp started later (1971 rather than 1970) and was less

FIGURE 8–6
Screening of paper companies by semilogarithmic plots

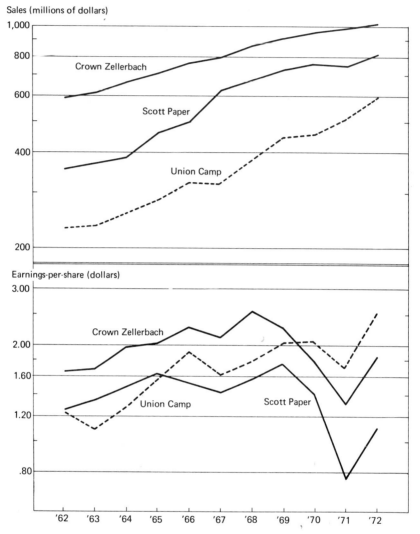

Sales (millions of dollars)

Earnings-per-share (dollars)

precipitous. Earnings per share for Scott Paper Company dropped by the greatest proportion.

If one had already concluded that the paper industry would be profitable in the future, a simple screening such as suggested in Figure 8–6 might suggest that Union Camp, rather than Scott Paper, was the company showing the greatest promise. On the other hand, if the price of Scott Paper common stock had dropped more than in proportion to its earnings, Scott Paper might be worth studying for a potential rise.

Specific evidence would be needed, however, to justify investing in Scott Paper Company on the assumption that its recent adverse performance would be reversed.

Because of the importance of analysis of the particular situation of a company as reflected in its financial statements, Chapters 9 and 10 are devoted entirely to this subject.

QUALITATIVE FACTORS IN COMPANY ANALYSIS

Financial statements and other statistics do not reveal all that must be known about a company. As with industry analysis, the investor able to identify some critical variable not readily quantifiable or perceived by other observers and yet important in early identification of probable future performance may often be able to make a corect investment decision in advance of general recognition of the investment merits of the company in question.

The key to early identification of improved future prospects is imagination in looking at the whole spectrum of relationships involving a given company within a particular industry and amid changing economic conditions. For this reason, checklists must inevitably be incomplete. Nevertheless, they are a starting point and they do illustrate the type of nonquantifiable variables that must be studied. Some of the more important of these factors are indicated below. Others are applications to a company of the same variables mentioned earlier in our brief discussion of industry analysis.

Quality of management

Corporate management should be capable and imaginative and should have established procedures for ensuring its collective perpetuation, even though individuals may enter and leave the management team. In one respect, the quality of management might be judged from the financial results it has produced. However, to say that a good earnings trend is evidence of top quality management is to follow circular reasoning if, later in the same analysis, good management so defined is used to forecast a good earnings trend. To avoid double-counting, management potential must be separated from the visible manifestations of its past activities. In this context, one must determine if the management has a firm grasp of key factors influencing its company and if it is keeping abreast of new trends, both in products and in management techniques. Does it have both short-run and long-run plans for the company against which actual results may be measured, and does it have the flexibility to adapt to unusual events? Is the board of directors composed in part of outsiders with a broad perspective, or is it made up entirely of corpo-

158

rate officers beholden to the chief executive for their jobs? Professional analysts evaluate the quality of management from interviews with managers, supplies, and customers of the firm in question as well as from contacts with competitors or other parties who know of the quality of the firm's managers. Individual investors are much more limited in their ability to evaluate management quality, although helpful articles do appear in business periodicals such as *Business Week, Forbes,* or *Fortune.*

Product reputation and sales potential

Products of the company should be highly regarded by the firm's customers, both for quality and for assurance that the most appropriate technology for each product has been used. Where relevant, the firm should have a reputation for constant product improvement (automobile manufacturers) or development of new products (electric appliances). In some instances this reputation can be measured by research and development expenditures as a percentage of sales; at other times a history of past product innovation may be most indicative.

Future sales potential is tied to more than a good product sold at an appropriate price. A growing demand for the product creates a better investment opportunity than does a stable demand or a demand that must be won by taking a share of the market from competitors. Furthermore, demand should not be vulnerable to external forces. If, for example, a major portion of demand is derived from a few very large industrial users, changes in the nature of their business may filter down to the supplier. The largest supplier of cyclamate sweetener to soft-drink manufacturers, for example, was a victim of the combination of federal restrictions on the sale of cyclamates and the drop in demand for that sweetener from all other users. Export sales to a major foreign market may suddenly disappear as that country seeks to develop a domestic capacity for making the good in question or is engulfed in a war or revolution. Any supplier to the defense or aerospace industry runs the risk that a change in the political situation will significantly reduce his business potential.

Product diversification

Diversification was shown in Chapter 3 to be the process of combining somewhat dissimilar assets into a portfolio as a means of reducing the variability of possible outcomes of the investor. Similarly, a firm can diversify across products and product lines so as to reduce the range of possible results that may occur under differing economic conditions and other environmental factors. Although one may argue that a firm should not attempt to diversify in this manner since investors can do that for themselves, there still may be reasons why a firm may choose to diversify across products.

One reason is that internal efficiencies may exist. These internal efficiencies might relate to production, as when one product can be produced cheaply as the by-product of another. Alternatively, efficiencies might relate to marketing, as when several products can be handled through the same distribution system. An example of product efficiencies might be the conversion by meat packers of animal by-products to fertilizer, while an example of distribution efficiencies would be the manufacture and sale of Minute Maid juices by the Coca-Cola Company. An ability to identify efficiencies of this sort is thus another qualitative factor that is part of the process of analyzing an individual company.

Socio-political status

Somewhat related to reputation of a firm's product is the reputation of the firm and its management. A history of forward-looking and successful product innovation, an imaginative marketing system, good relations with community and with employees, and a freedom from inappropriate social characteristics (such as having been identified as a racially discriminatory employer or as a heavy polluter) constitute a partial list of an endless array of characteristics that influence the probable future of a company and establish the parameters within which it must be judged.

Regulatory climate

Certain industries, such as public utilities and transportation companies, are dominated by regulators. These are treated later in Chapters 12 and 13. Other industries, not normally considered as regulated, are nevertheless sensitive to governmental regulation in certain aspects of their operations. Food manufacturers are subject to regulations on purity and on the use of additives. Pharmaceutical manufacturers must follow prescribed and lengthy testing procedures before being given permission to introduce a new drug to the general public. Automobile manufacturers are increasingly having to respond to new pollution and safety standards, and virtually all companies are now forced to assume greater warranty responsibility for the quality of their products than was required only a few years ago.

The economic success of any company depends in part upon its ability to satisfy the regulatory needs of a concerned public. Accordingly, more attractive investment opportunities are likely to be found among those companies most able to respond to changes in the regulatory environment without loss of earning potential.

SUMMARY

This chapter has provided an overview of the process by which a security analyst studies characteristics and attributes of particular industries and companies so as to identify potentially good investment opportunities. The major areas that must be studied by the security analyst include the reasonableness of stock price levels, the nature of particular industries, and those factors, both quantitative and qualitative, that are relevant in formulating a reasoned opinion about the future of a specific company.

SUGGESTED READINGS FOR CHAPTER 8

F. Amling. *Investments: An Introduction to Analysis and Management.* 2d ed. (Englewood Cliffs, N.J.: Prentice-Hall, Inc., 1970), Chapter 10.

B. Graham, D. L. Dodd, and S. Cottle. *Security Analysis: Principles and Technique.* 4th ed. (New York: McGraw-Hill Book Company, Inc., 1962), Chapter 7.

E. A. Helfert. *Techniques of Financial Analysis.* 3d ed. (Homewood, Ill.: Richard D. Irwin, Inc., 1972), Chapters 1–3.

J. A. Mauriello. *Accounting for the Financial Analyst.* rev. ed. (Homewood, Ill.: Richard D. Irwin, Inc., 1971), Chapters 1–2.

9

Financial statement analysis

ANALYSIS of the financial statements of a company is at the very heart of the process of investing for anyone who seriously considers investing in securities issued by corporations. An informed and meaningful set of conclusions can be deduced from the study of published financial statements only if one understands the nature and limitations of the information contained in the financial reports of a company, as well as the particular considerations that place the data into the sharpest possible perspective. It is the purpose of this chapter to explain the meaning of various measurable relationships that are obtained in a careful financial analysis. Chapter 10, which follows, will explore the assumptions, procedures, and conventions by which financial statements are created—and thus the accuracy with which accounting procedures portray reality.

REVIEW OF FINANCIAL STATEMENTS

Corporate progress and status are reported in three separate but basic statements. The first statement is the *balance sheet,* sometimes called the statement of financial position. The balance sheet indicates for a specific date (such as December 31 of a given year) the status of the company in terms of assets, liabilities, and net worth. *Assets* consist of all economic resources of value owned by the company and purchased for a measurable monetary amount. Under most conditions, assets are carried on the balance sheet at their acquisition cost or at some lesser figure; they are not written up to reflect any unrealized increase in observed current value. Liabilities and net worth represent the sources of the assets. Together they constitute a bundle of claims against the assets of the company. *Liabilities* are debt claims, usually for a precise quantity of dollars and often with an established maturity.

Net worth, also referred to as invested capital, stockholders' equity, book value, or simply equity, represents the ownership claims of stockholders. That portion, if any, of the net worth that is the claim of preferred stockholders is usually a fixed dollar amount, although if preferred dividends for prior years have not been paid, the amount due in liquidation to preferred stockholders might differ from the balance sheet claim. The remainder of net worth constitutes the claim of the common stockholders, who are the residual owners of the company. Although expressed as a dollar amount, the common stockholder claim is in fact a residual claim for any value that might remain after all other claims have been paid. It is also a claim against future earnings. Thus the dollar amount shown in the balance sheet has very little, if any, relationship to the "true" value (we have called it "investment value" in prior chapters) of the common stockholders' claim. A substantial portion of this book, in fact, is devoted to the process of determining the "true" investment value, as compared to the book value, of the claims of common stockholders. Book value is, at best, a weak indicator of investment value. Frequently it is of no use whatsoever in judging investment value.

The second major statement of significance in the analysis of a company's financial situation is the *income statement,* or the profit-and-loss statement, as it is sometimes called. An income statement is in fact a statement of revenues and expenses for an interval of time, such as a 12 month period ending on December 31. The statement explains the factors causing a change in the stockholders' well-being as measured by the net worth section of the balance sheet, during that time interval. In some presentations, the income statement stops short of accounting for all changes in stockholders' well-being, and a separate surplus reconciliation or retained earnings statement is added. A *retained earnings statement* shows how the retained earnings account (which is part of net worth) changes from one balance sheet to the next. In other presentations, the income statement itself includes, in addition to a calculation of net income for the time period, dividends and extraordinary charges, which together provide the information otherwise included in the surplus reconciliation.

A third statement, now required for all companies registered under the Securities Exchange Act of 1934, is a *statement of changes in financial position,* formerly called a *sources and application of funds statement.* This statement focuses broadly upon the derivation and use of corporate wealth during a time interval, and in particular on changes in the working capital position of the firm.

These three statements constitute the data source for financial analysis. To illustrate how the information can be used, the following sections of this chapter will study, for illustrative purposes, the consolidated financial statements of The Gillette Company. For purposes of exposition, the statements of 1967 will be compared with those of 1971. In fact, all years—if not all quarters—should be studied in a like manner and, in addition, the statements of Gillette should be compared with those of its closest competitors or with industry averages.

The basis of the illustrative analysis of Gillette that follows is a computer program developed at the U.C.L.A. Graduate School of Management.[1] The formats used in the remainder of this chapter follow those used in that computer program. The inputs and outputs of this computer

FIGURE 9–1
Inputs and outputs for a computerized system of financial statement analysis

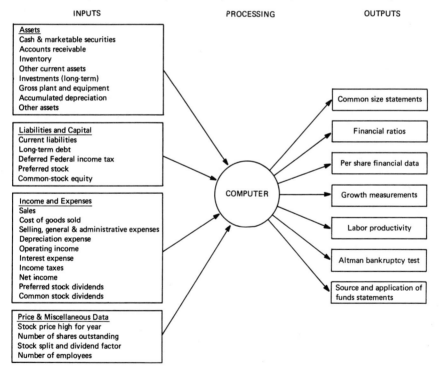

---

[1] The program is written in FORTRAN and has been used at the U.C.L.A. Graduate School of Management over the years with most models of I.B.M. computers. An earlier version of the program was described in David K. Eiteman, "A Computer Program for Financial Statement Analysis," *Financial Analysts Journal*, November–December, 1964, pages 61–68.

164

program, viewed as a processing problem, are shown in Figure 9–1. Four categories of inputs are used:

1. Asset items, taken from the balance sheet.
2. Liability and net worth items, taken from the balance sheet.
3. Income and expense items, taken from the income statement.
4. Miscellaneous data, including information on share prices and number of employees.

BALANCE SHEET ANALYSIS

Balance sheets for The Gillette Company are shown in Figure 9–2. The format and amount of data in this exhibit are revised and abbrevi-

FIGURE 9–2

THE GILLETTE COMPANY
Consolidated Balance Sheets
December 31, 1967 and 1971

Assets	1971	1967
Cash and marketable securities	$ 45,666,000	$ 46,187,000
Accounts receivable	140,452,000	65,628,000
Inventory	132,388,000	94,769,000
Other current assets*	0	0
Total current assets	$318,506,000	$206,584,000
Investments	990,000	1,797,000
Gross plant and equipment	253,320,000	146,961,000
Accumulated depreciation	–82,548,000	–52,212,000
Net plant and equipment	170,772,000	94,749,000
Other assets	65,184,000	46,146,000
Total assets	$555,452,000	$349,276,000
Liabilities and net worth		
Current liabilities	174,896,000	116,374,000
Long-term debt	70,090,000	40,159,000
Deferred federal income tax	11,800,000	3,700,000
Other liabilities and minority interest	2,176,000	2,322,000
Preferred stock	0	0
Common stock and paid-in capital	52,349,000	41,288,000
Retained earnings	244,141,000	145,433,000
Total liabilities and capital	$555,452,000	$349,276,000

* The format used here is identical to that used in the computer program, which is available to accompany this book. Therefore, the "other current asset" heading has been retained even though for Gillette the balance in this account is zero.

ated somewhat from the data as originally published by the company. Cash, for example, has been combined as a single line entry with marketable securities, and current liabilities are shown only as a total rather than by each separate component.

Every evaluation of financial statements necessitates the resolution of a certain dilemma. That is, a greater volume of input data can almost always be obtained, and thus greater and more detailed output is possible. In practice such expansion must be limited because collecting and recording data is expensive in terms of money and time, and the benefits of the additional data may not warrant the additional cost. In addition, an overwhelming volume of output may lead to less rather than greater understanding, simply because sheer quantity and lack of ability to focus on important relationships may prevent the analyst from fully interpreting the output.

Because the process of analyzing financial statements is oriented toward identifying meaningful relationships, rather than just toward processing a large quantity of data, the input information must be limited to that which can be meaningfully interpreted. It is an error to assume that volume of output can be substituted for informed interpretation. For that reason, we present the financial statements of Gillette in a compact form.

Common-size statements

The balance sheet data of Figure 9–2 may be reduced to percentage form, as in Figure 9–3, in order to focus attention on changes in the proportional mix of accounts, and also to identify significant variations for further consideration. Such a reduction of statements to this percentage form, frequently called a *common-size statement*, facilitates comparison

FIGURE 9–3

THE GILLETTE COMPANY
Common-size Balance Sheets
December 31, 1967 and 1971

Assets	*1971*	*1967*
Cash and marketable securities	8.2%	13.2%
Accounts receivable.	25.3	18.8
Inventory.	23.8	27.1
Other current assets.	0.0	0.0
Total current assets	57.3%	59.1%
Investments	0.2	0.5
Net plant and equipment.	30.7	27.1
Other assets	11.7	13.2
Total assets.	100.0%	100.0%
Liabilities and net worth		
Current liabilities	31.5	33.3
Long-term debt	12.6	11.5
Deferred federal income tax	2.1	1.1
Other liabilities	0.4	0.7
Preferred stock	0.0	0.0
Common stock, paid-in capital, and retained earnings	53.4	53.5
Total liabilities and capital	100.0%	100.0%

because the influence of growth is removed. Common-size statements may be of minimal value in making comparisons of companies in diverse industries. They also may have limited usefulness in comparing companies in similar lines of business because of variations and changes in accounting methods. The greatest advantage of common size statements is in making a time-trend analysis of a single company—or of companies already known to be virtually identical in economic characteristics.

Common-size statements for The Gillette Company portrayed in Figure 9–3 reveal a decline in proportional investment in cash and marketable securities from 13.2% of total assets in 1967 to only 8.2% in 1971. Clearly, The Gillette Company was less liquid in 1971 than four years prior. The analysis as such does *not*, however, reveal whether the company was normally liquid in 1967 and was illiquid in 1971 or whether the company was excessively liquid in 1967 and evolved to a position of normal liquidity.

Thus is illustrated both the basic strength and basic weakness of quantitative analysis: trends are quickly apparent, but the significance of these trends is a matter of judgment. The question as to the adequacy of Gillettes' cash position might be resolved by comparing the ratio of cash to total assets to that of other companies, or Gillette's management might be queried as to the cause of the indicated trend.

The truth of the matter is that a broad cross-section of U.S. companies have reduced their proportional investment in cash during the past several years. For example, *Fortune* magazine recently indicated that cash as a percentage of total corporate assets declined overall from 12.6% in 1963 to 5.9% in 1970 and then increased somewhat to 7.2% in 1971.[2] The downtrend resulted from more careful cash management by most U.S. companies, while the 1971 reversal was caused by a desire for more liquidity after the 1970 recession. Although the initial year of comparison is not the same, *Fortune*'s information would tend to indicate that Gillette has followed a national trend and was not excessively illiquid in 1971.

Other changes in the asset mix of The Gillette Company between 1967 and 1971 can be quickly identified from the presentation in Figure 9–3. Accounts receivable have increased proportionally from 18.8 percent of assets to 25.3 percent—a probable indication of weaker collection policies of the company, but possibly the result of changed competitive circumstances or of entry into new product lines that carry different credit terms than the original production of 1967. Furthermore, inventories have dropped in proportional significance; possibly technological improvements have been made that have increased the production process or have lessened the need to carry finished goods inventory of a

---

[2] "The Importance of Being Liquid," *Fortune*, June 1972, pages 49–50.

certain size. Alternatively, management simply may have been willing to operate with smaller level of inventory.

Current assets as a whole have diminished only slightly in relative importance, while net plant and equipment have risen slightly in relative importance. Investments in nonoperating assets (such as securities of nonconsolidated subsidiaries or, in the case of Gillette, sums due from employees under stock purchase and option plans) remain of very modest significance; a sudden enlargement or diminution of such investments or of other assets would be cause for further investigation.

Because the total percentage of assets must always equal 100%, a change in any one item, say an increase in current assets, must cause a decrease in some other items. In interpreting common-size statements, one must be careful not to count the same event twice, first as an increase in one asset category and then as a separate, apparently unrelated, decrease in some other asset category. The same caution must be applied in interpreting changes in the liabilities and equity side of the balance sheet.

The liabilities and equity side of the Gillette statements in Figure 9–3 shows a very constant pattern of financing. Although current liabilities have declined in relative importance from 33.3% to 31.5%, the change is slight and is offset by a slight increase in the relative importance of long-term debt. Total contractual debt, short- and long-term together, has remained very close to 44 percent over the period being studied. All other liability categories are of modest proportions, and the equity of the common stockholders has remained at approximately 53 percent.

Current asset proportions

Because a change within the current asset structure may at times be obscured by a disproportionately large increase in a fixed asset category, and because of the importance of efficient management of current assets to the near-term profitability of most manufacturing and merchandising companies, a valuable supplement to a common-size balance sheet is a common-size portrayal of current assets alone. This is shown in Figure 9–4. The data confirm what was apparent from Figure 9–3. That

FIGURE 9–4

THE GILLETTE COMPANY
Current Asset Proportions
1967 and 1971

	1971	1967
Cash and marketable securities	14.3%	22.4%
Accounts receivable.	44.1	31.8
Inventory	41.6	45.9
Other current assets.	0.0	0.0
Total	100.0%	100.0%

is, cash and inventory have diminished in relative importance while accounts receivable have risen in significance.

Capital structure proportions

As with current assets, it is sometimes desirable to identify specific changes in the capital structure of a company, both to see if the exposure of the enterprise to financial risk has changed with time and to identify the possibility of a change in management's attitude toward such risk. Such a tabulation of capital structure proportions for Gillette is shown in Figure 9–5.

FIGURE 9–5

THE GILLETTE COMPANY
Capital Structure Proportions
1967 and 1971

	1971	1967
Long-term debt	19.1%	17.7%
Preferred stock	0.0	0.0
Common stock and paid-in capital	14.3	18.2
Retained earnings	66.6	64.1
Total	100.0%	100.0%

The data reveal that Gillette has avoided any significant changes in its capital structure. Long-term (sometimes called funded) debt has increased slightly in importance, as has retained earnings, while contributed equity (common stock and paid-in capital in excess of par value) has diminished slightly. As was pointed out in Chapter 6, common stock and paid-in capital collectively represent the initial investment by common stockholders, while retained earnings represent their continuing reinvestment of earnings back into the company. One would surmise that the growth of Gillette has been financed in about constant proportions by increased debt and the retention of earnings, and not by the sale to the public of new shares of common stock. By conventional standards for incurring debt, which would permit most industrial companies to raise about 30 percent of their total capital structure from debt before the debt level was regarded as excessive, Gillette, with less than 20 percent debt, is shown to be financially conservative. Gillette now has the equity base to do additional debt financing should it wish to raise funds by selling more bonds.

An analyst must constantly be aware of data that might not show in the financial statements. In lieu of long-term debt, which does appear on the balance sheet, a company might enter into long-term financial leases. Such leases might in fact have financial implications identical to debt, in that lease payments approximate the combination of principal amortization and interest expense on debt, but the leases do not show on the balance sheet. Such a financing technique is sometimes called, for obvious reasons, "off balance sheet financing." An investor can identify the presence of leases by carefully reading footnote to the financial statements, or by noting lease payments on the income statement.

Because the financial implications of leases are similar to those of debt even though the debt quantity implicit in the lease is hidden from view, the analyst may wish to "capitalize" the lease. In other words, future lease payments, identified from footnotes to the financial statements, are discounted at an appropriate interest rate, and the present value total is added to the balance sheet as if it were debt. If such an adjustment is made, it is also necessary to add an equivalent sum to net fixed assets to reflect the equivalent additional "ownership" of assets.

INCOME STATEMENT ANALYSIS

Figure 9–6 presents income statement information for The Gillette Company for 1967 and 1971. As with the balance sheet data, certain

FIGURE 9–6

THE GILLETTE COMPANY
Statement of Income
Years Ended December 31, 1967 and December 31, 1971

	1971	1967
Sales	$729,687,000	$428,357,000
Cost of goods sold (excluding depreciation)	274,566,000	127,448,000
Gross profit	455,121,000	300,909,000
Selling and administrative expenses	315,224,000	190,763,000
Depreciation expense	18,365,000	8,993,000
Other operating expenses	–0–	–0–
Operating income	121,532,000	101,153,000
Interest expense	9,569,000	2,593,000
Income taxes	48,300,000	47,200,000
Other nonoperational charges (revenues)	1,264,000	–5,255,000
Net income	62,399,000	56,615,000
Dividends on preferred stock	–0–	–0–
Net to common stock	62,399,000	56,615,000
Dividends on common stock	40,999,000	34,432,000
Net addition to retained earnings	$ 21,400,000	$ 22,183,000

items have been rearranged to enhance the analytical potential. In its published income statement, Gillette does not report a separate line item for depreciation; presumably depreciation associated with product manufacture is included within Gillette's cost of goods sold figure, while depreciation on office equipment and other non-manufacturing assets is included under the heading, "administrative expenses." Analytically, it is desirable to separate depreciation, and in Figure 9–6 a compromise has been effected by subtracting the entire depreciation expense for the year (available from the statement of changes in financial position) from cost of goods sold and showing it as a separate expense line. Although admittedly a compromise necessitated by lack of complete data, this procedure is probably more meaningful than the alternative of combining depreciation with various cash expenses.

In another simplification, the heading "other nonoperational charges" has been used in Figure 9–6 to encompass both irregular, nonoperational, or extraordinary expenses (which would be subtracted) and irregular, nonoperational, or extraordinary revenue (which would be added). The entry in the income statement indicates the sum of these two items on a net basis. As seen, the net was negative (on balance, revenue) in 1967, but was positive (on balance, an expense) in 1971.

The income statements of Figure 9–6 have been reduced in Figure 9–7 to percentage or "common-size" form to cast sharper perspective

FIGURE 9–7

THE GILLETTE COMPANY
Common Size Income Statement
1967 and 1971—Data in Percent of Total Sales

	1971	1967
Sales	100.0%	100.0%
Cost of goods sold (excluding depreciation)	37.6	29.7
Gross profit	62.4%	70.3%
Selling and administrative expenses	43.2	44.5
Depreciation expense	2.5	2.1
Other operating expenses	–0–	–0–
Operating income	16.7%	23.6%
Interest expense	1.3	0.6
Income taxes	6.6	11.0
Other nonoperational charges (revenues)	0.2	–1.2
Net income	8.6%	13.2%
Dividends on preferred stock	0.0	0.0
Net to common stock	8.6%	13.2%
Dividends on common stock	5.6	8.0
Net addition to retained earnings	2.9%	5.2%

on variations between the year 1967 and 1971. The function of a common-size income statement is to compare expense levels to the sales revenue generated during an income period. Expenses, in turn, may be grouped into three classes: The first class consists of operating expenses payable in cash. Such expenses include direct labor, direct material (included together in cost of goods sold), and all other selling, general, and administrative expenses of a cash nature that were necessary to the functioning of the enterprise during the time period. An essential economic characteristic of these expenses is that their reduction, relative to sales, should be considered favorable. Moreover, general and administrative expenses are relatively fixed, and we should expect a percentage decline with increased sales. If a company can in fact decrease these expenses relative to sales, its operating efficiency can be increased. Care must be taken, of course, that any reduction in relative cash operating expenses is not a false economy, as for example if the research staff were fired in one year to make that year look better, while at the same time sacrificing potential improvements for the future.

In Figure 9–7, operating expenses payable in cash include cost of goods sold, which has increased significantly as a percent of sales since 1967; thus gross profit dropped significantly from 1967 to 1971. This would tend to indicate that The Gillette Company has been unable to keep costs under control or that it has been unable to advance prices in proportion to advances in manufacturing costs. Lower gross profit could also reflect price-cutting, entering into new product lines having lower profit margins, the expiration of patents, or more aggressive action by competitors.

On the other hand, selling and administrative expenses for Gillette have remained quite constant as a percentage of sales revenue. Apparently Gillette has not let these types of expenses, which in the short run relate more to the fixed expenses of being in business than to the variable expenses of changes in the volume of business, drift out of control.

The second class of expenses is noncash operating expenses, of which the most important is depreciation. Other expenses in this category include amortization (the periodic write-off of such outlays as goodwill or research and development) and depletion for companies exploiting natural resources. Because these are the costs of the capital consumed by operation, their magnitude in relationship to sales is also important. This relationship to sales, however, can also be altered for two other reasons: (1) the cost of capital consumed will increase, relative to production, if a company introduces a greater degree of automation and thus deliberately substitutes capital costs for the labor that was previously expended for the same job; (2) the magnitude of depreciation expense, relative to sales, might also increase or decrease because of an arbitrary change in the depreciable rate for an asset.

This type of juggling is more easily done with noncash operating expenditures, where the appropriate period of write-off must in any case be arbitrary, than with cash operating expenses, where outflows can be measured precisely. For this reason, depreciation and other noncash expenses should be judged separately relative to sales. Depreciation significance is discussed in greater detail in Chapter 10. In the case of Gillette, depreciation expense as a percentage of sales revenue is relatively low and did not change appreciably between 1967 and 1971.

Sales less both cash and noncash operating expenses leaves "operating income," an income figure that can be compared between companies without being influenced by the results of different tax rates or debt strategies or the results of miscellaneous other revenues or charges. In effect, operating income is the figure most useful in evaluating the efficiency of a company in manufacturing and distributing its product.[3] In the case of Gillette, operating income as a percentage of sales (sometimes referred to as the "operating income margin") dropped from 23.6% to 16.7%. In 1971, Gillette appeared to be a less efficient company than it had been in 1967. The *Wall Street Journal* of February 2, 1972, attributed this decline to the combination of increased competition in Gillette's traditional product, razor blades, with the high cost of diversifying to new fields, such as women's hair coloring, cosmetics, and colognes.

The third class of expenses are financial, and include interest and income taxes. The magnitude of interest expense, relative to revenue, is of a different significance from that of operating expense, for the most efficient operation may in fact incur more interest expense as an increased proportion of debt funds is used to finance operations. The level of interest expense is therefore more meaningful in relationship to the income available to pay interest than it is in relationship to sales. Therefore it is excluded from operating income. Income taxes are incurred in proportion to taxable income, rather than in proportion to sales, so they likewise are excluded from operating income and from comparison with sales. In the case of Gillette, income taxes have dropped proportionally to the drop in operating income margin, as would be expected if the company is taxed in a normal manner.

The significance of other nonoperational charges or of nonoperational revenue, in relationship to sales, is primarily by exception. Usually such items are a small part of the total earnings or expenses of a company. Should they assume major proportions, the analyst must recognize that total profitability is dependent upon events other than normal corporate operations, and he must seek out the significance of the activities that are subsumed under this nonoperational heading.

The remainder of Figure 9–7 shows dividends and net addition to retained earnings as a percent of sales. Although the drop in dividends as a percentage of sales is noted, stockholders would be far more con-

---

[3] An exception exists for some business that lease assets, thus including lease payments among operating expenses, while other firms being compared finance their own ownership of assets, thus incurring interest expense in lieu of lease payment. It is necessary to revise one type of statement to make it comparable with the other.

cerned with changes in dollar dividends that they receive, or in dividends as a percentage of current market price of the common stock. The decrease from 5.2% to 2.9% in the sales revenue retained by the company reveals that whatever expansion taking place in 1971 is financed to a lesser degree from retention of earnings and, therefore, to a greater degree from other sources.

FINANCIAL RATIOS

Additional perspective can be gained in financial statement analysis by reviewing financial ratios, many of which combine balance sheet data with income statement data. Seventeen key ratios for The Gillette

FIGURE 9–8
Key financial ratios (The Gillette Company, 1967 and 1971)

	1971	1967
Liquidity ratios		
1. Current ratio (times)	1.8	1.8
2. Quick ratio (times)	1.1	1.0
3. Cash turnover (days)	19.9	39.5
4. Receivable turnover (days)	64.5	48.6
5. Inventory turnover (days)	176.0	222.1
Efficiency ratios		
6. Earning power (percent)	22.9	34.3
7. Operating asset turnover (times)	1.4	1.5
8. Operating income margin (percent)	16.7	23.6
Profitability ratios		
9. Return on debt and equity (percent)	20.5	31.1
10. Return on common equity (percent)	21.9	33.3
11. Cashflow to common equity (percent)	28.3	38.6
Financial policy ratios		
12. Interest coverage (times)	12.6	41.0
13. Fixed charge coverage	−	−
14. Dividend payout (percent)	65.7	60.8
15. Effective tax rate (percent)	43.6	45.5
16. Accumulated depreciation (percentage of gross plant)	32.6	35.5
17. Net debt repaying ability (years)	2.5	1.7

Company are shown in Figure 9–8. For convenience of interpretation, these ratios are grouped by purpose, as follows:

1. Ratios analyzing liquidity.
2. Ratios analyzing operating efficiency.
3. Ratios analyzing the profitability of invested funds.
4. Ratios analyzing financial policies.

174

Liquidity ratios

Liquidity ratios are defined as follows:

1. Current ratio $= \dfrac{\text{Cash } (t) + \text{Marketable securities } (t) + \text{Receivables } (t) + \text{Inventory } (t)}{\text{Current liabilities } (t)}$

2. Quick ratio $= \dfrac{\text{Cash } (t) + \text{Marketable securities } (t) + \text{Receivables } (t)}{\text{Current liabilities } (t)}$

3. Cash turnover $= \dfrac{\text{Sales } (t)}{\dfrac{\text{cash } (t) + \text{marketable securities } (t) + \text{cash } (t-1) + \text{marketable securities } (t-1)}{2}}$, divided into 360

4. Receivables turnover
$= \dfrac{\text{Sales } (t)}{\dfrac{\text{Receivables } (t) + \text{Receivables } (t-1)}{2}}$, divided into 360

5. Inventory turnover
$= \dfrac{\text{Cost of goods sold } (t)}{\dfrac{\text{Inventory } (t) + \text{Inventory } (t-1)}{2}}$, divided into 360

The notation "(t)" indicates data input for the year for which the ratio is calculated, while the notation "$(t-1)$" indicates a data input for the immediately preceding year. Thus the denominator of ratio #3, cash turnover, is in fact *average* cash balance calculated as the average of the current year-end cash balance and the prior year-end cash balance. Should monthly or quarterly data be available, averages based on such data would be preferable to annual averages. When only one financial statement is available, thus precluding the possibility of using average denominators, all of the ratios explained in this chapter may be calculated with a single year-end value.

The current ratio measures the amount of liquid assets (current assets that are normally convertible into cash within one year) relative to currently existing claims payable within one year (current liabilities). With a current ratio of 1.8 in both 1967 and 1971, Gillette's liquidity position has not changed. Although the current ratio of 1.8 is slightly below the popular rule of thumb of 2 to 1, the difference is modest, and the validity of the 2 to 1 rule of thumb cannot be verified.

A high current ratio might appear for a company that was retaining, rather than writing off, a significant amount of inventory no longer salable. Therefore as a check on the current ratio, the quick ratio, also called "acid-test" ratio, is calculated by removing inventory from the numerator of the current ratio. Because inventory is different from firm to firm, and also because inventory is less liquid than either cash or accounts receivable, the quick ratio is really a better measure of liquidity for comparing firms in different industries. At 1.1 in 1971 and 1.0 in 1967, the quick ratio for Gillette does not reveal any deterioration of liquidity during the four-year interval.

The three current asset turnover ratios indicate what might be referred to as the "lingering time" within the company for each category. In 1971, for example, Gillette operated with a cash balance equal to almost 20 days of sales, down sharply from a cash balance equal to almost 40 days of sales in 1967. Receivables were equivalent to 64 days of sales, indicating that on the average the company had to wait 64 days from the date of a sale until sales proceeds were received in cash. This was a significantly longer wait than the 48 days wait experienced in 1967, and indicated a deterioration in the quality of accounts receivable. Inventory turnover indicates the average length of time inventory is held. For Gillette this ratio has dropped from 222 days to 175 days, indicating improved handling of inventory. In general, a shorter turnover interval for any of the current asset accounts indicates greater efficiency, although an extremely low ratio might call attention to the risk of running out of cash or inventory or failure to allow sufficient credit to attain the maximum profit from sales.

Efficiency ratios

These three ratios are derived from the three basic ratios of the famous DuPont System of financial control,[4] although the components are revised slightly to be more meaningful in comparing operating efficiency alone, rather than operating and financing efficiency combined. The three ratios are defined as follows:

6. Earning power $= \dfrac{\text{Operating income } (t)}{\dfrac{\text{Oper. assets } (t) + \text{Oper. assets } (t-1)}{2}}$

7. Operating asset turnover $= \dfrac{\text{Sales } (t)}{\dfrac{\text{Oper. assets } (t) + \text{Oper. assets } (t-1)}{2}}$

8. Operating income margin $= \dfrac{\text{Operating income } (t)}{\text{Sales } (t)}$

---

[4] For an explanation of the DuPont system of financial control, see J. Fred Weston and Eugene F. Brigham, *Managerial Finance*, (Holt, Rinehart and Winston, fourth edition, 1972), pages 29–33, or Robert W. Johnson, *Financial Management* (Allyn and Bacon, fourth edition, 1971), pages 37–45.

Operating income is as shown in Figure 9–6, while operating assets refers to all assets devoted to the major commercial activity of the company. In this instance, operating assets includes all assets except investments (which may be presumed to produce interest or dividend income, rather than sales and operating income).

Earning power indicates the rate of return the corporation is able to earn (before taxes, interest, and miscellaneous nonoperating revenues and expenses) on those assets devoted to generating sales revenue. This ratio indicates that Gillette's rate of earnings on operating assets dropped from 34% to 23% during a five year period. Clearly Gillette as of 1971 was not as profitable as it had been four years earlier. The ratio thus reveals fundamental changes in the corporation's profitable use of its assets.

Earning power (ratio #6) can be shown to be the product of operating asset turnover (ratio #7) and operating income margin (ratio #8) as follows:

$$\underset{(\text{ratio} \ \#\,6)}{\frac{\text{Operating income}}{\text{Average operating assets}}} = \underset{(\text{ratio} \ \#\,7)}{\frac{\text{Sales}}{\text{Average operating assets}}} \times \underset{(\text{ratio} \ \#\,8)}{\frac{\text{Operating income}}{\text{Sales}}}$$

In the case of Gillette, the decrease in earning power was caused primarily by the decrease in operating income margin—that is, in the profit retained from each dollar of sales. The operating income margin dropped from 23.6% in 1967 to 16.7% in 1971, while operating asset turnover declined slightly from 1.5 in 1967 to 1.4 in 1971. We shall explore further extensions of the earning power relationship in Chapter 11.

Profitability ratios

Profitability ratios measure the success with which the company employs all of the capital at its disposal, after interest, taxes, and any nonoperational charges or revenue. Two ratios that measure profitability are:

9. Return on debt and equity

$$= \frac{\text{Net income } (t) \ + \ \text{Interest expense } (t)}{\dfrac{\text{Total capital } (t) \ + \ \text{Total capital } (t - 1)}{2}}$$

10. Return on common stock equity

$$= \frac{\text{Net to common stock } (t)}{\dfrac{\text{Com. stk. eq. } (t) \ + \ \text{Com. stk. eq. } (t - 1)}{2}}$$

Return on debt and equity together (i.e., return on total permanently invested capital) is the annual rate of return earned on the investment of all permanent investors. For this purpose, long-term bondholders are regarded as "permanent" contributors to the corporate pool of capital, even though their investment does mature at some future date. The reason for doing so is an assumption that any maturing long-term debt is likely to be replaced with new long-term debt, so as to keep the capital structure at a constant mix over time. Gillette was able to earn 31.1 percent on the combined investment of bond and stockholders in 1967, but this ratio declined to 20.5 percent in 1971. It might be observed that a 20.5% rate of return on invested capital would probably delight most corporate managers, so the decline shown between 1967 and 1971 is of much greater moment from a time-trend point of view than from a comparative approach.

The impact of financial leverage, by which corporate management elects to use debt funds or preferred stock with an interest or preferred dividend rate lower than the implied cost of equity, is measured by ratio #10. Common stockholders of The Gillette Company earned a return of 21.9 percent on their invested capital in 1971, down from 33.3 percent in 1967. In both years, the return on common equity was slightly above the return on debt and equity together, indicating that the funds derived from bondholders (and preferred stockholders, if the company had had any) were used to earn more than their cost. The modest differential, in the case of Gillette, would appear to come primarily from the relatively small amount of debt in the capital structure (see Figure 9–5 above) plus the fact that the company has no preferred stock outstanding.

As was indicated earlier, depreciation is an expense the magnitude of which can be arbitrarily increased or decreased within a certain latitude. For that reason, there is a problem of comparability from one firm to another. Because the amount of depreciation deducted in calculating net income may be determined in an arbitrary manner, a helpful ratio to check the results of the basic profitability ratios is the ratio of "cash flow" to invested equity capital. This ratio is defined as follows:

11. Cash flow to common stock equity

$$= \frac{\text{Net to common } (t) + \text{Depreciation } (t)}{\dfrac{\text{Com. stk. eq. } (t) + \text{Com. stk. eq. } (t-1)}{2}}$$

Even if the amount of depreciation expense is changed from year to year or is calculated differently from one company to another, the sum of depreciation and net income, i.e., cash flow, is relatively more immune to arbitrary alteration. Thus ratio #11, the ratio of cash flow to common equity, serves as a check on the validity of ratio #10, return on common equity. In the case of Gillette, the decline in the two ratios from 1967 to 1971, indicate that the change in apparent profitability was not caused by any significant change in depreciation policies.

Financial policy ratios

Certain other ratios can be used to focus attention on a number of other relationships important for the investor. They are defined as follows:

12. Interest coverage
$$= \frac{\text{Net income } (t) + \text{Income taxes } (t) + \text{Interest expense } (t)}{\text{Interest expense } (t)}$$

13. Fixed charge coverage $= \dfrac{\text{Income available to pay fixed charges } (t)}{\text{Interest expense } (t) + \text{Lease payments } (t)}$

14. Dividend payout $= \dfrac{\text{Common stock dividends } (t)}{\text{Net to common stock } (t)}$

15. Effective tax rate $= \dfrac{\text{Income taxes } (t)}{\text{Net income } (t) + \text{Income taxes } (t)}$

16. Accumulated depreciation to gross plant
$$= \frac{\text{Accumulated depreciation } (t)}{\text{Gross plant } (t)}$$

17. Net debt-repaying ability
$$= \frac{\begin{array}{c}\text{Current liabilities } (t) + \text{Long-term debt } (t) \\ - \text{ Cash } (t) - \text{ Marketable securities } (t)\end{array}}{\text{Net income } (t) + \text{Depreciation expense } (t)}$$

Interest coverage indicates how many dollars of earnings are available, before taxes, to pay each dollar of interest expense. The ratio measures the safety of interest payments and is thus used to test the quality of a company's debt. Graham, Dodd, and Cottle suggest that interest coverage of seven or more times for industrial bonds is sufficient to be regarded as of high quality.[5] By this criterion, the bonded indebtedness of Gillette, interest on which was earned over 12 times in 1971, is of excellent quality.

A related test of protection is coverage of total fixed charges (ratio #13). As was mentioned earlier, the advent of leasing has led many companies to substitute, in effect, lease payments for interest and amortization of debt. Thus a coverage figure is sometimes calculated in which the numerator is the same as for interest coverage, but with lease payments added back to create a "pre–fixed charge" income. The denominator consists of interest expenses plus all fixed charges such as lease payments. Fixed charge coverage, so calculated, is an appropriate safety measure for bondholders. If fixed charge coverage is used by common stockholders to assess their residual position after the payment of fixed charges, it is also appropriate to add sinking fund charges into the de-

---

[5] Benjamin Graham, David Dodd, and Sidney Cottle, *Security Analysis, Principles and Technique*, (McGraw-Hill Book Company, fourth edition, 1962), page 348.

nominator. Payment of sinking fund charges is usually obligatory if earned, but nonpayment if not earned is not a cause for bankruptcy.

Either ratio #12 (interest coverage) or ratio #13 (fixed charge coverage) is usually satisfactory for measuring the trend of a single company over a period of time or for comparing companies about equally involved in leasing fixed plant and equipment. If, however, it is desirable to compare one company that leases its assets with another company owning assets financed by long-term debt, an adjustment is necessary to achieve comparability. The interest coverage ratio, calculated in the traditional way for the first company, measures coverage only of interest expense and not of debt amortization. To achieve comparability, the lease payments of the second company must be divided into that portion that constitutes substantive interest and that portion that constitutes substantive amortization. The substantive interest portion can then be added to interest expense, and the accounts of the two companies will have been reduced to a similar basis. Substantive interest portions of lease payment can be estimated first by calculating the present value of the leased assets at an appropriate current interest rate for long-term bonds of a company of the type being judged. The rate used to discount the stream of future lease payments can then be applied to the resulting present value to derive substantive interest for the initial year. Any portion of the present year's lease payment in excess of this substantive interest sum can be viewed as substantive principal amortization, and can be added to the denominator of ratio #13. In Figure 9–8, ratio #13 was not calculated due to lack of data.

Dividend payout, ratio #14 in Figure 9–8, indicated the proportion of each year's earnings distributed to common stockholders as cash dividends. With a payout ratio of 65.7 percent, Gillette's dividend policy is somewhat more generous than that of the majority of companies in the United States. For example, the average ratio for the 30 "blue-chip" companies in the Dow Jones Industrial Average is only 56 percent. Other things being equal, a high dividend payout stock is more attractive to seekers of current income, while a low dividend payout stock is assumed (sometimes incorrectly) to have potential for future growth.

Effective tax rate is calculated from public financial statements to verify that reported income tax expenses are within an appropriate and expected range. With an income tax rate of 48% on corporate income greater than $25,000, but with possibilities for variation due to capital gains or capital losses, varying tax treatment of consolidated foreign subsidiaries, special tax credits, and the like, a general range of from 45% to 50% is normal. Any *significant* deviation from this range should probably be investigated for the possibility that, even if current levels of pretax earnings are constant, after-tax earnings in the future might change because of the expiration of some particular short-lived tax advantage.

With a tax rate, from the public statement, of only 43.6% in 1971 and of only 45.7% in 1967, Gillette appears able either (1) to reduce income taxes below what they might normally be expected to be, or (2) to report for public purposes a level of earnings calculated by a more generous method than that used for tax purposes while not, at the same time, normalizing its tax expense.[6]

Accumulated depreciation as a percentage of gross plant and equipment, ratio #16, is a surrogate designed to reveal the *approximate* age of the plant and equipment. Figure 9–8 shows that to 1971 Gillette had accumulated depreciation equivalent to 32.6 percent of the cost of its plant and equipment. Although the rate of financial depreciation is not the same as the rate of physical depreciation, there is nevertheless a rough correlation between the two, especially if other indicators, such as ratio #11 (the ratio of cash flow to common equity) do not cast doubt on the consistency of the company's depreciation policies.

Net debt repayment ability indicates the time, in years, that would be needed to retire present debt obligations, both long-term and short-term, at present levels of earnings. Total debt is first reduced by present cash balances (including marketable securities) to obtain a net figure that must be repaid from operating cash flow. Operating cash flow, measured as the sum of net income plus depreciation, is then divided into the net debt figure to determine how many years would be needed under present conditions to completely retire that debt. The significance of the ratio lies in the fact that a sudden rise is a warning of danger from excessive debt *unless* future operating cash flows can be assumed to rise proportionally above present levels.

A repayment ability of two and a half years for Gillette, even though above the 1.7 figure for 1967, does not indicate that Gillette has incurred any undue financial risk by obligating itself for too great a magnitude of debt relative to its present cash generating ability.

PER-SHARE FINANCIAL DATA

For both screening and valuation purposes, it is useful to identify the characteristics of a single share of stock. Some of these, such as stock market prices, are not usually presented in annual reports and so must be obtained from external sources. The number of shares of

---

[6] Footnotes to Gillette's 1971 *Annual Report* indicate that they do in fact normalize because of the tax reduction caused through the use of accelerated depreciation. Thus the second hypothesis is wrong. The notes to the *Annual Report* further show that Gillette does not provide for federal income taxes on unremitted foreign earnings that have been either permanently invested or held for permanent investment. Because net income from operations abroad (excluding Canada) in 1971 amounted to 53% of consolidated net income, the lack of immediate U.S. taxes on that portion not remitted to the U.S. would seem to account for the tax rate of 43.7% calculated from the public statements.

common stock outstanding can usually be obtained from the balance sheet. These basic data are presented for the Gillette Company in the top portion of Figure 9–9.

FIGURE 9–9
Per-share calculation (The Gillette Company, 1967 and 1971)

	1971	1967
Stock price low for year	$34.75	$40.25
Stock price high for year.	$50.87	62.87
Average market price.	$42.81	51.56
Number of shares of common stock outstanding	29,287,000	28,909,000
Per-share calculations		
Earnings	$ 2.13	$ 1.96
Depreciation.	0.63	0.31
Cash flow	$ 2.76	$ 2.27
Dividends	$ 1.40	$ 1.19
Book value.	10.12	6.46
Sales	24.92	14.82
Price ratios		
Price-earning ratio (times)	20.09	26.33
Dividend yield (percent)	3.27	2.31
Price to book value (times)	4.23	7.98
Price to cash flow (times)	15.52	22.72
Net current assets to price (percent)	11.45	6.05

Per-share calculations, as shown in the center portion of Figure 9–9, indicate for a single share those characteristics of interest to most buyers. In addition to earnings and depreciation, which are sometimes totaled together as "cash flow," an investor might seek dividends, book value, or even sales per share. It will be noted that Gillette improved in all six of these measures between 1967 and 1971.

The ratio of sales per share of common stock bears further comment. During the several years that ended in 1970, many companies succeeded in boosting per share earnings by effecting mergers with other companies through an exchange of stock on a basis that increased per-share earnings by "purchasing" those earnings with a disproportionately small number of shares. Some stockholders, watching their reported earnings rise, did not realize that the increase was caused by a string of clever mergers and accounting adjustments, rather than by fundamental increases in the economic strength behind their shares of stock. Sales per share of common stock checks on this phenomenon, for if earnings per share are rising but sales per share are not, the possibilities for sustaining the rise in earnings are remote.

The bottom portion of Figure 9–9 relates certain of these characteristics to the average market price of a share of stock. In the sample calculation, average is taken as the mean of the high and low price for the year. However, other more representative averages, such as the mean of the 12 monthly highs and lows, may be used. Price-earnings ratios and dividend yields have already been discussed. The ratio of price to book value indicates how many dollars are being paid for each dollar of equity as recorded on the balance sheet. Because investment value is determined primarily from earning ability, rather than asset value, and because current values often differ significantly from the historic values recorded on balance sheets, this ratio may well exceed unity and may be in the interval of two to three.

However, if the ratio is an even higher multiple, as it was for Gillette at almost 8.0 times book value in 1967, careful scrutiny is warranted. If the present market price is justified by present earnings levels, and if book value is not excessively distorted by recent inflation, then earnings are usually high in proportion to the underlying assets. Although at first blush this is a desirable characteristic, it is likely to attract competition unless the company possesses unique attributes (patents, reputation, a skilled management team) that cannot be duplicated by a potential competitor. Lacking these unique attributes the company might be facing the advent of an increase in competition that will lower future earnings and thus market price. Of course, if the relatively high price is not supported by high earnings, a high ratio of price to book value is added warning of dangers in the present high stock price. This latter seems to be the case for Gillette.

The ratio of price to cash flow is a ratio used to supplement price-earnings ratios for companies where earnings are judged to be arbitrarily distorted by capricious depreciation accounting. The ratio is frequently used in analysis of petroleum producing companies.

The ratio of net current assets, defined in this instance as current assets less the sum of current and long-term debt, to price measures the vulnerability of the company to takeover for purposes of liquidation (sometimes called "raiding") rather than continued operations. This condition exists when the ratio exceeds 100 percent. At such a time, fixed assets could be abandoned and the company liquidated at a profit on the basis of its net current assets alone. The ratio is most useful in finding companies whose stock price has been excessively depressed because of poor earnings but whose assets alone have a substainable value. Such companies frequently recover or are absorbed on favorable terms into another company.

MEASURING GROWTH

As was seen from the valuation models of Chapter 6, anticipated growth is a critical variable in the valuation of common stocks. One indicator of potential future growth is the historic growth of past years. Such growth may be judged graphically, as was done in the previous chapter (Figure 8–6) where key financial characteristics were plotted on charts of semilogarithmic paper. An easy way of converting such data to approximate annual rates of growth is to plot, at the bottom of each sheet, several lines indicating the slope of a trend rising at 5%, 10%, 15%, and 20% per year. Such a chart is illustrated in Figure 9–10, in which earnings per share, net sales, and annual average market price (mean of the annual high and low) are plotted for Gillette. From Figure 9–10 one can guess that the annual increase of earnings per share was something less than 5%, while the rate of growth of net sales was almost 15%. There is no discernible long-run increase in the average

FIGURE 9–10
Sales, Earnings per share, and stock price range (The Gillette Company, 1966–1972)

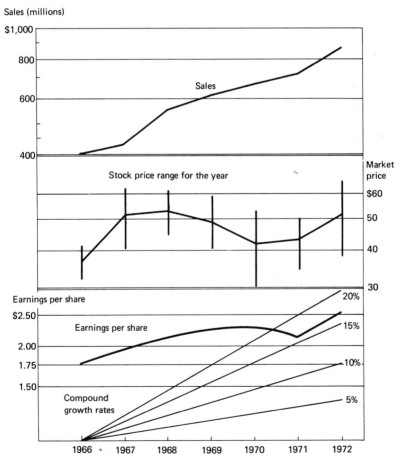

Sales (millions)

market price of the stock; in fact, starting in 1967 the trend was downward.

A more precise approach to measurement of growth is to calculate the slope of the least squares regression line that best fits the logarithms of the variables. This gives the annual average compound rate of growth of the variable. We shall discuss this procedure in detail in Chapter 11, along with other methods of forecasting. Such a calculation is presented in panel A of Figure 9–11 for seven important variables. We

FIGURE 9–11
Calculation of growth rates for The Gillette Company

A. *Compounded annual growth rates and correlation coefficients, 1966–1971*

	Growth rate per annum (percent)	Correlation coefficient
Earnings per share	4.24	0.8002
Net profit to common.	4.78	0.8149
Net sales.	13.74	0.9812
Dividends per share	4.10	0.8779
Average market price	0.18	0.0232
Book value per share	13.36	0.9876
Cash flow per share	6.68	0.9321

B. *Growth rate from previous year, percent*

	1971	1970	1969	1968	1967
Earnings per share	−5.66	0.56	4.84	9.38	11.76
Net profit to common.	−5.56	0.83	5.22	10.00	13.53
Net sales.	8.48	10.35	10.19	29.14	8.12
Dividends per share	0.12	−0.04	16.69	0.65	−0.72
Average market price	2.09	−15.17	−7.05	3.15	40.07
Book value per share	8.15	10.14	12.50	16.97	20.01
Cash flow per share	−2.16	4.72	6.14	11.73	12.32

C. *Change in growth rate from previous year, percent*

	1971–70	1970–69	1969–68	1968–67
Earnings per share	−6.22	−4.28	−4.54	−2.37
Net profit to common.	−6.39	−4.40	−4.78	−3.53
New sales	−1.88	0.16	−18.95	21.02
Dividends per share	0.16	−16.73	16.05	1.37
Average market price	17.26	−8.12	−10.20	−36.92
Book value per share	−1.99	−2.36	−4.47	−3.04
Cash flow per share	−6.88	−1.42	−5.59	−0.59

see that earnings per share have risen at an annual *average* rate of 4.24%, while net sales have been going upward at an annual average rate of 13.74%. The fact that earnings per share have been rising less rapidly than sales reflects the decrease in operating efficiency identified earlier.

One risk of complete quantification of growth rates is that perspective on variability is lost. For example, a calculated growth rate of 4.24% for earnings per share does not reveal whether that average growth rate is typical of most years or masks a number of very disparate annual performances. The variability problem must be resolved if historic data are to be used as a guide to the future. One approach is to study the apparent variability of the original data, such as in Figure 9–10. There we saw that the average growth rate for both earnings per share and for stock price range were poor indicators, for in recent years the trend has been downward, offsetting the favorable rise immediately after 1966.

An alternative approach is to calculate a statistical measure of variability. In panel A of Figure 9–11, the correlation coefficient of each variable with time is calculated. The reader will recall that correlation coefficients were introduced in Chapter 3 to measure the relative movements of pairs of investment assets. Any variable that increased *exactly* at the same rate each year would have a correlation coefficient of unity. Of the seven variables shown in Figure 9–11, book value per share and net sales have the highest correlation with time (0.9876 and 0.9812, respectively), indicating that their historic trend has been somewhat consistent from year to year. The correlation coefficient of 0.8002 for earnings per share indicates a weaker consistency, and of course the correlation coefficient of 0.0232 for average market price indicates that there has been virtually no consistent pattern for that variable over time.

A third approach to measuring variability of growth data is to plot year-to-year growth rates, as has been done in panel B of Figure 9–11. Here it can be seen, for example, that from 1966 to 1967 earnings per share of Gillette increased at 11.76%, and that thereafter the rate of increase diminished until 1971, when earnings per share declined 5.66%. Sharper perspective can be obtained by calculating the change in percentage points of each annual growth rate from the annual growth rate of the year before, such as in panel C of Figure 9–11. The advantage of this calculation is that a variable continuing to grow at a diminishing rate is revealed by the series of minus signs preceding the actual number. For example, even though earnings per share for Gillette were rising through 1970, the calculation of change in growth rate reveals that in every year the rate of growth was less than in the preceding year. An analyst working with data available in 1969 or 1970 might have anticipated the actual drop in earnings per share that occurred in 1971 as a continuation of the trend of constantly diminishing rates of increase.

MEASURING LABOR PRODUCTIVITY

American corporations presently are vulnerable to competition from abroad because of the interaction of rising wage rates in the United States and rising productivity in the industrial countries of Europe and in Japan. American industries that utilize a significant amount of unionized labor can remain viable companies and thus worthwhile investments only if labor elects to work harder for no increase in wages, if the United States shifts to a more protectionistic policy and excludes competitive imports, or if management can succeed in increasing the productivity of existing workers. Such techniques, which usually involve increasing the average investment in capital equipment per worker, are effective only if labor, in turn, does not bargain away all of the benefits.

One test of past successes in this area is to calculate several measures of labor productivity. Figure 9–12 indicates that between 1967 and 1971,

FIGURE 9–12
Employee productivity (The Gillette Company, 1967 and 1971)

	1971	*1967*
Number of employees	25,000	14,000
Sales per employee	$29,187	$30,597
Net income per employee	$ 2,496	$ 4,044
Net operating assets per employee	$22,178	$24,820
Stockholder equity per employee.	$11,860	$13,337

the number of employees of The Gillette Company increased from 14,000 to 25,000. However, the increase in number of employees was not matched by a correspondent increase in sales, for sales per employee dropped slightly, from $30,597 to $29,187. Even more important, the contribution of each employee to net income of the company dropped sharply, from $4,044 to $2,496 per employee. In the instance of Gillette, investment per employee, measured either in terms of net operating assets or in terms of stockholder equity, also dropped. Comparisons of this sort can lead to prognostications about the long-run viability of a company in a world of general increases in productivity.

BANKRUPTCY TEST

Professor Edward Altman has devised a quantitative test of impending bankruptcy within the next one to two years by the application of multiple discriminant analysis. His model was based on a sample of 66 manufacturing companies composed of pairs of similarly sized legally bankrupt and nonbankrupt companies.[7] The asset size of the companies ranged from $700,000 to $25,900,000. Although Professor Altman's test was derived from a sample of firms of smaller size than those normally traded on organized stock exchanges, both the methodology and the

---

[7] Edward I. Altman, "Financial Ratios, Discriminant Analysis and the Prediction of Corporate Bankruptcy," *Journal of Finance,* September, 1968, pages 589–609.

results can be valid in pinpointing comparative strengths and weaknesses from a review of corporate financial ratios.

Professor Altman predicts corporate bankruptcy from a "Z" value, determined by the following formula:

$$Z = 1.2x_1 + 1.4x_2 + 3.3x_3 + 0.6x_4 + 0.999x_5$$

where x_1 = Liquidity = Working capital/Total assets
   x_2 = Cumulative profitability = Retained earnings/Total assets
   x_3 = Earning power = Earnings before interest and taxes/Total assets
   x_4 = Leverage = Market value of equity/Book value of total debt
   x_5 = Activity = Sales/Total assets

According to this test, if a firm has a "Z" score of 3.0 or greater, it is almost certain to be in the "nonbankrupt" category. If the score is below 2.0, the firm has a very high probability of becoming bankrupt, and if the score is between 2.0 and 3.0, the outcome is not clear. If a single value were to be chosen as a borderline predictor between the two categories, it would be 2.67. This bankruptcy test is merely a check for most successful companies, but can be an important signal for firms beginning to experience difficulties.

Data in Figure 9–13 for Gillette indicate that the "Z" value is substan-

FIGURE 9–13
Bankruptcy test for The Gillette Company, 1967 and 1971

	1971	1967
Liquidity.	0.259	0.258
Cumulative profitability	0.440	0.416
Earning power.	0.217	0.305
Leverage	4.842	9.170
Activity	1.314	1.226
Z Value (weighted sum)	5.858	8.625

tially in excess of the minimum score, and thus suggest that Gillette is virtually immune from bankruptcy within the next few years. We do note that the "Z" score is lower for 1971 than for 1967.

STATEMENT OF CHANGES IN FINANCIAL POSITION

The sources and uses of funds statement was elevated to the status of a basic financial statement to be included in annual stockholders' reports and to be embraced in the auditor's opinion for all fiscal periods ending after September 30, 1971.[8] Their official designation was at that time changed to "statement of changes in financial position." We occasionally shall use the shorter name "funds statement" for simplicity.

Funds statements summarize significant financial changes that have occurred between the beginning and the end of a period of activity, thus giving an overall view of the financial management policies followed by that company. The format of a funds statement may vary. Perhaps the most common formulation is a source and application (or use) of funds, in which "funds" is defined as net working capital or net current assets. Another common formulation is an "all-inclusive" statement, in which current asset and current liability items are treated individually within the statement rather than combined under the heading of "working capital."

Statements of changes in financial position for Gillette, shown in Figure 9–14, show both an explanation of changes in working capital, permitting the analyst to focus on the basic components of financial strategy, and a supplemental tabulation explaining the detailed change in working capital components. Sources and applications are also presented on a percentage basis.

As can be seen in Figure 9–14, Gillette's working capital increased by $10,596,000 during 1971. Investment levels in cash and marketable securities and in receivables increased $10.5 million and $19.6 million. Part of this increase was financed by a $3.6 million decrease in inventory and part by a $15.9 million increase in current debt. The remainder, an increase of $10.6 million, had to be financed from other than changes in current assets and liabilities, and the Statement of Changes in Financial Position explains this increase. Such a statement classifies sources of funds into three general types:

1. Funds generated from operations, including net income plus any expenses deducted in determining net income that did not necessitate the payment of cash. Typically these are depreciation and amortization.
2. Funds generated from reductions in fixed assets or from the sale or other disposal of long-term investments.
3. Increases in the level of permanent capital, including the incurrence of long-term debt and the sale of shares of stock.

From Figure 9–14 it can be seen that the major sources of working capital for Gillette were funds from operations ($80.8 million, or 79.7%), of which the largest proportion, $62.4 million, came from net income. An increase in long-term debt provided some $12.9 million, while the sale and retirement of fixed assets provided $5.2 million. In general,

[8] Accounting Principles Board, *Opinion No. 19: Reporting Changes in Financial Position* (American Institute of Certified Public Accountants, March, 1971).

FIGURE 9–14

THE GILLETTE COMPANY AND SUBSIDIARIES
Statement of Changes in Financial Position
(thousands of dollars)
Years Ended December 31, 1967 and December 31, 1971

	1971		1967	
Source of working capital	$	%	$	%
Net income from operations.........	$ 62,399	61.6%	$ 56,615	48.0%
Depreciation, obsolescence, and amortization	18,365	18.1	8,993	7.6
Funds derived from operations	$ 80,764	79.7%	$ 65,608	55.6%
Stock option and purchase plans	1,519	1.5	7,131	6.0
Increase in long-term debt..........	12,876	12.7	39,887	33.8
Increase in equity resulting from pooling of interests.............	0	0.0	2,853	2.4
Sales and retirements of fixed assets	5,195	5.1	0	0.0
Other.....................	998	1.0	2,515	2.2
	$101,352	100.0%	$117,994	100.0%
Application of working capital				
Dividends declared	40,999	45.2	34,432	33.9
Purchase of fixed assets	31,261	34.4	28,838	28.4
Increase in other assets...........	8,620	9.5	5,172	5.1
Goodwill arising from acquisitions	6,902	7.6	32,445	1.9
Reduction of long-term debt	2,974	3.3	0	0.0
Other.....................	0	0.0	719	0.7
	90,756	100.0%	101,606	100.0%
Increase in working capital	10,596		16,388	
Summary of changes in working capital				
Increase (decrease) in cash..........	10,495		(1,687)	
Increase in receivables	19,598		15,562	
Increase (decrease) in inventories	(3,622)		32,295	
Total increase in current assets	26,471		46,170	
Less: Increase in current liabilities	15,875		29,782	
Increase in working capital	10,596		16,388	

Gillette has increased its working capital from internal sources (income plus noncash charges), rather than from external sources such as the sale of bonds or stock or liquidation of asset holdings. In 1967, it might be noted, an increase in long-term debt supplied 33.8% of funds.

Funds are applied for three basic purposes that are generally the opposite of the three types of sources:

1. Covering any operating deficits. Related to this category, which derives from the income statement, is the payment of cash dividends to stockholders. Although appropriately shown as an application of funds, dividend payments are occasionally shown as an offset to net income as a source of funds.

2. Funds used to increase fixed assets or other categories of assets,
3. Funds used to retire long-term debt or capital stock.

In the instance of Gillette, the largest use of funds (45.2% of total) was to pay some $41 million of dividends, while another $31 million was used to purchase fixed assets. Other uses included increases in prepaid and other assets and the "purchase" of goodwill through an acquisition. Only a very small proportion of available funds was used to reduce long-term debt.

Note that Gillette shows both an increase in long-term debt as a source of funds and a reduction of long-term debt as a use of funds. In many presentations, these changes would be netted together as a single net increase in long-term debt of about $9.9 million. This netting together is often preferred, since it helps the analyst focus his attention on the major financial policies the company is following.

Because sources of working capital exceeded the uses of working capital for Gillette, the result was a net increase in working capital of $10.6 million. Overall, the statement of sources and applications of funds for Gillette identifies the company's major financial policies to be to finance internally with some help from increasing long-term debt, and to use the funds for the payment of dividends and to expand both fixed assets and investment levels in cash and securities and in accounts receivable. The fact that receivables were increased by almost $20 million while inventory levels dropped slightly adds further emphasis to the observation that the company seems to be more involved in extending credit than in increasing inventory.

SUMMARY

Analysis of financial statements is a technique for obtaining perspective on the financial history of a company. The major financial statements used for analytical purposes are the balance sheet, the income statement, the statement of surplus reconciliation, and the statement of changes in financial position. One useful technique is to reduce the important statements to common-size form, in which total assets, total liabilities and net worth, and total net sales are expressed as 100% and all other items in the respective statements are expressed as percentages of these basic values. Another useful technique is to measure significant relationships in terms of the ratios of one item to another. Various ratios were suggested to measure liquidity, operating efficiency, profitability of invested capital, and various financial policies relating to interest coverage, dividend policy, tax expenses, depreciation policy, and the magnitude of total debt relative to ability to generate funds to repay that debt. Yet another set of ratios was suggested to relate market price to underlying per-share variables, such as earnings per share, dividends per share, and book value per share. Data available in financial statements were also used to calculate important growth rates and to measure the possibility of near-term bankruptcy. The funds statement also was shown to be a useful vehicle for examining the financial activities of a business firm.

SUGGESTED READINGS FOR CHAPTER 9

D. K. Eiteman. "A Computer Program for Financial Statement Analysis," *Financial Analysts Journal*, November–December, 1964, pages 61–68.

B. Graham, D. L. Dodd, and S. Cottle. *Security Analysis: Principles and Techniques*. 4th ed. (New York: McGraw-Hill Book Company, Inc., 1962), Part Two.

C. T. Horngren. *Accounting for Management Control: An Introduction*. 2d ed. (Englewood Cliffs, N.J.: Prentice-Hall, Inc., 1970), Chapters 3–4.

R. W. Johnson. *Financial Management*. 4th ed. (Rockleigh, N.J.: Allyn & Bacon, Inc., 1971), Chapter 4.

J. A. Mauriello. *Accounting for the Financial Analyst*. rev. ed. (Homewood, Ill.: Richard D. Irwin, Inc., 1971), Chapters 3, 4, 9, and 10.

J. F. Weston and E. F. Brigham. *Managerial Finance* (New York: Holt, Rinehart and Winston, Inc., 1972), Chapter 2.

10

Accounting adjustments

THE ULTIMATE RESULT of financial statement analysis is an overall assessment of a company's operations, progress, and status that allows an investor to make judgments about its likely future. Central to such assessment and prognosis are the earnings of the company in question. Unfortunately, considerable differences exist in accounting systems and procedures just as there exists widespread differences in type and size of companies whose securities might be considered for inclusion in the portfolio of an investor. As a result, both reported and projected earnings of a company in question can differ significantly depending on the particular accounting conventions employed. The purpose of this chapter is to explain some of these accounting variations and how they influence the earning of a particular company. This chapter is intended as a logical extension of our discussion of financial statement analysis in Chapter 9.

THE NATURE OF ACCOUNTING ADJUSTMENTS

Financial statements are the device by which corporate management reports to owners and creditors of a business. Owners and creditors, in turn, use the resultant statements to form opinions about the success or nonsuccess of management's stewardship of their funds. Financial statements themselves are probably the single most important item of information available to investors for measuring present performance and for using as a base for formulating opinions about probable future performance. This is not to negate the ultimate importance of other information about the company such as about its management team, its market prospects, or its position within the entire economy. Under most conditions, however, the financial statements constitute the base against which other more subjective items of information are judged.

Investors would undoubtedly be happier if accounting statements presented only objective facts, especially as they relate to calculating the almost magical figure that is the end result of the accounting process for most investors: earnings per share. As it happens, the accounting process must treat a number of variables in a subjective, often arbitrary, manner and the resultant earnings per share figure is thus equally subjective. So-called "generally accepted accounting principles" are in fact no more than accumulations of rules and procedures used in deriving company earnings as developed by consensus over an extended period of time. Because these rules and procedures are not uniform, one or another arbitrarily selected methods may be adopted that results in final earnings per share being either higher or lower than under some equally acceptable alternative calculation. Comparability between companies within a single industry is frequently obscured by differences in accounting treatment.

The informed investment analyst must be aware of the possibilities for arbitrary or inconsistent "twists" in the procedures by which company earnings are calculated. In this chapter, we identify a number of important variations in accounting treatment whereby a single event might be recorded, and call attention to alternative procedures that might have been followed. This discussion may appear to be skeptical of the accounting profession because it cautions against relying uncritically upon the end result of the public accountants' efforts, the audited financial statements of a corporate business, and the calculated earnings per share figure. Such a bleak interpretation should not be exaggerated. From the point of view of an investment analyst, the reliability of financial reports of U.S. companies in the 1970s is considerably improved from that of prior decades or other countries. One need only scan the pages of early editions of Benjamin Graham and David Dodd's Security Analysis: Principles and Techniques first published in 1934 by McGraw-Hill Book Company, to notice the number of inconsistent treatments that then abounded and that have now slipped from the ranks of current problems.

Much progress toward uniformity was made during the period 1962–1972 by the Accounting Principles Board of the American Institute of Certified Public Accountants, whose APB Opinions brought degrees of uniformity to the profession. In 1972, the Accounting Principles Board, which had consisted of 18 part-time members who were all Certified Public Accountants (C.P.A.'s) was replaced by the Financial Accounting Standards Board, of seven full-time members, including some who are not Certified Public Accountants and who represent other points of view, such as financial executives and Chartered Financial Analysts (C.F.A.'s).

Yet one more recent development indicates the ever progressing trend toward better disclosure of information that might call into question the reliability of audited financial statements. Disagreements have occurred between corporate management, which in reporting on its stewardship through financial statements wants to look as good as possible, and auditing firms of public accountants, which must affix their signatures attesting that these statements are prepared in accordance with "generally accepted accounting principles." Until recently, a firm could change its auditor with only management and the auditing firm understanding the reason. Since 1971 the Securities and Exchange Commission (S.E.C.) has required disclosure of disputes between auditors and corporate clients that lead to a change of auditors. Not only must a company report on reasons for a change in its auditors in its monthly 8–K report to the S.E.C. (see Chapter 19 for description of 8–K and 10–K reports), but the ousted auditor must also file a letter commenting on its view of the change.

The *Wall Street Journal* (February 23, 1972) reported that the first dispute involving a major company to come to light under the new disclosure rule involved a disagreement between Boothe Computer Corporation and its former auditor, Arthur Andersen and Company. At question was the value reported on Boothe's balance sheet of computers owned by Boothe and leased to its clients: If clients should cancel leases on a large scale, forcing Boothe to take back the equipment, the remaining values to Boothe would be significantly less than the amortized values at which Boothe was carrying the equipment. Arthur Andersen and Company, according to the *Wall Street Journal,* sought to insert a "subject" clause into its opinion, stating that the statements were satisfactory "subject to the effect of the outcome (which cannot now be determined) of future events with respect to rental revenues which the computer equipment will produce." Boothe disagreed that the value of the equipment might diminish because of lease cancellations, and in due course Arthur Andersen and Company was replaced by Touche Ross and Company.

The remainder of this chapter is devoted to explaining some (but not all) of the accounting variations by which earnings of a company may be arbitrarily reported at a higher or lower level within the procedural confines of "generally accepted accounting principles." One set of variations has to do with methods of recording investments in other companies. A second set of variations arises from the problems of determining when to recognize income, and a third set of variations derives from the timing of expense recognition. A fourth set of variations includes the need to understand the significance of fully diluted earnings per share and the importance of constantly watching for changes in the consistency of accounting treatment.

An investor or financial analyst needs to be aware of yet one further difference in approach between statements that satisfy his needs and those that comply with the objectives of corporate financial executives and their auditors. Quite correctly, the accounting profession has developed the concept of "materiality," which in essence states that if an event is of such minor significance that its effect on overall results is "not material," that event need not be stated and explained separately. Materiality is usually measured in relationship to total earnings. Thus a choice between techniques that might or might not add 4 cents to total earnings per share of $0.60 might well be determined to be immaterial.

Investors and financial analysts, however, tend to measure materiality in terms of the effect upon the *trend* rather than the *level* of earnings per share. This viewpoint is in keeping with the general focus on prospects for future growth. Thus if last year's earnings were $0.55 per share and this year's per share earnings were $0.60, and four cents of the total five cents increase came from an arbitrary accounting decision, this information would be most material to the investor. For if earnings rose five cents, the year-to-year growth rate was $0.05/$0.55 or approximately 9%. If "true" earnings rose only 1 cent, however, the annual growth rate was less than 2%. Under the latter condition, a totally different price-earnings multiple might be expected in the securities market. It is to be hoped that the new Financial Accounting Standards Board will give greater attention to "materiality" from the point of view of outside investors as reflected in this hypothetical example.

VARIATIONS IN ACCOUNTING FOR INVESTMENT IN OTHER COMPANIES

A company may own, as an asset, shares of common stocks of other companies. When 50% or more of the voting stock of another corporation is owned, that corporation is considered a *subsidiary* and, in most circumstances, its financial statements are consolidated with those of the parent. *Consolidation* means that subsidiaries and parent company are treated, for financial reporting purposes, as a single economic unit; the fact of separate legal entities is ignored.

If from 20% to 50% of the common stock of another company is owned, that company is regarded as an *affiliate* and it is carried on the parent books as a separate investment. Companies owned less than 20% are also carried on the parent books as investments. However, 20% or less ownership results in a different method of valuation on the parent books and such a company is not usually considered an affiliate.

Consolidation of subsidiaries

Units of a business may be organized as separate corporations rather than divisions for such reasons as minimizing tax expenses or limiting legal liability. In addition, if ownership of a particular unit is shared with another corporation or other owners, that unit will of necessity be organized as a separate corporate entity. When the substance of the arrangement, as distinct from the legal structure, is such that the parent and the subsidiary operate as a single economic organization, a consolidated financial statement presents a more meaningful statement to interested shareholders. In a consolidated statement, assets of the subsidiary are mixed with assets of the parent. Thus, for example, accounts receivable on the consolidated statement consist of receivables of the parent plus receivables of the subsidiary, less any intracompany receivables owed by one of the units to the other.

Parent companies are normally expected to consolidate statements of all subsidiaries owned 50% or more. This assumes that control is expected to be continuing rather than temporary and that the nature of the assets, liabilities, and operations is not so different from those of the parent that consolidation would be meaningless. An example of the latter would be a finance company owned by a manufacturing company parent; such a subsidiary would not be consolidated because the type of business is completely different. Foreign subsidiaries whose assets are not available for transfer to the United States need not be consolidated.

Consolidated statements are advantageous to investors in that the performance of the entire economic unit is presented. Two possible disadvantages are that (1) consolidation tends to obscure the individual performances of the various components that make up the consolidated unit, making it difficult to evaluate performance by product line for multiproduct companies, and (2) consolidation may obscure the significance of the treatment of the excess of book value of subsidiaries acquired over the asset cost of the subsidiaries on date of acquisition.

Measuring performance by product line

Prior to 1969, companies were not required to disclose results by product line. In that year, however, the Securities and Exchange Commission adopted a requirement that companies having annual sales in excess of $50 million must disclose sales revenue and operating profit or loss (before income taxes and extraordinary items) for each line of activity representing more than 10% of total revenues and net income or loss. For companies with less than $50 million in annual sales, a 15% measure of total activity is applied. In either instance, disclosure may be limited to the ten most important lines if more activities would qualify.

The significance of reporting profit by product line arises in the question as to whether a company can be worth more than the capitalized value of the sum of its various divisional earnings if one division is in fact losing money. Abandonment of that division, if possible, would enhance reported earnings of the remainder of the firm and hence the investment value of the common stock. In 1971, for example, Miles Laboratories discontinued a corn wet milling plant at Granite City, Illinois, thereby recording an extraordinary item that reduced after-tax earnings per share by $1.32 to $2.25. The effect of this discontinued operation on overall earnings for the six years prior to its discontinuation was as follows:

	Consolidated earnings per share as reported	Loss from discontinued operation	Earnings from continuing operations
1966	$ 1.92	$0.01	$ 1.93
1967	2.03	0.35	2.38
1968	2.41	0.05	2.46
1969	2.76	0.06	2.82
1970	2.01	0.11	2.12
1971	2.25	0.29	2.54
Total	$13.38	$0.87	$14.25

Note that in 1971 the corn wet milling plant caused a $0.29 per share loss from consolidated earnings from operation prior to the time of write-off, as well as the additional $1.32 loss when it was actually written off.

During the years from 1966 through 1970, annual reports of Miles Laboratories did not indicate the per-share significance of the loss-causing Granite City mill, although the 1971 report, issued after the mill was actually discontinued, did provide the figures above. Without knowing of the losses of the single division, an investor would presumably base his estimate of earning power upon the magnitude and trend of consolidated earnings per share. In fact, with abandonment of the losing division, the remaining company had higher earnings and was presumably worth more, assuming that the resulting earnings will continue into the future. In detecting investment opportunities of this type that might arise, it is well to realize that the value of the remaining operations of such a company may be greater than the value of the company as originally constituted—if the money-losing parts can be effectively separated.

Unfortunately, present rules provide for disclosure of only sales and operating profit by product line, but do not require disclosure of investment in operating assets by product line. Thus while it is advantageous to determine the contribution of each product line to corporate earnings potential in an absolute amount, a potential investor is unable to determine the contribution of each product line to return on invested capital.

In 1971, American Brands, Inc. reported net sales and operating income by product line as shown in Figure 10–1. Although American

FIGURE 10–1
American Brands, Inc. Sales and operating income by product line (millions of dollars), 1971

Product line	Net sales $	%	Operating income $	%	Operating income as % of net sales
Tobacco products, foreign	1,046.5	37.0	51.3	16.8	4.9
Tobacco products, domestic	997.4	35.3	187.4	61.3	18.8
Food products	349.3	12.3	6.4	2.1	18.3
Distilled beverages	135.5	4.8	17.6	5.8	13.0
Other (not specified)	109.5	3.9	11.1	3.6	10.1
Hardware	76.0	2.7	20.3	6.6	26.8
Office equipment and supplies	69.5	2.4	6.3	2.1	9.1
Toiletries	58.2	2.1	5.1	1.7	8.8
Intercompany adjustment	(14.6)	(.5)	–	–	–
Total	2,827.8	100.0	305.5	100.0	10.8

Brands sells more abroad than in the United States, a disproportionate amount of its profits are reported as earned domestically. Specifically, the company earns 4.9% on foreign tobacco sales and 18.8% on domestic tobacco sales. The company reports that it earns 26.8% on hardware sales, although these are significantly smaller in total amount.

Unfortunately the data are of limited benefit because the investor is not told what proportion of assets are required for each product line. The 18.8% domestic profit margin, which looks so good, might in fact be poor if a disproportionate investment is required to support domestic sales, and the 4.9% foreign profit margin might be excellent if it is attained at virtually no investment in assets. The reader of the financial statement can only speculate, since investment size is not provided.

Excess of purchase price over book value in mergers

The stock market boom of the late 1960's was partially induced by a number of "glamorous" mergers. Much of the glamour arose because of companies' ability to influence earnings per share after the merger by a choice of accounting methods. Acquisition of a new subsidiary prior to November 1, 1970, could be accounted for as either a pooling of interests or a purchase.

In a *pooling of interests*, the two enterprises are combined as if they had been a single unit. Assets and retained earnings of the acquired company are shown at book value on the resultant consolidated statement. If the subsidiary is acquired by issuing parent stock having a greater market value than the book value of the assets acquired, goodwill is not created. Rather the equity section of the resulting consolidated company simply reflects the fact that a greater number of shares of stock is outstanding.

In a *purchase,* on the other hand, the subsidiary's assets are transferred to the books of the parent company at fair market value. Retained earnings are not so transferred, however, and if the purchase price exceeds the value of the assets, an additional account labeled "goodwill" or, more precisely, "excess of purchase price over book value of assets acquired," is established.

The example in Figure 10–2 will illustrate these two possible methods. On May 16, 1969, Xerox Corporation acquired Scientific Data Systems

FIGURE 10–2
Xerox Corporation and Scientific Data Systems merger (May 16, 1969)

	Xerox*	SDS†	Pooling	Purchase
Assets	$905,704,125	$113,279,000	$1,018,983,125	$1,018,983,125
Goodwill				833,220,553
Total assets . . .			$1,018,983,125	$1,852,203,678
Liabilities	$388,090,734	$ 34,995,000	$ 423,085,734	$ 423,085,734
Capital stock	22,435,218		22,435,218	22,435,218
Stock issued‡	9,989,091		9,989,091	9,989,091
Paid-in capital	146,225,772		186,471,681	1,047,741,234
Retained earnings . . .	348,952,401	28,049,000	377,001,401	348,952,401
Total equity. . .			$1,018,983,125	$1,852,203,678

* Xerox Corporation, *Annual Report,* 1968, pp. 44 and 45.
† Scientific Data Systems, Inc., *Annual Report,* 1968, pp. 22 and 23.
‡ Xerox Corporation, *Annual Report,* 1969, footnote 1, p. 47, issued 9,989,091 shares of $1 par value common stock with a market price on May 16, 1969 of $91.25.

by issuing securities having a market value of $911,504,553 for a book value in assets, after deducting liabilities, of only $78,284,000. The merger was in fact treated as a pooling of interests, as shown in the third column of Figure 10–2. Total assets after the merger were recorded as $1,018,983,125. Had the acquisition been treated as a purchase, goodwill of $833,220,553 would have been created as follows:

Effective purchase price (9,989,091 shares of common stock with a market price on May 16, 1969, of $91.25)		$911,504,553
Less book value of assets acquired:		
Assets acquired	$113,279,000	
Less: liabilities	34,995,000	78,284,000
Excess of purchase price over book value of assets acquired (i.e., goodwill)		$833,220,553

Thus under the purchase method of merger accounting, total assets after the merger would have been $1,852,203,678—over 80% greater than under the pooling method.

The significance of the difference between the two methods is that under a pooling-of-interest approach, future depreciation is less because the assets are not written up and there is no amortization of goodwill. Future reported earnings per share will tend to be larger. If the acquisition is treated as a purchase, future depreciation will be larger if the acquired assets were in fact written up to their current fair market value. In addition, for all acquisitions after October 31, 1971, goodwill must be amortized over a period of time not to exceed 40 years. Treatment of goodwill for acquisitions completed prior to October 31, 1971, varies, with some companies amortizing (and thus lowering reported earnings per share) and others not amortizing.

Consider again the Xerox acquisition of Scientific Data Systems, illustrated in Figure 10–2. Earnings per share for 1968 (the year prior to the acquisition) and for 1969 (the year in which the acquisition occurred) under the pooling method and as estimated under the purchase method of accounting are shown below:

	Earnings per share		
Accounting method	1968	1969	Percent change
Pooling (method actually used)[1]	$1.68	$2.08	+23.8
Purchase (hypothetical)[2]	$1.75	$1.81	+ 3.4

Because Xerox used pooling, it was able to report a 23.8% increase in 1969 earnings over 1968 earnings. Had purchase accounting been used, the increase would have been only a modest 3.4%, after deduction of estimated amortization of goodwill.

The difficulties of comparing present earnings of companies that have been involved in acquisitions in past years is apparent from the great variety of treatment of goodwill. In their annual reports for the year ended December 31, 1971, Carnation Company, Beatrice Foods, Pet Incorporated, Esquire, Inc., and Penn-Dixie Cement Company, Inc., for example, reported that they were not amortizing goodwill acquired prior to November 1, 1970. Thus the earnings of these companies were reported relatively higher than the earnings of companies that were amortizing past goodwill, such as American Cement Corporation (20 to 30 years), Globe-Union, Inc. (over 20 years), Metromedia, Inc. (over 40 years), and General Motors (which began in 1970 to amortize over

[1] Xerox Corporation Annual Report 1969, page 41.
[2] 1968 earnings from Xerox Corporation Annual Report 1968 p. 43 and adjusted for stock split. 1969 earnings from Xerox Corporation Annual Report 1969 p. 41 and adjusted for amortization of goodwill.

ten years the goodwill of businesses acquired in and prior to 1943). This emphasizes that earnings per share of one set of companies may not be comparable with earnings per share of another set.

In 1970, the Accounting Principles Board issued an opinion that limited the conditions under which pooling accounting could be used and in effect required purchase accounting for most acquisitions.[3] Intangible assets must be recognized at cost as goodwill and must be amortized over a period of time not to exceed 40 years. Goodwill from acquisitions effected before November 1, 1970, however, need not be amortized. The new mandatory amortization of goodwill thus was not made retroactive. Because of the large number of acquisitions that took place between 1968 and 1970, a financial analyst must still be aware of possible variations in reported earnings per share caused by these earlier acquisitions.

Although amortization of goodwill is usually viewed as an act that reduces reported earnings per share, it is possible to have a series of events that arbitrarily increase earnings per share because of the amortization of what might be termed "negative goodwill". Such *negative goodwill* arises when a company pays *less* for assets acquired than their book value. Such a situation exists for Crane Company, which carried on its 1971 balance sheet an account, "Deferred Credit from Acquisition," of $9.8 million, down from $14.0 million in 1969. This account was being amortized as a reduction in cost of sales (and thus as an increase in income) over the seven years commencing in 1969. The annual increase in pretax earnings amounted to $2,633,000, or approximately $1.02 per common share. The contribution of this increase to pretax income can be seen in the following tabulation:

Year	Pretax income	Gain due to amortization of "negative goodwill"	Gain as % of pretax income
1969	$10,652,000	$1,074,000	10.1
1970	2,841,000	2,633,000	92.5
1971	13,458,000	2,633,000	19.5

Not only was almost 20% of 1971 pretax income caused by the reduction in "negative goodwill," but in 1970 the same technique supplied 92.5% of pretax income! In 1970, Crane Company also received an income tax credit, with the result that final net income after taxes was supplied

<hr>

[3] Accounting Principles Board, *Opinion Number 17: Intangible Assets* (American Institute of Certified Public Accountants, August, 1970).

65.6% from the tax credit, 31.9% from the deferred gain, and only 2.5% from normal, recurring operations of the company. Reported 1970 earnings per share of $3.15 per share thus were virtually meaningless as a guide to the earning power of the company or as a base from which to estimate the future benefits to be received by an owner of a share of common stock.

Nonconsolidated subsidiaries

Prior to 1971, corporations were permitted to account for nonconsolidated investments in other corporations by either of two methods. Under the *cost method,* only the original cost of the investment in shares of another company was shown on the balance sheet. Earnings of such investments appeared in the earnings of the parent company only when declared as cash dividends to the parent. Under the alternate *equity method,* the parent's full pro-rata share of the earnings of each nonconsolidated subsidiary was added to the carrying value of the investment. Such pro-rata share of earnings also appeared in the income statement, regardless of whether or not cash dividends were in fact declared. Although many exceptions existed, common practice was to use the equity method when the parent owned a majority or near-majority of the subsidiary's common stock and to use the cost method when less than half of the subsidiary was owned.

One significant consequence of this practice was that earnings of nonconsolidated investments could be hidden from public and investor view. Kaiser Industries Corporation, for example, used the cost method prior to 1971 to report its 38% ownership of Kaiser Aluminum and Chemical Corporation, its 37% ownership of Kaiser Cement and Gypsum Corporation, and its 22% ownership of American Motors Corporation.

During the period from 1961 through 1970, Kaiser Industries' equity in the undistributed earnings of these less-than-50% owned corporations was not included in Kaiser Industries' reported earnings per share, which were as shown in Column (C) of Figure 10–3. If Kaiser Industries' share of the "hidden earnings" of these nonconsolidated corporations, shown in Column (D) of Figure 10–3, had been included, actual earnings per share would have been revealed to be significantly higher. For example, as shown in Column (F) of Figure 10–3, 1965 earnings per share would have been increased by 350% and 1969 earnings per share would have been increased by 95%. These "hidden earnings" were reported for the first time in Kaiser Industries' 1971 *Annual Report.*

Effective with annual reports published after December 31, 1971, companies are required to use the equity method for reporting both profits and losses for all companies in which they hold investments and exert "significant" influence over the financial and operating policies

FIGURE 10–3
Kaiser Industries Corporation earnings per share calculations

Year	Earnings per share before extraordinary items (A)	Extra-ordinary items (B)	Earnings per share after extraordinary items (C) = (A) + (B)	Equity in undistributed earnings of less-than-50% owned corporations (D)	"Total" earnings per share (1971 method) (E) = (C) + (D)	Column (D) as % of column (C) (F)
1961	$0.21	$0.33	$0.54	$0.17	$0.71	32%
1962	0.13	–	0.13	0.25	0.38	192
1963	0.39	–	0.39	0.17	0.56	44
1964	(0.04)	0.14	0.10	0.28	0.38	280
1965	0.10	–	0.10	0.35	0.45	350
1966	0.78	–	0.78	0.68	1.46	87
1967	1.56	1.35	2.91	0.49	3.40	17
1968	1.37	–	1.37	0.43	1.80	31
1969	0.90	(0.33)	0.57	0.54	1.11	95
1970	0.55	0.29	0.84	0.12	0.96	14

Note: Losses shown in parentheses.
Source: 1971 Annual Report, Kaiser Industries Corporation.

of those companies;[4] the equity method was in fact used in many reports published at the end of 1971. In the absence of evidence to the contrary, ownership of 20% or more of the voting stock is considered to be significant and the equity method is to be applied retroactively to all investments in common stock held during any portion of the period for which results of operations are presented, regardless of the dates at which the investments were acquired. Exceptions to this application are common stock investments in foreign subsidiaries whose assets are not available for transfer to the United States; these investments may still be carried at cost.

In 1971, Kaiser changed to reporting its interest in nonconsolidated corporations on an equity basis, with the result that 1971 reported earnings per share were $0.50 (before extraordinary items), of which $0.12 constituted the contribution of less-than-50%-owned subsidiaries.

VARIATIONS IN TIMING THE RECOGNITION OF SALES REVENUE

Under the *accrual basis* of accounting, sales revenue is shown as occurring in the year in which the sale takes place, and the various

---

[4] Accounting Principles Board, Opinion No. 18: *The Equity Method of Accounting for Investments in Common Stock* (American Institute of Certified Public Accountants, 1971).

expenses of generating that sale are deducted in the same year. It would seem to be a simple matter of determining when a sale takes place, but in many industries the problem is quite complicated. Such complications lead to variations in timing the recognition of sales revenue and, in turn, to lack of comparability in reported earnings.

Current versus deferred recognition

When payment for a large portion of a sales price is to be made on an installment basis over many years, a question arises as to what segment of the transaction should properly be treated as current income. For certain industries, including land development companies, the problem is significant because the choice of accounting system becomes the prime determinant of what is reported to be current earnings.

Although land development companies have received the greatest notoriety, the problem arises in any industry with significant installment sales. For example, American Training Services operates vocationally oriented training schools for the maintenance of tractor-trailer and heavy equipment, hotel-motel management, and repair and replacement of brakes for personal and commercial vehicles. The full amount of a student's enrollment contract is recorded as a "sale" at the time the contract is signed, with the unpaid balance of the contract showing in the balance sheet as a contract receivable. Future costs of instruction, sales commissions, and certain general and administrative expenses are accrued and included in current liabilities. Most instructional costs, however, are treated as expenses in the current time period. The resultant balance sheet, expressed in both dollars and percentage form, is shown in Figure 10–4.

Because operating revenue is recorded at the time a sales contract is signed, both the resultant net income and earnings per share figures are "accurate" only if the provision for doubtful accounts (an estimate of what proportion of the company's receivables will not be collected) is correct. Under any set of conditions, that estimate must be made in the face of a considerable degree of uncertainty and must inevitably be regarded as an approximation. To illustrate the power of such an estimate, consider that in fiscal 1971 (twelve months ended February 28, 1971) American Training Services charged 23.0% of operating revenue as a provision for doubtful collections. Earnings per share in fiscal 1971 were 21¢. In fiscal 1972, the company increased its charge for doubtful accounts to 34.0% of operating revenue, but earnings per share rose, nevertheless, to 68¢.

If in 1972 the company had used the same 23.0% rate as used in 1971, pretax earnings would have increased $798,384 before taxes and just under $400,000 after tax. Earnings per share would have increased

FIGURE 10–4

AMERICAN TRAINING SERVICES, INC.
Balance Sheet
Feb. 29, 1972 (thousands)

Assets		$	%
Cash and certificates of deposit		423	11.2
Contracts receivable	3,874		
Less: allowance for doubtful collection	−1,234		
Net contracts receivable		2,640	70.0
Other receivables (government and franchise			
contracts)		275	7.3
Other current assets (supplies, etc.).		50	1.3
Total Current Assets.		3,388	89.8
Net property, plant and equipment.		345	9.2
Other assets		37	1.0
Total.		3,770	100.0%

Liabilities and stockholders' equity	$	%
Current liabilities	48	1.3
Accrued liabilities.	911	24.2
Provision for deferred income taxes.	1,018	27.0
Common stock and capital in excess of par value.	743	19.7
Retained earnings.	1,050	27.8
Total.	3,770	100.0%

Statement of Income
Year ended February 29, 1972

		$	%
Operating revenues		7,193	100.0%
Expenses:			
Operating expenses.		927	12.9
Advertising and selling.		1,865	25.9
Provision for doubtful accounts		2,445	34.0
General and administrative		536	7.5
Operating Income		1,420	19.7
Interest income	+14		
Provision for current income taxes	−45		
Provision for deferred income taxes	−661	692	9.6
Net Income . . . . $		728	10.1
Earnings per share on 1,075 shares of stock		$0.68	

approximately 36¢ to $1.04, up almost fivefold from 1971! In short, recognizing as sales contracts that may or may not be collected adds a very arbitrary and inprecise calculation to the income statement. When applied to sales the proceeds of which are realized over extended time periods, an alternative accounting procedure (used by American Training Services for income taxes) would be to report on a *cash basis*. Operating revenues would then show only when collected, and no estimate of doubtful collections would be needed.

This problem of accounting, which is essentially a question of when gross revenue is in fact obtained, appears also in the financial statements of other companies that sell on a long-term deferred payment basis. As was mentioned above, a prominent class is real estate and land development companies. The variety in treatment of current sales contracts as current sales revenue is apparent from the following tabulation of times when different land development companies record sales.[5]

Company	Criterion for recording a sale
General Development	After receipt of 5% of purchase price or a minimum down payment and two monthly payments.
Cavanagh Communities Corporation	After receipt of an amount equal to 3% of the sales price.
Dart Industries	After receipt of a 10% down payment.
Boise Cascade	After receipt of a 10% down payment.
McCulloch	After receipt of a 15% down payment.
Great Western United	After receipt of a 20% down payment.

Variations in reporting foreign earnings

With the advent of multinational expansion by U.S. corporations, the significance of foreign earnings has become of increased importance in two respects. A valid question must be raised as to the worth, in any valuation model, of foreign earnings as compared to domestic earnings. In addition, the advent of widespread foreign operations leads to the possibility of either foreign earnings being used to enhance U.S. earnings in years when domestic operations falter or the possibility that foreign operations will produce earnings that are not reported to U.S. stockholders.

First, we consider the use of foreign earnings to bolster total earnings. American corporate management often is growth-minded, for success in maximizing the market value of a company's shares of stock depends to a large degree on preserving a record of sustained growth. Foreign operations can come to the rescue of faltering consolidated operations by two techniques—recognition of exchange gains brought about by devaluation of the U.S. dollar relative to currencies of countries where foreign operations exist, and declaration of unusually large dividends from nonconsolidated foreign subsidiaries.

Although devaluation of the dollar relative to foreign currencies is a relatively new phenomenon, having occurred in 1971 (for the first time since the post–World War II international monetary system was established at Bretton Woods in 1944) and again in early 1973, it is nevertheless likely to be a continuing phenomenon of future years. Most

---

[5] *Business Week*, January 23, 1971, page 86.

current assets and current liabilities of foreign operations are denominated in foreign currencies and must therefore be translated into United States dollar equivalents in order to consolidate the foreign operations into the parent's financial statements. Therefore a gain will occur when the dollar loses value relative to the foreign currency and a loss will occur when the foreign currency devalues relative to the dollar.[6] Although this gain or loss will properly influence reported earnings per share, the significance of the gain or loss in terms of estimating future earnings is a separate matter.

An illustration of the possible effect of exchange gains occurred in the 1971 Annual Report of AMP, Incorporated, a manufacturer of electronic components and hardware, with operations in Puerto Rico, Argentina, Brazil, Australia, Japan, France, Great Britain, The Netherlands, Italy, West Germany, Spain, and Sweden. Approximately 50% of the net income of AMP, Inc. is earned abroad. Earnings per share before any gain on revaluation was reported by AMP as follows:

Year	Earnings per share (before revaluation)
1970	$2.00
1971	1.96

Thus, earnings per share from operations in 1971 declined 2% from the previous year. However, AMP also was able to report in 1971 an extraordinary gain of $0.08 per share "from the upward revaluation of major currencies in relation to the dollar, and the consequent translation of the current assets and the liabilities of (their) international subsidiaries at the new higher exchange rates." As a consequence, actual earnings per share were reported as follows:

Year	Earnings per share (after revaluation)
1970	$2.00
1971	2.04

In the letter to stockholders appearing in its annual report, AMP stated: "Earnings were up 2% to a new high of $25.0 million or $2.04 per share." Normal accounting treatment would have called for deferring the unrealized exchange gain as a reserve against which to charge future foreign exchange devaluation losses. Any person carefully reading these financial statements, however, would probably notice that $0.08 per share was "earned" because of the devaluation of the U.S. dollar, for this

---

[6] For a complete explanation of the accounting problems involved in translating foreign currency statements into dollars, see David K. Eiteman and Arthur I. Stonehill, *Multinational Business Finance*, (Addison-Wesley Publishing Company, 1973), Chapter 13.

fact was clearly called to the reader's attention in several places. *Fortune* magazine, in its listing of the 500 largest industrials (AMP was 426th), indicated 1971 earnings per share of $1.96, instead of the $2.04.

A comment was made in the introduction to this chapter about the accounting treatment of events not judged material in size. A foreign exchange gain of $0.08 might well be immaterial in relation to an earnings level of about $2.00. That small $0.08 component of earnings becomes very important to investors, however, when it is used to change a drop in earnings per share to a rise in earnings per share.

Second, we consider *hidden earnings*. Accounting principles do not require the consolidation of foreign subsidiaries or the reporting on an equity basis of foreign investments if recovery of the foreign assets is deemed questionable because of exchange and investment regulations imposed by the foreign government. Although the exact effect on foreign operations of Accounting Principles Board Opinion #18 remains to be determined, it is possible to hide the nature of foreign operations entirely. Martin Marietta, in its 1971 annual report, indicates an investment of $2.2 million in "foreign nonconsolidated subsidiaries and other investments." The comparable figure for 1970 was $3.3 million. The annual report further noted, "foreign nonconsolidated subsidiaries and other investments were carried at cost, which was less than the equity in these enterprises. Dividends from foreign nonconsolidated subsidiaries and other investments included in other income amounted to $208,000 in 1971 and $356,000 in 1970 and were less than the applicable earnings of the subsidiaries for each of those years." Martin Marietta failed to report the actual earnings of its nonconsolidated subsidiaries, and it furthermore did not disclose what and where they were. A stockholder or potential investor is unable to determine from the report if the hidden foreign investments are in fact worth significantly more than their original cost or if they are perhaps worthless, as might be the case if they were located in a war zone. Fortunately such hiding of foreign operations is now less frequent an occurrence than in previous years.

Nonnormal revenue

Nonnormal revenue may be defined as income received by a company from other than its normal business activity. Sometimes the expression "nonoperating" is used to describe this income. The significance of such income lies in the possibility that, although "nonoperational" by accepted definitions, such incomes might have a tendency to recur and thus should be considered as potentially part of an income stream that a buyer might capitalize. A second possibility is that nonnormal income is used to bolster sagging operational income and so disguise a true turn of events. We consider these two possibilities in turn.

For many years, Hilton Hotels has generated earnings from the sale of property, as can be seen from the following tabulation:

Year	Earnings per share from operations	Earnings per share from sale of property	Total earnings per share
1960	$0.93	$0.30	$1.23
1961	0.77	0.94	1.71
1962	0.72	1.55	2.27
1963	0.37	0.13	0.50
1964	0.62	(0.32)	0.30
1965	0.57	0.39	0.96
1966	0.98	0.05	1.03
1967	1.43	0.07	1.50
1968	1.68	0.28	1.96
1969	2.18	0.01	2.19
1970	1.88	0.00	1.88
1971	1.77	0.00	1.77
Average	$1.16	$0.28	$1.44

Over the last 12 years, earnings from the sale of property have equalled just over 24% of earnings from hotel operations. Such a large percentage cannot be ignored, athough it would be equally unwise to regard earnings from the sale of property as recurring, especially in view of the fact that nothing was earned from this portion of the business in 1970 and 1971, and virtually nothing in 1969.

A similar phenomenon was observable in airline companies in the 1950s when replacement of old aircraft by newer propeller planes and then by jet aircraft led major airlines to sell, usually at a profit, their older aircraft. As jet aircraft models stabilized in the 1960s, this source of nonnormal revenue ceased. With the advent of various new models of jet aircraft in the 1970s, one might hypothesize that additional nonnormal earnings will again be generated by airline companies. For example, The *Wall Street Journal*, on February 10, 1972, reported that Eastern Air Lines had for sale its fleet of 26 four-engined McDonnell Douglas DC-8 series jet aircraft, which it said had an anticipated total market value in excess of $100 million. The sale was part of Eastern's fleet simplification program, which would reduce Eastern's fleet to three basic aircraft, all having two or three jet engines, rather than four engines.

The significance of nonnormal earnings lies in the necessity of separating them from regular operating income in formulating an opinion about the future profitability of a company, and thus the benefits to be received by an investor. Under many circumstances, nonnormal income may properly be forecasted as an added increment of future earnings. In other circumstances, this may not be the case.

Nonnormal earnings may be used in many ways to bolster sagging regular earnings. One example, the recognition of foreign exchange gain, was mentioned earlier in conjunction with evaluation of foreign operations. Another example of using nonnormal revenue to bolster regular earnings came to light in a Securities Exchange Commission complaint filed against Occidental Petroleum Corporation.[7] According to the S.E.C., Occidental Petroleum realized gains from the sale of coal leases but did not disclose the extraordinary nature of these gains in its annual 1969 or interim 1970 statements. As a result of the S.E.C. complaint, Occidental's 1970 annual report segregated the amounts of 1969 and 1970 per-share earnings derived from the sale of coal lease rights. The disclosure revealed that Occidental would have suffered a year-to-year decrease in per-share earnings of 5%, rather than 2%, if the company had not gained from the lease rights sale. The effect on 1969 results was that sale of the coal lease rights contributed seven percentage points to the total 29% improvement in per-share earnings. *Barron's* observed that sales of coal lease rights contributed 6% of Occidental's 1969 earnings per share and 25% of the company's year-to-year gain in earnings per share.

VARIATIONS IN TIMING THE RECOGNITION OF EXPENSES

Operating businesses incur costs, which is to say that they give up one asset (usually cash) to acquire another asset such as plant, equipment, or inventory, or to acquire a valuable service such as labor. In order to determine the earnings of a company for a particular time period, it is necessary to *match* the incurred costs against the revenue produced. For some types of cost, such as salaries paid to clerks in a department store or utility bills paid during a year, the matching process is relatively simple: the cost is regarded as an expense of the time period in which it was incurred. Some other costs, such as the cost of acquiring items for inventory, are usually held until such time as the inventory item is sold. The cost of the inventory item then becomes an expense of the time period in which it was sold. Variations in the method of transferring the cost of inventory to expenses arise when particular costs cannot be traced through the inventory flow.

Among other important variations possible in reporting a particular cost as an expense of a specific time period are the treatment of pension fund costs, depreciation of fixed assets, treatment of the investment tax credit, and recognition of extraordinary items. Because of the importance of these items, they are explained in detail in the paragraphs that follow.

---

[7] *Barron's* July 17, 1972, page 5.

Pension fund accounting

Contributions to a pension fund represent an expense charged against revenue of each year to reflect that year's share of the cost of the pension that will be paid to each employee upon retirement. For a variety of reasons, the annual expense may vary and thus affect reported earnings per share.

One possible variation lies in the fact that some companies "fund" their pension liabilities, while others adopt a "pay-as-you-go" system. *Funding* means setting aside a sum of cash each year such that the accumulated cash plus interest earned thereon will equal the cost of supplying an annuity to each current employee at his or her retirement. Under the *pay-as-you-go* system, no expense is recorded for pensions for current employees, but the full amount of pension payments to retired employees is charged as an expense in the months and years of actual payment. If a company has a preponderance of young employees (possibly because it is a relatively new company) the effect of adopting a pay-as-you-go plan is to increase current earnings per share because current payments will be minimal. Young companies with dynamic growth prospects and a shortage of capital may find a pay-as-you-go system particularly advantageous, not only because they as yet have no retired employees, but also because the company's after-tax rate of return on any earnings retained in the business presumably is greater than the tax-free return that might be earned on the cash if turned over to trustees of a funded pension plan.

Another possibility for variation in the annual pension fund expense is a change in the *actuarial assumption,* which concerns the assumed rate of return on investment of the pension assets. An increase in this assumed rate allows a reduction in the amount of current pension fund expenses because the difference can, in effect, be made up by higher earning rates on the pension assets themselves. A third variation may arise from the manner in which capital gains earned on the pension assets are allowed to influence the need for additional funding.

The possible impact of such changes is illustrated in Figure 10–5, in which annual pension fund expense, number of employees, and pension fund expense per employee for United States Steel Corporation are shown. The per-employee calculation is a useful device to highlight a change in accounting policy that might not be detected from notes in the annual report itself. Five significant accounting changes in per-employee pension expense are denoted by letters.

Change (A). In 1958, U.S. Steel reduced its pension fund contribution per employee to $149 from a 1957 level of $517. The *Annual Report* for 1958 noted that "under business conditions and the reduced steel

FIGURE 10–5
Pension fund expenses per employee (United States Steel Corporation, 1953–1972)

Year	Total pension expense	Number of employees	Pension fund expense per employee	Accounting change
1953	$105,386,000	301,560	$349	
1954	102,132,000	268,142	381	
1955	115,473,000	272,646	423	
1956	125,207,000	260,646	480	
1957	140,193,000	271,037	517	
1958	33,296,000	223,490	149	(A)
1959	104,357,000	200,329	521	
1960	87,226,000	225,081	388	(B)
1961	85,451,000	199,243	429	
1962	38,787,000	194,044	200	(C)
1963	42,700,000	187,721	227	
1964	46,000,000	199,979	230	
1965	34,600,000	208,838	166	
1966	52,700,000	205,544	256	
1967	65,400,000	197,643	330	
1968	70,200,000	201,017	349	
1969	72,600,000	204,723	355	(D)
1970	104,800,000	200,734	522	
1971	62,100,000	183,940	338	(E)
1972	73,500,000	176,486	400	

operating rate existing in 1958, no payments (would) be made toward the funding of past service pension costs for the year and also that $67 million of the $297 million so provided in past years (would) be used to cover current service costs of non-contributory pensions . . ." U.S. Steel thus reduced its pretax pension expenses for the year 1958 by $97 million. After taxes, this amounted to an increase in per-share earnings of $0.87. In 1958, reported earnings per share fell 30%, from $7.33 (1957) to $5.13 (1958). Had it not been for the arbitrary change in pension fund accounting, 1958 earnings would have fallen to $4.26, a drop of 42% from the previous year. The change in procedure softened the impact of the reported decline.

Change (B). In 1960, actuarial service and mortality tables and the interest rate were redefined, reducing pension fund expenses for 1960 from $122,000,000 to $87,266,000, an expense reduction of $34,734,000. Assuming the 52% corporate income tax rate in effect in 1960, the change increased per-share earnings by $0.31. Reported earnings in 1960 were $5.16 per share, up 21% from $4.25 in 1959. Without the accounting change, earnings would have been approximately $4.85, up only 14%.

The accounting change accounted for one third of the reported growth in per-share earnings.

Change (C). In 1962, U.S. Steel adjusted interest factors and took into account a portion of the appreciation in the market value of the assets in the pension trust, reducing pension costs for 1962 from $81,687,000 to $38,787,000 on expense reduction of $42,900,000. Assuming a 52% corporate income tax rate, the arbitrary expense reduction added about $0.38 to per-share earnings. Reported earnings in 1962 were $2.56, down 16% from $3.05 in 1961. Had the change not been made, 1962 earnings would have been about $2.18, down 28%. In 1962, as in 1958, an arbitrary accounting change was used to hide the full magnitude of the decline in operating earnings.

Change (D). In 1969, interest factors were adjusted again, increasing net income by $14.4 million or $0.27 per share. U.S. Steel reported earnings per share of $4.01 in 1969, down 14½% from $4.69 in 1968. Without the change, 1969 earnings would have been only $3.74, a decline of approximately 20%.

Change (E). In 1971, U.S. Steel once again revised its interest factors, decreasing pension costs for 1971 from $104.7 million to $62.6 million, an expense reduction of $42.6 million. Assuming a 48% corporate income tax, this was a per-share increase in earnings of $0.41 per share. In 1971, reported earnings were $2.85 per share, up 5% from $2.72 in 1970. Without the accounting change, earnings per share would have fallen to $2.44, down 10%. The shift in accounting techniques converted a drop in earnings to a rise in earnings.

The power of a change in actuarial assumptions also can be seen from the 1971 Annual Report of Penn-Dixie Cement Corporation, which reported: "A change in actuarial assumptions, principally an increase in the assumed interest rate from 4% to 6% in 1970 with respect to two of the Company's plans, resulted in a decrease in pension expense for 1970 of approximately $665,000 and an increase in net income of $388,000." In 1968 and 1969, Penn-Dixie reported net income of over $4 million. In 1970, net income fell to $501,000, of which $338,000 was due to the change in actuarial assumptions and only $163,000 from normal operations as such. One is tempted to wonder if it was only coincidental that the change in actuarial assumptions was made in a year when earnings were abnormally low and needed (from a public image point of view) substantial bolstering. Since in 1970 Penn-Dixie paid dividends of $419,000, one consequence of the change in actuarial assumptions was that dividends paid did not exceed "earnings."

Unfunded past service costs is another example of variations in the recognition of expense. When pension benefits are increased, a company incurs added obligations of two types. First, pension fund contributions in the future must be increased to provide funds for the larger benefits. Second, the company incurs an obligation for unfunded past service costs equal to the sums of money that should have been contributed in past years to provide for the expanded benefits, but were not in fact so expensed. This unfunded past service cost is amortized over a future period of years, thus reducing future income. The number of years over which it is amortized, however, may vary substantially from company to company.

Vulcan Materials Company, for example, amortizes the charge "over the remaining pre-retirement years of the employees eligible for prior service credit." The company does not indicate the magnitude of the charge or the amount being amortized per year. Some companies minimize the impact on annual earnings by amortizing the charge over 40 years, the longest period allowed under generally accepted accounting principles. American Brands reports that as of year-end 1971, the actuarially computed value of vested benefits exceeded the total of pension fund assets by $53 million. This sum was being amortized over periods ranging from 19 to 39 years. Companies using a 40-year period include Brockway Glass Company and United Merchants and Manufacturers. At the other end of the spectrum, Union Electric Steel Corporation and Kaiser Cement and Gypsum Corporation amortize over 20 years, while Northrop amortizes over 10 years.

Some companies use still another variation in their treatment of unfunded past service costs. They expense only the interest on the unfunded costs, but not the principal amount. This policy is followed by, among others, Gamble-Skogmo, Inc., Metromedia, and Crane Company. This policy has the effect of lessening pension fund costs and maximizing earnings per share.

The significance of amortization rates for past service costs arises when the annual amortization is large in relationship to present earnings and when an amortization period is chosen so as to minimize the impact upon reported earnings. In addition, comparison of two or more companies otherwise similar is hindered if their policies of past service cost amortization vary significantly.

Depreciation

Depreciation is the process by which the cost of certain assets with long lives is assigned, year by year, to the gains they produce. A depreciable asset, such as a building or a piece of equipment, is best viewed at the time of purchase as a prepayment for future benefits. Net income in each of the future years (or other time periods, such as quarters) can be determined only by subtracting from the revenue of that time period an appropriate share of the original prepaid benefit. Net earnings in 1974, for example, can be determined only by subtracting from 1974 revenue a share of the prepaid benefits (physical assets) purchased in earlier years and used in 1974 to help generate sales.

Depreciation methods cause problems in evaluation of reported earnings per share for several reasons. One problem area derives from the uncertainty implicit in estimating the useful lifetime of depreciable assets and in the possibility that that lifetime, and thus annual depreciation expenses, will be different from what was originally anticipated. Another problem arises because of the use of different depreciation schedules for public accounting and for tax accounting purposes.

First, we consider changes in the depreciable life of fixed assets. Between 1968 and 1970, many American airlines extended the depreciable life of their aircraft, thus reducing annual depreciation expense and increasing annual reported earnings at a time when airline earnings were generally depressed. Typical of the airline accounting policies of this period were those adopted by Continental Airlines, Inc. in 1970. Continental extended the depreciable lives of its Douglas DC-9, Boeing 707, and Boeing 720B aircraft from 10 years to 12 years and of its Boeing 727 aircraft from 10 years to 14 years. This lengthening of depreciable lives had the effect of reducing 1970 depreciation expense by approximately $8.7 million and increasing net earnings by approximately $4.4 million. Earnings per share for Continental thus were increased by $0.38. Since reported earnings per share for 1970 were only $0.32, the effect of the change was to avoid reporting a loss of $0.06 per share. Because earnings in 1969 had been $0.29 per share, the company was able to state in the president's letter in the *Annual Report,* "Your company increased its earnings 16 percent to be one of the five trunk lines which operated at a profit. All other major air carriers sustained grievous losses in what was the worst year experienced by the United States' air transport industry."

Although the 16% increase by Continental was caused by the change in accounting methods, it must be noted in all fairness that by 1970 many other trunk lines had increased the depreciable life of their aircraft. Continental Airlines also pointed out that had the extended lifetimes been in effect in 1969, earnings per share in 1969 would have been $0.54 rather than $0.29. Thus the rise in earnings per share from 1969 to 1970 was illusory on any basis of comparability.

A second consideration is the method of depreciation being used. For purposes of calculating taxable income, Internal Revenue Service rules permit the use of various forms of *accelerated depreciation.* These rules allow a greater portion of the cost of an asset to be expensed in the early years of its life, and correspondingly a lesser portion in the later years of its life, since total depreciation may not exceed cost. The effect of the rules is to reduce taxable income and thus income

216

taxes in the early years and to increase taxable income and income taxes (assuming no change in tax rates) in later years. The shifting of the tax burden to later years was intended by Congress to spur expansion and modernization of capital equipment.

The significance of the tax gain can be seen in the hypothetical example portrayed in Figure 10–6, in which an asset costing $50,000 and

FIGURE 10–6
Tax significance of straight line versus double declining balance depreciation (equipment costing $50,000 with a 10-year tax life)

Year	Straight line	Double declining balance	Double declining balance over (under) straight line	50% of excess	Cumulative
1	$ 5,000	$10,000	$ 5,000	$2,500	$2,500
2	5,000	8,000	3,000	1,500	4,000
3	5,000	6,400	1,400	700	4,700
4	5,000	5,120	120	60	4,760
5	5,000	4,095	(905)	(452)	4,308
6	5,000	3,277	(1,723)	(862)	3,446
7	5,000	3,277	(1,723)	(862)	2,584
8	5,000	3,277	(1,723)	(862)	1,723
9	5,000	3,277	(1,723)	(862)	862
10	5,000	3,277	(1,723)	(862)	-0-
Total	$50,000	$50,000	-0-	-0-	-0-

presumed to have a useful life of ten years with no salvage value can be written off either on a straight line basis (10% of its original cost per year) or on a double-declining basis (20% of the remaining undepreciated cost per year). Because the double-declining method would leave a large residual to be written off in the tenth year, the example assumes a change to straight line depreciation of the remaining balance in the sixth year. The extra depreciation can be seen in the third column. If an income tax rate of 50% is assumed, the tax savings (larger payment in parentheses) are shown in the fourth column, and the cumulative tax delay is shown in the last column. Note that the effect of using accelerated depreciation is to delay the time of tax payment but not to reduce total tax payments over the life of an asset. This delay can have an important impact on the result of a present value calculation in determining investment value.

The significance to investors of the use of accelerated forms of depreciation for tax purposes lies in the variety of ways that companies using accelerated depreciation for tax purposes may elect to report to their shareholders. In general three possibilities exist, all illustrated in Figure

10-7. The three sets of calculations in this illustration assume purchase of the $50,000 asset described in Figure 10-6, that this is the only asset owned by the company, and that annual income before depreciation in each year is $40,000.

The company might report to the stockholders by the *tax method*, the same method used to report to the Internal Revenue Service. As can be seen, this method results in earnings rising from $15,000 in the first year to a high of $18,361 in years six through ten. Over the decade, total earnings are $175,000. The tax method is not normally used to report to stockholders of publicly held companies, although it may be used by smaller companies whose shares are traded infrequently in the over-the-counter market. The tax method is used to calculate annual tax payments for the two methods that follow.

The *flow-through method*, used by a number of publicly held companies, is one wherein depreciation is reported by the straight line method on public statements. Only actual tax liabilities are shown, however, with the result that the tax deferral allowed by the Internal Revenue Service "flows through" to increase reported earnings in the early years after assets are acquired. In later years, earnings are depressed by the larger-than-normal tax payments.

The *normalized method* is the most widely used of the three methods and is generally considered preferable. Under this method, both depreciation and tax expenses are shown as they would be without the use of accelerated depreciation. The difference between tax expense (accrued) and actual tax payments (from the tax method) is kept out of reported earnings and is shown as an increase or decrease in a liability account, "reserve for deferred income taxes." If a normalizing method is used, investors need make no adjustment for reported earnings per share. If either the flow-through or the tax method is used in the public reports, however, investors must be aware that the reporting method alone will cause earnings to change in future years. Accordingly the investor must adjust his concept of current normalized earnings as they relate to actual earnings of the present year, and as a basis for forecasting future earnings.

Investment tax credit

A *tax credit* is a direct reduction in taxes, as compared to a *tax deduction*, which is a reduction in taxable income. Assuming a 48 percent corporate income tax, a tax deduction increases after-tax income by 52% of the amount of the deduction, while a tax credit increases after-tax income by 100% of the amount allowed. Clearly tax credits are more valuable per dollar than tax deductions.

To encourage expansion and modernization, the federal government

FIGURE 10–7

Three depreciation reporting methods (equipment costing $50,000 with a 10-year tax life)

	1	2	3	4	5	6	7	8	9	10	Ten-year total
Tax method											
Income (before depreciation)	40,000	40,000	40,000	40,000	40,000	40,000	40,000	40,000	40,000	40,000	400,000
Depreciation (double declining balance)	10,000	8,000	6,400	5,120	4,095	3,277	3,277	3,277	3,277	3,277	50,000
Taxable income	30,000	32,000	33,600	34,880	35,905	36,723	36,723	36,723	36,723	36,723	350,000
Income tax (50%)	15,000	16,000	16,800	17,440	17,952	18,362	18,362	18,362	18,362	18,362	175,000
Net income	15,000	16,000	16,800	17,440	17,952	18,361	18,361	18,361	18,361	18,361	175,000
Flow-through method											
Income (before depreciation)	40,000	40,000	40,000	40,000	40,000	40,000	40,000	40,000	40,000	40,000	400,000
Depreciation (straight line)	5,000	5,000	5,000	5,000	5,000	5,000	5,000	5,000	5,000	5,000	50,000
Taxable income	35,000	35,000	35,000	35,000	35,000	35,000	35,000	35,000	35,000	35,000	350,000
Income tax (from tax method)	15,000	16,000	16,800	17,440	17,952	18,362	18,362	18,362	18,362	18,362	175,000
Net income	20,000	19,000	18,200	17,560	17,048	16,638	16,638	16,638	16,638	16,368	175,000
Normalized method											
Income (before depreciation)	40,000	40,000	40,000	40,000	40,000	40,000	40,000	40,000	40,000	40,000	400,000
Depreciation (straight line)	5,000	5,000	5,000	5,000	5,000	5,000	5,000	5,000	5,000	5,000	50,000
Taxable income	35,000	35,000	35,000	35,000	35,000	35,000	35,000	35,000	35,000	35,000	350,000
Income tax expense shown*	17,500	17,500	17,500	17,500	17,500	17,500	17,500	17,500	17,500	17,500	175,000
Net income	17,500	17,500	17,500	17,500	17,500	17,500	17,500	17,500	17,500	17,500	175,000
* Income Tax paid	15,000	16,000	16,800	17,440	17,952	18,362	18,362	18,362	18,362	18,362	175,000
Increase (decrease) in deferred Taxes	2,500	1,500	700	60	(450)	(862)	(862)	(862)	(862)	(862)	–0–
	17,500	17,500	17,500	17,000	17,500	17,500	17,500	17,500	17,500	17,500	175,000

included in the tax law of 1971 a tax credit provision, whereby a company is allowed to reduce its income taxes in any year by 7% of the cost of new assets purchased in that year. In effect, the government pays 7% of the cost of new assets purchased. The tax credit has no effect upon subsequent depreciation, which is allowed upon the full 100% of asset cost rather than upon only 93% of cost.

Determination of net income and thus of earnings per share for a company is made more difficult under the 7% tax credit provision because two alternate treatments are used for financial reporting purposes. Some companies choose to allow the tax credit to "flow through" so that the full 7% of asset acquisitions increases earnings in the first year. Other companies choose to amortize the tax credit over a period of time, usually ten years, thus normalizing or spreading the benefit over the time interval rather than using it to bolster first-year earnings alone. As a general matter, accountants would prefer to see the tax credit normalized since it results in less distortion of earnings on a year-to-year basis. Corporate directors, presumably hard pressed to improve earnings for the current year, often insist upon the flow-through method, which is also acceptable under "generally accepted accounting principles," even though from a potential investor's point of view it causes a company to appear significantly better than is warranted by its performance in that particular year. A related motivation of corporate directors in choosing a particular method is to stabilize earnings over time.

Variations in treatment can be seen from statements in the annual reports of Pet Incorporated and Carnation Company, both of which are engaged in dairy, milk products, and convenience and specialty foods. Pet, which uses the flow-through method, states, "The investment tax credit is recognized as a reduction of the provision for income taxes in the year in which the credits are available for tax purposes." On the other hand, Carnation states, "The accumulated reduction in income taxes resulting from application of the investment tax credit as permitted by the Internal Revenue Code in prior years, is being taken into income over the estimated useful lives of the related plant assets."

Pet Incorporated's use of the flow-through method in 1971 added approximately $750,000 to reported income of $16,253,000 (after deducting an extraordinary loss of $5,100,000 on various lines of business sold or closed). Without the flow-through method, Pet would have earned something over $15,000,000, and thus the use of flow-through increased 1971 earnings by about 5%. The level of Pet earnings would have to be reduced by this 5% if they had been calculated by the more conservative normalizing method used by their competitor, Carnation.

Interestingly, the annual reports of Pet and Carnation were both audited by Price Waterhouse and Company, illustrating the latitude allowed within generally accepted accounting principles even by the same public accounting firm. This example emphasizes the need for investors to be aware of variation in treatment allowed under "generally accepted accounting principles."

Extraordinary items

Accounting opinion and practice generally favor an *all-inclusive* concept of income statements, in which all extraordinary gains and losses are reflected in a special-items section of the income statement. An alternative but less desirable procedure is to recognize special items directly in the retained earnings account without showing them on the income statement. This last treatment is less desirable primarily because it tends to hide from public view the impact of special items, especially when they are losses. Extraordinary items might include (1) losses from sales of assets other than merchandise, such as equipment or investments in subsidiaries, (2) losses from one-time events, such as expropriations or storm or fire damage, (3) write-offs of various intangible assets, often including capitalized development expenses for a product that has failed to produce the anticipated revenue, or (4) losses from devaluations of foreign currency.

The significance to an investor of extraordinary items is twofold. First, such write-offs are often recognition that past time periods failed to carry a proportional share of expenses that should have been allocated to them. In one of the largest writeoffs of all time, Radio Corporation of America in 1971 wrote off $490 million as the cost of quitting its general-purpose computer business. After taxes the loss amounted to $250 million, or $3.36 per share of common stock, a sum equivalent to slightly more than the combined earnings of the two prior years. Such write-offs may or may not indicate the possibility of similar write-offs in future years. A loss due to an expropriation in a Latin American republic may simply call attention to the fact that the company is vulnerable to further political expropriation in other countries. Hurricane losses on the east coast of the United States, although not an annually recurring event, are nevertheless likely enough to cause question in an investor's mind as to the probability of eventual recurrence.

Second, some types of direct write-offs may free a company from a continued burden and so enhance the prospects for future reported profits. For example, in the third quarter of 1971, RCA earned $0.23 per share. These quarterly earnings included operations of the loss-producing computer division. Profits from continuing operations alone were $0.36. Thus, once RCA had decided to write off the computer division, an earnings level predicated upon third quarter earnings of $0.36 rather than $0.23 became a better base from which to estimate probable future performance.

OTHER VARIATIONS

Still other variations in accounting techniques produce possibilities for differing earnings-per-share calculations, even when all physical events are identical. Among these are shifting from last-in, first-out accounting for inventories to first-in, first-out treatment and the need to consider the significance of dilution upon earnings per share.

Inventory accounting—LIFO and FIFO

Reported earnings can be bolstered on a one time basis by a change in the method of transferring inventory costs to cost of goods sold in the income statement. In the early 1970s, a number of companies changed from last-in, first-out (LIFO) accounting to first-in, first-out (FIFO) accounting. By such a change, lower inventory costs were transferred to the income statement. The lower inventory costs represented the "first-in" costs of earlier years when the price level was lower. Because these "earlier" inventory items (on a cost basis, not a physical basis) were "sold" at the higher price levels of the 1970s, greater reported profits resulted. Among companies that made such a change in recent years have been Wilson & Company, a Ling-Temco-Vought subsidiary (1971); the J. I. Case Company subsidiary of Tenneco Inc. (1970); and Kaiser Aluminum (1971).

The magnitude of improvement possible by such a change can be seen from the 1970 statement of Chrysler Corporation. For the period from January 1, 1957, through December 21, 1969, the LIFO method of inventory valuation had been used for approximately 60% of Chrysler's consolidated inventory. Effective January 1, 1970, the FIFO method of inventory valuation was adopted for inventories previously valued using the LIFO method. This change in bookkeeping procedures changed a loss that would have been reported as $27.6 million under the old procedures to a loss of only $7.6 million. In other words, earnings were enhanced, or losses reduced, by $20.0 million or $0.40 per share. As a consequence of the change, inventories were written up by $150.0 million with, of course a concomitant improvement in the various liquidity ratios.

As a consequence of the change in accounting for inventory, Chrysler Corporation retroactively adjusted its books and also wrote up its retained earnings by $53.5 million. Also as a consequence of the change Chrysler incurred an additional tax liability of $52.8 million, representing taxes "saved" during the years when LIFO was being used, which would be repaid to the federal government over 20 years.

Lastly, the Chrysler switch of methods in 1970 meant that earnings for 1971 and subsequent years would be higher than would have been the case without the change of methods. Presumably Chrysler's stock price in post-1970 years would also be higher, reflecting the fact that most investors would not recall the change of methods and would continue to apply the same price-earnings multiple to the now higher earnings.

Fully diluted earnings per share

Earnings per share consist of the after-tax earnings of a company, less any dividends paid to preferred stockholders, divided by the number of outstanding shares of common stock. The number of shares outstanding at year-end is used in making some calculations, while average number of shares outstanding during the year is used in other instances. The variations between calculations based on year-end and average shares outstanding are seldom significant, unless the company sold a major issue of stock during the year.

To the extent that earnings per share are used to gauge an increase in the well-being of common stockholders, however, the possibility of dilution caused by the sudden creation of new shares of common stock not matched by a proportional increase in available earnings must be considered. Such increases in the number of shares come about through conversion of convertible debentures or of convertible preferred stock into additional shares of common, or through the exercise of common stock warrants by investors or stock options by company management. Calculation of earnings per share on a "fully diluted" basis means that the denominator (i.e., number of outstanding shares) is increased to a level reflecting the possible conversion into common stock.

Companies are required to calculate earnings per share on a fully diluted basis. Such a calculation for Crane Company, filed with their annual 10–K report to the Securities Exchange Commission, appears in Figure 10–8. In 1971, it will be seen, Crane Company reported earnings per share of $4.24. However, if all convertible securities had been converted, earnings per share would have been only $3.41.

Which earnings-per-share figure should an investor use in determining the investment value of a share of Crane common stock? Conservatism would suggest using only the "certain" amount of $3.41. A more aggressive approach would be to formulate an opinion as to the actual probability of conversion of the convertible securities.

In July, 1972, the Crane Company 5% Convertible Subordinate Debentures of 1993 were selling at $865 per bond; each debenture was convertible into 40 shares of common stock having an aggregate market value, at that time, of $775. Another issue of Crane 7% Convertible Subordinate Debentures, due in 1994, was selling at $770 per bond and was convertible into 34.78 shares of common stock having a market value of $612.50.

FIGURE 10–8

CRANE COMPANY
Annual Report for the year ended December 31, 1971
Computation of earnings per share
(in thousands of dollars)

	1967	1968	1969	1970	1971
Net income	$10,228	$10,998	$11,602	$8,255	$11,162
Preferred dividends	178	165	123	115	111
Net income applicable to common shareholders	$10,050	$10,833	$11,479	$8,140	$11,051
Common shares*	2,687	2,687	2,666	2,635	2,604
Net income per common share†	$3.75	$4.03	$4.30	$3.09	$4.24
Net income applicable to common shareholders	$10,050	$10,833	$11,479	$8,140	$11,051
Conversion of CF&I debentures: Add back interest, net of income tax	–	–	91	159	123
Increase in minority interest in CF&I net income	–	–	(414)‡	(414)	(258)‡
Conversion of Crane Co. debentures: Add back interest, net of income tax	–	308	1,175	1,564	1,446
Net income applicable to common shareholders, assuming conversion of debentures	$10,050	$11,141	$12,331	$9,449	$12,362
Common shares*	2,687	2,687	2,666	2,635	2,604
Add average shares reserved for conversion of Crane Co. debentures	–	233	796	1,167	1,024
Total common shares, assuming conversion of debentures	2,687	2,920	3,462	3,802	3,628
Net income per common share, assuming conversion of debentures†	$3.74	$3.82	$3.56	$2.48	$3.41

* In thousands of shares and adjusted for stock dividends.
† In dollars.
‡ Includes $128,000 in 1969 and $34,000 in 1971 for increase in minority interest in extraordinary credit.
　Extraordinary items per share computed by dividing the reported extraordinary item by applicable common shares as shown above except in the computation of the 1969 and 1971 extraordinary credits per share, assuming conversion of debentures, in which case the extraordinary credits as reported are reduced by $128,000 and $34,000 respectively, the increase in minority interest.
　In outstanding stock options were exercised as of the end of each year and the proceeds used to purchase Crane common shares on the open market, a net reduction in outstanding shares would result.
Source: Exhibit to Form 10–K filed with the Securities Exchange Commission

Not only would a loss be taken on conversion of either issue—a bond holder would be better off to sell than to convert the bond—but nothing would be gained from converting prior to maturity date since the bond prices would rise with any rise in the value of the underlying shares of stock.

Some incentive to voluntary conversion might arise if the current dividend yield on the stock exceeded the current yield on the bonds.

The 1993 issue provided for an annual interest payment of $50 per bond. At a 1972 dividend rate of $1.60 per year for the common stock, it would be necessary to have 31.25 shares of stock to obtain a current cash yield equivalent to the interest yield on the bonds. Because the bonds are convertible into more than 31.25 shares of stock, a holder could enhance his current yield by converting. Since he could enhance it even more, however, by selling the bond and buying shares of stock directly, conversion does not seem imminent.

As a result of these circumstances, an investor in 1972 with a horizon somewhat less than the 21 or 22 years remaining before the bonds mature might reasonably rely more on the $4.24 earnings than the $3.41. The investor should be aware, however, that conversion will eventually dilute the stock, and hence he should perhaps be somewhat conservative in his assessment.

SUMMARY

In determining investment value, investors rely to a great extent upon present earnings per share as a base from which to formulate expectations about future years. In addition, present market price at which any shares must be purchased is heavily influenced by the most recent earnings report of a company. It would be comforting to think that reported earnings per share were a "fact," but as this chapter has illustrated, there exists a great variety of techniques by which reported earnings per share may in fact be established at a higher or lower level than might otherwise be reported. This chapter has looked at some of these variations, which are summarized in the following table:

Variation	*Significance*
Measuring performance by product line	A losing product line that can be disposed of without affecting other product lines may permit total earnings (of the remaining product lines) to rise, enhancing total investment value.
Amortization of goodwill	Failure to amortize the excess of purchase price over book value in mergers effected prior to November 1, 1970, will arbitrarily increase earnings per share. (Goodwill acquired after November 1, 1970, must be amortized.)
Consolidation of subsidiaries	Nonconsolidation permits the hiding of subsidiary earnings, which may later be used to bolster parent earnings via a larger-than-usual dividend.
Current recognition of income to be received in later years	If a portion of such income is never received through default by the buyers, the technique permits present earnings to be unduly enhanced at the expense of future years.
Treatment of gains on foreign exchange	Gains recorded from translating foreign subsidiary statements into dollars in years when the dollar devalues may be used to enhance earnings per share.

Variation	*Significance*
Hidden earnings abroad	Nonconsolidation of some foreign subsidiaries effectively hides their earnings until such time as a dividend to the U.S. parent is declared.
Nonnormal revenue	Revenue from other than normal operations may or may not have sufficient probability of recurrence to warrant separate analysis.
Pension fund accounting	Variations in recording future pension fund obligations and changes in assumed interest rates may influence earnings levels.
Accelerated depreciation	Nonnormalization of the tax effect of using accelerated depreciation permits the reporting of higher earnings in the years immediately after large capital expenditures.
Investment tax credit	Flow-through, rather than amortization, is sometimes used to boost current earnings.
Extraordinary items	Even though accounted for in the nonoperating section of an income statement, this process of "taking a bath" all at once effectively obscures much of the true impact of such charges.
Inventory accounting	Shifting from LIFO to FIFO permits earnings to be calculated by a more favorable method, enchancing investment value in the eyes of those who accept reported earnings per share uncritically.
Dilution of earnings per share	Failure to perceive the significance of fully diluted earnings per share may lead an investor to buy shares of stock just before earnings are diluted by new shares issued for convertible securities.

The complexity of analysis, valuation and ultimate portfolio construction is underscored by this summary table. Nevertheless, understanding of allowable accounting adjustments is a necessary step in the process of investing.

SUGGESTED READINGS FOR CHAPTER 10

B. Graham, D. L. Dodd, and S. Cottle. *Security Analysis: Principles and Technique.* 4th ed. (New York: McGraw-Hill Book Company, Inc., 1962), Part Two.

C. T. Horngren. *Accounting for Management Control: An Introduction.* 2d ed. (Englewood Cliffs, N.J.: Prentice-Hall, Inc., 1970); Chapter 5.

J. A. Mauriello. *Accounting for the Financial Analyst.* rev. ed. (Homewood, Ill.: Richard D. Irwin, Inc., 1971), Chapters 5–8.

11

Forecasting future benefits

THE PRIMARY PURPOSE of investment analysis is to learn enough about a particular asset so that a confident judgment can be made about its relative attractiveness in the portfolio of the investor. In the case of securities, we have seen that this process begins, in most instances, with analysis of corporate financial statements and consideration of certain accounting adjustments. The end result of this initial step is a historical record of how the company has done during recent time, both before and after any unusual circumstances. Based on this record, the next step is to estimate or forecast the future benefits of owning the securities of the company, and to employ those estimates in security valuation. *Forecasting* becomes the link between the historical record of the past and projections of events in the future. Put another way, forecasting is the link between investment analysis and investment valuation. The purpose of this chapter is to explain, compare, and illustrate various methods of forecasting.

NATURE OF FORECASTS

What must be forecasted with regard to a particular security? One broad answer might be that forecasts should be made of all items appearing in the financial statements of the firm in question such as sales, expenses, profits, assets, and capital structure. A more precise answer might be that forecasts should be made of all those items called for in security valuation models, such as earnings, dividends, price-earnings ratios, growth rates, discount rates, and horizon lengths. The two answers clearly are related, for as will be shown presently, earnings per share depend directly on such items as margin, turnover, leverage, taxes, and book value. Dividends in turn depend on earnings and payout ratios, while future prices depend on dividends, earnings, and price-earnings ratios.

For discussing methods of forecasting, it is convenient to begin with the more direct path and focus on earnings, dividends, and other variables needed in the valuation models for common stocks. A logical starting point for such forecasts is the historical earnings record of the firm in question. To illustrate throughout, we shall use the common stock of Howard Johnson, a company familiar for their restaurants, motor lodges, and ice cream. The earnings record of Howard Johnson over the past decade has been as follows:

Year	Earnings per share
1961	$0.43
1962	0.48
1963	0.56
1964	0.79
1965	0.93
1966	0.94
1967	0.87
1968	0.96
1969	0.90
1970	1.14
1971	1.44

Rather than going into a detailed security analysis of Howard Johnson at this point, we shall assume that these values represent normalized earnings for the company over the eleven-year period 1961–1971. Our goal is to forecast earnings for the five-year horizon 1972–1976.

TYPES OF FORECAST

It is important to distinguish between two different types of forecasts: objective and subjective. If based solely on historical information, the forecasting process is said to be an *objective* process, and the result is an *objective* forecast. This is in contrast to a *subjective* forecasting process, which would not necessarily rely on just historical information, but on any available information, quantifiable or otherwise. Objective and subjective forecasts are not mutually exclusive, because a subjective forecast may well depend on historical information. In fact, a subjective forecast would logically begin where an objective forecast ends.

An example may help to clarify this distinction. Suppose we want to forecast the earnings of Howard Johnson for the year 1980. Using one of the forecasting methods to be discussed in this chapter, the annual earnings of Howard Johnson Corporation are forecast objectively to range between $3.00 and $3.50 per share for 1980. But suppose, hypothetically, we happen to know that a new management team specializing in production efficiencies and cost controls has decided to leave its existing company and join Howard Johnson in about a year. Aware of

228

their past accomplishments, we upgrade our forecast of earnings per share to be in the $3.60 to $3.90 range for the year. This, then, is a subjective estimate based on both past earnings numbers that are available and our nonnumerical, subjective feelings about the potential addition to management.

The distinction between objective and subjective forecasting is important because it focuses on the comparative advantage of security analysts over individual investors. That is, professional analysts are more likely than individuals to have access to information about changes in management, technological advances, and other developments within the firm and the industry. It also suggests that security analysts will never be replaced by computers, which certainly are faster than analysts in numerical calculations of historical growth rates and projections therefrom, but not capable of incorporating nonnumerical factors into subjective forecasts. Despite this important distinction, the remainder of this chapter will be devoted to various forecasting methods that are objective since they are based solely on historical information.

HISTORICAL GROWTH FORECASTS

One way to begin is to calculate the annual percentage increase or decrease for each year over some past horizon and to base forecasted earnings on a continuation of historical growth rates. Letting e_t represent earnings per share during period t, the percentage growth for that same period would be given by

$$g_t = \left(\frac{e_t - e_{t-1}}{e_{t-1}}\right)(100\%) = \left(\frac{e_t}{e_{t-1}} - 1\right)(100\%) \qquad (11\text{-}1)$$

The earnings per share of Howard Johnson increased from $1.14 to $1.44 during 1971, which is an annual growth of

$$[(\$1.44/\$1.14) - 1](100\%) = 26.3\%.$$

Annual growth rates for Howard Johnson over the past decade are calculated as follows:

Year, t	Earnings per share, e_t	Annual growth, g_t
1961	$0.43	—
1962	0.48	11.6%
1963	0.56	16.7%
1964	0.79	41.1%
1965	0.93	17.7%
1966	0.94	1.1%
1967	0.87	-7.5%
1968	0.96	10.3%
1969	0.90	-6.3%
1970	1.14	26.7%
1971	1.44	26.3%

We see that there were eight years of positive growth and only two years (1967 and 1969) of negative growth.

We can summarize these annual growth rates in different ways. The simple arithmetic average is given by the expression

$$g_a = \frac{1}{N} \sum_{t=1}^{N} g_t \tag{11-2}$$

while the geometric average is given by the expression[1]

$$g_g = \sqrt[N]{\prod_{t=1}^{N} (1 + g_t)} - 1 \tag{11-3}$$

For example, using only the last three years, we would obtain for the arithmetic average

$$g_a = \tfrac{1}{3}(-6.3\% + 26.7\% + 26.3\%) = 15.6\%$$

and for the geometric average

$$g_g = \sqrt[3]{(0.937)(1.267)(1.263)} - 1 = 14.5\%$$

Using longer past horizons of five and ten years for Howard Johnson gives

Data used	Arithmetic average, g_a	Geometric average, g_g
Five years	9.9%	8.9%
Ten years	13.8%	11.8%

Remembering that compounding is just the opposite of discounting, we can use the present value factors in Appendix A to estimate the compounded growth rate of a stream of earnings—or for that matter of any variable. Compounded growth would be given by g_c in the expression

$$\frac{e_0}{e_N} = \left(\frac{1}{1 + g_c}\right)^N \tag{11-4}$$

Notice in expression (11-4) that the compound growth rate does not reflect any of the intermediate values of earnings between the initial value e_0 and the terminal value e_N. Thus the calculated growth rate may not be a good indicator if either the first or last year is abnormal. Values

---

[1] The summation sign Σ was explained in Chapter 4 as a rule for adding a series of values. Similarly, the product sign Π is simply a rule that says to mulitply the particular values for all N periods being considered. The root sign $\sqrt[N]{}$ indicates that the Nth root is to be taken of the quantity underneath the sign.

of the right side of (11–4) for various N and g_c appear in the "discounted sum" columns of Appendix A. Again using the most recent three-year period 1969–1971 to illustrate, we would calculate the ratio

$$e_0/e_N = e_{1968}/e_{1971} = \$0.96/\$1.44 = 0.667$$

for Howard Johnson. Going across the $N = 3$ years row of Appendix A, we see that this calculated value lies about midway between the factor 0.675 for 14% and 0.658 for 15%, and thus we conclude that the compound growth rate $g_c = 14.5\%$.[2]

That this value of compound growth is identical to the geometric average result for the same three-period horizon is no coincidence. For by rearranging expression (11–3), we obtain

$$(1 + g_g)^N = \prod_{t=1}^{N} (1 + g_t) = \prod_{t=1}^{N} (e_t/e_{t-1}),$$

and then taking reciprocals of both sides gives

$$\left(\frac{1}{1 + g_1}\right)^N = \prod_{t=1}^{N} (e_{t-1}/e_t);$$

but the right hand side of the latter is just e_0/e_N for an N-period horizon, as it appears in expression (11–4). Hence, we have shown the exact equivalence $g_c = g_g$.

Letting $\hat{g}$ represent the growth rate that is expected to occur in the future, the forecasted value of earnings $\hat{e}_t$ in year t would be given by

$$\hat{e}_t = e_0(1 + \hat{g})^t \qquad (11\text{–}5)$$

where e_0 is the most recent value of earnings for the firm in question. For Howard Johnson, we would use $e_0 = \$1.44$, which is the 1971 level of earnings. The growth rate $\hat{g}$ should be the best estimate of future growth. If based only on past experience, it could be the arithmetic average g_a, the geometric average or compound growth g_c, a moving average of recent years, or some other average that has not been discussed here. Although compound growth has been shown to be superior to arithmetic average growth when evaluating past earnings, there is no particular reason to believe that using compound growth in expression (11–5) will

---

[2] Compound growth rates are also easily calculated with a slide rule using the log scales.

lead to more accurate forecasts than if the arithmetic average was used instead.

The following earnings forecasts $\hat{e}_t$ are obtained with expression (11–5) for Howard Johnson in the years 1972–1976 using both compound growth and arithmetic average of past annual growth rates, and also both five and ten years of historical earnings experience.

Year	Arithmetic average		Compound growth	
	Five years (9.9%)	Ten years (13.8%)	Five years (8.9%)	Ten years (11.8%)
1972	$1.58	$1.64	$1.57	$1.61
1973	1.74	1.86	1.71	1.80
1974	1.91	2.12	1.86	2.01
1975	2.10	2.41	2.03	2.25
1976	2.30	2.74	2.20	2.51

One quickly notes the wide range of forecasts that result. The range is much narrower for the early years, but grows as one goes out into time. For 1972, forecasts range from $1.57 to $1.64, while for 1976, the range is $2.20 to $2.74. And because the arithmetic average is greater than the geometric average, the forecasts are greater when arithmetic average is used instead of compound growth. Finally, the use of ten rather than five prior years leads to higher forecasts for the future. This is because there was steady growth for Howard Johnson during the earlier five years, while both upturns and downturns have occurred during the most recent five years.

FREEHAND FORECASTS

Another method of forecasting earnings that does consider the intermediate values is to construct freehand on semilog paper a "best-fit" line through the annual observations. The slope of the freehand line is equivalent to the compound growth rate over the period investigated If the freehand line happened to go through both the initial and terminal values of the series of observations, the resulting compound growth rate would be equivalent to that calculated with expression (11–4). Although there are subjective variations in lines constructed freehand through a series of plotted points, the growth rate estimated such a line may be considered superior to the previous method since all observations are reflected in drawing the line.

To illustrate, the historical earnings record of Howard Johnson over the period 1961–1971 is plotted on semilog paper in Figure 11–1. At the bottom of Figure 11–1 are several lines (representing compound growth rates from 3% to 25%) enabling one to estimate quickly by com-

FIGURE 11–1
Freehand forecasts of Howard Johnson earnings per share

Earnings per share (logarithmic scale)

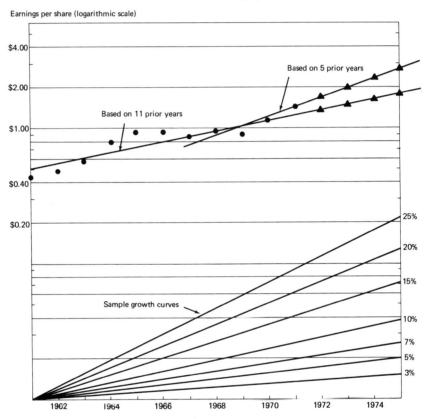

parison of slopes the growth rate of any freehand line that is drawn. We see that over the past eleven years, the earnings of Howard Johnson have experienced a cyclical pattern about an upward trend. By comparing slopes, we estimate a compound growth rate of 9%. But based on only the most recent five years of earnings for Howard Johnson, a freehand line indicates a much higher growth rate of about 17%.

In contrast to dots, which indicate historical earnings, triangles are used in Figure 11–1 to indicate forecasted earnings. The forecasts are merely extrapolations of the upward trend without speculation as to further cyclical developments. The two sets of forecasts, which can be read directly from the exhibits, are as follows:

	Freehand projections	
Year	Five years	Eleven years
1972	$1.68	$1.35
1973	1.97	1.50
1974	2.30	1.63
1975	2.70	1.80
1976	3.22	1.95

Again, we observe a diversity in forecasts that increases over time. And in comparing these freehand projections with the forecasts based on historical growth rates, we observe that freehand projections lead to lower forecasts when 11 prior years are used, but higher forecasts when only five prior years are used. Again, the primary determinant of this is that historical growth rates are applied to current earnings, while freehand projections employ current earnings as only a single observation. The 1972 forecast using 11 prior years of $1.35 is thus considerably below 1971 earnings of $1.44. In other words, forecasts based on freehand projections give weight neither to the cyclical nature of the earnings record nor to the most recent value of earnings.

LEAST-SQUARES FORECASTS

Freehand projections require a subjective judgment in fitting the straight line. In contrast, the method of least squares can be used to determine that line that best fits a set of observations in the sense of minimizing squared deviations from the line. If observations are made of variables X and Y, the equation of a straight line fitting the observations could be expressed as

$$Y = a + bX \qquad (11\text{--}6)$$

where a is the Y-intercept (i.e., the value when X is zero) and b is the slope of the fitted line. Letting X_i and Y_i denote the ith observation, and if there are a total of N observations, then one can use the following equations to calculate the intercept,

$$a = \frac{\Sigma Y_i \Sigma X_i^2 - \Sigma X_i \Sigma X_i Y_i}{N \Sigma X_i^2 - (\Sigma X_i)^2} \qquad (11\text{--}7)$$

and the slope

$$b = \frac{N \Sigma X_i Y_i - \Sigma X_i \Sigma Y_i}{N \Sigma X_i^2 - (\Sigma X_i)^2} \qquad (11\text{--}8)$$

respectively.

In our applications, we use earnings per share e_t instead of Y and time t instead of X. For the latter, it is convenient to simply let $t = 1$, 2, 3, etc., rather than using actual years $t = 1961, 1962$, etc. The following calculations are used to determine least-squares lines using, as before, both $N = 5$ and $N = 10$ prior years.

Year	e_t	t	t^2	$e_t \times t$
1962	$0.48	1	1	0.48
1963	0.56	2	4	1.12
1964	0.79	3	9	2.37
1965	0.93	4	16	3.72
1966	0.94	5	25	4.70
1967	0.87	6	36	5.22
1968	0.96	7	49	6.72
1969	0.90	8	64	7.20
1970	1.14	9	81	10.26
1971	1.44	10	100	14.40
1967–71 Total	5.31	40	330	43.80
1962–71 Total	9.01	55	385	56.19

Applying the least-squares equations, we obtain for five prior years

$$a_5 = \frac{(5.31)(330) - (40)(43.80)}{(5)(330) - (40)^2} = \frac{0.30}{50} = 0.006$$

and

$$b_5 = \frac{(5)(43.80) - (40)(5.31)}{(5)(330) - (40)^2} = \frac{6.6}{50} = 0.132$$

Using ten prior years in a similar manner, we would obtain

$$a_{10} = \frac{(9.01)(385) - (55)(56.19)}{(10)(385) - (55)^2} = \frac{378.4}{825} = 0.459$$

and

$$b_{10} = \frac{(10)(56.19) - (55)(9.01)}{(10)(385) - (55)^2} = \frac{66.3}{825} = 0.080$$

The equations using least squares can be summarized for five prior years

$$\hat{e}_t = 0.006 + 0.132t \tag{11-9}$$

and for ten prior years

$$\hat{e}_t = 0.459 + 0.080t \tag{11-10}$$

To use these equations as a means of forecasting earnings for Howard Johnson, we need only to substitute proper values of time t into expression (11–9) or (11–10): $t = 11$ would correspond to 1972, $t = 12$ for 1973, and so forth. Forecasts for the period 1972–76 using both five and ten prior years are as follows:

Year	t	Least-squares projections	
		Five prior years	Ten prior years
1972 11		$1.46	$1.34
1973 12		1.59	1.42
1974 13		1.72	1.50
1975 14		1.85	1.58
1976 15		1.99	1.66

When these forecasts are plotted in Figure 11–2, we again see the impact of historical values on future projections. From a statistical standpoint, it is always well to use as many observations as possible in making least-squares estimates and forecasts. In the present example, the inclusion of earnings for the earlier years 1962–66 serves to lower the earnings forecasts for 1972–76.

FIGURE 11–2
Least-squares forecasts of Howard Johnson earnings per share

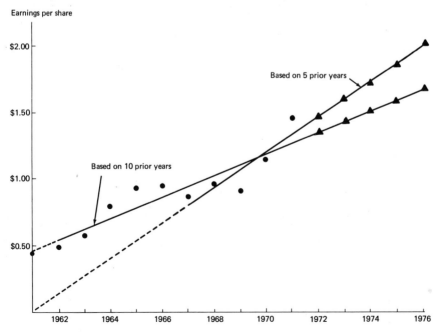

In summary, we have seen that different methods of forecasting earnings based only on historical data can lead to a range of possible forecasts for each year. The extent of historical data used also has been seen to be important. Furthermore, subjective information and judgments may lead to different forecasts than would be obtained objectively. There is no prescribed forecasting method or procedure for incorporating subjective judgments. The idea is to use whatever methods and procedures lead to the most accurate forecasts of company earnings in the future. Continuing our illustration of Howard Johnson, let us assume that earnings per share for the next five years are forecasted to be

Year	Forecasted earnings
1972	$1.60
1973	1.70
1974	1.80
1975	1.95
1976	2.20

Observe that these forecasts are within the range of values obtained in the foregoing discussion. The forecast depicts a continued growth in earnings for Howard Johnson as leisure time travel and appetites for quality ice cream continue to expand.

FORECASTING EARNINGS BY COMPONENTS

It can be shown that several of the financial variables identified in Chapters 9 and 10 are directly related to the earnings per share of a company. As a result, one method of forecasting is to work with the component variables that constitute earnings, rather than working with earnings itself. The advantage of this forecasting method is that it allows a careful comparison between companies since earnings changes can result from several possible sources. We proceed now to identify the component variables that constitute earnings per share.[3]

The following mnemonic abbreviations, reflecting typical items from the financial statements of firm j, will be defined and used in the development:

B_j = book value
e_j = earnings per share
EAT_j = after tax earnings
$EBIT_j$ = earnings before interest and taxes
L_j = leverage
LD_j = long term debt
M_j = margin

---

[3] This section is based on G. C. Babcock, "The Concept of Sustainable Growth," *Financial Analysts Journal*, May–June, 1970 pp. 108–14.

NS_j = net sales
NW_j = net worth
RNW_j = return on net worth
$RNW_j{}^*$ = after-tax return on net worth
ROI_j = return on total investment
SH_j = number of outstanding shares
T_j = turnover
U_j = tax factor (1 − federal income tax rate)

The result of this analysis is a detailed breakdown of earnings per share, which can be defined as

$$e_j = \frac{EAT_j}{SH_j}. \tag{11-11}$$

To achieve this result, we begin with return on investment, which can be defined as

$$ROI_j = \frac{EBIT_j}{LD_j + NW_j}, \tag{11-12}$$

where investment consists of the total long-term capitalization of the firm. But it also can be defined as the product of margin times turnover, as shown in Chapter 9. Margin reveals how successful a firm was in extracting profit from each dollar of sales. It is given by

$$M_j = \frac{EBIT_j}{NS_j}. \tag{11-13}$$

Turnover, on the other hand, measures how successfully the firm was able to use its total long-term capital in generating sale volume. That is,

$$T_j = \frac{NS_j}{LD_j + NW_j}. \tag{11-14}$$

Thus, return on investment can be shown to be

$$ROI_j = M_j T_j = \frac{EBIT_j}{NS_j} \times \frac{NS_j}{LD_j + NW_j}. \tag{11-15}$$

The degree of leverage in the firm reflects the capital structure that is employed. For our purpose here, it conveniently can be measured by the ratio of return on net worth to return on investment, as follows

$$L_j = \frac{RNW_j}{ROI_j}. \tag{11-16}$$

Using this, we can write return on net worth as

$$RNW_j = L_j ROI_j = M_j T_j L_j \tag{11-17}$$

or as the product of three factors: margin, turnover, and leverage. After-tax return on net worth $RNW_j{}^*$ is given by the product of four factors

$$RNW_j{}^* = M_j T_j L_j U_j,$$ (11–18)

where U_j is equal to unity minus the appropriate federal income tax rate for firm j.

Defining book value per share by

$$B_j = \frac{NW_j}{SH_j}$$ (11–19)

and using expression (11–11), we can also write after-tax return as the quotient

$$RNW_j{}^* = \frac{EAT_j/SH_j}{NW_j/SH_j} = \frac{e_j}{B_j}.$$ (11–20)

Equating expressions (11–18) and (11–20) and solving for earnings per share, we obtain finally

$$e_j = M_j T_j L_j U_j B_j$$ (11–21)

Earnings per share is thus shown to be a simple product of five important factors or components: margin, turnover, leverage, taxes, and book value.

Continuing the use of Howard Johnson as an illustration, their earnings for the years 1969–1971 can be broken down into the five components as follows

Year	Margin M_j	Turnover T_j	Leverage L_j	Tax factor U_j	Book value B_j	Earnings per share e_j
1969	0.069	2.801	1.036	0.503	$ 8.95	$0.90
1970	0.085	2.567	1.105	0.472	10.97	1.14
1971	0.106	2.141	1.030	0.499	12.52	1.44

We see that the increased margin for Howard Johnson over the three years was somewhat offset by a decreased turnover. Leverage was never very great for Howard Johnson and taxes remained fairly constant at about 50%. The major source of earnings increase was the growth in book value per share—that is, largely from retained earnings.

In general, increasing earnings per share necessitates an improvement in one or more of these five components. Management possesses no control over the tax factor except that as the firm's before-tax dollar earnings grow past $25,000, the effective tax rate increases significantly and the tax factor decreases. Margin can be increased, but improvement is limited somewhat by the nature of the industry and the actions of competitors. Turnover of fixed assets is limited by technology, but turnover of working capital (accounts receivable, inventory, etc.) can be improved by astute management. Leverage can be improved, although at some level, the interest rate on debt financing may be increased as creditors view the firm as becoming too risky. Of all five factors, therefore, only book value is a continuing source of improvement as seen for Howard Johnson over the period 1969–1971. The importance of book value, of course, has a direct bearing on the dividend policy selected by the firm.

The final step of this approach is to project each of the five components of earnings for subsequent years and to forecast earnings by simple multiplication. We shall not do so here.

FORECASTING DIVIDENDS

A series of valuation models for common stocks were compared and illustrated in Chapter 6. A central variable in all of those models was the stream of dividends expected to be received during the holding horizon. In some models, annual dividends per share D_t appeared directly, while in others, earnings per share e_t were adjusted by the firm's estimated payout ratio Q_t. The models are equivalent, of course, since $D_t = Q_t e_t$. Similarly, we could discuss the forecasting of dividends either directly, or by applying estimated payout ratios to forecasted earnings. Over many firms and many years of experience, the average payout ratio has been about 60%. The average payout varies considerably among industries, however, and one must examine each firm in question to see what its pattern, if any, has been. Because dividend policies vary greatly among firms, and because those policies change over time, one method may be better in some cases, while the second method is preferable in other cases.

The dividend payments by Howard Johnson over the period 1961–1971, as compared with their earnings record, were as follows:

Year	Earnings per share*	Dividends per share	Payout ratio
1961	$0.43	none	—
1962	0.48	none	—
1963	0.56	2% stock	—
1964	0.79	2% stock	—
1965	0.93	2% stock	—
1966	0.94	2% stock	—
1967	0.87	$0.05	6%
1968	0.96	0.18	18%
1969	0.90	0.22	24%
1970	1.14	0.24	21%
1971	1.44	0.24	17%

* Adjusted for indicated stock dividends and 100 % stock dividends in 1966 and 1969.

The board of directors of Howard Johnson made two major changes in dividend policy during that period. In 1963, they changed the policy from no dividends to stock dividends, and in 1967 they changed to cash dividends. Each of these three different types of dividend policy should be examined in terms of the firm itself and the valuation of its common shares.

No dividends were paid during 1961 and 1962, which were the first two years after Howard Johnson was incorporated. Many firms pay no dividends during their early years because retained earnings represent an important source of needed equity financing that is preferable to selling additional shares of common stock. Other firms, including many so-called growth companies, continue over time to pay no dividends to their common shareholders. In such cases, investors prefer the firm to reinvest earnings, which presumably lead to increased earnings and higher stock prices in the future. Moreover, capital gains resulting from higher stock prices are taxed at the capital gains rate, which is lower than the regular income tax rate on cash dividends. The offsetting disadvantage of non-dividend stocks, of course, is that investors must wait until they sell their common stock to receive any cash benefits from their investment. And trying to forecast stock prices several years in the future clearly is a more formidable challenge than forecasting next year's cash dividend.

Stock dividends are a false attraction to many investors. Although it appears that something of value has been distributed to each shareholder, this is an illusion. *Stock dividends*, represent nothing more than a bookkeeping transfer between two balance sheet accounts—from retained earnings to common stock and paid-in capital. But total assets, total equity, sales, and earnings capacity of the firm all are unchanged. And while the number of outstanding shares is increased by a stock dividend, the market price per share should decrease proportionally, and the total market value for each stockholder remains exactly the same. Because the market does not always make such adjustments instantaneously, there sometimes are short-term movements in stock price when stock dividends are announced. Usually, such movements can be attributed to changes in expectations for cash dividends or to general publicity for the firm caused by the news of the stock dividend.

In both 1966 and 1969, the board of directors of Howard Johnson announced a 100% stock dividend—or a two-for-one stock split as it is usually known. *Stock splits* also do not affect stockholder's market values since doubling the number of shares held is offset by halving the market prices. As is the case with stock dividends, announcement of stock splits may cause short-range price fluctuations if investors erroneously believe they are getting additional benefits. The major reason for a stock split by any company is simply to lower the market price to a level that presumably is more suitable for trading by investors. Ironically, brokerage commissions on a percentage basis are actually higher when stock prices are lower.

In 1967, Howard Johnson began to pay cash dividends to common stockholders. The per-share payment was small during 1967 and reached a rather constant level during 1969–1971, even though earnings continued to advance during that period. The payout ratio $Q_t = D_t/e_t$ has varied between 6% and 24% and there has been no definite trend in payout during the five years of cash dividends. Given the rather brief period of cash dividend history and the lack of a clear trend in the payout ratio, it would be difficult in the case of Howard Johnson to forecast dividends by applying estimated payout ratios to forecasted earnings. For other firms, however, the pattern of payout ratio over time is quite constant and payout ratios can be used to forecast dividends with some degree of accuracy.

Many investors and also corporate directors appear to place more emphasis on the long-term pattern of dividend payments as a continued announcement to the world of prosperity, than on the use of retained earnings as an important source of internal financing, and hence of future prosperity for the firm. Accordingly, those firms maintain a constant or increasing stream of dividend payments, even though earnings may fluctuate considerably. Dividend cuts are avoided, if at all possible. If a constant dividend payout ratio is maintained, dividends and earnings automatically move up and down in tandem. Notice that in 1969, Howard Johnson increased dividends even though earnings decreased.

The limited historical evidence of dividend payment suggests that Howard Johnson perhaps intends to maintain a policy of steady and/or increasing dividends despite cyclical patterns in earnings. This might take the form

Year	Forecasted earnings	Forecasted dividends
1972	$1.60	$0.24 (15%)
1973	1.70	0.30 (18%)
1974	1.80	0.30 (17%)
1975	1.95	0.40 (21%)
1976	2.20	0.40 (18%)

The resulting payout ratios, shown in parentheses, continue to vary from year to year, although the range of variability diminishes.

FORECASTING PRICE-EARNINGS RATIOS

Certainly the most difficult variable to forecast for any investment asset is the terminal sales price. The difficulty is twofold. First, we are forecasting a market value several periods or years from now, rather than in the immediate future. Second, we may be able to forecast future earnings with some degree of accuracy, but forecasting future price-earnings ratios is a more complicated matter since they reflect simultaneously the overall market level, industry developments, and market psychology—not to mention the individual characteristics of the particular firm. Price-earnings ratios, for example, may be related to the expectations that investors hold for the future growth rate of the firm in question. And while earnings per share may exhibit predictable trends and cycles over time, that may well not be the case for price-earnings ratios. Unusual externalities, such as Watergate, the middle-east war of 1973, and the energy crisis, also can have substantial impact on price-earning ratios over time.

To illustrate, we continue our examination of the common stock of Howard Johnson, as reflected in the following data for the same period being investigated:

Year	Earnings per share	Average price	Average P/E ratio
1961	$0.43	$12.43	28.9
1962	0.48	10.32	21.5
1963	0.56	11.03	19.7
1964	0.79	14.30	18.1
1965	0.93	20.65	22.2
1966	0.94	22.09	23.5
1967	0.87	24.01	27.6
1968	0.96	23.62	24.6
1969	0.90	23.13	25.7
1970	1.14	17.44	15.3
1971	1.44	31.10	21.6
Average.	$0.86	$19.10	22.6

Average price is the arithmetic average of the yearly high and low. During 1971, for example, the price of Howard Johnson ranged from just above $20 to slightly over $40, with an average of $31.10. The average price-earnings ratio for 1971 thus was $31.10/1.44 = 21.6.

Over the eleven years for which data are available, the price-earnings ratio for Howard Johnson ranged from 15.3 to 28.9 and averaged 22.6. During the past five years, the average price-earnings ratio was 22.9. So with the exception of 1970, which featured an overall market decline that affected most stocks, the price-earnings ratio for Howard Johnson has remained fairly constant. One possible forecast for a price-earnings ratio at the end of 1976 would be 23, the average over the past five years. Another approach would be to start with a base forecast of 23 and then increase or decrease depending on any other relevant information that might be available. For example, if there were ample evidence that a shorter work week and extended vacations would lead to increased demand for services of firms stressing leisure-time activities, one might increase the forecasted price-earnings ratio to 25 or so—thus predicting a greater popularity of leisure-oriented securities.

It is useful to test the sensitivity of a forecasted price-earnings ratio to the final determination of investment value. Using a discount rate of 10%, the present value of dividends forecasted above for the 1972–1976 horizon would be

Year	Forecasted dividend, $\hat{D}_t$	Weight, α_t	Weighted dividend, $\alpha_t\hat{D}_t$
1972	$0.24	0.909	$0.218
1973	0.30	0.826	0.248
1974	0.30	0.751	0.225
1975	0.40	0.683	0.273
1976	0.40	0.621	0.248
Present value of forecasted dividends.			$1.212

Earnings of $2.20 per share for the year 1976 have been forecasted earlier. The following calculations gives the present value of terminal share price for alternative price-earnings ratios, and the total investment value which includes the $1.212 present value of forecasted dividends.

Forecasted earnings	Forecasted P/E ratio, $\hat{Q}_t$	Forecasted terminal price	Weight, α_t	Present value of terminal price	Investment value
$2.20	17	$37.40	0.621	$23.222	$24.434
2.20	20	44.00	0.621	27.320	28.532
2.20	23	50.60	0.621	31.418	32.630
2.20	25	55.00	0.621	34.150	35.362
2.20	27	59.40	0.621	36.882	38.094

We see that investment value is quite sensitive to the forecasted P/E ratio as of 1976, even though the effect is discounted back to the present time. We also note that the present value of terminal price clearly dominates the present value of dividends. Finally, we note that the entire range of investment values for Howard Johnson is below the market price that existed throughout much of 1972. Apparently, the stock was overvalued despite our optimistic forecast of a price-earnings ratio. Only if earnings were forecasted as high as $3.00 per share would the resulting investment value begin to approach the current market price. In other words, given only objective information about Howard Johnson during the past decade, we would be somewhat confident that its common shares are currently overvalued. If availability of subjective information caused us to change our forecasts or earnings, dividends, and price-earn ings ratios, it is possible that different estimates of investment value would result.

SUMMARY

Forecasting is an important link between the several tasks of security analysis and the application of security valuation models. The important distinction between objective forecasts, based only on historical information, and subjective forecasts, which reflect additional information often of a nonquantifiable type, was stressed. With the common stock of Howard Johnson as an example, objective forecasts were made of earnings for the next five years using different methods for forecasting. We also reviewed a useful method of forecasting earnings per share based on certain component variables. Difficulties in forecasting future dividends were discussed. Finally, terminal price-earnings ratios at the end of five years were forecasted, and the sensitivity of investment value using these forecasts was illustrated.

SUGGESTED READINGS FOR CHAPTER 11

G. C. Babcock. "The Concept of Sustainable Growth," *Financial Analysts Journal*, May–June, 1970, pages 108–14.

S. E. Bolten. *Security Analysis and Portfolio Management* (New York: Holt, Rinehart and Winston, Inc., 1972), Chapters 5–6.

J. C. Francis. *Investments: Analysis and Management* (New York: McGraw-Hill Book Company, Inc., 1972), Chapter 10.

H. A. Latane and D. L. Tuttle. *Security Analysis and Portfolio Management* (New York: Ronald Press Company, 1970), Chapters 11–13.

part IV

Non-industrial securities

IN PART IV we expand our coverage of analysis and valuation to the securities of other than industrial corporations. It is important to do so because much of the literature of investments has focused almost exclusively on business firms that are product oriented or process oriented, and that require large investments in inventory and fixed assets. Chapter 12 is concerned with securities of public utilities, while Chapter 13 deals with securities of transportation companies. For both of these types of non-industrial securities, governmental regulation is an important characteristic that must be considered alongside of other operating characteristics. The next two chapters involve organizations that are financial in nature. Chapter 14 deals with financial institutions such as commercial banks, savings and loan associations, and insurance companies, and Chapter 15 is concerned with investment companies such as mutual funds, closed-end companies, and dual-purpose funds. Finally, Chapter 16 examines different types of firms that might be described as service organizations. Included among service organizations are firms whose dominant characteristic is equipment rental, and firms whose service is based on the specialized and/or professional capabilities of individuals. For firms of each type in Part IV, we review their important characteristics, examine their financial statements, and explore other unique features that should be considered in the process of investing.

12

Investing in public utilities

PRIVATELY OWNED public utility companies constitute one of the most important industries whose securities may be selected by investors. One reason for this is the vast size of the industry. In 1972, for example, the some 3,165 million shares of public utility common stocks listed on the New York Stock Exchange were almost 18 percent of the total 18,329 million shares listed, more than any other single industrial group. Moreover, transactions in common stocks of public utilities in 1972 constituted over ten percent of the total annual trading volume of 4,138 million shares, and again represented the largest single industry in magnitude.[1] In addition, the projected increases in energy consumption in the United States point toward the continued importance of utility securities. It seems clear that the utility industry will have to turn to the capital markets to raise many billions of dollars of new capital needed for expansion in the late 1970s and in the 1980s. In the past, the demand for electricity in the United States has doubled approximately every decade, a result both of increased population and increased usage per person. Should this rate of expansion continue as is expected, new investment in the next decade will have to equal total investment now existing. Thus present size and projected expansion create a situation in which securities issued by privately owned public utilities are and will continue to be a significant portion of the total pool of corporate securities available to investors. The purpose of this chapter is to explore the various characteristics and investment attributes of securities issued by public utilities.

---

[1] *Fact Book* (New York Stock Exchange, 1973) page 7.

OVERVIEW OF PUBLIC UTILITIES

Public utility companies of greatest interest to investors are electric power companies, telephone companies, gas distribution companies, and gas transmission companies. Water companies are now generally municipally owned in the United States and so are not of interest to investors. Transportation companies such as railroad and airlines also can be considered as utilities, but they are treated separately in Chapter 13 because their characteristics are significantly different. Because certain characteristics and attributes are similar to all public utilities, we shall concentrate in this chapter on the analysis of securities of electric power companies—with occasional reference to other types of utilities when appropriate.

As a group, the utilities to be considered here possess several basic economic characteristics that dominate the process of analysis. One such characteristic is that they are a "natural monopoly" and thus must be regulated. A natural monopoly arises when the inherent nature of the business is such that only one supplier can reasonably serve a given set of customers. More specifically, economies of scale are such that one firm can serve a market at a lower average cost than can several competing firms. It would be highly inefficient and almost twice as costly, for example, to construct two competing sets of electric power transmission lines through each neighborhood so that every household could select between the electricity offered by the two companies. Similarly, two telephone companies competing in the same geographical area would simply require a double investment in telephones, transmission wires, and switching equipment for every consumer within that area. As with electric power companies, a significant increase in physical capacity would be required to serve the same geographical area, and if the competing companies were both to survive in the long run, average costs would necessarily be higher because of a loss of economies of scale.

In spite of the characteristic of "natural monopolies," it should be observed that some competition does exist. Electric companies compete with gas companies as suppliers of energy for both businesses and homes. Telephone companies compete, to a degree, with telegraph companies and even with the United States Postal Service as a means of delivering communication. This aspect of competition exists independently of whether one or more electric or telephone companies are serving a given geographical area.

Since utilities can serve society best only when they are granted monopoly status for their own type of service, the various states and the federal government regulate the prices that may be charged the public so that public utilities do not abuse their monopoly status. The regulatory process by which utilities are granted an official monopoly status and are then regulated in terms of their attainable rate of earnings is thus one aspect of investing in public utilities that will be treated in this chapter.

A second important characteristic of utilities arises from the interaction of two operating aspects: (1) by their very nature utilities must possess a very large investment in fixed plant and equipment to serve their customers, and (2) utilities can not satisfy customers out of inventory. Both aspects, of course, have to do with the left-hand, or asset, side of the balance sheet of the public utility. Electric utility companies must invest in sufficient generating capacity to serve that one peak moment during the year when customers demand the most electric power. With the advent of air conditioning, this peak typically occurs on a hot July or August afternoon. It is not possible for the utility to generate electric power during the evening, or during the late winter and early spring months, accumulate that power in inventory, and then deliver during the peak demand period in summer. Telephone companies operate under a similar constraint; they must have sufficient lines available to handle whatever peak telephone load is demanded. Gas utilities are to a degree an exception, in that gas can be stored for later distribution. However, gas storage capacity in relationship to total demand is limited, and gas companies must still have distribution lines to ultimate customers adequate to handle peak demands.

A third basic characteristic of public utilities has to do with their mix of financing—or with the right-hand side of their balance sheets. The interaction of heavy investment in fixed plant and equipment already mentioned and a comparatively stable demand for their product or service have led utilities to finance their operations with a capital structure that, by the standards for most other industries, would be too heavy with debt. Yet given the comparatively stable nature of their business plus the fact that monopoly status is assured by law and rates are set by a governmental agency, utilities tend to finance with a large proportion of debt and a small proportion of equity. This process introduces a large degree of financial leverage, which has important implications to bondholders and stockholders for both risk and return.

REGULATION OF PUBLIC UTILITIES

Investors must attempt to judge whether regulatory authorities will permit increases in revenues, without an undue time lag, to offset increased operating and financial costs to the utility. That question is important not only for the present financial health of a utility, but for the utility's ability to attract new capital needed for expansion.

Privately owned public utilities operating within a single state are generally regulated by a state public utility or "public service" commission. Utility operations that extend across state lines, such as the long-distance operations of the American Telephone and Telegraph Company and various interstate gas transmission companies, are regulated by such federal agencies as the Federal Power Commission (power projects on navigable rivers, wholesale selling of electric energy in interstate commerce, and wholesale transmission and sale of natural gas) and the Federal Communications Commission (radio, television, and interstate and foreign telephone and telegraph services). For the type of utility service with which this chapter is concerned, most interstate sales are wholesale, with resale to households by a state-regulated utility company. All fifty states plus the District of Columbia have regulatory commissions. Of these 51 commissions, 48 have jurisdiction over gas utilities, 47 have jurisdiction over electric utilities, and 47 (not exactly the same commissions) have jurisdiction over telephone and telegraph companies.[2]

Entry into the industry

How does a company become a *regulated public utility*, and what rights and obligations are assumed when it does become "regulated"? Perhaps the most important right obtained by a public utility is protection against competition from an enterprise offering the same service within a prescribed service area. A utility receives a Certificate of Public Convenience and Necessity from the appropriate regulatory agency as well as, in some instances, a franchise from local governmental units. With its certificate and franchise, the utility obtains not only protection from competition, but also the right to use public property, such as streets, and the right of *eminent domain* to condemn private property when such property is necessary for the proper conduct of business. An example would be the taking of a strip of land for power lines or gas pipelines. Fair compensation must be paid for any property taken under the right of eminent domain. Regulated utilities also have the right to collect a reasonable price for their services, and they may not be forced to operate at a loss. They are not assured a profit, however, if no reasonable price will cover the cost of the service being provided.

In return for these rights, the utility obligates itself to satisfy the demands of the public. All who apply for service and are willing and able to pay must be served. Service must be safe and adequate, meaning that technical requirements for electrical voltage or gas pressure must be satisfied, and service must generally be available 24 hours per day. Rates to various classes of subscribers must be the same. In other words, a utility can not discriminate in price among customers within each sub-

[2] Charles F. Phillips, Jr., *The Economics of Regulation* (Richard D. Irwin, 1969) pages 91–95.

scriber class. A utility may establish different subscriber classes based upon variations in the type and cost of service provided to that type of customer. The price that the public utility charges for its service must be "just and reasonable" in that it reflects public interest as well as the interest of the corporation.

The significance to investors of the rights and obligations just described is the possibility that the profits of a utility may be squeezed between the operating costs of supplying all demand for its service and the price for its service set by a regulatory body. From the mid-1940s to the early 1970s such a concern was more apparent than real, for increased efficiency resulting from installation of larger generating plants, lower production costs per kilowatt of power generated, and improved coordination among public utilities led to economies that offset the inflation of those decades. With the exception of nuclear power, however, most such increases in efficiency now seem to have been realized. Thus, a reasonable prognosis for the years ahead is that increases in generating costs will necessitate rate increases by regulatory agencies. The process by which utility rates are established is the subject to which we now turn.

The rate base

State regulatory procedures establish a permissible level of earnings for a utility by allowing a percentage rate of return upon a *rate base* that purports to be a measure of the value of the assets used by or useful to that utility in serving the public. Dollar earnings permitted are therefore the product of the rate base and the allowed rate of return. These dollar earnings are calculated after depreciation and after income taxes, but before interest expenses. They thus constitute the dollar earnings available to total invested capital consisting of long-term debt and stockholders' equity.

The premise underlying this approach is that investors should be allowed a level of profit equivalent to one that would be earned in a competitive enterprise, while any benefits that might derive from the monopoly position of the utility should be preserved for the consumer. From the point of view of one who might invest in utility securities, an understanding of how the regulatory process might lead to greater or lesser levels of earnings is extremely important.

An increase in utility earnings could be caused either by an increase in the rate base or by an increase in the rate of return allowed on that base. The rate base itself could increase because of the inherent economic growth of the service area and the resulting greater investment in assets to serve that area, or it could increase because of a change in the procedure by which the utility commission measures the "value" of the assets that constitute the rate base. The allowed rate of return also could change because the utility commission itself determined that some other rate of return was appropriate, or because increases or decreases in utility operating costs were not matched by prompt adjustment of utility prices charged to the public.

A variety of methods are used by regulatory commissions to establish the asset valuation to be used as the rate base. Although the legal definition may vary from one jurisdiction to another, utility rate bases are typically original cost, reproduction cost, or some weighted average of the two. In all cases, the rate bases are calculated after deducting accumulated depreciation. *Original cost* is the actual cost, less depreciation, of putting the existing plant into operation. In practice, original cost is usually determined by taking the cost of the property as shown on the balance sheet of the utility, and accepting this "book cost" as reliable evidence of actual original cost unless evidence to the contrary is introduced.

Reproduction cost is the cost of replacing the existing utility plant at current prices, with an allowance for actual depreciation to date. This method is used only in Ohio, where this type of rate base is mandated by the state constitution. The resulting rate base is intended to reflect the current cost of reestablishing an identical plant, as distinct from the cost of providing identical service. These are likely to be different because of changes in technology.

A *weighted average* of both original cost and reproduction cost is used as a rate base in some jurisdictions, often under the name "fair value." The term "fair value" itself is derived from a famous United States Supreme Court decision in 1898, which held that a utility was entitled to earn a fair return upon the fair value of the property being used for the convenience of the public. The Supreme Court said that "in order to ascertain that value, the original cost of construction, the amount expended in permanent improvements, the amount and market value of its bonds and stock, the present as compared with the original cost of construction, the probable earning capacity of the property under particular rates prescribed by statute, and the sum required to meet operating expenses, are all matters for consideration, and are to be given such weight as may be just and right in each case."[3] Initial reaction to the many possible formulas for determining value was confusion. However, in ensuing decades the term "fair value" came to be interpreted as considering both original cost and reproduction cost. In some jurisdictions, both costs are considered, with the resultant rate base usually found to be equal to original cost. In other jurisdictions, however, rate bases are established between original cost and reproduction cost.

---

[3] *Smyth* v. *Ames*, 169 U.S. 466 (1898).

Because reproduction cost is generally higher than original cost, such a finding increases the rate base and thus contributes to increased profit levels.

In addition to applying various standards for the valuation of the rate base, regulatory commissions use a variety of discretionary measures to lower or raise a rate base derived in the first instance by one of the methods that have been described. Among these are the use of a rate base for a future period and the inclusion or exclusion, either in full or in part, of allowances for cash working capital, for materials and supplies, for plant under construction, and for plant held for future use. Cash working capital is not the usual concept of current assets minus current liabilities, but is rather an estimate of the amount advanced by investors to maintain operations between the giving of a service and the receipt of payment for that service. Cash funds held for the payment of future taxes may or may not be allowed as a portion of cash working capital. Investment in plant not yet completed also may or may not be included in the rate base.

The significance to investors of the type of rate base lies in the degree of legal compulsion upon utility commissions to provide rate increases in the face of inflation. In jurisdictions such as Ohio, which are committed to the use of reproduction cost, or in such "fair value" jurisdictions as Illinois, Indiana, Maryland, and Pennsylvania, which include some weight for reproduction cost, utilities generally are better able to keep abreast of inflation as the rate base increases. Investors should be aware, however, that factors other than rate base influence final utility earnings. Chief among these might be the degree of professionalism on a utility commission staff, the independence of the utility commission from political pressures, and the degree to which the commission sees its responsibility to the public in terms of preserving a financially healthy utility industry.

Rate of return

The second factor in the equation that expresses utility earnings is the allowed *rate of return*. As defined in another important court case, a fair rate of return is "equal to that generally being made at the same time and in the same general part of the country on investments in other business undertakings which are attended by corresponding risks and uncertainties."[4] The process by which the fair rate of return is established follows the traditional calculation of the cost of capital, in which the after-tax costs of different sources of financing are weighted by the relative importance of each source in the total capital structure.

---

[4] *Bluefield Water Works and Improvement Company* v. *Public Service Commission of the State of West Virginia et al.*, 262 U.S. 679, pages 692–93.

The use of a weighted-average procedure for determining an allowable rate of return for a public utility is illustrated in a California Public Utilities Commission decision on a rate application of Pacific Lighting Corporation.[5] In the weighted-average calculation, the cost rate for each source of financing is multiplied by the proportion that source represents in the total capital structure. An allowed rate of 8% was applied to the rate base of Pacific Lighting Corporation, a subsidiary of Southern California Gas Company.

Source of financing	Capital ratios	Cost rates	Weighted cost
Debt	50.0%*	5.80%	2.90%
Preferred stock	10.7	4.83	.52
Common equity	39.3	11.65	4.58
Total	100.0%		8.00%

* Includes 46.2 % long-term debt and 3.8 % short-term debt.

Regulatory procedure

In a utility rate case, allowable dollar earnings are established by multiplying the rate base by the allowed rate of return. The next step in the regulatory process is for the utility to suggest and for the commission to approve a schedule of rates for different services that will generate a gross revenue such that, after deducting all operating expenses including income tax, the allowable earnings will be achieved. Because a rate case may last from six months to two years, rate base, rate of return, and allowable rates are frequently established for a specified test period—perhaps the year immediately preceding the filing of the rate case. In the previous illustration of Pacific Lighting, the test year was 1972. The assumption is that by the time new rates actually become effective, both the rate base and the dollar earnings will be larger because of growth, but the allowed rate of return will be approximately correct. In some jurisdictions, such as California, the rate of return used in establishing rate schedules is slightly larger than that found to be "fair," the increase being caused by the need to compensate for the time delay or "regulatory lag" between rate case filing and completion.

What is the significance of understanding the regulatory procedure in the process of investing? First, investors should recognize potential changes in regulatory procedures, such as a change in jurisdiction from original cost to fair value. Such changes are usually determined in state supreme court decisions rather than by utility commissions themselves.

[5] Decision No. 80430 Before the Public Utilities Commission of the State of California in the matter of the Application of Southern California Gas Company, June 18, 1971, page 13.

Second, investors should realize that utilities in fair-value or reproduction-cost jurisdictions afford better protection against inflation than utilities in original cost jurisdictions. At times when inflation is not a problem, this advantage may be more conceptual than real. But when the
rate of inflation increases, the advantage can be very important.

A third significance lies not in the formal regulatory structure as
such, but in the signs that can be gleaned from watching that process
to determine how particular regulatory jurisdictions will respond to
changes in the financial needs of utilities. This would seem to be especially important during the remainder of the twentieth century, when
forecasts for expanded consumption of both electricity and gas indicate
great need for additional capacity. Because utilities have regulated
monopoly status, they have no alternative but to expand to meet increases in demand, and their financial health will be a critical variable
in determining the cost they pay for capital to increase capacity.

An inkling of what may be common in the years ahead occurred
between 1963 and 1973 for Pacific Telephone Company. Earnings failed
to advance as rapidly as interest expenses, with the result that interest
coverage fell from 8.72 times to 3.35 times. As a consequence, Standard
& Poor's Corporation in May 1973 lowered the quality rating of Pacific
Telephone bonds from AAA to AA. Existing bondholders experienced
a capital loss as their bonds dropped in market price to reflect the
new rating. In addition, interest charges on all new financing will be
higher than would otherwise have been the case, thus decreasing earnings to common stockholders. This condition will continue until rates
are raised to permit a sufficient improvement in the interest coverage
figure so that Standard & Poor's Corporation will raise their rating of
Pacific Telephone bonds.

A fourth significance, and again one not directly related to the
mechanics of rate base determination, lies in an analysis of regulatory
practice in granting rapid relief for changes in costs. If utility costs
such as labor and fuel rise without attendant rate relief, earnings will
be depressed. A cumbersome process that delays the time at which
relief can be granted will lengthen the period over which shareholder
earnings are depressed, even if eventual relief is assured by the mechanics of the regulatory process.

This regulatory lag is not only important for increases in operating
costs, but it also has an effect as the construction cost of new plant
and equipment rises. During most of the quarter century from the end
of World War II until 1970, technological improvements and economies
of scale in generating facilities offset the erosion of inflation, at least
for electric power utilities. Hence the average cost of a kilowatt-hour
tended to decline, and pressure for rate increases was moderated. Opportunities for cost saving in the decades ahead, excluding nuclear power

generation, seem more modest. This means that new plant and equipment will be more costly per kilowatt of generating capacity than plant and equipment installed in the recent past. Rate increases will be necessary to assure an adequate return on the required expanded investment in years ahead, and the slower the regulatory adjustment process, the more existing utility stockholders will suffer.

Some jurisdictions, it should be noted, have permitted frequent rate adjustments to reflect increases in costs over which the utility has no control by granting automatic fuel and tax adjustment clauses in their rate decisions. Thus noncontrollable increases in these cost items are automatically passed on to the consumer without additional rate hearings. This serves as an added protection to common stockholders of electric power companies.

OPERATING CHARACTERISTICS

The basic operating characteristic of a public utility is that a very large investment in assets is required to generate operating (sales) revenue. In 1971, the average turnover of net utility plant for 213 large, privately owned electric utilities in the United States was 0.291 times.[6] That is to say that annual sales revenue equalled 29.1% of the investment in net utility plant, or that an investment of $3.44 (derived from the reciprocal of 29.1%) was needed for public utilities to generate one dollar of sales in a single year. By comparison, General Motors Corporation (manufacturing) achieved a turnover of 1.55 times in 1971, while Sears, Roebuck and Company (retailing) had a 1971 turnover of 1.21 times.

Net plant turnover figures for four electric utilities representative

FIGURE 12–1
Significant operating characteristics of electric utilities, 1971

Characteristics	Class A and B electric utilities	Boston Edison Company	Houston Lighting and Power Company	Niagara Mohawk Power Corp.	Pacific Gas and Electric Company
Net plant turnover (annual operating revenue/ net utility plant)	0.29	0.31	0.31	0.32	0.57
Load factor (Average load/peak load)	–	59.9	64.0	62.5	64.2

[6] Aggregate data for all class A and B privately owned electric utilities. *Statistics of Privately Owned Electric Utilities in the United States, 1971.* Washington, D.C. 20426: Federal Power Commission, October 1972. Class A and B electric utilities include all those privately owned companies in the United States with annual operating revenues in excess of $1 million.

of various sections of the country are shown in Figure 12–1. As against the United States aggregate of 0.29 times, Boston Edison Company, in New England, achieved a turnover of 0.31 times, while Pacific Gas and Electric Company in the San Francisco Bay area achieved a much higher turnover, 0.57 times. Other things being equal, a utility with a relatively high turnover is more efficient, for it is able to generate more revenue per dollar of investment in utility plant. To some degree this might result from more modern plant and equipment, which because of technological advances in recent decades is less expensive per volume of output. The greatest differences in utility turnovers, however, are likely to spring from a company's ability to utilize a greater proportion of its plant on an around-the-clock basis. This characteristic is measured by the company's load factor.

Load factor is the ratio of average load for a year to peak load for that same year. Average load is total kilowatt-hour sales for the year divided by the number of hours in a year (8760), and is thus a measure of the *average* utilization of the utility plant. Peak load is the number of kilowatt-hours sold during the single hour in the year when customers demanded the most electricity. Because utilities agree to satisfy all demand for their services, they must build adequate capacity to satisfy their peak demand.

The nature of varying power demands is illustrated in Figure 12–2 showing weekly peak power demands for the city of Los Angeles during

FIGURE 12–2
Weekly peak power demands, Los Angeles, 1972

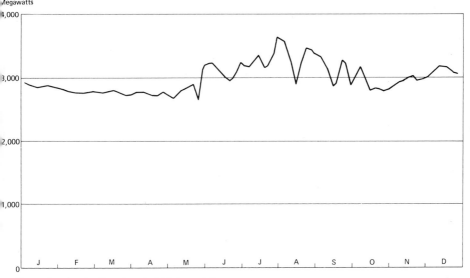

Source: Los Angeles Department of Water and Power

1972. Note that the peak power demand for the year occurred on July 31, 1972, when 3,630 megawatts of power were demanded. Assuming a generating capacity adequate to satisfy this demand, it is apparent from Figure 12–2 that during most of the year, and especially during the weeks from January through May, excess generating capacity was available. Because there would be virtually no cost to utilizing this idle capacity, power could be sold to other consumers during the slack periods at relatively low costs, provided it could be assured that those new consumers would not want electric power during a peak period. The success of a utility in filling up such slack periods with sale of its excess capacity is an indicator of efficiency, which can be measured by the load factor. The higher the load factor, the more efficient the operation.

Variations in electricity consumption occur during the course of a day, as well as over seasons of the year. Figure 12–3 shows hourly electricity consumption for the city of Los Angeles for July 31, 1972, the annual summer peak, and for Thursday, November 30, 1972, a typical winter day. On July 31, 1972, an hourly peak was reached at 2:00 P.M. On that day, temperatures in central Los Angeles reached 106 degrees, and the bulk of the peak demand may be ascribed to maximum air-conditioning power consumption. During the rest of the day, and particularly during the hours between midnight and 7:00 A.M., excess capacity existed. A typical winter day was Thursday, November 30, 1972. This was not the winter peak, nor was it Thanksgiving Day. During that day, a peak demand of approximately 2,960 megawatts was experienced at 6:00 P.M. The winter peak is normally experienced at about Christmas when a maximum of lights are burning both for decorative purposes and because of the small number of daylight hours. It will be noted that during the "typical" winter day of November 30, significant excess capacity was available not only during the early morning hours, but also during the regular daytime business hours.

Again, load factor measures a company's ability to utilize—to the maximum extent possible—generating capacity available during less-than-peak periods. Changes in standard of living over time have an important impact on load factors. For many years utilities experienced their system peaks in the winter. Electricity sold in the summer for air conditioning was an off-peak sale that did not require additional investment. Since the mid-1960s, however, most major urban utilities have experienced their system peak on a hot day in the summer, requiring additional investment to meet this peak and creating excess capacity during the winter months, which formerly were the peak demand. At the present time, sales for electrical heating tend to improve the load factor since such sales add little, if anything, to summer peak demands. Load-factor calculations for the four utilities also are included in Figure

FIGURE 12-3
Hourly load curves, Los Angeles, Monday, July 31, 1972 and Thursday,
November 30, 1972

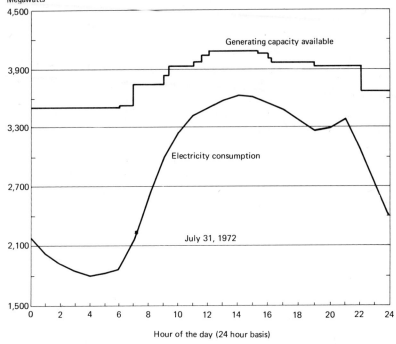

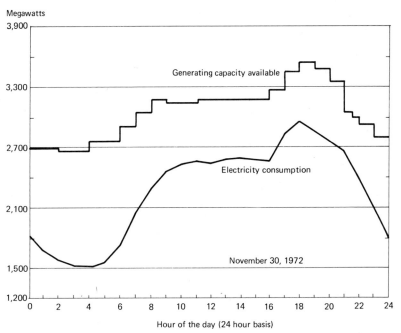

12–1. It can be seen that utilities in San Francisco and Houston have been able to achieve significantly better load factors than utilities in such a major eastern city as Boston.

Related to load factor is the *safety reserve margin*, a measure of the amount of excess generating capacity available over peak demands. This measure is the ratio of the difference between peak load and excess capacity to capacity of the system. If, for example, a utility had a system peak of 9,815,000 kilowatts and an operating capacity of 12,616,000 kilowatts, then that utility would have an excess capacity of the difference, 2,801,000 kilowatts. The company's safety margin would be 2,801,000 divided by 12,616,000, or 22.2%. Power demands could increase 22.2% either by population growth in the service area, or by a sudden unexpected rise in demand during an unusually intense heat wave, before the company's generating capability was exceeded. The United States average safety reserve margin is about 20%.

An example of the risk from too low a safety reserve margin is provided by Duke Power Company. In 1971 Duke Power Company had a peak load of 7,449,000 kilowatts, and a generating capacity of 7,652,000 kilowatts. Thus at its peak, Duke Power company was using 97% of its capacity and had a safety reserve margin of only 3%. Had electric power demand been 3% greater, Duke Power Company would have exceeded its capacity, necessitating either "brownouts" or the purchase of electricity from other generating systems. Since three percentage points is a very low margin of safety, the capacity factor may also be interpreted as signalling the need of Duke Power Company to go to the capital markets very soon for additional funds to finance an expansion of its capacity.

Finally, in an effort to sell electricity, especially during nonpeak periods, electric utilities offer different rates to various classes of users. Residential subscribers pay the highest rate per kilowatt-hour of electrical power. Although this class is the most stable source of revenue, it is also the most likely to demand power during a system peak, and thus is the group whose needs require additional investment in generating capacity. The percentage sales mix for various classes of users, both in terms of kilowatt-hour sales and in terms of dollar operating revenue generated, is shown for Class A and B electric utilities.

User class	Kilowatt-hour sales	Dollars of revenue
Residential.	32.7%	42.4%
Commercial	22.7	28.6
Industrial	40.4	24.8
Other.	4.2	4.2
Total	100.0%	100.0%

Commercial subscribers, which include stores, shopping centers, office buildings, schools, and hospitals, pay lower rates than other user classes because the bulk of their usage comes during off-peak hours. Industrial users, some of whom buy power on an interruptible basis, pay the lowest rates. They are the least stable source of revenue, but they contribute to an improved load factor. They also provide the largest demand for electrical power among the user classes reported here.

FINANCIAL ANALYSIS OF PUBLIC UTILITIES

Having discussed at length the operating and other characteristics of public utilities, we turn now to an examination of their financial statements. We begin with the balance sheet and then move to the income statement.

Utility balance sheets

The major characteristic of a public utility balance sheet is the proportionately large investment required in fixed plant and equipment. Figure 12–4 shows the composite balance sheet for 213 Class A and B privately owned electric public utilities in the United States at the end of 1971. These companies comprise all privately owned electric utilities in the United States with annual electric operating revenues of $1 million or more. They supply approximately 98% of the electricity generated by privately owned electric utilities in the United States, the remaining 2% being supplied by a large number of very small companies not reflected in the Federal Power Commission statistics. Privately owned electric utilities in the United States generated 77.5% of total national net generation in 1971.[7] The remainder was generated by municipal and other governmental utilities.

The aggregate balance sheet in Figure 12–4 shows that electric utility plant, less accumulated depreciation, constituted some 83.8% of total assets, while other utility plant (some electric utilities also are in the gas utility business) constituted an additional 7.4%. Thus 91.2% of total utility assets were invested in fixed plant and equipment. Current assets, by comparison, constituted only 6.0% of total assets.

Obviously, the chief asset-management task of public utilities revolves around their investment in long-term fixed plant and equipment, a characteristic that leads directly to the nature of financing used by utilities. Data in the bottom half of Figure 12–4 show that only 30.8% of total assets of class A and B privately owned electric utilities are financed

---

[7] *Statistics of Privately Owned Electric Utilities in the United States, 1971* Page VII, Washington, D.C. 20426: Federal Power Commission, October 1972. Data for private ownership include both Class A and B utilities and smaller utilities.

FIGURE 12–4

213 PRIVATELY OWNED ELECTRIC UTILITIES IN THE UNITED STATES
Composite Balance Sheet
December 31, 1971

	Millions of dollars	Percent of total
Assets		
Electric utility plant	104,300	
Less accumulated depreciation	22,006	
Net electric utility plant	82,294	83.8
Other utility plant	9,536	
Less accumulated depreciation	2,268	
Net other utility plant	7,268	7.4
Net utility plant	89,561	91.2
Net nonutility property, investments, and special funds	2,245	2.3
Cash and cash accounts	1,160	1.2
Receivables	2,528	2.6
Materials and supplies	1,688	1.7
Other current assets	511	0.5
Total current assets	5,887	6.0
Other assets	480	0.5
Total assets	98,173	100.0
Liabilities and capital		
Common stock	14,653	
Other capital stock items	5,422	
Retained earnings	10,129	
Total common stockholders equity	30,204	30.8
Preferred stock	9,266	9.4
Total stockholders' equity	39,470	40.2
Long-term debt	46,708	47.6
Current and accrued liabilities	7,918	8.0
Deferred credits and operating reserves	1,096	1.1
Contributions in aid of construction	557	0.6
Accumulated deferred income taxes	2,424	2.5
Total liabilities and capital	98,173	100.0

Source: *Statistics of Privately Owned Electric Utilities in the United States, 1971* (Federal Power Commission, Washington, D.C., October, 1972).

by the common stockholders, with an additional 9.4% financed by preferred stockholders. The largest single source of total financing is long-term debt, which supplies 47.6% of total financing. Current liabilities are relatively unimportant, corresponding to only 8.0% of total assets.

Thus is identified the prime characteristic of utility financing: large investments in fixed assets are financed almost entirely with securities of a type that might be included in an investor's portfolio. Over half of this permanent financing is in the form of long-term debt. When the proportion financed by preferred stockholders is included with debt, the highly leveraged position of the common stockholders is apparent. That is, public utilities adopt a risky capital structure in order to increase the return to common stockholders.

If an investor wishes to analyze the balance sheets of a public utility, his primary concern therefore will be with relationships between gross plant and equipment, accumulated depreciation, long-term debt, and the equities of the preferred and common stockholders. Three selected ratios based upon these balance sheet items are shown in Figure 12–5.

FIGURE 12–5
Balance sheet ratios for electric utilities, 1971 (percent)

	Class A and B electric utilities	Boston Edison Company	Houston Lighting and Power Company	Niagara Mohawk Power Corporation	Pacific Gas and Electric Company
Accumulated provision for depreciation / Total gross plant . . .	21.3	23.1	18.4	24.0	24.5
Net utility plant / Proprietary capital + long-term debt	103.9	113.4	106.7	103.9	100.4
Capital structure proportions:					
Long-term debt	54.2	56.8	56.6	55.5	53.8
Preferred stock	10.8	11.8	3.6	10.7	10.8
Common stockholders equity	35.0	31.4	38.8	33.8	35.4
Total capital structure	100.0	100.0	100.0	100.0	100.0

Source: Ratios for Class A and B electric utilities calculated from data in Figure 12–4. Ratios for individual companies: *A Regulated Electric Study, 1962–1971,* (Jefferson City, Missouri: Missouri Public Service Commission, October, 1972).

Included are ratios for the United States composite balance sheet of Figure 12–4, as well as corresponding ratios for the four large electric utility companies that we have been examining.

The first significant balance sheet ratio is the percentage of total company gross plant and equipment depreciated to date. This ratio gives a rough approximation of the average age and thus physical and technological condition of the plant and equipment, since a utility plant that has been further depreciated is probably older. Because of advances in technology, utility plants that are on balance newer are quite likely more efficient. The ratio also is influenced by two other variables. Hydroelectric plants possess significantly longer lifetimes than steam plants, and thus a company such as Pacific Gas and Electric Company (northern

California, including the San Francisco Bay area), which derives a greater portion of its power from hydroelectric plants, may have a different percentage depreciation than a company such as Houston Light and Power Company which generates a greater portion of its power from fossil fuel. The ratio will also be influenced by variations in the way utilities account for accelerated depreciation, a matter to be explained later. Figure 12–5 shows accumulated depreciation equal to 21.3% of gross plant for the composite of all electric utilities.

A second ratio measures the relationship between company net plant and long-term capital structure (long-term debt, preferred stock, and common stockholders' equity). A ratio of 103.9, such as for the U.S. composite, indicates that net plant is 3.9% greater than permanent capital. A company such as Boston Edison, with a net plant 13.4% greater than permanent capital, relies to a greater extent than most companies on the financing of net plant by current liabilities or deferred credits. For example, Boston Edison had $95 million of notes payable in 1971. At the other end of the spectrum of companies shown in Figure 12–5, Pacific Gas and Electric Company has financed virtually its entire net plant from permanent sources. To the extent that financing net plant from other than long-term sources might be regarded as risky, either because of a need to refinance or because such a policy limits access to short-term markets for emergency purposes, the balance sheet of Boston Edison would indicate a greater risk posture than that of Pacific Gas and Electric.

A third set of ratios of interest to investors is the capital structure proportions of the public utility. As can be seen in Figure 12–5, approximately 54% of the capital structure of the composite utility is derived from debt and just over one-third from common stockholders' equity. Variations among the five individual companies in Figure 12–5 are small, with the exception of Houston Light and Power Company, which has used more common stockholders' equity and less preferred stock than most utilities. Of concern to investors would be utilities that deviate significantly from the typical proportions indicated in Figure 12–5. A company that increased its financial risk disproportionately by incurring significantly more than 56% debt in its capital structure might be judged too risky for an investor. Such a company might also find the financing of necessary expansion difficult or unduly expensive, since further debt financing would be a virtual impossibility. In contrast, companies that have significantly less debt than normal are failing to use acceptable degrees of financial leverage to boost returns to their common stockholders. Investing in the common stock of such a company would not seem desirable unless the investor could foresee the probability of a change in financial policy, in which case a considerable one-time gain might result from a change in leverage.

Utility income statements

As was mentioned earlier in the chapter, the utility regulatory process does not *guarantee* a rate of return. Rather it simply provides for a fair rate of return if the utility is operated efficiently. An investor therefore must look at a utility's income statement to determine if that company is operating in an efficient manner. A company whose costs are increasing relative to revenue would be a risky investment because profits may be squeezed without sufficient or timely correction by the utility commission. Alternatively, a utility whose profit margins are increasing may prove a better-than-normal investment because the added profits will increase the benefits to stockholders either permanently (if the profit increase is not too great) or until such time as the regulatory commission orders a rate reduction. Additionally, such a utility has a built-in protective margin against future cost increases not matched by timely rate relief. Insofar as profit margins interact with utility regulation, the relationship might best be characterized as the establishment of boundaries beyond which utility profitability is not likely to be allowed to remain for any significant period of time. But within those boundaries, opportunities do exist for improved or deteriorating profit situations. Outside of the boundaries a time-lag in rate adjustment is likely.

A composite income statement for U.S. Class A and B privately owned electric utilities is shown in Figure 12–6. As can be seen, "operating expenses," i.e., those expenses necessary to the utility operations of the company, absorbed 79.2% of utility operating revenues, leaving an operating income margin of 20.8%. Other income, net of certain deductions including taxes, provided an additional 3.8 percentage points of gain, and interest expenses led to a deduction of 10.0 percentage points. When a small amount of extraordinary income was added, net income constituted 14.8% of operating revenues.

Of major importance in analyzing the income statement is the relationship of various operating expenses to operating revenue. In this context, "operating" expenses refer to all expenses necessary to utility operation, including the payment of income taxes, which is an expense that is deducted in the regulatory process. One type of operating expense is "operation" expense. *Operation expenses* are those incurred to generate electric power, including the fuel and labor expenses of operating steam plants, nuclear power plants, hydraulic plants, and other types of plants as well as the cost of power purchased from other utilities on an interchange basis. One element of risk in buying utility stocks is that these fuel and labor costs may rise and squeeze profits before adequate relief can be obtained through increased rates.

Significant income account relationships are shown in Figure 12–7 for the U.S. composite and for the four selected large utilities. Included

FIGURE 12–6

213 PRIVATELY OWNED ELECTRIC UTILITIES
IN THE UNITED STATES
Composite Income Statement
December 31, 1971

	Millions of dollars	Percentage of operating revenues
Utility operating revenues	26,027	100.0
Operating expenses		
Operation expense 12,204		
Maintenance expense. 1,681		
Depreciation and amortization 2,628		
Operating taxes 2,680		
Income taxes (including deferred) . . . 1,432		
Total operating expenses	20,625	79.2
Total utility operating income	5,402	20.8
Net other income	(+) 1,006	(+) 3.8
Interest charges	(–) 2,613	(–) 10.0
Extraordinary income, net of taxes. . . .	(+) 57	(+) 0.2
Net income	3,852	14.8
Preferred dividends	494	1.9
Common dividends	2,332	9.0
Increase in retained earnings.	1,026	3.9

Source: *Statistics of Privately Owned Electric Utilities in The United States, 1971* (Washington, D.C.: Federal Power Commission, October, 1972).

is a detailed breakdown of operation expenses and maintenance expenses, as well as a common-size picture of the entire income statement. Total operating expenses as a percentage of operating revenue, sometimes referred to as the operating ratio, measures the proportion of operating revenues consumed by the costs of operation. This ratio is an overall measure of efficiency. A company with a low operating ratio, such as Houston Lighting and Power, is basically more efficient than a company with a high operating ratio, such as Boston Edison. A sudden increase in operating expenses, say for added fuel costs, would have a much more severe impact upon Boston Edison's earnings than upon the earnings of Houston Lighting and Power. For example, an increase of ten percentage points in various operating expenses would absorb over two thirds of Boston Edison's operating income, which currently stands at only 14.8% of operating revenue. Houston Lighting and Power, however, has a much greater leeway; a similar ten percentage point increase would absorb less than half of Houston Lighting's 26.0% operating income margin.

Operation expenses are important because they are the largest single expense category and because they relate to the very basic efficiency

FIGURE 12–7

Income statement ratios for electric utilities, 1971 (percent)

	Class A and B electric utilities	Boston Edison Company	Houston Lighting and Power Company	Niagara Mohawk Power Corp.	Pacific Gas and Electric Company
Distribution of operating revenues					
Utility operating revenue	100.0	100.0	100.0	100.0	100.0
Operation expense	46.9	49.0	35.6	49.0	34.1
Maintenance expense.	6.5	6.5	6.7	8.1	5.9
Depreciation and amortization	10.1	8.7	9.7	10.4	12.7
Operating taxes	10.3	17.7	6.9	14.3	10.5
Income taxes	5.4	3.3	15.1	0.6	9.9
Total operating expenses.	79.2	85.2	74.0	82.4	73.1
Operating income.	20.8	14.8	26.0	17.6	26.9
Distribution of operation expenses					
Production.	69.6	66.0	62.2	69.2	58.9
Transmission	2.0	2.0	0.6	2.2	2.2
Distribution	6.8	9.6	7.2	5.5	12.8
Customer accounts	5.7	5.2	6.7	4.3	8.9
Sales	3.0	2.0	3.7	1.7	2.4
Administrative and general	12.9	15.2	19.6	17.1	14.8
Total operation expense	100.0	100.0	100.0	100.0	100.0
Distribution of maintenance expenses					
Production.	45.3	57.3	38.5	28.4	26.1
Transmission	8.2	1.0	4.6	9.8	10.8
Distribution	43.5	39.6	49.8	58.5	61.7
Administrative and general	3.0	2.1	7.1	3.3	1.4
Total maintenance expense	100.0	100.0	100.0	100.0	100.0

Source: Class A and B electric utilities, calculated from data in Statistics of Privately Owned Electric Utilities in the United States, 1971 (Washington D.C.: Federal Power Commission, October, 1972). Individual companies: A Regulated Electric Study, 1962–1971 (Jefferson City, Missouri: Missouri Public Service Commission, October, 1972).

of the utility in providing electric power for sale. For this reason, some analysts break operation expenses down into various subcategories, as is done in the second panel of Figure 12–7. From this example it can be seen that the basic efficiency of Houston Lighting and Power derives from its low cost of production. Transmission costs are also proportionately small, while the costs of servicing customers and of sales (advertising, etc.) are proportionately high. Administrative and general costs of Houston Lighting and Power are also proportionately high.

The second major cost group of concern to analysts is maintenance expense, since variations in this item may come about because of arbitrary maintenance decisions. The magnitude of maintenance expense in relationship to operating revenues measures the adequacy of expenditures to preserve the operating condition of the properties of the company. The significance of the ratio lies in the possibility that a company with as large a fixed investment as is typical for utilities could sustain profits for a limited period of time by deferring maintenance. Although such deferred maintenance would eventually have to be made up to prevent operating breakdowns or inefficiencies, over the short run the company would appear more profitable than was warranted.

From the percentage breakdown of maintenance expenses in the third panel of Figure 12–7 it can be seen that Niagara Mohawk spends proportionately more on the maintenance of its distribution system and less on the maintenance of its production plant. Boston Edison, at the other extreme, spends proportionately more to maintain production plant and less on distribution plant. Note that these calculations are based on total maintenance expense and must add to 100.0%. They do not by themselves imply too much or too little maintenance, a judgment that could be derived only from the ratio of total maintenance expense to operating revenue.

A third important operating expense is depreciation. Depreciation and amortization as a percentage of operating revenues provides a rough measure of the adequacy of charges for the wearing out or obsolescence of plant and equipment. Since plant and equipment has been seen to be the major asset of a utility, and since depreciation and amortization as such do not necessitate a cash expenditure, the magnitude of these expense items is important in judging the reasonableness of reported income. Variations in depreciation method can cause variations in apparent profitability not warranted by true operating circumstances.

Among the remaining operating expenses, taxes are an expense item that is largely beyond immediate control of the company. However the magnitude of the tax load, especially operating taxes, may be taken as an indication of the size of an externally imposed burden upon the company.

An additional item to observe in a utility income statement is the magnitude of other income, which consists, in order of importance on the composite income statement, of an allowance for funds used during construction, interest and dividend income, and miscellaneous nonoperating income. The allowance for funds used during construction represents the capitalizing of the interest cost of funds invested in that new construction prior to the time at which the new plant becomes operative. In effect it is an adjustment of the interest charge because a portion of that charge was in fact not a valid claim against current revenue. To the extent that any given utility has income from other sources, such as interest and dividend earnings or income from nonoperating activities (such as the sale of electric appliances), a portion of the company's operations is not true utility operations. Rather the company is operating as a private competitive business, and the profitability or possibility of loss of its nonutility ventures, if significant in size, should be judged separately.

Additional financial ratios

Among ratios of importance to investors are those that measure the rate of return earned upon the investment. Three such ratios are shown in Figure 12–8 for the same companies as before. While the ratios in Figure 12–8 are calculated on year-end balance sheet denominators,

FIGURE 12–8

Additional financial ratios for electric utilities, 1971

	Class A & B electric utilities	Boston Edison Company	Houston Lighting and Power Company	Niagara Mohawk Power Corporation	Pacific Gas and Electric Company
*Rate-of-return ratios**					
Return on net plant†	6.0%	4.7%	7.9%	5.6%	6.2%
Return on capital‡	7.4%	8.4%	8.9%	6.3%	7.2%
Return on common equity§	11.1%	11.8%	14.8%	9.1%	11.1%
Other financial ratios					
Common dividend payout ratio‖	69.4%	67.3%	45.5%	75.7%	59.2%
Interest coverage (pretax)#	2.5 times	2.4 times	4.9 times	2.5 times	3.4 times

* Rate-of-return ratios above are calculated on year-end denominators. Year-average denominators are equally appropriate.
† Operating income/Net plant.
‡ Income before interest/Total proprietary capital plus long-term debt.
§ Income available for common stock/Common stockholders' equity.
‖ Common stock dividends/Income available to common stockholders.
Income before interest charges plus income taxes/Total interest charges.

year-average denominators would be an equally appropriate approach. *Return on net plant* measures operating income as a percent of the utility's investment in net plant. It is an approximation of the rate-of-return calculation used in regulatory proceedings, the major difference being that the rate base denominator for rate proceedings may include additional adjustments for cash working capital, for contributions for construction, and for replacement cost of the plant. When compared with the average return for the composite utility of 6.0%, Boston Edison and Niagara Mohawk are seen to be less profitable than most utilities, while Pacific Gas and Electric and Houston Lighting are more profitable.

Return on capital is simply return before interest and taxes measured against total long-term capital. The same relative relationships hold as for rate of return on net plant, except that the return on capital for Boston Edison is comparatively high because that company finances a significant portion of its assets with notes payable, a current liability. Return on capital is higher than return on net plant for all companies for two reasons: the numerator is augmented by other income, and the denominator is diminished because net plant for all companies was greater than for long-term capital. This latter fact was identified in the second ratio in Figure 12–5.

Return on common equity shows the after-leverage rate of return, and is higher than return on capital because average interest costs are less than the before-tax return on capital. Should this return on capital drop below average interest costs, or should the company have a significant amount of new refinancing to accomplish in the very near future at levels of interest significantly above existing interest costs, the financial leverage might become a disadvantage. In 1971, however, the composite utility was able to lever its return of 7.4% on capital up to a 11.1% return on common stockholders' equity.

Common stockholders are also interested in the dividend payout of their company, for this ratio indicates what portion of earnings is to be realized in cash and what portion is reinvested for future growth. As shown by the fourth ratio in Figure 12–8, the composite utility pays out approximately 69% of its earnings in cash dividends, a payout ratio slightly higher than that of most industrial companies. Individual payouts ranged from a high of almost 76% for Niagara Mohawk to a low of 59% for Pacific Gas and Electric.

One last ratio is of concern to investors: interest coverage. It is of obvious importance to bond investors, for it is a major measure of the safety of their interest receipts. It is also of interest to common stockholders, for those owners would suffer if the company were unable to pay interest charges. To the extent that interest coverage remains barely adequate to pay interest but drops so low that the bonds of the utility are lowered in their rating, common stockholders suffer because new debt financing will have to be pursued at higher interest costs that might not be reflected in subsequent regulatory procedures. In addition, some bond indentures have provisions forbidding the sale of new bonds if interest coverage has dropped below some minimum level, such as two or three times interest charges. As reported in Figure 12–8, the composite utility had an interest coverage of 2.5 times, and most of the large utilities had coverages at least equal to this comparatively low level.

Variations among companies

For convenience of exposition, the data used in this chapter compare four separate companies and relate them to composite accounts for all Class A and B electric utilities. As a practical matter, there are variations among companies, such as in type of area, type of generating plant, and rate of growth of service area, that may invalidate intercompany comparisons. The same ratios, however, when observed as a trend over several years for a single company, may provide important additional perspective (unless, of course, that company has changed its method of accounting during the period under review).

Yet another reason exists for greater reliance on time-trend analysis for a single company than on intercompany comparisons. Various companies use different methods to calculate earnings. One variation involves treatment of the income tax savings that result from use of accelerated depreciation. Two rather different methods of accelerated depreciation, discussed and illustrated earlier in Chapter 10, are flow-through and normalized. Perhaps half of the utilities in the country use the flow-through method of reporting, either because they prefer this method or because the regulatory commission having jurisdiction has required them to adopt that method. In the *flow-through method* the tax deferral that results from the use of accelerated depreciation "flows through" to reported earnings, enhancing the apparent profitability of the utility during periods of rapid expansion, but also lessening the probability of rate increases. In later years, if the rate of expansion diminishes, the tax deferral will diminish and reported earnings will tend to deteriorate.

Conversely, in the *normalized method*, the tax deferral is kept out of reported earnings and shows as a deferred liability. Such companies will show lower earnings during periods of rapid expansion, but they are not susceptible to the future deterioration in earnings implicit in the flow-through method if or when the asset growth rate diminishes.

A second variation among companies is their treatment of the investment tax credit, which allows a reduction in current tax payments equal to 7% of current capital expenditures. Again, some utilities report on a flow-through basis, enhancing the current year's earnings by the full 7% tax credit, while others normalize by spreading the benefit over a period of years.

A third variation arises because of the treatment of an allowance for funds used during construction. At any given time, a certain proportion of the capital of a utility may be invested in plant under construction and, therefore, not yet producing revenue. Because several years may be needed to complete a generating facility, a large amount of capital may be so tied up. Some utilities reduce interest and other capital expenses by an estimate of the cost of the funds tied up in construction and increase the asset cost by this estimate. Such a procedure, which is similar to the idea of normalization, has the immediate effect of increasing reported earnings. The rate base is also increased, and the capitalized cost of the funds used during construction is depreciated over subsequent years. Other companies make no provision for the cost of funds used during construction, thus reducing reported earnings during periods of asset expansion. Comparisons of ratios for companies using different methods of treating these costs of funds used during construction may lead to inaccurate conclusions. This is especially true for ratios measuring the number of times interest charges are earned.

Increases in earnings per share

An increase in utility earnings per share can spring from advantageous financing as well as from changes in the regulatory climate. As the utility rate base increases because of additional investment in assets needed to serve increased demand, total earnings should rise. In part this rise in earnings may be the result of asset expansion financed by retained earnings, in part it may be caused by advantageous external financing, and in part it may result from increased financial leverage.

These three causes of increased earnings per share may be illustrated with a hypothetical example. Assume that a utility has a book value per common share of $10. Assume further that the utility is presently earning 12% on that equity and that as the company continues to grow it continues to earn 12% on the investment of its common stockholders. The utility has a dividend payout ratio of 50%. At the present time, each share of common stock will earn (12%) ($10.00) = $1.20, of which half, or 60 cents, will be paid in cash dividends. The other half of earnings will be reinvested, and next year's book value per common share will be $10.60. If earnings remain 12% on common equity, next years' earnings per share will be (12%) ($10.60) = $1.27. The reinvestment of earnings thus leads to a 6% increase in earnings per share.

Note that this increase is more assured for utilities than for industrial firms, because the regulatory process provides for a rate of return upon all capital, and as the utility grows the rate of return on incremental investment is likely to be the same as that already being earned on existing investment. In an industrial company, on the other hand, the rate of return on incremental investment may or may not be the same as before, depending on the particular industry and the unique characteristics of the industrial firm.

The above example can be expanded to illustrate the effect of financing part of required growth by the sale of new shares of common stock at a time when market price is above book value. If the utility presently has one million shares of common stock outstanding, total book value of equity will be 1,000,000 × $10 = $10,000,000.

Suppose that the market price of the utility's common stock is currently $15 per share, and that the company needs to expand its asset base by 15% to meet expected demand. The company will finance part of the expansion by selling $1,500,000 of additional common equity. The remainder of the expansion will be financed by debt so as to maintain the same capital structure proportions. At the present market price of $15 per share, 100,000 new shares must be sold. (Selling costs and commissions are ignored.) The new equity will appear as follows:

1,000,000 shares of existing equity.	$10,000,000
100,000 new shares sold at $15.00 per share	1,500,000
Total equity	$11,500,000
New number of shares	1,100,000

Assume that total equity continues to earn 12% because the regulatory process has not changed and because the degree of financial leverage has remained constant. New earnings would be 12% of $11,500,000, or $1,380,000. Earnings per share would now be calculated by dividing the $1,380,000 earnings by 1,100,000 shares to give $1.255. Earnings per share have risen from $1.20 to just over $1.25, without any reinvestment of earnings by the old stockholders. This expansion is caused by the ability of the utility to sell new shares of common stock at a price above the book value of existing shares. During periods when utility stock prices are at a high level, this phenomenon adds to the growth rate of utility earnings per share and tends to justify still higher prices for utility stocks. These higher prices, in terms of the ratio of price to book value, enable still additional, advantageous equity financing.

On the other hand, if stock prices are depressed below book value per share, additional financing will cause actual dilution of earnings per share and so further depress stock prices. An industrial company might not sell new shares of stock at a time when stock prices are depressed to avoid the forced dilution. But a public utility, by virtue of being a regulated monopoly, must expand to meet the demand of all customers in its service area. Because the utility may be forced to sell new shares of stock on the market at a time when stock prices are depressed, it may be forced to dilute its earnings per share simply because of the growth of the service area.

The above two examples show how growth in utility earnings may be achieved either by natural growth through retention of earnings or by advantageous equity financing at times when market price exceeds book value. In reality, both forces may be active at the same time. An additional potential cause of greater earnings per share arises from an increase in the degree of financial leverage implicit in the utility's capital structure. Assume for a moment that utility earnings are 10% on a rate base of $20,000,000 financed as follows:

Long-term debt (8%)	$10,000,000
Common stock equity (1,000,000 shares)	10,000,000
Total investment (approximate rate base)	$20,000,000
Allowed rate of return	×10%
Utility earnings granted by regulatory commission (before interest, after tax).	$ 2,000,000
Less interest expenses (8% × $10,000,000)	$ 800,000
Available to common stockholders	$ 1,200,000
Earnings per share	$ $1.20

Note in this example that an overall return of 10% allowed the utility to earn 12% on its stockholder's equity. This, again, is favorable leverage.

Assume now that this utility finances $3,000,000 of new assets entirely with 8% bonds. Assuming no change in the regulatory 10% rate of return allowed, earnings per share would be calculated as follows:

Long-term debt (8%)	$13,000,000
Common stock equity (1,000,000 shares)	10,000,000
Total investment	23,000,000
Allowed rate of return	×10%
Utility earnings granted by regulatory commission (before interest, after tax)	2,300,000
Less interest expenses (8% × $13,000,000)	1,040,000
Available to common stockholders	$ 1,260,000
Earnings per common share	$ $1.26

Note that the change in financial leverage has increased earnings per share from $1.20 to $1.26. Although an increase engendered by such a policy is theoretically possible for all utilities, it is in fact limited by two variables. The capital markets will not necessarily accept additional debt at the same interest cost, particularly if the utility has deviated from established and conventional capital structures, or if its interest coverage drops below some acceptable minimum. In this example, interest coverage after taxes dropped from 2.50 to 2.21.

The second constraint on a utility's increasing its degree of financial leverage is regulatory. The utility commission may refuse to allow the utility to sell additional bonds without also selling additional shares so as to maintain what the commission judges to be a proper capital structure.

SELECTING SECURITIES OF PUBLIC UTILITIES

The final step in selecting public utility securities for an investment portfolio is to apply the valuation framework discussed in Part II of this book to individual issues and thereby to determine if they are overvalued or undervalued. The final step also includes consideration of how the expected return and associated risk of an individual issue contribute to overall portfolio return and risk. Because this already has been discussed and illustrated, we shall here only highlight the important attributes of public utility securities from a portfolio perspective.

An important attribute to most investors is the income to be received from a given security. For a public utility bond, the income attribute can be measured by current yield and yield to maturity. For a public utility common stock, the current dividend yield can be measured. As illustrated in the following statistics the dividend yields of the four selected electric power utilities have tended to increase over recent time. They are also seen to have been greater than the average yield on the 500 stocks that comprise the Standard & Poor's Composite Stock Price Index. And as might be expected from the stable nature of the

utility business, the pattern of dividend yields for each electric power
utility was stable over time.

Year	Boston Edison Company	Houston Lighting and Power Company	Niagara Mohawk Power Corporation	Pacific Gas and Electric Company	Standard & Poor's Composite Index
1962	3.9%	1.8%	4.4%	3.2%	3.4%
1963	3.3	1.6	4.0	3.0	3.2
1964	3.3	1.6	3.7	3.3	3.0
1965	3.5	1.7	3.9	3.2	3.0
1966	4.3	2.1	4.7	4.0	3.4
1967	4.7	2.3	5.2	4.0	3.2
1968	4.9	2.5	5.3	4.1	3.1
1969	5.5	2.7	5.8	4.3	3.2
1970	6.3	3.0	6.9	5.2	3.8
1971	6.2	2.8	6.6	5.0	3.1
1972	6.6	2.7	6.7	5.7	2.7

Another important attribute of the common stocks of public utilities
is that they are usually considered to be more stable members of a
portfolio in terms of price movements. This, as we have seen in Chapter
3, is critical in a risk-reducing sense. Figure 12–9 compares the Standard
& Poor's Industrial Stock Price Index with the corresponding index for 35
electric power companies. We see that electric utility stocks generally
have followed the trend of the overall market but within a much narrower price range. The implication of this is that electric utility shares are
not likely to give investors as high a degree of appreciation during upward
markets, but they offer a degree of protection during downward markets.

A final aspect of the risk attribute of the common stock of public
utilities is the price-earnings ratios that they command in the stock
market. The following price-earnings ratios existed for the four illustrative electric power companies over the same period 1962–1972.

Year	Boston Edison Company	Houston Lighting and Power Company	Niagara Mohawk Power Corporation	Pacific Gas and Electric Company
1962	17.9	24.3	16.3	18.9
1963	19.2	27.9	18.2	19.0
1964	20.5	28.7	19.0	18.0
1965	19.3	27.0	17.6	17.8
1966	15.9	23.5	14.9	14.3
1967	14.4	22.1	12.5	14.0
1968	14.7	21.5	14.6	13.6
1969	12.4	18.0	12.5	13.4
1970	10.5	15.7	11.5	12.0
1971	10.8	16.1	11.3	11.8
1972	10.4	16.0	9.3	9.9

FIGURE 12–9
Relative price movements of utility stocks and industrial stocks, 1963–1972. (1941–1943 = 10; semi-log scale)

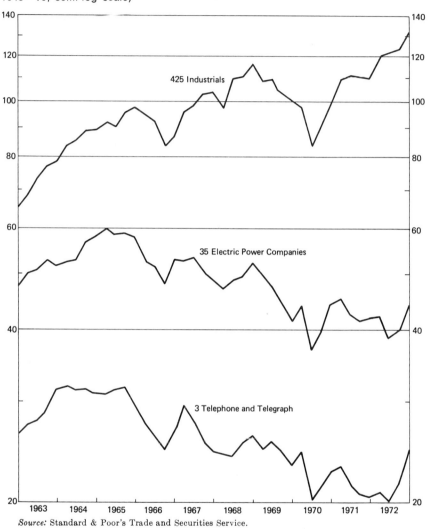

Source: Standard & Poor's Trade and Securities Service.

Here again we note differences among the four utilities but reasonable stability over time for each utility. We also note that price-earnings ratios overall tended to decrease over the eleven-year period.

An extrapolation of both dividend yields and price-earnings ratios into the future, tempered by subjective judgment based on many of the other characteristics and attributes considered in this chapter, is necessary in order to arrive at a measure of value for a particular security. Complex as this process may be, it is a key step in the process of investing in public utilities.

SUMMARY

Investment analysis of public utilities is strongly influenced by the fact that they are granted a market monopoly within a prescribed service area. Monopoly status is necessary because the large investment in fixed assets creates an economic situation in which one company can serve a market at lower average cost than could two or more competing firms. This monopolistic status leads to regulation of utilities by state public utility commissions or, in some instances, by federal regulatory agencies. This chapter has discussed in some detail those variables in utility operations of importance to those investing in utility securities. Formulation of opinions about the future benefits of a utility depends upon understanding the nature of the regulatory process, understanding the economics of a utility's operating situation as it pertains to supplying all customer demand from a utility plant that has a maximum capacity, and understanding the financial statements of a public utility. The stabilizing potential of public utility securities within a portfolio context was also noted.

SUGGESTED READINGS FOR CHAPTER 12

R. E. Badger, H. W. Torgerson, and H. G. Guthmann. *Investment Principles and Practices.* 6th ed. (Englewood Cliffs, N.J.: Prentice-Hall, Inc., 1969), Chapters 10 and 11.

D. Connors. "Fresh Look at the Electric Utilities," *Financial Analysts Journal,* November–December, 1970, pages 35–46.

D. K. Eiteman. "Independence of Utility Rate Base Type, Permitted Rate of Return, and Utility Earnings," *Journal of Finance,* March, 1962, pages 38–52.

B. Graham, D. L. Dodd, and S. Cottle. *Security Analysis: Principles and Techniques.* 4th ed. (New York: McGraw-Hill Book Company, Inc., 1962), Chapters 20–21.

D. A. Hayes. "Public Utility Returns on Equity," *Financial Analysts Journal,* September–October, 1970, pages 102–6.

R. S. Stich. "The Electric Utilities: A Second Look," *Financial Analysts Journal,* November–December, 1970, pages 47–51.

H. E. Thompson. "Capital Structure, Coverage Ratios, and the Rate of Return in Public Utilities," *Financial Analysts Journal,* January–February, 1973, pages 69–73.

13

Investing in transportation companies

TRANSPORTATION SECURITIES that are of interest to investors consist of those issued by airlines and railroads organized as common carriers. A *common carrier* is a transportation agency operating on a regularly scheduled basis under a *certificate of public convenience and necessity* granted by the government and requiring the carrier to serve without discrimination all who seek its services. Companies operating as common carriers include airlines, railroads, oil pipelines, truckers, barge lines, and merchant marine companies. Securities of trucking and barge companies are not generally traded in the securities markets since most of these companies are relatively small. United States merchant marine companies require subsidies in order to survive in competition with merchant marines from other countries. Thus securities of these latter three types of transportation companies are not of widespread interest to investors. Although securities of oil pipeline companies may be of interest to investors, we shall concentrate here on the securities of airlines and of railroads. The purpose of this chapter then is to explore the various characteristics and investment attributes of securities issued by airlines and railroads.

OVERVIEW OF TRANSPORTATION INDUSTRY

The trends in transportation of passengers by air, rail, and bus is shown in Figure 13–1. Intercity passenger travel is dominated by the airlines, which in 1971 carried over 106 billion passenger-miles, or 75% of the total intercity passenger-miles transported by common carriers. Motor buses were the second most important intercity carrier with 25

278

FIGURE 13–1
Intercity passenger travel in the United States by common carrier, 1961–1972

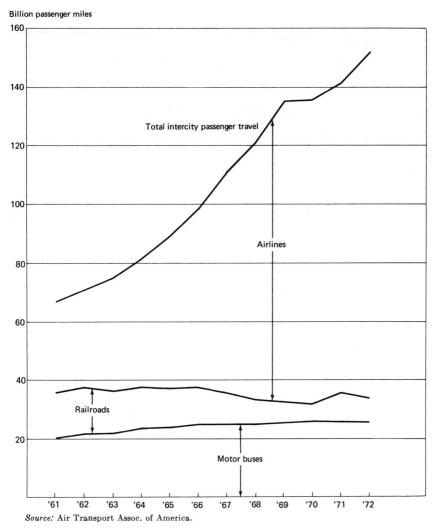

Billion passenger miles

Total intercity passenger travel

Airlines

Railroads

Motor buses

'61 '62 '63 '64 '65 '66 '67 '68 '69 '70 '71 '72

Source: Air Transport Assoc. of America.

billion passenger-miles or 18% of the total, while the once mighty railroads carried only 10 billion passenger-miles or 7% of the total. If urban
commuter statistics were added to these data the proportion for the
railroads and buses would be somewhat higher. It might also be noted
that all three types of common carrier carried only 10.8% of total intercity
passenger traffic; private automobiles accounted for the remaining 89.2%.

Trends in intercity freight transportation are depicted in Figure 13–2.
One of the largest carriers of intercity freight in terms of ton-miles

FIGURE 13–2
Distribution of intercity freight traffic (1961–1972)

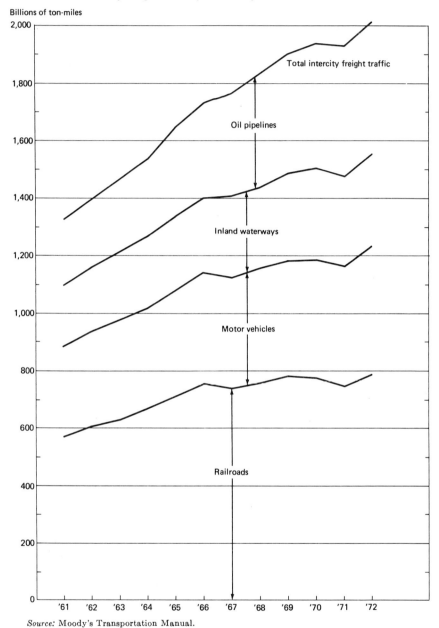

Billions of ton-miles

Total intercity freight traffic

Oil pipelines

Inland waterways

Motor vehicles

Railroads

'61 '62 '63 '64 '65 '66 '67 '68 '69 '70 '71 '72

Source: Moody's Transportation Manual.

(one ton of freight carried one mile) is the railroads. However the share of intercity freight carried by railroads has dropped from 43.0% in 1961 to 38.6% in 1971, as railroads have steadily lost their share of the market to competing transportation agencies. The share of motor vehicles in intercity freight traffic has also dropped, from 23.6% in 1961 to 21.9% in 1971. Although this might appear inconsistent with one's general observation of traffic in the United States, the drop in trucking by common carrier, as well as the drop in rail traffic, has to a very large extent been offset by increases in private non–common carrier trucking, statistics for which are not reflected in Figure 13–2. In terms of common carrier statistics alone, the diminished share of rails and trucking has been offset by traffic on inland waterways (15.8% in 1961, up to 16.0% in 1971) and oil pipelines (17.6% in 1961, up to 23.3% in 1971.) Not shown in Figure 13–2 is air freight, the proportion of which increased from 0.07% in 1961 to 0.18% in 1971. Although air freight traffic, by weight, is too small to be plotted in Figure 13–2, readers should be aware that the volume by *value* of merchandise carried would be significantly higher, since air freight is most effective for high-value, low-weight items.

CLASSIFICATION OF AIRLINES AND RAILROADS

United States air carriers are classified into various groups for general rate purposes and for statistical reporting. The *domestic trunk lines* are those carriers that fly regularly scheduled routes between the major cities of the United States. Since January, 1970, Alaskan and Hawaiian mileage has been considered domestic; prior to that date, traffic to both states was considered international. The domestic trunk lines consist of the domestic portion of domestic routes flown by the "big four" carriers (American, Eastern, United, and Trans World Airlines) and the domestic routes of Braniff, Continental, Delta, National, Northwest, and Western Airlines. Capital Airlines was a member of this group until absorbed by United Air Lines in June, 1961, as was Northeast Airlines until absorbed by Delta Airlines in August, 1972. Since January, 1970, the Hawaiian routes flown by Pan American World Airways also have been considered part of the domestic trunk statistics.

The *international carriers* operate over certificated routes between the United States and foreign countries. They consist of Pan American and Caribbean Atlantic—which, except for Pan American's Hawaiian traffic, are purely international carriers—and the international portions of the routes flown by American, Braniff, Delta, Eastern, National, Northwest, Trans World, United, and Western Airlines. Most international carriers fly in direct competition with foreign carriers, some of whose operations are financed or subsidized by foreign governmental owners.

282

Local service carriers, or regional lines, generally connect larger cities to smaller localities and so provide the means by which passengers may extend an air trip to a city or town too small to be served by a trunk line. Many regional carriers, however, operate on some routes in direct competition with the trunk lines, and the larger regional carriers are larger than the smaller trunk lines. The regional lines include Allegheny, Frontier, Hughes Airwest, North Central, Ozark, Piedmont, Southern, and Texas International Airlines.

All-cargo lines operate scheduled flights between designated cities in the United States and abroad for the purpose of carrying freight, express, and mail. They do not carry passengers except on a charter basis. The all-cargo lines are Airlift International, Flying Tiger, and Seaboard World Airlines.

FIGURE 13–3
Groupings of Class I U.S. railroads by geographical districts, 1972

Eastern District	*Southern District*	*Western District*
Akron, Canton & Youngstown	Alabama Great Southern	Atchison, Topeka & Santa Fe
Ann Arbor	Central of Georgia	Burlington Northern
Baltimore & Ohio	Cincinnati, New Orleans, & Texas Pacific	Chicago & North Western
Bangor & Aroostook	Clinchfield	Chicago, Milwaukee, St. Paul & Pacific
Bessemer & Lake Erie	Florida East Coast	Chicago, Rock Island & Pacific
Boston & Maine	Georgia	Colorado & Southern
Canadian Pacific (in Maine)	Georgia Southern & Florida	Denver & Rio Grande Western
Central of New Jersey	Illinois Central Gulf	Duluth, Missabe & Iron Range
Central Vermont	Louisville & Nashville	Duluth, Winnipeg & Pacific
Chesapeake & Ohio	Norfolk Southern	Fort Worth & Denver
Chicago & Eastern Illinois	Seaboard Coast Line	Green Bay & Western
Delaware & Hudson	Southern	Kansas City Southern
Detroit & Toledo Shore Line		Lake Superior & Ishpeming
Detroit, Toledo & Ironton		Missouri-Kansas-Texas
Elgin, Joliet & Eastern		Missouri Pacific
Erie Lackawanna		Northwestern Pacific
Grand Trunk Western		Oregon Electric
Illinois Terminal		St. Louis-San Francisco
Lehigh Valley		St. Louis-Southwestern
Long Island		Soo Line
Maine Central		Southern Pacific
Missouri-Illinois		Texas & Pacific
Monongahela		Toledo, Peoria & Western
Norfolk & Western		Union Pacific
Penn Central		Western Pacific
Pennsylvania-Reading Seashore		
Pittsburgh & Lake Erie		
Reading		
Richmond, Fredericksburg & Potomac		
Western Maryland		

Source: Operating and Traffic Statistics (Washington, D.C.: Association of American Railroads, June, 1973).

Another group of airlines for regulatory and statistical purposes is the *helicopter carriers,* of which three presently carry passengers from the major terminals in New York, Chicago, and San Francisco/Oakland to outlying points. Another category, labeled *other,* includes the two intra-Hawaiian carriers, Hawaiian and Aloha Airlines, plus five Alaskan carriers: Alaska, Kodiak, Reeve Aleutian, Western Alaska, and Wein Consolidated. Finally, a number of *supplemental carriers* operate on a charter basis to supplement the service of the certificated route carriers. Among these carriers are American Flyers, Capitol International, Interstate Airmotive, Johnson Flying Service, McCulloch International, Modern Air Transport, Air Transport, Overseas National, Purdue, Saturn, Southern Air Transport, Standard, Trans International, Universal, and World Airways. PSA (Pacific Southwest Airlines) is not included in any of the above groupings because it is entirely an intrastate carrier not subject to regulation by the Civil Aeronautics Board.

The Interstate Commerce Commission has classified railroads into two groups for statistical purposes. Class I railroads currently have annual operating revenues of $5 million or more, and Class II railroads have operating revenues of less than $5 million. Prior to January 1, 1965, the point of distinction had been $3 million, while prior to January 1, 1956, the dividing point had been $1 million. There were 67 class I railroads in 1972.

Railroads are also classified by geographical regions in the Eastern District, the Southern District, and the Western District, and statistics for these three districts are published by the Association of American Railroads in Washington, D.C. The Class I railroads that comprise each of these three districts are identified in Figure 13–3.

REGULATION OF TRANSPORTATION

Airlines and railroads are regulated by agencies of the federal government as well as by local and state governmental bodies. Federal regulation is of predominant importance to the earning power of these companies, however, while state and local regulation is of significantly lesser importance. In this respect, transportation companies differ from electric, gas, and telephone utilities, which are primarily regulated by state agencies.

Transportation companies resemble electric, gas, and telephone utilities in that they operate under franchises that grant certain routes. Transportation companies, however, do not have the type of monopoly position possessed by electric, gas, and telephone utilities. Rather they must compete with all other forms of transportation, including privately owned and operated motor vehicles. In addition there is often direct competition between similar types of carriers, especially in the airline industry where, for example, three domestic trunk carriers provide almost identical direct service between New York and Los Angeles and eight of the eleven domestic trunk lines (Pan American included) provide service from mainland cities to Honolulu, Hawaii.

Airline regulation

Airlines are regulated by a number of federal agencies, including the Federal Aviation Administration (FAA), established in 1958 to absorb several earlier regulatory agencies, and the Civil Aeronautics Board (CAB), created in 1938 and given its present name by presidential executive order in 1940. FAA regulation is basically operational in nature, and covers such factors as safety regulations, traffic control and navigation, environmental issues, and the construction, maintenance, and operation of the airways. CAB regulation is basically economic in nature, prescribing what routes may be flown, the rates that may be charged for various classes of service on those routes, and minimum levels of service that must be maintained. The CAB is required to foster competition to the degree necessary to develop soundly the airline industry. Thus while the CAB grants permanent route certificates to the various airlines, these routes are not exclusive and the airlines do not have a monopoly to the extent that public utilities may be deemed monopolies.

The basis of most CAB rate regulation is a decision as to what constitutes an appropriate rate of return upon invested capital, where invested capital means the sum of long-term debt and stockholders' equity of the carrier. For many years the CAB followed a criterion established in 1961: a 10.5% rate of return on investment was deemed "fair and reasonable." This rate of return reflected a general rate study which found that a reasonable rate of return for the "big four" trunk lines (American, Eastern, United, and Trans World Airlines) would be 10.25% and an 11.125% rate of return would be adequate for the remaining eight trunk carriers. These rates of return were weighted averages of the costs of the various components of the capital structure as shown in Figure 13–4. The weighted-average procedure is similar in concept to that used in setting a rate of return for electric power companies.

In 1971, the CAB raised the standard from 10.5% to 12.0%. Airline rate of return regulation generally has not been successful, as can be seen from a comparison of actual rates of return with the "fair and reasonable" levels of 10.5% and 12.0% established by the CAB. These data are shown in Figure 13–5. Only in 1965 have the major domestic trunk airlines earned a return equal to or above the standard set by the CAB in its 1961 general fare decision.

From an investment decision point of view, the significance of the

FIGURE 13–4
Rate of return for U.S. air trunk lines, 1961

Source of financing	Capital structure proportion	Component cost	Weighted cost
Big Four			
Debt	50%	4.5%	2.25%
Equity	50	16.0	8.00
			10.25%
Other Eight			
Debt	55%	5.5%	3.025%
Equity	45	18.0	8.10
			11.125%
All 12 trunk lines	–	–	10.50%

data in Figure 13–5 lies not in the adequacy or inadequacy of the CAB. "fair and reasonable" standard of 12.0%, nor even in the possibility that this standard might be raised. Rather the problem lies in the inability of the various airlines to approach this standard in reality. Therefore an evaluation of airlines must consider those operating and financial characteristics that might allow an airline to increase its rate of return up to or even above the CAB standard. Such an increase might come

FIGURE 13–5
Return on investment for domestic trunk airlines, 1961–1972

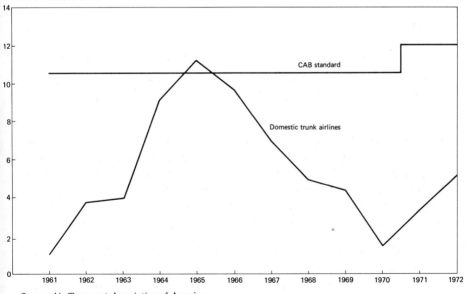

Return on investment (percent)

CAB standard

Domestic trunk airlines

Source: Air Transport Association of America.

about because of changes in CAB regulatory policy with respect to the degree of competition to be allowed on certificated routes between major traffic points.

Any increase in actual rate of return toward the CAB standard would presumably be accompanied by significant increases in common stock prices of the major airlines. Conversely one may speculate that existing common stock prices prior to any such increases reflect the current depressed level of airline earnings.

Railroad regulation

One of the goals of transportation regulation is to provide the United States with a healthy industry. Insofar as the airlines have consistently failed to earn a rate of return upon their investment that even approximates the CAB-determined "fair and reasonable" rate, airline regulation might be termed a failure. By a similar criterion, railroad regulation generally has been a disaster. The nature of this was clearly signalled by the failure in 1970 of the Penn Central Railroad and the threatened liquidation in 1973 of that railroad in the face of its continued inability to earn ongoing operating costs while in bankruptcy. Yet the Penn Central Railroad is the major rail transportation link in the northeastern part of the United States, which has the highest population density of all sections of the country.

Railroads are regulated by the Interstate Commerce Commission (ICC), established in 1887 and having jurisdiction over interstate commerce by motor carriers, water carriers, oil pipeline companies, and freight forwarders, as well as railroads. All common carriers under the jurisdiction of the ICC are required to establish just and reasonable rates and fares and to file these rate tariffs with the ICC. The ICC itself does not initiate rate decisions, but rather regulates and supervises rate schedules initiated by the carriers. The ICC may suspend any rate, and after hearnings and a proper finding, it may prescribe a new lawful rate.

In reviewing rate schedules, the ICC is bounded by a variety of criteria established in the laws. The ICC must take into consideration the inherent advantages of each form of transportation, the effect that proposed rates will have upon traffic movements, the need of the public for adequate and efficient service by the various common carriers at the lowest cost that is consistent with furnishing that service, and the need of the carriers for sufficient revenues to provide the service under an efficient management. All rates must be just and reasonable, and they may not be unfairly discriminatory or show undue preference among the various carriers.

In addition to its regulation of rates charged by common carriers, the ICC may investigate many aspects of the business of the companies under its authority. It prescribes the nature and frequency of the financial accounts to be maintained, and it regulates such diverse areas as safety requirements, construction and abandonments, mergers, consolidations, reorganizations, and fee sharing or splitting between two or more carriers. The ICC also exercises authority over the issuance of securities by carriers under its control, as well as the incurring of other financial obligations, guaranteeing or endorsing of debts of others, and entering into financial leases.

As with airlines, the immediate financial problems of railroads seem to be beyond the more technical aspects of rate regulation and to lie more in the domain of public policy. Railroads are likely to be good or bad investments in future years in accordance with such broad policy issues as freedom to adjust rates to meet nonrailroad competition, freedom to abandon routes where marginal income does not cover marginal costs, equitable reconciliation of the fact that railroad right-of-ways are heavily taxed by localities through which they pass while competing forms of transportation have their right-of-way provided by governmental units, and recognition and adjustment of the economic realities of railroad operations to the very strong wage and work-rule demands of organized railroad worker unions. Changes favorable to the railroads in the policies that have created financial problems for a number of U.S. railroads, especially in the northeastern part of the country, will lead to improved operating and financial characteristics and possibly to the reasonableness of railroad securities as investments. On the other hand, it may be that the errors of past U.S. transportation policy, combined with permanent changes in U.S. costs relative to possible railroad revenues, are such that railroad securities offer very little potential to investors.

OPERATING CHARACTERISTICS

The basic product that transportation companies sell is a perishable commodity that cannot be put into inventory and that ceases to exist with the passage of time, regardless of whether or not a customer has purchased it. That commodity is the movement of a unit of space from one location to another on a given day or series of days. If the unit of space is occupied by a passenger or by freight, the carrier receives revenue to offset the cost of moving the unit of space. Preferably, the revenue exceeds the costs involved. If the space is not occupied, almost all of the basic operating costs are incurred just as if the space had been sold. Except for very marginal costs, such as the cost of a passenger's meal, it costs an airline as much to fly an empty seat from San Francisco to Washington, D.C. as it costs to fly that seat with a passenger. A railroad, it is true, can remove empty cars from a train, but the train itself continues to run with approximately the same costs for fuel, labor, equipment, and right-of-way.

In financial terms, the transportation industry possesses a large degree of *operating leverage,* caused by large fixed costs that do not vary much in the short run, regardless of traffic, and low variable costs. From this economic characteristic arise those measures that are basic to evaluating various carriers. Because passenger traffic is of much greater importance than freight for the airlines, airlines will be discussed below in terms of analysis of passenger characteristics. Because what remains of railway passenger service has been transferred to Amtrak (the National Railroad Passenger Corporation), railroads will be considered in terms of analysis of freight. However, the general principles explained below can be applied with equal validity to the passenger or freight operations of all commercial common carriers.

Airline characteristics

Airline passenger operating characteristics revolve around seat-miles, which are their basic salable commodity. *Available seat-miles* is the number of seats available for the transportation of revenue-paying passengers multiplied by the number of miles those seats are flown. It is a statistical measure of airline passenger capacity. If an airline could fill every seat on every flight, that carrier would be operating at its full capacity. Available seat-miles are usually compared with *revenue passenger-miles,* a measure compiled by multiplying the number of revenue passengers by the number of miles they are flown.

The ratio of revenue passenger miles to available seat miles is called *revenue passenger load factor.* Expressed as a percentage it reflects the proportion of available seating capacity that the carrier has actually sold and utilized. Annual load factors for U.S. domestic trunk airlines and quarterly data for American Airlines and Eastern Airlines are shown in Figure 13–6. Because of the high fixed cost, low variable cost structure of airline operating expenses, profits increase significantly as carriers increase their load factors and decrease as the load factor falls. Figure 13–6 shows that for the airline industry as a whole, load factors have dropped steadily since their 1966 peak. Readers will also note the high correlation between the load factor statistics shown in Figure 13–6 and the return on investment statistics in Figure 13–5. The drop in load factor was caused in part by the recession of 1968–1970, in part by increases in the number of airlines awarded certificates to compete over certain routes that had proven profitable when flown only by one or two carriers, and in part by the arrival in the early 1970s of new widebodied aircraft with larger seating capacities just as traffic growth was diminishing.

FIGURE 13–6
Airline revenue passenger load factors, 1963–72

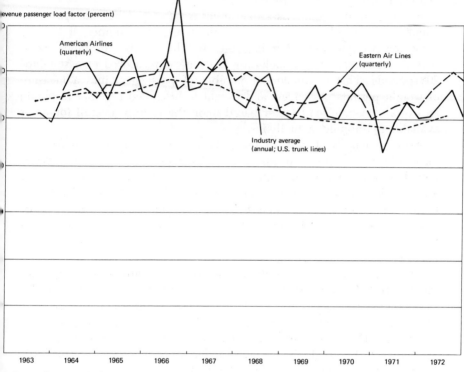

Source: Data in *Moody's Transportation Manuals.*

The quarterly data plotted in Figure 13–6 for American Airlines and for Eastern Air Lines indicate yet another aspect of airline efficiency, seasonal peaking. A predominantly east–west carrier, such as American Airlines, experiences its best load factor during the July–September period, while a predominantly north–south carrier in the eastern part of the nation, such as Eastern Airlines, tends have a more constant load factor. In some years Eastern's peak quarter has been January–March, when residents of the densely populated northeastern United States who are fleeing the cold and snow add sufficient traffic volume to improve the load factor statistics.

These seasonal patterns may be generalized under the word "peaking." Similar peaks and variations occur during days (most business travelers travel early in the morning or at dinner time), and weeks (end-of-week and beginning-of-week traffic exceeds middle-of-the-week traffic). The airlines must possess and schedule planes, personnel, and ground facilities to accommodate these peak demands, even though this capacity will be under-utilized during other periods of time. Various pricing and promotional plans, such as family plans, night coach flights, and special rates for flying during nonpeak hours are intended to raise the load factor and hence the profitability of the carriers.

A variation of revenue passenger-miles is *passenger revenue ton-miles*, which is the product obtained by multiplying the number of tons of passenger weight, including baggage, by the number of miles transported. Passenger weight including baggage is measured at a standard 200 pounds. This conversion of number of passengers into a measure of weight permits passengers and freight to be added together to obtain an overall revenue load factor based upon the ratio of overall ton-miles available to ton-miles actually flown.

Average length of trip, in miles, is a second statistic important in measuring the efficiency of air carriers. This statistic is primarily determined by the certificated route structure of each airline. Generally, the airline able to achieve longer average trips is likely to be more profitable because certain major passenger costs are constant per trip while revenue is proportional to the length of trip. The major costs of a constant or fixed nature include ticketing, security inspection, boarding, takeoff and landing fees, and air terminal costs.

Two statistics are looked at to evaluate trip length: the average distance traveled per flight, from takeoff to landing, and the average distance traveled by a passenger. The passenger distance is longer because many passengers remain with the aircraft through several takeoff/landing cycles. Data on average trip length for all U.S. domestic carriers are shown in Figure 13–7. The average length of flight for U.S. domestic trunk carriers in the year ended March, 1973, was 579 miles. The "big four," however, had a longer average flight, 650 miles, while the remaining trunk carriers operated on the average only 483 miles from takeoff to landing. The average local service carrier flew a much shorter average distance, 167 miles. Passenger trip length is proportional to flight length in these statistics.

Among individual domestic carriers, Pan American reported the longest average flight length because its only domestic route is from the Pacific Coast to Hawaii. Although this flight is long, it is not necessarily profitable because of the high degree of competition on that route. Average flight length for other trunk carriers ranged from 792 miles for TWA to 422 miles for Delta. Among the local service carriers, the range was from 205 miles for Allegheny to 142 miles for Piedmont.

Railroad characteristics

Investors interested in analysis of railroad statistics do not lack adequate data, for detailed railway statistics are collected and published by the Association of American Railroads in Washington, D.C. and by the Interstate Commerce Commission. The discussion that follows points

FIGURE 13–7
Average U.S. domestic airline flight lengths (twelve months ending March 31, 1973)

	Average length of flight (miles)	Average length of passenger trip (miles)
Total domestic operations, U.S. trunk carriers....................	579	794
Total, "Big Four"...............	650	834
Total, other trunk carriers and domestic flights of Pan American.........	483	731
Total, local service carriers.........	167	294
"Big Four"		
American	703	911
Eastern...................	472	591
TWA....................	792	1,045
United....................	702	878
Other		
Braniff...................	439	620
Continental	546	889
Delta....................	422	607
National..................	467	810
Northeast*................	474	671
Northwest................	509	762
Pan American..............	2,109	2,506
Western	562	773
Local service carriers		
Allegheny	205	296
Frontier..................	171	377
Hughes Air West	183	331
Mohawk..................	177	266
North Central..............	128	231
Ozark....................	150	276
Piedmont	142	278
Southern.................	144	283
Texas International............	173	303

Source: Air Carrier Traffic Statistics (Washington, D.C.: Civil Aeronautics Board, March, 1973).
* Northeast merged into Delta on August 1, 1972.

to only some of the highlights of available railroad data. Statistics for the period 1961–1972 are presented in Figure 13–8.

The basic salable commodity in the freight operations of railroads is a *ton-mile,* which represents the carrying of one ton of freight for one mile. Ton-miles may be compared with several operating and financial statistics to assess railroad efficiency and trends.

Average revenue per ton-mile, or ton-mile revenue, is the average amount received for hauling one ton of freight one mile. It is derived by dividing total freight revenue by the number of ton-miles hauled, and represents the average price received by the railroad. In 1972, the

FIGURE 13–8
Measures of railroad efficiency, Class I (freight only, 1961–72)

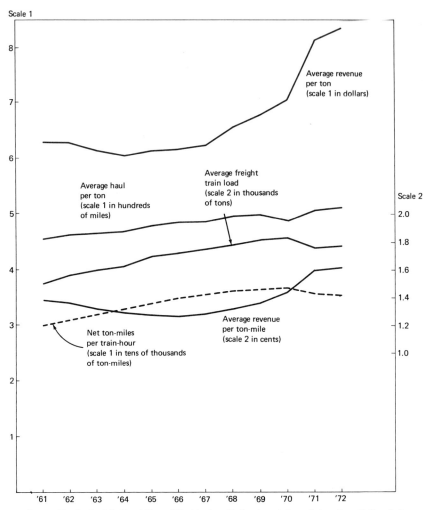

Source: *Yearbook of Railroad Facts* (Washington, D.C.: Association of American Railroads.)

average ton-mile revenue, as shown in Figure 13–8, was 1.620 cents, up from 1.374 cents in 1961 (and up from 1.076 cents in 1929). Interrailroad comparisons on the basis of revenue ton-miles are difficult because of the inherent differences between type of freight, type of terrain, etc., that exist for the different roads. Time-trend comparisons for individual railroads, however, are helpful in observing whether or not that railroad is successful in continually improving its operating situation.

Several other statistical measures of railroad efficiency are also shown in Figure 13–8. *Average revenue per ton* is the price received for freight without regard to distance carried. As can be seen, it has risen from $6.27 in 1961 to $8.35 in 1972. An increase in average revenue per ton can come about either because of tariff increases or because the railroad has successfully shifted the mix of its traffic into freight carrying a higher tariff per ton. Yet another variable in the mix of factors leading to increased railroad efficiency is the average number of miles each ton is hauled. For Class I railroads as a group, the *average haul per ton* increased from 452 miles in 1961 to 512 miles in 1972. Again, this trend is favorable in that railroads increase their effectiveness as they carry freight longer distances.

Still another measure of railroad efficiency is the average number of tons carried for each freight-train-mile. Increases in this *average load per train* are advantageous, in that railroads are relatively more efficient when carrying larger loads. The average trainload in 1972 was 1,774 tons, up from 1,495 tons in 1961. Yet another statistic is *net ton-miles per train-hour,* a measure of the hourly efficiency of a railroad. "Net tons" in this context refers to tons of freight, whereas the term "gross tons" refers to the weight of the freight and the freight cars combined. Net ton-miles per train-hour rose from 29,700 in 1961 to 35,400 in 1972.

As an approach to measuring the operatings efficiency of railroads, we suggest that efficiency ratios of the type plotted in Figure 13–8 be obtained from standard statistical sources such as *Moody's Transportation Manuals* and be compared on a time-trend basis for at least one decade and, where possible, with other railroads having similar operating characteristics and operating in the same section of the country.

FINANCIAL ANALYSIS OF TRANSPORTATION COMPANIES

Valuable perspective on historic trends and on intercompany comparisons may be obtained from an evaluation of the financial statements of both airlines and railroads. Such comparisons are facilitated by the very large quantity of uniformly reported data available for airlines and for railroads. In the following section an aggregate statement reflective of the industry as a whole will be compared with financial statements of two specific carriers for both airlines and railroads.

Airline statements

Detailed financial statements are published by the Civil Aeronautics Board in its monthly *Air Carrier Financial Statistics.* Figure 13–9 presents income statements in dollars and percentages for total U.S. domestic trunk airlines and for American Airlines and Eastern Air Lines. For trunk carriers as a whole, 88% of operating revenue is derived from passenger traffic. The proportions for American and Eastern are slightly higher. Other sources of revenue include freight, other transport activ-

294

FIGURE 13–9

U.S. DOMESTIC TRUNK AIRLINES
Revenues, Expenses, and Income
Twelve months ended June 30, 1972

	All U.S. domestic trunk airlines*		American Airlines		Eastern Air Lines	
	Millions of dollars	%	Millions of dollars	%	Millions of dollars	%
Operating revenues						
Passenger	6,354	88.3	1,054.0	89.4	836.5	90.4
Freight	448	6.2	85.2	7.2	39.9	4.3
Other transport	324	4.5	38.9	3.3	33.8	3.6
Nontransport	69	1.0	1.2	0.1	15.4	1.7
Total revenues	7,195	100.0	1,179.3	100.0	925.6	100.0
Operating expenses						
Flying operations	1,986	27.6	314.0	26.6	268.4	29.0
Maintenance	1,020	14.2	187.5	15.9	132.9	14.4
General services and administration	3,109	43.2	541.4	45.9	404.2	43.6
Depreciation and amortization	674	9.4	97.4	8.3	60.7	6.6
Total operating expenses	6,789	94.4	1,140.4	96.7	866.3	93.6
Operating profit	405	5.6	38.9	3.3	59.4	6.4
Interest expense	177		26.4		23.8	
Other nonoperating income and expense net	+37		+5.4		+3.7	
Net income before taxes	265	3.7	17.9	1.5	39.3	4.2
Income taxes	83		3.7		9.7	
Net income	181	2.5	14.2	1.2	29.5	3.2

Note: Totals may not add because of rounding.
* Including Pan American domestic operations.
Source: Air Carrier Financial Statistics (Washington, D.C.: Civil Aeronautics Board, June, 1972).

ities (such as express, mail, and charter flights), and nontransport revenue from services that are incidental to air transportation.

Operating expenses are incurred in the performance of air transportation, and include direct aircraft operating expenses as well as ground and indirect operating expenses. From an analytical point of view, the significance of operating expenses lies in their measurement of management efficiency. *Flying operations* are those expenses incurred directly in the in-flight operation of aircraft and expenses attached to the holding of aircraft and aircraft operational personnel in readiness for assignment to an in-flight status. For the trunk lines as a whole, flying operations expenses tend to run just over 27% of operating revenue.

Maintenance expenses are those outlays for preserving the operating quality of flight equipment. Included in the figure are both direct and indirect maintenance. *Direct maintenance* is the cost of labor, materials, and outside services consumed directly in periodic maintenance operations and the maintenance, repair, or upkeep of airframes, aircraft engines, other flight equipment, and ground property and equipment. *Indirect maintenance* consists of the overhead or general expenses of activities involved in the repair and upkeep of property and equipment, including inspection of equipment in accordance with prescribed operational standards. Also included are expenses related to the administration of stocks and stores, maintenance of operations records, and scheduling, controlling, planning, and supervising maintenance operations. Maintenance expenses are significant because they are subject to the discretion of management and are not immediately apparent either to the user of aircraft equipment or to an investor examining the financial statements of airlines.

General and administrative expenses are primarily of a corporate nature and are incurred in the performance of such general activities as purchasing, general financial accounting, legal activities, and other general operational administration. *Depreciation* is the periodic charge against revenue for the cost of airframes, aircraft engines, and other property and equipment. In the case of airlines, maximum depreciable lifetimes for flight equipment are established by the Civil Aeronautics Board. At the present time, for example, 85% of the cost of both airframes and engines may be depreciated over 12 years. Residual value thus is expected to be 15%.

Operating profit is the complement of *operating expenses,* since the two must add to equal 100% of *operating revenues.* Operating profit (or loss) is the economic result of the performance of air transportation. The magnitude of this item is the best indicator of overall operating efficiency of the carrier. Note in Figure 13–9, for example, that the operating profit of American Airlines is only 3.3%, lower than the 1972 average of the domestic trunk carriers, while the operating profit margin for Eastern is 6.4% and thus higher than average.

From operating profit is deducted interest expense, the net of any nonoperating income and expense (net nonoperating income is added), and income taxes. *Net income* is the final result available for shareholders. The greater efficiency of Eastern over American is apparent from comparing the 3.2% net income margin (as a percentage of sales) of Eastern with the 1.2% net income margin of American.

Condensed versions of the balance sheets for U.S. domestic trunk airlines and for American Airlines and Eastern Air Lines are shown in Figure 13–10. Here it can be seen that the major asset of air carriers is their net property, constituting 67.5% of total assets for all trunk carriers, slightly less for American, and only 56.7% for Eastern. The second most important category is current assets, which constitutes almost 20% for domestic trunk carriers as a whole. As expected, the proportion for

FIGURE 13–10

U.S. DOMESTIC TRUNK AIRLINES
Condensed Balance Sheet Data
June 30, 1972

	All U.S. domestic trunk airlines		American Airlines		Eastern Air Lines	
	Millions of dollars	*%*	*Millions of dollars*	*%*	*Millions of dollars*	*%*
Assets						
Current assets	1,965	19.2	271.4	15.8	259.0	22.2
Investments and special funds	1,028	10.2	180.4	10.5	215.6	18.4
Operating property and equipment at cost	10,824		1,688.7		1,095.1	
Less accumulated depreciation	−3,942		−563.5		−432.7	
Net operating property	6,882	67.5	1,125.2	65.5	662.4	56.7
Nonoperating property	111	1.1	87.3	5.1	0.4	0.0
Deferred charges	201	2.0	53.8	3.1	31.1	2.7
Total assets	10,187	100.0	1,718.1	100.0	1,168.5	100.0
Liabilities and equity						
Current liabilities	1,812	17.8	290.4	16.9	229.4	19.6
Noncurrent liabilities	4,364	42.8	668.7	38.9	534.4	45.7
Deferred credits	983	9.7	182.5	10.6	19.3	1.7
Preferred stock	24	0.2	—	–	21.7	1.9
Common stockholders' equity	3,004	29.5	576.5	33.6	363.7	31.1
Total liabilities and equity	10,187	100.0	1,718.1	100.0	1,168.5	100.0

Source: Air Carrier Financial Statistics (Washington, D.C.: Civil Aeronautics Board, June, 1972).

American is somewhat less, while the proportion for Eastern is greater than average.

In general, airlines finance about 43% of their assets with noncurrent liabilities, primarily long-term debt, and another 18% with current liabilities. Total debt amounts to 61% of total capital for trunk lines as a whole, with stockholders' equity responsible for about 30% of total capital. American Airlines has somewhat less debt than average, the difference being made up by a large deferred credit, the major portion of which is deferred federal income taxes. Eastern Air Lines, on the other hand, has a greater-than-average total of debt in its balance sheet and does not show any deferred credits. It should be noted that variations in the degree of leasing could invalidate comparisons based on balance sheets in which leased assets and obligations are not shown.

The profitability of air carriers is measured by the ratio of net income before interest to "adjusted investment." The numerator of this ratio is net income for the year with interest expense added back. The denominator of the ratio is the sum of the following seven accounts:

1. Long-term debt
2. Advances from associated companies
3. Advances from nontransport divisions
4. Other noncurrent liabilities
5. Unamortized discount and expense on debt (debit)
6. Preferred stock
7. Common stockholders' equity.

The sum of these accounts is then adjusted by subtracting equipment purchase deposits and capitalized interest. CAB statistics provide the ratio in two forms, with investment tax credit included and with investment tax credit excluded. The resulting ratio is not tailored to any particular needs, either regulatory or nonregulatory, and is thus not necessarily the exact ratio that would be used in a formal rate proceeding. It does conform in a general sense, however, to regulatory measures and is thus valuable as an overall indicator of both the level and trend of airlines earnings.

Rate-of-return ratios, as described above, are shown in Figure 13–11 for the ten trunk airlines. As can be seen, the range is very great, extending from 10.80% earned by Delta Air Lines to 3.29% for American Airlines. No carrier is earning the 12% rate of return deemed fair and reasonable by the CAB.

Railroad statements

Railroad financial statements can also be studied for trends of significance and differences between companies. Railroad accounts are kept

FIGURE 13–11
U.S. trunk airlines: ratios of net income before interest to adjusted investment (investment tax credit excluded; 12 months ended June 30, 1972)

Airline	Ratio
Delta	10.80%
National	9.17
Eastern.	7.91
Continental	7.84
Braniff	7.15
Northwest	6.84
Western.	6.28
Trans World	5.18
United	3.77
American.	3.29
Weighted average*	5.62%

* Incuding Northeast and domestic flights of Pan American. Weighted average is the sum of net income for all carriers divided by the sum of adjusted investment for all carriers.
Source: Air Carrier Financial Statistics (Washington, D.C.: Civil Aeronautics Board, June, 1972).

according to a uniform format prescribed by the Interstate Commerce Commission. Figure 13–12 shows a somewhat condensed version of the income statement for all U.S. Class I railroads, compared with statements for the Norfolk and Western Railway and for the Southern Pacific Transportation Company. It should be noted that the Southern Pacific Transportation Company, a common carrier that files reports as required with the Interstate Commerce Commission, is the major subsidiary of the Southern Pacific Company. The Southern Pacific Company is a holding company that owns, in addition to the Southern Pacific Transportation Company, other companies involved in land development, oil pipelines, leasing, and communications. Although a stockholder owns shares in the holding company, the process of analysis is keyed primarily to the major operating subsidiary. Therefore, the analysis that follows will be directed toward the statements of actual railway operating companies rather than holding companies.

Railroad earnings and dividends tend to fluctuate widely from year to year because of three characteristics: (1) the industry itself is cyclical in nature, with traffic volume very sensitive to changes in economic conditions; (2) the variability inherent in fluctuating traffic volume is magnified by the inherently large operating leverage of the railroads; i.e., railroad operating expenses tend to remain constant as operating revenue fluctuates; and (3) railroads utilize a large degree of capital structure leverage, inducing even greater changes in earnings for stockholders as traffic volume and operating income fluctuate.

FIGURE 13–12

U.S. RAILROADS
Income Statements
Year Ended December 31, 1971

	U.S. Class I railroads		Norfolk & Western Railway Company		Southern Pacific Transportation Company	
	Millions of dollars	%	Millions of dollars	%	Millions of dollars	%
Operating revenues						
Freight..................	11,786	92.9	700.8	96.3	1,001.4	97.3
Passenger	294	2.3	0.5	0.1	5.6	0.6
All other................	609	4.8	26.3	3.6	21.7	2.1
Total................	12,689	100.0	727.6	100.0	1,028.7	100.0
Operating expenses						
Maintenance of way and structures. .	1,813	14.3	83.3	11.4	140.5	13.6
Maintenance of equipment	2,351	18.5	135.1	18.6	203.5	19.8
Traffic expense	282	2.2	16.3	2.2	16.6	1.6
Transportation expense	4,890	38.5	253.8	34.9	383.7	37.3
Miscellaneous and general expense . .	719	5.7	39.1	5.4	60.5	5.9
Total................	10,055	79.2*	527.6	72.5*	804.8	78.2*
Net railway operating revenue......	2,634	20.8	200.0	27.5	223.9	21.8
Federal income taxes..........	108		4.3		9.5	
Other taxes	1,090		55.4		84.4	
Railway operating income........	1,544	12.2	140.3	14.3	130.0	12.6
Net equipment and joint facility rents..................	848		27.3		55.2	
Net railway operating income......	696	5.4	113.0	15.5	74.8	7.3
Other income	422		21.5		64.7	
Miscellaneous deductions	141		4.7		7.8	
Available for fixed charges	977	7.7	129.8	17.8	131.7	12.8
Fixed charges	601		49.4		38.8	
Contingent interest on funded debt .	29		2.7			
Net income (before extraordinary items)	347	2.7	77.7	10.7	92.9	9.0

* Operating ratio.

Analysis of the statements of railroads thus tends to focus on what will happen to income as revenues change. The significance of the various railway income and expense accounts can be highlighted by expression of the statements in common-size form, with total operating revenues equal to 100%. This is done in Figure 13–12.

In railroad parlance, *operating revenue* refers to the "sales" revenue of the company. The bulk of railroad operating revenue is derived from freight traffic, especially in recent years since passenger operations have been transferred to Amtrak. In 1971, almost 93% of railroad operating revenues for Class I roads came from freight, with only 2.3% from passenger traffic. Other sources of railway operating revenue included mail, express, and switching. The proportion of revenue from freight for the Norfolk and Western and for the Southern Pacific was higher than for all Class I roads, indicating even less dependence upon passenger traffic.

Operating expenses are those expenses necessary for the running of the railroad. One major approach to railroad evaluation is to compare each item of operating expenses to operating revenue in order to measure the distribution of the revenue dollar. *Maintenance* accounts are especially important because they are the items over which management may exercise the greatest discretion. The size of maintenance accounts reflects management's attitude toward maintaining the physical quality of way, structures, and equipment. By law, railroads must account for their maintenance expenses on a cash basis. Outlays in any year must be charged to that year and cannot be accrued and assigned to another year. This is termed "betterment" accounting to differentiate from "accrual" accounting. One of the major avenues open to management to conserve cash or to improve reported earnings is to delay or defer maintenance. An unusually low proportional expenditure for maintenance of way and structures over several years might indicate that the company was allowing its tracks, roadbed, or those buildings and structures directly involved in transportation to deteriorate. Low maintenance of equipment might reflect a deterioration in the quality of the railroad's rolling stock. The adequacy of maintenance expenses is important not only because management has control over this account, but because the economic results of too much or too little maintenance will not be visible in the operations or financial results (other than maintenance) of the railroad for a number of years. Yet eventually there must be a reckoning, and the railroad which has undermaintained for an extended period of years may have to undertake vast expenditures to return its property to normal operating condition.

In conjunction with the above point, it will be noted in Figure 13-12 that railroad income statements contain no depreciation. Under the betterment accounting procedures, railroads do not take depreciation on such items as roadbed or rolling stock. Rather the original cost of track, as an example, remains on the asset side of the balance sheet indefinitely, while the labor of putting that track in place and all costs of replacing the track are treated as current expenses at the time such replacement is made. In theory, annual replacement of, say, one twentieth of a railroad's rails, ties, and ballast on a cash expense basis would work out the same as if all roadbed expenses were capitalized and depreciated over a twenty-year period especially if the road was in a steady state where it repaired or replaced its physical properties at a regular rate. In fact, however, railroad management may make their income statement look better by not replacing roadbed or rolling stock that is wearing out. Only outlays that result in the "betterment" of the system, e.g. the extra cost of replacing 115-pound rail with 130-pound rail, are added to the asset values.

One consequence of such accounting, in addition to its income-distorting impact, is that assets listed at their original costs on the balance sheet may no longer be worth anywhere near that sum. Thus "book value" from railroad financial statements is an especially meaningless term.

Traffic expense records outlays to develop business. Included are expenses for advertising, traffic associations, stationery and printing, and the cost of superintendence. *Transportation expense* is the expense of actually operating the trains, and includes such costs as labor (for both train crews and station employees), fuel, train supplies, operation of signals and grade crossing protection, and service to locomotives. The magnitude of this item is important in judging the operating (train-running) efficiency of the railroad. *Miscellaneous and general expenses* include outlays for the operation of dining and buffet service, the salaries and expenses of general officers and of the management staff, pensions, general office supplies and expenses, and employees' health and welfare benefits.

Total operating expenses as a percentage of operating revenues is known as the *operating ratio*. This ratio, which has run at about 80% in most of the post–World War II period, shows the proportion of operating revenues consumed by those expenses necessary for the operation of the road. The ratio is useful in determining whether, over a period of years, management of the railroad is becoming more or less efficient in its control over operating costs, and the ratio can be used to compare one road to another if other variables are considered equal. Both of the railroads reported in Figure 13–12 had operating ratios of less than 80% and thus were more efficient than the average.

Subtraction of operating expenses from operating revenue leaves *net railway operating revenue*. From this sum are deducted taxes paid by railroads, the largest segment of which is payroll taxes, and the net costs of renting equipment and joint facilities to produce *net railway operating income*, the final measure of earnings of the company as a railroad. Net railway operating income is then adjusted with other income and miscellaneous deductions from nonrailway activities to produce income *available for fixed charges*, the income figure that is of greatest concern to bondholders. Various types of interest charges are subtracted from this figure to reach *net income*, the bottom line item of greatest interest to common stockholders. Net income may be reported either before extraordinary charges, as is shown in Figure 13–12, or after extraordinary charges. Again, both Norfolk and Western and Southern Pacific did better than average in 1971.

Railroad balance sheets are shown in Figure 13–13 in abbreviated form of the official ICC format. Data in Figure 13–13 reveal the capital-intensive nature of railroads, for over 75% of all assets are net transportation property, the roadbed and equipment of the carrier. In contrast,

FIGURE 13–13

TWO RAILROADS
Balance Sheets
December 31, 1971

	Norfolk & Western Railway Company		Southern Pacific Transportation Company	
	Millions of dollars	%	Millions of dollars	%
Assets				
Current assets.	195.6	8.9	289.7	11.
Special funds	10.3	0.5	6.8	0.
Investments	260.8	11.9	125.4	4.
Transportation				
Property–Cost	2,247.5		2,610.5	
Accrued Depreciation	–551.3		–646.9	
Net transportation property.	1,696.2	77.4	1,963.6	76.
Other assets and property	27.7	1.3	190.0	7.
Total assets	2,190.6	100.0	2,575.5	100.
Liabilities and equity				
Current liabilities	209.8	9.6	269.7	10.
Long-term debt	728.2	33.2	745.8	29.
Reserves	13.9	0.6	40.1	1.
Other liabilities	65.2	3.0	26.0	1.
Stockholders' equity	1,173.5	53.6	1,493.9	58.
Total liabilities and equity	2,190.6	100.0	2,575.5	100.

Source: Moody's Transportation Manuals.

current assets typically constitute only about 10% of total assets. On the liability and capital side of the balance sheet, we see that the major source of capital is stockholders' equity, constituting over half of all capital. Long-term debt is also important, averaging about one third of total capital, while other items, including current liabilities, are of modest overall significance. Briefly, the balance sheet of a railroad might be characterized as being dominated on the asset side by investments in fixed assets, and on the liability side by long-term sources of capital: bonds and stocks.

A number of ratios beneficial in evaluating the safety and profitability of a railroad from an investment point of view may be calculated from financial statement data. Four such ratios are compared in Figure 13–14.

Times fixed charges earned is obtained by dividing "available for fixed charges" by "fixed charges." Fixed charges include interest on debt

FIGURE 13–14
Selected railroad financial ratios, 1971

	U.S. Class I railroads	Norfolk & Western Railway Company	Southern Pacific Transportation Company
1. Times fixed charges earned (after tax)	1.63 times	2.63 times	3.39 times
2. Times fixed and contingent charges earned (after tax)	1.55 times	2.49 times	3.39 times
3. Margin of safety	3.59%	11.27%	9.95%
4. Rate of return on average net investment.	2.47%	6.55%	3.77%

Sources: Ratios 1 through 3 calculated from data in Figure 13–12. Ratio 4 for Class I railroads from *Statistics of Railroads of Class I* (Washington, D.C.: Association of American Railroads, October, 1972). For Norfolk & Western and Southern Pacific, calculated from data in *Moody's Transportation Manuals.*

as well as rent for leased road and equipment and amortization of discount on funded debt. The ratio gives a measure of the overall safety of the fixed charge claims. The Southern Pacific Transportation Company, for example, earned 3.39 times the amount of its fixed charges, while Class I railroads as a whole earned only 1.63 times. Clearly, payment of the fixed charges of the Southern Pacific is more reliable, in the event of a deterioration of railroad earnings, than is the payment of the average Class I railroad.

Times fixed charges earned is here calculated on an after-tax basis for two reasons: (1) the prescribed reporting format shows tax expenses as a deduction before the payment of fixed charges, and (2) the major portions of railroad taxes are payroll and state and local taxes, rather than federal income taxes. However it is not unreasonable to calculate the same ratio on a before-tax basis.

Times fixed and contingent charges earned adds to the denominator of the preceding ratio contingent interest on funded debt. Such interest would be payable on income debentures only if earned by the railroad. From the point of view of a bondholder, times charges earned is the most significant coverage, but from the point of view of either an income debenture holder or a shareholder, times fixed and contingent charges earned is a more meaningful ratio. The reason for this distinction is simply that the bondholder gets paid first.

Margin of safety is the percentage of gross revenue remaining after fixed and contingent charges but before federal income tax accruals. It is derived in Figure 13–14 by adding federal income tax accruals back to net income (to obtain an income-before-income-tax figure), and dividing this sum by operating revenue. Margin of safety is an alternative measure both of the safety of fixed and contingent charges and of the operating leverage inherent in the present level of net income. The margin of safety of 11.27% for Norfolk and Western shown in Figure

13–14, indicates that operating revenues could drop 11.27% with no attendant reduction in any expenses before the company would fail to earn its fixed charges or before net income would be reduced to zero. With a margin of safety of 11.27%, Norfolk and Western is clearly in a more secure earnings position than Class I railroads in general. Southern Pacific also has a very favorable margin of safety.

The presumption inherent in using the margin of safety to compare railroads is that operating expenses would not decline with a drop in operating revenue. Although this may be somewhat conservative, if operating revenues dropped because of short-run or unanticipated changes in traffic volume, such as might occur during a recession, operating expenses would in fact fluctuate very little. But if operating revenue were to decline because of a permanent change, such as abandonment of a portion of the rail line, operating expenses might decline as well.

The fourth ratio is *rate of return on average net investment*. In railroad parlance, this ratio has a specific definition. The numerator is net railway operating income (after taxes), the final measure of railroad earnings before miscellaneous nonrailroad income and deductions and before the subtraction of any return to invested capital (including interest). The denominator is the average for the year (year-end plus previous year-end divide by two) of the following three items:

1. Net transportation property (after accrued depreciation)
2. Cash
3. Materials and supplies.

This ratio thus measures after-tax earnings to invested capital as a percentage of the basic investment in railroad assets. Both the Norfolk and Western and the Southern Pacific have been successful in earning a higher return than has been earned by Class I railroads as a whole (Figure 13–14).

SELECTING SECURITIES OF TRANSPORTATION COMPANIES

As with public utilities and industrial corporations, the final step in selecting transportation company securities is to consider their investment attributes and apply the valuation framework. Throughout this chapter, we have considered the regulatory environment, operating characteristics, and financial statements of common carriers with which an investor must be familiar before he can make informed judgments about the benefits to be received from bonds and stocks issued by a particular carrier.

With respect to investing in the common stocks of transportation companies, the immediate benefits are cash dividends that are received.

Cash dividend yield to any single investor is a function of annual dividend received and the historic price paid per share. Thus, for any single stock a multitude of cash dividend yields are possible for each year, depending upon the price paid in some prior year for that stock. For example, Figure 13–15 indicates the cash dividend yield in each year from 1962 through 1972 for Southern Pacific Company for a shareholder who purchased the stock at the mean (of the annual high and low) price in each year and held through the remaining years. Because cash dividends rose in every year except 1970 (when they remained constant), realized dividend yield for each investor rose over the period. However, the series of dividend yields for an investor who purchased in a year of low prices, say 1962, 1967, or 1970, were considerably higher than the yields for those investors purchasing in such high-price years as 1964, 1965, or 1971.

The important point to remember in calculating anticipated dividend yield on a potential stock acquisition is that the yield is a function of the specific price paid by the investor as well as the anticipated dividend stream. Dividend yield tabulations that appear in such statistical sources as *Moody's* or *Standard & Poor's* are always *current yields* (this year's dividend divided by this year's price. Current yield is the top value in each of the columns in Figure 13–15; these were the only values presented in the similar exhibit of dividend yields for public utility stocks in the previous chapter. However, these are not necessarily the yields actually received by a given stockholder.

Using American and Eastern to illustrate airlines, and Norfolk and Western and Southern Pacific to illustrate railroads, we may calculate realized dividend yields for an investor who purchased at the mean market price of 1962:

Year	American Airlines	Eastern Air Lines	Norfolk & Western	Southern Pacific
1962	5.10%	0.00%	5.62%	4.60%
1963	5.10	0.00	6.13	5.18
1964	5.71	0.00	7.15	5.37
1965	6.42	0.00	6.64	5.56
1966	6.73	2.11	6.64	5.76
1967	8.05	3.68	6.13	5.87
1968	8.15	4.60	6.13	6.33
1969	8.15	3.49	6.13	6.91
1970	8.15	0.00	5.62	6.91
1971	4.08	0.00	5.11	7.48
1972	0.00	0.00	5.11	7.98

We see that in the late 1960s, American Airlines had the highest dividend yield, but that dividend cuts in 1971 and 1972 reduced the yield to

FIGURE 13–15

Annual realized dividend yields for an investor purchasing common stock of Southern Pacific Company at the annual mean market price of stock in the year indicated

Year dividend received	Purchase price	Annual dividend	Year stock was purchased										
			1962	1963	1964	1965	1966	1967	1968	1969	1970	1971	1972
1962	$26.06	$1.20	4.60%										
1963	33.12	1.35	5.18	4.08%									
1964	41.31	1.40	5.37	4.23	3.14%								
1965	40.37	1.45	5.56	4.38	3.25	3.59%							
1966	37.00	1.50	5.76	4.53	3.36	3.72	4.09%						
1967	31.06	1.53	5.87	4.62	3.43	3.79	4.17	4.93%					
1968	38.25	1.65	6.33	4.98	3.70	4.09	4.50	5.31	4.31%				
1969	38.44	1.80	6.91	5.43	4.04	4.46	4.91	5.79	4.71	3.63%			
1970	29.37	1.80	6.91	5.43	4.04	4.46	4.91	5.79	4.71	3.63	6.13%		
1971	41.06	1.95	7.48	5.87	4.37	4.83	5.32	6.28	5.10	3.93	6.64	4.75%	
1972	40.62	2.08	7.98	6.28	4.66	5.15	5.67	6.70	5.44	4.19	7.08	5.07	5.12%

zero in the latter year. The yield of Eastern Airlines was zero in most years because dividends were not paid except from 1966 to 1969. The Norfolk and Western dividend yield fell after 1964, as dividends were progressively cut, while the yield on Southern Pacific rose steadily as cash dividends were increased in almost every year.

Variations in annual dividend yield, when expressed in terms of an initial purchase price, point up the importance, over a period during which a stock is held, of accurately projecting future cash dividends. The Southern Pacific tabulation further illustrates the fact that even if an initial dividend yield (4.60% in 1962) seems so modest that the investor is tempted to direct all of his attention to anticipated price appreciation, continued dividend increases over a decade or so can raise the realized dividend yield to a respectable level (7.98% in 1972).

The second important benefit to investors who purchase common stock is the market price of their shares when they are sold. A major factor in this benefit is the price-earnings ratio established in the market for each common stock at the time of sale. Comparison of price-earnings ratios for the two airlines and two railroads can be examined for historical perspective. As with electric power utilities, the price-earnings ratios tended to decrease over the period 1962–72. There also was diversity over time for the carriers, especially Eastern Air Lines.

Year	American Airlines	Eastern Air Lines	Norfolk & Western	Southern Pacific
1962	23.6	NA	13.8	8.6
1963	11.6	NA	14.9	10.2
1964	10.9	NA	15.5	14.7
1965	12.9	9.9	13.4	13.2
1966	10.9	29.9	11.0	10.7
1967	16.3	23.2	12.5	11.5
1968	17.2	NA	13.0	11.7
1969	16.3	NA	10.8	11.3
1970	NA	37.8	11.0	10.2
1971	NA	67.6	10.6	10.7
1972	18.0	21.4	9.1	11.2

NA: Not applicable because earnings were negative for that year.

As always, it is important to evaluate each common stock being considered in a portfolio context. To illustrate this, Figure 13–16 traces Standard & Poor's price indices for twenty railroads and seven airlines over the same period of years, as compared with the Standard & Poor's Industrial Index of 425 stocks, which is used as a surrogate for the entire market. The railroad industry is seen to move in a relatively narrow range, but with movements rather closely paralleling the overall market. Airlines moved quite erratically, reaching relative high points in

FIGURE 13–16
Relative price movements of airline, railroad, and industrial stocks, 1963–72. (1941–43 = 10; semi-log scale)

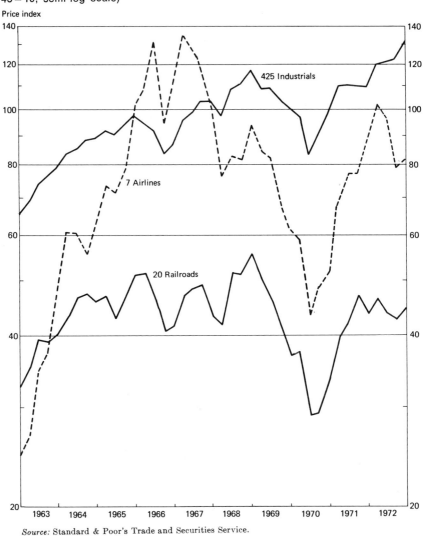

Price index

Source: Standard & Poor's Trade and Securities Service.

1966 and 1967. A careful reader will note that these highs were roughly coincident with the peak of load factors in 1966. A careful reader also may connect the stable price movements of all railroad stocks with their relatively stable dividend policy. For airlines that may or may not pay dividends, expectation for future earnings and future stock prices is the primary component of return, while dividends are the primary component of return from railroad stocks. Comparison of airlines and railroads within a portfolio context thus seems to underscore the tradeoff between return and risk in a rather dramatic fashion.

SUMMARY

Transportation company securities may be of interest to investors for two reasons. The industry is of major importance to the economy of the United States, and the industry possesses certain characteristics that might make transportation securities an appropriate component of a balanced portfolio. This chapter has looked at two of the major components of the transportation industry, airlines and railroads. Analysis of airlines has been used to indicate general aspects of analyzing any transportation service that moves people, while railroads have been used to indicate the general nature of analyzing freight transportation. Because both airlines and railroads are regulated by agencies of the federal government, an initial discussion was presented in which established classifications of air carriers and railroads were explained. This was followed with an explanation of the regulatory aspects of both segments of the industry. Because of the regulated nature of these industries and their vital importance to the economy, potential investors have access to considerable published data. Highlights of analyzing available operating statistics and financial statements of both types of carriers were explained and illustrated for selected carriers within each type of transportation company. The chapter concluded with a brief discussion of transportation securities within a portfolio context.

SUGGESTED READINGS FOR CHAPTER 13

R. E. Badger, H. W. Torgerson, and H. G. Guthmann. *Investment Principles and Practices* (Englewood Cliffs, N.J.: Prentice-Hall, Inc., 6th edition 1969), Chapter 12.

I. H. Benham. "Railroad-Based Conglomerates," *Financial Analysts Journal,* May–June, 1972, pages 43–53.

J. C. Clendenin and G. A. Christy. *Introduction to Investments* (New York: McGraw-Hill Book Company, Inc., 5th edition, 1969), Chapters 15 and 16.

G. H. Conklin. "The Airline Industry," *Financial Analysts Journal,* January–February, 1971, pages 40–43.

P. E. Dascher. "Penn Central Was Predictable," *Financial Analysis Journal,* March–April, 1972, pages 61–64.

A Davlin, Jr. "Trucking Companies: Have They Gained Institutional Standing?" *The Institutional Investor,* February, 1971, pages 42–43.

J. F. Lyons. "The Analysts: What Five of the Best Think about Airlines," *The Institutional Investor*, November, 1968, pages 42–48.

A. Roth. "The Railroads: What Will Diversification Mean to Earnings?" *The Institutional Investor*, October, 1968, pages 74–85.

S. Sealy. "How the Railroads Treat Analysts," *The Institutional Investor*, April, 1969, pages 74–76.

T. H. Vernon. "Air Carrier Return on Investment," *Financial Analysts Journal*, January–February, 1971, pages 44–53.

14

Investing in financial institutions

FINANCIAL INSTITUTIONS are businesses organized to provide some type of financial service to a particular group of clients or customers. Although many kinds of financial institutions provide a wide variety of specialized financial services, our interest here is limited to institutions organized as profit-seeking, stockholder-owned enterprises that issue securities to the public. We thus do not include those financial institutions organized on a mutual basis—i.e., those that are owned by their clients rather than by a separate group of stockholders. Our interest also is limited to those institutions that, as part of their overall operations, are engaged in investing funds that come to them from their creditors and from their stockholders. Frequently characterized as "financial intermediaries," these institutions raise funds, in part from their own stockholders and in part from a variety of clients and creditors, and invest the accumulated pool of funds in appropriate assets. The purpose of this chapter is to consider the overall and particular investment characteristics of four institutions so identified: commercial banks, savings and loan associations, life insurance companies, and fire and casualty insurance companies.

OVERALL CHARACTERISTICS OF FINANCIAL INSTITUTIONS

The four kinds of financial institutions covered in this chapter are of two general types. *Depository-type institutions* consist of commercial banks, "true" banks in one sense of the word, and savings and loan associations, not "true" banks in this sense, but rather institutions whose activities may appear to the potential investor similar to commercial banks. Commercial banks and savings and loan associations have as their general business the accepting of deposits or savings accounts for their clients and the investing of the resulting funds to produce an income that will cover operating expenses, allow for the payment of interest on the creditor-supplied funds, and provide a residual profit for the benefit of the stockholders. They differ in the composition of both their assets and their liabilities.

Insurance institutions covered in this chapter are also of two types. Life insurance companies receive funds from policyholders seeking protection against financial losses caused by death. These funds are combined with the aggregate investment of stockholders and are invested in a portfolio of securities that will ensure adequate liquidity to pay policy claims for those policyholders who die. Earnings on the invested funds cover a portion of the death claims, since the dollar amount of premium charged on most types of life insurance policy assumes a certain rate of return on the investment of the policyholders' premium payments. This rate of return is contractual, which means that the level of premiums is based upon an assumed percentage rate. If actual earnings exceed this contractual rate, the difference belongs to the owners of the insurance company, but if actual earnings are less than the contractual rate, the stockholders must make up the difference through less earnings for themselves. That portion of the earnings on the insurance company's portfolio that is not allocated for eventual payment of death claims is available to pay the operating expenses of the company and, if anything remains, as earnings attributable to the stockholders of the company.

Fire and casualty insurance companies, also called property and liability insurance companies, write insurance against the possibility of loss from a variety of causes other than death. They also are sometimes referred to just as nonlife companies. Included with fire insurance is coverage against losses due to windstorm and hurricane damage, explosion, water and flood damage, marine accidents, and automobile fire and collision. Casualty lines include workmen's compensation, automobile, and other types of liability insurance. Accident insurance and health insurance are written by both life and by fire and casualty companies, as well as by specialized accident and health companies.

As with life insurance companies, fire and casualty insurance companies combine premium receipts from policyholders with funds received from stockholders to create a portfolio with adequate liquidity to pay losses. Fire and casualty insurance companies, however, differ significantly from life insurance companies in two respects. Fire and casualty insurance policies typically last from three months to three years, after which they expire unless renewed. In contrast, most life insurance policies extend for many decades. The second difference is the variability of possible loss payments for fire and casualty companies as compared to life companies. Amounts paid out on fire and casualty losses are influenced by random events such as hurricanes, and the dollar amount paid is dependent in part upon the cost of replacing the damaged or destroyed asset. Such a cost increases with the cost of living and may vary with such uncertainties as the attitude of a court jury charged with assessing the amount of damages to be paid in a particular liability suit. By comparison, the dollar amount paid out on life insurance policies is fixed by the face of the policy, and the only variable is the time of death.

Commercial banks, savings and loan associations, and life insurance companies, which comprise a type of financial institution frequently called *financial intermediaries*, serve as a link between savers and borrowers. In effect, savers provide funds for the borrowers through the institutional intermediary, rather than by making direct loans or investments. The relative size of the various types of financial intermediaries in the United States is shown in Figure 14–1. At the end of 1972 commercial

FIGURE 14–1
Total assets of financial intermediaries in the United States, December 31, 1945 and 1972

	1945		1972	
	Billions of dollars	*Percent*	*Billions of dollars*	*Percent*
Commercial banks	$160.3	66.2%	$ 716.9	43.3%
Savings and loan associations	8.7	3.6	243.6	14.7
Life insurance companies	44.8	18.5	239.4	14.5
Mutual savings banks	17.0	7.0	100.6	6.1
Finance companies	4.3	1.8	73.7	4.4
Investment companies	1.3	0.5	59.8	3.6
Credit unions	0.4	0.2	24.8	1.5
Private pension funds.	2.8	1.1	123.7	7.5
State and local pension funds	2.7	1.1	72.2	4.4
Total.	$242.3	100.0%	$1,654.7	100.0%

Source: *1973 Savings and Loan Fact Book* (Chicago, Ill.: United States Savings and Loan League, 1973), page 53.

banks were the largest financial intermediary, with 43.3% of total assets. Savings and loan associations were the second largest type, with 14.7% of total assets, and life insurance companies were third, with 14.5% of total assets. These relative positions have changed since 1945, when life insurance companies had 18.5% of the assets of all financial intermediaries, and savings and loan associations had only 3.6% of total assets.

Fire and casualty insurance companies are absent from Figure 14–1 because they receive no funds from savers. That is, fire and casualty policies do not have the built-in savings components of most life insurance policies. Total assets under the control of stockholder-owned fire and casualty insurance companies at the end of 1972 were $49.3 billion, placing them as the fourth largest among the four financial institutions to be discussed here.

Only a part of the total ownership interest of all of the four types of U.S. financial institutions under consideration in this chapter is available to potential investors. There are, for example, almost 14,000 separate commercial banks in the United States. The great majority of these are owned and operated by local groups, and in most instances shares of common stock of these institutions are not available to the general public. In some instances, common shares might be available in local communities through private sale, in which case the procedures explained in this chapter for the publicly-held commercial bank stocks would apply.

At the end of 1972, there were 5,448 savings and loan associations in the United States, of which 4,783 operated as mutual institutions and only 665 operated as stockholder-owned organizations. Stockholder-owned savings and loan associations possessed $50,773 million of total assets, out of an industry total of $243,570 million. Thus ownership of only about 20% of the industry, as measured by total assets, is available to the investing public.

Of the 1,829 life insurance companies in business during 1972, stockholders owned 1,676 (about 92%). The remaining 153 were mutual insurance companies. Mutual life insurance companies, however, are generally older and larger than stockholder-owned companies, so that the mutual companies account for about two thirds of the assets of all U.S. life insurance companies.

More fire and casualty insurance companies are organized as mutual than as stockholder-owned, but a greater volume of insurance coverage is written by the stock companies. This is perhaps because property insurance is usually written for shorter periods of time. Additionally, as explained earlier, property-insurance losses are less easily predicted than life-insurance losses, especially on a short-term basis, because of the influences of catastrophes and of inflation. Stockholder-owned fire and casualty insurance companies have the advantage of a larger stockholder-supplied equity cushion, providing additional assets that could be liquidated in the event of major unanticipated losses. Thus the stockholder-owned form of company dominates the fire and casualty insurance business.

GENERAL PRINCIPLES IN THE ANALYSIS OF FINANCIAL STATEMENTS

Industry aggregate balance sheets for each of the four major types of financial institutions are portrayed in Figures 14–2, 14–6, 14–8, and

14–10. The format of these statements has been revised from the original version so as to emphasize those aspects common to all financial institutions.

Assets of financial institutions may conveniently be grouped into four types. Cash and cash-type holdings represent the first line of liquidity and provide funds for day-to-day operation. Other highly liquid types of investments, typically short-term government securities, represent the second line of liquidity. In commercial banks, this second line of liquidity is usually called "secondary reserves," and the term is an apt description of the need for this category of asset by all financial institutions. Investments of this type primarily contribute emergency liquidity; earnings (portfolio income) are of secondary importance. The third set of assets comprises those held primarily for earning purposes, with liquidity of secondary concern. The fourth classification of assets is of a miscellaneous nature, small in proportion to total assets, and includes such items as the physical premises and facilities in which the financial institutions work.

A first general approach to the analysis of all financial institutions is *asset leverage,* as measured by the proportional mix of the four asset types defined. Conservative managements are those that tend toward greater proportions of cash, cash-type, and highly liquid assets than is common for other institutions of the same type, while aggressive managements tend towards greater proportional holdings of less liquid investments that produce greater earnings. Analysis of financial institutions, therefore, begins with measurement of the risk-return trade-off selected by the management of a particular financial institution in relationship to the risk-return trade-off typical of institutions of that type.

A second general approach to the analysis of financial institutions, which might be termed *financial leverage,* deals with another risk-return trade-off adopted by management, this time on the liability side of the balance sheet. The major item on the right-hand side of the balance sheet of all financial institutions is what might be called "client-derived" liabilities that arise because of the normal operating relationship of the institution with its customers. An example would be the deposit liabilities of a commercial bank to its depositors. Customer-derived liabilities are of comparatively low cost to most financial institutions, but create risk in that they must eventually be repaid to the customer. A second category of liabilities have been labeled "other." These comprise an assortment of debts of the institution to various parties other than the normal clients. The third category is "stockholders' equity," which is the equity cushion from which any losses must be subtracted.

This second general approach to analysis of all financial institutions is measured by the proportion of client-derived liabilities to other liabilities and to stockholders' equity. A conservative management would be one that operated with a stockholders' equity proportion greater than typical for other companies in the same industry, while an aggressive management would take risks by accepting a greater proportion of liabilities relative to equity. The risk-taking propensity of any financial institution thus may be judged from both the asset side and the liability side of the balance sheet. A particular management could *offset* risks—for example, by adopting an aggressive posture in its asset mix (a high proportion of earning assets and low cash and liquid investments) while offsetting this position with a conservative mix on the liability side of its balance sheet (high equity in proportion to liabilities).

This possibility suggests another principle, in which "client-derived liabilities at risk" are measured against stockholders' equity. Although devised primarily for commercial bank analysis, this ratio is useful for all financial institutions. Client-derived liabilities at risk are those liabilities that would remain to be satisfied out of "less liquid investments" if cash and highly liquid investments are first used to pay off a portion of client-derived liabilities.

Finally, it should be noted that the major risk in the operation of a financial institution is that outflows of cash over a particular time period might exceed inflows of cash. Although the risk is derived from the *flows* of cash, the degree of protection against that risk rests on *stocks* (balance sheet values) of adequately liquid assets or adequate stockholders' equity relative to client-derived liabilities. Managers of all four types of financial institutions discussed in the remainder of this chapter are concerned with the risk of outflows of cash exceeding cash inflows. Astute investors should attempt to measure that degree of risk by the balance sheet ratios discussed above, as well as by other relationships unique to particular types of financial institutions.

COMMERCIAL BANKS

The basic and traditional business of commercial banks is accepting deposits from clients and investing funds so acquired in a variety of earning assets. These earning assets are of two types. One type is relatively safe and consists of U.S. Treasury securities and the securities of other U.S. governmental organizations as described in Chapter 5. As a general matter, these investments produce only minimal profit for the bank, but they do provide liquidity against possible deposit losses. The second type of investment consists primarily of loans to businesses and consumers, but also includes holdings of state and municipal bonds. This second type of asset produces greater returns, but is more risky because losses may be incurred, and because even solvent loans and good-quality state and municipal bonds are not easily converted into cash should the bank face liquidity problems.

In addition to these banking functions, commercial banks provide a variety of ancillary services, which for some banks are additional sources of important income. These include the operation of trust departments, the handling of corporate securities as transfer agents or registrars, the sale and redemption of travelers' checks, cashiers' checks, and bank drafts, the issuance of letters of credit for international trade and the acceptance of drafts drawn against these letters, the sale and redemption of federal, state, and municipal securities, and the operation of foreign exchange departments.

Since passage of the Bank Holding Company Act of 1970, many banks have additionally begun branching into other financial services that offer new and attractive opportunities for enhanced earnings. Although this section of this chapter deals with commercial banks from an investment point of view, the suggestions contained here should be supplemented with at least some understanding of the important subject of money and banking. This is especially true with regard to bank regulation and to the impact of general monetary conditions upon the operations of commercial banks.

Commercial banks are regulated by the Comptroller of the Currency, for national banks, and by appropriate state authorities, for state banks. In addition, banks belonging to the Federal Reserve System are regulated by the Board of Governors of the Federal Reserve System. Most banks have deposit insurance, which also subjects them to the supervision of the Federal Deposit Insurance Corporation.

Balance sheets of commercial banks

The major assets and liabilities of all United States commercial banks are shown in Figure 14–2. Individual banks publish quarterly balance sheets, which are available from the banks and are also published in local newspapers as required by law. As a general matter, the proportional mix of individual bank balance sheets can be compared with an aggregate balance sheet for the industry, such as that in Figure 14–2, in order to obtain perspective on how an individual bank compares with the industry. But it should be noted that an aggregate industry balance sheet gives dominant weight to large banks, and thus it may be less than a perfect guide for analyzing smaller local banks.

Asset leverage of banks may be measured by the proportional mix of assets. In Figure 14–2 it is seen that U.S. commercial banks had just over 15% of their assets in cash form at the end of 1971 and an additional 13% in highly liquid investments. Just over two thirds of total assets were in prime earning form: loans and bonds issued by states and municipalities. The other category accounted for the remaining 4%.

Increased asset leverage results when banks decrease the proportion of U.S. governmental securities in their portfolios and increase loans

FIGURE 14-2

Condensed assets and liabilities of all U.S. commercial banks December 31, 1971

Assets

	Millions of dollars	Percentage of total
Cash and cash-type holdings		
Currency and coin	$ 7,607	
Reserves with Federal Reserve Bank	24,483	
Deposits with other banks	26,535	
Items in process of clearing	38,721	
Total	$100,346	15.5%
Investments held primarily for liquidity		
U.S. Treasury Securities	65,368	
Securities of other U.S. Gov't. Agencies and Corporations	17,980	
Total	$ 83,348	12.9
Investments held primarily for income		
Obligations of states and subdivisions	82,644	
Other securities	4,360	
Federal funds & repurchase agreements	19,975	
Loans and discounts	330,562	
Total	$437,541	67.7
Other assets		
Bank premises, etc.	10,338	
Other assets	14,710	
Total	$ 25,048	3.9
Total assets	$646,283	100.0%

Liabilities and equities

Client-derived liabilities		
Demand deposits	$264,084	
Time deposits	278,826	
Total	$542,910	84.0%
Other liabilities		
Miscellaneous liabilities	49,456	
Reserves on loans and securities	6,458	
Capital notes & debentures	3,054	
Total	$ 59,068	9.1
Stockholders' equity		
Equity capital	44,405	6.9
Total liabilities and equity	$646,283	100.0%

Source: *Annual Report of the Federal Deposit Insurance Corporation 1971* (Washington, D.C.: Federal Deposit Insurance Corporation, June, 1972).

or holdings of state and municipal bonds. Such a shift would tend to increase both return and risk. Over recent decades, U.S. banks as a whole have moved strongly in the direction of increased asset leverage, as can be seen from the data in Figure 14-3. Taking the total bank portfolio of both investments and loans as equal to 100% (i.e., excluding

FIGURE 14–3
Loans and investments of U.S. commercial banks (proportional mix, 1950, 1960, 1970, 1972)

	December 1950	December 1960	December 1970	December 1972
U.S. government securities.	48.9%	30.4%	13.8%	11.7%
Other (primarily tax-exempt) securities	9.7	10.7	19.3	20.4
Total investments.	58.6%	41.1%	33.1%	32.1%
Commercial and industrial loans	17.5%	21.5%	25.2%	23.3%
Real estate loans	10.7	14.2	16.2	17.2
Consumer loans	6.1	10.3	12.0	12.4
Other loans	7.1	12.9	13.5	15.0
Total loans.	41.4%	58.9%	66.9%	67.9%
Total loans and investments.	100.0%	100.0%	100.0%	100.0%
Total loans in billions of dollars.	$124.8	$200.8	$446.8	$568.1

Source: Federal Reserve Bulletin.

cash items and other assets), U.S. governmental securities have declined from almost 49% of loans and investments in 1950 to about 12% in 1972. Holdings of other securities, of which tax-exempt securities predominate, have risen from just under 10% to just over 20%. The proportion of commercial and industrial loans (the traditional earning asset) has risen from 17.5% to 23.3%, and other types of loans have also risen proportionally, so that loans as a group have increased from 41.4% to 67.9%. While one might argue that the proportions of 1950 were distorted by the financing of World War II, the same general trends are apparent if 1960 is used as a starting date. Insofar as the past two and one half decades can be used as a guide, the policy of commercial banks clearly has been an aggressive movement toward boosting bank earnings through increased asset leverage.

On the liability side of the composite balance sheet of Figure 14–2, it will be noticed that banks are one of the most highly leveraged forms of business activity, having a total of 93.1% of resources derived from creditors and only 6.9% from stockholders. One important measure of bank risk-taking on the liability side of the balance sheet is the ratio of deposits to stockholders' equity. This ratio ($542.9/$44.4 = 12.2) has also risen during the quarter century since the end of World War II, indicating further the increased risk posture of American commercial banks.

Deposits, which represent the major source of bank capital, have also changed considerably in the past quarter century. Demand deposits are an "interest-free" source of borrowed money, although related costs do exist in that a proportion of demand deposits must be maintained in the form of nonearning reserve requirements. Greater sophistication by corporate treasurers in better management of their idle cash resources

320

has meant that demand deposits have failed to increase in proportion to total bank deposits. As can be seen in Figure 14–4, demand deposits have declined from 72% of total deposits in 1950 to just under 40% in

FIGURE 14–4
Deposits of U.S. commercial banks (proportional mix, 1950, 1960, 1970, 1972)

	December 1950	December 1960	December 1970	December 1972
Demand deposits, adjusted*	72.0%	62.2%	43.8%	39.7%
Time deposits	28.0	37.8	56.2	60.3
Total deposits	100.0%	100.0%	100.0%	100.0%
Total deposits in billions of dollars	$130.2	$190.4	$405.9	$516.7

* Adjusted for interbank deposits, U.S. Government deposits, and cash items in process of collection.
Source: Federal Reserve Bulletin.

1972. The offsetting factor has been an increase in time deposits, which consist of individual savings accounts plus certificates of deposit. Time deposits are interest-bearing, and the trend apparent in Figure 14–4 has meant that interest costs have come to be a major operating expense of commercial banks.

One consequence of this trend is that banks must compete with other financial institutions for funds at market rates to a greater degree than was true in past years. Bank profitability has become increasingly subject to a squeeze in which rising interest costs on a greater proportion of bank deposits may not be passed on to borrowers.

"Other liabilities" (i.e., nondepositor debt) has also grown in importance over recent years. The chief components of this classification vary significantly from period to period as banks respond to changing monetary conditions and regulations. Chief items within this category are Eurodollar borrowings, commercial paper, federal funds, borrowings from the Federal Reserve banks, and capital notes and debentures.

A composite measure of bank risk, which combines both asset leverage and financial leverage is the ratio of "deposits at risk" to stockholders' equity. This is the bank version of the general ratio of "client-derived liabilities at risk" to stockholders' equity that was mentioned earlier. Drawing from the industry composite balance sheet in Figure 14–2, the composite risk measure would be 8.09 times, calculated as follows:

Total deposits		$542,910,000
Cash and cash-type holdings	$100,346,000	
Investments held primarily for liquidity	83,348,000	183,694,000
Deposits at risk		359,216,000
Stockholders' equity		44,405,000
Ratio of deposits at risk to stockholders' equity		8.09 times

A ratio for an individual bank above eight times would indicate greater than average composite leverage risk, while a ratio below eight times would indicate less than average risk. A variation of this ratio, also frequently used, is the ratio of risk assets to capital funds, in which risk assets are defined as total assets less cash and U.S. governmental securities.

One additional ratio that is significant for banks as well as other financial institutions is "book value per share." Similar ratios calculated for nonfinancial businesses are of limited meaning because the "actual" value of assets will probably deviate significantly from book value. In the case of banks and other financial institutions, however, almost all assets are of a monetary nature and are thus valued on a basis that approximates current value. There is very little opportunity for a bank asset to have a value appreciably different from that at which it is carried. The major variant among bank assets, then, is their earnings generating potential rather than their face value as such. For this reason, book value, being the sum of common stock capital, surplus, and undivided profits divided by the number of common shares outstanding, gives a good measure of the liquid assets being acquired by the common stock investor.

In those instances when market price is significantly below book value, either some assets are of questionable quality or a potential for gain exists. When market price is significantly above book value, the investor is paying a premium for a package of monetary assets that could be justified only if the bank management was somehow capable of producing greater-than-normal earnings or growth from the assets at its command.

Income statements of commercial banks

Figure 14–5 reveals that banks receive the major portion of their operating income, some 63%, from interest and fees received on loans. Interest on all securities, including U.S., state, municipal, and other types, provides an additional 23.5% of revenue. The higher earning potential of loans, as compared to investments in securities, can be noted from the fact that loans and discounts (in Figure 14–2) constituted 51% of total assets but supplied 63% of operating income, while the aggregate of all securities constituted 29% of total assets but supplied only 23.5% of total operating revenue. Trust departments generate 3.5%, and service charges on deposit accounts provide 3.4% of total operating income. In the analysis of an individual bank, this mix may vary. For example, a particular bank might do a large and profitable trust business, which would raise the proportion of income received from this source significantly above that for the banking industry as a whole.

FIGURE 14–5

INSURED U.S. COMMERCIAL BANKS
Condensed Income Statement
Year ended December 31, 1971

	Millions of dollars	Percentage of total
Operating income		
Interest and fees on loans	$23,069	63.4%
Interest on U.S. Treasury securities.	3,387	9.3
Interest on state and municipal bonds	3,127	8.6
Other interest and dividends.	2,026	5.6
Trust department income	1,258	3.5
Service charges on deposit accounts	1,231	3.4
Other charges	2,266	6.2
Total operating income	$36,364	100.0%
Operating expenses		
Salaries, wages, and employee benefits.	$ 8,395	23.1%
Interest on deposits.	12,218	33.5
Other interest	1,377	3.8
Net occupancy expense of bank premises	1,410	3.9
Provision for loan losses	867	2.4
Other operating expenses	5,384	14.8
Total operating expenses	$29,651	81.5%
Income before income taxes and security gains or losses.	$ 6,713	18.5%
Less applicable income taxes.	1,689	4.7
Income before security gains or losses	$ 5,024	13.8%
Net security gains	213	0.6
Net income before extraordinary items	$ 5,237	14.4%
Extraordinary charges	1	
Minority interest in consolidated subsidiaries	0	
Net income	$ 5,236	$14.4%

Source: Annual Report of the Federal Deposit Insurance Corporation (Washington, D.C.: Federal Deposit Insurance Corporation, June, 1972).

Operating expenses are those outlays necessary for the operation of the basic banking business. The two largest operating expenses are salaries, wages, and associated employee benefits; and interest paid on deposits. Along with other operating expenses, total operating expenses amounted to 81.5% of bank operating income in 1971. This ratio, the "operating ratio," is a rough measure of bank efficiency. It is less than a perfect measure because variations among banks in the type of business they stress (consumer loans versus business loans, trust business versus international banking, etc.) or in their propensity to seek additional income at the expense of additional risk (variations in the mix of securities and loans in the asset side of the balance sheet) will cause variations between banks that may not have precise meanings. Time trends in the operating ratio for a single bank, however, do indicate changes that are worthy of further investigation.

One particular operating expense is worthy of additional emphasis;

the provision for loan losses. Based on an amendment to bank accounting and reporting regulations enacted in 1969, the item "provision for loan losses" has been included as an operating expense. Prior to 1969, this item was deducted after the calculation of net operating income. Thus net operating income calculations before 1969 are not comparable with those of 1969 and later years. The new laws provide for an experience-based reserve for loan losses determined by one of three methods elected by each bank: (1) a loss ratio determined by the average percentage of loan losses experienced during the previous five years, with such a moving average being applied to average loans out-standing during the year, (2) actual net losses (gross losses less any recoveries) incurred in the current year; or (3) the build-up of a five-year average starting with actual net losses in 1969. The first of these three methods is used by most banks. In all cases, however, the total loan loss reserve cannot exceed 2.4% of loans outstanding at the end of the preceding year. The significance of the provision for loan losses, when considered in conjunction with changes in the actual loan-loss reserve, is that an estimate of actual bad debt losses can be made which will serve as an index of the quality of the bank's loan portfolio. A loan portfolio of marginal quality during years of economic prosperity may be regarded as a signal of potential disaster should an economic recession take place.

The procedure in making this calculation is to take the year-beginning loan-loss reserve (from the balance sheet), add the provision for loan losses (from the income statement), and subtract the year-end loan-loss reserve (from the ending balance sheet). The resulting figure is actual loan losses for the year, which may be expressed as a percentage of year-average loans outstanding to determine what proportion were bad.

Bank operating income less operating expenses gives a residual figure entitled "income before income taxes and security gains or losses." From this is subtracted an estimate of what the bank's tax liability would be if its taxes were based solely on operating income and expenses and without regard to securities gains and losses and extraordinary items. This income measure is important because it is the best indicator of bank earning power on a regular continuing basis. Increases or decreases in bank earnings before security gains or losses and extraordinary items come about only because of improvement or deterioration in the bank's basic efficiency.

Security gains (as in 1971) are added or losses are deducted next. The timing of a loss or gain on a security transaction is determined primarily by management, and results in part from tax considerations, in part from short-run decisions to use funds for other purposes such as an increase in commercial loan demand, and in part from management decisions to influence the reported net income of the bank. In the long run, net income after securities transactions and extraordinary items may be a better estimate of basic bank earning ability, but in the short run this net income figure is so susceptible to wide fluctuations resulting from portfolio decisions and tax policies that the net income figure, from quarter to quarter or from year to year, is a poor measure of the consistency of bank profitability. In summary, then, income before security gains or losses is the best measure of bank performance for a particular year or other period of time, and it should be used as the appropriate earnings figure in assessing bank profitability.

From Figures 14–2 and 14–5 it is observed that U.S. commercial banks earned (before security gains or losses) $5,024 million on equity capital of $44,405 million, or a rate of return of 11.3%. However, the same earnings constituted only 0.8% of total assets of $646,283 million. This again points to the basic nature of the banking business: it is essentially a highly leveraged operation in which a modest return earned upon total assets is leveraged up by a very high proportion of debt, primarily in the form of customer deposits, to a reasonable rate of return upon stockholders' equity. The major factor affecting the rate of return is likely to be changes in the level of interest rates, which in recent years have fluctuated widely. Barring a significant change in regulatory philosophy, which might impose ceilings upon bank lending rates and thus remove the banking industry from being a viable and flexible financial institution within our economic system, banks tend to adjust the interest rates charged on loans to changes in the cost of their funds. Rates paid on various types of time deposits are competitive, so that if banks fail to pay within the same range that can be earned on U.S. Treasury bills, commercial paper, or savings accounts in savings and loan associations, they will be unable to maintain or increase their deposit base from which a return is generated.

Future trends for commercial banks

Up to the present commercial banks have operated primarily as middlemen in the financial flow process, charging borrowers a rate sufficient to pay for the cost of deposits and other borrowed funds, and raising or lowering this rate as money conditions change. As long as both loan and deposit terms are of short maturity, banks are not likely to be squeezed for any extended time by a rise in interest costs that they cannot pass along to those who borrow from the banks. On a short-term basis, however, they are often squeezed.

The risks that a bank faces and that should be studied by potential investors include a lengthening of loan maturities such that higher interest costs could not be quickly recouped; a rise in some other category of operating costs for a particular bank above national or regional averages, so that the bank experiences a cost squeeze; excessive asset leverage or excessive financial leverage; and the possibility of politically inspired legislation to "lower interest rates to benefit the consumer" that would have as a side effect the weakening of banking as a viable industry. Another important risk lies in changed patterns of competition between banks and savings institutions as a result of new regulatory procedures. This subject is discussed in the next section of this chapter.

Variations among banks in their levels of earnings and in their rates of growth are likely to arise primarily from variations in the profitability of various types of assets and the cost of various sources of capital. Traditional commercial banking, however, is being influenced by a new variable, the ability to expand into new nonbank activities via the device of bank holding companies. *Bank holding companies* had been used for many years as a device to achieve some of the advantages of branch banking in states where branch banking as such was not allowed. Traditional bank holding companies have owned and controlled a large number of individual commercial banks.

In 1967, the Union Bank of Los Angeles, having a strong position in real estate lending, sought to acquire Western Mortgage Company, the largest mortgage servicing company on the West Coast. To effect this acquisition without unduly penalizing earnings by the required amortization of the premium over book value ("goodwill") that would have been paid, Union Bank formed Union America, a one-bank holding company, which then acquired the stock of both the bank and the mortgage company. Other banks followed this lead, in part to diversify into activities not a traditional part of banking, and in part to raise capital through the sale of short-term paper by the holding company at a time when Regulation Q of the Federal Reserve System prevented regulated banks from paying competitive rates for funds.

Initially unregulated, one-bank holding companies were brought under Federal Reserve control in 1970 by an amendment to the Bank Holding Company Act of 1956. The amendment permits one-bank holding companies to engage in activities "closely related to banking or managing or controlling banks," including such activities as leasing, factoring, mortgage financing, consumer and commercial financing, providing financial advisory services for real estate investment trusts, supplying electronic data processing services, making certain types of equity investments in community rehabilitation and development corporations, and acting as an insurance agent or broker under certain limited conditions. It has not yet been determined if one-bank holding companies will be allowed to enter the savings and loan business. A decision permitting such entry would have major significance for the structure of deposit-type institutions in the United States.

With or without entry into the savings and loan business, the entry of many commercial banks into non-traditional fields via the one-bank holding company device means that those banks whose managements are likely to prove unusually successful in new fields in which they choose to specialize may well prove more profitable and more growth-oriented than banks that stay with traditional ways. These opportunities, however, are not without risk, and potential investors should assure themselves that banks venturing into new areas have competent and qualified management capable of successfully overseeing these new activities.

Banks, particularly those in major metropolitan areas, are also evolving away from their traditional mix of activities with greatly expanded activity in an area once preserved for just a few banks—international banking. Foreign deposits as a percentage of total deposits (in October 1972) for leading U.S. banks operating overseas were as follows:[1]

First National City Bank	46.2%
Morgan Guaranty	38.0
Chase Manhattan	34.3
Bank of America	33.1
Bankers' Trust	31.2
First National Bank, Chicago	29.8
Continental Illinois, Chicago	26.9
Manufacturers Hanover	24.6
Chemical Bank	21.0
Security Pacific	15.5

Initially serving their U.S. multinational corporate clients and operating in the Eurodollar market, U.S. commercial banks in recent years have sought foreign nonbank customers and have entered into a variety of merchant banking, money management, and equity investments in foreign banks and financial service companies. As with new and innovative activities within the United States, expanded international banking, if pursued successfully and with due attention to the need for exceptionally competent management, offers yet one more avenue for extra enhancement of bank earnings, and hence of potential return to investors.[2]

SAVINGS AND LOAN ASSOCIATIONS

The primary business of a savings and loan association is accepting savings from the public and investing the bulk of these savings in the financing of residential structures. As was seen in Figure 14–1, savings and loan associations are the second largest type of financial intermediary in the United States, second only to commercial banks. As a financial

[1] Andrew Brimmer, "Multinational Banks and the Management of Monetary Policy in the United States," *Journal of Finance*, May, 1963, p. 441.

[2] For further perspective on the services that international banks provide U.S. multinational firms, see David K. Eiteman and Arthur I. Stonehill, *Multinational Business Finance* (Addison-Wesley Publishing Company, 1973), Chapter 5.

institution, they are highly specialized and their operations are closely regulated. Savings and loan associations operate under either federal or state charters. All federal associations are mutual organizations, while state associations may be either mutual or stockholder-owned, depending upon state law. In the eastern part of the United States, mutual savings bank operate on a basis somewhat similar to that of mutual savings and loan associations.

Stock-type associations are the only type whose shares are available to investors, so it is with this type that this chapter is concerned. Of the 665 stock-type associations in the United States at the end of 1972, 99 were in California and 173 were in Texas.[3] In terms of assets, however, the California associations had $28,620 million of assets or 56% of the total of all stock associations. The California associations include the only publicly owned associations of sufficient size to be of interest to most investors.

The savings and loan industry is one in which careful analysis of prospects for the industry as a whole, including regulation and taxation, is of greater importance for successful selection of stocks than is detailed comparison between competing companies. For that reason, the remainder of this section will focus to a greater degee on ways of appraising the industry as a whole, with only secondary consideration being given to comparisons between individual companies.

Nature of the industry

The savings and loan industry is the major supplier of credit to residential mortgages. At the end of 1972, savings and loan associations held $187.1 billion of residential property mortgages out of the national total of $422.8 billion, or 44%. The second largest lender in the residential mortgage market was commercial banks. In terms of attracting savings, savings and loan associations held $207.3 billion of what might be called "over-the-counter" savings, or almost 35% of the national total of $596.4 billion. Savings and loans were the second-largest holder of over-the-counter savings, second only to commercial banks, which had $276.1 billion or 46% of the national total.

Over the last quarter century or so, the participation of savings and loan associations both in mortgage lending and in the attraction of savings deposits has increased very rapidly. With growth of the industry has come, in general, an increase in profitability of stock-owned associations. The dominant factor in future earnings increases for stock-owned associations, moreover, is likely to be continued growth. Growth for savings and loan associations depends, first, on their ability to attract

---

[3] All statistics on the savings and loan industry used in this section are from the *1973 Savings and Loan Fact Book* (Chicago: U.S. Savings and Loan League).

additional savings at competitive rates, and second, on their ability to expand their loan portfolios at rates that will cover the cost of savings plus operating expenses.

Traditionally savings and loan associations have paid a slightly higher rate for savings deposits than have their most similar competitor for this type of savings, the commercial banks. During the 1950s and much of the 1960s, the passbook savings account was the major savings instrument used by savings and loan associations. Individuals or companies having such passbook accounts could deposit or withdraw funds at any time, and interest was paid quarterly (for most California associations), semiannually, or annually, depending upon the policy of the association. As interest rates rose in the late 1960s and early 1970s, associations were threatened with "disintermediation," a process by which savers remove major portions of their savings from institutions and invest the funds directly. The major threat at this time came from the fact that interest levels on U.S. Treasury bills rose above the legal ceilings that savings institutions were allowed to pay on passbook accounts. As the minimum purchase size of Treasury bills at that time was $1,000, savers sensitive to interest rates began to remove funds from savings and loan associations and invest them directly in higher-yielding U.S. Treasury bills or other money-market instruments.

Subsequent legislation allowed savings and loan associations to raise the maximum rates paid on passbook accounts, to increase the frequency of compounding (thus increasing the effective yield), and to issue other types of savings documents in addition to passbook accounts. The result has been that certificates and special accounts paying higher rates than do regular passbook accounts increased from 11.7% of total savings in 1966 to 49.4% of total savings at the end of 1972.

On the savings side, future expansion and increased profits for the savings and loan industry will depend upon their ability to attract savings at competitive rates. Success will depend to a very large extent upon trends in interest rates because major and sudden increases in the level of interest rates in the United States and world economies is the event most likely to bring about a renewed period of disintermediation and again a necessary response. The response to any major change in interest levels, as well as to more slowly evolving competition from other types of institutions, lies primarily with regulatory bodies and only secondarily with the ability of individual associations to implement new types of savings arrangements allowed to them.

The second factor necessary for continued growth in savings and loan associations assets and thus in profits is a continuation of profitable lending opportunities. One variable is the type of loan that associations are allowed to make. At one time associations were limited exclusively to mortgages for the construction or purchase of residential property.

Changes in the laws in the early 1970s expanded the range of possible loans to such residential-related areas as "equipping" loans for ranges, dishwashers, refrigerators, draperies, central airconditioning, and built-in television sets. Savings and loan associations are also now allowed to finance the purchase of mobile homes and vacation homes, and they can invest up to 10% of their total loan portfolio outside of the state in which they are domiciled. Since 1971, savings and loan associations have also been able to make loans within 100 miles of any branch within their state; previously the limit was 100 miles from the principal office regardless of state boundaries. Possible future extension of savings and loan lending ability that would have an impact on the mix of earning assets and also serve to facilitate continued growth would be expansion of lending abilities to nonresidential areas, including consumer credit and business loans. As the spectrum of lending opportunities broadens, potential benefits should include improved diversification and improved liquidity.

Continued expansion of the traditional mortgage loan business depends upon several variables. Clearly a major factor is new housing starts. Turnover of existing loans as already-mortgaged property is sold and remortgaged is a second factor. Although most residential mortgages are written for an initial 20 to 30 year maturity, the average life of a mortgage loan is only 8 to 10 years, because homeowners move up to newer and/or more expensive homes as their level of affluence rises, because they are transferred or move on their own to another location as a result of ever-increasing job mobility, or because of such other events as unemployment, death, or divorce. Yet a third factor influencing the increased demand for mortgage funds is inflation and the population-induced rise in property values. Sequential sales of a single piece of property over the years typically are at higher and higher prices, so every change of ownership that leads to a newly written mortgage also leads to a greater dollar amount of mortgages. As was suggested earlier, a key factor in the analysis of savings and loan common stock is the probability that such increased funds as will be available from increased savings will also be employed profitably in an expanding loan portfolio.

Regulation of the savings and loan industry

The savings and loan industry possesses a central bank in the form of the Federal Home Loan Bank System, created in July, 1932. The System is organized much as the Federal Reserve System is for commercial banks. The Federal Home Loan Bank Board, situated in Washington, D.C., is an independent agency within the executive branch of the federal government. The Board is the center of the System and the locus of major policy decisions. The Federal Home Loan Bank System is organized into twelve regional Federal Home Loan Banks, which carry out the actual functions of the System in its dealing with member institutions. Members of the Federal Home Loan Bank System consist of individual savings and loan associations. All federally chartered associations are required by law to belong to the System, and membership is open on a voluntary basis to state-chartered associations as well as to mutual savings banks and life insurance companies. At the end of 1972, the System had 4,412 members, as follows:

Federally chartered associations.	2,044
State-chartered associations, insured by the Federal	
Savings and Loan Insurance Corporation	2,147
Other state-chartered associations	171
Mutual savings banks.	48
Life insurance companies	2
Total membership	4,412

At the end of 1972, there were 1,257 noninsured state-chartered savings and loan associations. Of these, 171 associations belonged to the Federal Home Loan Bank System and 1,086 associations did not belong.

The fundamental purpose of the Federal Home Loan Bank System is to provide a central credit facility to supplement the resources of its member institutions. In doing so, the System borrows funds in the national capital markets and lends these funds to the various member associations. The maximum legal loan to any individual association is limited to 50% of total savings balances; policy of the Federal Home Loan Bank Board, however, is to limit member borrowings to 25% of the association's total withdrawable savings balances unless the advances are for the purpose of meeting withdrawal demands of savers. The Federal Home Loan Bank Board also has authority to establish maximum rates that associations may pay on various types of savings.

A second organization whose activities have the substance of regulation in certain matters is the Federal Savings and Loan Insurance Corporation, created by Congress in 1934 to insure savings accounts at savings and loan associations. At the present time, individual savings accounts are insured for $20,000. At the end of 1972, membership in the Federal Savings and Loan Insurance Corporation consisted of all 2,044 federally chartered associations and 2,147 state-chartered associations. Insured savings and loan associations are subject to annual examinations to ensure their compliance with a body of regulations intended to protect both savers and borrowers.

For many years, savings and loan associations were in effect not subject to federal income taxes because they were able to transfer to loan-loss reserves sums equivalent to what would have otherwise been taxable net income. Changes in the tax laws in 1963 and again in 1969 revised the situation so that the allowable percentage of net income transferable to loss reserves (i.e., "tax free" earnings prior to deduction of loss provisions) decreases from 60% in 1969 to 40% in 1979. Thus the effective federal income tax rate on savings and loan associations is gradually being increased from about 19.2% in 1969 to about 28.8% in 1979, assuming a regular 48% corporate income tax rate. Associations are also subject to a 10% additional tax on certain "tax preference" items, primarily additions to the loan-loss reserves in excess of actual bad-debt experience. Tax rules with regard to additions to the loan-loss reserve stipulate that such additions can be made only if the reserve does not exceed 6% of loans outstanding, or if net worth including reserves does not exceed 12% of savings.

Balance sheets of savings and loan associations

A condensed statement of condition (balance sheet) for all savings and loan associations in the United States as of December 31, 1972, is shown in Figure 14–6. Cash and cash-type holdings constituted 1.1% of total assets, while investments held primarily for liquidity constituted an additional 8.9%. The loan portfolio of all institutions amounted to 86.3% of total assets, while other assets were 3.6% of the total. The major liability of savings and loan associations is savings deposits, which supplied 85.1% of total funds in 1972. Other liabilities provided an additional 8.9% of resources, while the stockholder equity cushion was only 6.1%.

The major operating risk of a savings and loan association arises from the dilemma that the major asset type, mortgage loans, is long-term in nature while the major liability, savings deposits, is short-term. The risk is less than might appear just from the balance sheet, however, because payments on mortgage loans are almost always made monthly, supplying a ready cash recovery of loan principal, even though the loan itself carries a final maturity of 20 to 30 years. Also, as mentioned, the maturity mix of savings deposits has been increased substantially in recent years with the advent of various types of fixed-maturity savings certificates. Liquidity is also less of a risk than might be apparent because of the existence of the Federal Home Loan Bank as a lender of last resort in the event of unanticipated savings withdrawals. Such safety is primarily for the benefit of savers rather than owners, however, for a set of conditions that would cause use of this emergency source would almost certainly cause losses for stockholders.

In addition to liquidity risk, the other asset-derived risk is that of bad loans. *Scheduled items* denotes mortgage loans contractually delinquent 90 days or more and real estate owned as a result of foreclosure, repossession, or deed in lieu of foreclosure. When data are available, scheduled items as a percentage of outstanding mortgage loans gives a good measure of basic loan quality.

332

FIGURE 14–6

ALL SAVINGS AND LOAN ASSOCIATIONS
Condensed Statement of Condition
December 31, 1972

Assets

	Millions of dollars	Percentage of total
Cash and cash-type holdings		
Cash on hand and in banks	$ 2,673	1.1%
Investments held primarily for liquidity		
Regulatory liquid investments	17,106	
Other legal investments	4,723	
	21,829	8.9
Investments held primarily for income		
Mortgage loans outstanding	206,367	
Other loans	3,921	
	210,288	86.3
Other assets		
Federal Home Loan Bank stock.	1,675	
Buildings and equipment.	3,300	
Real estate owned	600	
Other assets	3,205	
	8,780	3.6
Total assets.	$243,570	100.0%

Liabilities and equities

Client-derived liabilities		
Savings deposits.	$207,290	85.1%
Other liabilities		
Federal Home Loan Bank advances.	7,974	
Other borrowed money	1,873	
Loans in process	6,215	
All other liabilities	5,459	
	21,521	8.9
Stockholders' equity		
General and unallocated reserves	14,759	6.1
Total liabilities and equities	$243,570	100.0%

Note: Percentages may not add due to rounding
Source: *1973 Savings and Loan Fact Book* (Chicago: U.S. Savings and Loan League, 1973) page 94.

An alternate formulation of the same measure is the ratio of real estate owned and loans to facilitate (taken from the complete balance sheets filed with the Federal Home Loan Bank Board each quarter) to total assets. *Real estate owned* consists of property the title of which has been returned to the association, or of property in judgment, which has been foreclosed but is still subject to the defaulted borrower's right to redeem it for a specific time period. *Loans to facilitate* arise when an association disposes of property acquired through foreclosure on especially generous terms, such as low down payments, long maturities, or low interest rates. Both categories were individually less than 0.3% of total association assets at the end of 1972. Should the proportion for either rise above 0.3%, or should the combined proportion rise above 0.6% for a particular association, such as higher ratio would be an indicator of a loan portfolio of questionable quality.

Income statements of savings and loan associations

An aggregate income statement for the savings and loan industry for 1972 is shown in Figure 14–7. This statement is based on the combined results of both mutual and stock associations, and certain terms

FIGURE 14–7

ALL SAVINGS AND LOAN ASSOCIATIONS
Condensed Statement of Income
Year ended December 31, 1972

	Millions of dollars	Percentage of total revenue
Revenues		
Interest on mortgage loans.	$12,998	83.1%
Loan commissions and fees	923	5.9
Other sources	1,720	11.0
Total revenue	$15,641	100.0%
Expenses		
Salaries and wages	$ 1,138	7.3%
Other operating expenses	1,369	8.7
Interest on savings accounts	10,306	65.9
Interest on other borrowed money	489	3.1
Total expenses	$13,302	85.0%
Operating income	$ 2,339	14.9%
Nonoperating charges, net of non- operating income and including federal income taxes	$ 590	3.7%
Net income, transfers to reserves, and undivided profits	$ 1,749	11.2%

Source: 1973 Savings and Loan Fact Book (Chicago: U.S. Savings and Loan League, 1973), pages 103–105. Certain dollar amounts derived by application of data published in percentage form only.

have been revised from the original source to reflect better the realities of savings and loan operations. Some 83.1% of total revenue was derived from interest earned on mortgage loans, while an additional 5.9% came from mortgage loan fees, commissions, and premiums. The remaining 11.0% of income came from "other sources."

The biggest single expense of the industry was interest paid on savings accounts, which absorbed 65.9% of revenue. Interest on other borrowed money, such as advances from the Federal Home Loan Banks, absorbed 3.1% of revenue, while wages and salaries accounted for 7.3% of revenue. Other operating expenses took 8.7% of revenue, and the sum of income taxes and all nonoperating charges and gains resulted in a net expense of 3.7%.

For the industry as a whole, net income, including transfers to reserves and undistributed profit, amounted to 11.2% of total revenue. This residual is available for the payment of cash dividends to stockholders only to the extent that it is income after payment of income taxes. That is, dividends cannot be paid from any portion of the tax-free transfer of earnings to loss reserves.

Legislative reform for banks and savings institutions

The present regulatory system for banks and savings institutions was to a very large extent created after the financial failures of the 1930s. Public concern with protecting depositors from loss has been the dominant philosophy, and the operating details of the regulations have tended to prevent direct and open competition between banks and various types of savings institutions. One example would be Regulation Q of the Federal Reserve System, which establishes maximum rates of interest that may be paid on savings accounts, and which has been used to keep the rates that commercial banks may pay on passbook savings accounts below the rate payable by savings institutions.

There is a strong likelihood that the basic regulatory philosophy will change in the years ahead, primarily because of fundamental changes within our financial system. The impact of the computer on established procedures for data and information processing has been fundamental, as has been the trend toward use of credit cards rather than cash or checks to handle many personal transactions. Higher interest rates have unsettled traditional savings patterns because rates of interest allowed on savings accounts were not allowed to rise to market levels. Availability of other attractive money market instruments such as U.S. treasury bills, governmental agency securities, commercial paper, and bankers' acceptances has tended to increase the competition for savings dollars.

Fundamental reform has been proposed by the President's Commission on Financial Structure and Regulation, more commonly called the "Hunt Commission" after its chairman, Reed O. Hunt. The Hunt Commission was appointed to look at the possibility that depository institutions were being overregulated with attendant damage to the long-run vitality of that industry. The recommendations of the Hunt Commission, if carried out, would have a major impact upon competition between depository institutions within the United States and of course would have important consequences for the owners of those institutions. The major proposals would give broader flexibility to mutual savings banks and savings and loan associations in establishing their assets and liabilities. They would be allowed to make short-term consumer loans and thus reduce their present dependency upon the long-term mortgage market. They would be allowed to issue credit cards and to offer checking accounts. These changes, it is hoped, would lessen the vulnerability of savings institutions to sudden loss of deposits when the level of interest rises by allowing them greater managerial flexibility.

In return for this greater flexibility, savings institutions would lose the protective shelter of Regulation Q and would lose some of the special income tax advantages that they hold vis-a-vis commercial banks. Under the proposed reforms, all lenders would be granted certain tax credits on mortgage loans, meaning that commercial banks could compete in the mortgage loan market on the same basis as the savings institutions. Some bankers believe that the gains to banking would be greater than the loss of exclusive control of checking accounts because the trend in our economy is away from the use of checks and toward increased use of credit cards. In addition, elimination of Regulation Q would allow banks greater freedom to compete directly on an interest rate basis for passbook savings accounts.

The hypothesis that underlies the recommedations of the Hunt Commission is that the trend in the United States is likely to be toward "one stop" financial services for the typical household. A single institution conceivably could hold the mortgage on the family home and the loan on the automobile, could finance personal credit needs through personal loans or by allowing overdrafts on checking accounts or credit cards, and could provide computer-based facilities for the transfer of funds for such diverse household transactions as paychecks, shopping expenses, and the payment of utility bills. If both commercial banks and savings institutions are given freedom to compete for supplying this broad range of financial services, the consumer will be served. Competition between banks and savings institutions is likely to increase, however, with significant results for investors who purchase the common shares of either or both types of depository institutions.

LIFE INSURANCE COMPANIES

Life insurance companies agree to provide financial protection against death for an indefinite period that lasts until the death of the insured. Financial statements of all types of companies, including manufacturing and retailing, as well as financial, are provisional because they constitute periodic reports about what can be measured with finality only on final liquidation of the enterprise. With the passage of time, the assumptions under which the periodic reports were prepared may prove to be wrong. The very long-lived nature of life insurance contracts gives even greater emphasis to the provisional nature of periodic financial statements for life insurance companies. The major liabilities of life insurance companies, and thus the major determinant of eventual profitability, are promises to pay sums of money at indefinite future dates based upon probabilities of death. All insurance company financial statements must be viewed with the thought that future events may well render current periodic reports, after the fact, to have been wrong.

Underwriting operations of life insurance companies

Underwriting is the process by which an insurance company determines whether and on what basis it will accept an application to insure a particular type of risk. Life insurance is sold to persons wishing to provide financial protection to some beneficiary, usually a family but on occasion a business or other parties who would otherwise experience a financial loss in the event that the person died prematurely. Because all persons die eventually, the basic business of the life insurance company is underwriting the risk associated with premature death. The first step in the underwriting process involves determining expected length of life from mortality tables, which have been compiled over many years and which give the ratio of deaths to those living at each age. The second step is to assure that an adequately large number of policies is sold so that actual death experience among the many policyholders of each age group approximates the assumptions based on the mortality tables. The third step in the underwriting process involves determining what premiums the insured must pay to the insurance company so that total premium receipts in each year, plus possibly a portion of earnings upon the portfolio, are adequate to pay the death benefit claims expected in that year. The fourth step is one wherein the company determines the "load," or amount of operating expenses that must be added to the premium to pay the ongoing costs of the insurance business itself and to provide any underwriting (as distinct from investment) profit.

Life insurance companies sell a wide variety of policies, all of which are combinations of three basic types: term insurance, straight life insurance, and annuities. The simplest type of life insurance is a *term policy*, in which the policy runs for a stated period, perhaps five to ten years, after which it expires. Payment is made to the beneficiary only if the insured dies within the term. An *individual straight life*, also called *ordinary life* or *whole life*, policy provides insurance coverage for a person's entire life unless the policy is terminated by lapse (failure to pay the premium) or surrender for its cash value. *Annuities* are insurance

contracts that guarantee a regular current income for life or for a specified period of years. An annuity for life is, in some respects, the reverse
of a straight life policy.

The basic nature of a term policy can be explained with reference
to a one-year policy issued to a 23-year-old person. According to the
Commissioners 1958 Standard Ordinary Mortality Table (one of a
number of tables used by insurance companies), during the period
1950–1954 there were 1.89 deaths per thousand persons 23 years old.
If the company wrote $1,000 policies on 100,000 persons 23 years old
on the assumption that their mortality experience would duplicate that
of the table, the company would anticipate that 189 of these persons
would die in the ensuing year. Looking only at insurance, the company
would have to collect $189,000 from its 100,000 policyholders in order
to have funds to pay $1,000 for each of the 189 expected deaths. Thus
the "pure" premium would be $1.89 per insured person.

Most individuals want insurance coverage over a major portion if
not the entirety of their life. Term insurance, described earlier, expires
at the end of the term and a new policy must be taken out if continued
coverage is wanted. One potential difficulty in obtaining a new term
policy to replace an expired term policy is that insurance companies
usually require medical examinations for those whom they insure so
as to protect themselves against adverse selection by applicants who
know they will soon die. As a person ages, he might become unable
to pass a physical examination. This difficulty can be circumvented by
taking out renewable term insurance, in which the policy can be renewed
or extended without further medical examination. This is possible because if the renewable provision was stated in the initial policy, there
can be no adverse selection several years later at the date of potential
renewal.

Term insurance presents another difficulty for the insured, for as
he grows older his premium will rise. Continuing with our earlier example of a one-year term policy, rather than the more common five- and
ten-year policies, the annual "pure" premium would rise with each decade of age as follows:

Age	"Pure" premium for one-year term policy of $1,000
23	$ 1.89
33	2.32
43	4.53
53	10.89
63	26.57
73	63.26
83	139.38
93	289.30
99	1,000.00

As the insured aged, he would find it increasingly difficult to pay the increasing premium costs. To avoid rising premiums on sequential term policies, one can take out straight life insurance. Under such a policy, a level or constant premium is paid each year until death, at which time the benefits are paid to the beneficiary. The level premium will be higher than the term premium in early years, but lower than the term premium in later years.

The use of level premium plans causes life insurance companies to become investment companies as well. The substance of the level premium plan is that a portion of the premium goes to pay the equivalent of the term premium, while the remainder is invested in a "savings account" for the policy holder. This savings account, technically called the *policyholder's reserve*, earns interest at a contractual rate established at the time the policy is written. As the policyholder's reserve builds up over the years through additional premiums plus earnings on past accumulations, it is necessary to "purchase" smaller and smaller amounts of term insurance. At the end of 30 years, for example, the pure premium per $1,000 of insurance would have risen to $10.89. If by this time, however, the policyholder's reserve had increased to, say, $600, it would be necessary to purchase only $400 of pure term insurance at a premium cost of 40% of $10.89 or $4.35. By the end of the policy period, the "savings account" would have grown to $1,000, and the death benefit payment would amount to giving to the beneficiary the $1,000 balance in the insured's "savings account."

The level premium type of insurance policy provides funds for the portfolio of the insurance company. Even a term policy written for five or ten years has itself a level premium over this interval and thus has, to a modest degree, a policyholder's reserve during some of this interval. In any event, the insurance company is receiving funds that it must invest and on which it is calculating an imputed interest rate to add to the reserve of the policyholder. If the insurance company can earn more on the funds than it has contracted to add to the policyholder's reserve, the difference belongs to the stockholders of the company. This is offset, of course, by the fact that if the funds should earn less than the contractual rate, earnings on the stockholders' equity cushion would have to make up the difference. As a general matter, contractual rates are established below what the company thinks it will be able to earn. In recent years, the contractual rate has been 3% or $3\frac{1}{2}\%$, while insurance companies have earned a net rate (after imputed income taxes) of about $5\frac{1}{2}\%$.

Balance sheets of life insurance companies

An aggregate balance sheet for all United States life insurance companies, as of year-end 1972, is shown in Figure 14–8. Account headings

FIGURE 14–8

ALL UNITED STATES LIFE INSURANCE COMPANIES
Aggregate Balance Sheet
December 31, 1972

Assets

Cash and cash-type holdings
Cash . . . . $ 1,918   0.8%
Investments held primarily for liquidity
Government securities   11,372   4.7
Investments held primarily for income
Corporate bonds   86,140
Corporate stocks   26,845
Mortgages   76,948
Real estate.   7,295
Policy loans   18,003
                          Total. $215,231   89.8
Other Assets
Miscellaneous assets . . . . $ 11,209   4.7
                          Total assets. $239,730 100.0%

Liabilities and equities

	Millions of dollars	Percentage of total
Client-derived liabilities		
Policy reserves–life	$128,257	
Policy reserves–health	4,347	
Policy reserves–annuities	55,387	
Policy reserves–other	4,155	
Total.	$192,146	80.2%
Other liabilities		
Policy dividends.	11,061	
Other obligations	17,568	
Special surplus funds	3,264	
Total.	$ 31,893	13.3
Stockholders' equtiy		
Unassigned surplus	13,967	
Capital (stock companies)	1,724	
Total.	$ 15,691	6.5
Total liabilities and equities	$239,730	100.0%

Source: *Life Insurance Fact Book 1973* (New York: Institute of Life Insurance, 1973), pages 66, 67, 70.

again have been regrouped under the standard format used earlier for both banks and for savings and loan associations. From Figure 14–8 it can be seen that life insurance companies keep a very small portion of their assets (less than 1%) in the form of cash, and only a modest 4.7% in the form of investments held primarily for liquidity. This is because insurance companies are exposed to limited risk that cash demands will be significantly different from those anticipated. Mortality payments for large groups of people tend to be very predictable, and in addition the trend of the past two centuries has been toward longer lifetimes.

Thus policies written on historical mortality experience have always proved somewhat better than anticipated. Perhaps the largest risk of cash drains deviating from what was anticipated arises because policyholders may borrow against their cash values. That is, they may "withdraw" a portion of their "savings account" in the form of a loan. The unpredictable nature of this demand necessitates some attention to liquidity in the corporate asset mix.

The bulk of insurance company assets are in investments held primarily for income, the most common forms being corporate bonds, mortgages, corporate stocks, and real estate. Yet another category of assets is policy loans. As was mentioned, these arise when a policyholder borrows back from the insurance company all or a portion of his policyholders' reserve. He is essentially borrowing his own funds, and should he die before repaying the loan, the loan is deducted from the policy payment. Such a loan thus is absolutely safe from the viewpoint of the life insurance company. It should be noted that if the insured person wishes to cancel his policy, he can recover its "cash value," which is nothing more than the "savings account" accumulated from a portion of his premium payments.

The major entry on the right side of the aggregate balance sheet is client-derived liabilities, in this instance the reserves on various types of insurance policies. Although life insurance reserves are the largest, other reserves exist because of annuities and other types of insurance. Some 80.2% of the assets of life insurance companies are financed by policy reserves—i.e., by funds contributed by policyholders and held and invested for them by the company. The policyholders' reserves are an estimate of the liabilities due to policyholders for mortality costs of future years, based upon assumptions inherent in mortality tables, upon contractual rates of interest allowed in the contract provisions of individual policies, and upon legal requirements imposed by regulatory authorities. Thus the basic business of the life insurance company might be characterized as investing these funds, with the benefits of that investment process going in part to the policyholders (the contractual rate) and in part to stockholders (the residual). Other liabilities, such as claims in the process of settlement, policyholder dividends, and miscellaneous liabilities, provide 13.3% of total resources, and stockholders' equity (stock companies) or unassigned surplus (mutual companies) constitutes 6.5% of the total.

Income statements of life insurance companies

Aggregate income and expense categories for all U.S. life insurance companies in 1972 are shown in Figure 14–9. Approximately three fourths of total income was derived from premium receipts, of which life insur-

FIGURE 14–9

ALL UNITED STATES LIFE INSURANCE COMPANIES
Aggregate Income and Expense Accounts
1972

	Millions of dollars	Percentage of total
Income		
Life insurance premium receipts	$24,678	41.9%
Annuity premiums	5,503	9.4
Health insurance premiums*	14,318	24.3
Total premium receipts	$44,499	75.6%
Investment income	12,127	20.6
Other income	2,222	3.8
Total income	$58,848	100.0%
Distribution of income		
Benefit payments in year	$31,014	52.7%
Additions to policy reserve funds	13,182	22.4
Additions to special reserves and surplus funds	1,353	2.3
Total benefits and benefit-related expenses	$45,549	77.4%
Commission to agents	$ 4,237	7.2%
Home and field office expense	5,767	9.8
Total operating expenses	$10,004	17.0%
Taxes	$ 2,648	4.5%
Dividends to stockholders of stock life insurance companies	647	1.1
	$ 3,295	5.6%
Total expenses	$58,848	100.0%

* Includes some premiums for workmen's compensation and auto and other liability insurance.
Source: Life Insurance Fact Book, 1973 (New York: Institute of Life Insurance, 1973), pages 59–63.
(Dollar expenses estimated by application of published percentage to total income.)

ance premiums were the single most important source. Investment income constituted 20.6% of total income. The major expense item was benefit payments for the year, followed by additions to policyholders' reserves, that is, allocations for benefits expected to be paid in future years. Additions to special reserves and surplus funds, constituting in part a "net profit" figure for mutual life insurance companies, was 2.3%. Operating expenses required 17.0% of total income and income taxes took 4.5%. For all life insurance companies (mutual and stock combined), dividends to stockholders of stock life insurance companies were reported as 1.1% of total income. However, for stock companies alone the corrected figure was 2.3%. The aggregate industry figures of Figure 14–9 do not show the profitability of stock companies as a separate group of companies.

The method by which stock life insurance companies calculate and report their earnings is currently in a state of flux, which causes some confusion from the point of view of investing. The basic problem arises because for many years regulatory bodies have been concerned primarily with the solvency of life insurance companies. Therefore they prescribed what was in effect a cash method of accounting for certain expenses. Perhaps the most important of these was the cost of issuing a policy, including the commission to the salesman. Other first-year costs are the cost of underwriting (to determine the price and the nature of the policy), the cost of any medical examination, and the various administrative expenses of issuing the policy and setting up the necessary records. Virtually all of these costs are incurred on a cash basis in the year in which the policy is written. On the other hand, the benefits in the form of premiums earned (i.e., "sales") are derived over the entire term of the contract.

Statutory accounting, a form of cash (as distinct from accrual) accounting used by most regulatory bodies, prescribes that all these heavy first-year costs be treated as expenses in the year the policy is written. Because the writing of a new policy incurs more costs than the initial premium, new policies have the effect of making the insurance company appear unprofitable.

Two alternative approaches to life insurance accounting have been proposed in recent years. The Association of Insurance and Financial Analysts (AIFA) has proposed a method that has been adopted by A.M. Best Company, the leading publisher of insurance reference books; and the American Institute of Certified Public Accountants (AICPA) has released an audit guide that contains generally accepted accounting principles for audited reports starting in 1972. Both the AIFA and the AICPA methods provide for proportional amortization against premium income of the large costs incurred in the first year that a policy is written. Differences between the AIFA method and the AICPA method are less conceptual than procedural, and tend to concern themselves with which specific expenses should be amortized, what particular method of amortization should be used, and what the period of amortization should be.

Another issue treated by the AIFA and the AICPA approaches is the calculation of and adjustment for reserves. As was mentioned earlier, the legal reserve measures the extra portion of the early year premiums that have been set aside and allocated to pay future death benefits. Note that the benefit itself is paid from assets; the reserves are only the recording of a claim in effect to earmark a portion of the assets against this claim. Insurance companies have used a variety of methods to establish reserves on each policy and to determine total reserves for the company. These policies have tended toward conservatism, including expensing first-year costs, and the use of conservative interest rates assumed to be earned upon policyholders' reserves. As a consequence, a portion of what is called policyholders' reserve is really stockholders' equity.

Calculation of the appropriate adjustments is a task beyond the abilities of any except actuarily trained accountants. An investor should be aware, however, that earnings and net worth, as reported in a life insurance company's annual report, may bear no relationship to earnings and net worth as reported in another company's report or as determined for other types of companies by "generally accepted accounting principles." The guiding principle for those not prepared to develop for themselves the special expertise needed to convert life insurance financial statements from their present cash accounting basis to a more meaningful accrual basis should be to select a single reliable and qualified source that has recalculated life insurance statistics by a uniform method. As was mentioned, the A.M. Best Company is the most highly regarded U.S. statistical corporation specializing in insurance reporting, and its statistics are now determined consistently by the AIFA method.

Qualitative factors

Difficulties in determining "true" life insurance company earnings should not obscure the fact that stock of a life insurance company may prove a successful investment because of the strength of the intangible aspects of its situation. Long-run success depends in part upon the ability of the company to grow, even though the industry's unique cash-accounting rules may cause that growth to penalize earnings at first. Growth depends in part upon the geographic areas in which the company can sell insurance, as well as upon the strength and professional expertise of its sales force. The ideal life insurance company would sell policies over a wide portion of the country and to a diverse population, employing a sales force possessing professional expertise. Such a company may be difficult to identify, but a potential investor can at least note its training program, the number of agents who are Chartered Life Underwriters (C.L.U.'s), and the nature of renewal commissions and fringe benefits provided agents. The latter increase the probability that agents will remain with the company instead of transferring their allegiance to a competitor.

Growth of the market is also related to increases in population, especially that segment of the population between ages 25 and 34, which is the major market for new policies, and to rises in personal income, which permit the purchase of more life insurance.

Company management is always a major factor. Management should be profit-oriented, rather than interested just in maximizing company size. Although aggressive attention to sales is essential, it is not sufficient if the management is so sales-oriented (perhaps because management are all ex-salesmen) as to overlook the profit needs of the stockholders. Short of talking with managers in order to ascertain their orientation, a potential investor can examine the profit margins of a particular company—both over time and as compared to other life insurance companies.

FIRE AND CASUALTY INSURANCE COMPANIES

Fire and casualty insurance companies provide financial protection against the loss of one's own property or against liabilities that might arise as the result of injury or loss of property to other people. The fire and casualty insurance business differs from the life insurance business in several very important respects. Perhaps the major difference is that losses or loss payments cannot be easily predicted. Whereas actual mortality experience for life companies hews to historical experience, property and casualty losses vary substantially from year to year. Some variation is purely random, while other variation is caused by natural catastrophes. Still other variables are inflation, which increases the monetary loss with the passage of time, and the unpredictability of juries charged with awarding damages in suits involving personal liability.

As part of a policy of diversifying the fluctuating nature of losses on various types of policies, fire and casualty companies tend to write insurance on a wide variety of lines within the property-casualty group. Historically there had been a division, with "fire" or "property" companies writing insurance protection against risk of loss from fire, theft, windstorm, earthquake, and collision. Such policies covered homes and buildings as well as automobiles, ships, and personal possessions. "Casualty" companies, on the other hand, tended to specialize in protection against liabilities that might arise from automobile bodily injury, other types of accidents, or health, fidelity, and surety losses. At the present time, the ideal fire and casualty company would write a diversified portfolio of policies in many different areas so as to better assure itself that adverse events in one year or in one line of insurance business would not unduly hurt the entire company. Companies also reinsure risks they have underwritten with other companies, passing along to another insurance carrier a portion of both the risk and the premium, so as to further spread the risk of loss from unusually large policies or from policies written in a single geographic area.

Maximum rates on some individual lines of insurance are determined by state regulatory bodies. For many years there was a lag in adjustment of rates to actual loss experiences, so that certain individual insurance lines (especially automobile and homeowners) often went through cycles of profitable years followed by unprofitable years. As a result, income from portfolio investments has tended to be relatively more important for fire and casualty insurance companies than for life insurance companies. Recently there has been a trend toward the adoption of flexible rating structures in various states. Under these new approaches, insurance companies may file rates with the state commissioner and then simply use the new rates unless the commissioner objects. These new systems now account for about half of the total premium volume for the industry, and their use has helped shift the industry away from the volatile feast or famine pattern of past decades.

Balance sheets of fire and casualty insurance companies

An aggregate balance sheet for 840 stock fire and casualty insurance companies operating in the United States as of year-end 1971 is shown in Figure 14–10. As can be seen, cash and cash-type assets are a relatively small fraction (9.8%) of total assets, while U.S. government bonds, held primarily for liquidity, constitute an additional 6.7% of assets. The division between assets held primarily for liquidity and those held primarily for income is somewhat less clear for the fire and casualty industry than for the other types of financial institutions to which this framework has been applied in this chapter. Thus the decision that the U.S. governmental bonds are primarily for income may be considered somewhat arbitrary. But even with this arbitrary classification, securities held for income purposes constitute 77.0% of total assets. Included in this grouping are significant portions of common stocks, representing 34.8% of total assets.

In this respect, fire and casualty insurance companies differ significantly from life companies, which hold a much smaller proportion of assets in common stock form. Specifically, common stocks constitute only 11.2% of total assets for life insurance companies (Figure 14–8). In addition, individual fire and casualty insurance companies vary widely in the proportion of assets held in common stock form. Thus is identified one significant aspect of the analysis of fire and casualty companies: the investor is acquiring not only an equity position in a diversified portfolio, but that portfolio may contain a significant proportion of common stocks, making it subject to both the risks and the potential gains that accrue from direct ownership of common stocks. This is the "asset leverage" referred to in the introductory section of this chapter.

Other important categories of assets held primarily for income include municipal bonds, which benefit fire and casualty insurance companies because most such companies pay regular corporate income taxes. The yield from a tax-free municipal bond is equivalent to a taxable yield some 1.92 times (the reciprocal of a 52% retention rate) as large. Preferred stocks are also important holdings for fire and casualty companies because only 15% of the dividends declared by United States corporations

FIGURE 14–10

840 STOCK FIRE AND CASUALTY INSURANCE COMPANIES
Aggregate Balance Sheet
December 31, 1971

Assets

	Millions of dollars	*Percentage of total*
Cash and cash-type holdings		
Cash	$ 1,841	
Premiums receivable	3,693	
	$ 4,841	9.8%
Investments held primarily for liquidity		
U.S. Government Bonds	$ 3,292	6.7
Investments held primarily for income		
Municipal bonds	$ 6,380	
Other bonds.	12,713	
Common bonds.	17,188	
Preferred stocks.	1,566	
Mortgages	135	
	$37,982	77.0
Other assets		
Real estate.	$ 689	
Other assets	2,530	
	$ 3,219	6.5
Total.	$49,333	100.0%

Liabilities and equity

Client-derived liabilities		
Reserve for losses and adjustment expenses.	$16,190	
Unearned premiums	12,155	
	$28,345	57.4%
Other liabilities		
Commissions and taxes.	$ 1,045	
Other liabilities	2,635	
	$ 3,680	7.5
Stockholders' equity		
Capital paid up	$ 1,910	
Net surplus	12,120	
Voluntary reserves	3,278	
	$17,308	35.1
Total.	$49,333	100.0%

Source: *Best's Aggregates and Averages, Property-Liability 1972* (Morristown, N.J.: A. M. Best Company, 1972), page 52.

become taxable to a corporate holder. Thus the effective income tax rate on both preferred and common stock dividend income is $(0.15 \times 0.48) = 7.2\%$. When the 7.2% corporate tax paid on dividends from domestic corporations is compared to the 48% tax rate paid on interest received from corporate or United States government bonds, the advantage of having a significant portion of corporate stocks, both preferred and common, in the portfolio of a fire and casualty insurance company is apparent.

Liabilities of fire and casualty companies consist of reserves for losses and adjustment expenses (sums due on losses but not yet paid) and unearned premiums. Together these client-derived liabilities constitute 57.4% of total liabilities and equity. Other liabilities constitute 7.5%, and the stockholders equity cushion is 35.1%.

The management of a fire and casualty insurance company can vary the risk-return position of the company by increasing or decreasing the proportion of common stocks in the asset mix. It can also vary the risk-return trade-off by variations in the amount of insurance business written with a given net worth. This later variation is the financial leverage referred to earlier in this chapter. A measure of equity leverage appears in the ratio of client-derived liabilities to stockholders' net worth. The industry as a whole has $28.3 billion of client-derived liabilities for an equity of $17.3 billion, or a ratio of the former to the latter of 1.6. A larger ratio would indicate greater risk.

The creation and significance of the *reserve for unearned premiums* for a fire and casualty insurance company can be best explained with reference to a hypothetical example of a company that writes a single policy. Unlike most life insurance policies, fire and casualty policies are usually written for a comparatively short period of time, usually one to three years. We will assume that a single policy with a $1,000 premium is written on July 1 for a period of two years. We will further assume that the policy is a profitable one, with 50% of the premium going to pay losses, 45% going to pay expenses, and with 5% of the premium, or $50, constituting the underwriting profit of this particular policy. The significance of the example lies in the way that fire and casualty insurance companies must account for this particular policy over portions of the three calendar years that it is in effect. This accounting is shown in Figure 14–11.

Insurance accounting procedures prescribe that the revenue ("sales") gain on the policy be allocated to the years in which the premiums are earned. Thus in the first (half) year, premiums written is reduced by the $750 portion of the premium that "belongs" to subsequent years. Hence in the first year, premiums earned are $250, while in the second and third year premiums earned are $500 and $250 respectively. Losses are assumed to be 50% of premiums and to occur over the time interval

FIGURE 14–11
Accounting for a single twoyear policy with a $1,000 premium sold on July 1st of an initial year

	First year	Second year	Third year
Premiums written	$1,000	$ 0	$ 0
less increase in reserve for unearned premiums	– 750	+ 500	+ 250
Premiums earned	$ 250	$500	$250
Losses incurred (50% of premiums earned)	125	250	125
Expenses incurred (45% of premiums written)	450	0	0
Statutory underwriting profit (loss)	$ (325)	$250	$125

that the policy is in effect. This is a realistic asumption because losses on a large group of policies do tend to be spread over the period of coverage. Thus the losses over the three years are, respectively, $125, $250, and $125. Underwriting costs are assumed to be 45% of the premium value of the policy. In fact, the major portion of these costs occur and are paid at the time the policy is written. As with life insurance policies, underwriting costs are dominated by salesmen's commissions and by the cost of putting the policy on the books of the company. Current practice is to show these costs as expenses in the year in which they are paid. Thus in the hypothetical example, the cost of $450 is shown as an expense in the first year, while the second and third years bear no portion of this cost. The result, as can be seen from Figure 14–11, is that the single profitable (by definition) policy produces an underwriting loss of $325 in the first year followed by profits of $250 and $125 in the second and third year. The overall profitability of the policy is the sum of these three numbers, or $50.

Several conclusions derive from this example. On the balance sheet, the liability "reserve for unearned premiums" is a true liability to the extent that future losses will be charged against it. However, these losses will absorb only a portion of the reserve, perhaps 50% as in the example. The remainder of the reserve is in substance stockholders' equity, although not labeled as such. This is because the remainder of the reserve consists of 5% profit and a 45% reserve against underwriting costs that have already been written off in prior accounting periods. One facet of the analysis of the balance sheets of fire and casualty companies thus involves a detailed estimate of what portion of the reserve for unearned premiums is in fact stockholders' equity. This adjustment is usually made by assigning for investment analysis purposes (including calculation of "adjusted" book value per share) a percentage of the reserve for unearned premiums to stockholders' equity. An appropriate percentage is the "expense ratio" for that company, as explained in the following section.

Income statements of fire and casualty insurance companies

Another facet of conventional analysis of the fire and casualty insurance industry is to adjust income statements to determine "true" earnings. To generalize from the simple example given above, a fire and casualty insurance company that is writing more new business than it wrote in prior years will tend toward a statutory underwriting loss because the first-year costs of putting the new business on the books will be charged against the current year while a portion of the premium revenue will be earned only in future years. Thus an expanding company will tend to show less profit than it would if accrual accounting were used. Conversely, an insurance company that is not writing new policies as rapidly as old policies are expiring will tend to show an underwriting profit, since current revenue from premiums earned need not bear any share of underwriting expenses.

This problem is resolved by the calculation of four ratios that will be illustrated with data from Figure 14–12, an aggregate income statement for the industry.

FIGURE 14–12

840 STOCK FIRE AND CASUALTY INSURANCE COMPANIES
Aggregate Income and Disbursements
Year ended December 31, 1971

		Millions of dollars
Net premiums written		$24,841
less increase in reserve for unearned premiums		1,037
Premiums earned		$23,804
Losses incurred	$13,809	
Adjustment expenses incurred	2,072	
Total losses		$15,881
Underwriting expenses incurred.		7,230
Other items (bail bond fees, etc.) net.		14
Net underwriting gain		679
Net investment gain		3,417
Net income before policyholder dividends and income taxes		4,096
Policyholder dividends	218	
Income taxes	450	
Total dividends and taxes		668
Net income		$ 3,428

Source: Best's Aggregates and Averages, Property-Liability 1972 (Morristown, N.J.: A. M. Best Company, 1972), page 53.

1. The *loss ratio* is the ratio of losses and loss-related expenses to premiums earned. In the aggregate income statement of Figure 14–12, this is $15,881 million divided by $23,804 million, or 66.7%.
2. The *expense ratio* is the ratio of underwriting expenses to premiums written. In Figure 14–12 this is $7,230 million divided by $24,841 million, or 29.1%.
3. The *combined loss and expense ratio* is the sum of the loss ratio and the expense ratio as separately calculated. For Figure 14–12, this is 66.7% plus 29.1%, or 95.8%.
4. The *combined underwriting gain (or loss) ratio* is 100% minus the combined loss and expense ratio, or for Figure 14–12, 4.2%.

The combined underwriting gain ratio gives the percentage of premiums written that will eventually become underwriting profit over the life of the various policies, without regard for the mixed accrual accounting (for revenue) and cash accounting (for expense) procedures actually used in the statutory corporate accounts. Of course this ratio is in part a prediction of the future, since it will in fact prove valid only if future losses remain at their present level in relationship to premiums earned. As was indicated earlier, there is a tendency for actual fire and casualty losses to fluctuate from year to year because of a variety of external factors.

Although the combined underwriting ratio is a better predictor of actual underwriting results when the business is expanding or contracting, it does not report on the investment earnings on the company's portfolio of securities, which are shown separately as investment income. As can be noted in Figure 14–12, this amount for the industry is $3,417 million divided by $679 million, or 5.03 times the magnitude of underwriting earnings.

A typical adjustment to actual underwriting earnings for a fire and casualty company is to increase reported earnings by a percentage of the increase in unearned premium reserves equal to the expense ratio. In Figure 14–12, the aggregate industry income statement, the premium for unearned reserves was increased by $1,037 million. The expense ratio of 29.1% implies that a sum equivalent to 29.1% of this increase has already been deducted as an expense, and that therefore 29.1% of the increase is an addition to the "hidden surplus" inherent in a portion of the reserve. If this increase in hidden surplus had been reported as income, it would have been taxed. Thus the addition to earnings resulting from the adjustment should be reduced by the probable tax charge. Using a 48% tax rate, 52% of 29.1% of the increase in the reserve for unearned premiums, or

$$(52\%)(29.1\%)(\$1,037 \text{ million}) = \$156.9 \text{ million}$$

could reasonably be added to current year's earnings. Such an adjustment would be useful in comparing the profitability records of several fire and casualty insurance companies.

Qualitative factors

Many of the comments on the qualitative aspects of life insurance companies are equally applicable in the evaluation of fire and casualty insurance companies. In particular, the loyalty of the various agents, many of whom will be Chartered Property and Casualty Underwriters (C.P.C.U.'s), will be a decisive factor in the long-run ability of the company to attract new and profitable business. A company that writes its policies through a large number of agents is perhaps in a fundamentally more sound position than a company whose business is written by a few large agents. Should the latter decide to place business with another company, the first company would suddenly lose a significant portion of its policy-generating ability.

Other factors of importance in the evaluation of insurance companies include the mix of coverages written. A wide range of coverages is less susceptible to sudden loss than is a range of coverage limited to a few speciality lines, such as automobile or home owners. The desirability of a wide range may be offset if the company becomes so expert in a special line, such as insurance on liquefied petroleum gas (L.P.G.), marine insurance, or insurance on elevators, that it can obtain a major portion of this coverage without excess exposure to the risk of loss. It might be noted, for example, that the loss ratio on steam boiler insurance is very low, primarily because companies specializing in this type of insurance have developed a very thorough program of safety inspection. The safety inspection program does, however, raise the expense ratio.

SELECTING SECURITIES OF FINANCIAL INSTITUTIONS

The trends of stock prices for the four types of financial institutions covered in this chapter are shown in Figure 14–13. As compared with Standard & Poor's Industrial Index for all stocks, prices of New York bank stocks have moved in the same general direction but with less volatility. Fire and casualty insurance company stocks have moved in a similar pattern. Life insurance stocks have generally dropped during the decade, although the level of life insurance stock prices is almost fourfold the level of the composite index. Stocks of savings and loan associations have exhibited greater-than-normal volatility during the decade. All financial institutions, it will be noted, tended to drop to a 1966 low and to rise, with varying degrees of irregularity, thereafter. Such considera-

FIGURE 14–13

Relative price movements of financial-institution and industrial stocks, 1963–72. (1941–43 = 10; semi-log scale)

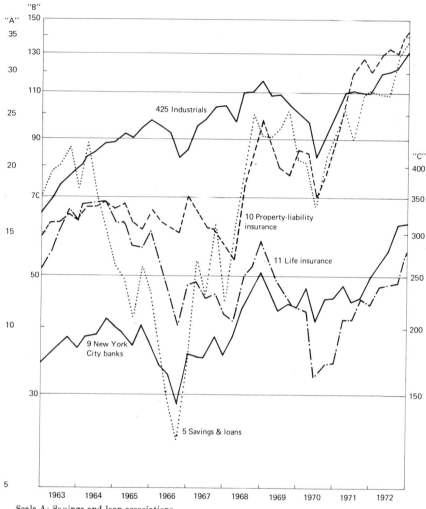

Scale A: Savings and loan associations.
Scale B: Industrials, property-liability insurance, banks.
Scale C: Life insurance.
Source: Standard & Poor's Trade and Securities Service.

tions are important as an investor considers the role of financial institutions within the context of an entire portfolio.

Our basic valuation model can be applied to the stocks of financial institutions. During the decade 1963 through 1972, earnings per share, adjusted by Moody's in the case of insurance companies, rose. Average annual current dividend yields for three large companies within each classification of institution are shown in Figure 14–14. While this selection of companies cannot be considered a valid statistical measure of the

FIGURE 14–14
Average dividend yields for selected financial institutions

Year	Commercial banks	Savings and loan associations	Life insurance companies	Fire and casualty insurance companies
1963	3.0%	0.0%	0.8%	2.6%
1964	2.7	0.0	0.7	2.7
1965	3.0	0.0	0.9	2.8
1966	3.6	0.0	1.1	3.0
1967	3.6	0.0	1.5	3.3
1968	2.9	0.0	1.7	3.5
1969	3.3	0.0	2.0	4.4
1970	3.8	0.0	2.5	5.5
1971	3.4	0.0	2.2	4.2
1972	2.8	0.3	2.1	4.3
Average	3.2	0.0	1.6	3.6

Source: Three largest institutions in each category, by deposits for banks and savings and loan associations and by assets for insurance companies, reported in Moody's *Handbook of Common Stocks.* Banks: BankAmerica Corporation, First National City Corporation, and Chase Manhattan Corporation. Savings and loan associations: Great Western Financial Corporation, First Charter Financial Corporation, and Imperial Corporation of America. Life Insurance companies: Aetna Life and Casualty Company, Connecticut General Insurance Corporation, and Lincoln National Corporation. Fire and casualty insurance companies: Continental Corporation, INA Corporation, and United States Fidelity and Guaranty Company.

industry as a whole, it nevertheless gives a rough guideline for the largest companies within the industry. Commercial bank stocks tend to sell in a range that produces a dividend yield very close to the decade average of 3.2%. Years in which bank dividend yields exceeded this average figure by a significant margin, such as 1966, 1967, and 1970, were years in which bank stocks dropped as part of a general market decline. This is apparent from the stock price indexes plotted in Figure 14–13. From a valuation point of view, it would not be unreasonable to expect a bank stock to yield a dividend return in the vicinity of 3.2%.

None of the three savings and loan associations paid any cash dividends until 1972, when one of the companies paid a dividend equal to 1% of the average stock price of that year. Obviously savings and loan associations are not purchased for current yield, and the valuation of savings and loan stocks by the discounted future cash flow approach suggested in Chapter 6 would revolve around successful prediction of future prices.

Dividend yields on life insurance company stocks have been generally low, averaging 1.6% over the decade. In the last half of the decade, the yield was slightly higher than in earlier years because life insurance stocks dropped in price. Dividends for life companies tend to be a relatively small proportion of adjusted earnings. Given the change in accounting procedures adopted by life insurance companies in 1973, it would be unwise to assume that future dividend yields and price-earnings would necessarily follow the pattern of the past. Dividend yields on fire and casualty insurance company stocks have averaged 3.6% over the decade, with the trend being toward higher yields during the later years of the decade.

The other important determinant of investment value is probable future price-earnings ratios. Past price-earnings ratios, which provide a starting point for this estimate, are shown in Figure 14–15. The decade

FIGURE 14–15
Average price-earnings ratio for selected financial institutions

Year	Commercial banks	Savings and loan associations	Life insurance companies	Fire and casualty insurance companies
1963	18.1	11.4	23.3	27.2
1964	18.5	12.6	26.1	28.1
1965	16.3	8.9	20.3	22.1
1966	12.6	10.9	14.4	17.7
1967	12.8	14.8	13.1	16.7
1968	14.5	16.9	14.0	18.7
1969	14.6	15.9	15.8	16.7
1970	11.9	13.1*	14.8	12.0
1971	12.5	12.4	11.4	12.3
1972	14.1	12.4	9.9	10.1
Average	14.6	12.9	16.3	17.1

* Based on two associations only.
Source: Based on same institutions as in Figure 14–14.

average price-earnings ratio for the three large banks was 14.6. The average price-earnings ratio for savings and loan associations was somewhat lower, 12.9, while the average for life insurance companies was 16.3 and, for fire and casualty companies, 17.1. The average price-earnings ratios for the two types of insurance companies dropped by more than half during the decade. Thus the decline in insurance company stocks apparent in Figure 14–13 came about because of dropping market prices in relationship to earnings, rather than because of a fall in actual earnings per share.

Because financial institutions' assets are primarily of a monetary nature, the concept of book value (for banks and savings and loan associations) is a meaningful term. Capital funds per share (for life insurance companies) and liquidating value per share (for fire and casualty companies) are similar concepts and are used in the same way. The equity of the common stockholders, by whatever name, represents a share in a portfolio of monetary assets whose values are in fact close to the measured book value. For this reason, the reasonableness of stock prices for financial institutions is often measured in relationship to the underlying per-share assets. The ratio of price to book value, capital funds, or liquidating value per share, for the four types of institutions is shown in Figure 14–16. Banks have tended to sell at a premium over

FIGURE 14–16
Average price-to-book-value ratios for selected financial institutions

Year	Commercial banks	Savings and loan associations	Life insurance companies	Fire and casualty insurance companies
1963	1.7	1.8	2.3	1.0
1964	1.9	1.4	2.7	0.9
1965	1.7	0.9	2.2	0.8
1966	1.4	0.7	1.8	1.2
1967	1.4	0.9	1.4	0.8
1968	1.7	1.3	1.6	0.9
1969	1.7	1.5	1.8	1.1
1970	1.5	1.2	1.6	0.9
1971	1.6	1.4	1.6	1.1
1972	1.9	1.6	1.6	1.0
Average.	1.6	1.3	1.9	1.0

Source: Based on same institutions as in Figure 14–14.

book value, and the average for the three banks portrayed was 1.6 times book value. Savings and loan associations have tended to sell somewhat closer to book value, with a decade average of 1.3 times. In three years (1965–1967), they averaged less than book value. If the stock price indices of Figure 14–13 are reviewed, it will be noted that these years would have been the most advantageous time to buy shares of these companies. Life insurance companies have an average 1.9 times their capital funds per share, with the trend showing a steady decline. Fire and casualty insurance companies have averaged close to their liquidating value per share.

In general, one could conclude that when financial institutions sell below their book value (or some other measure of invested assets per share), they offer a greater-than-normal potential for recovery because of the inherent value of the underlying assets. In this respect, financial institutions differ from most other types of business, for in other types of business the balance-sheet values attributed to assets may not have the inherent value that monetary assets possess.

SUMMARY

Financial institutions play an important role of intermediation within our economic system. Of interest to investors are the securities of institutions such as commercial banks, savings and loan associations, life insurance companies, and fire and casualty insurance companies. The financial statements of these four types of institutions were compared using a common balance-sheet framework. Assets were categorized as (1) cash and cash-type, (2) investments held primarily for liquidity, (3) investments held primarily for income, and (4) other. Liabilities and equities were categorized as (1) client-derived liabilities, (2) other liabilities, and (3) stockholders' equity. Specific measures of asset leverage and financial leverage were identified for each type of institution. Future charges and problems of regulation were discussed for each type. Finally, the benefits for each type of institution were reviewed as inputs to a valuation model and for considering a particular security for possible inclusion in the portfolio of an investor.

SUGGESTED READINGS FOR CHAPTER 14

J. W. Bowyer, Jr. *Investment Analysis and Management.* 4th ed. (Homewood, Ill.: Richard D. Irwin, Inc., 1972), Chapters 14–15.

J. C. Clendenin and G. A. Christy. *Introduction to Investments.* 5th ed. (New York: McGraw-Hill Book Company, Inc., 1969), Chapters 18 and 20.

D. K. Eiteman and A. I. Stonehill. *Multinational Business Finance* (Reading, Mass.: Addison-Wesley Publishing Co., Inc., 1973), Chapter 5.

D. A. Hayes. *Investments: Analysis and Management.* 2d ed. (New York: Macmillan Company, 1966), Chapters 20–21.

L. D. Jones. *Investment of Policies of Life Insurance Companies* (Cambridge, Mass.: Division of Research, Harvard University, 1968).

R. A. Lyon. *Investment Portfolio Management in the Commercial Bank* (New Brunswick, N.J.: Rutgers University Press, 1960).

15

Investing in investment companies

THE DISTINCTION between investing directly in stocks, bonds, and other investment assets and investing indirectly through the portfolios of institutional investors was explained in Chapter 1. Examples of institutional investors include insurance companies, commercial banks, a variety of savings institutions, investment management and advisory companies, and brokerage firms. Examples of the portfolios managed by these institutional investors include insurance company portfolios, trust funds, university endowments, foundations, pension funds, and mutual funds. Each of these types of institutional portfolios involves billions of dollars under professional management, and each is an important segment of the total money management industry. Because of their growth and popularity in recent years and also because of data availability, we proceed now to take a closer look at investment companies. The purpose of this chapter is to identify the general characteristics of investment companies, to consider the unique aspects of investing in different types of investment companies, and to explore the problem of selecting attractive investment company shares.

CHARACTERISTICS OF INVESTMENT COMPANIES

An *investment company* is a corporation whose shares are sold to investors, with the proceeds of those sales being invested in a portfolio of investment assets—notably common stocks and other securities. The portfolio of assets is managed for a fee by an investment management company. Examples of investment companies to be discussed in this chapter are mutual funds, closed-end companies, and dual-purpose funds. Investment companies have three important characteristics that should be identified and explained: aggregation, diversification, and management.

Aggregation is the pooling of the investable wealth of many individual investors into a single portfolio of considerable size. Because the objectives and policies of each investment company are usually well stated in its prospectus, advertisements, and other public sources of information, only those investors who agree with those objectives and policies are likely to buy the shares of a particular investment company. This means that the owners of each investment company tend to have common investment objectives, and investment policies of that investment company can be implemented accordingly. Furthermore, the large size of the investment company portfolio means that securities and other investment assets can be bought and sold at lower transaction costs per invested dollar than would be possible if the investor purchased by himself. Size, particularly in the case of security portfolios, also means that investment company management can have access to considerable research from brokerage firms as a result of the large commissions generated by the professional manager.

Another favorable characteristic that results from the large size of the investment company portfolio is *diversification*. We saw in Chapter 3 that total portfolio risk decreases rather sharply until the number of securities approaches the critical range of ten to fifteen. Few individual investors are able to hold that many securities without resorting to odd-lot (less than one hundred share) transactions. The number of individual holdings varies greatly among investment companies but typically is well above this critical range. In other words, owners of investment companies are almost always assured adequate diversification—at least in terms of number of assets held. Because many portfolio managers tend to diversify across industries or among different types of investment assets, owners of investment companies usually are assured of reasonable levels of diversification, certainly far greater than they could achieve by themselves.

The third characteristic is *management*. Because individual investors seldom have the time, experience, or access to the amount of research available to institutional investors, individuals are presumably at a distinct disadvantage—vis-à-vis professional portfolio managers—as fas as their overall capability to manage their investable wealth. But while aggregation and diversification tend to be favorable characteristics almost without exception, there is really no evidence that professional managers have been able to produce results better than that of the market itself, and thus to justify the management fees that are paid by investors to the management company. Yet one might argue that the fees are justifiable if, by themselves, individual investors somehow manage to do worse than the overall market. Emphasis on the achieved performance of institutional portfolios, or the lack thereof, has intensified in recent years. Part of this emphasis is due to improved methods of measurement, some of which will be explained and illustrated in Chapter 21. But despite questionable performance by institutional investors, many individuals may still feel more comfortable if their wealth is managed professionally.

In summary, aggregation and diversification are rather clear-cut characteristics of investment companies that make them attractive as investment assets. The value of management, the third characteristic of investment companies, is less certain, yet still important to many individuals as they consider alternative investment opportunities. All three characteristics should be kept in mind as we proceed to more detailed examination of different types of investment companies.

INVESTING IN MUTUAL FUNDS

Mutual funds are by far the most popular type of investment company. They are also called *open-end* investment companies because they offer new shares for sale and must be prepared to redeem outstanding shares at all times. Investors receive a return on their investment in mutual fund shares from three sources: distributions of dividends earned by the assets in the fund (less all expenses incurred), distribution of capital gains realized by the fund, and changes in the net asset value of the fund. The latter reflects unrealized capital gains, since it is based on the market values of all assets held by the fund.

The market value of assets held by any mutual fund—and hence also that of the totality of mutual funds—tends to vary significantly over time. The following tabulation presents data since 1941 on all mutual funds that are members of the Investment Company Institute.[1]

Year	Number of funds	Market value of total assets (billions of dollars)	Number of shareholders accounts (millions)
1941	68	$ 0.4	0.29
1951	103	3.1	1.11
1956	135	9.0	2.52
1961	170	22.8	5.32
1966	182	34.8	7.70
1967	204	44.7	7.90
1968	240	52.7	9.08
1969	269	48.3	10.39
1970	356	47.6	10.69
1971	392	55.0	10.90
1972	410	59.8	10.64

[1] *Investment Companies* (Wiesenberger Services, Inc., 1973), p. 19.

One quickly notes the steady growth over the past thirty years of number of funds, total assets, and number of investor accounts holding mutual fund shares. We see that in 1972 the average fund size was $59.8 billion divided by 410, or $146 million, while the average account of an investor was $59.8 billion divided by 10.6 million, or $5,642. An individual with investable wealth of $5,642 could not expect to attain a level of diversification beyond four or five securities without incurring excessive brokerage commissions—thus reinforcing our earlier observation about diversification as an important characteristic.

Mutual funds have a variety of different objectives. One way to illustrate this, together with other features of mutual funds, is to identify the categorization schemes used in three of the important sources of mutual fund data. The sources are *Forbes, Fundscope,* and Wiesenberger.

Forbes is a popular financial magazine published twice a month ($12 per year). The annual August 15 issue includes ratings of achieved performance and/or other information for a large number of investment companies. A total of 567 were categorized in the August 15, 1973 issue as follows[2]

Category	Number of funds
Stock funds (load)	148
Stock funds (no load)	37
Funds for investing abroad	6
Closed-end investment companies	19
Balanced funds (load)	31
Balanced funds (no load)	7
Bond and preferred stock funds	8
Exchange funds	21
Dual funds	18
New mutual funds (not yet classified)	237
New closed-end companies (not yet classified)	35

Certain terms in this exhibit should be defined. A *load* fund is one for which the investor pays a percentage fee when he purchases the mutual fund shares. This charge is intended as compensation for the sales effort rendered by the organization that sells the mutual fund shares, and is thus somewhat analogous to a brokerage commission.

The Investment Company Act of 1940 allows a maximum "load" or sales charge of 9% of the public offering price, although most mutual funds charge a somewhat lower figure, frequently 8% to 8.5%. The sales charge is levied as a percentage of the *offering price,* and the offering price minus the dollar sale charge is the net asset value of the mutual fund. *Net asset value* is the actual dollar investment in securities. If the offering price for a certain mutual fund were $12.00 per share and the applicable sales charge were 8%, net asset value would be 92% of the offering price, or $11.04 per share. Since net asset value is often

---

[2] *Forbes,* August 15, 1973.

quoted for a mutual fund, the offering price can be found by reversing the above calculation. Of a total $1,000 investment in shares of that mutual fund, the loading charge is $80, while $920 is actually invested in the shares of other companies. The effective percentage thus is $80 divided by $920, or 8.7% for small mutual fund purchases.

A *no-load fund* is one for which the investor pays no sales charge, although no-load funds sometimes levy a small charge (say, one percent) for redemption of shares. A *balanced fund* is a mutual fund that holds preferred stocks and bonds in addition to common stock in an attempt to reduce risk, but without undue sacrifice of long-term growth. This is in contrast to a *stock fund* whose holdings consist mainly of common stock. An *exchange fund* is a mutual fund for which investors during the period 1960–67 were able to obtain shares by exchanging other securities and thereby postponing the payment of capital gains taxes. This type of tax-free exchange has not been approved by the Internal Revenue Service since 1967.

A *closed-end investment company* differs from a mutual fund in that it does not sell or redeem shares at all times, but rather it has a fixed number of outstanding shares. Shares of closed-end companies are bought and sold in organized securities markets as are other listed stocks and bonds, rather than being bought and sold by the fund itself. A *dual fund* is a special type of closed-end company whose aggregate portfolio of investments provides distinct benefits to two classes of owners. Closed-end companies and dual funds will be examined later in this chapter.

Fundscope is a monthly publication that deals exclusively with mutual funds. The annual April issue ($20 cost), "Mutual Fund Guide," contains a wealth of useful information on mutual funds, their performance, and their sponsoring management companies. Their categorization scheme for 378 funds is somewhat more detailed than Forbes's as follows[3]

Category	Number of funds
Growth funds: diversified common stock	97
Growth funds: hedge funds	4
Growth funds: insurance stock funds	4
Growth funds: performance funds	129
Growth funds: specialized funds	8
International securities	5
Growth with income: diversified common stocks	36
Growth with income: flexibility diversified	11
Income and growth: diversified common stock	15
Income and growth: flexibility diversified	15
Balanced funds	22
Income funds	20
Bond and preferred stock funds	9
Not yet classified	3

---

[3] *Fundscope*, April, 1973.

There are new terms here also. A *hedge fund* is a mutual fund whose management utilizes sophisticated strategies, often involving both long and short positions in the same company, for increasing capital appreciation and reducing risk. A *performance fund* is a mutual fund whose holdings often include more volatile and usually lesser known issues in an attempt to enhance the return that is achieved, particularly in the short run.

Each year, Wiesenberger Services, Inc., publishes *Investment Companies*, usually referred to in this book simply as "Wiesenberger." This source ($55 per year) is considered by many to be the leading single source of mutual fund data. In addition to extensive statistical information on mutual funds and other types of investment companies, Wiesenberger contains an excellent overview of the mutual fund industry, its historical growth, and the regulatory climate in which investment companies must operate. The categorization scheme of Wiesenberger for funds is presented here.[4] It is interesting to note that certain of the category definitions include volatility—a risk measure discussed at some length in Chapters 3 and 4.

Category	Number of funds
Large growth funds	24
Smaller growth funds: maximum capital gains, high volatility	146
Smaller growth funds: long-term growth of capital and income, above-average volatility	69
Other diversified common stock funds: growth and current income, average volatility	42
Other diversified common stock funds: growth and current income, with relative stability, below-average volatility	20
Balanced funds	22
Income funds	38
Specialized funds: insurance and bank stocks	4
Specialized funds: international issues	4
Specialized funds: public utility stocks	1
Specialized funds: convertible bonds and preferred stocks	3
Specialized funds: bonds	8
Tax-free exchange funds	21

We have reviewed three different categorization schemes in order to reveal the various differences that exist among mutual funds as far as size, objectives, and extent of specialization in their portfolios. A concise summary (as of December 31, 1972) with respect to total assets under management for a larger sample of 604 mutual funds is taken from Wiesenberger,[5] first according to size

---

[4] *Investment Companies* (Wiesenberger Services, Inc., 1973).

[5] *Investment Companies* (Wiesenberger Services, Inc., 1973), p. 49.

		Combined assets	
Size of fund	Number of funds	thousands of dollars	percentage of total
Over one billion dollars.	14	$23,231,600	37.2
$500 million–$1 billion	14	9,958,800	15.9
$300 million–$500 million	22	8,309,200	13.3
$100 million–$300 million	67	10,941,500	17.5
$50 million–$100 million	66	4,820,200	7.7
$10 million–$50 million	183	4,425,600	7.1
$1 million–$10 million	170	738,500	1.2
Under one million dollars	68	31,100	0.1
Total	604	$62,456,500	100.0

and then according to type of fund.

		Combined assets	
Type of fund	Number of funds	thousands of dollars	percentage of total
Common stock:			
Maximum capital gain	184	$ 8,899,400	14.3
Growth	175	20,203,300	32.3
Growth and income	111	20,348,900	32.6
Specialized	15	381,200	0.6
Balanced	25	6,823,300	10.9
Income	50	3,611,900	5.8
Tax-free exchange.	21	1,209,000	1.9
Bond and preferred stock	23	979,500	1.6
Total	604	$62,456,500	100.0

Here, the total assets under management at the end of 1972 are in excess of $62 billion. Furthermore, we see that a majority of mutual funds have assets in the range $1 million to $50 million; a majority also have objectives of either maximum capital gains or overall growth.

Current information on mutual fund shares is frequently seen in the financial sections of newspapers. Usually bid and ask quotations are reported. The *bid* quotation is the net asset value per share, that is, the price at which the mutual fund will redeem any outstanding shares. It is calculated by dividing the current market value of the fund's portfolio holdings by the number of shares outstanding at that time. The *ask* quotation is the amount that a buyer must pay to obtain a share of the mutual fund. The ask quotation is greater than the bid quotation by the amount of the loading charge. Bid and ask quotations are equal in the case of a no-load mutual fund.

Many of the other pertinent features are included in the *prospectus* for each fund, which is prepared for both existing and potential buyers of mutual fund shares. The prospectus identifies the investment objectives and policies of the mutual fund as well as any investment restrictions that exist. As an illustration of these and other features, we shall examine Investors Stock Fund, whose total assets of over $2.6 billion make it the second largest mutual fund in existence. It is managed by Investors Diversified Services, Inc., a professional management company that also manages Investors Mutual Fund—the single largest mutual fund, with assets of over $3.0 billion. Primary objectives of Investors Stock Fund are "capital appreciation on an investment basis over a long term and a reasonable income consistent with the investment policies of the Fund." The Stock Fund invests only in marketable securities, and it limits portfolio turnover by not trading for short-term profits. It does not sell securities short or purchase on margin. The Fund may not invest more than 5% of its total assets in the securities of any single corporation, and it may not acquire more than 10% of the outstanding common stock of any single corporation. There are also a number of additional restrictions that pertain to the activities of the officers of Investors Stock Fund.

The prospectus also explains the loading charges paid by the investors in a particular mutual fund. The loading charges for Investors Stock Fund are as follows

Transaction size	Stated sales charge	Effective charge
Less than $15,000	8%	8.7%
$15,000 to $20,000	7.5%	8.1%
$20,000 to $25,000	7%	7.5%
$25,000 to $50,000	6%	6.4%
$50,000 to $100,000	4%	4.2%
$100,000 to $200,000	2.5%	2.6%
$200,000 to $400,000	2%	2.1%
$400,000 to $700,000	1.5%	1.5%
Over $700,000	1%	1.0%

These percentages apply to the cumulative investment of an investor, so that the charge decreases if the investor continues to purchase the shares of Investor Stock Fund over time. Each point at which the sales charge is reduced ($15,000 in the first step above) is technically called a *break point*.

Investors indirectly also pay an annual management fee to the investment management company. For example, Investors Stock Fund pays management fees to Investor Diversified Services according to the following schedule:

Assets under management	percentage	thousands of dollars*
Annual fee		
First $250 million	0.5%	$1,250
Next $250 million	0.47	1,175
Next $250 million	0.44	1,100
Next $250 million	0.41	1,025
Next $250 million	0.38	950
Next $250 million	0.35	875
Next $250 million	0.32	800
Remaining assets	0.30	—

* At maximum of that step

Usually management fees are calculated and paid monthly at a rate equal to one twelfth of the indicated annual fee. The management fees paid in 1971 by Investors Stock Fund totalled $7,343,000!

There are a variety of procedures, again explained in detail in the prospectus, whereby individuals can systematically accumulate an investment in mutual fund shares over time. For example, either or both of the dividend distributions and capital gains distributions can be taken as additional shares rather than cash. Mutual funds must permit the investor to reinvest his capital gains distributions at net asset value; i.e., without a sales charge. Dividend income may be reinvested at net asset value (no sales charge) or at the public offering price (including sales charge), depending on the policy of the particular mutual fund.

Most mutual funds also enable investors to accumulate fund shares through systematic and regular investment of modest sums of money. While the minimum investment for an initial purchase may be $500, an *accumulation plan* permits the investment of smaller sums, often $25 to $50, on a regular monthly or quarterly basis. Although there is no legal obligation on the investor to adhere to his accumulation plan, the systematic procedure tends to encourage savings and investment by individuals who might not do so otherwise.

There are two types of accumulation plans that differ in how the sales charge is handled. A *contractual accumulation plan* is one wherein the investor agrees to make payments for a stated period of time, say $100 per month for ten years. Moreover, one half of the first year's total payment may be deducted to pay a portion of the sales charge for the ten-year contractual period. For this reason, contractual plans are sometimes called "front-end load" plans. In contrast, a *voluntary accumulation plan* is one wherein the regular sales charge is levied on each purchase of mutual fund shares.

In both types the investor may discontinue his systematic purchases at any time. The difference between the two types is shown in the following comparison.

At the end of	Contractual accumulation plan		
	Amount invested in shares	Sales charge	Total payment
1st year.	$ 600	$600	$ 1,200
10th year.	11,040	960	12,000

At the end of	Voluntary accumulation plan		
	Amount invested in shares	Sales charge	Total payment
1st year.	$ 1,104	$ 96	$ 1,200
10th year.	11,040	960	12,000

Obviously, an investor who does not complete the ten-year plan will be worse off under a contractual accumulation plan since the sales charge for the full ten years is paid in advance. Even if the investor does complete the plan, his principal builds up earlier in a voluntary accumulation plan and thus becomes a larger initial base for earnings and capital appreciation. As a result, contractual accumulation plans are prohibited by law in some states and have been questioned on a national basis.

Most mutual funds also allow their shareholders to arrange for monthly or quarterly withdrawal of a constant dollar amount from their fund holdings. Under a *withdrawal plan,* all dividends and capital gains distributions are reinvested in additional fund shares, and a periodic check is sent to the investor upon liquidating a portion of his total holdings. Withdrawals may consist of both regular income and capital gains. If withdrawal exceeds the amount of reinvested dividends and capital gains, the amount of the original investment will be reduced.

When a single management company manages two or more mutual funds, investors are often given the option of transferring their investment from one fund to another in the same group of funds at little or no cost. For example, shareholders of Investors Stock Fund may transfer to Investors Mutual Fund and the other four funds included in the "Investors Group" in such a manner. Conversion is made at net asset value without a sales charge, although a fixed administrative fee, perhaps $5, may be charged. Such a conversion is regarded for tax purposes as the sale of one fund and the purchase of another. Free conversion can be used as a tax shelter. Assume an investor purchases $10,000 of a particular fund with an 8% load, thus receiving shares having a net asset value of $9,200. These shares may immediately be converted into shares of another fund in the group, with the result of an $800 capital loss for tax purposes. The effect of this conversion is to permit the investor to deduct the full sales charge against current taxable income. For a person in the 50% tax bracket, the purchase of one fund followed by immediate conversion into another cuts the effective sales charge in half.

We have already indicated that the typical mutual fund makes two types of periodic payments to its owners. On the one hand, virtually all of the income earned on the assets of the mutual fund is passed on to owners as a dividend distribution. Federal taxes are not paid by the mutual fund, but by the individual investors on the dividend distributions that they receive. The mutual fund also distributes to owners the proceeds of capital gains that are realized over time from the portfolio; the shareholder pays capital-gains taxes on such distributions. Dividend and capital-gains distributions are thus periodic benefits to mutual fund shareholders, while changes in net asset value are analogous to stock price changes for direct investors. During 1972, net asset value per share for Investors Stock Fund rose from $20.39 to $22.72; dividend distributions were $0.48 per share and capital-gains distributions were $0.29 per share. The investor also pays capital-gains taxes on any realized appreciation when he sells mutual fund shares.

Finally, it is important to note that a mutual fund keeps track of both its portfolio of investments and its collective ownership on a *per-share* basis. At least once per trading day, an accurate calculation is made of the total market value of all assets held, the total number of outstanding shares, and hence of the net asset value per share. At the end of October 31, 1972, for example, the total assets of Investors Stock Fund were $2,693,315,889, and there were 126,128,567 outstanding shares; hence the net asset value of the Fund was $21.354 per share. As mentioned, all sales and redemptions are based on the current net asset value per share. And as we shall see, it is convenient to examine fund performance on a per-share basis.

INVESTING IN CLOSED-END COMPANIES

Another type of investment company is the *closed-end company*. As mentioned above, the capitalization of a closed-end company is relatively constant over time, just as is that of any other corporation. The shares of such closed-end companies are listed on the organized stock exchanges alongside the shares of General Motors, Eastman Kodak, and hundreds of other corporations. Apart from this trading distinction, the three characteristics—aggregation, diversification, and management—are similar for closed-end companies and mutual funds.

Compared to the large universe of mutual funds, the number of closed-end investment companies is not large. In contrast to a total asset value of $62.5 billion reported earlier for 604 mutual funds, the total assets under management by the less-than-50 closed-end companies was $6.7 billion at the end of 1972.[6] Justification for examining closed-end companies in some detail here is that the closed-end structure has been used for other types of investment assets.

Nineteen of the closed-end companies for which data are available over the past decade are identified in Figure 15–1. Of this sample, twelve

FIGURE 15–1
Characteristics of selected closed-end investment companies

Closed-end company	Category	Total assets (12/31/72)	Market*
Adams Express	Diversified	$210.0 million	NYSE
American-South African	Specialized	111.5	NYSE
Carriers & General	Diversified	25.0	NYSE
Central Securities	Nondiversified	51.7	ASE
Consolidated Investment Trust	Diversified	97.4	OTC
Dominick Fund	Diversified	68.8	NYSE
General American Investment	Diversified	140.9	NYSE
International Holdings	Diversified	124.0	NYSE
Japan Fund	Specialized	139.9	NYSE
Lehman Corporation	Diversified	641.8	NYSE
Madison Fund	Diversified	336.8	NYSE
National Aviation	Specialized	119.2	NYSE
Niagara Shares	Diversified	131.7	NYSE
Petroleum Corporation	Specialized	96.0	NYSE
Standard Shares	Nondiversified	97.8	ASE
Surveyor Fund	Diversified	173.7	NYSE
Tri-Continental Corporation	Diversified	849.3	NYSE
United Corporation	Nondiversified	160.8	NYSE
U.S. & Foreign Securities	Diversified	172.4	NYSE
Sample Average	–	$197.3 million	–

* Abbreviations: NYSE—New York Stock Exchange; ASE—American Stock Exchange; OTC—over-the-counter market.
Source: Investment Companies (Wiesenberger Services, Inc., 1973).

are categorized as *diversified* investment companies, which means that at least 75% of their total assets must be invested in the securities of other companies. Others in the sample are categorized as either *nondiversified* companies or *specialized* companies. The average amount of assets under management was $197.3 million, which is somewhat larger than the average size of mutual funds. And we note that, with

[6] Investment Companies (Wiesenberger Services, Inc., 1973), p. 12.

but two exceptions, shares of the closed-end investment companies are traded on the New York Stock Exchange.

Investors in closed-end companies also receive a return on their shares from three sources. As is the case for mutual funds, closed-end companies make dividend distributions and capital-gains distributions to share-holders. The third source is changes in the market price of the shares themselves. Investors pay taxes on these three sources of return just as do investors in mutual fund shares.

The major difference then between investing in mutual funds and investing in closed-end companies is that mutual fund shares sell at their net asset value, while closed-end shares sell at a price determined by the market. There is, of course, a corresponding net asset value for closed-end shares since holdings of a closed-end company are comparable to those of a mutual fund. Because the holdings of a closed-end company are highly liquid in the sense of usually being securities listed on the organized exchanges, one would expect the market prices of closed-end shares to approximate the per share value of their underlying net assets.

But this is not the case. In some instances, closed-end shares sell at a premium above net asset value. In a larger number of instances, closed-end shares sell at a discount from net asset value. Moreover, there are considerable differences in the premium and discounts among the closed-end companies, and the premiums and discounts vary over time. Letting P_t represent the market price for a closed-end company at the end of period t, and N_t the corresponding net asset value, we then can define

$$U_t = \frac{P_t - N_t}{N_t} \qquad (15-1)$$

as the market premium at the end of the period t. If U_t is negative, the closed-end fund is said to be selling at a discount. Figure 15–2 includes premiums (or discounts) for the sample of nineteen closed-end companies at the end of each year in the period 1965–1972. The range extends from a premium of 77% for American–South African in 1967 to a discount of 33% for U.S. & Foreign Securities in 1965. Overall, there was an average premium in only the two years 1968 and 1969, and for only five closed-end companies over the eight-year period. The overall average was a discount of 5%.

The phenomenon of premiums and discounts has never been explained in any satisfactory manner. Possible explanations are the potential tax liability on unrealized capital gains, associated management costs, lack of a selling effort, realized management performance, or expectations for future management performance. Perhaps the best explanation of the overall discount of all closed-end companies over all years is simply

FIGURE 15–2
Premiums and discounts of diversified closed-end investment companies

Closed-end fund	1965	1966	1967	1968	1969	1970	1971	1972	Average
Adams Express	-12%	-6%	-6%	10%	6%	-6%	-15%	-14%	5%
American-South African	5	12	77	54	-15	37	10	-6	22
Carriers & General	-11	-19	-21	-12	-14	-18	-20	-17	17
Central Securities	-11	9	-3	31	58	37	14	-31	13
Consolidated Investment Trust	-21	-10	-1	1	-4	-2	-2	-4	-5
Dominick Fund	-19	-20	-5	-4	-8	-18	-25	-29	-16
General American Investment	-7	-11	1	14	8	-8	-12	-4	2
International Holdings	-21	-25	-16	-5	-10	-18	-23	-27	18
Japan Fund	-27	-32	-9	5	6	11	7	-8	-6
Lehman Corporation	-11	-9	16	23	16	14	-8	-13	4
Madison Fund	2	18	19	32	48	16	-3	-19	14
National Aviation	-2	14	33	26	-15	-12	-15	-27	0
Niagara Shares	-8	-12	-11	8	12	5	-13	-7	-3
Petroleum Corporation	6	0	-3	7	4	-3	-14	-4	-1
Standard Shares	-16	-21	-20	-6	-13	-24	-23	-25	-19
Surveyor Fund	-14	-13	-13	10	10	-8	-28	-19	-9
Tri-Continental Corporation	-23	-25	-6	-4	-2	-5	-14	-19	-12
United Corporation	-24	-20	-12	-7	-14	-15	-26	-28	-18
U.S. & Foreign Securities	-33	-29	-17	-7	-11	-3	-7	-3	-14
Average	-13%	-10%	0%	9%	3%	-1%	-11%	-16%	-5%

that of uncertainty to the investor. In other words, there is no assurance to the investor that he can sell his closed-end shares for their asset or liquidation value—as he can in the case of a mutual fund. The premium-discount phenomenon thus adds another component of risk to investing in closed-end shares, even though in most other respects the situation is similar to that of mutual funds. This added risk is well documented by shares of Central Securities, which sold at a 14% premium at the end of 1971 but fell to a 31% discount one year later.

INVESTING IN DUAL-PURPOSE FUNDS

In 1967, a special type of closed-end investment company, the so-called "dual fund," came into existence. A *dual-purpose* or *dual fund* is an investment company that offers benefits to two distinct types of investors: those who are interested solely in income, and those who are interested solely in capital gains. The investable wealth of both types of investors is pooled into a common portfolio of securities. The *income shares* receive all dividend income from the total portfolio, while an equal number of *capital shares* receive all capital gains. Each investor thus receives the type of benefit that he desires from twice the investable wealth that he is able to allocate to the dual fund. In other words, both types of shares enjoy specialized benefits from a leveraged investment.

At present, there are seven dual funds in existence. Their identities and asset sizes are as follows. The average dual fund is seen to be

Dual fund	Total assets (December 31, 1972)
American Dualvest	$ 44.5 million
Gemini Fund	54.7
Hemisphere Fund	22.3
Income & Capital Shares	36.9
Leverage Fund of Boston	64.4
Putnam Duofund	26.8
Scudder Duo-Vest.	118.7
Sample Average	$ 52.6 million

considerably smaller than of either the average mutual fund or the average closed-end investment company. To further discuss the investment characteristics of this interesting type of investment company, it is useful to distinguish the two types of shares that are available.

To some observers, the *income shares* of dual funds represent an excellent vehicle for those investors who are interested primarily in dividend income. Pertinent information on such income shares is presented in Figure 15–3. Dividend yield, based on the year-end market prices of the seven funds, ranges from 6.3% to 8.2% and averages 7.4%. While this is considerably higher than the dividend yield to mutual fund shares,

FIGURE 15–3
Income shares of dual-purpose funds

Fund	Market price (December, 1972)	Yield	Call date	Call value
American Dualvest	$13.00	6.7%	June, 1979	$15.00
Gemini Fund	14.50	8.2	Dec., 1984	11.00
Hemisphere Fund	7.00	7.9	June, 1985	11.44
Income & Capital Shares	11.00	8.2	Mar., 1982	10.00
Leverage Fund of Boston	13.13	7.4	Jan., 1982	13.73
Putnam Duofund	17.00	7.4	Jan., 1983	19.75
Scudder Duo-Vest	8.38	6.3	April, 1982	9.15

or to individual common stocks for that matter, it should be remembered that income shares receive *only* the income from a leveraged investment base. On the other hand, income shares are to be redeemed at indicated call values on dates ranging from June, 1979, to June, 1985. Five of the income shares were selling (as of the end of 1972) below their corresponding call values, thus ensuring investors at least some appreciation in addition to their dividend income. For example, an investor who bought Hemisphere Fund for $7.00 per share at the end of 1972 could expect appreciation by June, 1985, of $11.44 − $7.00 = $4.44 per share. This represents a compound growth rate of 4.1% per year, in addition to the 7.9% dividend yield, or a total expected pre-tax return of 12%.

Market premiums (or discounts) of *capital shares* are indicated in Figure 15–4. We note that the average discount of 15% is three times

FIGURE 15–4
Premiums and discounts of dual-purpose fund capital shares

Fund	1967	1968	1969	1970	1971	1972	Average
American Dualvest	−21%	−7%	−4%	−3%	−20%	−29%	−14%
Gemini Fund	−6	−7	−1	−9	−21	−28	−12
Hemisphere Fund	−17	−24	0	42	0	−15	−2
Income & Capital Shares	−16	−2	9	−16	−28	−36	−15
Leverage Fund of Boston . . .	−20	−25	−15	−20	−27	−28	−23
Putnam Duofund	−13	−15	−4	−14	−35	−33	−19
Scudder Duo-Vest	−15	−20	−19	−4	−30	−33	−20
Average	−15%	−14%	−5%	−5%	−23%	−20%	−15%

greater than the average discount of the closed-end investment companies as reported in Figure 15–2. Moreover, five of the seven capital shares have consistently sold at substantial discounts. One possible explanation of the larger discounts on capital shares is simply that investors are less familiar with dual funds than with the older, larger, and better known types of investment companies.

SELECTING SHARES OF INVESTMENT COMPANIES

In the case of individual securities, we have suggested that individual selections be made within a proper portfolio· perspective by analyzing the prospects of a particular company and identifying the benefits that are likely to accrue to investors who own its bonds or shares of common stock. Valuation, we have suggested, should be based on discounting those future benefits with an appropriate discount rate that reflects their relative riskiness.

For mutual funds, closed-end companies, and dual funds, it would be difficult if not impossible to proceed in a similar manner because future benefits to an investment company reflect the future benefits of all the individual securities that are held as well as the many portfolio changes that may be made by the management of the company.

Clearly, if an investor does not hold a favorable view about the long-run prospects for common stocks in general, he would be well advised to avoid selecting investment companies whose policy is to purchase and hold common stocks. The only exception to such a generality would be the case in which the investor held strong views about the ability of the professional manager to choose individual issues whose performance would run counter to the market as a whole. Because there do not appear to be a large number of issues that consistently outperform the market, we remain skeptical that there are many such professional managers. Because of their large holdings, one might expect prices of investment company shares to stay very close to the overall market. This is confirmed in Figure 15–5, where we compare a price index for closed-end companies with the Standard & Poor's Industrial Price Index.

Accordingly, there does not appear to be any systematic method for selecting investment company shares that does not depend heavily on an appraisal of *past performance*. In fact, we suggest that investment company shares be selected by measuring past performance over a period of years sufficiently long so that "luck" and short-range fluctuation of the securities markets do not seriously influence the achieved results. The remainder of the chapter is devoted to methods of assessing past performance. We shall focus on mutual fund performance, recognizing that shares of closed-end companies and dual funds possess the added uncertainty of market premiums and discounts.

All professionally managed portfolios have come under closer scrutiny in recent years, and a good deal of criticism has been voiced about their performance. Mutual funds have received an inordinate amount of attention and also criticism—mainly because the mutual fund industry

374

FIGURE 15–5
Relative price movements of closed-end investment companies and industrial stocks, 1963–1972. (1941–1943 = 10; semi-log scale)

Price index

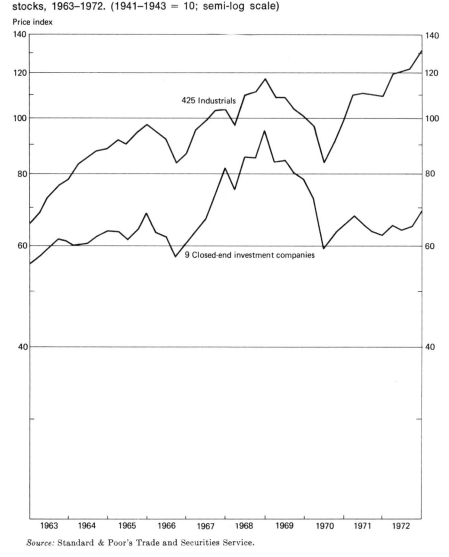

Source: Standard & Poor's Trade and Securities Service.

is far more exposed to the public than are other segments of the money management industry. Another reason for the increased attention given to mutual fund performance in recent years has been the emergence of better methods of measurement and comparison. While certain of the more sophisticated methods will be explained in Chapter 21, it is useful here to review the more popular methods of performance measurement.

One popular method of measuring the achieved performance of a mutual fund, or any other investment asset for that matter, is to calculate return on investment. To make this calculation, it is necessary to define the following variables, which determine the components of return on investment:

N_t = net asset value per share at the end of period t.
D_t = dividend distribution per share during period t.
G_t = capital-gains distribution per share during period t.

Dividend and capital-gains distributions are cash payments to fund shareholders, while net asset value is a measure of the continuing investment being made by the mutual fund. For example, value of N_t, D_t, and G_t for Investors Stock Fund over the past decade are as follows

Year, t	Net asset value, N_t	Dividend distribution, D_t	Capital gains distribution, G_t
1962	$17.19	$0.4025	$0.1025
1963	19.19	0.4350	0.4000
1964	21.06	0.4925	0.3800
1965	22.25	0.5500	0.3160
1966	19.04	0.5950	0.4000
1967	22.28	0.5925	0.4900
1968	22.42	0.5675	1.1000
1969	19.29	0.4950	0.8800
1970	18.01	0.4750	0.0000
1971	20.39	0.4950	0.1550
1972	22.72	0.4800	0.2900

We note that dividend distributions have remained relatively constant over time while capital-gains distributions have been sporadic. Net asset value per share actually ended the period only slightly higher than it was at the end of 1965. In other words, the generous increase in net asset value during 1972 was not a consistent characteristic.

The achieved *return* for any year should reflect both dividend and capital gains distributions and also the change in net asset value for each share. We can calculate the percentage annual return, R_t, in year t as follows

$$R_t = \frac{(N_t - N_{t-1}) + D_t + G_t}{N_{t-1}} \times 100 \qquad (15\text{--}2)$$

Net asset value at the beginning of the year is used as the investment base. The three components of return are appreciation of net asset value, dividend distributions, and capital-gains distributions. Values of R_t, including its three components, for Investors Stock Fund are as follows

Year	Dividends	Capital gains	Appreciation	Total return
1963	2.5%	2.3%	11.6%	16.4%
1964	2.6	2.0	9.7	14.3
1965	2.6	1.5	5.7	9.8
1966	2.7	1.8	−14.4	−9.9
1967	3.1	2.6	17.0	22.7
1968	2.5	4.9	0.6	8.0
1969	2.2	3.9	−14.0	−7.9
1970	2.5	0.0	−6.7	−4.2
1971	2.7	0.9	13.2	16.8
1972	2.4	1.4	11.4	15.2
Geometric mean	2.6%	2.1%	2.8%	7.5%

Although the average dividend distribution and the average capital-gains distribution are about the same, the latter fluctuated more over the decade examined. Annual appreciation (or depreciation) was even more volatile over the ten years, ranging from 22.7% in 1967 to —9.9% in 1966. Total return was positive in seven of the ten years, and the geometric mean return was 7.5% annually. It is interesting to note that mutual fund salesmen are not allowed to publicize rates of return wherein capital gains distributions and dividend distributions are added, as has been done in the numerator of expression (15–2).

On the basis of annual return as given by expression (15–2), individual funds can be evaluated and comparison can be made among groups of funds. We have already seen that the 1972 return per share of Investors Stock Fund was 15.2%. Figure 15–6 includes the annual returns for the ten mutual funds (with assets greater than $10 million) that achieved the highest return during the single year 1972. Each of the ten funds in Figure 15–6 had a return for 1972 at least twice as great as the average return of all mutual funds. Two of the ten were no-load funds, while the other eight were load funds.

It was argued earlier that selecting a mutual fund on the basis of only one year of performance may not be a reasonable strategy—particularly if the investor is planning to hold the mutual fund shares for a much longer horizon. Instead, it may be preferable to base mutual fund selection on achieved performance over longer horizons, thus reflecting different types of market conditions. Three methods will be discussed: *dollar accumulation, aggregate percentage return,* and *performance ratings.*

FIGURE 15–6
Mutual funds with best percentage return during 1972

Rank	Mutual fund	Percentage return	Asset size*
1	Templeton Growth	64.1%	$ 13.0 million
2	International Investors	55.8	12.7
3	Omega Fund.	44.3	45.3
4	Putnam Voyager	39.0	44.6
5	Twentieth Century Growth	37.8	15.4
6	Putnam Vista	35.0	102.4
7	Life Insurance Investors	34.3	90.3
8	Janus Fund (no-load).	33.0	30.9
9	Sudden Development (no-load)	30.4	33.8
10	Chemical Fund	29.9	834.6
	Sample average	40.4%	$122.3 million

* As of September 29, 1972.
Source: Arthur Lipper Corporation.

For evaluation and comparisons of performance over longer horizons, there are two important considerations that must be made. The first is how to handle the dividend and capital-gains distributions that occur during the longer horizon. The second is how to reflect the loading fees that are incurred for load funds. The three sources of information on mutual funds mentioned earlier in the chapter treat these considerations in slightly different ways. To illustrate, we shall present performance comparisons over the decade 1963–1972 for another sample of ten mutual funds.

Figure 15–7 presents the ten funds (according to *Fundscope*) that had the highest dollar accumulation at the end of 1972, assuming that $10,000 was invested in each fund at the beginning of 1963. Where applicable, loading fees reduced the initial investment. Both dividend

FIGURE 15–7
Mutual funds with best dollar accumulation, 1963–1972

Rank	Mutual fund	Accumulated value	Asset size*
1	Rowe Price New Horizons (no load)	$67,327	$510.7 million
2	Enterprise Fund	49,383	414.1
3	Invest Fund	41,814	371.1
4	Security Equity	41,657	133.7
5	Scudder Special (no load)	38,478	217.6
6	Ivy Fund (no-load)	37,866	62.5
7	Chemical Fund	37,334	928.3
8	Investors Research	36,994	6.9
9	Johnston Mutual Fund (no-load)	36,829	332.5
10	Axe-Houghton Stock.	35,424	88.2
	Sample Average	$42,311	$306.6 million

* As of December 31, 1972.
Source: Fundscope, April, 1973, p. 245.

and capital-gains distributions are assumed to be reinvested in the shares of the particular mutual fund. The average dollar accumulation of the ten funds in Figure 15–7 was $42,311—as compared with the median value of $22,475 for all mutual funds. Although the effect of loading charges is reduced somewhat in performance comparisons over longer horizons, four of the best performers were no-load funds. We also note that the average size of assets under management for this sample was over twice as large as that for the sample in Figure 15–6. Chemical Fund is the only mutual fund that appears in both samples.

Figure 15–8 presents returns over extended horizons (according to

FIGURE 15–8
Percentage return of mutual fund sample over selected horizons through 1972

Mutual fund	Two years 1971-72	Four years 1969-72	Six years 1967-72	Eight years 1965-72	Ten years 1963-72
Rowe Price New Horizons (no-load).	86.8	52.5	250.1	492.5	561.1
Enterprise Fund.	31.2	−28.8	122.9	230.2	420.5
Invest Fund	35.5	18.6	70.9	135.5	348.9
Security Equity	47.4	−0.3	84.9	259.9	339.0
Scudder Special (no-load)	35.4	3.8	117.8	185.1	265.8
Ivy Fund (no-load)	34.1	−15.4	132.7	95.4	268.8
Chemical Fund	57.2	53.8	111.6	160.1	280.6
Investors Research	49.4	32.6	92.1	198.1	286.6
Johnston Mutual Fund (no-load).	57.7	47.8	105.3	163.9	242.1
Axe-Houghton Stock.	25.9	−7.5	83.9	151.3	267.9

Source: Investment Companies (Wiesenberger Services, 1973).

Wiesenberger) for the same ten mutual funds. Aggregate returns over the decade are expressed as a percentage of net asset value at the beginning of each horizon. They are not annual returns. All horizons extend to the end of 1972. Capital gains distributions are assumed reinvested, but total dividend income over the horizon is simply added to the terminal net asset value. Treatment of dividend distribution is the difference between the measurements of performance by *Fundscope* and by Wiesenberger.

Though it is not directly evident from Figure 15–8, many of the high performers during the past decade achieved much of that performance during the mid-sixties, notably 1965–67. For some, performance during that period was high enough to offset substantially lower returns during the subsequent years. Although one might quarrel with the way in which dividend distributions are added with no adjustment for timing, the return measure used in Figure 15–8 does provide a common benchmark for comparing the performance of a group of mutual funds.

Performance ratings (according to *Forbes*) for the same ten funds are presented in Figure 15–9. The *Forbes* ratings are different from the measurement schemes of *Fundscope* and of Wiesenberger in that letter grades (A+ to F) are assigned both for "rising markets" and "declining markets." Specific rising and declining markets are defined as follows.

Rising markets	Declining markets
June 30, 1962–February 9, 1966	February 9, 1966–October 7, 1966
October 7, 1966–November 29, 1968	November 29, 1968–May 26, 1970
May 26, 1970–January 11, 1973	January 11, 1973–June 30, 1973

The achieved performance of each fund that is rated by *Forbes* is compared to all funds of a similar category in each of the six market periods. Performance is averaged for each fund for three up-markets and for three down-markets. The following letter ratings are assigned to each fund based on its ranking against other funds: A+ for the top 12.5 percent, A for the next 12.5 percent, B for the next 25 percent, C for the next 25 percent, and D for the lowest 25 percent. The F rating is reserved for funds that did especially badly during a down market. Rankings of performance are thus transformed to these five grade ratings according to a fund's ability or inability to consistently outperform other funds of a similar category. The overall market, as represented by the *Forbes* Stock Average receives C ratings in both rising and declining markets according to this system.

We see in Figure 15–9 that all ten mutual funds received B or higher

FIGURE 15–9
1972 performance ratings of mutual fund sample

Mutual fund	Rising markets	Declining markets
Rowe Price New Horizon (no-load)	A+	D
Enterprise Fund	B	F
Invest Fund	A+	F
Security Equity	A	F
Scudder Special (no-load)	B	F
Ivy Fund (no-load)	A	F
Chemical Fund	A	A
Investors Research	A	B
Johnston Mutual Fund (no-load)	B	C
Axe-Houghton Stock	B	D

Source: "1972 *Forbes* Mutual Fund Ratings," *Forbes* (August 15, 1973).

ratings in rising markets, while their corresponding ratings during declining markets were often C or worse. Such a pattern of inconsistent performance is observed for most mutual funds. Because of the restrictiveness of their stated objectives and policies, and/or because of the inflexibility resulting from large size, mutual funds as a group have not been able to adapt favorably their portfolios to changing market conditions during the past decade. Chemical Fund was in fact the only mutual fund in the *Forbes* 1973 ratings to receive an A rating in both rising and declining markets. Further explanation of this phenomenon using the concept of portfolio volatility will be offered in Chapter 21.

As mentioned at the outset of this section, the authors believe that selecting investment company shares necessarily must depend on an assessment of past performance. Carefully deciding upon an investment objective enables the investor to narrow his search to a particular category of investment company shares. For mutual funds, the performance ratings of *Fundscope* and of Wiesenberger can be used to identify professional managers that seem to have made more successful investment decisions over time. And finally, for those investors who believe that they can predict major movements and changes in movement of the securities market, the performance ratings of *Forbes* can be used to identify mutual funds that have done better in particular types of markets. Because of loading charges, however, a strategy of switching from one fund to another in anticipation of changing market movements must likely be restricted to no-load funds or to switching from one fund to another within a group of funds offering a transfer option.

SUMMARY

We have examined investment companies as one vehicle whereby individuals are able to invest indirectly in the securities of many companies. Aggregation, diversification, and management, three characteristics of investment companies, were explained in some detail. Special attention was placed on investing in mutual funds because of their popularity and the aggregate value of their assets under management. Closed-end investment companies have a fixed capitalization, and their shares are traded on the organized stock exchanges, occasionally at premiums but more often at discounts from their net asset values. Dual funds are a type of closed-end company that offer distinct types of benefits from a common portfolio to two classes of shareholders. Sources of information on mutual funds, including the prospectus, *Fundscope*, Wiesenberger, and *Forbes*, were reviewed. Components of return to mutual fund shares include dividend distributions, capital-gains distributions, and appreciation of net asset value. Comparisons of realized performance, based on both percentage return and dollar accumulation, were illustrated with a sample of mutual funds. It was suggested that selecting investment company shares should include a careful evaluation of past performance.

SUGGESTED READINGS FOR CHAPTER 15

I. Friend, M. Blume, and J. Crockett. *Mutual Funds and Other Institutional Investors: A New Perspective* (New York: Twentieth Century Fund, Inc., 1970).

Investment Companies (New York: Wiesenberger Services, Inc., 1973).

D. L. Markstein. *How to Make Money With Mutual Funds* (New York: McGraw-Hill Book Company, Inc., 1969).

S. B. Mead. *Mutual Funds: A Guide for the Lay Investor* (Morristown, N.J.: D.H. Mark Publications, General Learning Corp., 1971).

J. P. Shelton, E. F. Brigham, and A. E. Hofflander, "An Evaluation and Appraisal of Dual Funds" *Financial Analysts Journal*, May–June, 1967, pages 131–39.

Wharton School of Finance and Commerce, University of Pennsylvania. *A Study of Mutual Funds* (Washington, D.C.: Government Printing Office, 1962).

16

Investing in service organizations

THE PREVIOUS four chapters have dealt with investing in the securities of various nonindustrial corporations that frequently receive attention of one sort or another in investment literature. One type of nonindustrial corporation that has not received much attention is those business organizations engaged in providing services rather than producing or distributing physical commodities. While our economy is recognized as highly industrialized, observations of that economy and forecasts of its future often conclude with statements about its evolution into a high service orientation. One somewhat disturbing aspect of understanding an economy increasingly dominated by service organizations is that the fields of finance and investments have continued to be dominated by thought and research attuned to industrial activity.

One characteristic that differentiates service from industrial businesses is that success of service organizations usually is less dependent upon a physical asset base, and instead is more dependent upon people, their ideas and imagination, than is the case with industrials. Nonetheless, investment analysis has been dominated with measuring rate of return on asset investment by firms. This was evident in Chapter 9 of this book as well as in certain of the preceding chapters of Part IV. Efficient use of invested capital has continued to be the cornerstone of investment analysis procedures, with particular focus on measurement according to the familiar DuPont expression:

Return on investment = Asset turnover × Profit margin.

Because of this, a cynic might conclude that techniques of investment analysis are finally catching up with the industrial revolution in which the three factors of production were land, labor, and capital. A fourth factor of production within an economy increasingly dominated by service organizations is personal characteristics, either in the form of skills and abilities or in the form of entrepreneurship. The purpose of this chapter is to explore the process of investing in the securities of organizations whose success is relatively more dependent upon people, their abilities, and their ideas, than upon the presence of good physical location (land), adequate manpower (labor), and modern production facilities (capital). It will be noted that while this chapter is written from the viewpoint of analyzing service oriented businesses, a great many of the suggested approaches are equally applicable to analysis of small businesses.

IDENTIFYING THE SERVICE SECTOR

The increasing importance of the service sector has been discussed by many writers. In *Future Shock*, for example, Alvin Toffler contends

> Much excitement has accompanied the discovery that once a techno-society reaches a certain stage of industrial development, it begins to shift energies into the production of services, as distinct from goods. Many experts see in the services the wave of the future. They suggest that manufacturing will soon be outstripped by service activity in all the industrial nations—a prophecy already on its way toward fulfillment.[1]

Such a trend is readily seen from a cursory examination of U.S. national income accounts over the past two decades.

Year	Gross national product (GNP) (billions)	Personal consumption (billions)	Total services (billions)	Services as percentage of GNP	Services as percentage of personal consumption
1972	$1,155.2	$726.5	$309.2	26.8	42.6
1970	977.1	617.6	262.6	26.9	42.5
1960	503.7	325.2	128.7	25.5	39.6
1950	284.8	191.0	62.4	21.9	32.7

During the decades since the end of World War II, the services component of personal consumption expenditures (which measures the service component of gross national product from the consumption rather than the production side) has increased from 21.9% of gross national product to 26.8%. If the consumption of services is measured relative to personal consumption expenditures, the increase is from 32.7% to 42.6%.

---

[1] Alvin Toffler, *Future Shock* (Random House, Inc., 1970), page 221.

In order to analyze the relative merits of investing in service organizations as distinguished from industrial firms, it is necessary to cultivate a feel for the nature and scope of the service sector. In so doing, we for the moment include public utilities and transportation firms within the industrial category because they are asset-heavy firms.

To better understand the scope of the service sector, the authors of this book recently tabulated fifty different establishments along a single street in a suburb of Los Angeles. They are classified into five categories in Figure 16–1 according to the dominant characteristic of the business with respect to the consumer.

FIGURE 16–1
Classification of fifty establishments

Dominantly physical commodity (22)

1. Artist supplies store
2. Bicycle store
3. Bookstore
4. Clothing store
5. Delicatessen
6. Drugstore
7. Furniture store
8. Furrier
9. Gas station
10. Hardware store
11. Health food store
12. Ice cream store
13. Jewelers shop
14. Lighting store
15. Liquor store
16. Nursery (gardening)
17. Paint store
18. Pet store
19. Stationery store
20. Supermarket
21. Tire store
22. Variety store

Nonprofit organizations (4)

23. Church
24. Kindergarten
25. Post office
26. Public library

Financial services (2)

27. Bank branch
28. Insurance agency

Dominantly equipment rental (9)

29. Bowling alley
30. Car wash
31. Data processing company
32. Dry cleaners shop
33. Laundromat
34. Miniature golf course
35. Motel
36. Tavern
37. Theater

Dominantly human capability (13)

38. Barbershop
39. Employment agency
40. Escrow company
41. Locksmith's shop
42. Medical offices
43. Realty company
44. Restaurant
45. Stockbroker's office
46. Swimming pool maintenance store
47. Tailoring shop
48. Television repair shop
49. Travel agency
50. Veterinary office

Most of the establishments might be described as retail, and a first category of 22 firms specifically were engaged in selling a *physical commodity* to the public. A second category included four establishments (church, kindergarten, post office, and public library) that offered some type of service to the public but were not profit-oriented businesses. A third category included the small outlets of two financial institutions such as were discussed in Chapter 14.

The remaining 22 firms are clearly service organizations within the scope of interest here. Of these 22, a fourth category of nine firms had as the dominant characteristic the effective *rental of equipment* to the public. In each instance, the customer is allowed the temporary use of certain physical facilities that he would not normally purchase on his own. There is no tangible product: hence the service classification. Perhaps the premier industry within this category (though not in the sample of Figure 16–1) is automobile rental. Its success lies in providing short-term use of an automobile to an individual whose need is only temporary. An investment in physical assets is clearly a part of this business, and to a degree success may be measured by return on investment. Effective use of the asset base is more a matter of personal service and convenience, however, than of the physical characteristics of the automobile itself. Also within this equipment-rental category are firms not immediately thought of as renting their equipment. The essence of a dry cleaning establishment is that the customer obtains use of the dry cleaning machinery for the few minutes necessary to clean his clothes. In a car wash, the customer is renting the washing machinery for the short time needed to scrub his own vehicle. In a movie theater, the customer rents a seat for about two hours, while in a tavern he rents the seat until he slumps out of it or decides to leave under his own power.

Put another way, success in these pseudo-rental operations depends, at the customer level, more on the physical assets being utilized than upon the personal services obtained therewith (singing bartenders being an exception). From another point of view, however, success of the industry depends upon the intellectual effort that inspired the operation. In this context, success of the car-wash industry has sprung from the conceptualization and engineering that produced machinery to satisfy a need previously filled largely by schoolboys working on Saturday mornings. The resultant "technological unemployment" of schoolboys highlights another characteristic of what we have termed the pseudo-rental service industry. Success has sprung to a large extent from increasing the degree of automation so that the basic need-fulfillment desired, a washed car or a tabulation of accounting data, can be provided more economically by short-term access to capital equipment rather than by longer use of labor.

The remaining category of thirteen firms in Figure 16–1 has as the dominant characteristic the *human capability* of one or more individuals. Frequently, he is the entrepreneur. While people are obviously involved in all fifty establishments of the survey, success of the business is uniquely tied to the ability of individuals to satisfy the particular needs of customers in this particular category. A barber is successful, not because he has the most modern barber chair or because his scissors are the sharpest, but because the artistry of his work is judged good or bad in a qualitative sense by the customer, who either returns for future haircuts or seeks another barber. The same is true for repairmen, restaurateurs, and various professional people who set themselves up in service business.

Alternative dimensions can also be used to describe and differentiate various service organizations vis-à-vis industrial and other nonindustrial types of firms. For example, the extent of investment in fixed assets for establishments listed in Figure 16–1 ranges from high (motel) to low (locksmith's shop). Number of employees ranges from high (restaurant) through low (barbershop) to virtually none (laundromat). The level of training and technical expertise ranges from high (data processing company) to low (car wash). And the extent of governmental regulation ranges from high (bank branch) to low (tailoring shop). These dimensions, in conjunction with the material covered in Chapters 12–15, permit us to make a more extensive classification of all business firms whose securities are available as potential investments. It is well to review the classification, summarized in Figure 16–2, as based on major economic characteristics.

FIGURE 16–2
Characteristics of selected types of business firms

Type of business	Invest- ment in fixed assets	Invest- ment in inventory	Size of personnel force	Profes- sionalism of personnel force	Govern- mental regu- lation
Other-than-service organizations					
Manufacturing firms	High	High	High	Low	Low
Retail and wholesale firms	Low	High	Low	Low	Low
Public utility companies	High	Low	Low	Medium	High
Transportation companies	High	Low	Variable	Variable	High
Financial companies	Low	Low	Low	Low	High
Service organizations					
Dominantly equipment rental	Medium	Low	Low	Low	Low
Dominantly human capability	Low	Low	Low	High	Low

Manufacturing firms are characterized by relatively high investment in fixed assets and in inventory. Typically they possess a relatively large work force of a relatively low level of professionalism, although it is usually possible for the management of manufacturing firms to shift resources from labor to fixed assets by selecting more capital-intensive production processes. Economic success, and therefore success in investing is likely to depend upon the efficiency of the investment in fixed assets and upon the proper control of the investment in inventory and other current assets. In many instances, success will depend upon the wisdom with which management varies the mix of labor and capital. Government regulation is of minor importance.

Retail and wholesale firms are dominated by their high investment in inventory and in other current assets, and economic success of such firms is related primarily to the efficiency with which they generate profit relative to their total current assets. Fixed assets tend to be of lesser importance, although in the case of certain types of retail outlets, geographic location may be a critical variable. "Good" geographic location may require added capital costs, especially for new firms, or it may be an accident of historical location. The labor force is typically small in relation to the volume of business generated, and a high degree of professionalism is not necessary. Government regulation is a minor factor in the affairs of these firms.

Public utilities and *transportation companies* are characterized by a very high investment in fixed assets relative to the volume of business generated. Inventories and other current assets are of modest significance. The labor force is small for utilities and some types of transportation (freight), although it may be high for transportation companies serving passengers, such as the airlines. In this respect, success of the airlines may involve some of the attributes that this chapter ascribes to service industries. Government regulation of both public utilities and transportation companies is very intense as we have seen, and economic and investment success depends upon the interaction of government regulation with the twin requirements of a large asset base and the need to develop and sustain an adequate volume of business activity.

Financial companies include a variety of types previously identified as deposit and savings organizations and insurance companies. Such organizations have modest investment in fixed assets and virtually nothing in inventory. Their major asset commitment is a heavy investment in various types of securities and loans. The labor force is small in proportion to the dollar volume of business, and a considerable portion of labor activity is at a low level of professionalism. Government regulation is high.

If the above groups constitute the nonservice sector, what then is the service sector? For all of the nonservice categories, a heavy investment in some type of asset is essential, be it fixed assets, inventory, or monetary securities. As a general matter, a heavy investment in some type of asset is not essential for service organizations. In some cases, a medium degree of asset investment is essential, though business success depends more upon other variables than upon the physical characteristics of this asset. An example would be a restaurant. It is essential to invest in tables, chairs, and kitchen equipment, as well as the physical premises.

On the other hand, success depends more upon the quality of the food and atmosphere (sometimes in reverse order) than upon the fact that the electronic range, let us say, is the most modern of its type. In other cases, such as a real estate broker's business, physical assets are virtually inconsequential to the ability to enter the business or to success therein. It is also possible in the case of many service organizations to lease the necessary assets rather than owning them outright.

It is also seen in Figure 16–2 that service organizations dominated by equipment rental differ in two important respects from service organizations dominated by human capability. First, those businesses whose success depends upon individual capabilities usually have a low if not negligible investment in fixed assets. Second, their personnel force usually is characterized by a higher level of professionalism, even though the number of individuals involved may be low. Finally, we see in Figure 16–2 that governmental regulation is low for both types of service organizations.

An alternative classification of service organizations is between those that are primarily oriented to the consumer, and those that are primarily technology-oriented. Consumer-oriented firms may be further subdivided into those where the customer seeks a product or product-related service, such as repair of his automobile or television set, or the shortening of his hair, or where the customer seeks passive forms of entertainment, as in a theater or tavern, or more active pleasures, as from golfing or bowling. Technology-oriented firms would be those whose output is of an intangible nature, and might include research and development firms, business consultants, engineering design firms, book publishers (who typically contract the physical printing to another firm), and accounting and legal firms.

Service industries can be identified by yet another characteristic, the basic *entry hurdle* for firms within the industry. This characteristic cuts across those used in Figure 16–2. The major entry hurdle for manufacturing, merchandising, utilities, and transportation companies is raising sufficient financial capital to enter the business on a size made necessary by the technological economies of scale. Another entry hurdle for utilities, transportation companies, and financial institutions is regulatory. Franchises or licenses from a governmental body are essential before business can commence. This regulatory hurdle may be qualifications as to who will be allowed to enter the industry, compliance with a variety of regulations intended to protect society, or zoning that imposes a location limitation.

On the other hand, the dominant entry hurdle for service organizations is human. Can a person or persons be found who can lead the business firm to success? In the dominantly human category this person will typically be the one who provides the service (i.e., the barber.

the stockbroker, or the repairman). In the dominantly equipment rental category, this leadership may be provided by a management team with sufficient imagination to conceptualize and organize a way in which customers can have convenient and inexpensive short-term access to the benefits of certain physical facilities.

The above paragraphs have attempted to identify the service sector of the economy in terms of the relatively lesser importance of fixed operating assets and tangible products and the relatively greater importance of human capital. Another classification has been the attractiveness to the customer of the human abilities of the employees of the firm or of the rental (including pseudo-rental) services supplied by the firm. Yet another classification has been on the dominant hurdle to entry. It should be noted also that some industries may well include firms in two or more of the types of businesses that have been mentioned. For example, the tennis industry consists of manufacturing and retailing (tennis balls, racquets, and sports clothing), equipment-rental service (tennis courts), and human-capability service (tennis instruction).

A more quantitative classification of business firms can be obtained from a study of the asset mix of four broad sectors and of selected industries within each sector as of year-end 1972. Data for this purpose is presented in Figure 16–3 for manufacturing, wholesaling, retailing, and service firms, as well as for three illustrative subgroups within each of these major classifications.

The asset mix of manufacturing firms again is seen to be dominated by a proportionally heavy investment in fixed assets, with additional necessary investment in accounts receivable and inventory. Wholesaling and retailing firms differ in that investment in fixed assets is proportionally less, while investment in inventory is proportionally more. Accounts receivable remain at about the same level of importance as for manufacturing firms.

The asset mix of service firms is also dominated by investment in fixed assets, although the variation among components is greater. Fixed assets are large in proportion to total assets primarily because inventory is almost never of much importance. The significance of accounts receivable depends enormously upon the industry. Those firms that provide a service against a billing, such as engineering and architectural firms, are concerned with receivables, while those that operate on a cash-and-carry basis, such as laundries, dry clearners, and theaters, have very little investment in receivables.

Something not revealed by the comparisons in Figure 16–3 is the volume of business and resulting profit that are attained in proportion to the underlying assets. In Figure 16–4, sales as a percentage of assets and before-tax profits as a percentage of assets are presented for the same sectors and industries. Surprisingly, average asset turnover for a

Percentage balance sheet breakdown for selected sectors and industries, 1972

Sector and industry (number of firms)	Assets					Sources				
	Cash and equiv- alent	Accounts receiv- able	Inven- tory	Net fixed	Total assets	Bank credit	Accounts payable	Other accruals	Long- term financ- ing	Total sources
Manufacturing (2,213)	6.3%	25.6%	25.9%	42.2%	100.0%	6.5%	12.3%	11.4%	69.8%	100.0%
Meat packing (138)	5.6	27.4	25.5	41.5	100.0	14.5	13.7	12.2	59.6	100.0
Electronic components (212)	6.8	27.8	33.1	32.3	100.0	8.3	13.1	12.3	66.3	100.0
Miscellaneous plastic parts (135)	6.3	25.2	34.0	34.5	100.0	4.9	11.9	11.4	71.8	100.0
Wholesaling (2,143)	5.8%	29.6%	40.7%	24.9%	100.0%	9.9%	24.2%	10.5%	55.9%	100.0%
Radios, refrigerators and appliances (142)	6.0	34.8	43.1	16.1	100.0	9.4	30.2	10.7	49.7	100.0
Wine, liquor, and beer (293)	6.1	26.7	44.6	22.6	100.0	13.3	29.8	11.5	45.4	100.0
Building materials (359)	6.3	31.9	27.4	34.4	100.0	11.8	16.4	11.4	60.4	100.0
Retailing (2,045)	8.1%	21.8%	42.2%	27.9%	100.0%	7.6%	18.5%	11.7%	67.7%	100.0%
Hardware (145)	5.9	19.2	47.7	27.2	100.0	8.0	16.4	8.5	67.1	100.0
Drugs (182)	7.9	10.8	57.9	23.4	100.0	3.6	23.5	9.9	63.0	100.0
Jewelry (141)	3.9	26.0	48.9	21.2	100.0	10.7	13.5	15.6	60.2	100.0
Services (2,066)	9.0%	25.4%	6.0%	59.6%	100.0%	7.4%	11.6%	14.8%	66.7%	100.0%
Engineering and architectural (233)	8.6	43.9	7.5	40.0	100.0	6.0	9.0	20.9	64.1	100.0
Laundries and dry cleaners (90)	9.0	16.8	9.6	64.6	100.0	3.1	17.0	12.3	72.6	100.0
Management consulting and public relations (90)	13.3	38.4	4.6	43.7	100.0	6.1	8.0	24.5	61.4	100.0

Source: *Annual Statement Studies* (Robert Morris Associates, 1973 edition).

FIGURE 16–4
Sales and profits in comparison to assets for selected sectors and industries, 1972

Sector and industry (number of firms)	Ratio of sales to assets	Before-tax profit as percentage of assets
Manufacturing (2213).	1.95	8.1%
Meat packing (138).	6.32	3.9%
Electronic components (212)	1.49	9.6%
Miscellaneous plastic parts (135)	1.59	10.8%
Wholesaling (2143)	3.27	6.9%
Radios, refrigerators, and appliances (142)	2.68	6.6%
Wine, liquor & beer (293)	3.91	6.7%
Building materials (359)	2.59	7.5%
Retailing (2045)	2.61	6.9%
Hardware (145).	2.53	7.3%
Drugs (182)	2.90	8.8%
Jewelry (141)	1.66	6.2%
Services (2066)	1.27	5.6%
Engineering & architectural (233)	2.23	9.3%
Laundries and dry cleaners (90)	2.11	3.2%
Management consulting and public relations (90)	1.92	7.5%

Source: *Annual Statement Studies* (Robert Morris Associates, 1973).

sample of over 2,000 firms is smaller for the services sector than for any of the other three sectors. Before-tax profit as a percent of assets is also lowest for the services sector.

These low percentages seem to come about for two reasons. First, although service industries are not what we have identified as asset-heavy industries, they nevertheless do possess the ability to increase human productivity with investment in labor-saving equipment. Thus the asset base for several of the dominantly human capability types of business may be larger than first hypothesized because of investment in expensive tools, such as oscilloscopes for automobile mechanics and computers for management consultants.

A second reason springs from the basic DuPont formula: the apparently lower-than-expected asset turnover for service firms may be offset by larger-than-expected profit margins. This appears to be the case, and will be discussed later in this chapter.

AVAILABILITY OF SECURITIES

Our concern in this book is with the process of investing. Service industries are therefore of practical interest to us only if they issue securities that can be purchased and included within a portfolio. Of

the service establishments identified in Figure 16–1, many of those classified as dominantly human are essentially the personal investments of
the proprietor or partners, rather than corporations that issue publicly
marketable securities amenable to inclusion within the portfolio of an
investor. The same is generally true with the dominantly rental (including pseudo-rental) establishments such as those in Figure 16–1. But
it is well to note an evolutionary process wherein businesses that traditionally were privately owned and operated are increasingly becoming
part of national franchise operations that permit the entry of public
capital. This process started with the franchise food business in the
1950s. Twenty years ago it would have been difficult to invest, via securities traded on organized stock exchanges, in hamburger stands, fried-
chicken outlets, or pancake houses. Today, however, one can buy stock
in McDonald's, Kentucky Fried Chicken, or International Industries and
effectively include within one's portfolio an investment in those particular
types of business.

A more recent trend has been the national franchising of real estate
brokerage companies, which until the early 1970s were typically organized only as local community businesses. The process of innovation,
combined with the synergism that may result from national combinations
of local businesses, may provide in the decades ahead increased opportunities for investment in the service sector.

In view of such a trend, it is not surprising that groups of firms
have tended to be identified as belonging to the service sector. Because
of the way in which firms are grouped, however, there is by no means
a clear cut consensus as to the composition of the service sector. To
illustrate this at a general level, Figure 16–5 identifies different types
of businesses that are classified as being service industries by Robert
Morris Associates, the source of the financial statement data in the preceding two figures. We see that many of the businesses included in
Figure 16–5 were also observed in the informal survey presented earlier
in the chapter. On the other hand, the popular magazine *Business Week,*
in its quarterly survey of corporate performance, includes a much narrower set of firms in its service category: leasing, vending machines,
wholesaling, real estate builders and developers, etc. Also to illustrate
the lack of consensus at a particular level, Denny's Restaurants is classified into "leisure time" by *Business Week,* "travel services" by Value
Line, "retailing–food" by Standard & Poor's, and just "services" by Merrill
Lynch, Pierce, Fenner and Smith, Inc.

A second set of available securities in the service sector are those
issued with a legal impairment of their marketability. Included within
this group is what is commonly called *letter stock.* Shares of such stock
are sold to a limited number of public investors who have established
that they are professionally capable of making such investment decisions

FIGURE 16–5
Types of businesses classified as services by Robert Morris Associates

Accounting, auditing, and bookkeeping	Janitorial
Advertising agencies	Laundries and dry cleaners
AM radio stations	Linen supply
Auto repair shops	Local trucking and storage
Auto and truck rental and leasing	Long distance trucking
Bowling alleys	Management, consulting, and public relations
Cable TV	Membership sports and recreation clubs
Car washes	Motels, hotels, and tourist courts
Commercial research and development laboratories	Nursing, convalescent, and rest homes
Data processing	Outdoor advertising
Direct mail advertising	Photographic studios
Engineering, architectural, and surveying	Real estate agents and brokers
Equipment rental and leasing	Real estate holding companies
Farm product warehousing and storage	Refrigerated warehousing
Funeral service and crematories	Refuse systems
General warehousing and storage	Telephone communication
Hospitals	Transportation on rivers and canals
Insurance agents and brokers	Travel agencies
Intercity and rural highway transportation	TV stations
	Water utility companies

Source: *Annual Statement Studies* (Robert Morris Associates, 1973).

and that they have sufficient wealth to take the risk of investing in a company whose securities might not be judged suitable for the great mass of investors. Letter stock arises because of the nature of securities regulation by state and federal agencies in the United States. Federal securities regulation in the United States is based upon the principle of "full disclosure." In order to make an offering of securities to the general public, a registration statement must be filed with the Securities and Exchange Commission in Washington and a condensation of this information in the form of a "prospectus" must be delivered to each person who buys the stock. Preparation of the requisite registration statement is an expensive process that has the effect of foreclosing entry to the national securities markets of smaller firms, so an exemption from the regular procedure is available for offerings of less than $500,000. This exemption allows public sale, termed a "Regulation A Offering," of qualified issues if an "offering circular," containing information on the issue and the issuer, is made available to all buyers. The offering circular, which is less detailed than a prospectus, is filed with the S.E.C. along with copies of all sales material (advertisements, radio and TV scripts, etc.), and the S.E.C. may suspend the Regulation A offering if it finds that any provision of the law has been violated.

State securities laws are based upon a different principle: the state must protect innocent buyers from being deceived by unscrupulous salesmen who would offer "the blue sky" for sale if given the opportunity. Therefore most state securities laws provide for obtaining approval of a designated state official before a public offering can be made. A typical law requires a state commissioner of corporations to make a finding that the proposed issuance of securities is fair, just, and equitable and that the securities that are to be issued or the method by which they are to be issued will not work a fraud upon the purchaser of those securities. Such a finding must be made *before* any securities may be offered for sale to the general public, and thus every offering of securities possesses, to some degree, the mark of approval of a public official.

Legal restrictions such as these increase the difficulty of raising venture capital for new, risky firms, including those in the expanding service sector of the economy. As a consequence, the device of *letter stock* has been developed, in which new securities may be sold to professional investors of demonstrated sophistication and bargaining power, who are experienced and able to inquire into and assume the risks involved. To prevent the subsequent resale of these securities, which are judged to have above-average risk, to an unsuspecting and innocent general public, such shares are typically stamped or overprinted with a legend that prevents their resale except as approved (on a transaction-by-transaction basis) by the appropriate state authority. The restriction may remain in effect until removed by approval of an application of the corporation, or for a stated period of time, say five years after the initial sale. In either instance, a limitation is imposed on the marketability of the stock. Because there is no general market that trades in letter-stock securities, they cannot be said to have a market value. Although they can be valued by such techniques as discounted future benefits, as discussed in Part II of this book, lettered securities cannot be compared to listed common stocks on a basis of price-earnings ratios—simply because they have no market price. In addition, firms of this type often have no earnings, especially during their early years.

Why would an individual consider purchase of letter stock or other shares, the marketability of which is limited by law? The answer lies in the evolution of a typical business from inception to recognized success as a major national or international business firm. Great financial reward accrues to those investors who commit their funds early in the evolutionary process, if the business is in fact destined to become a large, successful organization. This phenomenon, of course, is in no sense unique to service companies. Rather it is part of the process of investing in new, emerging firms, whatever their industrial grouping. It is our hypothesis, however, that many of the more interesting investment opportunities in emerging firms in the remainder of this century will lie within the service sector.

The typical historical evolution of a business firm begins with its organization as an individual or family-owned enterprise. Initial success will depend, in most instances, upon the personal characteristics of the founder, who often performs all of the management functions himself. Securities of such enterprises are not usually available to the general public.

If this new business is successful, expansion follows, constrained in many instances by limited availability of capital. Additional capital may be needed for fixed assets and inventory, in the case of manufacturing and mercantile firms, or to pay operating costs and wages, in the case of a human-capability service firm. In either instance, the firm soon reaches the limits of additional expansion from family-owned resources and seeks to sell securities to the general public. Because the firm may be unseasoned as a business venture, or perhaps because the quantity of new capital needed at that time does not warrant a public offering, shares may be sold on a limited basis to friends and relatives or to investors known in the local community. Such shares are typically in letter-stock form as described above. These shares possess several important attributes: they are nonmarketable, or of very limited marketability, because general marketability is constrained by law. They are also highly risky, because many rapidly growing small businesses fail. Their inherent worth is also difficult to assess because the business itself may limit the financial data available to the general public. On the other hand, if the business is successful, such investments prove very profitable. In terms of our discussion in Chapter 3, these securities possess a very small probability of very great success.

A path by which holding of such investments may come to be considered a success involves the eventual offering of the securities to the general public. At such a time, the past success of the firm, now an established historical fact, and the addition of complete marketability to securities previously of impaired marketability, mean that the market price will be substantially above what was paid by the investor who purchased during the period of limited marketability. An investor who can enter the evolutionary process at the intermediate stage, during which shares are being sold on a limited basis, and hold those shares until after the company grows to a size that warrants its "going public" will typically find that he has made a most successful investment.

One risk of this scenario must be noted. Shares of common stock in comparatively young, rapidly growing firms are usually marketed on their expected future growth. This will be true for letter-stock shares, as well as for smaller national offerings under Regulation A and for smaller intrastate offerings sufficiently large to warrant sale without the letter-stock restriction. Although sold on a promise of future growth, the process by which an investor "escapes" from such a commitment of funds is seldom specified. Cash recovery following purchase of nonmarketable equity securities of small companies can come from only three sources. First, cash dividends may be received—although dividend payments typically are small or nonexistent for rapidly growing, small firms because they desperately need capital for continued expansion. Second, there may be a sudden increase in market value if the firm successfully goes public. The decision to go public is usually complicated because it involves both overall market conditions and the willingness of original owners to relinquish control in order to attract new investors. The outside investor has little leverage by which to force a firm to go public if the majority stockholders are not interested in this alternative.

A third possibility for escape is for the rapidly growing firm to merge into another firm whose securities are publicly traded. In this eventuality, the stockholder exchanges his shares of limited marketability for fully marketable shares of the acquiring firm. Success in this method of liquidation depends upon the same variables as in going public, including especially the willingness of the dominant original stockholders to take this action. In many instances such dominant stockholders do not want to surrender the personal control of the company or even its identification with their own name, even though the financial aspects of the merger may be desirable.

Lacking payment of cash dividends, going public, or a merger with a publicly traded firm, the investor who enters the evolutionary development of a small firm is a prisoner of that commitment, regardless of the financial success of the firm itself. This circumstance serves to reiterate the risky nature of investing in small businesses, many of which are service organizations of one type or another.

FINANCIAL STATEMENT ANALYSIS

Corporate balance sheets list the assets and liabilities of the enterprise and are one of the two major financial statements used by security analysts to obtain historical perspective on the developments within a corporation. For manufacturing and merchandising concerns, the asset side of the balance sheet is a fairly accurate representation of the economic resources at the disposal of the firm. Variations in the accuracy of this portrayal, although important, do not obscure the basic fact that the balance sheet generally describes to a reasonable degree the capital committed to the venture. For this reason, efficiency of an industrial firm is often measured in terms of a rate of return earned upon assets (using the left side of the balance sheet) or upon invested capital (using the capital structure components on the right side of the balance sheet).

Balance sheets of service companies, especially the dominantly human type, possess less validity as a base from which to measure efficiency, primarily because a significantly greater proportion of the valuable resources of a service company do not appear in any compilation of its assets. The list of "missing assets" that follows may be applied, it is true, to manufacturing and merchandising companies, and indeed it should be. Its great significance, however, is that a very large proportion of valuable resources controlled by service companies are not "assets" in the technical sense.

Perhaps the greatest missing asset is human capital. To the extent that business success is a function of the skills and abilities of the people whose activities are joined together under the corporate banner, the balance sheet fails in its basic purpose of providing a base from which to judge success in the use of economic resources.

Assets leased by the firm are a second important class of assets conspicuously absent from the balance sheet. Although of significance for the measurement of results of all businesses that lease assets, the fact that many assets used by service industries, including store buildings and offices, are leased as a matter of normal practice means that the balance sheet asset tabulation does not measure the economic resources devoted to corporate activities. For example, a firm such as Howard Johnson (used for illustration in Chapter 11) that leases most of its buildings and facilities has a balance sheet that greatly understates the value of the asset base being used.

Yet a third category is "goodwill" as it is understood in a general sense—the reputation of a business unit among its customers that serves to bring those customers back. Where reputation or goodwill is based upon the development of a satisfied clientele over an extended period of time and in a situation in which other assets that would constitute part of a physical product are missing, the existence of goodwill is extremely important in assuring financial success. The importance to a consumer of locating the right lawyer, the best plumber, or the restaurant with the finest chef means that possession of that quality—reputation—is, in the true meaning of the word, an asset that cannot be depicted on the balance sheet. A fourth type of unlisted asset is backorder for products, a category as important for manufacturing as for service, but possibly of greater importance in proportion to other assets for some service firms such as architects and consultants.

Thus financial statement analysis based on balance sheets is of limited usefulness. What remains is analysis based upon income statements alone. This means that in assessing the financial success of businesses whose activities are primarily service in nature, the various relationships between the expenses of operating a business and the revenue that is generated are paramount. Two techniques are suggested: common-size income statement analysis and break-even analysis.

398

Common-size income statements

Common-size analysis of income statements was discussed in Chapter 9 for industrial companies, and the same general principles hold here. The basic measure of success is comparatively low operating expenses in relation to operating revenues or, if one prefers, comparatively large income margins. These may be measured either over time for a single business unit or across a spectrum of several businesses involved in the same type of activity. It is worthy of note that reliance on common size statements and upon income margins is, in effect, reliance on half of the DuPont expression mentioned at the outset of this chapter. While we are able to formulate opinions about cost efficiencies, we lack a procedure for forming judgments about efficient use of the resources at the command of the firm. Nevertheless, this partial measure is valid if we assume that the expenses of acquiring the nonasset resources (such as the salary expenses of acquiring the human resources) are competitive rates determined in a free market place. That is, one is inclined to assume that the expenses of hiring engineers for an aerospace design firm are the true expenses of that resource, for engineers tend to change jobs in pursuit of the highest salary. The imputed wages paid to the owner-operator of a corner grocery store, however, are very likely to be much lower than what that owner-operator could earn if he entered the general labor market. This is especially true if the owner-operator works much longer hours than he would tolerate as a full-time employee working for someone else. What we are suggesting is that common-size analysis of income statements is better for those companies that bid for all of their economic resources in a competitive market, but is poorer for those companies that have a noneconomic claim on some of their resources.

Figure 16–6 presents common-size income statements for the same four sectors and selected industries that have been reflected in earlier exhibits of this chapter. For many of the specific industries within the service sector, "cost of sales" is not calculated, and thus all the expenses are included in "other expenses." As a result, the average cost of sales is only 8.1% for over 2,000 service organizations—as compared to 75.8% for manufacturing, 80.3% for wholesaling, and 69.8% for retailing. Before-tax profit as a percentage of sales is also seen to be greater for the services sector. In other words, the profit margin is greater for service organizations than for firms in other sectors of the economy.

Break-even charts

The other analytical technique is *break-even analysis.* This analytical approach is of particular usefulness in assessing prospects for financial

FIGURE 16–6
Common-size income statement for selected sectors and industries, 1972
(percentages of sales)

Sector and industry (number of firms)	Cost of sales	Other expenses	Before-tax profits
Manufacturing (2,213)	75.8%	18.6%	5.6%
Meat packing (138)	91.3	8.1	0.6
Electronic components (212)	69.8	24.5	5.7
Miscellaneous plastic parts (135)	74.5	20.0	5.5
Wholesaling (2,143)	80.3	16.6	3.1
Radios, refrigerators, and appliances (142)	82.8	14.2	3.0
Wine, liquor, and beer (293)	85.1	12.5	2.4
Building materials (359)	80.4	16.3	3.3
Retailing (2,045)	69.8	26.1	4.0
Hardware (145)	69.8	25.0	5.2
Drugs (182)	70.9	24.8	4.3
Jewelry (141)	68.1	27.6	4.3
Services (2,066)	8.1	85.1	6.8
Engineering and architectural (233)	62.2	31.6	6.2
Laundries and dry cleaners (90)	25.7	72.6	1.7
Management consulting and public relations (90)	–	91.9	8.1

Source: Annual Statement Studies (Robert Morris Associates, 1973).

success and thus for investment success of a service organization. The usefulness springs from the fact that break-even analysis is based upon data from an income statement but is useful in predicting levels of profit as a function of the volume of business that is achieved. To illustrate the basic nature of break-even analysis, as applied to a service company, let us assume that we are looking at a franchised food-service outlet of the drive-in or walk-in type that specializes in fried froglegs. We shall call our company Louisiana Fried Froglegs.

Louisiana Fried Froglegs sells a lunch-sized service for $1.25, including the basic frogleg serving (prepared according to the secret recipe of its founder, Colonel Sandhurst), cole slaw, and a beverage. Each serving has costs as follows:

Fresh froglegs	$0.25
Spices, oil, other condiments	.25
Beverage and cabbage	.25
Total costs per serving	$0.75

Variable costs for the outlet are $0.75 times the number of lunches sold during the quarter. In addition, the Louisiana Fried Froglegs outlet incurs fixed expenses of $25,000 per quarter for such items as the salaries of all personnel, rent and utilities for the uniquely designed building, specialized cooking equipment, advertising, and payment of a fixed franchise fee to the parent organization.

The relationship between these expenses and the revenue of $1.25 per serving are shown in Figure 16–7. Output in terms of number of lunches served per quarter is shown on the horizontal axis, and dollars of revenues and expenses are plotted on the vertical axis. Maximum capacity with the present physical facilities is 80,000 lunches per quarter,

FIGURE 16–7
Break-even analysis for Louisiana Fried Froglegs

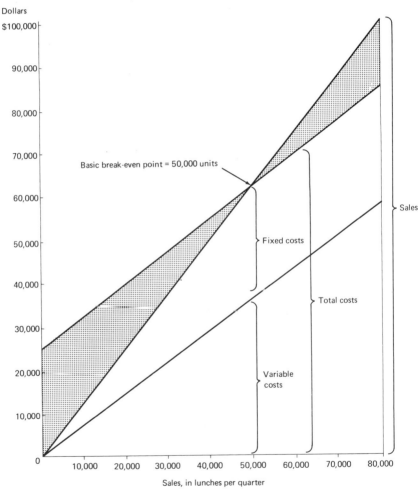

Note:
  Selling price—$1.25 per lunch.
  Variable cost—$0.75 per lunch.
  Fixed cost—$25,000.

so the analysis covers the range of possibilities from zero to 80,000 lunches. Beyond 80,000 lunches per quarter, it would be necessary to build a larger facility, which would necessitate a new level of fixed costs and the drawing of a new break-even chart.

At every level of output, fixed expenses are $25,000. In addition, variable costs are $0.75 per lunch sold, and this cost is added to fixed costs. For example, if 70,000 lunches were sold, fixed costs would be $25,000 and variable costs would be ($0.75) (70,000) = $52,500. Total cost would be the sum of variable costs ($52,500) and fixed costs ($25,000) or $77,500. On the other hand, sales revenue at every level of output would be $1.25 times the number of lunches sold. At a volume of 70,000 lunches, sales revenue would be ($1.25) (70,000) = $87,500. Profit at this volume of lunch business would be revenue of $87,500 minus expenses of $77,500, or $10,000.

The importance of break-even analysis lies in the shaded triangles of Figure 16–7. These triangles, formed by the space between the total cost line and sales revenue line, indicate potential profit or loss at every possible level of output for the sales outlet and its existing capacity. The point where the lines cross over is known as the *basic break-even point*. For the Louisiana Fried Froglegs outlet, this is 50,000 units, which means that the outlet must sell at least 50,000 lunches per quarter if it is to be a financial success. Arrangement of income statement data in this format is especially useful for analysis of service industries because it reduces the unknown factor in the generation of profits to an estimate of the probable level of sales. In the instance of an investor interested in the profit-generating potential of a fried frogleg food outlet, the essential question reduces to whether or not more than 50,000 lunches per quarter can be sold. This would be determined by quantitative analysis of the reputation of froglegs as a new lunch food, plus restaurant and other competition within the immediate geographic area.

A logical extension that is particularly germane to a new business is shown in Figure 16–8, where we will assume that of the $25,000 total fixed charges per quarter, $10,000 is depreciation of the special cooking equipment and other fixtures that must be purchased by the food outlet. Since depreciation is not a cash payment, but rather an accounting entry, a *cash break-even point* can be located at that sales level where sales revenue just equals the total cash payments that must be made during the quarter. In the case of Louisiana Fried Froglegs, we see that the cash break-even point is 30,000 lunches per quarter. Often in the case of a small service business, the owner-operator cannot expect to make a profit during the first few months while he is building sales up to a normal level. But if he can expect sales beyond the cash break-even point, then he will at least have enough sales revenue to pay all the bills.

402

FIGURE 16-8
Cash break-even analysis for Louisiana Fried Froglegs

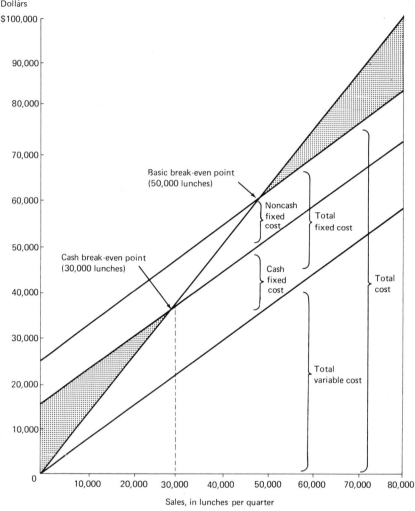

Note:
  Selling price—$1.25 per lunch.
  Variable cost—$0.75 per lunch.
  Cash fixed cost—$15,000.
  Depreciation—$10,000.

Another logical extension that is germane to more seasoned businesses is shown in Figure 16–9. Here the idea is to determine the sales volume necessary for a specified level of profit. This determination is accomplished by adding the profit requirement to fixed and variable costs, and locating the *profit break-even point,* where the total is just equal

FIGURE 16–9
Profit break-even analysis for Louisiana Fried Froglegs

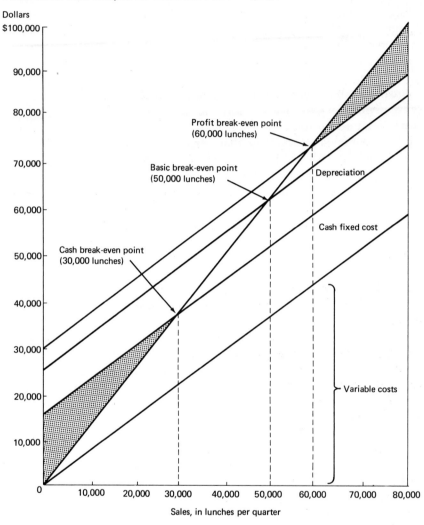

Dollars

Profit break-even point
(60,000 lunches)

Basic break-even point
(50,000 lunches)

Depreciation

Cash fixed cost

Cash break-even point
(30,000 lunches)

Variable costs

Sales, in lunches per quarter

to sales revenue. Suppose a profit of $5,000 per quarter is set as a target for Louisiana Fried Froglegs. We see in Figure 16–9 that this profit would be achieved at a volume of 60,000 lunches per quarter. For higher volume, profit of course would exceed $5,000 per quarter. For many of the service organizations identified in this chapter and also for many small businesses, break-even analysis (including the basic, cash, and profit versions) is a useful technique for better understanding profit-volume relationships.

SELECTING SECURITIES OF SERVICE ORGANIZATIONS

As with all purchases of common stocks, investments in service organizations should be valued through the discounted cash flow model of Chapter 6. Application of this model to actual service organizations presents several problems. Perhaps the greatest of these is that earnings of service organizations of the type previously identified as dominantly human capability arc in many instances tied to the personal abilities of an individual who is a major force in the business's activities. Any forecast of future earnings and thus of future dividends is in fact a forecast of the continued presence of that person or team of persons. This personal element adds a high degree of risk to the forecast, a risk for which a conservative investor must compensate by a greater discount rate or by using the most conservative estimate of future earnings and dividends. Moreover, book value or asset value in liquidation is not likely to provide a floor for valuation, since earnings are not usually a function of those assets.

Service organizations of the type previously identified as equipment rental or pseudo-equipment rental are more amenable to valuation by the techniques applied to industrials because the assets do have a value of their own and do function as a base from which earnings are generated.

If an attempt is made to value service organizations by more traditional approaches, such as application of conventional price-earnings multipliers to current or anticipated future earnings, a problem arises because of wide variations between levels of multipliers for various types of service organizations. Insofar as "service" is considered an industry, we have seen that one dominant characteristic of the industry is its heterogeneity. The diversity of business activities and of price-earnings ratios for the decade 1963–1972 for a selected group of companies that might be considered service organizations within the context of this chapter is shown in Figure 16–10.

Average price-earnings ratios for the decade range from highs of 34.1 for the Marriott chain of hotels, food service, and airline catering operations, and of 34.0 for Pinkerton's, a company of historic fame as a supplier of private protective services, to lows of 10.5 for Twentieth Century-Fox Film Corporation and of 14.0 for Allied Maintenance Corporation. High ratios for individual years ranged from 92.6 for Burns International Security Services and 63.8 for Walt Disney Productions, while lows ranged from 6.1 for Twentieth Century-Fox Film and 8.1 for American Building Maintenance.

Even within groupings by related activities, the ranges are great. Hilton Hotels had a decade average price-earnings ratio of 17.4, while Holiday Inns averaged 30.0. Servomation Corporation averaged 19.5,

FIGURE 16–10
Price earnings ratios for selected service organizations, 1963–1972

Company	Decade average	Highest year	Lowest year
Cleaning and maintenance			
Allied Maintenance Corporation 14.0		29.6	8.9
American Building Maintenance Industries* 21.1		38.7	8.1
Food vending			
ARA Services 27.6		34.8	20.1
Servomation Corporation 19.5		26.7	14.7
Restaurants			
Denny's Incorporated† 29.1		52.7	10.7
Howard Johnson Company 22.7		29.2	15.3
McDonald's Corporation† 30.5		60.8	15.9
Protective services			
Burns International Security Services. 28.7		92.6	11.8
Pinkerton's Incorporated‡ 34.0		40.3	22.5
Broadcasting			
Capital Cities Communications, Inc. 17.6		24.5	14.0
Columbia Broadcasting System, Inc. 18.9		28.5	14.2
RCA Corporation 22.1		27.8	17.6
Truck leasing			
Leaseway Transportation Corporation 15.3		21.8	10.6
Ryder Systems 18.9		29.1	11.7
Motion pictures and related activities			
Disney (Walt) Productions 26.5		63.8	8.9
MCA Incorporated § 16.2		26.1	11.4
Twentieth Century-Fox Film Corporation‖ 10.5		16.2	6.1
Loew's Corporation# 14.8		25.4	8.6
Hotels and other accommodations			
Hilton Hotels Corporation 17.4		27.2	8.8
Holiday Inns, Inc. § 30.0		48.4	20.7
Marriott Corporation 34.1		52.9	16.7
Publishing			
Book-of-the-Month Club 13.8		22.5	9.8
Dow Jones and Company 31.5		45.1	20.0
Grolier Inc. 14.4		18.0	10.5
Times-Mirror Company 20.5		27.3	16.4

* Seven years, 1966–72, only.
† Eight years, 1965–72, only.
‡ Six years, 1967–72, only.
§ Nine years, 1964–72, only.
‖ Excludes 1969 and 70.
Excludes 1969.
Source: Moody's Handbook of Common Stocks.

while its competitor in the food vending machine business, ARA Services, averaged 27.6. Grolier, Inc., an encyclopedia publisher, averaged 14.4, while Dow Jones and Company, a newspaper publisher, averaged 31.5. Clearly it is impossible to generalize to any significant degree about "typical" values for companies within the service sector.

In spite of problems such as these, securities of service organizations are likely to become increasingly important components of investment portfolios in future years as the service sector of what has been termed the "post-industrial society" evolves to increased significance. Valuation of service organizations is likely to proceed along traditional lines, either using discounted future cash benefits or in application of traditional price-earnings multipliers as modified by expectations and/or popularity. The wide diversity of investment securities within the service sector should make such securities attractive for inclusion in diversified portfolios.

SUMMARY

The essence of this chapter has been to point out that there exists an ill-defined group of companies linked only by a thread of providing some degree of service to their customers. The dominant trait of these service organizations is that a heavy investment in assets is not a major economic characteristic, although it may be important to a degree for some. Service organizations can possibly be grouped into two types: (a) rental and pseudo-rental companies, and (b) companies whose major economic trait is the provision of human-generated services to customers. Neither of these types of service companies has been well analyzed in the literature of business finance or investments, and this chapter is but a preliminary approach to further understanding the securities of this growing category of business activity.

SUGGESTED READINGS FOR CHAPTER 16

J. Balog. "The Health Care Industry," *Institutional Investor*, May, 1970, pages 62–65 and 90–96.

R. F. Greeley. "The Business Service Companies," *Institutional Investor*, April, 1970, pages 62–65 and 96–97.

L. R. Johnson. "The Computer Software Companies," *Institutional Investor*, March, 1970, pages 58–61 and 93–100.

W. L. Paternotte. "The Food Service Companies: How Many Stars Do They Rate?" *Institutional Investor*, August, 1973, pages 93–98.

part V

Investor activities

IN EARLIER CHAPTERS, we covered portfolio construction, investment valuation, and investment analysis. Now in Part V, we examine a number of topics that have to do with investors' implementing the decisions that culminate the process of investing. Chapter 17 reviews various markets in which securities and other investment assets are traded. Next, we examine in Chapter 18 a number of procedures whereby investors select securities firms, open accounts at these firms, and place orders for buying or selling stocks and bonds. We also review the different transaction costs that are involved in implementing investment decisions. Chapter 19 considers the entire spectrum of information sources available to investors as they deliberate on various investment opportunities. Included are sources on company history and organization, recent financial history, forecasted earnings, and investment recommendations. Chapter 20 deals with the important subject of timing as being central to the process of investing. Topics such as technical analysis, dollar cost averaging, and formula planning are explained and illustrated. Finally, in Chapter 21, we consider alternative methods of evaluating the achieved performance of an ongoing portfolio over time. Alternative measures of return and risk are developed and illustrated to measure the performance of an investor's portfolio and to serve as a basis for future investment decision-making.

17

Operations of markets

SECURITIES MARKETS are systems of trading created to facilitate investor buying or selling of stocks, bonds, and other securities. Within the United States there exist organized stock exchanges, organized bond exchanges, the over-the-counter market, and what is commonly called the "money market." The purpose of this chapter is to describe these exchanges and markets, to review the functions of brokers, dealers, and other participants in security markets, and to explain the nature of security transactions.

TYPES OF MARKETS

An *organized stock exchange* is a physical entity whose members meet face to face and, by means of a two-sided auction process, buy or sell securities for their customers. Trading is limited to a list of securities formally "listed" or "admitted to trading" on that exchange. In contrast, the *over-the-counter market* is based upon a sophisticated communications network that transmits information about prices at which securities firms will buy or sell securities with other securities firms physically scattered about the country. Actual transactions are effected between participating securities firms by telephone or teletype. Although some trading occurs in securities also listed on stock exchanges, the majority of over-the-counter transactions are in securities not traded upon an exchange.

Securities markets provide a valuable service to those who wish to buy or sell securities. A greater benefit, however, may be to society as a whole, for the availability of organized procedures for trading in stocks and bonds expands the number of investment alternatives available to individuals and financial institutions, thereby enlarging the total pool of capital available to finance productive enterprises. The auction nature of securities markets furthermore provides an efficient method for allocating funds among competing sectors in a free economy. Securites markets also provide important signals, through security prices and yields, to business managers about how well they are making decisions and running their organizations.

All transactions on organized stock exchanges and a very large proportion of over-the-counter transactions are in "already-issued" securities; i.e., in securities already owned by investors who are now selling to other investors. Because such transactions between existing security holders do not provide new capital to the issuer of the security, they are frequently referred to as *secondary market* transactions to differentiate them from *primary market* transactions, in which business or governmental units initially offer new securities to the public to raise new capital for productive purposes. Primary offerings are all handled in the over-the-counter market. It is generally accepted that sales of new securities in the primary market are made possible, to a large extent, because buyers have confidence that they can resell the securities, should they wish to do so, in a dependable secondary market. Thus the economic health of primary and secondary markets is interrelated.

Another expression, *third market*, is sometimes used to refer to over-the-counter trading in stocks listed on the New York Stock Exchange or other organized exchanges. Such trading typically occurs between large institutional investors who seek to acquire or dispose of large blocks of stock at lower commission costs or at prices not influenced by the size of the transaction. Third market trades usually are arranged by a securities firm that is not a member of an organized exchange.

Finally, the expression *fourth market*, is used to refer to transactions negotiated directly between institutional investors that bypass all financial intermediaries.

ORGANIZED STOCK EXCHANGES

When the term *stock market* is mentioned, most investors probably think of the New York Stock Exchange, on which about 71% of all share trading on organized exchanges occurs. There are, however, a total of twelve operating exchanges in the United States. The relative importance of these exchanges can be seen from Figure 17–1, which indicates both market value and share volume of trading for the year 1972.

Two of these exchanges, the New York Stock Exchange and the American Stock Exchange (both located in New York City), are truly

FIGURE 17–1

Stock trading on U.S. securities exchanges (market value and share volume for 1972)

Exchange	Market value		Share volume	
	Thousands of dollars	Percentage of total	Thousands of shares	Percentage of total
New York	159,700,186	78.3	4,496,187	71.4
American	20,452,646	10.0	1,103,222	17.5
Midwest	8,427,981	4.1	228,751	3.6
Pacific	8,023,893	3.9	248,490	3.9
Philadelphia-Baltimore-Washington	5,274,083	2.6	143,105	2.3
Boston	1,562,151	0.8	38,472	0.6
Detroit	362,390	0.2	9,808	0.2
Cincinnati	103,439	0.1	2,324	*
National (New York City)	112,091	0.1	15,743	0.2
Spokane	4,498	*	9,258	0.1
Intermountain (Salt Lake City).	2,362	*	3,841	*
Honolulu.	2,122	*	271	*
Total	204,027,807	100.0	6,299,473	100.0

Note: Totals do not add because of rounding.
* Less than 0.05 percent.
Source: Statistical Bulletin (United States Securities and Exchange Commission, February 21, 1973) page 68.

national exchanges. The remaining exchanges are commonly called *regional exchanges*, although a very high proportion of their transactions involve securities that are also traded on the New York or American Stock Exchanges. Because most U.S. stock exchanges operate under rules and procedures more or less similar to those of the New York Stock Exchange, the next discussion focuses on that largest organized exchange.

The New York Stock Exchange (the "Exchange") was formed in the decades following the Revolutionary War. There had been no pressing need for an organized stock market in American colonies because securities were neither issued nor traded in America. Capital financing of colonial businesses was arranged in London.

The outbreak of the revolution cut the colonies off from their traditional British capital markets and also led the Continental Congress and the various states to issue bonds and notes to finance the war effort. In 1781 the Bank of North America was established in Philadelphia; in 1784 shares of the bank of New York were first sold; and in 1791 the first Bank of the United States was chartered. The shares of these banks, plus Treasury bonds issued under Alexander Hamilton to refinance the war debts of the

Continental Congress and of the 13 states, created a supply of securities, and a securities exchange was formed in Philadelphia in 1790.

Ten years later a group of New York securities brokers formed an association and pledged themselves "not to buy or sell from this day for any person whatsoever, any kind of public stock at a less rate than one quarter per cent commission on the specie value." Thus was born the antecedent of the New York Stock Exchange. During sunny days trading was conducted outdoors under a buttonwood (sycamore) tree, and when the weather turned bad the associated brokers moved into the nearby Tontine Coffee House to continue their activities. In 1817 a formal constitution was adopted, along with the name "New York Stock and Exchange Board," which was changed eventually to "New York Stock Exchange."

Today the New York Stock Exchange is a corporation governed by a 21-member Board of Directors. Ten directors are elected from among the principal executives of securities firms, and ten are elected from the public. These directors elect a full-time chairman, who becomes the 21st member of the board.

The Exchange itself neither buys nor sells securities. Nor does it set security prices. Rather, security trading is conducted between individual members of the Exchange with the Exchange providing facilities, clerical help, statistical reporting, and rules and procedures designed to provide equal opportunity and protection to all investors. The Exchange owns its own building at 11 Wall Street on lower Manhattan Island, and all trading is conducted on the *floor* of this building.

Transactions on the floor of the Exchange can be executed only between members of the Exchange. These 1,366 members are said to own *seats* on the exchange, although physical seats have not been present on the trading floor for almost a century. Rather "seat" is a synonym for ownership of a share of stock in the New York Stock Exchange, Incorporated. A seat is the private property of a member and may be transferred by sale, by gift, or by bequest. The privileges of membership after acquiring a seat, however, may be exercised only by those persons meeting the high qualifications of the Exchange and approved by the Exchange. A successful applicant for the privileges of membership must be a citizen of the United States, be over twenty-one years of age, be in sound financial condition, and have a satisfactory business, social, and educational record.

The secretary of the Stock Exchange maintains a file of written bids and offers for seats on the Exchange, and new members other than those acquiring seats by gift or inheritance must purchase a seat at the going offering price. The price at which seats are bought and sold is directly related to the health of the securities industry, as can be seen from Figure 17–2 in which each vertical line represents the price range for that year.

FIGURE 17-2
Seat prices on the New York Stock Exchange, 1928-1972

Thousands of dollars

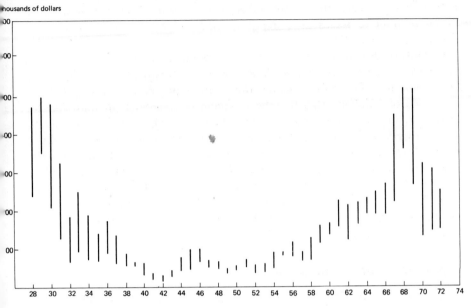

Membership on the Exchange is available only to natural, as distinct from corporate, persons. However, members may join together to form member firms. At the end of 1972 there were 569 such member firms, 269 partnerships and 300 corporations.

LISTINGS OF SECURITIES ON THE NEW YORK STOCK EXCHANGE

Only *listed securities* may be traded on the floor of the New York Stock Exchange. To have its stock listed, a company must satisfy certain specific requirements of the Exchange and agree to keep the investing public informed about its affairs. Eligibility for listing is based on such matters as the degree of national interest in the company, the company's relative position and stability in its industry, and whether the company is engaged in an expanding industry with prospects of maintaining its position. Before a security can be admitted to trading on the Exchange it must also be registered with the Securities and Exchange Commission under provisions of the Securities Exchange Act of 1934.

In addition to these general requirements, the Exchange requires a company applying for listing to have at least 2,000 stockholders owning 100 or more shares. The company must have at least 1,000,000 shares publicly held with a market value in excess of $16 million. Demonstrated earnings power before federal income taxes and under competitive conditions must have been at least $2.5 million for the latest fiscal year and $2.0 million for each of the preceding two years. At the end of 1972, the number of issues of common stock listed on the New York Stock Exchange was 1,478.

Operating procedures of the various regional exchanges (but not of the New York or American Stock Exchanges) provide for dual listing of some securities and for unlisted trading in others. *Dually listed stocks* are those of companies that have applied for and been approved for listing on one or more regional exchanges as well as on one of the two national exchanges. *Unlisted trading* privileges are granted by a regional exchange so that its members can trade in a stock that is listed on one of the major exchanges. Unlisted trading may take place only in stocks that have been formally admitted to listing on another exchange. No security is dually listed on both the New York Stock Exchange and the American Stock Exchange, and these two exchanges do not admit stocks to unlisted trading privileges.

TYPES OF MEMBERSHIP ACTIVITY

A member of the New York Stock Exchange may use his membership for whatever purpose he chooses within the rules of the Exchange. As of May, 1973, the 1,366 members of the Exchange were functioning in the following capacities, which will be explained below:

Commission brokers	740
Independent brokers (two-dollar brokers)	132
Registered traders	53
Specialists	383
Odd-lot dealers	10
Inactive members	48
Total	1,366

Commission brokers act as agents for the general public. By themselves or in conjunction with other commission brokers, they may form commission brokerage firms, which in turn maintain one or more offices about the country where registered representatives (also called account executives or brokers) execute orders received from the public. These offices are connected by private wire to the trading facilities of the Exchange, and the partner or stockholder of the brokerage firm, who is himself a member of the Exchange, works on the floor executing orders for the firm's clients. The commission schedules used by commission brokers are discussed in the next chapter. Of the 740 commission brokers indicated above, 25 handle bond transactions exclusively.

Independent brokers, also called *two-dollar brokers,* execute orders for other members of the Exchange in return for a floor commission. At one time this commission was $2 per 100-share transaction; hence the nickname. At present two-dollar brokers receive a scaled-down special commission that allows them to earn a portion of the commission paid by the public to the commission broker.

Two-dollar brokers exist because commission brokers sometimes receive more orders than they can handle at one time. In addition, a member may be ill or away from the floor for some other reason, and since an employee of a member commission broker may not function in that member's absence, a two-dollar broker will fill in for the missing member.

Registered traders are Exchange members who buy or sell for their own account and profit (or loss). They do not come into contact with the public, and they do not execute orders for other members of the Exchange. In effect they buy a seat and pay the additional costs of membership in order to be able to execute their own transactions on the floor personally and without the usual brokerage commissions.

Registered traders are subject to a number of restrictions that prevent their trading activities from conflicting with orders from the public. Among such restrictions are a prohibition against executing trades for their own account in any security for which they have executed a public order during the same day. There are also several situations in which registered traders must yield on the floor to orders placed by the public.

The registered trader category was established in 1964 to preserve the benefits of a system of floor trading (by *floor traders*) that preceded the new classification, while eliminating the grounds for some criticisms of floor trading. Floor trading activities are believed to contribute to the existence of a better market for investors by narrowing the spread between the price at which some members seeks to buy (the *bid* price) and the price at which other members are willing to sell (the *ask* or *offer* price). In addition, registered traders provide reserve buying power so that large blocks of stock can be traded quickly on the floor at a minimum price variation from previous sales. Registered traders occasionally have been criticized because their position on the floor allegedly gives them a competitive advantage over the general public.

A *specialist* is a member with a specific task of maintaining a continuously "fair and orderly" market in certain stocks assigned to him. Each common stock traded on the Exchange is assigned to a specialist, and each specialist is typically responsible for from six to fifteen issues. In conducting his activities on the floor, the specialist sometimes acts as a broker for other brokers and sometimes acts as a dealer for his own account. In contrast to a broker who effects a security transaction between buyer and seller without owning the security, a *dealer* actually owns securities. Because the specialist's operations are at the very heart of the market operations of the Exchange, they will be discussed in more depth in the next section of this chapter.

An *odd-lot dealer* is a member who stands ready to buy from or sell to customers of commission brokers any number of shares less than one hundred. Such a unit is considered an *odd lot* to differentiate it from a *round lot* or *full lot*, which in almost all cases consists of 100 shares. Only round lots are traded on the floor of the Exchange, so investors trading in less than 100 shares must transact their business with an odd-lot dealer. Such transactions are arranged indirectly through a commission broker. At the present time all odd-lot dealers on the Exchange work together for a single firm, Carlisle DeCoppet and Company.

An odd-lot dealer automatically buys all odd lots offered at the market and sells all odd lots sought at the market. To a large extent his purchases and sales offset each other, but should he accumulate an inventory or find himself in a short position (obligated to deliver more shares than he owns), he may buy or sell a round lot on the floor of the Exchange to balance his position.

To purchase or sell odd lots, the customer pays his broker a commission that is $2.00 less than the commission calculated on a round lot of 100 shares. The odd-lot dealer gets no part of this commission, but gains income from the difference between the prices at which he purchases shares and the prices at which he sells them. When a customer places a market order to buy an odd lot, it is understood that he will pay a price equal to the price of the next effective round-lot transaction executed on the floor, plus an *odd-lot differential* equal to $\frac{1}{8}$ of a point (12$\frac{1}{2}$ cents) per share. Similarly, when a customer seeks to sell an odd lot, it is understood that he will receive a price equal to the price of the next effective round-lot transaction executed on the floor, less the $\frac{1}{8}$ of a point odd-lot differential. Prior to 1972, the odd-lot differential on stocks selling above $55 per share was $\frac{1}{4}$ of a point. Note that the odd-lot dealer does not receive the differential directly on each transaction. Rather the differential is one of several factors that influence the prices at which the dealer buys and sells.

To illustrate the working of the odd-lot system, assume that an investor places an order with his commission broker to buy 30 shares at the market. The order is passed to the odd-lot dealer, who holds it until a round-lot transaction occurs. If the round-lot transaction occurs at 52\frac{1}{8}$ per share, the odd-lot dealer sells 30 shares to the commission broker's customer at 52\frac{1}{4}$ per share. The odd-lot system thus enables small investors to buy or sell shares in small quantities without encumbering the regular round-lot trading mechanism with small orders.

A *block positioner* is a new classification of member created in 1972 to handle transactions in quantities of a single stock having a market value of $200,000 or more. The need for the block positioner category developed in recent years as large financial institutions evolved into a dominant force in the stock market. Special trading procedures are followed that permit an Exchange member certified as a block positioner to cross (i.e., to match a specific buy order with a specific sell order) a large block of stock on the Exchange at a specific clean-up price that is outside of the current quotation. Before a block can actually be crossed under these procedures, the specialist in the issue must buy 100 shares at the bid price, thus permitting all public "buy" orders on his book also to be executed at the benefit from the lower clean-up price.

OPERATIONS OF THE SPECIALIST

At the very core of auction procedures on the floor of the Exchange lie the operations of that type of member called a specialist. Only through the specialist are other members able to carry on their business with assurance that the market will function on a continuous basis and that some semblance of continuity will be maintained between sequential transactions.

As a broker's broker, the specialist accepts—from commission brokers—limit orders for execution at prices away from the present price. Suppose that a commission broker receives an order to buy a particular stock at 45 at a time when that stock is being traded at 52. Clearly it would be impractical for that commission broker to remain at the trading post for the hours or days that might elapse before the trading range dropped to 45. In fact, the stock might never trade that low. Under such circumstances, the commission broker hands the order with a price limit to the specialist, who enters it in his "book" and, if possible, executes it on behalf of the commission broker whenever feasible.

The specialist's book, sample pages of which are shown in Figure 17–3, consists of a series of pages for each price interval in the stock. Limit orders for other brokers are recorded opposite the desired price and in the order received. For example, in Figure 17–3, the specialist has received and is holding orders to buy 200 shares of the stock for broker Hofflander at a price of 40⅛ and 300 shares at the same price for broker Krouse. Buy orders from other brokers at lower prices would be recorded higher on the page (as the orders for Mason and Eaton) or on earlier pages in the book.

Sell orders received above the present market are recorded on the right side of the book. Figure 17–3 shows an order being held to sell 200 shares for broker Zwick at 40¾ and an additional 100 shares for broker Mayers at 40⅞. Sell orders at still higher prices would appear on later pages on the book.

FIGURE 17-3
Pages from a specialist's book

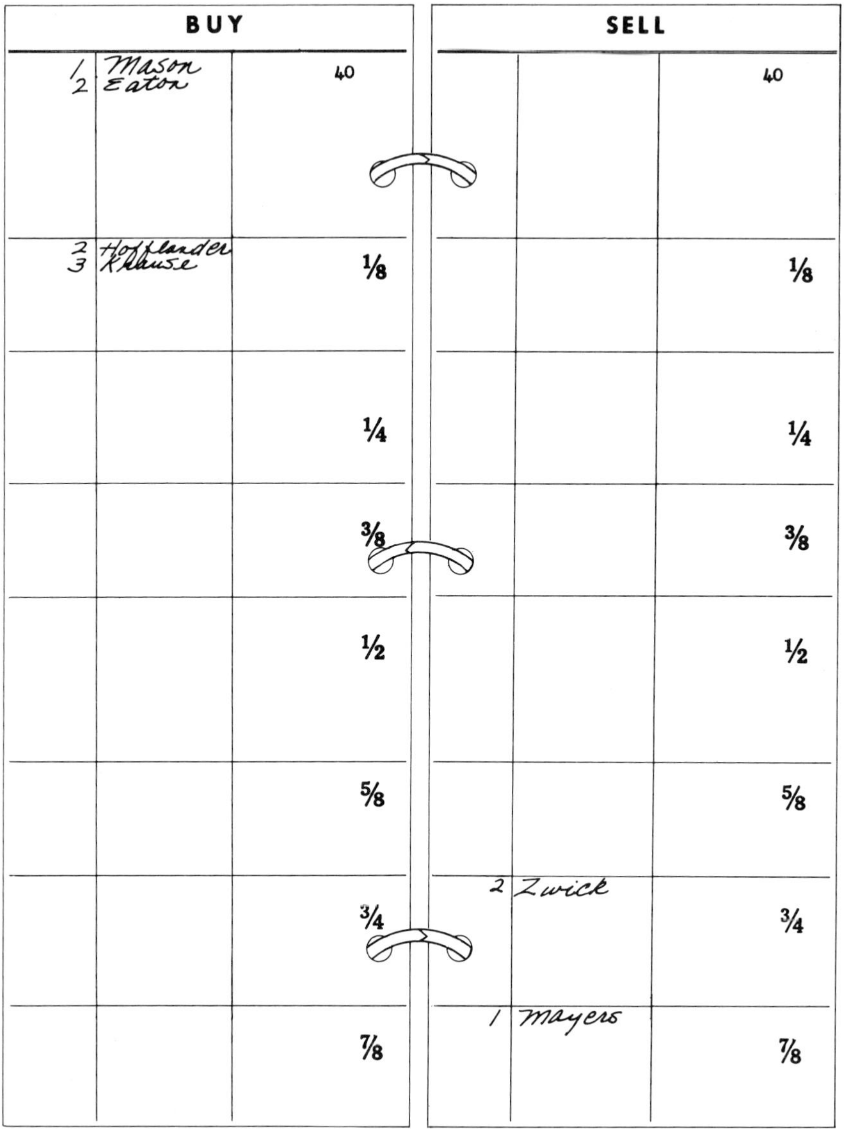

	BUY			SELL	
$\frac{1}{2}$ Mason Eaton		40			40
$\frac{2}{3}$ Hofflander Krause		$\frac{1}{8}$			$\frac{1}{8}$
		$\frac{1}{4}$			$\frac{1}{4}$
		$\frac{3}{8}$			$\frac{3}{8}$
		$\frac{1}{2}$			$\frac{1}{2}$
		$\frac{5}{8}$			$\frac{5}{8}$
		$\frac{3}{4}$	2 Zwick		$\frac{3}{4}$
		$\frac{7}{8}$	1 Mayers		$\frac{7}{8}$

The specialist is obligated to execute these orders as soon as possible; i.e., if someone offered to sell 100 shares at a price of $40\frac{1}{8}$, the specialist would have to buy these for the account of broker Hofflander to satisfy part of Hofflander's order for 200 shares.

The New York Stock Exchange has a number of rules to assure

that customers' orders are fairly treated. The rule of *priority*, for example, states that when two or more bids are made at the same price (both Hofflander and Krouse bid at 40⅛), the bid clearly established as having been entered first receives priority. If no bid is clearly entitled to priority, the rules of *precedence* apply. That is, if all the various buy bids are for amounts of stock less than the amount offered, the bid for the largest number of shares has precedence over the others and will be filled first. Bids for amounts of stock greater than the amount offered have precedence over bids for amounts of stock less than the amount offered. If several bids are made for an amount of stock greater than the amount offered, the rule of *parity* applies; the bids are considered to have equal claim and the issue is settled with a toss of a coin. The rules of priority, precedence, and parity apply to both buy and sell transactions. Additional rules limit activities of all members when buying for their own account.

The second major activity of the specialist is to maintain a fair and orderly market by trading for his own account to the extent necessary. In fulfilling this obligation the specialist acts as a dealer for his own account. This obligation comes into play when there is a temporary disparity between supply and demand. Public investors in the United States have come to expect a continuous market in which immediate execution of a market order is assured unless some major crisis has interrupted trading. A stockholder wishing to sell his shares at the market at 10:15 in the morning should not have to wait until the next public order to buy is received, possibly at 2:15 in the afternoon. The specialist bridges this gap in continuity by buying for his own account when public orders are not at hand, and later selling the same shares to fill public buy orders if sell orders are not at hand. The obligation to maintain a fair and orderly market also includes entering the market as either buyer or seller to ensure that the spread between bid and ask quotations is not too large, and trading in the market so that each transaction in sequence is not at too great a price interval from the previous transaction. Of course the amount of price change between sequential transactions that is reasonable will depend upon market and business conditions of the moment, as well as upon the floating supply of outstanding stock.

The specialist is obligated to supply on request a quote (bid and ask) and size of market (number of shares bid for and offered) in each stock assigned to him. If asked for a quote on the stock whose book is illustrated in Figure 17–3, the specialist might conceivably say "40⅛ for 500; 200 at 40¾," which means that he stands willing to buy 500 shares at $40⅛ per share and to sell 200 shares at $40¾ per share. This quote is directly from orders in his book and would not involve any transaction for his own account. Alternatively, the specialist might decide that the spread of $\frac{5}{8}$ (62½¢) between the bid and ask prices on his book is too wide to constitute a fair and orderly market. Then he would enter either a bid or an ask for his own account to narrow the spread. Perhaps he would bid 40⅝ (for his own account) and offer shares at 40¾ (for broker Zwick), to narrow the spread to $\frac{3}{8}$ (37½¢).

The Exchange requires a specialist unit (a minimum of three specialists working together as a team) to have sufficient capital to carry a 5,000-share position in each common stock assigned to it. The unit must have minimum net liquid assets of $500,000 or 25% of the total position it is required to be able to hold, whichever is greater. Specialists may use their own funds to satisfy their capital needs or they may arrange for subordinated credit from banks or other members of the Exchange.

NATURE OF A SECURITIES TRANSACTION

Transactions occur on the floor of the Exchange in response to orders placed by public investors with commission brokerage firms. A transaction consists of two separate events: (1) the making of an oral agreement on the floor of the Exchange calling for future delivery of a certain number of shares against payment of a specified sum of money; and (2) settlement of this transaction at a later date by physical delivery of the shares and actual payment of the monetary obligation.

Settlement for most transactions on the New York Stock Exchange takes place in the fifth business day following the transaction and is effected through the facilities of the New York Stock Exchange Stock Clearing Corporation. Through the clearing procedure, all transactions are netted out; i.e., a brokerage firm obligated to pay $10,000,000 to a number of other firms and at the same time obligated to receive, say, $8,000,000 from another group of firms, including possibly some of the same firms, settles its obligation by making a single payment of $2,000,000 to the Clearing Corporation. Transfer of stock certificates is currently being replaced by a computerized Central Certificate Service, in which physical certificates are kept on deposit and "transferred" by a bookkeeping entry.

To illustrate a security transaction, suppose that Mr. Sierra in Mount Whitney, California, wants to buy 100 shares of Ultra-Super Corporation common stock at the market, i.e., at the best price obtainable at that moment. Mr. Sierra places his order by telephone with a local registered representative of a New York Stock Exchange member firm, which acts as a commission broker. The order will be sent by private wire or teletype either directly to the floor of the Exchange or to the New York office of the firm, which will forward it to the Exchange floor. On the

Exchange floor a clerk will receive the order and hand it to the member firm's floor broker. This floor broker will go immediately to the trading post to which Ultra-Super Corporation has been assigned. There are 22 such posts, and every listed stock is assigned to one such post.

At the post, the floor broker will ask the specialist in the issue for the *market;* that is, for the *bid* and the *ask* quotations. The *bid* is the highest price at which the specialist or the public will buy 100 shares of the stock, and the *ask* is the lowest price at which the specialist or the public will sell 100 shares. Suppose the specialist replies that the common stock of Ultra-Super is bid $62\frac{1}{8}$ and asked $62\frac{5}{8}$. The broker knows he can buy at $62\frac{5}{8}$, since the specialist is willing to sell at this price. He also knows he cannot buy at $62\frac{1}{8}$, since the specialist already is trying to buy at that price. Note that the floor broker has not yet revealed whether he intends to buy or sell—or is just seeking information.

Instead of buying immediately at $62\frac{5}{8}$, the floor broker may try to obtain a better price for his customer. Perhaps he will announce his willingness to pay $62\frac{1}{4}$ for 100 shares. If no one in the crowd at the post accepts this bid, he may bid $62\frac{3}{8}$. The floor broker makes these bids in the hope that another floor broker will arrive at the post with a market order to sell, and that a transaction can be executed between the specialist's bid and ask. If no broker accepts his $62\frac{3}{8}$ bid, the floor broker may try $62\frac{1}{2}$. If no stock is offered from the crowd at this price, the floor broker will take the stock from the specialist at $62\frac{5}{8}$.

As soon as a price for the transaction of 100 shares of Ultra-Super is agreed upon, an Exchange employee assigned to the post as a reporter records the price and number of shares traded on a punched card and places the card in an optical scanner located nearby. Information on the transaction is fed immediately into the Exchange's computers, from which it is disseminated as public information to the thousands of ticker tapes and desk-top display units in brokerage houses about the country. Computerized information on transactions is also used for the Exchange's surveillance system, which monitors all trades and identifies any unusual price movements for subsequent study to ensure that the specialist is in fact maintaining a fair and orderly market.

At the same time that the particular transaction is being reported to the public via the computer, the two members who agreed upon the trade note the name of each other's firm and notify their own offices that the order has been executed. This information is used to arrange clearing of the 100 shares of Ultra-Super on the fifth business day after the trade. In addition, the office of the floor broker will notify the registered representative from whom the order came so that he in turn may inform Mr. Sierra. The following day a written confirmation of the transaction will be mailed to the customer.

BOND TRADING ON THE NEW YORK STOCK EXCHANGE

Most bond trading in the United States is conducted in the over-the-counter market. However, about 2,000 bond issues are listed and traded on the New York Stock Exchange, and in recent years bond volume on the Exchange has been rising rapidly. Bonds are traded in the "bond room," a separate section of the trading floor. A small number of active issues are traded much as stocks are traded, but the majority of bonds are traded by a *cabinet* method in which bids or offers are transcribed onto cards and filed for each issue in order of price. Information on these cards is available to all members. A broker wishing to complete a bond transaction executes his order against the best bid or offer filed in the cabinet. The Exchange is currently developing and implementing a system to provide electronic storage, retrieval, and matching of orders in nonconvertible cabinet bonds and to provide quotations for all bonds traded.

Bond prices are quoted on the Exchange as a percentage of par value. Thus a quoted price of 92 means 92 percent of par value, or $920 for a $1,000 bond. For all $1,000 bonds with a market value of $100 or more, the brokerage commission per transaction is $2.50 per bond.

THE OVER-THE-COUNTER MARKET

We have seen that an organized stock exchange, such as the New York Stock Exchange, is a *centralized, formal, auction* market. Before the establishment of organized exchanges, securities were purchased and sold over the counter of various bank offices. As organized exchanges came into existence, trading in unlisted stocks continued to be called "over-the-counter" even though transactions were no longer negotiated directly over a counter. Today the over-the-counter market is a *decentralized, informal, negotiated* market involving about 5,000 broker/dealer securities firms throughout the country. About 50,000 different issues are traded in the over-the-counter market, as compared with about 6,000 issues (including bonds) traded on all of the organized exchanges. About 11,000 over-the-counter issues have a sufficiently wide public ownership to warrant regular quotations in the over-the-counter market.

In addition to stocks of many thousands of comparatively smaller industrial corporations, all mutual fund shares are traded in the over-the-counter market, as are most U.S. government securities, municipal securities, and corporate bonds. Stocks may be traded over the counter because they are primarily of local interest, because there is not a sufficient volume of orders to justify an exchange listing, because the corporate officers prefer to have a securities firm with an active interest in the stock make a market in their shares, because the company does not wish to comply with the more stringent disclosure requirements of the exchanges, or because the company is simply not large enough in terms of total earnings to qualify for listing.

Most over-the-counter transactions are effected through the combination of a computer-based quotation system, called NASDAQ (pronounced "nazdak") and telephone or teletype execution of actual orders. NASDAQ consists of a central computer, located in Trumbull, Connecticut, and connected to a nationwide network of terminals located in the offices of brokerage houses, financial institutions, and securities firms "making a market" in the various over-the-counter issues. The terminals themselves resemble television screens, and a user of the service can query the system by punching certain instructions into his own terminal.

There are three levels of NASDAQ terminals, which correspond to three types of service available from the system. Level–1 subscribers are typically offices of brokerage firms that want to know the latest average bid and ask quotations of over-the-counter stocks for their customers. Level–2 terminals provide a list of all market-makers in a stock and their individual bid and asked prices. On request, the terminal provides quotes of five market-makers ranked according to the best current bid. By punching a "MORE" button, the terminal provides the next best five bids, followed by as many additional sets of five as are necessary to display all current quotes. Level–2 terminals are usually located in the trading rooms of broker/dealer firms, and from such terminals individual traders determine which market-maker to telephone to arrange an actual transaction.

Level–3 terminals are in the trading rooms of market-makers. Such terminals provide all information available in the system and also allow any securities firm "making a market" to enter, change, or retract its own quotations in the system. The phrase "making a market" means that the firm is willing to buy (at an indicated bid price) or sell (at a higher offer or asked price) some specified number of shares for its own account. The difference between the bid and ask price is known as the "spread," and in general a larger percentage spread indicates less activity in the stock and a smaller spread indicates greater activity. For example, if a certain common stock were quoted at "35 to three-quarters" (bid at $35; offered at $35.75), the spread of 75¢ would be 2.14% of the bid price. If another common stock were quoted at "20 to five-eighths" (bid at $20; offered at $20.62½), the spread of 62½¢ would be 3.12% of the bid price. Even though the spread for the second stock is less than the spread for the first stock, the probability is that there is more market activity in the first stock because the spread is a smaller percentage of the bid price. Presumably dealers are willing to quote the narrower spread for the first stock because a larger volume of activity lessens the chance of incurring a lost on an inventory position.

Quotations for less widely traded over-the-counter securities are published in the National Quotations Bureau, Inc.'s daily "Pink Sheets." These pages, printed on pink paper for issues with a national interest and on other colors of paper for various regional issues, list bid and ask quotations for many thousands of issues not quoted on the NASDAQ system.

Actual trading in the over-the-counter market is not done through the NASDAQ information system, but rather is carried out by telephone between the trading departments of the various securities firms. To illustrate the process, assume that a customer places an order with his securities firm to purchase 100 shares of an over-the-counter stock at the present market price. The registered representative who receives the order forwards it to the trading department of his firm, where a trader queries NASDAQ to determine which other securities firms in the country are making a market in that particular stock. Having located the market-maker offering the stock at the lowest price, the trader telephones directly to that market-maker and negotiates the purchase.

Under most conditions, the trader will buy the shares for the account of his securities firm and then resell the same securities to the customer at a price that includes a markup deemed "fair and reasonable" under rules established by the National Association of Securities Dealers. Under normal circumstances a 5% markup is considered fair and reasonable, so that if the securities firm purchased the shares from the market maker at $33, the shares would be resold to the customer at about ($33)(1.05) = $34.65 per share. Transactions on the over-the-counter market are generally made on such a "dealer" basis, with the dealer acting as a principal in the transaction, buying and then reselling the shares to the customer at a slight markup over cost. A dealer does not charge a commission because his profit comes from the markup that is added. From the standpoint of the investor, however, there is little difference between a transaction through a broker or through a dealer since he effectively pays for the service of execution in either case.

GOVERNMENTAL REGULATION OF THE SECURITIES INDUSTRY

About a quarter of a century ago, the stock market began what is commonly known as the "great crash." From a September 7, 1929, high of 25.38, Standard & Poor's industrial stock price index dropped to a June 30, 1932, low of 3.52. Approximately 86 percent of the value of stocks disappeared!

Various securities laws were passed by the federal government as a result of this crash and of the abuses in the securities industry discovered in subsequent investigations. In addition to regulation by the federal government, portions of the securities industry are also regulated by state governments through so-called "blue sky" laws. The National Association of Securities Dealers (N.A.S.D.) and the various organized stock exchanges also have a legal basis for self-regulation through authorization created by federal laws. Federal regulation of the securities industry derives from the federal government's jurisdiction over interstate commerce. As a general matter the selling and transfer of securities within a single state does not come under federal jurisdiction.

Certain federal securities legislation applies to specific situations. For example, the Public Utility Holding Company Act of 1935 was passed for the purpose of restricting the widespread development of utility holding companies, which had led to financial abuses during the late 1920s. The Investment Company Act of 1940 provides the legal basis for the organization and operation of both closed-end and mutual fund types of investment companies, and the Investment Advisors Act of 1940 requires the registration of those persons who seek to serve the general public as expert advisors in investment matters.

In contrast, there are three basic federal laws that apply to the securities industry in general, and they will be explained briefly below. These are the Securities Act of 1933, the Securities Exchange Act of 1934, and the Maloney Act of 1938, which is in fact an amendment to the Securities Exchange Act of 1934.

Securities Act of 1933

The first federal law dealing expressly with securities was the Securities Act of 1933, passed for the purpose of providing ". . . full and fair disclosure of the character of (newly issued) securities and to prevent frauds in the sale thereof." Thus the statute is concerned with the issuance of new securities and not with trading activity in already outstanding issues.

The 1933 Act requires that all new issues of securities and most secondary offerings be registered with the federal government unless the securities are of a type specifically exempt from the registration requirement. "Exempt" securities include issues of the U.S. government, of states and municipalities, and securities sold only within a single state (intrastate issues). Securities of certain foreign and world organizations are also exempt. In addition, offerings of less than $500,000 (so called Regulation A offerings) are exempt from the regular registration requirement.

The 1933 Act makes it unlawful to offer for sale any security (except *exempt* issues) "by any means or instrument of transportation or communication in interstate commerce or the mails" unless a proper registration statement has been filed with the Securities and Exchange Commission and is in effect. The 1933 Act further provides that no *registered* security may be offered for sale to an investor without "prior or concurrent" delivery of an effective prospectus meeting the requirements stated in the Act.

In substance, a prospectus is a summary of the most important portions of the registration statement, and in fact the body of the prospectus is usually incorporated into the registration statement itself. The front page of the prospectus, an illustration of which is shown in Figure 17–4, contains a description of the securities, information on the selling price, underwriting discounts and commissions, and proceeds to the company. Also named is the leading underwriter. The informational content of a prospectus will be discussed in Chapter 19.

An essential attribute of the federal regulatory philosophy is that the federal government does not pass judgment upon the accuracy or adequacy of the statements made in the registration statement or the prospectus. Furthermore the federal government does not approve or disapprove of any offering. Rather the statute is intended to cause "full and fair disclosure" of all material facts; and officers, lawyers, and accountants who sign the registration statement are personally liable and possibly guilty of fraud if their statements are inaccurate or misleading.

The Securities Exchange Act of 1934

The "Act of '33," as the Securities Act of 1933 is frequently called, relates only to new issues and to certain secondary offerings. In contrast, the Securities Exchange Act of 1934 (the "Act of '34") provided for ". . . the regulation of securities exchanges and over-the-counter markets operating in interstate and foreign commerce and through the mails, to prevent inequitable and unfair practices on such exchanges and markets, and for other purposes."

Specifically, the 1934 Act created the Securities and Exchange Commission (S.E.C.) as the body to administer the federal securities laws. All stock exchanges (except for a few small exchanges with limited volume) were required to register with the S.E.C., and all stocks traded on those exchanges were also required to be registered with the S.E.C. As a consequence of this law, periodic and complete financial information for all listed securities was required to be made public information. The Securities Exchange Act of 1934 also declared it unlawful for any person to engage in any "manipulative or deceptive device or contrivance." Inequitable and unfair acts and practices on exchanges, over-the-counter markets, and in securities transactions in general were declared illegal.

Regulation under the 1934 Act extended to the over-the-counter

FIGURE 17–4
Front page of a prospectus

PROSPECTUS

$75,000,000

Pan American World Airways, Inc.

7½% Convertible Subordinated Debentures, due January 15, 1998

The Debentures will be convertible into Capital Stock of the Company on and after January 16, 1975 and prior to maturity, unless previously redeemed, at a price per share equal to 80% of the average of the daily mean between the high and low sales prices for the Capital Stock on the ten consecutive trading days ending on January 15, 1975, provided that the conversion price per share may not be less than $7.00 nor more than $13.50. The Debentures may not be redeemed prior to February 1, 1976. Sinking Fund payments will begin on January 15, 1983. The Debentures are subordinated to all Superior Indebtedness which at December 31, 1972 amounted to $745,245,000. The Indenture does not restrict the incurrence of additional Superior Indebtedness. See "DESCRIPTION OF DEBENTURES".

The price of the Capital Stock on the New York Stock Exchange from January 3, 1972 through January 16, 1973 ranged from a low of $8⅝ to a high of $17¾. On January 16, 1973, the last sale on that Exchange was at $9⅛ per share. See "MARKET PRICE OF CAPITAL STOCK".

SEE "INTRODUCTORY STATEMENT" ON PAGE THREE FOR RISK FACTORS TO BE CONSIDERED BY POTENTIAL INVESTORS.

Application has been made to list the Debentures on the New York Stock Exchange.

THESE SECURITIES HAVE NOT BEEN APPROVED OR DISAPPROVED BY THE SECURITIES AND EXCHANGE COMMISSION NOR HAS THE COMMISSION PASSED UPON THE ACCURACY OR ADEQUACY OF THIS PROSPECTUS. ANY REPRESENTATION TO THE CONTRARY IS A CRIMINAL OFFENSE.

	Price to Public (1)	Underwriting Discounts and Commissions (2)	Proceeds to Company (1) (3)
Total.................................	$75,000,000	$1,125,000	$73,875,000
Per Unit.........................	100%	1.50%	98.50%

(1) Plus accrued interest from January 15, 1973 to date of delivery.
(2) The Underwriting Agreement contains provisions under which the Company has agreed to indemnify the Underwriters against certain liabilities, including liabilities arising under the Securities Act of 1933.
(3) Before deducting expenses payable by the Company estimated at $410,000.

The Debentures are offered hereby, subject to prior sale, to withdrawal, cancellation or modification of the offer without notice, to delivery to and acceptance by the Underwriters, to the approval of their counsel and of counsel to the Company, and to certain further conditions. It is expected that delivery of the Debentures will be made at the office of Lehman Brothers Incorporated, New York, New York, on or about January 24, 1973, against payment therefor in New York funds.

Lehman Brothers
Incorporated

The date of this Prospectus is January 17, 1973

---

market, because all securities brokers and dealers not members of registered stock exchanges (and thus not regulated through the process of regulating exchanges) were required to register directly with the S.E.C. The only exceptions were brokers or dealers engaged exclusively in intrastate business. A broker/dealer's application for registration could be denied, or his existing registration revoked, for making false or misleading statements in his registration application, for having been convicted within the past ten years of a felony or misdemeanor involving a securities transaction, for having been enjoined by a court from engaging in the securities business, or for having willfully violated any of the federal securities acts. Minimum capital requirements were established for broker/dealer firms, and certain books and records were required to be maintained and made available to the S.E.C. upon request.

The Maloney Act of 1938

One facet of federal regulation of the securities markets has been to permit, to the maximum extent possible, self-regulation by industry organizations. The organized stock exchanges were clearly capable of such self-regulation, but no central organization existed for the informal trading conducted in the over-the-counter market. Thus in 1938 Congress passed the Maloney Act, which became Section 15A of the Securities Exchange Act of 1934. The Maloney Act provided for the formulation of trade associations within the securities business for the purpose of self-regulation, and for the registration of such trade associations with the S.E.C.

Only one trade association has been formed under the Maloney Act, The National Association of Securities Dealers (N.A.S.D.). Virtually all securities firms in the United States belong to this association. The N.A.S.D. maintains its importance through a provision that members may give preferential rates and discounts only to other members. All dealings with nonmembers, including nonmember financial institutions and securities firms, must be made at the same rates and discounts as are available to the general public. Thus loss of N.A.S.D. membership effectively prevents a securities firm from buying at "wholesale" or "inter-dealer" prices and thus from operating at a profit.

Blue Sky Laws

In 1911 the State of Kansas passed the first state securities law. State securities laws came to be called "Blue Sky Laws" because of a comment that their intent was to prevent "speculative schemes which have no more basis than so many feet of blue sky."[1] Some state laws simply prohibit the fraudulent sale of securities and prescribe penalties for such sales. Other laws require registration of new issues and of broker/dealer firms and their registered representatives. Some state laws follow a full-disclosure philosophy, similar to that incorporated in the federal statutes, while other states require approval of a new issue before it can be offered for sale.

---

[1] *Hall* v. *Geiger-Jones Co.*, 242 U.S. 539.

The law of the State of California, rewritten in 1968, is an example of the approval type of philosophy.[2] New issues of corporate securities offered in California must generally qualify by one of three methods: (1) qualification by coordination is available if a registration statement has also been filed with the S.E.C.; (2) qualification by notification is available for securities of certain companies already registered with the S.E.C. and traded nationally; and (3) qualification by permit is required for all other offerings. In granting a permit, the California Commissioner of Corporations must issue an opinion that the proposed issuance is "fair, just and equitable."

THE MONEY MARKET

Although the expression "over-the-counter market" is used in this book to refer to trading in stocks and bonds that does not occur on an organized stock exchange, there is yet another type of over-the-counter market. This system is commonly called the *money market,* although it is not a single market as such, and "money" in the sense of currency or demand deposits is not traded. Instead, the type of obligation traded is a high-quality, short-term debt obligation, and the market itself is an interconnecting network of telephones and teletypes.

The money market is dominated by trading in U.S. government securities, including 90-day Treasury bills. Approximately 20 firms act as dealers in the U.S. government securities markets, either buying and selling for their own accounts (as *principals* or *dealers*) or acting as *agents* for other buyers or sellers such as commercial banks or securities firms. Money-market transactions are effected on the basis of individual negotiation between buyer and seller, with or without use of a middleman. Such transactions are usually initiated by telephone or teletype, and confirmed in writing.

Quotations in U.S. government securities are expressed in *yields* for discount issues, such as U.S. Treasury bills. For example, a Treasury bill, which has a $1,000 maturity in 90 days, might be quoted 6.75 "bid" and 6.65 "ask." This implies that the dealer will purchase the bill at a discount of 6.75% per annum below the $1,000 maturity value. Because the bill matures in 90 days ($\frac{1}{4}$ of a year) the actual discount would be ($1,000)(0.0675)(0.25) = 16.87\frac{1}{2}$. Thus the bid price of the bill would be $1,000 — 16.87\frac{1}{2}$ = 983.12\frac{1}{2}$. The dealer would sell the same security at a (higher) price such that the discount to maturity earned by the dealer would be only 6.65% per annum.

Quotations for coupon issues, such as U.S. Treasury notes and bonds,

---

[2] For a complete explanation of the new California law in nonlegal terminology, see David K. Eiteman and Franklin Tom, "The New California Blue Sky Law," *California Management Review,* Winter, 1969, pages 5–12.

are typically quoted on a *price* basis per $100 of maturity value. Fractions of a full percent are expressed in 32nds of a percent. Thus a quoted bid of 84.22 means a price of $84^{22}\!/_{32}$ percent of maturity, or $84.6875 per $100 of maturity value. Since the bond will in fact have a one-thousand-dollar maturity, the price would be $846.87½.

Money market trading occurs in other short-term debt instruments. *Federal funds* refers to money that is immediately available in the form of a check drawn upon a deposit at a Federal Reserve bank. Federal funds trading usually occurs between banks that belong to the Federal Reserve System. Typically banks with excess reserves "sell" these reserves, via telephone, to banks with temporary reserve deficiencies. The transfer is made through an entry on the books of the Federal Reserve bank, and no physical transfer of money is needed. The transfer is usually for one day, with the buyer paying the seller one day of interest in a separate transaction.

Other money-market instruments also are available. *Commerical paper* traded in the money markets consists of unsecured short-term notes issued in bearer form by large, well known business firms. Bearer-form securities do not have the name of the owner on the certificate, nor does the issuer maintain a registry of owners. Rather possession is evidence of ownership. A dollar bill is an example of a bearer instrument. Negotiable *certificates of deposit* (CD's) are negotiable receipts issued by a commercial bank for time deposits having a specific maturity. The claim to the deposit may be traded in the open market prior to maturity. *Bankers' acceptances* are also banks' promises to pay certain sums at a designated maturity. They differ from certificates of deposit in that acceptances arise from the financing of international trade. As with certificates of deposit and commercial paper, bankers' acceptances are freely traded in the money market during the weeks or months prior to their maturity. Quotations for these various money-market instruments appear daily in the *Wall Street Journal.*

SUMMARY

This chapter has described the major securities markets of the United States, with especial attention given to those markets in which corporate stocks and bonds are traded. Chief of these is the New York Stock Exchange, whose trading volume accounts for over 78% by dollar value of all stock trading on organized exchanges. Public trading through the facilities of the New York Stock Exchange is carried out by its members, most of whom choose to specialize in certain activities, such as commission brokerage or being specialists, registered traders, floor brokers, odd-lot dealers, or block positioners. The manner by which a transaction is executed on the floor of the Exchange was explained, as was the organization and operation of the over-the-counter market. A brief overview of federal and state securities regulations that relate to securities trading was presented, and the operation of the U.S. money market was described briefly.

SUGGESTED READINGS FOR CHAPTER 17

W. J. Baumol. *The Stock Market and Economic Efficiency* (Bronx, N.Y.: Fordham University Press, 1965).

J. B. Cohen, E. D. Zinbarg, and A. Zeikel. *Investment Analysis and Portfolio Management.* Rev. ed. (Homewood, Ill.: Richard D. Irwin, Inc., 1973), Chapter 2.

W. J. Eiteman, C. A. Dice, and D. K. Eiteman. *The Stock Market.* 4th ed. (New York: McGraw-Hill Book Company, Inc., 1966), Chapters 1–4 and 10–13.

D. K. Eiteman and F. Tom. "The New California Blue Sky Law," *California Management Review,* Winter, 1969, pages 5–12.

C. D. Ellis. *The Second Crash* (New York: Simon and Schuster, Inc., 1973).

"Outlook for the Securities Industry," Supplement to the *Journal of Financial and Quantitative Analysis,* March, 1972, pages 1687–1705.

S. Robbins. *The Securities Markets: Operations and Issues* (New York: The Free Press, 1966).

18

Investment procedures

PLACING ORDERS to buy or sell shares of common stock or other types of marketable securities culminates the process of investing. To place such orders, an investor must select a securities firm and choose a registered representative of that firm who will be responsible for handling the details of his transactions. The investor should also familiarize himself with certain technical aspects of his relationship with a securities firm. He should have some understanding of the various types of accounts he may open. He should understand the nature of stock quotations, and he should appreciate the potential gains and risks from trading on margin or from selling short. This chapter is devoted to those technical aspects and investment procedures necessary for an investor to move toward implementation of his investment decisions.

SELECTING A SECURITIES FIRM

Several characteristics of a securities firm may be important to an investor seeking to buy or sell securities. Under most conditions, he is likely to desire a firm with membership on the New York Stock Exchange and with access to other exchanges and to the over-the-counter market. He will certainly want a firm that is in strong financial condition and that is efficient and accurate in executing his orders. He may want a firm that can provide him with dependable investment suggestions, and he will definitely want a firm with whose employees he can establish a relationship of confidence and trust. Because brokerage fees are constant for all orders under $300,000, the cost of the service as such is not likely to be a criterion.

In seeking a satisfactory securities firm, the investor is likely to find his personal ability to make an assessment limited. How, for example, can he evaluate the financial strength of the brokerage house, the quality of its investment advice, or the dependability of the firm's employees? Fortunately, competition within the brokerage industry works to the advantage of the investor, for he may transfer his business from one securities firm to another at any time he thinks such a change will be advantageous. He may, in fact, carry accounts in several brokerage firms concurrently and direct his orders to those firms that seem to be doing the best job for him. While this tactic allows for the benefits of competition, it should be noted that, as the volume of business at any single firm diminishes, the investor is likely to receive less in the way of attention. And even though the investor may change firms, the time and nuisance involved in such a shift are such that some preliminary attention should be devoted to the traits of securities firms and their employees. Investors whose activities are relatively modest are likely to find a continuing relationship with a single firm more advantageous.

As a practical matter, a new investor should probably select a securities firm that is a member of the New York Stock Exchange. Although several well known national firms that were members of the New York Stock Exchange have gone bankrupt in recent years, it is nevertheless true that capital requirements and dependable surveillance of customer practices are at a much higher level of consistency for New York Stock Exchange member firms than for nonmember firms. Customers of New York Stock Exchange member firms that have gone bankrupt have so far been protected by an emergency fund created by all members of that Exchange. Moreover, the New York Stock Exchange has rigorous standards, which it attempts to maintain and improve, and it has a reputation—built over many years—of dealing fairly with all parties. Commission brokerage firms that belong to the New York Stock Exchange also belong to the National Association of Securities Dealers, which provides not only added surveillance of firms' activities but assures access to the many securities traded on the over-the-counter market.

Within the securities firm, the investor will deal primarily with a registered representative, termed "account executive" in many firms, who is an employee of the firm and who will be responsible for giving the investor such information and advice as he may seek, for properly executing the investor's orders, and for handling all other details of the relationship between securities firm and investor. An investor is likely to want a registered representative with whom he can establish an effective personal rapport and who will be available when the investor wishes to place orders. He will certainly want a registered representative interested in handling a client with the volume and type of business the investor is likely to generate; this attribute is best discerned by the potential investor informing the registered representative of the general type of business he will be creating and then seeing if the registered representative appears interested in having such a client.

Although New York Stock Exchange member firms are the industry leaders as far as the nation as a whole is concerned, there do exist a number of high-quality firms that do not belong to that Exchange. Some of these specialize in certain activities, such as third-market transactions, investment banking, or marketing mutual funds at local levels. Others belong only to regional exchanges or confine their activities to the over-the-counter market. The authors of this book have a general predilection that a novice investor should deal with a New York Stock Exchange member firm; nevertheless, other firms might be appropriate at times. It would appear extremely foolish, however, for an investor to associate with any securities firm not a member of the National Association of Securities Dealers, since firms not members of the N.A.S.D. have little or no status in the brokerage industry.

The expression "securities firm" has been used in the above discussion to refer to what are sometimes called "broker/dealer" firms. These are firms that execute orders on behalf of the investing public. Such securities firms should not be confused with "investment advisors," which are registered with the federal government (under the provisions of the Investment Advisors' Act of 1940), are in the exclusive business of selling investment advice, and do *not* execute orders for the public. Investment advisory firms are not eligible for membership in the N.A.S.D. Securities firms, investment advisory firms, and a potpourri of other organizations constitute what is referred to somewhat loosely as the *securities industry.*

Quality of investment advice may be a desirable attribute of a firm. An investor should be aware that a registered representative is not usually a security analyst. Rather he is a trained professional salesman who passes on to his clients the recommendations of the research department of his firm. One can assess the past research quality of a firm by asking to see past reports prepared for customers of the firm. One can also inquire as to the professional status of the research department, including the number of persons on the research staff who are Chartered Financial Analysts (C.F.A.'s), a designation of professional competence earned by passing three rigorous, professionally oriented examinations on all aspects of analyzing securities. The C.F.A. designation is comparable in many respects to the C.P.A. designation of accountants.

Related to the question of investment advice is the question of the major emphasis and interest of the firm. Some firms have a worldwide reputation for giving careful attention to the needs of investors of modest means, while other firms prefer to specialize in wealthy or institutional clients. Some firms emphasize mutual funds, while others devote their main efforts to common stocks. Some firms, and some registered representatives, are primarily interested in short-term profits from trading activity, while other firms tend to emphasize long-term investments. Some firms approach the stock market primarily from a technical point of view, seeking investment opportunities from scrutiny of past trading patterns, while others follow a more fundamental approach (such as that proposed in this book) based upon analysis of economic conditions within the nation, the industry, and the particular company. Some firms and some registered representatives divide their time and attention between stocks, options, and commodities, or even devote their major effort to commodities, while others eschew anything except corporate securities. Still others specialize in municipal bonds, in foreign securities, or in shares of real estate developments.

Most important to an investor in selecting a firm and a registered representative is to match his investment goals with the major interests of the firm and the registered representative with whom he will deal. An investor interested in long-term appreciation based upon fundamental analysis will sooner or later become disenchanted with a registered representative whose only interest in taking short-term speculative positions. Conversely, an investor with a speculative bent will be unhappy with a firm that emphasizes only conservative approaches.

The obligation to seek a correct matching of goals and interests belongs, at least in part, to the investor, for few securities salesmen will turn down a potential client who appears to represent a source of sales volume because most salesmen are compensated with a portion of the brokerage commission on the volume of business they generate. Prior to opening an account, an investor should visit several local brokerage houses, meet a registered representative in each, and ask what type of recommendations that registered representative would recommend for him based on the investor's personal characteristics and existing holdings. In such a visit, the investor would be unfair if he did not give the registered representative a concise statement of his own situation and goals.

There are, of course, other approaches to selecting a good securities firm. One is to seek recommendations from friends or acquaintances whom one trusts. If entering a new community, one can seek advice from a banker. The investor for whom investment advice is less important, because he has developed his own analytical abilities, may well be less concerned with the investment advice or personal abilities of the registered representative than would another investor for whom astute suggestions by the registered representative constitute an important part of the securities firm–investor relationship.

OPENING AN ACCOUNT

Once a satisfactory securities firm and registered represenatative are located, it is necessary to open an account. This involves filling out a signature card and/or identification card. Both the New York Stock Exchange and the National Association of Securities Dealers have rules requiring their members to learn the essential facts about their customers, including residence, occupation, citizenship, social security number, and credit references. In part, this requirement ensures that recommendations given the customer are appropriate for his or her circumstances, and in part it protects the firm against swindles perpetrated by strangers seeking to open accounts and to trade without any intention or ability to pay for transactions.

Accounts are of two basic types: cash accounts and margin accounts. *Cash accounts* are intended for those who wish to buy securities and pay cash. Final payment for a cash purchase must be made within five business days or seven calendar days from the trade date. If full payment is not received from the customer within the prescribed number of days, and if no extension of time has been sought by the customer, the securities firm is required by law to cancel the trade or to liquidate any unpaid portion of the trade, and the account must be restricted for 90 days. To trade in a *restricted account,* the investor must deposit 100% cash before purchasing any stock.

Stock sale through a cash account is regulated by the Securities and Exchange Commission, which requires that whenever a broker executes a sell order (other than a short sale) for a customer, and the broker has not obtained possession of the securities within ten business days after the settlement date, the broker must immediately close the transaction by purchasing the securities for the customer's account. Because settlement date is the fifth business day (or the seventh calendar day) after the trade date, the effect of the S.E.C. rule is to require that certificates be in the physical possession and control of the broker by the fifteenth business day after the date of transaction.

A *margin account* is opened when the investor intends to deposit only a portion of the funds needed to make a purchase, with the remainder of the funds being borrowed from the broker. Margin accounts are also used for short selling, which will be explained later in this chapter. Only securities that are listed on a major stock exchange or that appear on an approved list of over-the-counter stocks may be purchased in a margin account. Opening a margin account necessitates signing a "customers agreement and loan consent" form granting the securities firm the right to retain possession of the physical certificate, to use it as collateral for loans from banks, or to lend it to itself or to other securities firms.

Depending upon state laws, a variety of other types of accounts may be required in particular situations. In some states a married woman may not open an account without approval of her husband. Accounts opened in the name of corporations or of partnerships may require special forms, as may accounts opened by investment clubs or by trustees. Accounts in which the registered representative is given discretion as to the selection, timing, amount, or prices to be paid or received also require certain written authorization. Commodities, such as wheat or cotton, are traded in separate commodity accounts opened for that purpose.

CUSTODY OF CERTIFICATES

Orders placed in a cash account may specify that certificates for stock purchased be registered in the investor's name and delivered to him, usually by registered or certified mail a month or so after the transaction. Alternatively, the investor may specify that the certificates be left in the custody of the brokerage house. Such certificates are registered in *street name,* which means in the name of the brokerage firm itself, and are kept in a vault by the brokerage firm. Dividends received by the brokerage firm on such securities are passed on by check to the owner or are credited to the owner's account. Securities held in custodial accounts by member firms of the New York Stock Exchange are insured up to $50,000 against physical loss by the Securities Investor Protection Corporation.

Leaving certificates with a brokerage firm eliminates the necessity of renting a safe-deposit box for their safe custody. In addition, the shares can be sold by phone without having to make the physical transfer of the certificates to the brokerage office. Yet another advantage is that a regular monthly statement from the broker provides the investor with a complete and accurate record of his holdings, both for his personal needs and for preparing his income tax returns. An example of a monthly statement from a brokerage firm is included later in this chapter. A possible disadvantage of leaving certificates with a brokerage firm is that sale of the shares must be handled by the same firm that made the purchase. In effect, an investor is to some extent locked into a particular brokerage office and may find it psychologically difficult to transfer his business elsewhere should he wish to do so.

Having securities held in the custody of the brokerage firm may prove especially advantageous when the investor is travelling for extended periods of time, for it is possible to enter orders on a "give up" basis at other brokerage firms that are members of the same exchange. Suppose, for example, that an investor with an account at the Van Kurt Brokerage Company is in a town or country where Van Kurt has no office. He may enter the office of any member firm of the New York Stock Exchange, tell them he has an account with Van Kurt, and place an order. After verifying that he does indeed have such an account, the other member firm will place the order with instructions that the securities or cash is to be "given up" to Van Kurt. The transaction will be confirmed in the investor's Van Kurt account and will appear in the regular statement he receives monthly from that firm.

When certificates are physically kept by the investor, he may from time to time find it necessary or convenient to mail his certificate to his broker rather than deliver it personally. A certificate that is being delivered against a sale must be endorsed in exactly the same manner as it is registered on the face. Such an endorsed certificate is a negotiable instrument and should be sent only by registered mail. An alternate way to deliver certificates by mail is to mail the unendorsed certificate and to mail at a separate time a "stock power of attorney," which allows the party named in the stock power to transfer ownership.

TYPES OF ORDERS

Having opened an account, the investor will next be concerned with placing orders. There are in fact a large variety of order types to serve the many special needs of particular investors. All orders are of two basic types: "buy" orders and "sell" orders. Sell orders, in turn, may be either "long" or "short." Motivation for a particular buy or sell order should, of course, be based on the major activities of the process of investing—investment analysis, investment valuation, and portfolio construction—that have been discussed throughout this book.

A *buy order* usually is entered in the belief that the stock price will rise after purchase, enabling the buyer to sell at a later time at a profit. Buy orders are also entered because the dividend yield from the security makes it an attractive holding from the purchaser's point of view. A person buying stock or holding stock in anticipation of either price appreciation or dividend income is said to have a "long position," meaning that he is the legal owner of the shares.

A *sell order* may be entered in the belief that the stock will decline in price, or it may be entered because the investor has found another stock that he believes to be an even better holding than stock already owned. A stockholder who sells stock he owns is "liquidating a long position"; as was indicated above, he must deliver the certificate to his broker within a few days of the sale. Such a sale is often called a *long sale*. Another type of sell order is called a *short sale*. In a short sale, a person sells shares that he does not own. Short sales are explained in detail later in this chapter.

Within the basic classification of orders as buy or sell, a variety of order types are possible to carry out the wishes of the investor. Unless otherwise indicated, the types of orders described below are applicable both in buying and selling securities.

A *market order* is to be executed as soon as possible after reaching the floor and at the best obtainable price. Market orders are generally used when assurance of execution is more important than quibbling over a possible small improvement in price that might be obtained with some other type of order. Any market order that cannot be filled during the day is cancelled at the end of that day.

A *limit order* (also called *limited order*) contains a specific price limit. An example would be, "buy 100 shares of PDQ common stock at 35." The commission broker would attempt to buy 100 shares of PDQ at the lowest price obtainable, but in no event would he pay more than $35 per share. If the limit order could not be executed immediately, it would be left with the specialist for later execution, as was described in Chapter 17.

A *stop order* is an order that is held in abeyance until it is triggered by a transaction at a stated price. It then becomes a regular market order. For example, a customer orders "sell 100 PDQ at 58, stop" at a time when PDQ is selling at about $60. The stop order will be held by the specialist until the market declines and a round-lot transaction occurs at or below $58 per share. The stop order is then "elected"; that is, it becomes a market order for execution immediately at the best price obtainable. This price might be $58 per share, or it might be slightly above or below $58 since, after the triggering transaction at 58, the market could fall or rise on the next trade.

A *stop buy order* can be used to enter the market if prices start to rise. For example, the investor does not know if the price of a stock will reach 60, but he believes that if it does reach 60 it will then continue to rise to 80. He enters a stop buy order at 60 (when the market is, say, 55). If the market does rise to 60, perhaps because of an announcement of an innovative product, the investor's broker automatically buys the security for him.

A *stop sell order* can be used to leave the market near the beginning of a decline. For example, the investor does not know if the price of the stock, currently at 50, will decline to 40, but he believes that if the 40 price is reached then all is lost and the stock will plummet to 20. Hence he enters a stop sell order at 40. If the stock does drop to 40, his broker sells him out and saves him the loss that would result from his holding the shares while they fall to 20. On the American Stock Exchange, stop orders are not accepted. Stop limit orders, however, are acceptable.

A *stop limit order* is created when a stop order is combined with a limit order. For example, "sell 100 PDQ at 40 stop, limit 38" instructs the broker that when a transaction occurs at 40, he is to attempt to sell 100 shares of PDQ stock at the best price obtainable but in no instance lower than a price of 38. A stop limit order is sometimes used to avoid the risk that the stop order will be executed at a price considerably lower (for a sell order) or higher (for a buy order) than the stop price that elected the order. In placing a stop limit order, the investor is acquiring protection against a market that is moving very rapidly in the wrong direction. On the other hand, if the limit is exceeded immediately after the electing transaction, the investor may lose the basic safety he was seeking by the use of a stop order.

Orders may be placed with a variety of time-limit instructions. A *day order*, if not executed, expires at the end of the day on which it was entered. Unfilled market orders automatically expire at the end of the day, but limit orders will remain outstanding unless accompanied by a notation that they are valid for one day only. A *good 'till cancelled order* (GTC), also called an *open order*, remains valid until it can be executed or until cancelled by the customer. However the Exchange requires that outstanding GTC orders be reconfirmed every April and October to ensure that the customer has not forgotten them. Many brokerage houses mail monthly notices of outstanding open orders to their clients for the same purpose. Registered representatives will also accept orders with other time limits, such as good for one week, good until the end of the month, etc. These orders are sent to the specialist as open orders, and it is the responsibility of the commission broker to cancel them if they have not been executed by the designated expiration date.

Orders are sometimes marked *at the close,* which means that the order is to be executed at or as near to the close of trading hours as is possible. Orders marked *at the opening* or *at the opening only* are to be executed only at the opening of trading hours. If they cannot be executed at that time, they are cancelled.

Other types of orders are used in specific situations. An *all or none order* (AON) is to be executed in its entirety or not at all. For example, a regular order to buy 400 shares at a price of, say, 50, is in fact an order to buy 100, 200, 300, or 400 shares at that price. Part of the order would be filled at the limit if the entire amount could not be filled. The all or none order instructs the floor broker to buy the entire order or nothing. The broker will attempt to buy the entire lot sought for as long as is necessary or until the all or none order expires.

Related to an all or none order is a *fill or kill order.* A fill or kill order is to be executed in its entirety immediately when it reaches the trading post. If it can not be filled at that moment, it is to be cancelled. Thus a fill or kill order possesses all of the attributes of an all or none order, plus the fact that if it can not be executed at once it must be cancelled. The fill or kill order would be used when the investor wanted to try to amass a block of stock at once, but did not wish to wait to see if the shares could be acquired at a later time. Also related to the all or none order and the fill or kill order is an *immediate or cancel order.* Such an order is to be executed in whole or in part as soon as it reaches the trading floor, but if executed in part, the unfilled portion is to be cancelled.

An *alternative order,* also called an *either/or order,* is an order to do either of two alternatives. For example, a customer might instruct his broker: "buy 100 shares of Ford at 50 at once or, if this can not be done, then buy 200 shares of Chrysler at the market." Such an order gives the investor the option of first trying one tactic (buy Ford at 50) and then, if the first strategy fails, immediately shifting to a second tactic (buy Chrysler).

Under most conditions, outstanding limited orders to buy and outstanding stop orders to sell are reduced by the amount of an ordinary cash dividend when the stock is traded ex-dividend. For example, an outstanding order to buy 100 shares at 25 is changed automatically to an order to buy 100 shares at 24½ if a $0.50 dividend is paid. An order may be designated *do not reduce* (DNR) if the customer does not want his order price changed when the stock is traded ex-dividend in anticipation of an ordinary cash dividend. Outstanding orders will, however, be reduced for other distributions such as stock dividends or rights.

A *not held order* is an order in which the broker is relieved of all responsibilities with respect to the time and price or prices of execution. In other words, the broker will not be held liable for missing the market or for executing the order. Not held orders also are sometimes marked *disregard tape* or *take time.*

A *scale order* specifies the total number of shares to be purchased or sold, and the amount to be bought or sold at specific price variations. By such an order the customer might instruct his broker to buy, for example, 100 shares at 50, another 100 at 51, another 100 at 52, etc., up to the total number of shares required.

MARGIN TRADING

Trading on margin refers to the practice of purchasing stock with borrowed funds. Both federal law and Exchange rules require that an investor buying on margin advance a certain portion of the purchase price in cash. This cash portion is known as the "margin." The remainder of the purchase price is paid for with credit obtained from the broker's firm. In order to open an account in which stocks will be purchased on margin, the Exchange requires an initial deposit of $2,000 or its equivalent in securities.

Federal regulation of margin transactions is implemented through Regulation T of the Board of Governors of the Federal Reserve System, which states that only securities listed on a major stock exchange, or appearing on a list of some 470 over-the-counter stocks specifically approved for margin purchase, may be bought on margin. Under Regulation T, anyone buying these stocks on margin must provide a cash down payment, or *initial margin* equal to a specified percentage of the purchase price. The required percentage is changed from time to time as part of the Federal Reserve System's regulation of credit in the economy, and has varied from as low as 55% to as high as 80% in the early 1970s.

Under a separate *maintenance margin* requirement, imposed by the Exchange and by its commission brokerage firms, an investor must maintain after purchase a cash equity in the transaction equal to a certain percentage of the current market value of that security. The Exchange requires a maintenance margin of 25%, and individual commission brokerage firms often apply higher maintenance margins, especially if the price of the stock is relatively volatile.

To illustrate the interworkings of the various margin requirements, suppose that an investor purchases $10,000 of a stock at a time when initial margin requirements are 55%. The investor puts up $5,500 against his $10,000 purchase, as required by Regulation T, and borrows the $4,500 remainder of the purchase price from his broker. The broker will charge the investor interest on this loan, or "debit balance" as it is usually called, at a rate slightly above the rate of interest charged on brokers' call loans with New York banks. Interest is charged on the average daily debit balance for each day there is a debit balance in the account.

Continuing the example, suppose that the stock purchased for $10,000 now drops in value to $6,000. Because the debt remains at $4,500, the equity (margin) has now been reduced to $6,000 minus $4,500, or $1,500. At this point the remaining margin ($1,500) is exactly equal to 25% of the remaining value of $6,000, and the Stock Exchange would require the deposit of additional margin should the stock fall further. A request for additional margin is termed a *margin call*. If the investor cannot provide the necessary additional equity, the stock is sold, the loan is repaid, and any remaining proceeds are returned to the investor.

To carry the example one step further, suppose that the stock fell in value to $5,500. Equity (margin) has been reduced to $5,500 − $4,500 = $1,000; and the remaining margin of $1,000 is equal to 18.18% of the remaining value of $5,500. A cash deposit of $375 would be needed to bring the margin up to $1,375, the Exchange minimum of 25% of $5,500. An alternate procedure would be to sell $1,500 of stock and apply the proceeds against the debit balance. Total value would then be $4,000 ($5,500 of original value less the $1,500 sold), the equity would remain $1,000, and the margin would now be 25%.

Note that four times as much stock would have to be sold ($1,500) as additional cash deposited ($375) to bring the account up to minimum margin.

Why would an investor choose to purchase on margin? Suppose that, in the above example, the stock rose (instead of declined) in value from $10,000 to $15,000. An investor who purchased for cash would earn $5,000 on his investment of $10,000, for a 50% gain. An investor who purchased on margin would also have a profit of $5,000 on sale after repaying his loan. However, his own investment was only $5,500, the initial margin, so his rate of profit would be $5,000 divided by $5,500, or 90.9%. The possibility of leveraging up one's rate of return with the use of borrowed money makes margin trading attractive to investors seeking large returns for large risks. The risk of losing more rapidly should stock prices fall makes margin trading unattractive to others.

Figure 18–1 is an illustrative monthly statement for the margin account

FIGURE 18–1
Monthly statement of a margin account

DATE	BOUGHT OR RECEIVED	SOLD OR DELIVERED	DESCRIPTION	PRICE	DEBIT	CREDIT
			US FDS BALANCE JULY 27	M	4818 65	
7 30			200 DENNYS INC	* DIV		12 00
8 1			100 CTY INVESTNG CO	* DIV		15 00
8 1			100 STANRAY CORP	* DIV		15 00
8 1			100 VCA CORP	* DIV		11 00
8 10			200 OHIO ART	* DIV		10 00
8 24			INT TO 8 24 FOR 35 DAYS		46 32	
			BASED ON AVG RATE&DR BAL			
			OF 10.550% & $4516			
			US FDS CLOSING BALANCE		4801 97	
		100	CITY INVESTING CO			
		200	DENNYS INC			
		30	MOBIL OIL CORP			
		200	OHIO ART CO			
		400	SHAREHOLDERS CAPICAL	CASH		
		100	STANRAY CORP			
		100	V C A CORP			
		200	DEL E WEBB CORP			

of a customer of Merrill Lynch, Pierce, Fenner and Smith, Inc. The eight common stocks that were held in the account as of the end of August, 1973, are identified on the bottom half of the statement. The "Cash" indicated that Shareholders Capital (an over-the-counter issue) does not qualify for the margin account, and thus does not enter into the margin calculations. In other words, the monthly statement really reflects a margin account for seven issues and a cash account for Shareholders Capital.

At the top of the statement, we note that the loan from Merrill Lynch to the customer was $4,818.65 at the beginning of the month. The market value of the portfolio at that time (excluding Shareholders Capital) was approximately $10,200 and thus the customer's margin was $10,200 — $4,818.65 = $5,381.35, or about 53% of the market value. While this is below the 65% initial margin requirement existing in 1973, it is above the maintenance margin requirement. Interest totaling $46.32 at 10.55% on a daily balance of $4,516 was charged to the account during August. This charge was offset by crediting the $63 of cash dividends paid on five of the common stocks. No stocks were bought or sold during the month, and thus the ending balance was $4,818.65 — $46.32 + $63.00 = $4,801.97.

SHORT SELLING

A short sale occurs when a person sells shares that he does not own. Because the buyer in any transaction expects to receive a certificate for the shares which he purchases, a short seller must deliver shares even though he does not own any. This delivery is accomplished through the securities firm that executed the order; the securities firm will arrange to "borrow" a certificate for the needed number of shares, and this certificate will be delivered against the short sale. All sell orders sent to the floor of the exchange must be marked "long" or "short."

Brokerage firms obtain the shares to be borrowed from stock held in margin accounts of their other customers. It will be recalled that one of the conditions of opening a margin account, described at the beginning of this chapter, was the signing of a loan consent form granting the securities firm the right to retain possession of the physical certificates and to, among other things, loan them to itself or to other securities firms.

A short sale is usually entered in the hope that a subsequent market decline will enable the short seller to "cover his position" at a profit, by buying at a later date and at a lower price the shares needed to deliver against his original short sale. The nature of a short sale operation may be illustrated with an example that occurred in late 1972 and early 1973.[1] Common stock of Bowmar rose from an October,

1972, low of about $10 to a February, 1973, high of $31.75 per share. At this price, many investors thought that a decline was probable because intense competition in pocket calculators, the major product of Bowmar, would narrow profit margins and cause earnings to decrease.

An investor having such beliefs could sell 100 shares of Bowmar short at $31.75 in February, 1973. Ignoring commissions, the sale would net proceeds of $3,175.00, which would be placed in the investor's account on a restricted basis. That is, the investor could not withdraw these funds. In addition, the investor would have to make a cash deposit in his account equal to 65% of the amount of short sale, or $2,063.75. This additional cash deposit is a margin contribution determined by the initial margin requirement of 65%

Assume that the investor's beliefs proved to be correct and Bowmar common stock fell to $15 per share. At that price the investor would buy 100 shares for $1,500 and use the purchased shares to repay the loan of certificates arranged by his broker. His profit on the short transaction (ignoring commissions) would be as follows:

Proceeds from short sale (100 shs × $31.75)	$3,175.00
Cost of shares purchased (100 shs × $15.00)	−1,500.00
Profit	$1,675.00
Rate of profit on investment of $2,063.75.	81.1%

Such profit obviously is not without risk, for if the stock had risen in price the short seller would have been forced to put more money into the account or to cover at a higher price, causing a loss. For example, if the price of Bowmar had risen to $52⅜, the purchase of 100 shares would have cost $5,237.50. Such a purchase would have used all of the sales proceeds ($3,175.00) plus an additional $2,062.50. The original investment of $2,063.75 would have been virtually wiped out.

A long sale can be executed on the floor of the Exchange at any time. However, the time of execution of short sales is restricted to prevent "bear raids," a practice in which groups of investors precipitate a market decline by selling a volume of shares that they do not own, hoping to buy back after regular investors have been stampeded into selling their shares. To prevent this type of manipulation, short sales can be executed only after an up-tick or zero up-tick transaction. An *up-tick* designates a transaction at a price higher than the preceding transaction, while a *zero up-tick* refers to a transaction at the same price as the preceding trade but above the last preceding different price. An up-tick is also referred to as a *plus-tick*. The effect of this rule is that stocks can be sold short only in a rising market. Thus sequential short sales can not be used to drive the price of a stock down continually.

---

[1] *Business Week*, March 3, 1973, page 47.

If the last change in the price of the stock were downward, i.e., if there were a *down-tick* or a *zero down-tick*, the short seller would have to wait until natural market demand caused the price to rise again before he could again sell short.

On occasion an investor will enter a short sell order to sell shares in which he has a long position. Such a transaction is called a *short sale against the box*, the box presumably referring to the safe-deposit box in which the seller is keeping his long shares. Selling against the box establishes the amount of profit in the long transaction, since any further price rise will cause a loss in the short transaction equal to the gain in the long position, while any subsequent price decline will cause a loss in the long position matched by a gain in the short transaction. However, the *time* (as distinct from the amount) of profit is established only when the short sale is covered, usually by delivering the shares held long.

To illustrate, assume that on December 1 an investor owned 100 shares of stock worth $45 per share or $4,500. The shares were purchased for $10 per share, so if sold the investor would have a taxable gain of $35 per share. For reasons related to other income, he would much prefer to take his profits and pay his taxes next year. The company is in trouble, however, and the investor is convinced that by early January the price of the stock may be back down to $10 per share. This investor could sell short against the box on December 1, receiving in his account sales proceeds of $4,500. These sales proceeds are not taxable income, since the short sale has not been covered. On January 2, the investor can deliver his long shares against his short sale, thus converting the $4,500 received in December into revenue. At this time he would have taxable profits of $3,500, the excess of the sales proceeds over his $1,000 investment cost. The amount of this profit would not be influenced by whether or not the price of the stock on January 2 was $10 per share or, for that matter, $70 per share. Any gain or loss on the long position would be exactly offset by a loss or gain on the short sale.

QUOTATION INFORMATION

All securities firms possess some sort of electronic device to obtain current information on the prices at which stocks are being traded. In some houses this information will be obtained from units that resemble desk-top calculators. The Level-1 NASDAQ system described in Chapter 17 is one such unit that makes available current quotations for over-the-counter stocks. Other units are manufactured and leased by private quotation services, such as Scanlon Electronics, Teleregister Corporation, and Ultronics Systems Corporation, to provide similar information for both listed and over-the-counter stocks. One such unit is shown in Figure 18–2. Although the hardware may differ, the systems

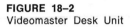

FIGURE 18–2
Videomaster Desk Unit

are generally similar in that a symbol for the particular stock, frequently a one- to three-letter abbreviation called a *ticker symbol,* is entered into the machine along with a request for certain types of information. Perhaps the price of the last transaction plus the current bid and ask quotation are sought. The response appears either on a small television-type screen or on a number display unit. Some units provide answers on slim strips of paper tape so that the information is not lost when the machine seeks information on the next company. The various desk units query central computer storage files, which obtain their information from the computer system of the New York Stock Exchange.

A number of brokerage houses have a seating area that resembles a small theater facing a wall of black or grey panels, each of which has a set of adding machine-type numerical indicators. These indicators constitute an electronic quotation board, which is connected to the computer.

Yet a third system of reporting, in use in many brokerage offices, is the ticker tape. Modern versions of this presentation provide for a large visual display on an electric screen such as the Ultrascope shown in Figure 18–3.

On such a presentation, the "ticker symbol" abbreviations of stock names appear, followed by information on the number of shares traded

FIGURE 18–3
Section of ticker tape

and the price per share. The section of tape shown in Figure 18–3, for example, reports the following transactions, which occurred on the floor in the indicated sequence:

200 shares of High Voltage Engineering (ticker "HVE") were traded at $13.37½ per share. The "2" in front of the "s" indicates that two round lots, or 200 shares, were exchanged.

300 shares of Travelers Corporation (ticker symbol "TIC") were traded at $37.50 per share.

300 shares of John Hancock Insurance (ticker symbol "JHI") were traded at $21.62½ per share.

100 shares of Bunker Ramo Corporation (ticker symbol "BR") were traded at $12.12½. When a single round lot of 100 shares is traded, no indication of share volume appears.

100 shares of National Gypsum Company (ticker symbol "NG") were traded at $21.62½ per share.

200 shares of Pargas Inc. (ticker symbol "PAG") were traded at $24.25 per share.

100 shares of Atlantic Richfield (ticker symbol "ARC") were traded at $71.25 per share.

100 shares of American Telephone and Telegraph (ticker symbol "T") were traded at $46.12½ per share.

400 shares of American Chain and Cable (ticker symbol "ACN") were traded at $25.37½ per share.

Note that on transactions of 100 shares, the tape carries no indication of volume: one hundred shares is assumed. On round-lot transactions from 200 shares through 900 shares, only the first digit is shown, followed by the letter "s" to indicate hundreds. Thus "2s" means two hundred shares. On trades of 1,000 shares or more, the full number of shares is shown to avoid confusion.

TRANSACTION COSTS

Various examples in this chapter have been based, for simplicity, upon the assumption that there are no costs of transactions. In fact, there are two clear costs: commissions must be paid for executing an order, and taxes must be paid.

Commission schedules for round-lot orders on the New York Stock Exchange are illustrated in Figure 18–4. The basic commission schedule

FIGURE 18–4
Commission schedules for the New York Stock Exchange

(a)   On orders of 100 shares (one round lot) the rates are as follows:

Money involved	Percentage of money involved	Plus stated amount
Under $ 100	As mutually agreed	–
$ 100, but under $ 800	2.0%	$ 6.40
$ 800, but under $2,500	1.3%	$12.00
$2,500 and above	0.9%	$22.00

Notwithstanding the foregoing, the commission on any order for 100 shares shall not exceed $65.

(b)   On multiple round-lot orders the rates are as follows:

Money involved	Percentage of money involved	Plus stated amount
Under $ 100	As mutually agreed	–
$ 100, but under $ 2,500	1.3%	$12.00
$ 2,500, but under $20,000	0.9%	$22.00
$20,000, but under $30,000	0.6%	$82.00
$30,000 to and including $300,000	0.4%	$142.00

Plus a charge for each round lot of 100 shares within the order as follows:
First to tenth round lot . . . . $6.00 per round lot
Eleventh round lot and above . . . . $4.00 per round lot
Notwithstanding the foregoing, the commission on each round lot within a multiple round-lot order cannot exceed the commission for a 100 share order computed as in (a) above. The price to be used in calculating the single round-lot commission referred to above is the lowest price at which any round lot within the order was executed.

(c)   The commission on any portion of an order exceeding $300,000 can be negotiated between broker and customer.

has three components: One schedule applies on orders of 100 shares, or one round lot, and is based upon the amount of money involved. A separate schedule is used for multiple round-lot orders, and is based upon a lower percentage of the amount of money involved plus a charge for each round lot within the order. A third component of the basic commission schedule is the provision that commissions on any order exceeding $300,000 may be negotiated between securities firm and customer.

The commission on an odd-lot order is two dollars less than the commission on a single round-lot order, and in addition may not exceed $65 per order. An odd-lot order as mentioned in Chapter 17 has an additional cost component in that an odd-lot differential of 12½¢ (⅛ of a point) per share is added to or subtracted from the per-share price by the odd-lot dealer.

Taxes are of two types: transfer taxes are levied by the State of New York, and federal and state income taxes must be paid on any profit from securities transactions. The New York State transfer tax for residents of that state ranges from 1¼¢ per share sold, while the tax for out-of-state residents not employed in New York is less. The transfer tax on a securities transaction is quite small relative to either brokerage commissions on shares sold or to the income taxes that may result from owning securities.

Income taxes are levied on income from securities by the federal government and by some of the states. Federal income taxes, as they relate to securities, consist of income taxes payable upon ordinary current income, such as dividends and interest received, and upon net short-term capital gains. In this tax context, short-term capital gains refers to the profit incurred when a security is sold above its cost within six months of the date of purchase. Federal income taxes levy the same tax rate upon ordinary income (dividends and interest) and short-term capital gains. The first $100 of dividends ($200 for a married couple) is exempt from the federal income tax.

Long-term capital gains—that is, profit from the sale of a security held longer than six months—are taxable at a rate equal to the lower of (1) half of the regular income tax rate that might apply, or (2) 25%. If the taxpayer's long-term capital gains exceed $50,000, then the capital-gains tax rate increases up to a maximum of 35%.

Within any taxable year, gains are calculated net of any losses. Short-term gains and short-term losses are netted against regular income. Long-term gains and long-term losses are also netted, with only a net long-term gain being taxable. Half of net long-term capital losses incurred after January, 1970, may be subtracted from ordinary income only to the extent of $1,000 per year, with any remaining net long-term loss carried foward to future years at the rate of $1,000 per year. Thus since 1970 a tax payer needs $2 of net long-term loss to offset $1 of ordinary income.

Transaction costs probably do not receive adequate attention in the process of investing. With respect to brokerage commissions, an investor should always be aware of the size of commissions relative to the amount of capital being invested. For those individual investors who buy and hold over extended horizons, the average percentage commission charge is not great. But for those individuals who buy and sell shares repeatedly throughout the year, brokerage commissions can reach a significant total (or percentage) relative to the market value of the securities held. Institutional investors, on the other hand, have the advantage of lower percentage brokerage commissions since they buy and sell larger quantities of shares. Nevertheless, individuals whose wealth is managed by institutional investors should be aware of the level of portfolio turnover, since brokerage commissions increase with turnover.

Taxes are of less concern to institutional investors since they are either tax-exempt (pension funds and foundations) or they simply pass the taxes on to individuals (trust funds and mutual funds). But for individuals, taxes can have a significant impact on investment decisions and their timing. For example, we have seen in this chapter how an investor can convert a short-term gain into a long-term gain by selling against the box. An investor can also plan his selling decisions so as best to combine short-term and long-term gains and losses. Yet another consideration is the locked-in effect of capital gains, an extremely important topic whose discussion we shall defer to Chapter 20.

SUMMARY

This chapter has been concerned with the procedures by which an investor implements his investment decisions. The need to select a securities firm appropriate for the investment operations of the investor was discussed, types of accounts that might be opened were explained, and procedures for custody of certificates were mentioned. A variety of order types that may be used to place orders for execution on an exchange were explained, as were such specialized investment operations as margin trading and short selling. Brokerage office hardware that can be used to obtain price quotations and other information about current stock trading was described. Lastly, brokerage commissions and taxes resulting from securities transactions were reviewed.

SUGGESTED READINGS FOR CHAPTER 18

C. A. D'Ambrosio. *A Guide to Successful Investing* (Englewood Cliffs, N.J.: Prentice-Hall, Inc., 1970), Chapter 6.

Mr. Dollar Investor. *My Stockbroker Is a Bum* (Jericho, N.Y.: Exposition Press, Inc., 1971).

W. J. Eiteman, C. A. Dice, and D. K. Eiteman. *The Stock Market.* 4th ed. (New York: McGraw-Hill Book Company, Inc., 1966), Chapters 6–7 and 14–15.

452

L. Engel. *How to Buy Stocks.* 5th ed. (New York: Bantam Books, Inc., 1972).

J. C. Schreiner. "Graphical Comparison of Actual and Proposed Brokerage Commission Schedules," *Financial Analysts Journal,* July–August, 1971, pages 75–84.

D. E. Vaughn. *Survey of Investments* (New York: Holt, Rinehart and Winston, Inc., 1967), Chapter 8.

19

Sources of information

INFORMATION is at the very heart of the process of investing. Any individual or institution confronted with the need to make informed investment decisions must be aware of the many sources from which various bits of information may be gleaned and formed into patterns that ultimately will suggest particular investment relations. In this chapter, we shall identify a number of sources of information, discuss the nature of each source, its availability, cost, and reliability, and indicate how investors might use that source.

IMPORTANCE OF INFORMATION

The importance of information has been stressed repeatedly throughout this book. In Chapter 2, the process of investing was defined as the analysis of information about various investment alternatives and the making of decisions that are consistent with the objectives of investors. The schematic diagram in Figure 2–1 identified a series of detailed steps within the major activities: investment policy, investment analysis, investment valuation, and portfolio construction. Accomplishing each of those steps requires information about investors, about investment assets, or about the economic environment within which those assets are bought and sold. Each ultimate portfolio decision, as suggested in Chapter 3, necessitates information about individual preferences and information about investment possibilities—both defined in terms of various attributes such as return and risk.

In Part II, we began to focus on specific information needed to judge the investment attractiveness of different assets. The suggested procedure, it will be recalled, is to calculate the investment value of an asset as the discounted present value of future cash benefits to be received by the potential investor. Depending on whether the asset is a bond, a stock, or some other form of investment, future cash benefits can be interest receipts, cash dividends and capital gains, or other cash flows, respectively. The appropriate discount rate for each benefit reflects both the timing and riskiness of that benefit. Estimates by investors of future cash benefits and discount rates are based on the best information available. Special problems of estimating the future benefits associated with security investments were discussed in Part III. Such estimates involve analysis of information, from financial statements or other available sources, about each company whose securities are being considered. Because these statements and sources contain historical information, the process also involves the forecasting of future benefits, generally using historical information as a point of departure. These problems were further discussed in the several applications to nonindustrial securities treated in Part IV.

What we have done is to concern ourselves with various procedures and techniques for processing information in order to make better portfolio decisions. Only occasionally, as in Chapter 10, have we paused to question the reliability of the information that was being processed. Scarcity of information is seldom a problem to investors. What is a problem to investors, instead, is trying to sort through many different types of information from varied sources, determining the validity of that information, and then trying to decide how that information can best be used in making investment decisions.

As opposed to what we have done in other chapters, we focus here on information rather than the process of investing. Because the two are so closely related, however, it is well to use a specific example of an investment opportunity—Holiday Inns, Inc., which has common stock, preferred stock, and corporate bonds outstanding. As potential investors in the securities of Holiday Inns, we shall be interested in learning what we can from available sources of information. After briefly identifying industry and economic sources, we shall consider detailed sources dealing with Holiday Inns. Sources of information on investment companies were reviewed in Chapter 15 and will not be included here.

INFORMATION AS BASIS FOR PROJECTIONS

At the outset, it is important to emphasize one aspect of information that has motivated considerable debate in the literature of investments. The question of whether or not one should use historical information to make future estimates about investment opportunities was briefly discussed in Chapter 11. If based solely on historical information, the estimation process is said to be an *objective* process. This is in contrast to a *subjective* estimation process that would not necessarily rely only on historical information, but would use any available information. Objective and subjective estimation are not mutually exclusive, but rather a subjective estimation may or may not include objective information.

The debate then has to do with whether stock market prices and hence security returns follow definite trends or not. The findings of a plethora of sophisticated research studies collectively suggest that hour-to-hour, day-to-day, and even week-to-week changes in prices seem to follow a random walk.[1] That is, they appear *not* to follow definite trends but rather to be better described by some underlying probability distribution. If these findings are valid, then it should not be possible to use past price changes to estimate future price changes for any given security. An objective estimation process for security prices, therefore, would have little validity according to this evidence. In addition to recognizing the serious doubt cast by this concept on the credibility of technical, or charting, approaches to investment timing, we must explore the implications of random-walk theory to the determination of investment value for a security.

A first observation is that the horizon in determination of investment value typically is several periods or years, a length of time much longer than that suggested in the random-walk literature. A second observation is that investment value as usually defined depends mainly on earnings and dividends, and on security price only at the end of the investment horizon. This in turn suggests the need for examining trends in dividends and earnings, as well as trends in stock prices.

Although evidence concerning changes in earnings is not as strong as that for security prices, it can be said that both earnings and prices are dependent on a multitude of factors that differ from security to security as well as over time. Dividends, on the other hand, are a direct result of decision-making by the board of directors of the company. Cash dividend payments are made from the cash generated within the firm. If the dividend policy of the firm is to pay out a constant fraction of that year's earnings, the pattern of dividends follows closely the pattern of earnings. By varying the payout fraction, however, the pattern of dividends may be made quite different from that of earnings. By observing the dividend patterns of hundreds of publicly-held firms over many years, one finds that payout fractions do vary and, on the average, dividend patterns are much more stable than earnings patterns.[2] And as mentioned in Chapter 11, the directors of a large number of firms appear

---

[1] Empirical evidence on the random-walk phenomenon and also the broader subject of efficient markets is reviewed in Chapter 20.

[2] See Keith V. Smith, "The Increasing Stream Hypothesis of Corporate Dividend Policy," *California Management Review*, Fall, 1971, pages 56–64.

to follow a policy of keeping dividends constant from year to year and increasing dividends only when they foresee no difficulty in maintaining the larger payments in the immediate future.

As a result, historical dividend payments often provide an excellent basis for forecasting future dividends. In fact, the dividend policy of many boards of directors is clearly stated in the annual reports of their firms. Earnings and prices are not a direct policy decision of the board, however, and additional variables together with subjective judgment are needed in order to forecast these components of return. And because of the horizon generally reflected in decision-making, we must not ignore the importance of historical information in forming the basis for forecasting the future benefits that accrue to investors.

TYPES OF INFORMATION

A beginning investor quickly finds that there are numerous sources of information that he may examine before making final decisions. As added perspective for our coverage of sources of information, it may be useful to identify a number of different categories of information that are available.

First, the investor must distinguish between primary and secondary sources. The President of PQR Pharmaceutical mentions during a luncheon speech that the research group of his company is working on a new approach to developing a cure for the common cold. The rumor spreads and by the next morning, it is announced on a television broadcast in that city that a cold cure is imminent from PQR. While listeners to the broadcast have obtained information from a secondary source, some may carelessly respond as if it were primary in nature. Unfortunately, there is much more information available from secondary sources than from primary sources of information.

Second, the investor must distinguish between factual and evaluative sources of information. One investment advisory service reports that the net asset value of DEF Mutual Fund grew from $8.80 to $9.10 per share. Another advisory service reports that investors in DEF Mutual Fund fared better than the Dow Jones Industrial Average but not as well as those in the rival GHI Mutual Fund. Again, investors may respond differently because the sources are different. In the former case, only facts were provided, while in the latter case, facts were augmented by evaluations. There certainly is nothing wrong with evaluations, and in fact they may prove useful to investors. The problem is simply that different evaluations often can be made from the same set of facts.

Third, general and particular sources of information must be distinguished. On the way home from work, an investor hears on his automobile radio that the stock market declined for the sixth straight day because of unsettling developments in the international money markets. This concerns the investor because he recently increased the size of his stock portfolio, especially his holdings of PQR Pharmaceutical. But when he arrives home and examines the newspaper, he sees that the stock of PQR Pharmaceutical continues to sell at its five-year high. Thus he is disturbed by general information, while simultaneously being delighted by particular information.

Cost and physical location of investment information are factors which allow a fourth and fifth categorization of information. Considerable factual information about securities is available free in libraries, while financial information in newspapers, on radio, or on television is virtually free. Other kinds of both factual and evaluative information are available from market letters and investment advisory services whose costs range from a few dollars to several hundred dollars per year. Other more-detailed and forward-looking information may be available only from company management. Professional investors may have occasional access to such information, but small investors generally do not, or they receive the information from a secondary source at some later time. Some investment advisory services and other more specialized information may be available in university libraries or in the offices of large brokerage firms. But geography may prohibit investors in remote locations from conveniently availing themselves of these sources.

Cost, physical location, and other constraints clearly prohibit all investors from having the same information at the same time about all securities. Nevertheless, we proceed now to examine a number of sources of information in more detail with respect to what we can learn about Holiday Inns, Inc.

INDUSTRY AND ECONOMIC INFORMATION

In the remainder of this chapter, we shall review sources of information on individual securities, using Holiday Inns, Inc. as an illustration. Coverage will include company history and organization, S.E.C. information, recent financial history, forecasted earnings, current price and volume, and investment recommendations. In making our review, we will be paralleling the logical sequence that one might follow in appraising a security, estimating its investment value, and reaching a final decision to buy, hold, or sell. What we should do first, however, is to consider the important steps of economic analysis and industry analysis.

Economic analysis is used to appraise the overall economic and market system in which firms produce and distribute commodities and services, and in which the securities of those firms are bought and sold. Economic analysis is thus a broad activity that can be conducted at several levels. Accordingly, there are a range of informative sources that can be examined by individuals and institutions in order to learn more about the economy.

Later in the chapter, we shall mention the *Wall Street Journal, Barrons,* and the *New York Times* as three daily sources of price and volume data for large numbers of securities. These popular financial newspapers also are a source of general information on the current status of the economy and of prognoses of future developments. Some of these prognoses are purely economic, while others are closely tied to the politics of the day and the continuing debate about the relative merits of fiscal and monetary policies. Similar information is also found in periodic magazines of business and finance such as *Business Week, Fortune,* and *Forbes.* There are also articles of varying depth and sophistication dealing with economic analysis in a number of academic journals such as the *American Economic Review* and the *Journal of Finance.*

Current statistical information on various aspects of the economy is available from time to time in other financial newspapers and magazines. On a regular basis, detailed statistical data is found in the *Federal Reserve Bulletin,* which is published by the Board of Governors of the Federal Reserve System, and the *Survey of Current Business,* which is published by the U.S. Department of Commerce. Statistical indices of national output, industrial production, employment, interest rates, money supply, and many others—from these sources—enable one to track the economy and thereby provide a perspective for analyzing securities.

Industry analyses also are useful as background information. Articles on particular industries and particular companies within those industries appear periodically in the financial newspapers and magazines already identified. Industry analyses also appear regularly in the *Financial Analysts Journal* and the *Institutional Investor,* two publications widely read by professional investors and others in the securities industry. In addition, trade publications are a useful source of information on particular industries.

Standard & Poor's Corporation also provides Industry Surveys ($176 per year) as one of their services. Holiday Inns is classified into their "retailing–food" industry, which includes supermarkets, restaurants, and food service. Each Survey includes a brief look at the total industry and also at each subset as far as past demand and the prospects for future sales. It also includes comparative company analyses for the past decade on several variables. For example, the retailing–food industry report includes capital expenditures, sales, profit margins, net income, dividends, and price-earnings ratios for seven firms: Denny's Restaurants, Gino's, Host International, Howard Johnson, International Industries, Marriot Corporation, and McDonald's Corporation. Unfortunately, Holiday Inns is not included. A supplemental report includes some comparative data for eleven firms (including Holiday Inns) having restaurant chains as part of their activity. The comparative statistics are presented as Figure 19–1.

Among the most important sources of industry analyses are the research departments of the large brokerage firms. Institutional investors constitute the market for a large share of their brokerage business, and brokerage firms must provide useful research in order to attract that business. Most research departments are organized by industry, and analysts are assigned to cover one or more industries. As a result, analysts often spend several years or even entire careers becoming experts in their assigned industry. The research reports of brokerage firms differ in both format and depth. Many of these are made available in summary form to individual investors. We shall see subsequently that recommendations of securities, and hence industries, differ between brokerage firms. Individuals thus must be careful in deciding which firm or which analysts to believe and follow. A good track record is essential for security analysts of brokerage firms.

COMPANY HISTORY AND ORGANIZATION

Many investors are interested in how a particular company got started and how it has grown and changed over time, as well as in learning something about its current arrangement and organization. A good summary of that information is provided in *Moody's Manuals,* a series of annual volumes covering industrial firms (two red volumes), transportation companies (green), public utilities (brown), banks and financial institutions (black), and governmental securities (blue). In addition to the large annual volumes, up-to-date information is provided in loose-leaf supplements for each series. The current annual cost of the *Moody's Manuals* is $435. Cost of the industrial volumes alone is $200 per year.

Holiday Inns, Inc. is included in *Moody's Bank & Finance Manual* as part of the real estate section. Information from the 1971 *Manual* is included here as Figure 19–2. We observe that Holiday Inns was incorporated in 1954, and its major business is owning, leasing, and operating motels. At the beginning of 1970, there were 260 inns owned, with 41,659 rooms, and 904 inns leased on a franchise basis, with 117,228 rooms. Holiday Inns also operates subsidiary businesses, both domestic and international, including Continental Trailways, a leader in bus transportation.

Other information about Holiday Inns available from *Moody's Manuals* is an identification of the Board of Directors and corporate management, the location of the corporate headquarters, consolidated financial statements for recent years, and detailed characteristics of the firm's capital structure. We see that one component of the company's long-term debt is a $30 million issue of first mortgage bonds due in 1995, which pay $9\frac{1}{2}\%$ interest annually, are callable at designated premiums prior to maturity, and of which $2.25 million are redeemed each year with

FIGURE 19–1
Illustration of Industry Survey

*STATISTICAL POSITION OF COMMON STOCKS IN THE FOOD RETAILING INDUSTRY

	INTERIM OR ANNUAL OPERATING DATA										**ANNUAL EARNINGS — $ Per Share				$ DIVS. PER SH.		1973			
	No. of Months	§Sales 1972	§Sales 1973	% Change	§Net Income 1972	§Net Income 1973	% Change	Earns. $ Per Sh. 1972	Earns. $ Per Sh. 1973	Year Ends	1969	1970	1971	A1972	Paid 1972	¶Indic. Rate	1973 Price Range	5-31-73 Price	†Price Earns. Ratio	‡Yields %
GROCERY CHAINS																				
■ Acme Markets, Inc.	12 Mar.	1,861.6	2,025.3	+ 8.8	12.43	3.60	− 71.0	3.57	1.03	Mar.	[1]3.62	[1]4.30	[1]3.57	[1]P1.03	[15]1.50	1.00	26 - 17⅜	18	17.5	5.6
■ Albertson's, Inc.	3 Apr.	147.0	190.1	+29.3	1.50	2.15	+ 43.3	0.24	0.34	Jan.	[1]0.74	[1]0.83	[1]0.98	[1]1.18	[15]0.34½	[5]0.36	17⅜- 13¼	14	11.9	2.6
■ Allied Supermarkets	40 Wks.	[2]745.8	779.4	+ 4.5	[2]1.32	1.67	+ 26.5	[2]0.30	0.32	June	[1]d1.03	[1]d1.25	[1]0.31	[1]...	Nil	Nil	5½- 3	4	...	Nil
■ Borman's Inc.	12 Jan.	379.5	404.4	+ 6.6	0.48	0.71	+ 47.9	0.16	0.24	Jan.	[1]1.55	[1]0.41	[1]0.16	[1]0.24	Nil	Nil	6 - 3	4	16.7	Nil
■ Colonial Stores	12 Wks.	166.4	175.4	+ 5.4	2.02	1.89	− 6.4	0.46	0.43	Dec.	1.76	1.97	2.34	2.09	1.00	1.04	22¼- 16¼	17	8.1	6.1
■ First Natl. Stores	12 Mar.	[2]842.6	849.3	+ 0.1	[2]d1.57	0.26	....	[2]d1.15	0.19	Mar.	[1]1.76	[1]2.55	[1]d1.15	[1]P0.19	Nil	Nil	22¼- 16¾	17	††	Nil
■ Fisher Foods	12 Wks.	132.7	180.1	+35.7	1.71	1.99	+ 16.4	0.29	0.32	Dec.	0.81	0.93	1.21	1.40	0.19¾	0.20	18½- 10	11	7.9	1.8
■ Food Fair Stores	28 Wks.	1,100.0	1,100.0	....	7.40	4.30	− 41.9	0.97	0.56	[6]July	[1]1.44	[1]1.45	[1]0.20	[1]...	[15]0.54	[7]0.20	9⅞- 7	7	...	2.9
■ Grand Union Co.	12 Feb.	1,304.4	[3]1,379.7	+ 5.8	14.02	[3]8.99	− 35.9	2.16	[3]1.40	Feb.	[1]2.30	[1]2.42	[1]2.16	[3]1.40	0.80	0.80	16⅞- 11⅜	12	8.6	6.7
■ Great Atl. & Pac.	12 Feb.	5,508.5	6,368.9	+15.6	14.62	d51.28	....	0.59	d2.06	Feb.	[1]2.15	[1]2.02	[1]0.59	[1]d2.06	[8]0.60	Nil	19 - 9¾	12	...	Nil
■ Jewel Cos., Inc.	13 Wks.	[4]431.0	460.8	+ 6.9	[4]7.44	4.04	− 45.7	[4]0.63	0.54	Feb.	[1]3.22	[1]3.36	[1]3.60	[1]3.84	[15]1.63	1.66	55⅛- 33⅛	35	9.1	4.7
■ Kroger Company	12 Wks.	[2]835.7	928.1	+11.1	[2]9.99	3.61	− 63.9	[2]0.74	0.27	Dec.	2.84	3.00	2.71	1.73	1.30	1.30	24⅜- 15⅞	16	9.2	8.1
■ Lucky Stores, Inc.	3 Apr.	468.5	530.9	+13.3	6.87	7.20	+ 4.8	0.22	0.23	Jan.	[1]0.78	[1]0.91	[1]0.99	[1]0.97	[15]0.49¼	[9]0.54	16⅜- 10¾	12	12.4	4.5
■ Munford, Inc.	13 Wks.	33.8	40.4	+19.5	0.21	0.25	+ 19.0	0.08	0.09	Dec.	0.78	0.76	1.03	1.20	0.24	0.28	14⅛- 7¼	8	6.7	3.5
■ National Tea Co.	12 Mar.	1,088.3	1,089.8	+ 0.1	8.92	d9.09	....	1.18	d4.74	Mar.	[1]1.30	[1]1.01	[1]1.18	[1]Pd4.74	[10]0.40	Nil	7⅞- 4⅜	5	...	Nil
■ Penn Fruit Co.	24 Wks.	172.0	154.6	−10.1	1.31	d1.14	....	0.92	d0.86	Aug.	[1]1.11	[1]1.84	[1]0.26	[1]...	Nil	Nil	8¼- 3¾	4	...	Nil
■ Pueblo Int'l., Inc.	12 Jan	467.1	495.2	+ 6.0	6.51	d0.70	....	1.44	d0.15	Jan.	[1]1.63	[1]1.30	[1]1.44	[1]d0.15	[15]0.29	[11]0.28	6⅜- 3½	4	...	7.0
■ Safeway Stores	12 Wks.	1,325.8	1,468.9	+10.8	18.02	18.01	....	0.70	0.70	Dec.	2.01	2.70	3.14	3.55	1.35	1.40	44⅛- 30½	31	8.7	4.5
■ Southland Corp.	3 Mar.	276.2	303.0	+ 9.7	2.51	2.88	+ 14.7	0.18	0.18	Dec.	0.95	1.11	1.26	1.32	0.22½	0.24	32¼- 14½	18	13.6	1.3
★ Stop & Shop Cos.	12 Jan	907.7	[3]994.5	+ 9.6	3.56	[3]6.40	+ 79.8	1.13	[3]2.03	Jan.	[1]2.40	[1]1.80	[1]1.13	[3]2.03	[15]0.90	0.90	20⅛- 13¾	15	7.4	6.0
■ Supermarkets General	12 Jan.	976.2	[3]1,194.4	+22.4	9.90	[3]4.18	− 57.8	1.16	[3]0.50	Jan.	[1]0.80	[1]0.95	[1]1.16	[3]P0.50	[15]0.20	0.20	14¼- 6⅛	7	14.0	2.9
■ Weis Markets	3 Mar.	55.5	63.3	+14.1	2.46	2.48	+ 0.8	0.40	0.41	Dec.	1.22	1.42	1.59	1.61	0.4784	0.50	21¾- 14½	15	9.3	3.3
■ Winn-Dixie Stores	40 Wks.	1,391.9	1,559.9	+12.1	28.39	30.97	+ 9.1	1.44	1.54	June	[1]1.45	[1]1.73	[1]1.98	[1]E2.10	[15]1.16	1.20	41¾- 33½	36	17.1	3.3
FOOD WHOLESALERS																				
■ Fleming Cos.	16 Wks.	[2]251.5	282.8	+12.4	[2]1.90	2.21	+ 16.3	[2]0.36	0.42	Dec.	0.95	0.93	1.02	1.20	0.50	0.50	12⅛- 9¾	10	8.3	5.0
■ Malone & Hyde	36 Wks.	353.5	402.0	+13.7	4.60	5.22	+ 13.5	0.78	0.88	June	[1]0.90	[1]1.04	[1]1.17	[1]E1.35	[15]0.29½	0.32	35¼- 20⅞	25	18.5	1.3
■ Scot Lad Foods	39 Wks.	448.3	466.9	+ 4.1	3.98	3.53	− 11.3	1.80	1.62	June	[1]1.68	[1]2.10	[1]2.42	[1]...	[15]0.57½	0.58	21⅞- 9½	11	...	5.3
■ Super Valu Stores	12 Feb.	[3]1,021.9	1,220.4	+19.4	[3]8.03	8.45	+ 5.2	[3]2.08	2.19	Feb.	[1]1.32	[1]1.52	[3]2.08	[1]2.19	[15]0.76	0.76	24⅞- 16	17	7.8	4.5
RESTAURANTS																				
■ Denny's Inc.	9 Mar.	131.7	148.4	+12.7	2.87	4.10	+ 42.9	0.39	0.55	June	[1]0.81	[1]0.40	[1]0.52	[1]E0.75	0.04	[12]0.04	20¾- 9¾	11	14.7	0.4
■ Gino's, Inc.	3 Mar.	26.3	33.0	+25.5	0.57	0.82	+ 43.9	0.12	0.17	Dec.	0.83	0.95	0.41	1.09	Nil	Nil	30¼- 16⅝	17	15.6	Nil
■ Hardee's Food Systems	6 Apr.	42.6	61.9	+45.3	0.94	1.07	+ 13.8	0.29	0.32	Oct.	[1]0.27	[1]0.55	[1]0.76	[1]...	[15]0.16	0.16	22 - 9⅞	12	...	1.3
■ Holiday Inns	3 Mar.	172.7	193.8	+12.2	6.71	7.36	+ 9.7	0.22	0.24	Dec.	1.15	1.29	1.36	1.38	0.26⅞	0.30	42⅞- 19	20	14.5	1.5
■ Host International	3 Mar.	32.3	36.1	+11.8	0.87	1.00	+ 14.9	0.16	0.18	Dec.	0.98	1.04	1.01	1.01	0.36	0.36	26⅜- 11¾	12	11.9	3.0
■ Howard Johnson	3 Mar.	69.5	78.2	+12.5	2.50	3.21	+ 28.4	0.12	0.15	Dec.	0.45	0.57	0.72	0.90	0.13	0.16	34⅞- 16⅛	17	18.9	0.9
■ International Indus.	6 Feb.	40.2	44.6	+10.9	0.52	0.43	− 17.3	d0.07	d0.09	Aug.	1.34	d5.32	d0.15	...	Nil	Nil	4⅞- 1½	2	...	Nil
■ Marriott Corp.	28 Wks.	[2]207.6	269.0	+29.6	[2]7.97	10.06	+ 26.2	[2]0.28	0.34	July	[1]0.42	[1]0.50	[1]0.50	[1]E0.75	Nil	[13]...	41 - 25	27	36.0	[13]...
■ McDonald's Corp.	3 Mar.	83.4	121.3	+45.4	6.70	10.44	+ 55.8	0.17	0.27	Dec.	0.39	0.49	0.69	P0.94	Nil	Nil	76⅞- 58	64	††	Nil
■ Pizza Hut	12 Mar.	47.0	64.5	+37.2	2.13	3.50	+ 64.3	0.75	1.11	Mar.	[1]0.42	[1]0.43	[1]0.75	[1]P1.11	Nil	Nil	36 - 14¼	17	15.3	Nil
■ Ponderosa System	12 Wks.	[2]13.8	23.9	+73.2	[2]1.08	2.21	+104.6	[2]0.25	0.50	Feb.	[1]0.17	[1]0.49	[1]0.88	[1]P1.40	Nil	Nil	86¼- 40	49	35.0	Nil
★ Sambo's Restaurants	3 Mar.	3.5	5.2	+48.6	1.11	1.71	+ 54.1	0.13	0.18	Dec.	0.22	0.29	0.44	0.64	0.03	0.067	30⅜- 18	18	28.1	0.4
FOOD SERVICE & VENDING																				
■ ARA Services	6 Mar.	418.6	476.2	+13.8	12.85	14.49	+ 12.8	2.20	2.48	Sept.	[1]3.62	[1]3.95	[1]4.53	[1]E5.00	[15]1.19	1.22	155¼-113	125	25.0	1.0
★ AAV Companies	12 Feb.	47.8	72.8	+52.3	1.31	1.55	+ 18.3	0.99	1.16	Feb.	[1]0.76	[1]0.81	[1]0.99	[1]P1.16	[15]0.20	0.20	12⅞- 5½	6	5.2	3.3
★ Automatic Service Co.	6 Mar.	28.7	35.4	+23.3	0.38	0.51	+ 34.2	0.48	0.56	Sept.	[1]0.90	[1]0.64	[1]0.92	[1]...	[15]0.20	0.20	8¾- 4⅞	5	...	4.0
■ Interstate United	40 Wks.	123.1	143.0	+16.2	0.75	2.38	+217.3	0.25	0.81	June	[1]0.72	[1]0.55	[1]0.55	[1]E1.10	Nil	Nil	11⅝- 6	7	6.4	Nil
■ Macke Co.	6 Mar.	69.1	80.0	+15.8	1.47	1.77	+ 20.4	0.48	0.57	Sept.	[1]0.60	[1]0.17	[1]0.99	[1]E1.20	[15]0.30	[5]0.31	12⅞- 7⅛	8	6.7	3.9
■ Servomation Corp.	9 Mar	224.0	242.4	+ 8.2	7.08	8.08	+ 14.1	1.29	1.48	June	[1]1.40	[1]1.56	[1]1.79	[1]E2.00	[15]0.48½	0.52	26⅞- 12¾	15	7.5	3.5
Szabo Food Svces.	6 Mar	30.9	31.8	+ 2.9	0.52	0.61	+ 17.3	0.43	0.51	[14]Sept.	[1]0.26	[1]d0.01	[1]0.69	[1]...	Nil	Nil	14 - 6	7	...	Nil

■N.Y.S.E. ★A.S.E. *Adjusted wherever necessary for stk. splits & divs. **Based on primary earns. d–Deficit. †Based on actual or preliminary 1972 earns. or actual, preliminary or estimated 1972-73 earns. ††–Ratio over 50. ‡Based on indicated rate. ¶Based on latest quarterly dividend payment. §Millions of dollars. A–Actual. P–Preliminary. E–Estimated. [1]Of foll. cal. yr. [2]Restated. [3]53 Wks. [4]12 Wks. [5]Excl. extras. [6]Yrs. ended Apr. 30 prior to 1970. [7]Plus 2% in stk. semi-annually. [8]Directors 1-4-73 omitted divds. [9]Plus 3% stk. payable 7-22-73. [10]Directors 10-27-72 omitted divds. [11]Excl. spl. [12]Pd. annually. [13]2½% in stk. payable 6-15-73. [14]1970 & prior yrs. end. Dec. 31. [15]Pd. in 1972-73 fiscal yr.

NOTE—Net income and earnings per share are shown before special charges and special credits.

Information has been obtained from sources believed to be reliable, but its accuracy and completeness and that of the opinions based thereon, are not guaranteed. Printed in the United States of America.

FIGURE 19–2
Illustration of Moody's Manuals

MOODY'S BANK & FINANCE MANUAL

HOLIDAY INNS INC.

History: Incorporated in Tennessee Apr. 30, 1954 as Holiday Inns of America, Inc., present name adopted May 22, 1969.

In Feb., 1967, acquired Nat Buring Packing Co., Memphis meat packer for 70,000 common shares.

In Feb., 1968, acquired 80% interest in World Travel International, Memphis.

In Aug. 1968 acquired Bianco Manufacturing Co. for 18,618 common shares and Johnson Furniture Co. for 31,858 common shares.

On Feb. 27, 1969 merged TCO Industries, Inc. Each TCO common share was exchanged for 5/8 share of Holiday Inns common plus 1/2 share of Holiday Inns special convertible stock. Each share of TCO preferred was exchanged for 1/4 share of Holiday Inns common and 1/5 share of Holiday Inns special convertible stock.

In June 1969 acquired Marl Dinettes, Inc. (sold in 1970) by issue of 10,000 common shares and International Foam Corp. by issue of 7,367 common shares.

In Feb. 1970 acquired Bus Terminal Restaurant Management Corp., Norfolk, Va., operators of a chain of 42 restaurants located in bus terminals.

On Feb. 5, 1970, exchanged over 1,500,000 common shares for shares of several corporations that held franchises for 74 Holiday Inns. Under the agreement, company exchanged one com. sh. for each $5 of inns net earnings through Dec. 31, 1969. Part of shs. were issued upon completion of the inns' 1969 audits, and issuance of remaining shs. was to be based upon earnings of the inns for next 3 years.

In Jan. 1971, acquired certain assets and operations of Albert Parvin & Co. and Dohrman Co. for undisclosed terms.

Business: Owns or leases motels and licenses others to contract and operate motels, known as Holiday Inns.

At Jan. 2, 1970 system comprised 260 company owned inns with 41,659 rooms and 904 franchised inns with 117,228 rooms.

Through Continental Trailways, Inc. conducts long-line and local motor bus operations in the Mid-West, Mid-South, southwest, Far west and East coast.

Subsidiaries are engaged in ocean cargo transportation between New Orleans and other U. S. Gulf ports and east coast of South America and West Coast of Africa, operation of restaurants, writing of all lines of insurance and real estate development.

Foreign Expansion: In fiscal 1969, company opened 300-room Inn at Marrakech, Morocco, 366-room Inn at Acapulco, Mexico. In 1970, a license arrangement was effected for establishment of a chain of Inns with a minimum of 6,900 rooms in Australia, New Zealand, American and Western Samoa, and Fiji Islands.

In addition, a 646-room facility was opened in 1969 on Waikiki Beach in Hawaii.

Subsidiaries: Inn Keepers Supply Co., wholly owned, sells items for construction and operation of motels; Merchants Hotel Supply, Inc.; Coffee Host, Inc.; Holiday Press, Inc.; Holiday Manufacturing Co., Camden, Ark., Holiday Industries, Hernando, Miss., Hi-Air; General Data Corp.; General Innkeeping Acceptance Corp. (non-consolidated subsidiary); Holiday Containers, Inc.; Johnson Furniture Co.; Bianco Manufacturing Co., Holiday Inn Food Processing Co.

Nat Buring Packing Co., Memphis Meatpackers and Phenix Carpet Mills, Phenix, Ala., were acquired in 1967.

An 80% interest in World Travel International, Inc., Memphis, was acquired in Feb., 1968.

Officers

Kemmons Wilson, Chairman
W. E. Johnson, Vice-Chairman
W. B. Walton, President

Senior Vice-Presidents

F. W. Adams	C. H. Dixon
L. M. Clymer	E. B. McCool
C. M. Collins	J. B. Temple

Vice-Presidents

W. L. Andrews	Hugh Jones
H. G. Arrison	J. B. Luton
R. T. Ashman	W. J. Mann
J. C. Barksdale	W. P. Poteete
C. B. Bland, Jr.	L. M. Price
W. W. Bond, Jr.	R. K. Rasmussen
H. E. Bower	W. T. Roane
J. H. Carney, Jr.	C. B. Robinson
H. W. Champ	R. E. Shultz
J. H. Cleghorn	E. G. Sims
D. W. Cudd	R. E. Smith
L. E. Duerksen	R. H. Thurmond
J. M. Greene, Jr.	R. T. Wells
R. L. Hall	J. L. Yeager
F. K. Jeffrey	

W. C. Marsh, Secretary
Ora Wood, Asst. Secretary
F. W. Adams, Treasurer
R. H. Thurmond, Controller

Directors

Kemmons Wilson	W. N. Clarke
W. E. Johnson	F. G. Currey
W. B. Walton	C. B. Harrison
E. B. McCool	R. A. Lile
C. M. Collins	L. K. McKee
L. M. Clymer	M. E. Moore
J. B. Temple,	A. B. Morgan
C. H. Dixon	Ralph Owen
F. W. Adams	R. M. Scott, Jr.
W. W. Bond, Jr.	R. E. Slater
J. E. Brown	

Auditors: Harris, Kerr, Forster & Co.

Annual Meeting: Third Wednesday in Nov.

No. of Stockholders: Dec. 31, 1969: Preferred, 1; special conv., A, 3,500; common, 35,000.

No. of Employees: Dec. 31, 1969, 32,000 (approx.).

Office: 3736 Lamar Ave., Memphis, Tenn. 38118.

Consolidated Income Account, years ended:

Sales & Income:	Jan. 2,'70	Dec. 31,'69
Inns, etc.	$247,509,146	$143,943,657
Supply & mfg.	113,478,430	85,079,970
Travel & trans.	168,148,240	167,482,596
Other	9,563,306	8,356,155
Total	538,699,122	[4] 404,862,378
Costs & expenses	319,148,733	247,510,379
Selling, etc. exp.	102,527,937	74,047,343
Rent	14,642,551	6,505,565
Interest, etc.	15,451,250	9,503,250
Deprec. & amort.	27,336,499	22,914,292
Income taxes	27,580,032	18,658,132
[2] Extraord. credits	1,051,392	1,549,991
Net income	33,066,512	[4] 27,272,408
Prev. retain. earn.	89,659,785	26,759,002
Retain. earn. acq.	9,955,205	45,615,626
Preferred divs.	708,353	747,765
Common divs.	4,595,966	3,067,482
Com. divs. acq. cos.	132,466	3,574,296
Pfd. divs. "pool. co."	------	504,102
[1] Distrib. of shs.	------	93,606
Stock dividend	1,903,618	------
Ret. earn. 12-31	125,341,099	89,659,785
Earn. com. share	$1.19	[4] $2.13
[3] Aver. shares	27,241,694	12,426,828

[1] Fgn. sub. pooled co. [2] Incl. gain from sales of prop. [3] Reflects full conv. A spec. stk. to com. and exercise of empl. stk. options. [4] Adj. figures reflect acq. of cos. acq. in "pool. of int.": Total sales and inc. $467,849,727; net income, $30,033,678; earn. com. sh. $1.08 on 27,172,516 aver. shs., reflect full conv. A spec. stk. and exercise empl. stk. options and 2-for-1 stk. split 5/69.

Consolidated Balance Sheet, as of Dec. 31:

Assets:	Jan. 2,'70	Dec. 31,'68
Cash	$34,233,429	$29,500,824
Receivables, net	57,029,203	40,158,069
Inventories	19,427,027	17,484,373
Accrued oper. diff.	4,181,928	4,370,332
Oth. curr. assets	17,269,203	7,180,395
Deposits	*dr*5,069,087	*dr*5,444,008
Restrict. fds.	9,023,522	6,549,702
Notes receivable	2,253,631	------
Inv. & advs. subs.	3,559,693	3,282,281
Inv. & advs. affil.	4,941,252	5,472,401
Oth. inv. & advs.	4,121,864	267,258
[1] Net property	378,544,366	294,550,066
Construction	26,790,806	22,313,307
Prop. not in use	6,563,602	3,431,227
Def. charges, etc.	8,857,165	7,079,916
Other assets	3,539,032	5,607,612
Total	$575,266,636	$441,803,755
Liabilities:		
Accts. & notes pay.	$33,369,685	$24,177,339
Income taxes	7,430,424	4,003,585
Dividends pay.	1,174,881	2,143,687
Debt due	43,251,369	18,884,163
Long term debt	223,792,526	176,262,220
Unterm. voy. rev.	2,563,000	1,766,932
[2] Oth. def. credits	14,926,497	15,963,872
Deferred inc. tax	10,750,761	3,927,576
Oth. curr. liabil.	20,494,535	19,279,049
Pfd. sink. fund	2,297,000	------
Minority interest	530,258	454,795
5% pfd. stk. ($100)	11,130,500	14,094,500
Spec. stk. A ($1.125)	1,617,747	1,662,105
Common stk. ($1.50)	37,881,873	17,141,391
Capital surplus	43,000,445	52,805,970
Retained earnings	125,341,099	89,659,785
Stockhold. equity	218,971,664	175,363,751
Reacquired stk.	4,285,964	423,214
Net stkhold. eq.	214,685,700	174,940,537
Total	$575,266,636	$441,803,755
[1] Depr. & amort.	$176,911,073	$148,211,668

[2] Excess of book val. over inv. in sub. Delta S. S. Lines, Inc.

Long Term Debt: Holiday Inns, Inc. first 9½s, due 1995:

AUTH.—$30,000,000; outstg., June 10, 1970, $30,000,000.

DATED—June 15, 1970. DUE—Dec. 15, 1995.

INTEREST—J&D15.

TRUSTEE—First National City Bank, NYC; Blair A Powell, individual trustee.

FIGURE 19–2 (*continued*)

MOODY'S BANK & FINANCE MANUAL

DENOMINATION—Fully registered, $1,000 and authorized multiples thereof.
CALLABLE As a whole or in part, on at least 30 days' notice, to each Dec. 14, incl., as follows:

1971..	109.50	1972..	109.00	1973..	108.50
1974..	108.00	1975..	107.50	1976..	107.00
1977..	106.50	1978..	106.00	1979..	105.50
1980..	105.00	1981..	104.50	1982..	104.00
1983..	103.50	1984..	103.00	1985..	102.50
1986..	102.00	1987..	101.60	1988..	101.20
1989..	100.80	1990..	100.40	1995..	100.00

Not callable, however, prior to June 15, 1980 from moneys borrowed at an interest cost less than 9.50%. Also callable for sinking fund (which see) at par.
SINKING FUND—Annually, each Nov. 15, 1976-94, cash (or bonds) to redeem $2,250,000 bonds; plus similar optional payments.
SECURITY—Secured by a first lien on property excluding permitted encumbrances, including (1) liens for taxes, assessments or other governmental charges not then delinquent, (2) mechanics', laborers', materialmen's and similar liens, (3) all liens, encumbrances and exceptions to title existing prior to the date and time specified in any titled insurance binder relating to the property in question known to the title insurance company and not appearing as exceptions to title in such insurance binder; (4) rights of lessors; (5) zoning restrictions, easements, rights of way, exceptions, reservations, restrictions, conditions, limitations, covenants, adverse rights or interests and any other defects or irregularities in title, not having a material adverse effect on any portion of the mortgaged property in respect to its use as an inn; and (6) any lien for the satisfaction or discharge of which a sum of money deemed adequate by trustee is on deposit with trustee.
DIVIDEND RESTRICTION—Co. may not pay cash divs. on or acquire capital stock in excess of consolidated net income after Jan. 2, 1970 plus net proceeds from sale of stock or debt converted into stock after such date plus aggregate of consolidated net tangible assets represented by all property other than cash acquired after Jan. 2, 1970 in consideration of the issuance of stock plus $20,000,000.
RIGHTS ON DEFAULT—Trustee, or 33⅓% of bonds outstg. may declare principal due and payable (30 days' grace for payment of interest).
INDENTURE MODIFICATION — Indenture may be modified, except as provided, with consent of 66⅔% of bonds outstg.
LISTED—On New York Stock Exchange.
PURPOSE—Proceeds of bonds and warrants for construction, acquisition and improvement of inns.
OFFERED—$30,000,000 bonds and 330,000 common purchase warrants in units, each unit consisting of $1,000 bonds and 11 warrants to purchase common at $24.75 a share, at $1,000 a unit (proceeds to Co., $980.00 a unit) on June 10, 1970 thru Smith, Barney & Co., Inc., Equitable Securities, Morton & Co., Inc., Lehman Brothers, and Merrill Lynch, Pierce, Fenner & Smith, Inc. and associates.
PRICE RANGE—(x.w.) 1970, 105½-96.

Commitments and Contingent Liabilities: At Jan. 2, 1970, company had entered into contracts and commitments or contemplated doing so in the amount of $70,000,000 to complete construction. Involved were 10 new owned domestic, 9 new foreign Inns, and 13 new leased inns with a total of 10,466 rooms. Mortgage loan and other financing is anticipated upon completion of this construction.

Long Term Debt: First Mortgages: Outstanding, Jan. 2, 1970 (company and subsidiaries), $154,058,098, interest, 3% to 10%; varying maturities to 1994.

Contracts: Outstanding, Jan. 2, 1970, $16,631,811.

Other Long Term Debt: Outstanding Jan. 2, 1970, $96,353,986 comprising (1) $7,320,000 5½% U. S. Government insured Merchant Marine bonds callable at premiums ranging from 105.18% in 1969 to 100% in 1985, annual sinking fund payment of $452,000 (2) $18,568,000 6-6½% sinking fund notes due to Jan. 1983, (3) $9,004,151 4-11% secured notes due to Jan. 1971. (4) $6,118,622 4¼-9½% unsecured notes due to Mar. 1, 1985. (5) $14,673,613 5.7% equipment obligations due to July 1974. (6) $2,069,600 deb. 6-10%, due to Jan., 1979 (7) $26,000,000 commercial paper, 8½-9½%, due to Jan., 1990. (8) $12,000,000 8½% revolving credit agreement.

Cash dividends on common stock are limited to consolidated net income, as defined, accumulated after June 30, 1966 plus $1,000,000, minus all preferred stock dividends payable after June 30, 1966. Consolidated retained earnings deemed to be free of such restrictions totaled $108,866,800 at Jan. 2, 1970.

Capital Stock: 1. Holiday Inns Inc. 5% cumulative preferred stock, par $100:
AUTHORIZED—150,000 shares; outstanding, Jan. 2, 1970, 134,275 shares, pursuant to agreement with Gulf Oil Corp., see below.

Preferred Sale Agreement—Loan Guaranty: On July 9, 1963, stockholders approved creation of 150,000 par $100 shares of 5% cumulative preferred stock which company agreed to sell to Gulf Oil Corp. on or before Dec. 31, 1965, for investment. Proceeds used to acquire existing licensee-owned Inns and for new sites and construction thereon.

Gulf Oil Corp. has also agreed to guarantee up to $25,000,000 of company's first mortgage loans on newly acquired or constructed Holiday Inns or Holiday Inns Jr. provided such guaranteed loans do not exceed 25% of total amount of such loans and provided maximum guarantee on any loan may not exceed 70% of cost of the Inn to which it is applicable. Gulf's commitments were contingent on sale of 400,000 common shares and on approval by stockholders of creation of preferred.

2. Holiday Inns, Inc. stock dividend conv. special stock, Ser. A; par $1.125:
AUTH.—All series, 5,000,000 shs.; outstg., 1,365,805 shs.; in treasury, 72,192 shs.; par $1.125.
PREFERENCES—Has preference over com. as to assets.
DIVIDEND RIGHTS—Entitled to non-cumulative stock divs. at the annual rate of $1.70 of market value of com., per ser. A sh., payable M&N1.
DIVIDEND RECORD — Paid stock dividends (in Co. common stock) as follows:

	May 1	Nov. 1
1969	0.062449%	0.021574%
1970	[1]......	[1]......

[1] Payable in com. at rate of $0.85 of market value of com. Market price for May dividend based on $41.29; for No. 2 dividend, $27.89.
LIQUIDATION RIGHTS—In liquidation, entitled to conversion price, if involuntary; if voluntary, prices as follows (per sh., plus divs.) to each Nov. 1, incl.: 1969, $65; 1970, $73; 1971, $81; 1972, $89; 1973, $97; thereafter, $105.
VOTING RIGHTS—Has ¾ vote per sh. Consent of majority of ser. A stock needed to change terms adversely.
CALLABLE—As a whole or in part after 61 calendar months from date of issuance on at least 30 days' notice, at $105 a sh. plus divs. Redemption price may be paid in cash or com.
SINKING FUND—None.
CONVERTIBLE—Into com. at any time (if called, on or before 3rd business day prior to redemption date) initially at rate of 1½ com. shs. for each spec. sh. No adjustment for divs. Cash paid in lieu of fractional shs., or, holder may either purchase additional fractional interest to make up a full sh. or sell fractional interest to which he is entitled. Conversion privilege protected against dilution. Conversion right will be suspended between declaration date of cash divs. on Co. com. and business day next following record date for such divs.
PREEMPTIVE RIGHTS—None.
TRANSFER AGENTS—First National Bank, Memphis, Tenn. and Chemical Bank, NYC.
REGISTRARS—National Bank of Commerce, Memphis and Bank of New York, NYC.
LISTED—On New York Stock Exchange.
PURPOSE—Issued in connection with merger TCO Industries, Inc. into Co.
PRICE RANGE—1970, 63¼-28½; 1969, 70-48.

3. Holiday Inns Inc. common, par $1.50:
AUTHORIZED—60,000,000 shares; outstanding Jan. 2, 1970, 25,067,638 shares; in treasury, 186,944 shares; reserved for conversion of special stock, 2,048,708 shares; reserved for options, 587,960 shs.; reserved for delayed compensation plan, 30,000 shares; par $1.50.

Par changed from $1.50 to $1.80 Nov. 2, 1962 by charging capital surplus; from $1.80 to $1.50 Nov. 30, 1962 by 6-for-5 stock split; $1.50 par shares split 2-for-1 Sept. 11, 1967 and June 3, 1969.
DIVIDEND RESTRICTION—See Long Term Debt above.

DIVIDENDS—(Calendar years):

1958...	[1]	1959-60	[1]	1961-62	nil
1963...	$0.05	1964...	0.22½	1965...	0.32½
1966...	0.42½	1967...	0.37½		

After 2-for-1 split:

1967...	0.07½	1968...	0.31¼	1969...	0.18¾

After 2-for-1 split:

1969...	0.10	1970...	0.21⅛	[2]1971..	0.05⅝

[1] Paid stock dividend: 1958, 5%; 1959-60, 4%.
[2] To Feb. 1.
VOTING RIGHTS—Has one vote per share (non-cumulative).
PREEMPTIVE RIGHTS—None.
TRANSFER AGENTS—First National Bank, Memphis, Chemical Bank, NYC, Bank of America N. T. & S. A., Los Angeles and Continental Illinois National Bank & Trust Co., Chicago.
DIVIDEND DISBURSING AGENT—First National Bank, Memphis.
REGISTRARS—National Bank of Commerce, Memphis, Bank of New York, United California Bank, Los Angeles, and Harris Trust & Savings Bank, Chicago.
LISTED—On New York, Pacific Coast, Mid-West and Philadelphia-Baltimore-Washington Stock Exchanges.
OFFERED—(120,000 shares) at $9.75 per share Aug. 20, 1957, by Equitable Securities Corp., Nashville, and associates, and (100,000 shares) at $16 per share Feb. 25, 1959.

(127,647 shares) at $33 per share Dec. 15, 1960 by Equitable Securities Corp., Nashville, and associates. Offering did not represent company financing.

(420,047 shares) at $18.25 a share on May 15, 1963 by Equitable Securities Corp., Nashville, and associates. Proceeds of 400,000 shares for company account used to reduce bank notes; for construction and other purposes.

PRICE RANGE—	1970[1]	1969	1968[2]	1967	1966
High..........	42⅞	47⅜	80⅞	58	45
Low..........	19¾	34	39¼	38¾	25⅝

[1] After 2-for-1 split; before, 86¾-65.
[2] After split; before, 82⅞-40.

Warrants: Outstg., warrants to purchase 330,000 common shares at $24.75 a share. Warrants expire June 18, 1975. Issued in registrable form. Warrant Agent: First National City Bank, NYC. See also first 9½s, 1995, above.

a sinking fund payment. Also outstanding is $11 million of cumulative preferred stocks plus about 25 million shares of common stock.

Information appearing in the annual *Moody's Manuals* generally would be used as a way of gaining initial perspective about a particular company. It seldom would be used as the only source prior to making a decision because the information is strictly historical. The information generally is quite reliable. The $435 price would be prohibitive to most investors, but fortunately the *Manuals* often are included in the business or reference sections of large public libraries.

Similar information, both in content and format, appears in *Standard & Poor's Corporation Records* for a large number of companies in which there is public interest. Included are companies listed on the New York and American Stock Exchanges, as well as larger unlisted firms and regional exchange companies. Total assets of any company included must not be less than $1,000,000. The company history, organization, and other information is kept in several loose-leaf binders and thus may be updated periodically. The *Corporation Records* are available at a cost of $442 per year and generally may be found in public libraries.

S.E.C. INFORMATION

The Securities and Exchange Commission (S.E.C.) is a source of extensive information for all companies whose securities are widely held. Apart from its annual report to shareholders which will be discussed presently, each firm coming under the jurisdiction of the S.E.C. is required to submit an annual 10–K report to that federal agency. While the format of shareholders' annual reports varies considerably from firm to firm, all 10–K reports follow basically the same format. Each firm's report must be filed within 90 days after the end of its fiscal year. As shown on the cover sheet of Holiday Inns' 10–K report in Figure 19–3, its fiscal year ends December 31, and thus is identical to the calendar year. The following information is required:

Item 1. Nature of the business including products and services, markets, backlog of orders, patents, licenses, research and development, and number of employees.

Item 2. Summary of operations for each of the past five years.

Item 3. Location and characteristics of all properties owned or leased.

Item 4. Parents and subsidiaries of the reporting firm including percentages of securities held.

Item 5. Pending legal proceedings of which the firm is a party or its property is the subject.

Item 6. Increases or decreases in outstanding securities including the nature and terms of each transaction.

FIGURE 19–3
Illustration of 10–K report

SECURITIES AND EXCHANGE COMMISSION
WASHINGTON, D. C. 20549

FORM 10-K

ANNUAL REPORT
Pursuant to Section 13 of the
Securities Exchange Act of 1934

For the Fiscal Year Ended December 31, 1971. Commission File No. 1-4804

HOLIDAY INNS, INC.
(Exact name of registrant as specified in its charter)

Tennessee	I.R.S. No. 62-0524913
(State of incorporation)	(I.R.S. Employer Identification No.)

3742 Lamar Avenue
Memphis, Tennessee 38118
(Address of principal executive offices)

Registrant's telephone number, including area code: (901) 362-4001

Securities registered pursuant to Section 12(b) of the Act:

Title of each class	Name of each exchange on which registered
Common Stock, Par Value $1.50 per share	New York Stock Exchange Midwest Stock Exchange Pacific Coast Stock Exchange Philadelphia-Baltimore-Washington Stock Exchange
Stock Dividend Convertible Special Stock, Series A (Stock Dividend at rate of $1.70 market value of Common Stock)	New York Stock Exchange
9½% First Mortgage Bonds due December 15, 1995	New York Stock Exchange

Securities registered pursuant to Section 12(g) of the Act:

Warrants to Purchase Common Stock expiring June 18, 1975
(Title of Class)

Indicate by check mark whether the registrant has filed all annual, quarterly and other reports required to be filed with the Commission within the past 90 days and in addition has filed the most recent annual report required to be filed. Yes ✓. No___.

Item 7. Approximate number of equity security holders.
Item 8. Executive officers of the firm.
Item 9. Indemnification of directors and officers.
Item 10. Financial statements.
Item 11. Principal security holders and holdings of management.
Item 12. Directors of the firm.
Item 13. Remuneration of directors and officers.
Item 14. Options granted to management to purchase securities.
Item 15. Interest of management and others in certain transactions.

Space prohibits an illustration of all these items for Holiday Inns, but it should be clear from the list that the annual 10–K report is an excellent source of information on the firm and its management. Additional detailed information of a seasonal or special nature is provided in current 8–K reports.

Another important source of information required by the S.E.C. is the prospectus, which is furnished to potential buyers of a new issue of securities by a firm. The prospectus contains many of the items listed above, including detailed information on how the new security issue is related to the existing capital structure of the firm. The front page of a typical prospectus was shown earlier in Figure 17–4. If Holiday Inns were making a new offering of common stock, a "tombstone" advertisement to that effect would appear in the Wall Street Journal and other financial publications. The actual prospectus could be obtained from any of the underwriting brokerage houses. A preliminary prospectus, sometimes called a "red herring" prospectus, bears the heading "preliminary prospectus" in red at the top and a cautioning paragraph, also in red, shown printed sidewise along the left edge. Such a preliminary prospectus will be replaced eventually by a final prospectus without the red inscriptions and with certain final information that was omitted from the preliminary version.

RECENT FINANCIAL HISTORY

Although considerable financial information is provided by Moody's, the S.E.C., and periodically in prospectuses, there are other sources that allow investors an opportunity to trace the recent financial history of a particular company. Of interest are variables such as assets, sales, margins, earnings, dividends, and market prices. Four sources that contain such information will be compared: Standard & Poor's Stock Reports, Moody's Handbook of Widely Held Common Stock, Value Line Ratings and Reports, and the company's own annual report.

Standard & Poor's Corporation, which is a subsidiary of McGraw-Hill, Inc., makes available a wealth of information about potential investments in the securities of United States companies. One of the more popular of their services is a two-page report for each of a large number of common and preferred stocks. The Standard & Poor's stock reports are organized alphabetically within each of three sets of loose-leaf reports corresponding to stocks traded on the New York Stock Exchange ($250 per year), the American Stock Exchange ($250 per year), and in the over-the-counter markets ($188 per year). The reports are updated frequently.

Figure 19–4 is the report on Holiday Inns dated June 13, 1972. Appearing on the front side of the report are recent operating developments, recent earnings and dividend results, plus the prospects for the Company both in the near term and in the long term. Holiday Inns is expected to continue its growth in lodging business and its expansion into other travel-related services.

On the back side of the report is additional information about company operations, as well as a description of the existing capital structure of the firm. A ten-year summary of pertinent statistics from the income statement and the balance sheet, some of which are converted to a per-share basis, is also presented. These per-share statistics allow one quickly to trace the growth of the firm and the cyclical nature of the business over time. For Holiday Inns, we see that sales revenues, assets, and earnings have grown rapidly during the past decade. Dividends have increased steadily but at a much lower rate. The trend in market prices of Holiday Inns common stock, reflecting a price-earnings ratio between 12 and 41, has consistently been above the trend of the Standard & Poor's Industrial Stock Price Index.

Similar information is provided in a quarterly publication, Moody's *Handbook of Widely Held Common Stocks* ($50 per year). A single page contains data on each firm, such as in Figure 19–5 for Holiday Inns. Comparing this second-quarter, 1972, report with the previous exhibit, we see that the numbers often are identical from the two sources, with differences usually due to the handling of special situations. For example, Moody's reports earnings per share of $0.82 in 1967, while Standard & Poor's reports only $0.62—the latter number excluding extraordinary items according to a footnote reference.

Stock dividends and stock splits also influence the reporting of earnings per share. Fortunately, Moody's, Standard & Poor's, and other sources of information adjust the prior earnings record of a company for each stock dividend and stock split so that consistent records of earnings, dividends, and cash flow are reported. During the decade 1962–1972, the earnings per share of Holiday Inns, adjusted in this manner, have increased from $0.15 to $1.36, which reflects an annual compound growth rate of 24.7%.

Value Line ($330 per year) also presents a single page summary for each company as part of its service. The Holiday Inns report dated

FIGURE 19–4
Illustration of Standard & Poor's Stock Reports

HIA¹

Holiday Inns

1143

Stock —	Price Jun. 7'72	Dividend	Yield
COMMON..........................	54⅛	²$0.27½	²0.5%
SERIES A SPECIAL STOCK............	80	³$1.70	³2.1

RECOMMENDATION: Holiday Inns and its licensees operate over 1,300 lodging establishments, and the company is engaged in related travel, manufacturing and service activities. Continued expansion, both domestic and international, and possible acquisitions enhance long-range potentials. However, the growth rate has slowed considerably in recent periods, and with uncertainties raised by the foreign expansion program, the shares seem somewhat fully priced at current levels.

X Charted on special comparable scales, values not shown.

¹TOTAL REVENUES (Million $)

Quarter:	1972	1971	1970	1969
March..............	⁴172.7	⁴155.3	136.7	111.5
June.................		181.9	156.2	136.2
Sept.................		196.1	171.1	150.2
Dec.................		175.3	140.6	141.9

Revenues for 1971 rose 17% from those of 1970, reflecting increases in all areas of operations. Margins were penalized by a decline in occupancy levels and heavy start-up expenses related to new properties; total income was up 12.6%. Pretax income gained 12%. After taxes at 44.9%, against 43.7%, net income advanced 9.8%, before special credits of $0.05 and $0.02 a share, respectively.

For the quarter ended March 31, 1972, revenues increased 11%, year to year, aided by strong gains in the Products and Inns and Restaurants divisions. Higher occupancy levels offset a slight decline in the Transportation division, and pretax earnings moved ahead 32%. Taxes were at 44.2%, versus 38.4%, and net income advanced 19%. Results for the 1971 period excluded a special credit of $0.16 a share.

COMMON SHARE EARNINGS ($)

Quarter:	1972	1971	1970	1969
March..............	⁴0.22	⁴0.19	0.16	0.13
June.................		0.42	0.40	0.39
Sept.................		0.52	0.48	0.45
Dec.................		0.23	0.25	0.18

PROSPECTS

Near Term — Revenues for 1972 should show a sizable advance from the record $708 million of the preceding year. Continued growth in all three major areas, aided by some acquisitions, should contribute to the gain. Increased travel expenditures would also be beneficial.

Margins should be well maintained as innkeeping operations are made more efficient and costs are spread over a larger sales base. Although occupancy levels are expected to pick up, operating expenses, particularly labor costs, should also increase. Share earnings for 1972 are likely to approximate $1.55, up from the $1.36 of the prior year, which was before $0.05 special credits. Dividends have been raised to $0.06¾ quarterly.

Long Term — Included in aggressive expansion plans is the opening of some 500 inns in Europe by 1980. Expansion moves and further integration of travel services should provide greater revenues and profits.

RECENT DEVELOPMENTS

At the end of 1971 there were 1,371 inns (290 operated by the company) and 200,532 rooms (51,755), including 9 European inns. An additional 387 inns (26 foreign) and 72,529 rooms were under construction or planned.

Trav-L-Parks, a nationwide system of recreational vehicle camping parks being developed and licensed by Holiday, opened its first 11 facilities in 1971.

Recent agreements have been signed to acquire Show Biz, Inc., which is engaged in the entertainment business, Osceola Operating Corp., an operator of tourist facilities in Florida, La Crosse Motels, licensee of a Holiday Inn and Chambers-Godfrey, which process and sells cured hams.

The company's overseas subsidiary in April, 1972 placed privately $18 million of seven-year notes.

DIVIDEND DATA

Payments in the past 12 months were:

Amt. of Divd. $	Date Decl.	Ex-divd. Date	Stock of Record	Payment Date
0.06¼.	Jun. 19	Jun. 28	Jul. 2	Jul. 31'71
0.06½.	Sep. 18	Sep. 27	Oct. 1	Nov. 1'71
0.06¼.	Dec. 10	Dec. 17	Dec. 24	Feb. 1'72
0.06⅝.	Mar. 17	Mar. 18	Mar. 30	May 1'72

¹Listed N.Y.S.E.; also listed Midwest and Pacific Coast S Es. & traded Boston, Detroit & Phila.-Balt.-Wash S Es.   ²Indicated rate.   ³Payable semi-annually in Holiday Inns common stock.   ⁴Incl. cos. acq. in 1972 on a pooling-of-interests basis.

STANDARD N.Y.S.E. STOCK REPORTS   STANDARD & POOR'S CORP.
Reproduction in whole or in part without written permission is strictly prohibited. All rights reserved.
Published at Ephrata, Pa. Editorial & Executive Offices, 345 Hudson St., New York, N.Y. 10014

Vol. 39, No. 114   Tuesday, June 13, 1972   Sec. 12

FIGURE 19–4 (*continued*)

1143 HOLIDAY INNS, INCORPORATED

[3]INCOME STATISTICS (Million $) AND PER SHARE ($) DATA

[1]Year Ended Dec. 31	Total Revs.	% Total Inc. of Revs.	Total Inc.	Depr. & Amort.	Net bef. Taxes	[4]Net Inc.	[4]Earns. (Common Share ($) Data[2])	Divs. Paid	[1]Price Range	Price-Earns. Ratios HI LO
1972—	-----	---	-----	----	----	----	---	0.13⅛	55⅝-43⅜	-----
1971—	707.88	18.1	128.19	36.37	73.64	40.60	[5]1.36	0.24⅜	50⅝-34⅜	37-25
1970—	604.56	18.8	113.87	32.12	65.61	36.97	[5]1.29	0.21⅞	42⅞-19¾	33-15
1969—	539.83	19.1	103.23	27.70	60.15	32.30	[5]1.15	0.19⅜	47⅜-32½	41-28
1968—	467.85	18.7	87.56	25.35	50.22	28.67	[5]1.03	0.15⅝	40½-19⅝	39-19
1967—	319.21	19.5	62.13	19.50	34.10	18.75	0.82	0.13¼	29-10	35-12
1966—	119.38	18.8	22.44	4.84	13.29	7.12	0.41	0.09⅜	11¼-6⅜	27-15
1965—	71.21	20.0	14.26	3.96	7.27	4.08	0.29	0.06⅞	8¼-4⅛	29-15
1964—	57.11	19.9	11.37	3.41	5.26	2.93	0.21	0.03¾	5¼-3⅝	25-18
1963—	48.20	21.8	10.53	3.16	4.58	2.47	0.18	Nil	6¼-4⅛	35-23
1962—	29.57	24.3	7.18	1.87	3.84	1.79	0.15	Nil	7-3⅜	46-24

[3]PERTINENT BALANCE SHEET STATISTICS (Million $)

[1]Dec. 31	Gross Prop.	Capital Expend.	Cash Items	Inventories	Receivables	Current Assets	Current Liab.	Net Workg. Cap.	Cur. Ratio Assets to Liab.	Long Term Debt
1971—	751.52	119.39	38.20	23.34	64.50	136.05	102.86	33.19	1.3-1	284.63
1970—	662.88	85.66	40.90	21.19	57.62	133.44	95.13	38.30	1.4-1	287.27
1969—	596.37	68.04	34.41	19.45	56.70	128.25	109.33	18.92	1.2-1	227.22
1968—	533.95	83.25	34.72	18.84	44.97	105.55	83.53	22.02	1.3-1	215.53
1967—	395.43	115.15	27.15	12.70	32.69	76.48	59.32	17.16	1.3-1	135.17
1966—	139.94	31.77	12.04	6.02	15.10	34.45	25.44	9.01	1.4-1	77.83
1965—	103.49	24.55	3.71	3.75	8.05	16.69	14.24	2.46	1.2-1	53.88
1964—	78.94	14.82	7.13	4.28	8.19	20.26	15.37	4.89	1.3-1	47.20
1963—	64.12	12.26	7.47	3.49	6.31	17.85	10.63	7.23	1.7-1	44.97
1962—	51.85	32.41	5.62	1.19	4.67	12.22	8.16	4.07	1.5-1	36.67

[1]Yrs. ended June 30 prior to 1967. [2]Adj. for stock splits of 6-for-5 in Nov. 1962, 2-for-1 in Sept. 1967 & 2-for-1 in June 1969. [3]Incl. TCO Industries aft. 1966. [4]Bef. spec. crs. equal to $0.05 a sh. in 1971, $0.02 in 1970, $0.04 in 1969 & $0.05 in 1968; in prior yrs. nominal amts. (less than $0.01) a sh. incl. in earns. [5]Based on com. shs. & com. sh. equivalents (series A spec. stk.).

Fundamental Position

Holiday Inns and its subsidiaries and licensees constitute the largest chain lodging operations in the nation. TCO Industries, involved in bus transportation (Continental Trailways), related businesses and steamship operations, was merged in early 1969.

At December 31, 1971 a total of 1,371 inns (1,001 licensed) were in operation, containing 200,532 (148,777) rooms. Inns are located throughout the U. S., Canada and Europe, with heaviest concentrations in the eastern half of the U. S. and Canada. Facilities vary in size from 48 rooms to 646, with a large number having 100 to 150 rooms. In 1971, the chain's occupancy rate declined to 68.1% from the 70.2% of 1970 (73.4% in 1969).

Revenues for 1971 were divided as follows: inns and restaurants 51%; supply and manufacturing 19%; travel and transportation 29%; and the balance from miscellaneous sources. Licenses are sold for an initial fee, and continuing royalties are received thereafter. Although accounting for some 3% of revenues, the contribution of licensing income to profits is substantially greater.

Through various companies in the Products division, Holiday conducts supply and manufacturing operations. These include the production of furniture, equipment and related items for hotels, restaurants, offices and other institutional establishments. A commercial press for institutional printing and a construction company are also operated. The Food Service International subsidiary caters to industrial customers.

Continental Trailways operates the second largest intercity bus system in the U. S. and accounts for about 85% of TCO's revenues. About 3,340 buses operate along 69,200 route miles. Subsidiaries have interests in real estate development, insurance, restaurants and foreign and domestic travel tours.

Delta Steamship Lines, 99%-owned by TCO, operates 12 vessels under the U. S. flag. Service extends to the East Coast of South America and the West Coast of Africa.

A Government suit alleging violation of Custom Laws by TCO was filed in 1969. Penalties in substantial amounts are sought.

Finances

At December 31, 1971, minimum annual leases totaled $13,688,000, plus additional rentals based on a percentage of income, which amounted to $26,830,000 in 1971.

In April, 1971 the company sold 800,000 common shares at $44.50 each.

CAPITALIZATION

LONG TERM DEBT: $302,634,362, incl. $12,122,500 of 8% debs. conv. into com. at $35 a sh.

5% CUM. PREFERRED STOCK ($100 par); 73,008 shares (held by Gulf Oil Corp.).

SERIES A SPECIAL STOCK: 1,057,426 shares ($1.125 par); init. conv. into 1.5 com. shs.; $1.70 ann. divd. payable in Holiday common.

COMMON STOCK: 28,136,224 shs. ($1.50 par); some 14% controlled by directors.

OPTIONS: To purchase 660,036 shares.

WARRANTS: To purchase 325,373 shares. (Terms and trading basis should be checked in detail.)

Incorporated in Tenn. in 1954. **Office**: 3742 Lamar Ave., Memphis, Tenn. 38118. **P.**—W. B. Walton. **Secy.**—W. C. Marsh. **Trea.**—[illegible] W. Adams. **Dirs.**—K. Wilson (Chrmn), F. W. Adams, J. F. Brown, W. N. Clarke, L. M. Clymer, C. M. Coll[illegible], F. G. Currey, C. H. Dixon, C. B. Harrison, W. E. Johnson, R. A. Lile, E. B. McCool, L. K. McKee, M. E. Moore, A. B. Morgan, R. [illegible], R. M. Scott, Jr., R. F. Slater, J. B. Temple, W. B. Walton. **Transfer Agents**—First National City Bank, NYC; First National Bank of Memphis, Bank of America NT&SA, Los Angeles, Continental Illinois Nat'l. Bank & Trust Co., Chicago. **Registrars**—Bank of New York, NYC; National Bank of Commerce in Memphis, United California Bank, Los Angeles; Harris Trust & Savings Bank, Chicago.

FIGURE 19–5
Illustration of *Moody's Handbook*

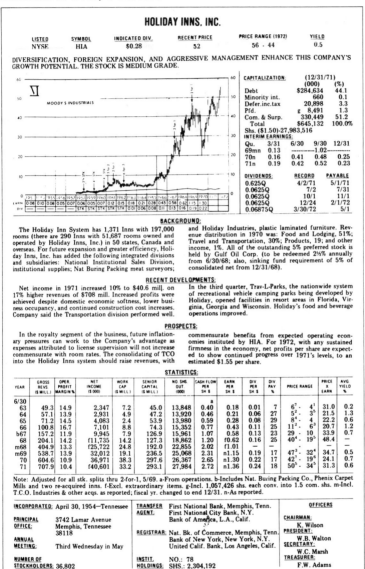

June 30, 1972 is presented as Figure 19–6. Much of the same type of information as that from Moody's and Standard & Poor's is included. Again, differences appear in certain items such as earnings per share depending on whether extraordinary items are included or not. Value Line reports 1971 earnings of $1.40 per share for Holiday Inns, which

470

FIGURE 19–6
Illustration of Value Line reports

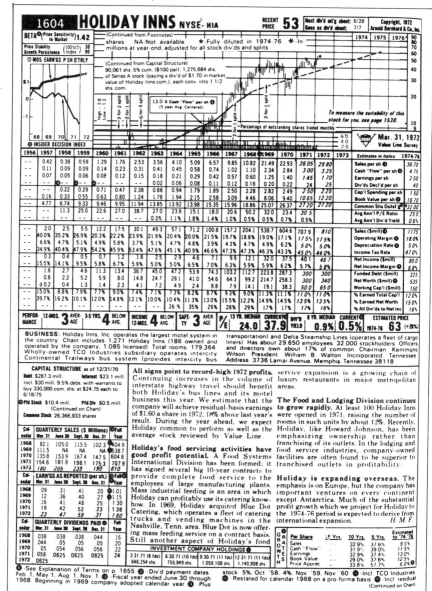

includes an extraordinary component, while $1.36 was reported in the other two sources that have been discussed.

Value Line also includes certain information not found in either Moody's or Standard & Poor's. First, Value Line presents historical growth rates for sales, cash flow, earnings, book value, and stock price. Annual growth of all these variables has been greater than 28% for Holiday Inns over both the past five and the past ten years. Second, a beta value of 1.40 was reported for Holiday Inns at the extreme upper left hand corner of the report. In Chapter 3, beta (or volatility) was defined as the slope of a firm's characteristic line, which relates the return on a security to the return from the entire market. Value Line estimates beta by regressing the weekly percentage change in stock price for the firm on the average weekly percentage change in price for all stocks included in the survey. A five-year period is used in the regression analysis. Third, Value Line forecasts values of a number of financial variables for the next year (1972) and also for the next three to five years (1974–1976). Fourth, Value Line reports for each firm the quarterly holdings by investment companies during the past year. We see that ten mutual funds held approximately 756,000 shares at the end of June, 1971, while 12 funds held 1,150,000 shares at the end of March, 1972. The latter represented about 4% of the 28.1 million shares outstanding at that point in time.

Last but certainly not least as a source of recent financial history is the annual report of the company in question. Although the content of material and format of presentation differs significantly between firms, most firms present a financial review of the past few years. Such a five-year summary, appearing in the 1971 *Annual Report* of Holiday Inns, is included as Figure 19–7. The annual report also includes, of course, a wide range of other information concerning the company, its recent developments, and oftentimes its optimistic plans for the future.

COMPUTERIZED DATA SOURCES

As everyone knows, the electronic computer has become an essential tool within our complex and growing society. It is not surprising, therefore, that the computer has become of importance to the investment community. In addition to computerized data sources, numerous computer programs exist that can be used to analyze investment data. The high cost of computerized data sources and analysis programs has tended to limit their use to institutional investors. For now, we simply review some of the better known computerized sources of financial and investment data.

Investors Management Sciences, a subsidiary of Standard & Poor's Corporation, provides a number of computer-oriented services of interest

472

FIGURE 19–7
Illustration of one page in an annual report

Holiday Inns, Inc. and Consolidated Subsidiaries

Five Year Financial Review

	1971	1970	1969	1968	1967
Revenues					
Historical	707,876,910	604,556,276	538,699,122	404,862,378	157,197,936
Restated for Poolings of Interests	707,876,910	604,556,276	539,834,149	466,783,357	369,532,526
Income Before Income Taxes					
Historical	73,643,846	65,613,278	59,592,152	45,930,540	18,977,552
Restated for Poolings of Interests	73,643,846	65,613,278	60,150,575	50,531,622	38,520,045
Earnings Applicable to Common and Series A Stock					
Historical	41,591,807	36,881,111	32,358,159	26,524,643	9,187,942
Restated for Poolings of Interests	41,591,807	36,881,111	32,648,388	29,478,718	20,097,001
Earnings Per Share					
Historical	1.41	1.31	1.19	1.07	.58
Restated for Poolings of Interests	1.41	1.31	1.18	1.08	.79
Depreciation and Amortization*					
Historical	39,987,026	37,430,168	31,826,501	25,040,141	7,533,752
Restated for Poolings of Interests	39,987,026	37,430,168	29,008,955	27,932,875	24,253,481
Additions To Fixed Assets					
Historical	119,393,893	85,657,985	67,320,940	68,559,002	37,826,467
Restated for Poolings of Interests	119,393,893	85,657,985	68,041,343	83,429,909	127,748,744
Working Capital					
Historical	33,194,414	38,301,786	19,053,809	24,762,162	7,902,536
Restated for Poolings of Interests	33,194,414	38,301,786	18,922,425	21,469,727	14,414,548
Total Assets					
Historical	764,229,439	676,350,011	575,226,636	441,803,755	198,943,350
Restated for Poolings of Interests	764,229,439	676,350,011	580,769,651	516,370,306	432,313,810
Long-Term Debt					
Historical	284,634,362	287,270,816	223,792,526	176,262,220	103,179,851
Restated for Poolings of Interests	284,634,362	287,270,816	227,221,129	219,638,919	169,049,915
Stockholders' Equity					
Historical	338,939,817	258,333,201	214,685,700	174,940,537	64,284,808
Restated for Poolings of Interests	338,939,817	258,333,201	215,181,171	187,853,883	165,688,224
Average Common Shares Outstanding					
Historical	29,510,052	28,189,619	27,241,964	12,426,828	7,980,746
Restated for Poolings of Interests	29,510,052	28,189,619	27,614,870	27,337,351	25,393,439

*Includes other charges not affecting working capital

to investors. The best known of these services is *Compustat,* a computer-readable library of annual and quarterly data tapes. Coverage includes 60 data items for up to twenty years for each of several hundred industrial and public utility firms. The data include adjustment factors for stock splits and stock dividends so that growth rates over time can be calculated on a per-share basis. Although the Compustat tapes contain occasional errors and incomplete data, the information generally is considered reliable. The tapes are being used for research by numerous universities and financial institutions.

Complementing Compustat are data tapes provided by the University of Chicago Center for Research in Security Prices (CRSP) and those provided by Investors Statistical Laboratories (ISL). The former include monthly closing prices since 1926 of all common stocks traded on the New York Stock Exchange. The ISL tapes, on the other hand, include daily prices (high, low, and closing) and volume for all New York and American Stock Exchange stocks plus approximately 1,900 over-the-counter issues. Data are available from 1962 for the listed exchanges and from 1968 for the over-the-counter issues. Collectively, the Compustat, CRSP, and ISL tapes provide a gigantic data base on which academic and institutional researchers have based a plethora of empirical studies.

Computerized data bases also are available from other sources. For example, *Fortune* magazine makes available almost twenty years of data from its annual survey, "500 Largest U.S. Industrials."

FORECASTED EARNINGS

In Part II of this book, we saw that future earnings play a central role in the determination of investment value. We also devoted considerable attention in Part III to a careful measurement of the earnings record of a firm with due regard to accounting adjustments and nonrecurring components of earnings. In addition, we reviewed a number of procedures for forecasting earnings for subsequent years. It would seem natural in our comparison of sources of information that we would mention possible sources of forecasted earnings.

A logical starting point is the company itself. While earnings already achieved typically are reported quarterly in the *Wall Street Journal* and other newspapers, forecasted earnings appear more sporadically. Reports are made by corporate officers to security analysts and financial reporters, or they may be included in financial statements sent to stockholders. For example, the following six-month earnings report appeared in the *Wall Street Journal* on July 27, 1972:

HOLIDAY INNS, INC.		
6 Month June 30:	*1972*	*1971*
Shr earns	$.61	a$.60
Revenues	372,235,602	337,531,241
Income	18,473,211	17,820,019
Spec gain		b3,608,704
Net Income	18,473,211	c21,428,723
Com shares	20,102,752	29,172,174

a-Based on income before special credit. b-From sale of options. c-Equal to 72 cents a share.

The annual report of a company seldom includes a specific forecast of earnings for the coming year, but often a general statement will be included. In the letter to shareholders, which introduces the Holiday Inns 1971 *Annual Report,* the Chairman, Vice Chairman, and President state:

> We are hopeful that the trends of the last quarter of the year will continue, enabling us to report record high sales and earnings again for 1972.

In this particular statement, investors should be careful to distinguish between total dollar earnings and earnings per share. It is possible for a growing company to have an increase in dollar earnings but not necessarily an increase in earnings per share—particularly if the company has sold additional common shares during the year to finance company growth, or has achieved growth through mergers implemented by an exchange of shares of common stock.

Forecasted earnings are also provided as addenda to certain of the financial summaries as reported in the prior section. The following 1972 earnings forecasts for Holiday Inns are noted from Figures 19–4, 19–5, and 19–6, respectively:

Source	*1972 Earnings per share forecast*
Standard & Poor's	$1.55
Moody's	1.55
Value Line	1.60

Part of the difference in such forecasts may arise because the forecasts are not made at the same time.

The research departments of large brokerage firms and other investment advisory services also provide earnings forecasts. For example, Merrill Lynch, Pierce, Fenner and Smith, in a discussion of several firms within the services industry, suggested that:

> Holiday Inns profits this year should gain more sharply than they have in the last two years. Earnings this year should equal or exceed $1.65 per share. On a longer-term basis, annual earnings should grow at a rate of 15% or somewhat more.

One useful summary of several such forecasts is provided in a weekly publication, *Standard & Poor's Earnings Forecaster.* One page of the January 14, 1972 issue, which includes Holiday Inns, is presented as Figure 19–8. We see that 1972 forecasts lie in the $1.65–1.70 range.

CURRENT PRICES AND VOLUME

In order to determine whether a security is overvalued or undervalued, it is necessary to compare the investment value of the security

FIGURE 19–8
Illustration of earnings forecasts

22

STANDARD & POOR'S EARNINGS FORECASTER

COMPANY & FISCAL YEAR END / ESTIMATOR	DATE OF ESTIMATE OR REVIEW	A-1970	E-1971	E-1972
•HARSCO CORP.(Dec)		2.03		
S&P	*		1.90	—
•HART SCHAFFNER & MARX(Nov)		R1.30	RA1.18	
S&P	*			RQ1.55
•HAWAIIAN ELECTRIC(Dec)		Rp2.14 / RQp2.04		
Sutro & Co.	#		RQ2.00	—
•HAYES-ALBION(Jul)		j1.47	A0.78	
United Business Service	Jan 3			1.60
S&P	*			1.85
•HAZELTINE CORP.(Dec)		0.52		
S&P	*		d0.40	0.50
HEALTH-TEX(Dec)		1.06		
Hornblower & Weeks	Jan 3		1.35	1.50
United Business Service	Jan 10		1.35	—
•HECLA MINING CO.(Dec)		z0.76		
Shearson, Hammill & Co.	Nov 17		0.65	—
S&P	*		j0.70	0.70
HEILEMAN (G.) BREWING(Dec)		Rp1.37		
Robert W. Baird & Co.	Dec 7		R1.40	R1.60
Fredrick & Co., Inc., (Milw.)	Nov 10		R1.40	R1.60
United Business Service	Sep 7		R1.50	—
•HEINZ (H.J.) CO.(Apr)		R2.41 / RQ2.33	RA2.53 / RQA2.50	
Bache & Co.	**			R2.75
Moore, Leonard & Lynch	Dec 15			R2.75
United Business Service	Dec 27			R2.70
S&P	*			R2.75
•HELENA RUBINSTEIN, INC.(Dec)		1.69		
United Business Service	Jan 10		1.80	—
•HELLER (WALTER E.) INTL.(Dec)		Rj1.60 / RQj1.48		
Frederick & Co., (Milw.)	Nov 10		R1.85	—
Shuman, Agnew & Co.	Dec 6		R1.90	R2.10
United Business Service	Sep 7		R1.85	—
S&P	*		R1.85	R2.05
•HELME PRODUCTS(Dec)		z1.14		
Harris, Upham & Co.	Dec 1		1.50	1.75/1.85
Thomson & McKinnon, Auchincloss	Nov 22		1.50	—
Walston & Co.	Dec 22		1.50	1.70
S&P	*		1.45	1.70
•HELMERICH & PAYNE, INC.(Sep)		R1.72	RA2.07	
Thomson & McKinnon, Auchincloss	Nov 22			R2.25
S&P	*			R2.30
HENREDON FURNITURE INDS.(Mar)		1.83	A1.45	
Wheat & Co.	Nov 10			1.90
•HERCULES, INC.(Dec)		2.51		
United Business Service	Sep 16		2.65	—
H. N. Whitney, Goadby & Co.	Dec 13		2.60	—
S&P	*		2.85	3.15
HERFF JONES CO.(Jun)		Rjz0.87 / RQjjz0.85	RzA1.24 / RzA1.21	
First Columbus Corp.	Nov 8			R1.35
•HERSHEY FOODS CORP.(Dec)		p1.41		
Abraham & Co.	Nov 16		1.80	—
S&P	*		1.60	1.80
HESS'S INC.(Jan)		R1.44	RA1.48	
Butcher & Sherrerd	Nov 23			R1.00
DeHaven & Townsend, Crouter & Bodine	Dec 20			R1.10
Moore, Leonard & Lynch	Dec 28			R1.00
Reynolds Securities, Inc.	Nov 11			R1.25
•HEUBLEIN INC.(Jun)		†Rj1.42	†RjA1.65	
Parker/Hunter, Inc.	Jan 3			‡1.80
Parker/Hunter, Inc.	Dec 21			‡1.80
United Business Service	Nov 29			‡R1.85
S&P	*			‡R1.80
†-Excl. Kentucky Fried Chicken.				
‡-Incl. Kentucky Fried Chicken.				

COMPANY & FISCAL YEAR END / ESTIMATOR	DATE OF ESTIMATE OR REVIEW	A-1970	E-1971	E-1972
•HEWLETT-PACKARD(Oct)		z0.90	A0.89	
Bache & Co.	**			1.05/1.10
Harris, Upham & Co.	Dec 1			1.00
E. F. Hutton & Co.	Nov 22			1.15
S&P	*			1.10
HEXCEL CORP.(Dec)		R0.64		
Bateman Eichler, Hill Richards	Dec 20		R0.95	R1.15
•HIGH VOLTAGE ENGINEERING(Dec)		jd1.00		
Hornblower & Weeks	Dec 1		Nil	0.25
S&P	*		d0.05	0.25
▲HILLENBRAND INDUSTS.(Nov)		2.53		
Parker/Hunter, Inc.	Nov 30		2.50	2.70
•HILTON HOTELS(Dec)		R1.94		
S&P	*		R1.85	—
HITACHI LTD.(ADS)		†c2.94	†c2.27	
Nomura Research Institute	Dec 16			†c1.74
†-12 Months Sept.				
•HOBART MFG.(Dec)		2.03		
W. D. Gradison & Co.	Dec 3		2.50	2.90/3.00
Prescott, Merrill, Turben	Dec 20		2.40	2.80
United Business Service	Nov 8		2.40	—
S&P	*		2.60	2.90
•HOERNER-WALDORF(Oct)		R2.12 / RQ1.95	RA1.79 / RQNR	
Piper, Jaffray & Hopwood	Dec 30			RQ2.00/2.20
S&P	*			R2.15
•HOFFMAN ELECTRONICS(Dec)		Rj0.36		
Bateman Eichler, Hill Richards	Dec 22		R0.80	R1.25
S&P	*		R0.75	R0.90
•HOLIDAY INNS INC.(Dec)		Rjp1.30		
Bache & Co.	**		R1.45	R1.70
Morgan, Keegan & Co.	Nov 9		R1.40	—
Research Institute	Nov 15		R1.40/1.45	R1.65
United Business Service	Sep 16		R1.45	—
S&P	*		R1.45	—
•HOLLY SUGAR(Mar)		d1.59	A0.72	
S&P	*			0.80
•HOMESTAKE MINING(Dec)		j0.61		
S&P	*		0.45	0.50
HON INDUSTRIES(Dec)		†1.03		
Piper, Jaffray & Hopwood	Nov 29		1.05	—
†-52 Wks. ended Jan. 2, 1971.				
HONDA MOTOR CO.(ADS)		†c1.95	†c2.11	
Nomura Research Institute	Dec 16			†c2.23
†-12 Months Aug.				
•HONEYWELL, INC.(Dec)		jp3.34		
Bache & Co.	**		3.40	3.70
Hornblower & Weeks	Jan 3		3.00	4.00
Piper, Jaffray & Hopwood	Nov 29		3.45	4.00
United Business Service	Jan 3		3.50	4.25
H. N. Whitney, Goadby & Co.	Dec 13		3.10	3.45
S&P	*		j3.25	j3.65
†-Pro-forma for merger of General Electric Computer Components Co.				
HONOLULU GAS(Dec)		j1.36		
Sutro & Co.	#		1.55	—
•HOOVER BALL & BEARING CO.(Jul)		p1.82	A1.85	
Shearson, Hammill & Co.	Nov 17			2.30
Walston & Co.	§			2.70
Watling Lerchen & Co.	Nov 8			2.40
S&P	*			2.45
HOOVER CO.(Dec)		2.71		
E. F. Hutton & Co.	Nov 22		2.85	3.10
Prescott, Merrill, Turben	Dec 20		2.90	3.20
United Business Service	Dec 27		2.85	—
•HORIZON CORP.(May)		R4.06	RA5.48	
Shearson, Hammill & Co.	Dec 30			R6.50
United Business Service	Jan 10			R6.50
▲HOSKINS MFG.(Dec)		1.62		
Watling, Lerchen & Co.	Nov 8		1.50	—

EXPLANATION OF SYMBOLS—• Listed NYSE, ▲ Listed AMEX, A-ACTUAL, E-ESTIMATE, P-PRELIMINARY, R-PRIMARY EARNINGS PER SHARE, RQ-FULLY DILUTED EARNINGS PER SHARE. OTHER SYMBOLS SEE INSIDE FRONT COVER.

with its current market price. A number of sources publish the market prices of a large number of stocks and bonds on a daily or weekly basis. These sources also include the volume of transactions as buyers and sellers interact in the secondary markets for outstanding securities. Current price and volume information are organized by market such as New York Stock Exchange, American Stock Exchange, the several regional exchanges, and the over-the-counter market. Most daily newspapers, especially those serving large metropolitan areas, publish price and volume information. All include New York Stock Exchange stocks. Some extend coverage to include full American Stock Exchange and various regional exchange prices, while others present only samples of stocks from the American Stock Exchange, the regional exchanges, and the over-the-counter markets. Bond coverage is infrequent in the financial sections of daily newspapers.

The *Wall Street Journal* is a comprehensive source of price and volume information for both stocks and bonds. The *Wall Street Journal* is a business and financial newspaper published five days a week in three geographical editions. Figure 19–9 includes price and volume information

FIGURE 19–9
Illustration of stock quotations

THE WALL STREET JOURNAL, Friday, August 18, 1972

New York Stock Exchange Transactions

Thursday, August 17, 1972

--1972-- High	Low	Stocks Div.	Sales in 100s	Open	High	Low	Close	Net Chg.
60	33¾	Hilton Hotl 1	87	37	37¾	37	37¾	+ ⅛
5	3⅜	HMW Ind	3	3⅞	4	3⅞	4	+ ⅛
69	60⅛	Hobart 1.20	18	67½	67½	67½	67½	− ¼
38	27⅜	HoernWal .97	10	35⅝	35⅝	35⅜	35½	− ⅛
31⅞	16⅛	Hoff Electrn	52	26¾	28½	26¾	28	+1¼
55⅝	39½	HolidyInn .27	297	40⅜	40¾	40¼	40¾	+ ⅜
19¼	13⅞	HollySug .40e	7	14⅝	14⅝	14½	14½	+ ⅛
30⅞	18	Homestke .40	59	26⅝	27⅛	26⅜	26⅞	+ ¼
170¾	127⅞	Honywll 1.30	106	157½	159⅝	157½	159¼	+ ¼
42¾	32	HoovrBl 1.20	37	41¼	42⅜	41⅛	42⅜	+ ⅞
44¼	27½	Horizon Cp	271	27½	27¾	26½	26⅞	− ⅝
30¼	21¼	Hospit Affil	62	24	24	23⅞	24	.....
43¼	35½	HospitCp Am	34	43⅛	43⅜	42⅜	42⅞	+ ⅛
42¼	32¼	Host Intl .36	6	34¾	34⅞	34¾	34⅞	− ⅛
16⅜	12⅞	Houdaille .60	14	13⅛	13⅜	13	13⅛	+ ⅛
25½	19⅝	Houg Miff .40	72	22½	22½	22¼	22½	+ ¼
29⅞	12¼	House Fabric	78	14	14⅞	14	14⅞	+ ¾
57⅛	48	HousehF 1.30	55	52⅞	53⅝	52⅞	53⅜	+ ⅝

for a sample of stocks on the New York Stock Exchange as reported on Friday, August 18, 1972. The sample of stocks, listed alphabetically as usual, ranges from Hilton Hotels to Household Finance and includes our illustrative firm. We see that on Thursday, August 17, 1972, the market price of Holiday Inns common stock opened at $40⅜ per share, and ranged during the day from a low of $40¼ to a high of $40¾, which was also its closing price for the day. This closing price was up ⅜ of a dollar from the closing price of August 16. Compared to its annual price range of $39½ to $55⅝, we find that Holiday Inns was trading near its 1972 low. Sales on August 17 for Holiday Inns amounted to 29,700 shares. In addition to this daily information, which summarizes how investors viewed Holiday Inns on August 17, the *Wall Street Journal* includes announcements of earnings and dividends, information about investment companies, commodity markets, and government securities, articles on the economy, industries and individual companies, and extensive advertising.

Many investors follow the fortunes of their security investments from day to day by examining market prices reported in the *Wall Street Journal* or the financial sections of their daily newspapers. Among the daily newspapers, the *New York Times* has the most comprehensive coverage of financial news and developments as well as price and volume data. Other investors prefer to watch their investments at less frequent intervals. An excellent summary of price and volume information on a weekly basis appears in *Barron's,* which like the *Wall Street Journal* is published by Dow Jones & Co., Inc. Although the format of price and volume data is similar to that already illustrated, *Barron's* also includes recent information on dividends and earnings for each company whose stock is included. The weekly listing of stocks in *Barron's* usually is more complete than that of the *Wall Street Journal,* particularly if certain issues are not widely traded. For example, the preferred stock of Holiday Inns seldom is shown in the *Wall Street Journal* but is reported in *Barron's.*

Extensive coverage of bonds is also included in *Barron's.* Figure 19–10

FIGURE 19–10
Illustration of bond quotations

July 31, 1972 BARRON'S

LISTED BOND QUOTATIONS

1972 High	1972 Low		Sales $1,000	Weekly High	Weekly Low	Last	Net Chg.
115½	87½	HiltnHot 5½s95	87	90	87½	87½	−2¼
62	58½	HockVal 4½s99	1	59¼	59¼	59¼	.....
115	94½	HoernrWa 5s94	45	102½	102½	102½	−1
112½	109⅝	HolidInn 9½xw	116	111¾	111	111	− ¾
85⅜	79	Honywl 5.60s92	7	83¼	83	83¼	+ ¼
92	89½	Honeywell 4s76	45	91	90½	90½	− ½
108	97	Host Int 5¼s94	20	105	105	105	−2½
109½	106⅛	HouseFin 9s7 6	35	108	106¾	106¾	− ¾
108½	105⅛	HousFin 8¾s75	68	106½	105⅛	105¼	− ⅝
86	80⅛	HousFin 4⅞s81	24	85½	85	85½	+ ½
87½	84	HouseFin 4s78	12	86⅜	86⅜	86⅜	.....

includes July 31, 1972, quotations for a sample of corporate bonds traded on the New York Exchange. The sample ranges from the 5½% bonds of Hilton Hotels due in 1995 to the 4% bonds of Household Finance due in 1978. The latter is one of four outstanding debt issues of House-hold Finance. Bond quotations are in percentages of their face value (without use of a "%" sign), so a quote of 90½ for a $1,000 bond means that the bond traded at $905. For Holiday Inns, 116 bonds were traded during the week of July 24–28 in the price range of $1,110 to $1,117.50. The closing transaction was at the price $1,110, down $7.50 from the previous week's close. The 1972 price range is also shown. In addition to the extensive statistical section, *Barron's* includes in-depth articles on the economy and the securities markets. There is also a large number of advertisements, many offering investment advice of one type or another.

INVESTMENT RECOMMENDATIONS

After examining the history and organization of a particular firm, its recent financial history, forecasted earnings, and current price and volume information, the investor begins to form judgments about the advantages and disadvantages of holding the securities of that firm in his portfolio. Apart from his own personal judgments, the investor may be interested in comparing his final opinion with other recommendations. For Holiday Inns, we can illustrate the nature of investment recommen-dations as given by some of the professional sources that have already been identified.

Moody's recommendation, included as part of their one-page sum-mary, is brief and straightforward:

> Diversification, foreign expansion, and aggressive management enhance this company's growth potential. The stock is medium grade.

Standard & Poor's recommendation for Holiday Inns contains more detail:

> Continued expansion, both domestic and international, and possible acquisitions enhance long-range potentials. However, the growth rate has slowed considerably in recent periods, and with uncertainties raised by the foreign expansion program the shares seem somewhat fully priced at current levels.

Value Line includes its recommendations for Holiday Inns along with recommendations for about 1,400 common stocks on a weekly basis. The particular page for Holiday Inns of the June 16, 1972, issue is in-cluded as Figure 19–11. In addition to the current market price (54), projected market price for the period 1974–1976 (63), current dividend yield (0.5%), and other pertinent information, Value Line includes four distinct rankings of all 1,400 stocks into five categories. The four rankings (1 to 5 in decreasing desirability) are probable market performance

FIGURE 19–11
Illustration of Value Line ratings

		NAME OF STOCK	Ticker Symbol	Recent Price	Potential Value 1974–76†	Next 12 mos.	To 1974 1976‡	In c o m e	S a f e t y	Est'd Yield next 12 mos.%	Est'd Div'd next 12 mos.	Est'd Earns. 12 to 9-30-72	Current P/E Ratio	Qtr. Ended	Earns. Per Sh.	Year Ago	Qtr. Ended	Latest Div'd	Year Ago
	1637	GULF LIFE HOLDING .	GHC	52	68	2	4	4	4	1.5	.80	5.60	9.3	—	—	—	3/31	.39	.25
1523	349	GULF, MOBILE & OHIO	GFO	103	To be merged into Illinois Central														
407	379	GULF OIL	GO	24	49	3	1	1	1	6.3	1.50	2.77	8.7	3/31	.67	.70	6/30	.375	.375
	380	GULF OIL CANADA LTD. b	GOC	31*	29	3	5	3	2	1.9 ○	.60	1.34	23.1	3/31	.38	.25	9/30	.15	.15
	1032	GULF RESOURCES & CHEM.	GRE	7	16	5	1	5	5	Nil	Nil	d.34	—	3/31	d.02	.14	3/31	—	—
	654	GULF STATES UTIL.	GTU	18	34	4	2	1	2	5.8 ¶	1.04	1.44	12.5	3/31	.20	.24	6/30	.26	.26
35	1237	GULF & WESTERN IND.	GW	40	48	1	4	4	4	1.5	.61	3.34	12.0	4/30	.01	.66	9/30	.15	.125
	908	GULTON INDUSTRIES	GUL	12	24	2	1	5	5	Nil	Nil	d10	—	2/29	d.13	d1.11	3/31	—	—
	723	HACKENSACK WATER	HWA	35	57	4	3	1	1	6.3	2.20	3.31	10.6	3/31	.42	.40	6/30	.55	.55
	1172	HALLIBURTON CO.	HAL	95	89	3	5	4	3	1.2	1.11	3.52	27.0	3/31	.74	.64	6/30	.263	.263
	1572	HALL (W.F.) PRINTING	HPG	56	66	1	4	2	3	3.3	1.82	4.38	12.8	3/31	1.63	.86	6/30	.62	.55
		HAMILTON WATCH CO.	HMW	Name changed to HMW Industries Inc.															
	841	HAMMERMILL	HML	17	36	5	1	3	2	2.9	.50	.48	35.4	3/31	.06	.15	6/30	.125	.25
	909	HAMMOND CORP.	HMD	9¾	24	3	1	2	4	4.1	.40	.85	11.5	3/31	d.17	.09	6/30	.10	.10
	1377	HANDLEMAN CO.	HDL	30	45	3	3▲3	3		2.3	.68	1.65	18.2	1/31	.52	.51	6/30	.17	.17
	1065	HANDY & HARMAN	HNH	17	30	4	3	2	4	4.2	.72	.95	17.9	3/31	.29	.14	6/30	.18	.18
	1412	HANES CORP.	HNS	19	35	3	2	3	4	2.6	.50	1.69	11.2	3/31	.38	d.04	6/30	.125	.125
876	1033	HANNA MINING CO.	HNM	64	69	3	4	3	2	2.4	1.35	3.44	16.3	3/31	.32	.31	6/30	.338	.325
	1573	HARC'RT, BR'CE JOV'NOVICH	HBJ	43	86	3	2	5	3	2.3	1.00	2.63	16.3	3/31	d.32	d.26	9/30	.25	.25
	1686	HARRIS BANKCORP INC.	HSVG	52	81	4	3	2	1	1.9	2.00	5.68	9.2	3/31	1.26	1.51	6/30	.50	.44
	1173	HARRIS-INTERTYPE	HI	55	72	5	4	3	2	1.8	1.00	2.22	24.8	3/31	.50	.61	6/30	.25	.25
	1066	HARSCO CORP.	HSC	22	35	3	3	2	2	4.5	1.00	2.23	9.9	9/31	.40	.40	6/30	.25	.25
	1413	HART SCHAFFNER & MARX	HSM	28	44	4	3	3	1	2.9	.80	1.50	18.7	2/29	.40	.30	6/30	.20	.20
	655	HAWAIIAN ELECTRIC	HE	25	46	2	2	1	1	6.0	1.50	2.31	10.7	3/31	.51	.47	6/30	.36	.36
	153	HAYES-ALBION CORP.	HAY	20	30	3	3	1	3	5.3	1.05	1.96	10.2	4/30	.46	.12	6/30	.25	.25
	910	HAZELTINE	HZ	11	17	2	3	5	5	Nil	Nil	.09	—	3/31	.01	d.11	3/31	—	—
348, 746	1414	HCA INDUSTRIES, INC.	HCA	17	15	○	5	5	5	Nil	Nil	d.05	—	1/31	d.72	d.45	3/31	—	—
	1034	HECLA MINING	HL	22	27	3	1	5	4	Nil	Nil	.70	24.3	3/31	.16	.16	6/30	—	—
	1289	HEINZ (H.J.)	HNZ	43	46	3	5	1	1	2.4	1.04	2.96	16.0	1/31	.45	.37	6/30	.26	.25
	585	HELENE CURTIS	HC	7	21	3	1	5	5	Nil	Nil	.22	31.8	2/29	d.11	d.90	3/31	—	—
	1774	HELLER (WALTER, E.) INT'L	HLR	30	42	3	3	3	3	2.5	.76	2.12	14.2	3/31	.46	.42	6/30	.20	.19
35	1125	HELME PRODUCTS	HPI	17	40	3	1	3	4	2.4	.40	1.55	11.0	3/31	.32	.34	9/30	.10	.097
	381	HELMERICH & PAYNE, INC.	HP	34	44	2	4	4	4	0.9	.30	2.30	14.8	3/31	.39	.25	6/30	.15	.10
	1760	HEMISPHERE FUND (cap.)	HEM	4¹,	8	2	2	5	5	Nil	Nil	—	—	12/31	3.76(a)	2.47(e)			
	515	HERCULES INC.	HPC	64	78	3	4	3	3	2.0	1.26	3.02	21.2	3/31	.75	.49	6/30	.26	.25
	1290	HERSHEY FOODS	HSY	24	38	3	2	2	2	4.6	1.10	1.76	13.6	3/31	.50	.45	6/30	.275	.275
1525	330	HEUBLEIN, INC.	HBL	60	66	2	4	2	2	1.5	.87	2.00	30.0	4/30	.36	.33	9/30	.22	.2125
	205	HEWLETT-PACKARD	HWP	67	65	2	5	4	3	0.3	.20	1.10	60.9	4/30	.31	.23	6/30	.10	.10
	911	HIGH VOLTAGE ENGIN'RN'G	HVE	11	45	2	1	5	5	Nil	Nil	d.06	—	3/31	d.04	d.03	6/30	—	—
	1603	HILTON HOTELS	HLT	39	90	4	1▲3	3		2.6	1.00	2.10	18.6	3/31	.46	.42	6/30	.25	.25
	204	HMW INDUSTRIES INC.	HMW	4¾	12	4	1	5	5	Nil☆	Nil	d.10	—	4/30	d.07	d.03	3/31	—	—
	912	HOBART MFG. CO.	HOB	68	63	4	5	3	1	1.9	1.28	2.62	26.1	3/31	.47	.59	6/30	.30	.30
	863	HOERNER-WALDORF CORP.	HWC	37	45	2	4	3	3	2.6	.98	2.40	15.4	4/30	.62	.39	9/30	.245	.225
42	913	HOFFMAN ELECTRONICS	HEC	27	41	3	4	4	4	0.5	Nil	1.35	20.0	3/31	.22	.19	3/31	—	—
	1604	HOLIDAY INNS INC.	HIA	54	63	3	4	4	3	0.5	.275	1.52	36.2	3/31	.22	.19	6/30	.069	.0625
	1035	HOLLINGER MINES LTD. b	HOL	43*	40	4	5	2	2	3.7	1.60	2.53	17.0	3/31	.42	.34	6/30	.40	.40
	339	HOLLY SUGAR	HLY	15	27	2	2	3	3	1.3 2.7	.20-40	1.10	10.0	3/31	.66	.18	6/30	.20	—
	1036	HOMESTAKE MINING	HM	29	30	3	5	4	5	1.4	.40	.61	47.1	3/31	.17	.17	6/30	.10	.10
	980	HONEYWELL, INC.	HON	150	201	3	4	4	2	0.9	1.37	4.31	34.6	3/31	.60	.40	6/30	.325	.325
	154	HOOVER BALL & BEARING	HBB	37	43	3	4	2	3	3.2	1.20	3.20	11.6	4/30	.90	.71	6/30	.30	.30
	1317	HORMEL (GEO. A.) & CO.	HRL	20	30	5	3	2	2	3.8	.78	1.25	16.0	4/30	.14	.57	6/30	.195	.180
	1605	HORN & HARDART CO.	HOR	8¼	16▲3	2	5	5		Nil	Nil	d2 13	—	3/31	.36	d1.41	3/31	—	—
	1606	HOSPITAL CORP. OF AMER.	HSP	49	79	2	3	5	5	Nil	Nil	1.31	37.4	3/31	.36	.29	6/30	—	—
	1607	HOST INTERNATIONAL, INC.	HII	34	44	3	4	3	3	0.0	.36	.98	39.8	3/31	.34	.03	9/30	.09	.09
	155	HOUDAILLE INDUSTRIES	HM	14	21	4	3	2	3	4.3	.60	1.25	11.2	3/31	.44	.39	6/30	.15	.15
	1574	HOUGHTON MIFFLIN CO.	HM	24	30	2	4	4	4	1.8	.42	.98	24.5	3/31	.44	d.40	6/30	.10	.10
	1775	HOUSEHOLD FINANCE	HFC	52	64	3	4	3	1	2.3	1.20	3.19	16.3	3/31	.79	.68	6/30	.30	.30
	656	HOUSTON L'T & POWER	HOU	45	71	2	3	1	1	3.0	1.36	3.15	14.3	3/31	.47	.38	6/30	.16	.16
	427	HOUSTON NATURAL GAS	HNG	55	69	2	3	3	1	1.7	.76	2.75	16.4	1/31	.78	.62	6/30	.16	.14
	1608	HOWARD JOHNSON	HJ	55	58	2	5	4	4	0.5☆	.24	1.59	34.6	3/31	.23	.16	6/30	.06	.06
	1067	HOWMET CORP.	HW	15	36	2	1	1	4	4.7	.70	1.61	9.3	3/31	.47	.35	6/30	.175	.175
	1754	HUBBARD REAL ESTATE INV.	HRE	21	25	3	4	1	2	7.0	1.48	1.50	14.0	1/31	.39	.41	9/30	.37	.37
	1037	HUDSON BAY M'NG b	HD	23*	34	3	3	2	2	3.5 ○	.80	1.67	13.8	3/31	.45	d.01	6/30	.20	—
	842	HUDSON PULP & PAPER	HPAPA	31	52	4	2	4	2	0.5	.15	1.09	28.4	4/30	.40	.39	9/30	.10	.100
	1474	HUGHES & HATCHER	HGH	12	16	3	4	2	3	3.3	.40	.89	13.5	4/30	.15	.05	6/30	.10	.10
	516	HUNT (PHILIP A.) CHEM.	HCC	20	24	2	4	4	4	0.8	.16	.53	37.7	3/31	.12	.09	6/30	.04	.03
	657	IDAHO POWER	IDA	31	41	2	2	1	1	5.5 ¶	1.70	2.77	11.4	3/31	.76	.74	6/30	.425	.40
	781	IDEAL BASIC	IDL	16	29	1	2	2	3	4.4	.70	1.43	11.2	3/31	.35	.21	6/30	.175	.15
484	1512	IDEAL TOY CORP	IC	25	38	4	3	5	3	Nil☆	Nil	1.17	21.4	4/30	.17	.15	3/31	—	—
1396, 1523	267	ILLINOIS CENTRAL IND.	IL	33	50	3	2	2	2	3.6	1.18	3.10	10.6	3/31	.83	.64	9/30	.295	.295
	658	ILLINOIS POWER	IPC	31	50	4	3	1	2	7.1	2.20	2.61	11.9	3/31	.91	.98	6/30	.55	.55
18	1714	IMPERIAL CORP. OF AMER.	ICA	13	30	4	1	5	5	Nil	Nil	1.62	—	3/31	.35	.26	3/31	—	—
	1002	IMPERIAL INDUSTRIES	IMPR	13	30	ø	1	5	5	Nil	Nil	1 25	10.4	3/31	.26	.03	6/30	—	—
	382	IMPERIAL OIL b	IMO	39*	34	2	5	4	2	1.5 ○	.60	1.11	35.1	3/31	.20	.20	9/30	.15	.125
	1638	INA CORP.	NA	51	75	4	3	4	2	2.8	1.45	4.05	12.6	3/31	.95	.77	6/30	.35	.35
	1761	INCOME & CAP. SHS (cap.)	ICS	10	23	2	1	5	3	Nil	Nil	—	—	3/31	14.64(e)	15.38(e)			
	428	INDIANA GAS CO.	IGC	25	53	3	1	1	2	6.0	1.72	3.00	8.3	3/31	2.66(e)	2.88(e)	9/30	.43	.43
	659	INDIANAPOLIS P'W'R & L'T	IPL	26	48	2	2	1	1	6.0	1.56	2.64	9.8	2/29	.72	.51	9/30	.39	.375
C16	1445	INDIAN HEAD, INC	IHD	26	50	3	2	2	3	3.2	.82	2.70	9.6	3/31	.45	.36	9/30	.20	.20
	1687	INDUSTRIAL NAT'L CORP.	INB	36	43	1	4	3	1	2.6	.94	2.36	13.3	3/31	.66	.49	9/30	.235	.15
	1174	INGERSOLL-RAND	IR	69	90	5	4	3	2	3.0	2.08	4.05	17.0	3/31	.95	.90	6/30	.52	.50

during the next year, probable market performance during the period 1974–1976, income, and safety. The five categories contain 100, 300, 600, 300, and 100 stocks, respectively. On these four characteristics, Holiday Inns is ranked 3, 4, 4, and 3 in the order indicated. In other words, Holiday Inns is ranked into the middle category for 12-month performance and safety, but into a lower-than-average category for both 3–5 year performance and income.

There are at least two distinct advantages of the Value Line recommendations. First, by ranking a large number of common stocks that collectively represent a wide spectrum of investment opportunities, an individual can compare a particular stock of interest with others in that industry or others that he is considering. To facilitate such comparisons, Value Line suggests the use of a weighted average computation. Points are assigned to each of the five possible rankings as follows:

Ranking	Assigned points
1 (best)	10
2	8
3	6
4	4
5 (worst)	2

Then the individual investor allocates a total of 100 percentage points to the four categories in order to reflect the relative importance of each. The ranking points and relative percentages are then used to compute a single numerical (weighted-average) score for each stock being considered.

Suppose we are interested in comparing Holiday Inns with Howard Johnson, both of which are in the leisure-oriented business and both of which have been used in this book for illustrative purposes. The four Value Line rankings for Howard Johnson are 2, 5, 4 and 4, respectively. Suppose further that we are interested in the four rankings according to the following: 12-month performance (60%), safety (25%), 3–4 year performance (10%), and income (5%). The weighted-average computations for the two common stocks would be given by

Characteristic	Impor- tance	Holiday Inns			Howard Johnson		
		Rank- ing	Points	Weighted	Rank- ing	Points	Weighted
12-Month performance	60%	3	6	360	2	8	480
3–5 Year performance	10%	4	4	40	5	2	20
Income	5%	4	4	20	4	4	20
Safety	25%	3	6	150	4	4	100
Total score	100%			570			620

The total score turns out to be higher for Howard Johnson, mainly because it received a ranking of 2 on 12-month performance as compared to a 3 for Holiday Inns. Similar computations could be made for any number of stocks in a similar fashion and using any set of relative weights. By asserting his own set of relative percentages, an individual thus can use the Value Line rankings as a basis for actually constructing a portfolio. Alternatively, many individuals may prefer to use the weighted-average technique as a convenient way of screening a large number of common stocks down to a smaller group for which further security analyses can be conducted.

The second advantage of the Value Line recommendations is that we are told how the rankings are made. The *12-month performance* ranking for a particular stock is based on three component rankings. First, a nonparametric value is calculated, which includes recent earnings and price relative to a sample average for all 1,400 common stocks, as well as recent price relative to a 52-week average price for the stock. Second, relative valuation is measured by current to historical price-earnings ratios. Third, earnings momentum is measured as the year-to-year change in quarterly earnings relative to that for the sample.

The *3–5 year performance* ranking is based on the relationship of current price to investment value. For Value Line, the latter depends on an estimate of cash flow four years hence and a cash flow multiplier that reflects both historical experience and trend. The income ranking is based on expected dividend yield during the next twelve months. Finally, the safety ranking is based largely on past growth of cash flow and past price stability, with some attention to capital structure and the nature of the industry in which the particular firm competes. Although these four descriptions of Value Line rankings have been brief, they serve to emphasize the many variables involved and the complexity of interrelationships that are considered.

To illustrate that all recommendations may not be the same, we consider the analysis of Holiday Inns by Merrill Lynch, Pierce, Fenner and Smith. The qualitative evaluation which appeared as part of their Research Discussion #30 on service issues included the passage:

> We believe that future operating prospects for the company are favorable and expect profit gains in coming years of about 15%. . . . During the past year, Holiday Inns common has lagged other growth lodging shares. In our opinion, the stock is undervalued.

Merrill Lynch also recommends Holiday Inns as a "Buy" both in the intermediate term and in the long term. Although these recommendations may appear not to be consistent with those of Value Line, one must be careful in making such comparisons since different variables, horizon lengths, and other assumptions are involved. Nonetheless, this brief comparison does serve to emphasize the care that individuals must use in assessing potential investments using information from several sources.

Investment recommendations on individual securities also are made available as part of numerous investment advisory services. Few are as extensive (or as expensive) as Value Line, but their expense does not diminish their popularity. Financial newspapers and magazines are replete with advertisements of services that presumably will help the individual investor. A recent single issue of *Barron's* contained over seventy individual advertisements offering advice on mutual funds, commodities, special situations, and other "sure-success" opportunities. An individual who had answered all those advertisements would have spent over $300 just for the "introductory offers." The point of all this is that there are extensive investment recommendations available to investors. Both the price and quality of these recommendations vary considerably, and an individual interested in such information must select carefully.

SUMMARY

We have seen the range of information sources that are available to individual and institutional investors. We have traced through the steps of security analysis and illustrated where different types of information might be found at each step. We have compared the different sources along such dimensions as availability, cost, reliability, and usage. Above all, we have tried to stress the important point that there really is no shortage of information, albeit a shortage of "good" information may exist. Whereas some sources are strictly factual, there are other sources that include investment recommendations as well.

SUGGESTED READINGS FOR CHAPTER 19

J. B. Cohen, E. D. Zinbarg, and A. Zeikel. *Investment Analysis and Portfolio Management* (Homewood, Ill.: Richard D. Irwin, Inc., 1973), Chapter 3.

W. J. Eiteman, C. A. Dice, and D. K. Eiteman. *The Stock Market*. 4th ed. (New York: McGraw-Hill Book Company, Inc., 1966), Chapter 24.

J. C. Francis. *Investments: Analysis and Management* (New York: McGraw-Hill Book Company, Inc., 1972), Chapter 7.

K. V. Smith. "The Increasing Stream Hypothesis of Corporate Dividend Policy," *California Management Review*, Fall, 1971, pages 56–64.

C. N. Stabler. *How to Read the Financial News* (New York: Harper and Row, 1965).

D. E. Vaughn. *Survey of Investments* (New York: Holt, Rinehart and Winston, Inc., 1967), Chapter 11.

20

Investment timing

Managing an ongoing investment portfolio is difficult for many reasons. As seen in Chapter 19, one such reason is that many diverse, often contradictory, sources of investment information and advice are available to individual and institutional investors. We also have seen the complexity of activities such as security analysis, security valuation, and portfolio construction, which must be based on available information. And we have seen that important questions must be answered, such as *which* investment assets should be considered, *whether* to buy or sell, and *what* dollar amounts should be allocated to each investment. The purpose of this chapter is to discuss yet another critical question that complicates the investing process: namely, *when* to buy or sell investment assets. Although discussion of investment timing is appropriately included in this final part of the book devoted to implementing investment decisions, the central question of when to buy or sell permeates the entire process of investing.

NATURE OF TIMING

A popular investment maxim that would seem to constitute a ready answer to the problem of investment timing is to "buy low and sell high." While it is difficult to disagree generally with this maxim, it requires further study in order to be of practical help to investors. We must examine what is meant by low and by high, we must decide whether the maxim refers to assets, to portfolios, or to entire markets, and we must specify an allowable degree of precision in order to implement the maxim. Before pursuing answers to these and other related questions, however, we should review the nature of timing as it has been reflected throughout this book.

One dimension of investment timing concerns the different types of investment assets that were identified in Chapter 1. There is no particular difficulty in timing decisions to increase or decrease dollar investments in cash, except for possible loss in purchasing power over time. Other fixed-principal investments possess a definite value at a specified future date, and timing decisions are complicated when buying or selling occurs prior to that maturity. Problems of timing are more intense with respect to variable-principal securities that have no maturity and for which terminal value for an individual holder is thus not known with certainty. Timing decisions for certain nonsecurity investments are even more difficult because of fluctuating values, varying degrees of illiquidity, and lack of market and other varying kinds of information to evaluate those investments.

A second dimension of timing centers around the concept of investment value discussed in Chapter 4. The reader will recall that the market price of a particular asset fluctuates from day to day and week to week, but generally it is expected to trend toward investment value, which is defined as the present value of all future cash benefits accruing to that asset. This approach is often referred to as *fundamental analysis*. The question of proper timing for that asset, therefore, would seem to depend on two opinions: the degree to which investment value is expected to change as a result of either new information or revised expectations for the asset in question, and the rate at which market price is expected to converge toward investment value.

A third dimension of timing is inherent in the portfolio perspective strongly suggested in Chapter 3. In other words, as investors try to decide when to buy or sell investment assets, they should not do so strictly on the merits of individual assets, but rather on how those assets will interact in an entire portfolio. Unfortunately, the efficient portfolio model described and illustrated in Chapter 3 is a single-period model that does not reflect timing over an extended horizon.

Consideration of cash flow constitutes a fourth dimension of timing both for individual and institutional investors. For individuals, decisions to make changes in their overall portfolios of investable wealth may be based on needs and wants external to the portfolio itself—such as a larger apartment, a new automobile, a graduate education, or a vacation. Decisions by individuals may be based solely on the merits of assets in the portfolio or of assets to be added. A similar pattern of both internal or external factors also holds for institutional portfolios. Timing decisions for the portfolios of pension funds depend on inflows from employers and active employees and on forecasted outflows to retired employees. Total value of mutual fund portfolios increases with sale of new shares or decreases as existing shares are redeemed. And the timing of investment decisions by trust departments depends upon the cash flows unique to personal trust funds and estates.

Further dimensions of timing can be related to other attributes of investment assets. For example, brokerage firms often publish lists of suggested year-end tax switches, whereby investors presumably can take advantage of the fact that capital gains are taxed at a lower rate than dividend income. Existing stockholders of a particular company may be confronted with an immediate decision to increase their dollar holdings via a rights offering and thereby maintain their proportional ownership in the particular firm. Investors may be faced unexpectedly with a tender offer that if exercised gives them an immediate increase in their total wealth if their shares are sold. And, as we shall see in the next chapter, timing is an important aspect to consider in the evaluation of portfolio performance.

Also in connection with timing decisions, there are two specific terms that should be understood. *Portfolio turnover* for some portfolio over a given period is typically defined as the lesser of (*a*) assets sold or (*b*) assets purchased, divided by (*c*) the average market value of the portfolio during that period. In some instances, turnover acts as a constraint for decision-making; usually turnover simply results from the decisions that were made. The other term, which has a negative connotation, is churning. *Churning* usually is taken to mean revision of a portfolio for purposes other than maximizing the wealth of the portfolio owner. For example, brokers have sometimes been accused of churning certain accounts in order to generate larger brokerage fees.

A final dimension of timing from the viewpoint of an investor is that it is a relative concept. It does an individual no good to discover astutely an undervalued security and proceed to make an investment in that security if other investors do not eventually make the same discovery and take similar action. Optimal timing is somehow to lead the pack in spotting attractive buy situations and in identifying early sell situations. Although popular lore suggests that individuals generally tend to trail (rather than lead) insititutions in moving into and out of the market, recent evidence on the achieved performance of mutual funds and pension funds casts some measure of doubt on such a view.

All of this suggests that timing decisions are both important and complex for all types of investors. Subsequent sections of this chapter are devoted to particular aspects of timing as related to investment decision-making. We begin with broad aspects such as market forecasting and formula planning, move then to technical analysis and methods used to accumulate positions in particular assets, and finally to considerations of timing in selling investment assets.

MARKET FORECASTING

The popular maxim "buy low and sell high" applies not only to individual assets, but also to entire markets of assets. A key presumption in the latter case is that prices of all assets in a particular market tend to move together over time. While certainly this presumption is less than perfect, there is some empirical evidence that common stock prices, at least, tend to move together. In Chapter 8, for example, we saw that popular indices of stock activity (such as the Dow Jones Industrial Average, the Standard & Poor's Composite Index, and the New York Stock Exchange Index) move together rather closely. If there are somewhat definite trends to prices within a given market, such as the New York or American Stock Exchanges, then there would be justification for discussing market forecasting—either as a prelude to more detailed analyses of particular securities, or in trying to decide when to shift investable wealth among different types of assets such as stocks, bonds, and real estate. Also mentioned in Chapter 8 was the idea that attention to market conditions may be worthwhile if for no other reason than to avoid buying or selling securities at clearly inappropriate times.

Unfortunately, identification of major trends and changes in those trends in past years is far easier than to forecast future trends and changes. Figure 20–1 indicates three rising markets and two declining markets over the period 1962–1972 as used by *Forbes* in preparing its performance ratings for mutual funds.[1] Figure 20–1 also includes four rising and four declining markets over the shorter period 1968–1971 as used by Wiesenberger in calculating price volatilities for mutual funds. This comparison reveals that a classification of some past period into distinct markets depends on the span of intervals of time over which the various movements are measured. For example, mid-1971 was part of a declining market according to Wiesenberger, but it was in the middle of an extended rising market according to *Forbes*. One reason for this is the presence of different types of stock market trends such as long-term (or primary) trends, shorter-term (or cyclical) trends, and finally week-to-week and day-to-day fluctuations. The truth of the matter is that in mid-1971, there was considerable uncertainty as to what direction the overall market was likely to take in the immediate future. Admittedly, there are many points in time when this is the case. In other words, forecasting market directions and changes in direction is by no means an easy or straightforward task.

In Chapter 8, we discussed levels of the stock market as related to underlying economic factors such as dividend yields, price-earnings ratios, and book values. We also reviewed Barron's Confidence Index,

---

[1] The *Forbes* performance ratings were discussed in Chapter 15.

FIGURE 20–1
Rising and declining markets over recent decade

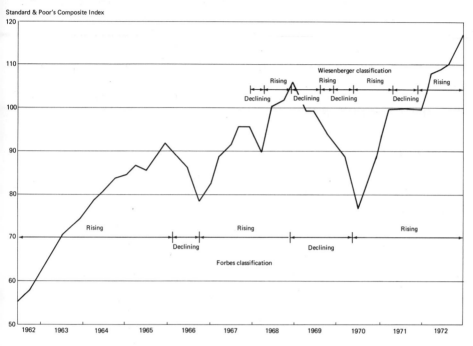

Standard & Poor's Composite Index

which relates bond yields to stock yields. Another approach to market forecasting is to use market averages directly. The *Dow Theory,* perhaps the best known of such direct approaches, utilizes the Dow Jones Industrial Average (30 stocks) and the Dow Jones Transportation Average (20 stocks) to identify major changes in market direction. One variation (of many) is that a rising (bull) market changes to a declining (bear) market when both the Industrial and Transportation Averages "break through" their respective low points in previous declining markets. Conversely, a declining market changes to a rising market when the two averages "break through" their respective high points of previous rising markets. The Dow concept in these aggregate market signals is that the stock averages must exhibit adequate momentum in order for one to confidently forecast rising or declining markets. Clearly, such signals are intended mainly for forecasts of primary market trends, rather than for secondary or shorter trends.

Market forecasting methods based on investor type and strategy type also exist. The *odd-lot theory* suggests that individual investors who buy and sell stocks mainly in odd lots are inherently unsophisticated in their analyses and are likely to make poor timing decisions and thereby lag the overall market, which is dominated by presumably more sophisticated institutional investors. High levels of odd-lot volume during a rising market thus signal the possible end of that market, while high odd-lot volume during a declining market may signal the resumption of a rising market. On the other hand, the *short-interest theory* contends that higher levels of short selling relative to average volume signal a future rising trend since short sales eventually must be covered. Conversely, lower levels of short selling relative to average volume constitute a bearish signal.

FORMULA PLANNING

If overall market trends can be forecasted with some degree of accuracy, then investors can presumably make profitable shifts between types of investment assets. A *formula plan* is nothing more than a predetermined decision guideline for taking advantage of forecasted major market shifts. The idea is to establish a plan that reduces the difficulty of forecasting as market uncertainty unfolds over time. Formula planning also is based on the dual premises that (1) variable-principal investments—notably common stock—offer greater returns during rising markets, while fixed-principal investments are preferable during declining markets, and (2) the stock market is likely to experience both rising and declining phases over time.

Formula plans exist in both fixed-ratio and variable-ratio versions. To illustrate, suppose that an investor decides to allocate his initial investable wealth of $10,000 between common stocks and savings during the next two years. Suppose further that the stock market, as measured by the Standard & Poor's Composite Index, is forecasted to range between a low of 70 and a high of 130 during the next two years. The market is at an initial level of 100.

In a *fixed-ratio plan,* the proportional allocations to common stock and savings are held fixed over time. That is, the investor's holdings are adjusted to the fixed proportions at each review point—which is quarterly in the illustration. The investor decides that 70% in stock and 30% in savings are suitable for his purposes. The initial commitment to stocks thus would be $7,000 with the remaining $3,000 placed in a savings account that pays 1.5% quarterly. At the end of each quarter, stocks would be bought or sold (with savings decreased or increased appropriately) so that the 70%–30% mix is re-established.

To illustrate appropriate adjustments according to the fixed-ratio formula plan, assume that the market declines during the first two quarters and then rises somewhat steadily during the next six quarters as shown in the following calculation. No transaction costs are assumed, and we ignore the effect of dividends from the stock portfolio. At the end of the first quarter, the overall market has dropped 10% to 90, the market value of the stock portfolio fell 7.1% to $6,500, and the savings account increased 1.5% to $3,045. The total wealth of $9,545 ($6,500 + $3,045) is then reallocated as follows: (70%) ($9,545) = $6,682 to stocks and (30%) ($9,545) = $2,863 to savings. This adjustment is accomplished by withdrawing $182 from savings and purchasing shares of common stock. The same type of adjustment is made at the end of each quarter. In three instances, stock is purchased, while in the other five instances, stock is sold.

Quarter	Standard & Poor's Index	Before adjustment			Appropriate adjustments	After adjustment		
		Market value	Savings account	Total wealth		Market value	Savings account	Total wealth
0	100	–	–	–	–	$7,000	$3,000	$10,000
1	90	$6,500	$3,045	$ 9,545	Buy $182 stock	6,682	2,863	9,545
2	85	6,100	2,906	9,006	Buy $204 stock	6,304	2,702	9,006
3	95	6,800	2,743	9,543	Sell $120 stock	6,680	2,863	9,543
4	110	8,000	2,906	10,906	Sell $366 stock	7,634	3,272	10,906
5	120	8,250	3,321	11,571	Sell $150 stock	8,100	3,471	11,571
6	120	7,850	3,523	11,373	Buy $111 stock	7,961	3,412	11,373
7	125	8,760	3,463	12,223	Sell $114 stock	8,656	3,577	12,223
8	140	9,960	3,631	13,591	Sell $446 stock	9,514	4,077	13,591

Total wealth value is $13,591 at the end of two years, thus representing a $3,591 increase over the initial wealth level. Had the investor simply held the initial mix of $7,000 stock and $3,000 savings unchanged for eight quarters, it would have grown to $10,165 stock and $3,379 savings, or a total wealth of $13,544. The formula plan thus added wealth of $47. If transaction costs had been included in the calculation, a buy-and-hold strategy would have done better than the fixed-ratio formula plan.

Several observations should be made of this illustration. First, the savings account always increases at the same 1.5% rate, while the common stock investment either increases or decreases. Moreover, the rate of appreciation (or depreciation) for a specific stock or portfolio is not necessarily the same as that of the market—as measured by any stock price index. Second, additional stock is bought when the market declines, but shares are sold as the market rises. Although this may appear contrary to common sense to some readers, we must remember the two premises, mentioned earlier, on which the formula adjustments are made over time. Third, it was possible to adjust the portfolio at the end of the eighth quarter, even though the stock market advanced beyond the 130 maximum level that had been forecasted for the two-year period. Finally, the illustration says nothing about which common stocks should be purchased. That is, formula planning is used in allocating wealth to investment categories rather than to particular securities.

In contrast, a *variable-ratio plan,* the proportional allocations are varied corresponding to different levels of the market. Suppose that the investor establishes the following target proportions corresponding to the 70–130 forecasted range of the market index.

Standard & Poor's Composite Index	Target Proportions Common Stock	Savings
70–79	85%	15%
80–89	80%	20%
90–99	75%	25%
100–109	70%	30%
110–119	65%	35%
120–130	60%	40%

The idea here, of course, is to vary the proportions to take better advantage of the unique characteristics of stock and savings as the market changes directions.

Continuing the illustration, the appropriate adjustments according to the variable-ratio formula plan can be calculated in a similar manner. Achieved quarterly returns for the common stock investments are exactly the same as before in order to provide a meaningful comparison of the two different formula plans.

Quarter	Standard & Poor's Index	Before adjustments Market value	Savings account	Total wealth	Appropriate adjustments	After adjustments Market value	Savings account	Total wealth
0	100	–	–	–	–	$7,000	$3,000	$10,000
1	90	$6,500	$3,045	$ 9,545	Buy $658 stock	7,158	2,387	9,545
2	85	6,534	2,423	8,958	Buy $632 stock	7,166	1,792	8,958
3	95	7,729	1,819	9,548	Sell $568 stock	7,161	2,387	9,548
4	110	8,576	2,423	10,999	Sell $1,427 stock	7,149	3,850	10,999
5	120	7,726	3,908	11,634	Sell $746 stock	6,980	4,654	11,634
6	120	6,764	4,724	11,488	Buy $129 stock	6,893	4,595	11,488
7	125	7,585	4,664	12,249	Sell $236 stock	7,349	4,900	12,249
8	140	8,456	4,973	13,429	?	?	?	?

Total market value for the variable-ratio formula plan is $13,429 at the end of two years, just slightly less than in the previous case of the fixed-ratio formula plan. Nevertheless, there are important differences in the two cases. The most obvious is that the variable-ratio plan leads to more extreme adjustment (and hence higher portfolio turnover) at the end of each quarter. As the market declines, greater dollar allocations are made to common stock; as the market rises, greater dollar allocations are made to savings. The idea again of this more extreme plan is based on a belief that the market experiences both rising and declining phases over time. The second difference is that the variable-ratio formula plan provides no guideline when the market index moves above 130. What are the target proportions when the market reaches 140, or perhaps 150 during the third year?

Although the rationale for formula planning is appealing intuitively, the apparent simplicity can certainly be misleading. Formula plans often are thought to be a means of avoiding emotional factors in the process of investing. Our illustration, it is hoped, points at certain fallacies of such arguments.

One variation is to base a variable-ratio plan on the long-run trend line fitted to historical data for the overall market. One might, for example, hold 70% stock and 30% savings when the market is within 10% of its historical trend line, shift to 80% stock and 20% savings when the market drops more than 10% below the trend line, and so forth. The major advantage of such a scheme is that the proportional mix is not distorted by the long-run growth of the economy, as the break-points are adjusted with the passage of time.

TECHNICAL ANALYSIS

As mentioned early in this chapter, a fundamental analysis of investment alternatives assumes that market prices fluctuate about investment value as they tend to converge toward that value. Opportunities for return depend jointly on the extent to which market prices deviate from investment values and on the rate of convergence of market prices toward investment values. Although buy and sell decisions presumably should be made when such return opportunities are attractive enough, there is no explicit treatment of timing in fundamental analysis.

An alternative approach is *technical analysis.* It can be defined as the art of studying the past market performance of stock prices and timing buy and sell decisions on the recognition of formations or patterns that occur. Technical analysis is based on the belief that market prices quickly reflect all available information, but that new information is not available to all investors simultaneously. "Insiders" and institutional investors would be expected to receive certain types of information before the same information would reach (or be recognized by) individual investors. Moreover, formations and patterns in stock prices would be expected as information eventually spreads to all investors. While the goal of fundamental analysis is to forecast correctly the future benefits associated with a given investment, the goal of technical analysis is to recognize formations and patterns that have a recurring historical significance. By accurately recognizing a particular formation or pattern, the technician (or chartist) can make and implement an appropriate

492

buy or sell decision. Two somewhat different methods of analyzing historical price trends, as used by technicians, will be explained and illustrated.

The most popular method is *bar charting*, which requires the price range and closing price of the stock for each interval over time. Bar charting also may include trading volume for each interval. While the interval may be a day, a week, a month, or even longer, most chartists prefer to use shorter intervals in order to spot emerging trends more quickly. The following price and volume data are for Extraordinary Electronics during a recent four-week period.

Date	High price	Low price	Closing price	Volume
February 5	$57\frac{1}{2}$	$54\frac{1}{8}$	$54\frac{3}{8}$	31,900
February 6	$58\frac{1}{4}$	$54\frac{1}{8}$	$57\frac{1}{4}$	45,300
February 7	$60\frac{5}{8}$	$57\frac{1}{2}$	$60\frac{5}{8}$	38,600
February 8	$63\frac{7}{8}$	$61\frac{1}{8}$	$63\frac{7}{8}$	79,600
February 9	64	$59\frac{5}{8}$	$59\frac{3}{4}$	49,100
February 12	59	$56\frac{1}{8}$	$57\frac{1}{4}$	49,200
February 13	60	$58\frac{1}{4}$	$59\frac{3}{8}$	38,600
February 14	$61\frac{3}{4}$	$58\frac{5}{8}$	$59\frac{7}{8}$	46,100
February 15	$63\frac{5}{8}$	$59\frac{1}{4}$	$63\frac{1}{4}$	62,500
February 16	65	$62\frac{5}{8}$	$63\frac{1}{2}$	71,900
February 19	$67\frac{1}{4}$	$64\frac{1}{2}$	$67\frac{1}{4}$	90,200
February 20	$67\frac{1}{2}$	$66\frac{3}{8}$	$66\frac{7}{8}$	84,800
February 21	$67\frac{1}{8}$	$65\frac{1}{2}$	$65\frac{7}{8}$	60,900
February 22	$67\frac{7}{8}$	64	$67\frac{7}{8}$	42,000
February 23	$71\frac{1}{2}$	$68\frac{1}{4}$	$71\frac{1}{2}$	87,400
February 26	$72\frac{3}{4}$	$69\frac{1}{4}$	$70\frac{3}{8}$	54,500
February 27	75	$69\frac{1}{2}$	$74\frac{7}{8}$	58,400
February 28	$75\frac{3}{8}$	$72\frac{1}{4}$	$72\frac{3}{8}$	48,600
March 1	$74\frac{5}{8}$	$72\frac{3}{8}$	74	36,900
March 2	75	$72\frac{1}{2}$	$72\frac{3}{4}$	25,800

Figure 20–2 is a weekly bar chart for Extraordinary Electronics, while Figure 20–3 is a daily bar chart for the same firm. Each bar in the chart is a vertical line extending from the low price to the high price for the given interval. The closing price is marked with a horizontal tick. Both bar charts reveal the general upward trend of market price during the four-week period, although the daily bar chart indicates the finer fluctuations that occurred.

One type of information that chartists attempt to glean from bar charts is support levels and resistance levels that occur as part of extended stock price trends. A *support level* is a barrier to subsequent price decline, while a *resistance level* is a barrier to subsequent price advance. The idea of a support level is that there is adequate demand for the stock at that price so that it is unlikely that the arrival of selling orders will push the price lower. Support levels might be identified

FIGURE 20–2
Weekly bar chart for Extraordinary Electronics

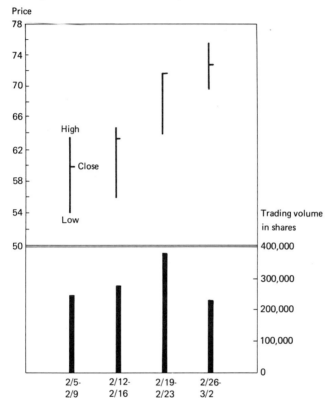

as shown in the upward trend at the left in Figure 20–4. The opposite argument is made for resistance levels as illustrated at the right of Figure 20–4.

A second type of information that technicians seek from their bar charts includes various signals of imminent price movements in a definite upward or downward direction. Familiar price patterns that reportedly provide such signals include those called head-and-shoulders, triangles, ascending bottoms, descending tops, wedges, flags, rectangles, pennants, sauce pans, bowls, and many others. Some of these patterns together with their forecasted price movements and timing decisions, are presented in Figure 20–5.

For each recognizable pattern, the chartist usually has a rationale of why that particular pattern provides the indicated signal. Consider the "triple top" in Figure 20–5. When prices rise to a point, decline, rise again to the same point, decline, and so forth, a multiple top is identified. Chartists usually contend that the more tops the formation

494

FIGURE 20–3
Daily bar chart for Extraordinary Electronics

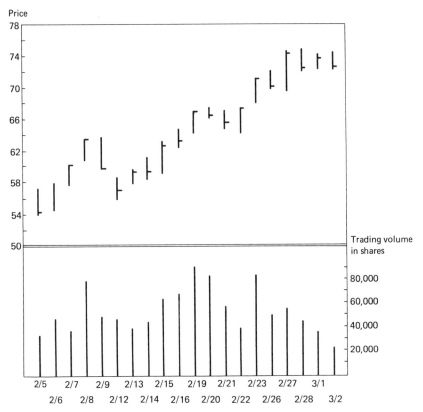

includes, the sharper will be the future decline. Conversely, double, triple, and multiple bottoms are inverse formations that presumably signal the beginning of a sizable uptrend in stock prices.

An alternative method of analyzing stock price trends is *point-and-figure charting*, which aggregates the time dimensions and focuses on significant upward and downward trends. Figure 20–6 is a point-and-figure chart for Extraordinary Electronics over the same four-week period. An "X" represents a price rise of $1, while a "O" represents a price decline of $1. A movement to the right in a new column indicates a change in price trend, and it is independent of the passage of time. Only rises and declines of $3 are indicated, in order to focus on important price movements. Until prices change by at least enough to continue a rising or declining trend, or to change a trend, no additions are made to the point-and-figure chart. So in contrast to bar charting, which records all price activity, point-and-figure charting records only significant

FIGURE 20–4
Illustration of support and resistance levels

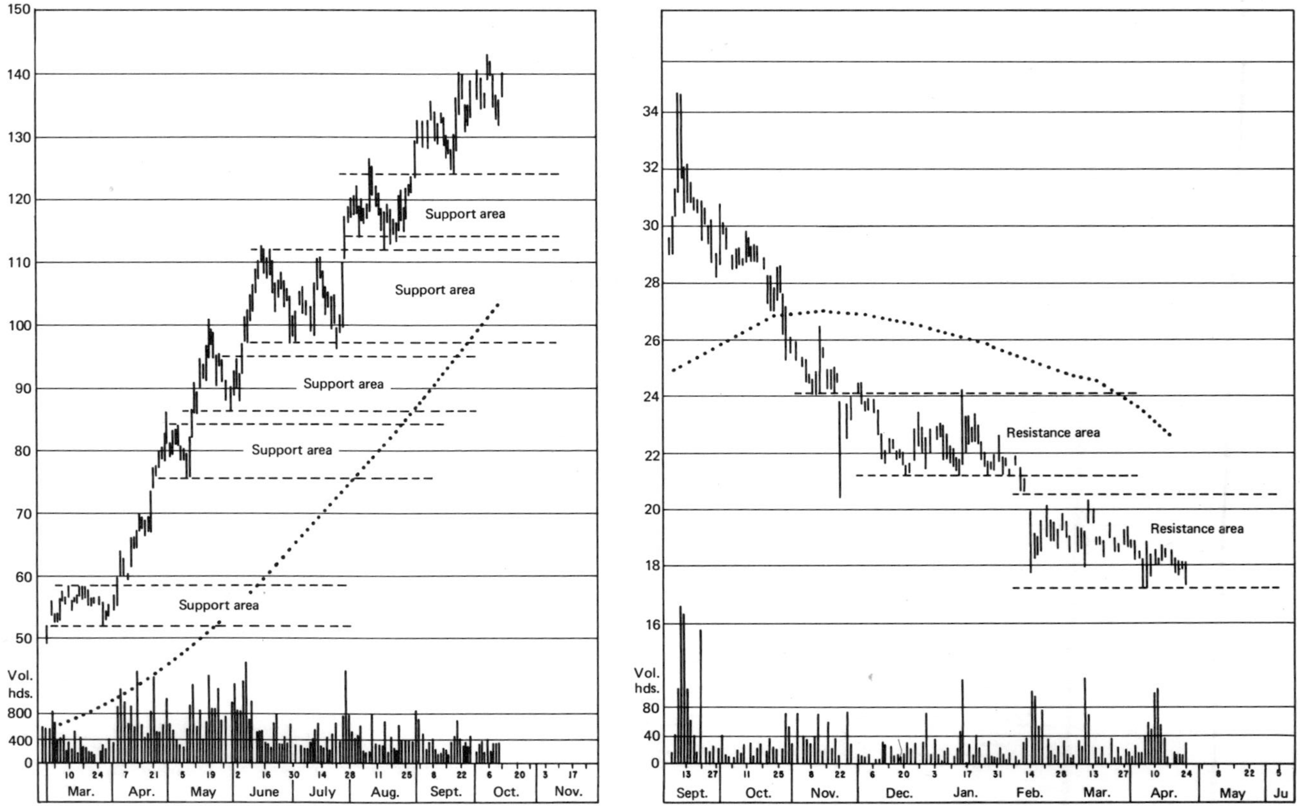

496

FIGURE 20–5
Selected buy and sell signals for bar charting

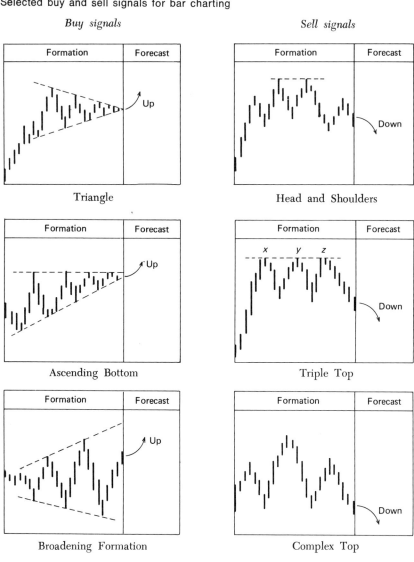

Buy signals

Triangle

Ascending Bottom

Broadening Formation

Sell signals

Head and Shoulders

Triple Top

Complex Top

price changes. Advocates of point-and-figure charting would argue that only important price information is reflected in their charts.

Beyond that basic distinction, technicians using point-and-figure charts essentially seek the same two types of information as do those using bar charts. That is, they attempt to identify levels of support and resistance and signals of imminent price movements in definite upward or downward directions. Many of the formations and patterns

FIGURE 20–6
Point-and-figure chart for Extraordinary Electronics

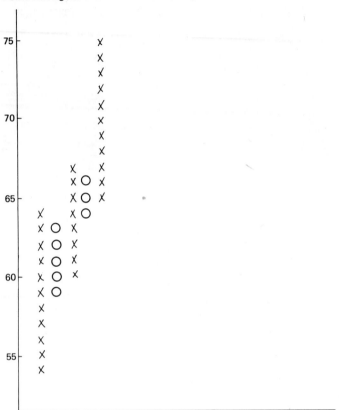

that were mentioned in connection with bar charting also appear in discussions of point-and-figure charting. Figure 20–7 illustrates the use of point-and-figure charts to identify buy or sell signals.

EFFICIENT MARKETS

Our cursory discussion and illustration of charting techniques—vis-à-vis the extended treatment of fundamental analysis in this book—reflects our feelings (and undoubtedly those of many academicians) on the relative importance of the two different approaches to security analysis. Before leaving the subject of technical analysis as one possible approach to investment timing decisions, we should review the findings of certain empirical studies that cast doubt on the validity of a technical approach. The contention of many economists and other academicians is that the

498

FIGURE 20–7
Buy and sell signals from point-and-figure charts

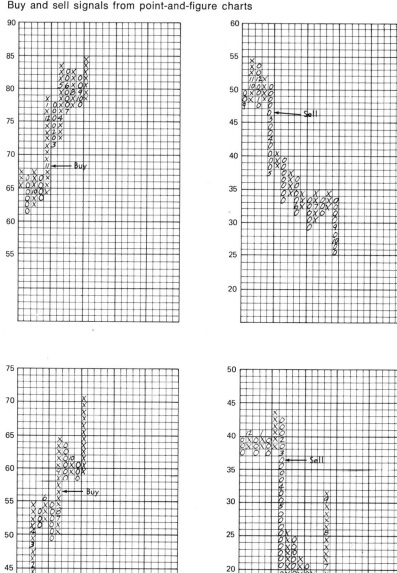

markets for common stocks and other securities are amazingly efficient in reflecting all available information about those securities. Brief mention of capital market theory was made in Chapter 4. The contention of this theory differs from that of technicians who believe that markets are indeed efficient, but that not all information is immediately available to all investors—and hence price trends will occur. The implication of the *efficient markets hypothesis* is that an examination of stock price formations and patterns is not likely to lead to achieved results that are consistently better than naive strategies of simply buying and holding portfolios of high-quality common stocks. In a word, the efficient market hypothesis, if true, invalidates a technical approach to security analysis and ensuing portfolio selection.

Empirical studies of the efficient market hypothesis have been classified according to the extent of formation reflected.[2] First, *weak-form* tests of the hypothesis center on changes in the stock prices and associated trading volumes of securities to see if there are trends or whether the changes appear to come from certain recognizable probability distributions. The weak form of the efficient market concept is more well known as the *random-walk hypothesis*, which has been widely debated by both academicians and practitioners. Second, the *semi-strong form* of the hypothesis contends that stock prices efficiently reflect all publicly available information. And third, the *strong form* of the hypothesis is that the market reflects all information, regardless of whether it is publicly available or not. Empirical studies to date present heavy support for the weak form of the efficient market hypothesis, but less for the stronger forms of the hypothesis.

It should also be noted that empirical evidence on market efficiency also casts doubts on the usefulness of fundamental analysis as well. It suggests that many individuals and institutions probably should not devote extensive resources in searching for undervalued or overvalued investment opportunities. Skillful analysts with quick access to information about the technology of a particular industry and unusual insight about the unique problems and management capabilities of particular companies may be able to spot profitable buy and sell situations on a somewhat consistent basis. But if the markets for securities are indeed efficient in reflecting available information, then resources of most investors would be better devoted to understanding the risk level of individual securities and portfolios of securities, and hence the returns that would be expected for those risk levels. The empirical evidence reviewed above also casts suspicion on portfolio management strategies that result in

---

[2] Origin of the classification scheme presented here, plus an excellent summary of the relevant literature, is found in E. F. Fama, "Efficient Capital Markets: A Review of Theory and Empirical Work," *Journal of Finance*, May, 1970, pages 383–417.

high degrees of portfolio turnover. It would seem that achieved returns from well diversified portfolios held unchanged over extended periods present rather formidable challenges for those investment strategies that result in high turnover and associated transaction costs.

On the other hand, some investors probably have done very well with their investments by using a technical approach. Whether these chartists can continue to generate above-average results without undertaking a high degree of risk would seem to be doubtful. But if enough investors engage in charting and particularly if they reach similar decisions, they are likely to have an impact on market prices. Moreover, many institutional investors engage the services of professional chartists to augment their fundamental analyses. It would appear that as a supplement to fundamental analysis, various methods of technical analysis may be useful in adding support to certain investment decisions and their timing. It would also appear that technical analysis applied to the entire securities markets occasionally may be useful as a supplement to detailed fundamental analysis of individual securities.

DOLLAR COST AVERAGING

Formula planning and technical analysis are methods wherein investors actively attack the question of investment timing in buying and selling securities by trying to forecast future directions of the entire market or of individual securities. In contrast, *dollar cost averaging* is a method whereby investors passively deal with timing as part of a continuing program of acquiring securities. It consists of buying a fixed amount of securities at regular intervals. By fixing the dollar commitment (it can be any amount) during each period, the investor effectively buys more shares at lower prices and fewer shares at higher prices, thus reducing his average cost per share over time.

To illustrate dollar cost averaging, assume that regular $600 purchases are made by an investor every three months of the common stock of Western Industries, which sells at $50 per share at the beginning of the year, drops in price to a low of $30, and then recovers to its original price by year-end. Purchases are summarized in the following schedule

Date	Amount invested	Price per share	Number of shares purchased	Total holdings	Total market value
January 1	$600	$50	12	12	$ 600
April 1	600	40	15	27	1,080
July 1.	600	30	20	47	1,410
October 1	600	40	15	62	2,480
December 31	—	50	—	62	3,100

Because total purchase cost was $2,400, the investor had experienced appreciation of $3,100 minus $2,400, or $700 by the end of the year, even though beginning and ending prices were identical. We also note that his average purchase cost was $2,400 divided by 62, or $38.71 per share, which is lower than the average price of Western Industries shares of $40 on the four purchase dates. This is a direct result of dollar cost averaging.

For the case of dollar cost averaging with steadily rising prices, the purchase schedule for Western Industries shares would be as follows

Date	Amount invested	Price per share	Number of shares purchased	Total holdings	Total market value
January 1	$600	$50	12	12	$ 600
April 1	600	60	10	22	1,320
July 1.	600	60	10	32	1,920
October 1	600	75	8	40	3,000
December 31	—	75	—	40	3,000

Again, the average purchase cost of $2,400 divided by 40, or $60 per share is less than the average price of Western Industries shares of $61.25 on the four purchase dates. For the case of increasing prices, the paper profit at year-end of $3,000 minus $2,400, or $600 is actually less than the previous case since fewer shares are purchased at higher prices.

And for the case of dollar cost averaging with steadily declining prices, the purchase schedule for Western Industries shares would be

Date	Amount invested	Price per share	Number of shares purchased	Total holdings	Total market value
January 1	$600	$50	12	12	$ 600
April 1	600	40	15	27	1,080
July 1.	600	30	20	47	1,410
October 1	600	20	30	77	1,540
December 31	—	30	—	77	2,310

Once again, dollar cost averaging causes the average purchase cost of $2,400 divided by 77, or $31.17 per share to be less than the average price of Western Industries shares of $35 on the four purchase dates. But here the investor has a paper loss of $2,400 minus $2,310, or $90 at the end of the year.

To summarize, dollar cost averaging always results in a lower average cost per share because the dollar commitment is constant at each point of puchase. The amount of capital gain or loss, however, depends on the overall change in price level for the particular security—and in particular on the market price at the end of the acquisition period as related to the lowest purchase price during the period. Dollar cost averaging can be applied to individual securities, to mutual funds and other investment assets, or to entire portfolios of investment assets. Ultimate success of an investment program is enhanced by dollar cost averaging but depends also on ability to select particular assets and on the overall price patterns that emerge for those selected assets.

TIMING AND SELLING

The process of investing involves both buying and selling decisions, but much of the literature of investments deals almost exclusively with buying. In concluding our discussion of investment timing in this chapter, it is imperative that we examine this asymmetric coverage of investment decision-making, consider possible reasons why selling is often given but scant attention, and identify some of the variables that should be included in selling decisions.

The fundamental approach to security and investment valuation as presented in Chapter 4 suggests that undervalued securities should be bought, while overvalued securities should be sold. Nevertheless, we would argue that much of the detailed discussion of financial statement analysis, accounting adjustments, and security valuation models that appear in textbooks, journals, and other publications—as well as in the content of investment courses—focuses on trying to find undervalued opportunities. Even comparisons of two or more investment assets on a relative basis often would seem to be biased toward "asset A is a more preferable *buy* than asset B" rather than toward "asset C is a more preferable *sell* than asset D." While technical analysis perhaps has been less negligent in this regard, there would still seem to be more discussion of how price formations and patterns can be used to signal buy decisions than to signal sell decisions. At a very practical level, many readers may have noticed that telephone calls from brokers are considerably less frequent during declining markets when sell decisions presumably should be made.

Why is this? First, a skeptic of this asymmetric viewpoint might argue that over the last four or five decades, there have been many more months of stock market advance than months of stock market decline, and hence buy decisions are more frequent than sell decisions. One might counter-argue that poor portfolio results are much more likely to be caused by incorrect sell decisions than by ill-advised buy decisions, and hence there is need for greater discussion of investment selling.

A second and probably more revealing reason for lack of attention to investment selling is that it usually connotes that previous buy decisions have proven unprofitable over time. Psychology is central to the process of investing, and hence human nature—being as it is—perhaps causes many investors to ignore those securities that do poorly in favor of those that do well. The investment stories and results swapped by friends at cocktail parties inevitably dwell on successes rather than failures. It may not be easy for a broker to call a customer and recommend selling an issue that he brought to the attention of the customer a few weeks or months earlier. In sum, the whole tone of selling decisions is negative and backward-viewing—rather than positive and forward-looking as in the case of buy decisions amid a major market advance.

A third reason for neglected treatment of investment selling is simply that it may be *more complex* than investment buying. An individual who has $2,000 cash to invest in a common stock will be right or wrong depending on the accuracy of his analysis and decision (or that of his recommending broker) and on how the future unfolds. If future prospects are equally likely, then chances of a successful buy decision are "50–50." But for an individual who owns a particular stock and contemplates selling it and then reinvesting the proceeds in another stock, the chances of a successful two-way decision—again in view of equally likely future prospects—are really "75–25" against the individual. In other words, he must be right both in selling and then subsequently in buying. Our rationale for connecting the sell and buy decisions in this fashion is simply that individuals tend to invest in this fashion. Recommended lists of year-end tax switches by brokerage firms are prepared in this spirit.

A fourth reason, also relating to the complexity of sell decisions, is based on the presence of transaction costs. Brokerage fees, as discussed in Chapter 18, are applicable both to the buying and selling of securities. But in selling a security that has been held for some time, the investor really should not neglect the "locked-in" pressure of capital-gains taxation. By postponing the sale of a stock whose price has advanced since its initial purchase, the investor continues to invest the total market value, rather than having it decreased by the amount of the capital gains tax that becomes payable for the tax year during which the stock is sold. The amount of the capital gains tax is in essence an interest-free loan from the government as long as the selling decision is postponed.

Suppose the individual's initial investment of $2,000 (100 shares at $20 per share) has grown to $5,000 during the past few years. The capital gain is $5,000 minus $2,000, or $3,000, and the capital gains tax in the event of a sale is ($3,000)(25%), or $750. Thus, the investor either continues to hold the $5,000 in the original 100 shares, or he has available $5,000 minus $750, or $4,250 for purchasing another security after the original shares are sold. If the investor believes those shares to be overvalued and that their price may fall in the near future, he may decide to sell the shares and protect his capital gain. But the longer the original shares are held, and assuming their price continues to increase, the larger is the amount of the effective free loan from the government. The investor continues to keep 75% of all further gains on this "loan" portion. If, on the other hand, an investor has a capital loss, then postponing the sell decision delays the added benefit of reducing taxable income on other capital gains when the capital loss is realized. Clearly sell decisions are complicated because of the tax situation involving those shares that may be sold.

SUMMARY

Investment timing is an important aspect of the process of investing. The nature of timing was carefully discussed and various approaches to timing decisions were described and illustrated. Included were market forecasting, formula planning, technical analysis, and dollar averaging. Recent evidence—on the efficiency of security markets in reflecting information—that casts doubt on the validity of technical analysis was reviewed. We also explored reasons why selling decisions have received less attention than buying decisions in the literature of investments.

SUGGESTED READINGS FOR CHAPTER 20

F. Amling. *Investments: An Introduction to Analysis and Management.* 2d ed. (Englewood Cliffs, N.J.: Prentice-Hall, Inc., 1970), Chapter 21.

J. B. Cohen, E. D. Zinbarg, and A. Zeikel. *Investment Analysis and Portfolio Management.* Rev. ed. (Homewood, Ill.: Richard D. Irwin, Inc., 1973), Chapter 13.

P. H. Cootner (ed.). *The Random Character of Stock Market Prices* (Cambridge, Mass.: M.I.T. Press, 1964).

R. D. Edwards and J. Magee. *Technical Analysis of Stock Trends.* 5th ed. (Springfield, Mass.: John Magee, Inc., 1966).

W. J. Eiteman, C. A. Dice, and D. K. Eiteman. *The Stock Market.* 4th ed. (New York: McGraw-Hill Book Company, Inc., 1966), Chapters 22–23.

E. S. Emory. *When to Sell Stocks* (Homewood, Ill.: Dow Jones-Irwin, Inc., 1973).

E. F. Fama. "Efficient Capital Markets: A Review Of Theory and Empirical Work," *Journal of Finance,* May, 1970, pages 383–417.

J. C. Francis. *Investments: Analysis and Management* (New York: McGraw-Hill Book Company, 1972), Chapters 18–19.

C. Holt and J. P. Shelton. "The Financial Implications of the Capital Gains Tax for Investment Decisions," *Journal of Finance,* December, 1961, pages 559–80.

H. A. Latane and D. L. Tuttle. *Security Analysis and Portfolio Management* (New York: Ronald Press Company, 1970), Chapter 14.

A. J. Lerro and C. B. Swayne, Jr. *Selection of Securities: Technical Analysis of Stock Market Prices* (Morristown, N.J.: D. H. Mark Publications, General Learning Corp., 1970).

B. G. Malkiel. *A Random Walk down Wall Street* (New York: W. W. Norton & Company, 1973).

21

Performance evaluation

OUR BOOK ENDS with a chapter on performance evaluation, even though that topic should not be construed as the final step in the process of investing. Rather, evaluation of a group of investment assets held in a portfolio should be viewed as a regenerating activity from which many of the steps discussed in this book are repeated once again. As pointed out in Chapter 2, investing is a continuing process over time whether it is done by individuals or institutions. Whereas the evaluation of portfolio performance may seem straightforward at first glance, it turns out that there are certain problems in measurement and comparison that must be handled carefully in order to reach proper conclusions about the status and progress of a portfolio, and thereby form a basis for subsequent investment decisions. The purpose of this chapter is to place performance evaluation in proper perspective and to compare alternative methods for measuring the return and risk of a portfolio.

RATIONALE FOR EVALUATION

In Chapter 3, we used the illustration of a portfolio of investment assets held by a university professor and his wife. Each of the four asset types—savings, mutual fund, trust fund, and variable annuity—was itself noted to be a portfolio of investment assets under professional management. Market value of their total portfolio was $14,800. Let us suppose that one year later, the total market value of their portfolio was $15,400, and that market value grew to $19,250 at the end of two years. Why would we (or they, for that matter) be interested in such a result?

First, the professor and his wife are anxious to know the status of their investable wealth since it represents the potential for a higher standard of living in the community, college education for their children, and an eventual European vacation for them. If their wealth level grows sufficiently, they will be able to do many things that they have planned and worked for during the past years. If not, they will have to alter their timetable, or somehow provide for additional sources of wealth.

Second, by being aware of how their portfolio of investments has fared during the past year, the professor and his wife will be able to appraise the management of each segment of the total. While the savings account earns at a prescribed rate, returns to the mutual fund, the trust fund, and the variable annuity are dependent upon the abilities of professional management. The value of the latter three is subject to changing conditions in the security markets and each is likely to experience a performance different from that of the savings account. In addition, each segment presumably is subject to a change in management if that performance is not acceptable.

Third, the professor and his wife hope to add to their portfolio from time to time. Evaluation of performance will constitute, therefore, a major factor in subsequent decisions as to the amount and disposition of any additional capital.

NATURE OF EVALUATION

Just how well then have the professor and his wife done? Total portfolio value rose $600 during the first year (from $14,800 to $15,400) and $3,850 during the second year (from $15,400 to $19,250). Whereas a dollar increase of $600 during the first year may or may not seem reasonable to the professor and his wife, a dollar measure of performance is inadequate for several reasons. For example, a change in portfolio value from $80,000 to $80,600 also would give a dollar increase of $600. Yet it is clear that that result would not be considered as good as that for the family because over five times as much capital was employed in order to generate that dollar increase. This suggests that performance measurement should somehow reflect the amount that is invested over time. A common practice is to calculate the percentage return on a portfolio that is achieved over some period.

Alternatively, suppose that portfolio value rose from $14,800 to $25,100 in the first year, but then it dropped to $19,250 during the second year. Although the end result ($19,250) is the same, it seems unlikely that the university professor and his wife would feel the same about those two patterns of performance. They would have yet another feeling if they had been able to withdraw $3,000 at the end of the first year and still end up with a market value of $19,250 at the end of the second year. In other words, intermittent cash flows into or out of the portfolio cannot be ignored in evaluating performance. The possibility of different performance patterns over time suggests that performance measurement should somehow reflect the variability of achieved returns over time.

The careful reader will begin to see certain parallels between evaluation (*ex post* or after the fact) of portfolio performance, as we have begun to describe here, and the expectations (*ex ante* or before the fact) for return that were at the heart of portfolio choice as discussed in Chapter 3. One important difference is that expected return, either for an investment asset or for a portfolio of assets, reflects an entire probability distribution of possible return outcomes, while realized or achieved return is a single observation. And while variance or standard deviation of possible returns was suggested as one measure of risk encountered by an investor, the variability of achieved returns is really a quite different concept. If variability of returns is stable over time, as has been suggested in some academic studies, then ex post variability may be a reasonable estimate of ex ante risk faced by an investor. Conversely, many investors may feel that there is no such thing as ex post risk, and that only achieved return is important. Subsequent sections of this chapter will deal with measures of return and of risk-adjusted return for a portfolio.

It is not enough just to evaluate the achieved return, and possibly the ex post risk, of the entire portfolio. For in order to serve as a basis for changing portfolio objectives, portfolio holdings, or even portfolio managers, it is necessary to have a measure of performance for each segment of the portfolio. The university professor and his wife should want to know how the aggregate growth in market value to $19,250 at the end of two years is attributable to each of their four investment assets: savings account, trust fund, mutual fund, and variable annuity. The return on the savings account is predictable, while that of the other three segments is not. If the trust fund and variable annuity accounted for the majority of the dollar increase in the portfolio, while the mutual fund remained at about the same net asset value, then the professor and his wife might decide to make a change to another mutual fund or perhaps even some other investment asset. And although the trust fund, the mutual fund, and the variable annuity each is a portfolio itself, different evaluation methods may be necessary depending on the cash flow for each, and also the nature of the contractual arrangement with the professional management in each instance.

It also is not enough to evaluate the realized performance of each portfolio segment. For in order to make judgments about the performance of each segment, it is necessary to have benchmarks for comparisons. We are told that the small portfolio of John and Alice Jones "outperformed" the Dow Jones Industrial Average. We read about a famous senator throwing darts at a *Wall Street Journal* and using the resulting portfolio as a comparison standard. Or we learn that Better Mutual

Fund did worse than several other funds in its category. In evaluating the performance of an individual or institutional portfolio, it is important that an appropriate benchmark be chosen. It is also important that each comparison be made with due regard for such transaction costs as brokerage commissions, taxes, and loading charges.

BANK ADMINISTRATION INSTITUTE RECOMMENDATIONS

We have touched on certain aspects of performance evaluation. Before proceeding to a more-detailed examination of performance measurement and comparison, let us review the recommendations of a well-known report that was concerned with the performance evaluation of pension funds, the fastest-growing segment of the money management industry.

The Bank Administration Institute (BAI) was organized in 1924 as a nonprofit corporation to provide assistance to banks through programs of education and research and development. A major interest of the research division of BAI in recent years has been investment performance. In 1966, a distinguished Advisory Committee of academicians, under the chairmanship of Professor James H. Lorie of the University of Chicago, was commissioned to study various methods for evaluating pension fund performance and to make recommendations as to preferred methods. Working in conjunction with a Steering Committee, which represented the banking community, the Advisory Committee published its findings and recommendations in 1968.[1] This pioneering effort has had a pronounced impact on the investment community in standardizing the methods of performance measurement and comparison, as well as increasing the sophistication of evaluation methods currently being used. Though the report was written for pension funds, its findings are applicable to evaluation of all types of portfolios. Accordingly, it is appropriate to summarize the major recommendations of the BAI study.

1. Measurement of performance should be in two dimensions: rate of return and risk.
2. Rates of return should be based on income and on changes in the market value of assets held. For measuring the success of the portfolio manager in making investment decisions, a time-weighted rate of return should be used. For measuring the overall performance of the portfolio, a dollar-weighted rate of return should be used.[2]

---

[1] James H. Lorie, et al., *Measuring the Investment Performance of Pension Funds* (Park Ridge, Illinois: Bank Administration Institute, 1968). The BAI recommendations are not inconsistent with an earlier study, Peter O. Dietz, *Pension Funds: Measuring Investment Performance* (New York: The Free Press, 1966), and, in fact, elaborate on several issues of performance measurement introduced in that study.

[2] Time-weighted and dollar-weighted returns, as well as measures of risk, will be discussed in subsequent sections of this chapter.

3. Measurement of rates of return and of risk should be based on calculations for calendar quarters in order to facilitate interfund comparisons.
4. Although it is not clear what is the best method of measuring risk, variability of the time-weighted quarterly rate of return in general, and the mean-absolute-deviation in particular, are recommended until better methods are developed.
5. For diagnostic purposes, the investment assets of portfolios should be classified as follows: common stocks and warrants, convertible securities, cash and short-term fixed-income securities, long-term fixed-income securities, assets directed by the trustor, and other assets such as real estate and commodities.
6. The group of portfolios used as a basis for comparisons should be as large as possible.
7. Further research should be conducted, particularly in the concept and measurement of risk.

The reader will note that certain aspects of performance evaluation discussed so far in this chapter follow somewhat the BAI recommendations. This is not surprising because of the importance of the BAI report. The reader also will note that the BAI recommendations are stronger for the return attribute than for the risk attribute. The final BAI recommendation, in fact, identifies the need for further research on risk.

EVALUATION OF RETURN

We have already noted that an evaluation of the total portfolio of the university professor and his wife should focus on its four segments. Nevertheless for purposes of discussing the measurement of portfolio return, we shall assume here that their portfolio consists of only a single segment—say an investment account managed by the trust department of the local bank. How did they fare then, if total market value of their investment account grew from $14,800 to $15,400 after one year and then to $19,250 at the end of the second year? Since only the three annual market values are given, we must limit our evaluation to an annual basis. While semiannual or quarterly intervals would form the bases for more accurate measurements of performance, annual data is the only possibility in many instances including the present illustration.

The return achieved during any given year t is defined as the ratio of ending market value M_t to beginning market value M_{t-1}, where ending market value includes dividends, interest, or other cash flows, as well as appreciation of principal. In evaluating mutual fund performance, for example, annual return to each share would reflect dividend and capital-gain distributions plus growth in net asset value. Specifically, annual return may be written as the *wealth relative*,

$$Y_t = \frac{M_t}{M_{t-1}} = \frac{M_{t-1} + (M_t - M_{t-1})}{M_{t-1}} = 1 + \frac{M_t - M_{t-1}}{M_{t-1}}.$$

From this, we see that annual return is the ratio of successive market values, but that it also is equivalent to *one* plus the percentage increase in market value. For the two years of our example, achieved returns were

$$Y_1 = \$15,400/\$14,800 = 1.04 \text{ and } Y_2 = \$19,250/\$15,400 = 1.25,$$

or increases of 4% the first year and 25% the second year.

Expression (21–1) can be evaluated before or after the transaction costs associated with the given portfolio. The effective loading charge would reduce the first year return from an investment in mutual fund shares, while brokerage fees would reduce the return from security investments for any period in which stocks or bonds were bought or sold. Taxes also have an impact on the periodic cash flows to the investor, and on the terminal cash flow when the portfolio is liquidated. We shall ignore transaction costs in the present discussion, but consider them again later in the chapter.

The key step in evaluating return is properly combining annual (or periodic) returns into a single aggregate measure of return for the entire horizon. In our example, we must combine the 4% and 25% into a measure of annual return achieved over the two-year horizon. Computationally, it is convenient to work with the wealth relative (Y_t), rather than the equivalent percentage returns $(Y_t - 1)$.

Two possibilities for an aggregate measure are the arithmetic average and the geometric average of annual returns. Both of these measures were identified and illustrated in Chapter 11. Arithmetic mean return over an horizon of T years would be given by

$$Y_{ave} = \frac{1}{T}\left(\sum_{t=1}^{T} Y_t\right), \tag{21-2}$$

while geometric mean return would be given by

$$Y_{geo} = \sqrt[T]{\prod_{t=1}^{T} Y_t}. \tag{21-3}$$

For our example, we would calculate the arithmetic mean return to be

$$Y_{ave} = \frac{1.04 + 1.25}{2} = 1.145,$$

which is equivalent to 14.5% per year. The geometric mean return for the same performance would be

$$Y_{geo} = \sqrt{(1.04)(1.25)} = 1.140,$$

or 14.0% per year. The arithmetic mean for any set of positive wealth ratios is always greater than the geometric mean of the same set because equal weight is given to the earlier periods when the investment base is smaller.

Another example can be used to show that the geometric mean return is a more accurate measure of performance than the arithmetic mean return. Suppose $Y_1 = 2.00$ and $Y_2 = 0.50$, which means that wealth doubles the first year and then falls 50% in the second year. The arithmetic mean return is

$$Y_{ave} = (2.00 + 0.50)/2 = 1.25,$$

which is equivalent to a 25% annual increase over two years. Intuition suggests that this is a nonsensical answer since the investor who starts with $M_0 = \$10,000$ ends up with $M_2 = \$10,000$, even though in the interim $M_1 = \$20,000$. The geometric mean return, however, would be

$$Y_{geo} = \sqrt{(2.00)(0.50)} = 1.00,$$

or a zero annual return, which is the correct answer. Henceforth, we shall *not* use the arithmetic mean return because it is inferior to the geometric mean as a measure of performance.

Performance evaluation is further complicated if there are cash flows into or out of the portfolio during the investment horizon. Suppose that at the end of the first year, the professor and his wife decide to spend a portion of their investable wealth and take an extended vacation in Europe. They withdraw $4,000 of the $15,400 from their investment account, and the remaining $11,400 continues under management by the trust department. At the end of the second year, this investment grows to $14,250. The annual returns for this case are

$$Y_1 = \$15,400/\$14,800 = 1.04 \text{ and } Y_2 = \$14,250/\$11,400 = 1.25.$$

These annual returns are deliberately identical to the previous case when there was no withdrawal.

The geometric mean return is found to be

$$Y_{geo} = \sqrt{(1.04)(1.25)} = 1.140$$

or, as before, 14% per year. Since this measure is independent of the $4,000 withdrawal which was made, it indicates how well the trust department accomplished their fiduciary responsibility on behalf of the professor and his wife. It is a *time-weighted* measure of performance, and in accord with the recommendations of the Bank Administration Institute should be used in evaluating the managerial ability of the trust department.

It is not really a good measure of how well the university professor and his wife fared, however, because the $4,000 withdrawal is not reflected. We need yet another measure to do that. The proper choice is the internal-rate-of-return, Y_{int}, which was defined in Chapters 4–6 as that discount rate that makes the present value of all future cash benefits just equal to the cost of the investment. In our two-year example, the cash benefits were the $4,000 cash withdrawal at the end of the first year and the $14,250 market value at the end of the second. The cost of the investment was just the original market value of $14,800.

Remembering that the internal-rate-of-return can be obtained in an iterative fashion, we first try 14% as follows:

Benefit	Weight (14%)	Weighted benefit
$ 4,000	0.877	$ 3,508
14,250	0.769	10,958
Total		$14,466

The present value of $14,466 using 14% is less than the $14,800 cost, and hence a 14% rate is too high. Additional iterations yield

Discount rate	Discounted present value	Comment
14%	$14,466	Rate too high
10%	15,407	Rate too low
12%	14,909	Rate too low
13%	14,698	Rate too high
12.5%	14,813	Approximate solution

and we see that $Y_{int} = 12.5\%$, which is less than $Y_{geo} = 14\%$. The internal rate of return is less than the geometric mean return because there was less capital invested during the second year, when the portfolio manager achieved an annual return of 25%. Because it reflects the exact benefits and timing to the investor, the internal-rate-of-return is a *dollar-weighted* measure, and in accord with the recommendations of the Bank Administration Institute should be used to measure the performance achieved by the portfolio of the professor and his wife.

In summary then, the internal-rate-of-return of 12.5% indicates how well the university professor and his wife did over the two-year period, while the geometric mean return of 14% reflects the management results of the trust department over the same horizon. If there are no cash flows to or from the portfolio, then the dollar-weighted and time-weighted returns are identical. But if interest or dividends are paid to investors, or if there are cash additions or withdrawals, then dollar-weighted return is different from time-weighted return.

The calculation of dollar-weighted return over a horizon of two or more periods requires only beginning and ending market values for the entire horizon, plus all intermediate cash flows. Calculation of time-weighted return for the same horizon, however, requires a market value for the portfolio at the time of each cash flow into or out of the portfolio. This information was available in our simple illustration, and both dollar-weighted and time-weighted returns were easily calculated. For certain large institutional portfolios, such as trust funds and pension funds, total market value typically is not determined at the time of each cash flow. This means that time-weighted returns can only be approximated for those portfolios. This problem does not exist for mutual funds, because their per-share determination necessitates a market valuation whenever shares are sold or redeemed. In other words, the per-share values for mutual funds lead directly to time-weighted returns.

EVALUATION OF RISK-ADJUSTED RETURN

Suppose, quite unrealistically, that the professor and his wife, after the fact, have their choice of four possible patterns of performance over the two-year horizon. Each of the four possibilities is described by three wealth levels M_0, M_1, and M_2

Pattern	Initial wealth, M_0	First year, M_1	Second year, M_2
1.......	$14,800	$15,400	$19,520
2.......	14,800	12,700	19,520
3.......	14,800	25,100	19,520
4.......	14,800	16,870	19,520

All four patterns begin and end the same. The first pattern has already been evaluated. The second pattern includes a decrease followed by a sharp increase, while the third pattern is just the opposite. The fourth pattern has a somewhat higher level of wealth after the first year as compared with the first pattern.

Each of the four patterns also can be described by the two annual wealth relatives $Y_1 = M_1/M_0$ and $Y_2 = M_2/M_1$

Pattern	First year return, Y_1	Second year return, Y_2
1..........	1.040	1.250
2..........	0.858	1.538
3..........	1.700	0.765
4..........	1.140	1.140

We note that $Y_1 = Y_2 = 1.14$ (or 14%) for the fourth performance pattern. The two annual returns are quite different ·for the other three patterns. The immediate question is whether the professor and his wife are indifferent to varying annual returns, when the end result is the same. Admittedly, no one can predict how the professor and his wife really feel toward any investment. And while many readers may feel that interim results are not important—and that only the final result should be considered—many other readers may prefer a more stable pattern of annual returns over time. Moreover, a more stable pattern of achieved returns may be construed as an ex post (after the fact) realization of the ex ante (before the fact) risk that was faced by the investor at the time when investment decisions were made and the performance pattern began. If this is the case, then it becomes desirable to consider somehow the variability of achieved returns over the investment horizon as one component of performance evaluation. The measures of risk discussed in Chapter 3 are logical choices in doing this. We shall, in fact, consider two different measures of *risk-adjusted rate of return* that reflect the variability of return as well as an aggregate measure of portfolio return.

To illustrate the two measures of risk-adjusted return, it is convenient to compare the performance patterns of two portfolios over time. Because more data are available for mutual funds than for other professionally managed portfolios, we shall compare the performance of two mutual funds over a ten-year period. One of the two is Better Mutual Fund, which has previously been mentioned, while the other is Giant Growth Fund. Their annual percentage rates of returns—based on dividend distributions, capital-gains distributions, and changes in net asset values—over the last ten years are as follows:

	Annual rate of return		
Year	Better Mutual Fund	Giant Growth Fund	Market Return Index
1	6%	3%	4%
2	8	11	8
3	-4	-3	-4
4	15	13	14
5	1	-6	-1
6	1	6	1
7	15	21	16
8	20	22	20
9	11	15	11
10	9	8	10

Also included is the corresponding rate of return for the stock market as a whole for each year. The characteristic lines for these two mutual funds, based on plotting fund rates of return against market rate of return, are shown in Figure 21–1. (Characteristic lines were explained

FIGURE 21–1
Characteristic lines for two mutual funds

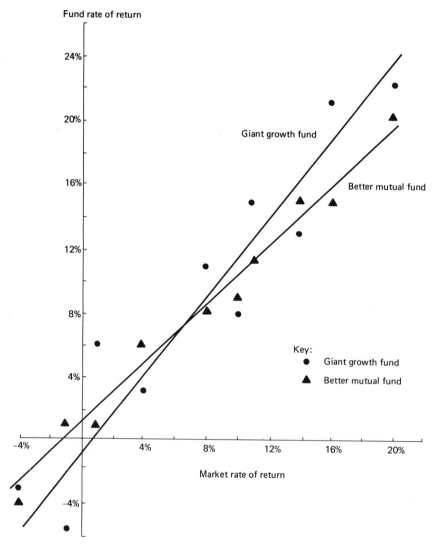

in Chapter 3.) Other relevant parameters are included in the following summary.

Parameter	Better Mutual Fund	Giant Growth Fund
Geometric mean return, Y_{geo}	8.0%	8.6%
Standard deviation, S.	7.2%	9.2%
Volatility, β	0.92	1.22

We see immediately that Giant Growth Fund would be ranked higher than Better Mutual Fund on the basis of geometric mean return.

Two possible measures of risk-adjusted rate of return are based on excess annual return $(Y_{geo} - i)$, where i is the return on a risk-free investment such as a savings account and Y_{geo} is the geometric mean of annual returns. One possibility is a return-variability measure

$$\theta_{var} = (Y_{geo} - i)/S \qquad (25\text{--}4)$$

where S is the standard deviation of annual returns. A second possibility is a return-volatility measure

$$\theta_{vol} = (Y_{geo} - i)/\beta \qquad (25\text{--}5)$$

where β is the volatility of annual return as related to market return. The reader will recall from Chapter 3 that variability S reflects total variation, while volatility β reflects only the systematic (or nondiversifiable) component of variation. Both measures θ_{var} and θ_{vol} are risk-adjusted measures of return, and both can be used to rank the performance of two or more portfolios. For both, the higher the measure, the better the achieved performance of the portfolio in question.

Letting $i = 5\%$ be the risk-free rate, we can calculate θ_{var} and θ_{vol} for the two mutual funds of our illustration. We obtain

Performance measure	Better Mutual Fund	Giant Growth Fund
Return-variability, θ_{var}	0.417	0.391
Return-volatility, θ_{vol}	3.26	2.95

and for both risk-adjusted measures, the performance of Better Mutual Fund would be ranked higher than the performance of Giant Growth Fund. In other words, performance rankings of the two funds reverse when evaluation incorporates risk.

During the decade of the sixties, the performance of mutual funds and pension funds received increasing attention both by academicians and investors. Recognition of the need to consider risk as well as return in the evaluation of portfolio performance was an important development during that decade. It enabled investors to understand better why superior performance was achieved by some portfolio managers but not by others. We turn now to a closer look at portfolio performance achieved by mutual funds during the past decade.

PERFORMANCE AND VOLATILITY

In Chapter 15, the ratings of mutual fund performance by *Forbes* were explained and illustrated. We observed briefly that very few funds have been able to perform well in both rising and declining markets. Based on the discussion of performance evaluation in this chapter, it is now possible to understand the apparent inconsistency in performance over time. Toward that end, it is convenient to examine carefully the performance of a sample of fifteen mutual funds. Because *Forbes* uses only a small number of fund categories, a sample of funds was selected using categories employed by Wiesenberger, another important source of mutual fund data. The sample funds are identified in Figure 21–2.

FIGURE 21–2
Identification of mutual fund sample

Funds	Assets*	Wiesenberger category	Number of funds in category
1. Delaware Fund	$ 530	Large growth funds.	24
2. Putnam Investors Fund	527		
3. Fairfield Fund	49	Smaller growth funds; maximum capital gains; volatility generally high.	146
4. Ivy Fund (no-load)	63		
5. Knickerbocker Growth Fund	11		
6. Pioneer Enterprise Fund	7		
7. Value Line Special Situations	137		
8. American Growth Fund	17	Smaller growth funds; long-term growth of capital and income; volatility moderately above average.	69
9. Keystone S-3	198		
10. Stein Roe & Farnham Stock Fund (no-load)	202		
11. Channing Common Stock Fund	30	Other diversified common stock funds; growth and current income; volatility average.	42
12. Investors Stock Fund	2,806		
13. Windsor Fund	554		
14. Guardian Mutual Fund (no-load)	63	Other diversified common stock funds; growth and current income, with relative stability; volatility below average.	20
15. Pine Street Fund (no-load)	58		

* Asset size of each fund in millions is shown at end of 1972.
Source: Investment Companies (Wiesenberger Service, Inc., 1973).

Note that the categories defined by Wiesenberger reflect fund size, fund objectives, and fund volatility. Balanced funds, income funds, specialized funds, and tax-free exchange funds were not represented in our sample because their objectives are considerably different and specialized.

Size of each fund, as measured by millions of dollars of net assets managed at the end of 1972, is also indicated. For the sample, size ranged from $7 million for Pioneer Enterprise Fund to $2,806 million for Investors Stock Fund, which was then the second largest mutual fund in existence. Average size for the sample was $350 million. Excluding Investors Stock Fund, the average size of the sample was $175 million, which was approximately the average size of all mutual funds at that time. Finally, four of the mutual funds in the sample were no-load funds, while eleven funds charged a sales loading charge at the time of purchase. All in all, the sample of fifteen funds seemed to be representative of the total universe of mutual funds.

Figure 21–3 includes *Forbes* ratings for the sample of mutual funds over the past five years. These ratings were examined both for consistency over time and for differences between performance in rising and declining markets. First, the ratings for each fund were quite consistent over the five years, during both rising and declining markets. This is not surprising since the ratings in any year covered about ten prior years, and performance in the current year was added to that of the previous nine years reflected in earlier ratings. The only change in rating of more than a single level occurred for Windsor Fund in 1971 when a C rating followed an A rating in 1969 and 1970. For several of the funds, ratings were similar in all four years.

Second, the ratings for most funds were markedly different in rising markets than in declining markets. Several funds such as Knickerbocker Growth and Value Line Special Situations consistently were rated A+ or A in rising markets but D or F in declining markets. For other funds, notably Guardian Mutual and Pine Street, higher ratings consistently were recorded for declining markets than for rising markets. One concludes from observing Figure 21–3 (or by examining all the *Forbes* ratings) that virtually no fund consistently performed well over the five-year period relative to all other funds, in both rising and declining markets. The closest exception to this was Putnam Investors Fund as seen in its 1973 ratings. In those few instances where a fund received an A or B for both types of markets, that fund was typically a new or small fund. Again, Putnam Investors Fund was a notable exception. Furthermore, high ratings in both types of markets usually did not continue over time.

In other words, fund performance was consistent, but only in distinct types of markets. If an investor mainly sought diversification and was content with average performance over all types of markets, then any one of many large, established funds would have proved sufficient. But the investor was faced with something of a dilemma if he desired above-average performance. Even if there was evidence suggesting that one should not have expected above-average performance, it is likely that many investors would nevertheless have tried to do so.

The performance phenomenon in Figure 21–3 can be explained in part by examining the respective volatilities of the fifteen mutual funds. As previously mentioned, the concept of volatility has received consider-

FIGURE 21-3
Selected *Forbes* ratings, 1969–1973

Mutual fund	Rising markets					Declining markets				
	1973	1972	1971	1970	1969	1973	1972	1971	1970	1969*
1. Delaware Fund	B	B	B	A	A	D	D	D	D	D
2. Putnam Investors Fund	B	B	C	D	D	A	B	B	B	B
3. Fairfield Fund	A	A+	A	A	A	F	F	F	F	D
4. Ivy Fund	A	A	A	B‡	B‡	F	F	F	F	D
5. Knickerbocker Growth Fund	A	A+	A+	A+	A+	F	F	F	F	D
6. Pioneer Enterprise Fund	A+	A	A	A	A	F	F	F	F	D
7. Value Line Special Situations	B	A	B	A+	A+	F	F	F	F	D
8. American Growth Fund	B	B	B	A	A	C	D	D	D	C
9. Keystone S-3	A+	A+	A+	A	A	D	D	D	D	C
10. Stein Roe & Farnham Stock Fund	B	B	B	B	B	C	C	C	C	C
11. Channing Common Stock Fund	D	D	C	C	C	C	B	B	B	C
12. Investors Stock Fund	D	D	D	D	D	C	C	C	C	C
13. Windsor Fund	B	C	C	A	A	C	B	C	C	C
14. Guardian Mutual Fund	C	C	C	C	C	B	B	B	B	B
15. Pine Street Fund	D	D	D	D	D	B	A	A	A	A

* F-ratings were not used in 1969 survey, with D being the lowest category.
‡ Fund was not in existence during all markets, hence highest ratings not allowed.
Source: Forbes, August 15, 1973.

able treatment in investment literature and has become, as well, a fashionable term used by investment practitioners. And we have seen that the categorization scheme of Wiesenberger's includes volatility as one of defining characteristics. Wiesenberger also reports estimates of price volatility during both rising and declining markets for a large number of mutual funds. Whereas total fund return is a more suitable measure of performance, price return (i.e., price appreciation) is a good surrogate for total return because of the overall stability of dividend and capital gains distributions for most funds. Volatility estimates appearing in the 1973 edition of Wiesenberger are based on the following dates:

Declining markets	*Rising markets*
1. November 29, 1968 to July 29, 1969	2. July 29, 1969 to November 10, 1969
3. November 10, 1969 to May 26, 1970	4. May 26, 1970 to April 18, 1971
5. April 28, 1971 to November 23, 1971	6. November 23, 1971 to January 11, 1973
7. January 11, 1973 to February 27, 1973	

As compared to the *Forbes* ratings of performance, which span six markets over a decade, the Wiesenberger estimates of volatility span seven markets, but over a period of just over four years.[3]

Average price volatilities during the four rising and the four declining markets for the sample of fifteen mutual funds are presented in Figure 21–4. Ideally, a fund would be characterized by a high (aggressive)

FIGURE 21–4
Selected Wiesenberger volatilities in rising and declining markets

	Mutual fund	*Rising markets*	*Declining markets*	*All markets*
1.	Delaware Fund	0.91	1.24	1.10
2.	Putnam Investors Fund	1.46	0.82	1.09
3.	Fairfield Fund	1.27	1.70	1.51
4.	Ivy Fund	1.03	1.36	1.22
5.	Knickerbocker Growth Fund	1.48	1.56	1.53
6.	Pioneer Enterprise Fund	1.22	1.38	1.31
7.	Value Line Special Situations	1.21	1.98	1.65
8.	American Growth Fund	0.69	0.90	0.81
9.	Keystone S-3	1.23	1.23	1.23
10.	Stein Roe & Farnham Stock Fund	1.31	1.02	1.14
11.	Channing Common Stock Fund	0.69	1.09	0.92
12.	Investors Stock Fund	1.08	0.99	1.03
13.	Windsor Fund	0.93	0.96	0.95
14.	Guardian Mutual Fund	0.90	0.99	0.95
15.	Pine Street Fund	0.78	0.96	0.88
	Average	1.08	1.21	1.15

Source: Investment Companies (Wiesenberger Services, Inc., 1973).

---

[3] Rising and declining markets according to both *Forbes* and Wiesenberger were identified in Figure 20–1 of the previous chapter.

volatility during rising markets, but a low (defensive) volatility during declining markets. Among the sample, only Putnam Investors Fund achieved those ideal characteristics. Still, there are certain other funds that have a significantly higher volatility during rising markets, but they are not defensive during declining markets. For over half of the funds in Figure 21–4, however, average volatility either was comparable in the two types of markets, or was actually lower during rising markets. For the entire sample of fifteen mutual funds, average volatility was actually higher during declining markets than during rising markets. Such findings, which again are based solely on price volatilities, also extend to larger samples of mutual funds. From these results, combined with recent empirical studies of volatility from the academic community, one must conclude that volatilities are stable over time, thus suggesting that fund managers have not been able to adjust their portfolios favorably as rising and declining markets materialize. Hence performance ratings typically are not high in all markets. In other words, as a market peak approached, portfolio managers were not able to revise their portfolio holdings from aggressive to defensive issues in anticipation of the subsequent market decline.

PERFORMANCE AND TRANSACTION COSTS

These observations of fund volatility and mixed performance ratings might be explained on the basis that fund managers simply were not able to recognize or predict major changes in the overall security markets. While there certainly have been times when the markets were neither clearly rising nor clearly declining, there have been more times when the direction of the markets was rather evident. A more plausible explanation of the findings in Figures 21–3 and 21–4 is the presence of transaction costs.

Although economists often posit a world devoid of transaction costs, the securities markets are a clear example of the unreality of such an assumption. Transaction costs clearly influence both individual and institutional investors. Consider initially the transaction costs faced by the managers of a large institutional portfolio such as a mutual fund. First, brokerage fees must be paid on all shares bought or sold for the fund. Because total assets are in the millions of dollars, and given negotiated commissions on large volume trades, each individual transaction is likely to incur the minimum percentage commission—often less than one percent of the total market value. Nevertheless, a complete change in fund holdings from aggressive to defensive at the earliest signs of a shift to a declining market could cause brokerage fees amounting to hundreds of thousands of dollars for even an average-size mutual fund.

Second, taxes must be considered. Dividend income distributed to shareholders of the fund is taxed as ordinary income to those shareholders. Price appreciation of securities held in the fund is not taxed, however, until the capital gains are realized and distributed to fund shareholders. As noted in Chapter 20, in delaying the realization of a capital gain, the investor in essence delays the tax payable—which is tantamount to an interest-free loan from the government—and this provides a greater investment base. But since taxes are paid by investors rather than by the fund itself, it is unlikely that they significantly constrain the implementation of decisions by the fund manager. Taxes should not be ignored, however, as an important transaction cost to individual investors. Performance measures illustrated earlier in the chapter thus were overstated because they did not reflect transaction costs, especially the unrealized tax liability on capital gains.

Third, and more germane to our discussion here, are market costs of large transactions by an institutional portfolio. A mutual fund such as Delaware Fund or Investors Stock Fund simply cannot accumulate or liquidate a major position in a security without consideration of how that transaction is likely to influence the market price of that security. Buying a large block of a given security tends to increase the market price, while selling a large block tends to depress the market price. Once a large fund decides on a portfolio change, it often will take several weeks or even months to implement that decision. Often overlooked in discussions of mutual fund performance is the critical role of traders who must implement buy and sell decisions at the most favorable market prices.

Transaction costs to individual fund shareholders also must be considered. Indirectly, shareholders pay the brokerage commissions on all fund transactions. Taxes on dividend-income and capital-gains distributions, which have already been mentioned, are passed on to individuals and thus are outside of the control of fund management once the particular fund shares are owned. What can be controlled by an individual, however, is the loading charge when those shares are purchased. Figure 21–5 indicates the percentage loadings applicable to shares of the fifteen mutual funds as stated in their respective prospectives. Each loading charge is expressed as a percentage of the offering price. The same loading charges expressed as a percentage of the amount invested are even higher. For example, 8.5% of offering price is equivalent to 9.3% of invested wealth. There is, of course, no loading charge for the four no-load funds in the sample. The maximum stated percentage loading, which pertains to small investments in fund shares, is 8% or more (or over 9% of invested principal) for each of the other eleven funds. The minimum percentage loading, which pertains to large investments in fund shares, drops off considerably in each case.

For small investors, the maximum loading would almost always apply. An investment of $1000 in a load fund buys $920 or less in net assets, but a full $1000 in the case of a no-load fund. This initial transaction

FIGURE 21–5
Loading charges for selected mutual funds

Mutual fund	Maximum loading	Minimum loading
1. Delaware Fund	8.5%	1.0%
2. Putnam Investors Fund.	8.5%	1.0%
3. Fairfield Fund.	8.5%	1.0%
4. Ivy Group	None	None
5. Knickerbocker Growth Fund	8.7%	1.7%
6. Pioneer Enterprise Fund	8.5%	0.5%
7. Value Line Special Situations	8.75%	1.0%
8. American Growth Fund	8.5%	0.0%*
9. Keystone S-3	8.75%	1.0%
10. Stein Roe & Farnham Stock Fund	None	None
11. Channing Common Stock Fund.	8.5%	1.0%
12. Investors Stock Fund.	8.0%	1.0%
13. Windsor Fund	8.5%	1.0%
14. Guardian Mutual Fund	None	None
15. Pine Street Fund	None	None

* On purchases exceeding $200,000.

cost to small investors places load funds at a distinct disadvantage relative to their no-load counterparts. If fund shares are held over long horizons, the annualized effect of the loading charge decreases. And, as mentioned in Chapter 15, investors have some flexibility in switching their investment from one fund to another within a group of funds under common management. Nevertheless, for horizons of only a year or two, the loading charge makes it very difficult for an investor to break even, let alone to make a reasonable return on his investment. As emphasis on performance has increased during recent years, not surprisingly so has the interest in no-load mutual funds.

To summarize, transaction costs constrain fund managers from adapting their portfolio holdings to major changes in direction of the securities markets. In addition, most funds identify in their prospectuses a major investment policy that reflects at least some degree of aggressiveness or defensiveness. To make widespread changes in portfolio holdings would be to change these investment policies. As a result, the volatilities of most mutual funds tend to be stable over time, and hence performance is seldom above average in all types of markets. Transaction costs also constrain individual investors from undue revisions of their security portfolios, or from switching from one fund to another. This again suggests the importance of reflecting transaction costs in performance evaluation.

PERFORMANCE COMPARISONS

So far, we have discussed measures of return and risk-adjusted return that can be used in evaluating a portfolio of investment. We also have analyzed the apparent inability of mutual funds consistently to out-perform other funds or the overall market. The latter necessiated performance comparisons, an important aspect of investing that we now examine in more detail.

Investment performance cannot effectively be evaluated in isolation. In order to make judgments about how well an individual fared or how well a manager made decisions, performance benchmarks or comparison standards are needed. Many benchmarks exist and performance comparisons can be made under countless combinations of horizon lengths, transaction costs, and reinvestment assumptions. Some benchmarks are realistic while others are purely hypothetical. Furthermore, the more complete the benchmark or standard, the wider the scope of the ensuing evaluation. Finding, for example, that Better Mutual Fund advanced more than the market during February is less informative than discovering that Better Mutual Fund outperformed the market in three of the last four years, as well as for the total four-year horizon. And calculating, as we did, that Better Mutual Fund outperformed Giant Growth Fund, on the basis of risk-adjusted return, gives less information to a potential investor that to inform him that Better Mutual Fund outperformed fifteen other funds out of a total sample of twenty growth funds that were examined. With such aspects in mind, we now review four distinct types of performance standards.

The first type of performance standard includes measures of the overall market. Although it is impossible actually to buy the entire market, it is possible through proper diversification to construct a portfolio of investment assets that has characteristics resembling that of the market itself. At least this is more nearly true of large institutional portfolios such as mutual funds and pension funds than of small, individual investors. While the New York Stock Exchange Index is a complete measure of all common stocks listed on that largest exchange, it surprisingly is seldom used as a benchmark for performance comparison of common stock investments. The Standard & Poor's Composite Index, which is an accurate representation of the overall market for listed common stocks, is used occasionally. The most frequent benchmark for evaluation of common stocks is the Dow Jones Industrial Average, which reflects only thirty issues and is not as representative of the total market in either sample or weighting. Persistent popularity of the DJIA is undoubtedly more psychological than rational, buttressed by the ready availability of the DJIA in the *Wall Street Journal* and other financial publications.

Another possible disadvantage of using market measures in performance comparisons is that the market is not a managed portfolio. Instead, it reflects a buy-and-hold strategy over the investment horizon. But because buy-and-hold strategies incur no transaction costs, they often become rather formidable benchmarks for comparison with managed portfolios. Certainly, a mutual fund or other managed portfolio should simply buy and hold unless a more active policy of revision leads to an improvement in performance after all transaction costs have been reflected.

This is dramatically illustrated by the performance comparisons in Figure 21–6. The second column indicates the compounded growth of

FIGURE 21–6
Growth of $10,000 in three types of investment assets

Year-end	Savings account	Mutual funds	DJIA
1949	$10,000	$10,000	$ 10,000
1950	10,500	11,089	12,323
1951	11,025	12,734	14,930
1952	11,576	14,166	17,026
1953	12,155	14,150	17,307
1954	12,763	20,233	25,961
1955	13,401	23,805	32,715
1956	14,071	25,604	34,968
1957	14,775	23,023	31,988
1958	15,514	32,088	44,278
1959	16,290	36,198	53,075
1960	17,105	37,403	49,756
1961	17,906	46,911	60,858
1962	18,858	41,484	56,186
1963	19,801	48,519	67,706
1964	20,791	54,866	80,297
1965	21,831	66,256	91,604
1966	22,923	62,785	77,228
1967	24,069	84,294	91,865
1968	25,272	99,138	98,903
1969	26,536	85,100	87,372
1970	27,863	78,616	94,930
1971	29,256	94,008	104,153

$10,000 at 5%, such as might be paid by a savings-and-loan association or a commercial bank, over the period 1950–1971. The third column indicates how a $10,000 investment in mutual fund shares would have grown over the same two decades. The mutual fund growth, based on the average performance of all mutual funds and reflecting a loading charge of 8.5%, ended with a value of $94,008, which is over three times the ending value of $29,256 for the savings account. This evidence has been used in advertising copy by the mutual fund industry.[4] But the fourth column of Figure 21–6 reveals that a $10,000 investment in the Dow Jones Industrial Average would have grown to $104,153 over the same period.[5] The equivalent compound annual growth rates over the

[4] For example, *Wall Street Journal*, August 9, 1972.
[5] *Growth Stock Outlook*, October 15, 1972.

22-year horizon were 5% (savings), 10.7% (mutual funds), and 11.3% (DJIA). This interesting finding does not mean, of course, that all mutual funds have performed worse than the market, but it does serve to dilute the advertising claim being made by the mutual fund industry. It also emphasizes the formidability of a buy-and-hold investment strategy, and it assumes that the investor could actually buy the "market."

The second type of performance standard is based on random chance. The idea is that a managed portfolio ought to perform as well or better than a portfolio selected randomly from some universe of investment assets. Using a set of darts, a pair of dice, or a table of random numbers, a randomly selected portfolio can be constructed at virtually no cost. And while it could be otherwise, random portfolios typically are held unchanged throughout the investment horizon. The results achieved by random portfolios have been reported in a number of empirical studies. One of these is based on the extensive study made at the University of Chicago of all NYSE-listed stocks over several decades. The median return (Y_{int}) for over 150 million combinations of randomly selected portfolios and investment horizons was 9.8%.[6] Perhaps the major disadvantage of using the performance of randomly generated portfolios as a comparison standard is that many investors psychologically may not be prepared to entrust their investment selections to a pair of dice or a set of darts.

The third type of standard reflects the performance of other managed portfolios. For example, we might compare Better Mutual Fund with other funds. Or we might compare the trust fund of the university professor and his wife with other trust funds. The advantage of this type of standard over either market or random performance is one of reality, since the portfolios actually exist and are being managed over time under conditions resembling that of the portfolio in question. Another advantage is that the set of comparison portfolios can be carefully selected so as to be similar in objectives and investment policies. The performance data for mutual funds available in sources such as *Forbes, Fundscope,* Lipper, and Wiesenberger are all of this type. Unfortunately, performance data for pension funds, trust funds, and other managed portfolios generally are not available, thus prohibiting performance comparisons.

The fourth type of performance standard is seldom mentioned and is quite different from the three that have been discussed. It involves comparing the performance of a given portfolio at the end of an investment horizon against the expectations that the investor or portfolio manager had at the beginning of the same horizon. For example, suppose

[6] Lawrence Fisher, "Outcomes from 'Random' Investments in Common Stocks Listed on the New York Stock Exchange," *Journal of Business,* 38:149–161, April, 1968.

the professor and his wife expected a 10% annual return on their trust fund at the start of the two-year horizon. Their realized performance of 14% per year after two years would compare favorably with that particular expectation. Conversely, the 8% annual performance of Better Mutual Fund over a decade would compare unfavorably with a similar 10% expectation by owners of those shares.

Comparisons based on this type of standard are unique to the particular portfolio. Rankings of portfolio performance are not possible since there is likely to be a different expectation for each investment asset that is held. And, of course, there is no reason to believe that all investors should have the same expectations, or even that those expectations are particularly rational.

The fourth type of performance standard brings us to the final point —and that is the use of performance evaluation and comparisons as a basis for change. Investing is an ongoing or continuing process, as suggested in Chapter 2. Each step of the process of investing must be repeated time and time again, since people change, their needs change, and, we hope, their investable wealth increases. In addition, investment opportunities change over time. The setting of objectives, the analysis and valuation of investment assets, and the ultimate construction of portfolios of investment assets should all reflect the past performance that has been achieved, as well as future needs and opportunities that are identified.

Hence, the pivotal role of performance evaluation. Rather than completing his study with this chapter, the reader should sense the importance of returning to earlier chapters and to the discussion of other steps in the process of investing.

We end with two suggested guidelines for investors who choose to do so. First, investors should force themselves to write down their objectives for each investment asset before that decision is actually implemented. The investor also should write down as part of this plan, the rules he will employ as time progresses and asset prices rise or fall. In other words, when will he sell, when will he buy, or when will he revise his rules? Second, investors should periodically force themselves to evaluate, again in writing, the performance of their portfolio of investment holdings. Some of the methods discussed in this chapter should prove helpful.

Both suggested guidelines require writing, a difficult task for some. The first guideline should help the investor to make and implement decisions with less emotional involvement. The second guideline should provide the investor with an assessment of his progress and the basis for continuing decision-making. Even as they travel through Europe, the university professor and his wife should give at least some thought to their future plans and upon their return to a continuation of their process of investing. Who knows, perhaps, if successful, they will be able to tour South America on a subsequent vacation.

SUMMARY

We have reiterated the importance of performance evaluation as a central step in the process of investing. Because of their impact on performance measurement in recent years, the recommendations of the Bank Administration Institute on pension fund evaluation were reviewed. Dollar-weighted and time-weighted measures of return were explained and illustrated. Risk-adjusted measures of return based on both intertemporal variability and volatility were also explained and illustrated. Using these concepts, the inconsistent performance of mutual funds was analyzed and partial explanations offered. Also reviewed were four different types of comparison standards that can be used as part of performance evaluation. The chapter concluded with two guidelines for investors, one involving the setting of investment objectives, and the second involving the evaluation of performance as a pivotal step in the process of investing.

SUGGESTED READINGS FOR CHAPTER 21

P. O. Dietz. *Pension Funds: Measuring Investment Performance* (New York: The Free Press, 1966).

L. Fisher and J. H. Lorie. "Rates of Return on Investment in Common Stocks: The Year-by-Year Record, 1926–1965," *Journal of Business,* July, 1968, pages 291–316.

L. Fisher. "Outcomes for 'Random' Investments in Common Stocks Listed on the New York Stock Exchange," *Journal of Business,* April, 1968, pages 149–61.

H. A. Latane and D. L. Tuttle. *Security Analysis and Portfolio Management* (New York: Ronald Press Company, 1970), Chapter 28.

J. H. Lorie, et. al. *Measuring the Investment Performance of Pension Funds* (Park Ridge, Ill.: Bank Administration Institute, 1968).

K. V. Smith. *Portfolio Management* (New York: Holt, Rinehart and Winston, Inc., 1971), Chapters 8, 10–11.

J. L. Treynor, "How to Rate Management of Investment Funds," *Harvard Business Review,* January–February, 1965, pages 63–75.

appendix A

Time value of money tables annual compounding and discounting

Time value of money, based upon an initial one dollar and annual compounding or discounting

TIME HORIZON	INTEREST RATE = 1.00%			INTEREST RATE = 2.00%			INTEREST RATE = 3.00%			TIME HORIZON
	COMPOUND SUM	DISCOUNTED SUM	DISCOUNTED ANNUITY	COMPOUND SUM	DISCOUNTED SUM	DISCOUNTED ANNUITY	COMPOUND SUM	DISCOUNTED SUM	DISCOUNTED ANNUITY	
1	1.010	0.990	0.990	1.020	0.980	0.980	1.030	0.971	0.971	1
2	1.020	0.980	1.970	1.040	0.961	1.941	1.061	0.943	1.913	2
3	1.030	0.971	2.941	1.061	0.942	2.884	1.093	0.915	2.829	3
4	1.041	0.961	3.902	1.082	0.924	3.808	1.126	0.888	3.717	4
5	1.051	0.951	4.853	1.104	0.906	4.713	1.159	0.863	4.580	5
6	1.062	0.942	5.795	1.126	0.888	5.601	1.194	0.837	5.417	6
7	1.072	0.933	6.728	1.149	0.871	6.472	1.230	0.813	6.230	7
8	1.083	0.923	7.651	1.172	0.853	7.325	1.267	0.789	7.020	8
9	1.094	0.914	8.566	1.195	0.837	8.162	1.305	0.766	7.786	9
10	1.105	0.905	9.471	1.219	0.820	8.982	1.344	0.744	8.530	10
11	1.116	0.896	10.367	1.243	0.804	9.787	1.384	0.722	9.253	11
12	1.127	0.887	11.254	1.268	0.788	10.575	1.426	0.701	9.954	12
13	1.138	0.879	12.133	1.294	0.773	11.348	1.469	0.681	10.635	13
14	1.149	0.870	13.003	1.319	0.758	12.106	1.513	0.661	11.296	14
15	1.161	0.861	13.864	1.346	0.743	12.849	1.558	0.642	11.938	15
16	1.173	0.853	14.717	1.373	0.728	13.577	1.605	0.623	12.561	16
17	1.184	0.844	15.561	1.400	0.714	14.292	1.653	0.605	13.166	17
18	1.196	0.836	16.397	1.428	0.700	14.992	1.702	0.587	13.753	18
19	1.208	0.828	17.225	1.457	0.686	15.678	1.753	0.570	14.324	19
20	1.220	0.820	18.044	1.486	0.673	16.351	1.806	0.554	14.877	20
21	1.232	0.811	18.856	1.516	0.660	17.011	1.860	0.538	15.415	21
22	1.245	0.803	19.659	1.546	0.647	17.658	1.916	0.522	15.937	22
23	1.257	0.795	20.454	1.577	0.634	18.292	1.974	0.507	16.443	23
24	1.270	0.788	21.242	1.608	0.622	18.914	2.033	0.492	16.935	24
25	1.282	0.780	22.022	1.641	0.610	19.523	2.094	0.478	17.413	25
30	1.348	0.742	25.806	1.811	0.552	22.396	2.427	0.412	19.600	30
35	1.417	0.706	29.407	2.000	0.500	24.998	2.814	0.355	21.487	35
40	1.489	0.672	32.833	2.208	0.453	27.355	3.262	0.307	23.115	40
45	1.565	0.639	36.092	2.438	0.410	29.490	3.782	0.264	24.519	45
50	1.645	0.608	39.194	2.692	0.372	31.423	4.384	0.228	25.730	50

Time value of money, based upon an initial one dollar and annual compounding or discounting

TIME HORIZON	INTEREST RATE = 4.00%			INTEREST RATE = 5.00%			INTEREST RATE = 6.00%			TIME HORIZON
	COMPOUND SUM	DISCOUNTED SUM	DISCOUNTED ANNUITY	COMPOUND SUM	DISCOUNTED SUM	DISCOUNTED ANNUITY	COMPOUND SUM	DISCOUNTED SUM	DISCOUNTED ANNUITY	
1	1.040	0.962	0.962	1.050	0.952	0.952	1.060	0.943	0.943	1
2	1.082	0.925	1.886	1.102	0.907	1.859	1.124	0.890	1.833	2
3	1.125	0.889	2.775	1.158	0.864	2.723	1.191	0.840	2.673	3
4	1.170	0.855	3.630	1.216	0.823	3.546	1.262	0.792	3.465	4
5	1.217	0.822	4.452	1.276	0.784	4.329	1.338	0.747	4.212	5
6	1.265	0.790	5.242	1.340	0.746	5.076	1.419	0.705	4.917	6
7	1.316	0.760	6.002	1.407	0.711	5.786	1.504	0.665	5.582	7
8	1.369	0.731	6.733	1.477	0.677	6.463	1.594	0.627	6.210	8
9	1.423	0.703	7.435	1.551	0.645	7.108	1.689	0.592	6.802	9
10	1.480	0.676	8.111	1.629	0.614	7.722	1.791	0.558	7.360	10
11	1.539	0.650	8.760	1.710	0.585	8.306	1.898	0.527	7.887	11
12	1.601	0.625	9.385	1.796	0.557	8.863	2.012	0.497	8.384	12
13	1.665	0.601	9.986	1.886	0.530	9.394	2.133	0.469	8.853	13
14	1.732	0.577	10.563	1.980	0.505	9.899	2.261	0.442	9.295	14
15	1.801	0.555	11.118	2.079	0.481	10.380	2.397	0.417	9.712	15
16	1.873	0.534	11.652	2.183	0.458	10.838	2.540	0.394	10.106	16
17	1.948	0.513	12.166	2.292	0.436	11.274	2.693	0.371	10.477	17
18	2.026	0.494	12.659	2.407	0.416	11.689	2.854	0.350	10.828	18
19	2.107	0.475	13.134	2.527	0.396	12.085	3.026	0.331	11.158	19
20	2.191	0.456	13.590	2.653	0.377	12.462	3.207	0.312	11.470	20
21	2.279	0.439	14.029	2.786	0.359	12.821	3.400	0.294	11.764	21
22	2.370	0.422	14.451	2.925	0.342	13.163	3.603	0.278	12.042	22
23	2.465	0.406	14.857	3.071	0.326	13.488	3.820	0.262	12.303	23
24	2.563	0.390	15.247	3.225	0.310	13.799	4.049	0.247	12.550	24
25	2.666	0.375	15.622	3.386	0.295	14.094	4.292	0.233	12.783	25
30	3.243	0.308	17.292	4.322	0.231	15.372	5.743	0.174	13.765	30
35	3.946	0.253	18.665	5.516	0.181	16.374	7.686	0.130	14.498	35
40	4.801	0.208	19.793	7.040	0.142	17.159	10.286	0.097	15.046	40
45	5.841	0.171	20.720	8.985	0.111	17.774	13.764	0.073	15.456	45
50	7.107	0.141	21.482	11.467	0.087	18.256	18.420	0.054	15.762	50

Time value of money, based upon an initial one dollar and annual compounding or discounting

TIME HORIZON	INTEREST RATE = 7.00%			INTEREST RATE = 8.00%			INTEREST RATE = 9.00%			TIME HORIZON
	COMPOUND SUM	DISCOUNTED SUM	DISCOUNTED ANNUITY	COMPOUND SUM	DISCOUNTED SUM	DISCOUNTED ANNUITY	COMPOUND SUM	DISCOUNTED SUM	DISCOUNTED ANNUITY	
1	1.070	0.935	0.935	1.080	0.926	0.926	1.090	0.917	0.917	1
2	1.145	0.873	1.808	1.166	0.857	1.783	1.188	0.842	1.759	2
3	1.225	0.816	2.624	1.260	0.794	2.577	1.295	0.772	2.531	3
4	1.311	0.763	3.387	1.360	0.735	3.312	1.412	0.708	3.240	4
5	1.403	0.713	4.100	1.469	0.681	3.993	1.539	0.650	3.890	5
6	1.501	0.666	4.767	1.587	0.630	4.623	1.677	0.596	4.486	6
7	1.606	0.623	5.389	1.714	0.583	5.206	1.828	0.547	5.033	7
8	1.718	0.582	5.971	1.851	0.540	5.747	1.993	0.502	5.535	8
9	1.838	0.544	6.515	1.999	0.500	6.247	2.172	0.460	5.995	9
10	1.967	0.508	7.024	2.159	0.463	6.710	2.367	0.422	6.418	10
11	2.105	0.475	7.499	2.332	0.429	7.139	2.580	0.388	6.805	11
12	2.252	0.444	7.943	2.518	0.397	7.536	2.813	0.356	7.161	12
13	2.410	0.415	8.358	2.720	0.368	7.904	3.066	0.326	7.487	13
14	2.579	0.388	8.745	2.937	0.340	8.244	3.342	0.299	7.786	14
15	2.759	0.362	9.108	3.172	0.315	8.559	3.642	0.275	8.061	15
16	2.952	0.339	9.447	3.426	0.292	8.851	3.970	0.252	8.313	16
17	3.159	0.317	9.763	3.700	0.270	9.122	4.328	0.231	8.544	17
18	3.380	0.296	10.059	3.996	0.250	9.372	4.717	0.212	8.756	18
19	3.617	0.277	10.336	4.316	0.232	9.604	5.142	0.194	8.950	19
20	3.870	0.258	10.594	4.661	0.215	9.818	5.604	0.178	9.129	20
21	4.141	0.242	10.836	5.034	0.199	10.017	6.109	0.164	9.292	21
22	4.430	0.226	11.061	5.437	0.184	10.201	6.658	0.150	9.442	22
23	4.740	0.211	11.272	5.871	0.170	10.371	7.258	0.138	9.580	23
24	5.072	0.197	11.469	6.341	0.158	10.529	7.911	0.126	9.707	24
25	5.427	0.184	11.654	6.848	0.146	10.675	8.623	0.116	9.823	25
30	7.612	0.131	12.409	10.063	0.099	11.258	13.267	0.075	10.274	30
35	10.676	0.094	12.948	14.785	0.068	11.655	20.413	0.049	10.567	35
40	14.974	0.067	13.332	21.724	0.046	11.925	31.409	0.032	10.757	40
45	21.002	0.048	13.606	31.920	0.031	12.108	48.326	0.021	10.881	45
50	29.457	0.034	13.801	46.901	0.021	12.233	74.355	0.013	10.962	50

Time value of money, based upon an initial one dollar and annual compounding or discounting

TIME HORIZON	INTEREST RATE = 10.00% COMPOUND SUM	DISCOUNTED SUM	DISCOUNTED ANNUITY	INTEREST RATE = 11.00% COMPOUND SUM	DISCOUNTED SUM	DISCOUNTED ANNUITY	INTEREST RATE = 12.00% COMPOUND SUM	DISCOUNTED SUM	DISCOUNTED ANNUITY	TIME HORIZON
1	1.100	0.909	0.909	1.110	0.901	0.901	1.120	0.893	0.893	1
2	1.210	0.826	1.736	1.232	0.812	1.713	1.254	0.797	1.690	2
3	1.331	0.751	2.487	1.368	0.731	2.444	1.405	0.712	2.402	3
4	1.464	0.683	3.170	1.518	0.659	3.102	1.574	0.636	3.037	4
5	1.611	0.621	3.791	1.685	0.593	3.696	1.762	0.567	3.605	5
6	1.772	0.564	4.355	1.870	0.535	4.231	1.974	0.507	4.111	6
7	1.949	0.513	4.868	2.076	0.482	4.712	2.211	0.452	4.564	7
8	2.144	0.467	5.335	2.305	0.434	5.146	2.476	0.404	4.968	8
9	2.358	0.424	5.759	2.558	0.391	5.537	2.773	0.361	5.328	9
10	2.594	0.386	6.145	2.839	0.352	5.889	3.106	0.322	5.650	10
11	2.853	0.350	6.495	3.152	0.317	6.207	3.479	0.287	5.938	11
12	3.138	0.319	6.814	3.498	0.286	6.492	3.896	0.257	6.194	12
13	3.452	0.290	7.103	3.883	0.258	6.750	4.363	0.229	6.424	13
14	3.797	0.263	7.367	4.310	0.232	6.982	4.887	0.205	6.628	14
15	4.177	0.239	7.606	4.785	0.209	7.191	5.474	0.183	6.811	15
16	4.595	0.218	7.824	5.311	0.188	7.379	6.130	0.163	6.974	16
17	5.054	0.198	8.022	5.895	0.170	7.549	6.866	0.146	7.120	17
18	5.560	0.180	8.201	6.544	0.153	7.702	7.690	0.130	7.250	18
19	6.116	0.164	8.365	7.263	0.138	7.839	8.613	0.116	7.366	19
20	6.727	0.149	8.514	8.062	0.124	7.963	9.646	0.104	7.469	20
21	7.400	0.135	8.649	8.949	0.112	8.075	10.804	0.093	7.562	21
22	8.140	0.123	8.772	9.934	0.101	8.176	12.100	0.083	7.645	22
23	8.954	0.112	8.883	11.026	0.091	8.266	13.552	0.074	7.718	23
24	9.850	0.102	8.985	12.239	0.082	8.348	15.179	0.066	7.784	24
25	10.835	0.092	9.077	13.585	0.074	8.422	17.000	0.059	7.843	25
30	17.449	0.057	9.427	22.892	0.044	8.694	29.960	0.033	8.055	30
35	28.102	0.036	9.644	38.574	0.026	8.855	52.799	0.019	8.176	35
40	45.258	0.022	9.779	65.000	0.015	8.951	93.051	0.011	8.244	40
45	72.889	0.014	9.863	109.529	0.009	9.008	163.987	0.006	8.283	45
50	117.388	0.009	9.915	184.562	0.005	9.042	289.000	0.003	8.305	50

Time value of money, based upon an initial one dollar and annual compounding or discounting

TIME HORIZON	INTEREST RATE = 13.00% COMPOUND SUM	DISCOUNTED SUM	DISCOUNTED ANNUITY	INTEREST RATE = 14.00% COMPOUND SUM	DISCOUNTED SUM	DISCOUNTED ANNUITY	INTEREST RATE = 15.00% COMPOUND SUM	DISCOUNTED SUM	DISCOUNTED ANNUITY	TIME HORIZON
1	1.130	0.885	0.885	1.140	0.877	0.877	1.150	0.870	0.870	1
2	1.277	0.783	1.668	1.300	0.769	1.647	1.322	0.756	1.626	2
3	1.443	0.693	2.361	1.482	0.675	2.322	1.521	0.658	2.283	3
4	1.630	0.613	2.974	1.689	0.592	2.914	1.749	0.572	2.855	4
5	1.842	0.543	3.517	1.925	0.519	3.433	2.011	0.497	3.352	5
6	2.082	0.480	3.998	2.195	0.456	3.889	2.313	0.432	3.784	6
7	2.353	0.425	4.423	2.502	0.400	4.288	2.660	0.376	4.160	7
8	2.658	0.376	4.799	2.853	0.351	4.639	3.059	0.327	4.487	8
9	3.004	0.333	5.132	3.252	0.308	4.946	3.518	0.284	4.772	9
10	3.395	0.295	5.426	3.707	0.270	5.216	4.046	0.247	5.019	10
11	3.836	0.261	5.687	4.226	0.237	5.453	4.652	0.215	5.234	11
12	4.334	0.231	5.918	4.818	0.208	5.660	5.350	0.187	5.421	12
13	4.898	0.204	6.122	5.492	0.182	5.842	6.153	0.163	5.583	13
14	5.535	0.181	6.302	6.261	0.160	6.002	7.076	0.141	5.724	14
15	6.254	0.160	6.462	7.138	0.140	6.142	8.137	0.123	5.847	15
16	7.067	0.141	6.604	8.137	0.123	6.265	9.358	0.107	5.954	16
17	7.986	0.125	6.729	9.276	0.108	6.373	10.761	0.093	6.047	17
18	9.024	0.111	6.840	10.575	0.095	6.467	12.375	0.081	6.128	18
19	10.197	0.098	6.938	12.056	0.083	6.550	14.232	0.070	6.198	19
20	11.523	0.087	7.025	13.743	0.073	6.623	16.366	0.061	6.259	20
21	13.021	0.077	7.102	15.667	0.064	6.687	18.821	0.053	6.312	21
22	14.714	0.068	7.170	17.861	0.056	6.743	21.645	0.046	6.359	22
23	16.626	0.060	7.230	20.361	0.049	6.792	24.891	0.040	6.399	23
24	18.788	0.053	7.283	23.212	0.043	6.835	28.625	0.035	6.434	24
25	21.230	0.047	7.330	26.462	0.038	6.873	32.919	0.030	6.464	25
30	39.115	0.026	7.496	50.949	0.020	7.003	66.211	0.015	6.566	30
35	72.067	0.014	7.586	98.098	0.010	7.070	133.174	0.008	6.617	35
40	132.777	0.008	7.634	188.879	0.005	7.105	267.860	0.004	6.642	40
45	244.633	0.004	7.661	363.670	0.003	7.123	538.761	0.002	6.654	45
50	450.719	0.002	7.675	700.213	0.001	7.133	1083.640	0.001	6.661	50

Time value of money, based upon an initial one dollar and annual compounding or discounting

TIME HORIZON	INTEREST RATE = 16.00%			INTEREST RATE = 17.00%			INTEREST RATE = 18.00%			TIME HORIZON
	COMPOUND SUM	DISCOUNTED SUM	DISCOUNTED ANNUITY	COMPOUND SUM	DISCOUNTED SUM	DISCOUNTED ANNUITY	COMPOUND SUM	DISCOUNTED SUM	DISCOUNTED ANNUITY	
1	1.160	0.862	0.862	1.170	0.855	0.855	1.180	0.847	0.847	1
2	1.346	0.743	1.605	1.369	0.731	1.585	1.392	0.718	1.566	2
3	1.561	0.641	2.246	1.602	0.624	2.210	1.643	0.609	2.174	3
4	1.811	0.552	2.798	1.874	0.534	2.743	1.939	0.516	2.690	4
5	2.100	0.476	3.274	2.192	0.456	3.199	2.288	0.437	3.127	5
6	2.436	0.410	3.685	2.565	0.390	3.589	2.700	0.370	3.498	6
7	2.826	0.354	4.039	3.001	0.333	3.922	3.185	0.314	3.812	7
8	3.278	0.305	4.344	3.511	0.285	4.207	3.759	0.266	4.078	8
9	3.803	0.263	4.607	4.108	0.243	4.451	4.435	0.225	4.303	9
10	4.411	0.227	4.833	4.807	0.208	4.659	5.234	0.191	4.494	10
11	5.117	0.195	5.029	5.624	0.178	4.836	6.176	0.162	4.656	11
12	5.936	0.168	5.197	6.580	0.152	4.988	7.288	0.137	4.793	12
13	6.886	0.145	5.342	7.699	0.130	5.118	8.599	0.116	4.910	13
14	7.988	0.125	5.468	9.007	0.111	5.229	10.147	0.099	5.008	14
15	9.265	0.108	5.575	10.539	0.095	5.324	11.974	0.084	5.092	15
16	10.748	0.093	5.669	12.330	0.081	5.405	14.129	0.071	5.162	16
17	12.468	0.080	5.749	14.426	0.069	5.475	16.672	0.060	5.222	17
18	14.462	0.069	5.818	16.879	0.059	5.534	19.673	0.051	5.273	18
19	16.776	0.060	5.877	19.748	0.051	5.584	23.214	0.043	5.316	19
20	19.461	0.051	5.929	23.105	0.043	5.628	27.393	0.037	5.353	20
21	22.574	0.044	5.973	27.033	0.037	5.665	32.323	0.031	5.384	21
22	26.186	0.038	6.011	31.629	0.032	5.696	38.142	0.026	5.410	22
23	30.376	0.033	6.044	37.006	0.027	5.723	45.007	0.022	5.432	23
24	35.236	0.028	6.073	43.296	0.023	5.746	53.108	0.019	5.451	24
25	40.874	0.024	6.097	50.657	0.020	5.766	62.668	0.016	5.467	25
30	85.850	0.012	6.177	111.062	0.009	5.829	143.368	0.007	5.517	30
35	180.313	0.006	6.215	243.497	0.004	5.858	327.591	0.003	5.539	35
40	378.719	0.003	6.234	533.852	0.002	5.871	750.361	0.001	5.548	40
45	795.438	0.001	6.242	1170.439	0.001	5.877	1716.640	0.001	5.552	45
50	1670.691	0.001	6.246	2566.117	0.000	5.880	3927.243	0.000	5.554	50

Time value of money, based upon an initial one dollar and annual compounding or discounting

TIME HORIZON	INTEREST RATE = 19.00%			INTEREST RATE = 20.00%			INTEREST RATE = 21.00%			TIME HORIZON
	COMPOUND SUM	DISCOUNTED SUM	DISCOUNTED ANNUITY	COMPOUND SUM	DISCOUNTED SUM	DISCOUNTED ANNUITY	COMPOUND SUM	DISCOUNTED SUM	DISCOUNTED ANNUITY	
1	1.190	0.840	0.840	1.200	0.833	0.833	1.210	0.826	0.826	1
2	1.416	0.706	1.546	1.440	0.694	1.528	1.464	0.683	1.509	2
3	1.685	0.593	2.140	1.728	0.579	2.106	1.772	0.564	2.074	3
4	2.005	0.499	2.639	2.074	0.482	2.589	2.144	0.467	2.540	4
5	2.386	0.419	3.058	2.488	0.402	2.991	2.594	0.386	2.926	5
6	2.840	0.352	3.410	2.986	0.335	3.326	3.138	0.319	3.245	6
7	3.379	0.296	3.706	3.583	0.279	3.605	3.797	0.263	3.508	7
8	4.021	0.249	3.954	4.300	0.233	3.837	4.595	0.218	3.726	8
9	4.785	0.209	4.163	5.160	0.194	4.031	5.560	0.180	3.905	9
10	5.695	0.176	4.339	6.192	0.162	4.192	6.727	0.149	4.054	10
11	6.777	0.148	4.487	7.430	0.135	4.327	8.140	0.123	4.177	11
12	8.064	0.124	4.611	8.916	0.112	4.439	9.850	0.102	4.278	12
13	9.596	0.104	4.715	10.699	0.093	4.533	11.918	0.084	4.362	13
14	11.420	0.088	4.802	12.839	0.078	4.611	14.421	0.069	4.432	14
15	13.589	0.074	4.876	15.407	0.065	4.675	17.449	0.057	4.489	15
16	16.171	0.062	4.938	18.488	0.054	4.730	21.114	0.047	4.536	16
17	19.244	0.052	4.990	22.186	0.045	4.775	25.547	0.039	4.576	17
18	22.900	0.044	5.033	26.623	0.038	4.812	30.912	0.032	4.608	18
19	27.251	0.037	5.070	31.948	0.031	4.843	37.404	0.027	4.635	19
20	32.429	0.031	5.101	38.337	0.026	4.870	45.259	0.022	4.657	20
21	38.591	0.026	5.127	46.005	0.022	4.891	54.763	0.018	4.675	21
22	45.923	0.022	5.149	55.206	0.018	4.909	66.263	0.015	4.690	22
23	54.648	0.018	5.167	66.247	0.015	4.925	80.178	0.012	4.703	23
24	65.031	0.015	5.182	79.497	0.013	4.937	97.015	0.010	4.713	24
25	77.387	0.013	5.195	95.396	0.010	4.948	117.389	0.009	4.721	25
30	184.673	0.005	5.235	237.375	0.004	4.979	304.474	0.003	4.746	30
35	440.695	0.002	5.251	590.665	0.002	4.992	789.725	0.001	4.756	35
40	1051.652	0.001	5.258	1469.764	0.001	4.997	2048.337	0.000	4.760	40
45	2509.608	0.000	5.261	3657.240	0.000	4.999	5312.836	0.000	4.761	45
50	5988.801	0.000	5.262	9100.375	0.000	4.999	13780.078	0.000	4.762	50

Time value of money, based upon an initial one dollar and annual compounding or discounting

TIME HORIZON	INTEREST RATE = 22.00%			INTEREST RATE = 23.00%			INTEREST RATE = 24.00%			TIME HORIZON
	COMPOUND SUM	DISCOUNTED SUM	DISCOUNTED ANNUITY	COMPOUND SUM	DISCOUNTED SUM	DISCOUNTED ANNUITY	COMPOUND SUM	DISCOUNTED SUM	DISCOUNTED ANNUITY	
1	1.220	0.820	0.820	1.230	0.813	0.813	1.240	0.806	0.806	1
2	1.488	0.672	1.492	1.513	0.661	1.474	1.538	0.650	1.457	2
3	1.816	0.551	2.042	1.861	0.537	2.011	1.907	0.524	1.981	3
4	2.215	0.451	2.494	2.289	0.437	2.448	2.364	0.423	2.404	4
5	2.703	0.370	2.864	2.815	0.355	2.803	2.932	0.341	2.745	5
6	3.297	0.303	3.167	3.463	0.289	3.092	3.635	0.275	3.020	6
7	4.023	0.249	3.416	4.259	0.235	3.327	4.508	0.222	3.242	7
8	4.908	0.204	3.619	5.239	0.191	3.518	5.589	0.179	3.421	8
9	5.987	0.167	3.786	6.444	0.155	3.673	6.931	0.144	3.566	9
10	7.305	0.137	3.923	7.926	0.126	3.799	8.594	0.116	3.682	10
11	8.912	0.112	4.035	9.749	0.103	3.902	10.657	0.094	3.776	11
12	10.872	0.092	4.127	11.991	0.083	3.985	13.215	0.076	3.851	12
13	13.264	0.075	4.203	14.749	0.068	4.053	16.386	0.061	3.912	13
14	16.182	0.062	4.265	18.141	0.055	4.108	20.319	0.049	3.962	14
15	19.742	0.051	4.315	22.314	0.045	4.153	25.196	0.040	4.001	15
16	24.085	0.042	4.357	27.446	0.036	4.189	31.242	0.032	4.033	16
17	29.384	0.034	4.391	33.759	0.030	4.219	38.741	0.026	4.059	17
18	35.849	0.028	4.419	41.523	0.024	4.243	48.038	0.021	4.080	18
19	43.735	0.023	4.442	51.073	0.020	4.263	59.568	0.017	4.097	19
20	53.357	0.019	4.460	62.820	0.016	4.279	73.864	0.014	4.110	20
21	65.096	0.015	4.476	77.269	0.013	4.292	91.591	0.011	4.121	21
22	79.416	0.013	4.488	95.041	0.011	4.302	113.573	0.009	4.130	22
23	96.888	0.010	4.499	116.900	0.009	4.311	140.831	0.007	4.137	23
24	118.203	0.008	4.507	143.787	0.007	4.318	174.630	0.006	4.143	24
25	144.208	0.007	4.514	176.858	0.006	4.323	216.541	0.005	4.147	25
30	389.751	0.003	4.534	497.907	0.002	4.339	634.816	0.002	4.160	30
35	1053.379	0.001	4.541	1401.758	0.001	4.345	1861.042	0.001	4.164	35
40	2846.971	0.000	4.544	3946.368	0.000	4.347	5455.871	0.000	4.166	40
45	7694.508	0.000	4.545	11110.207	0.000	4.347	15994.547	0.000	4.166	45
50	20795.949	0.000	4.545	31278.586	0.000	4.348	46889.965	0.000	4.167	50

Time value of money, based upon an initial one dollar and annual compounding or discounting

TIME HORIZON	INTEREST RATE = 25.00%			TIME HORIZON
	COMPOUND SUM	DISCOUNTED SUM	DISCOUNTED ANNUITY	
1	1.250	0.800	0.800	1
2	1.562	0.640	1.440	2
3	1.953	0.512	1.952	3
4	2.441	0.410	2.362	4
5	3.052	0.328	2.689	5
6	3.815	0.262	2.951	6
7	4.768	0.210	3.161	7
8	5.960	0.168	3.329	8
9	7.451	0.134	3.463	9
10	9.313	0.107	3.571	10
11	11.641	0.086	3.656	11
12	14.552	0.069	3.725	12
13	18.190	0.055	3.780	13
14	22.737	0.044	3.824	14
15	28.421	0.035	3.859	15
16	35.527	0.028	3.887	16
17	44.408	0.023	3.910	17
18	55.510	0.018	3.928	18
19	69.388	0.014	3.942	19
20	86.735	0.012	3.954	20
21	108.418	0.009	3.963	21
22	135.523	0.007	3.970	22
23	169.404	0.006	3.976	23
24	211.754	0.005	3.981	24
25	264.693	0.004	3.985	25
30	807.775	0.001	3.995	30
35	2465.125	0.000	3.998	35
40	7522.934	0.000	3.999	40
45	22958.090	0.000	4.000	45
50	70062.250	0.000	4.000	50

appendix B

Time value of money tables periodic compounding and discounting

8% compound sum of one dollar

TIME HORIZON	ANNUAL COMPOUNDING	SEMIANNUAL COMPOUNDING	QUARTERLY COMPOUNDING	MONTHLY COMPOUNDING	CONTINUOUS COMPOUNDING	TIME HORIZON
1	1.C8C	1.082	1.082	1.083	1.C83	1
2	1.166	1.170	1.172	1.173	1.174	2
3	1.260	1.265	1.268	1.270	1.271	3
4	1.36C	1.369	1.373	1.376	1.377	4
5	1.469	1.48C	1.486	1.490	1.492	5
6	1.587	1.601	1.608	1.613	1.616	6
7	1.714	1.732	1.741	1.747	1.751	7
8	1.851	1.873	1.885	1.892	1.896	8
9	1.999	2.02f	2.040	2.049	2.054	9
1C	2.159	2.191	2.208	2.220	2.226	1C
11	2.332	2.370	2.390	2.404	2.411	11
12	2.518	2.563	2.587	2.603	2.612	12
13	2.720	2.772	2.8CC	2.819	2.829	13
14	2.937	2.599	3.031	3.053	3.065	14
15	3.172	3.243	3.281	3.307	3.320	15
16	3.426	3.508	3.551	3.581	3.597	16
17	3.7CC	3.794	3.844	3.876	3.896	17
18	3.996	4.104	4.161	4.2CC	4.221	18
19	4.316	4.439	4.504	4.549	4.572	19
2C	4.661	4.8C1	4.875	4.926	4.953	2C
21	5.C34	5.193	5.277	5.335	5.366	21
22	5.437	5.617	5.712	5.778	5.813	22
23	5.871	6.075	6.183	6.257	6.297	23
24	6.341	6.571	6.692	6.777	6.821	24
25	6.848	7.107	7.244	7.339	7.389	25
3C	1C.C63	10.520	1C.765	1C.934	11.023	3C
35	14.785	15.572	15.995	16.285	16.445	35
4C	21.724	23.C50	23.768	24.266	24.533	4C
45	31.920	34.119	35.318	36.154	36.599	45
5C	46.9C1	50.505	52.480	53.863	54.6CC	5C

8% discounted sum of one dollar

TIME HORIZON	ANNUAL COMPOUNDING	SEMIANNUAL COMPOUNDING	QUARTERLY COMPOUNDING	MONTHLY COMPOUNDING	CONTINUOUS COMPOUNDING	TIME HORIZON
1	0.926	0.925	0.924	0.923	0.923	1
2	0.857	0.855	0.853	0.853	0.852	2
3	0.794	0.790	0.788	0.787	0.787	3
4	0.735	0.731	0.728	0.727	0.726	4
5	0.681	0.676	0.673	0.671	0.670	5
6	0.630	0.625	0.622	0.620	0.619	6
7	0.583	0.577	0.574	0.572	0.571	7
8	0.540	0.534	0.531	0.528	0.527	8
9	0.500	0.494	0.490	0.488	0.487	9
10	0.463	0.456	0.453	0.451	0.449	10
11	0.429	0.422	0.419	0.416	0.415	11
12	0.397	0.390	0.387	0.384	0.383	12
13	0.368	0.361	0.357	0.355	0.353	13
14	0.340	0.333	0.330	0.328	0.326	14
15	0.315	0.308	0.305	0.302	0.301	15
16	0.292	0.285	0.282	0.279	0.278	16
17	0.270	0.264	0.260	0.258	0.257	17
18	0.250	0.244	0.240	0.238	0.237	18
19	0.232	0.225	0.222	0.220	0.219	19
20	0.215	0.208	0.205	0.203	0.202	20
21	0.199	0.192	0.189	0.187	0.186	21
22	0.184	0.178	0.175	0.173	0.172	22
23	0.170	0.165	0.162	0.160	0.159	23
24	0.158	0.152	0.149	0.148	0.147	24
25	0.146	0.141	0.138	0.136	0.135	25
30	0.099	0.095	0.093	0.091	0.091	30
35	0.068	0.064	0.063	0.061	0.061	35
40	0.046	0.043	0.042	0.041	0.041	40
45	0.031	0.029	0.028	0.028	0.027	45
50	0.021	0.020	0.019	0.019	0.018	50

12% compound sum of one dollar

TIME HORIZON	ANNUAL COMPOUNDING	SEMIANNUAL COMPOUNDING	QUARTERLY COMPOUNDING	MONTHLY COMPOUNDING	CONTINUOUS COMPOUNDING	TIME HORIZON
1	1.120	1.124	1.126	1.127	1.127	1
2	1.254	1.262	1.267	1.270	1.271	2
3	1.405	1.419	1.426	1.431	1.433	3
4	1.574	1.594	1.605	1.612	1.616	4
5	1.762	1.791	1.806	1.817	1.822	5
6	1.974	2.012	2.033	2.047	2.054	6
7	2.211	2.261	2.288	2.307	2.316	7
8	2.476	2.540	2.575	2.599	2.612	8
9	2.773	2.854	2.898	2.929	2.946	9
10	3.106	3.207	3.262	3.300	3.320	10
11	3.479	3.603	3.671	3.719	3.743	11
12	3.896	4.049	4.132	4.190	4.221	12
13	4.363	4.549	4.651	4.722	4.759	13
14	4.887	5.112	5.235	5.320	5.366	14
15	5.474	5.743	5.892	5.995	6.050	15
16	6.130	6.453	6.631	6.755	6.821	16
17	6.866	7.251	7.463	7.612	7.691	17
18	7.690	8.147	8.400	8.577	8.671	18
19	8.613	9.154	9.454	9.665	9.777	19
20	9.646	10.286	10.641	10.891	11.023	20
21	10.804	11.557	11.976	12.272	12.429	21
22	12.100	12.985	13.479	13.828	14.013	22
23	13.552	14.590	15.171	15.582	15.800	23
24	15.179	16.393	17.075	17.558	17.815	24
25	17.000	18.420	19.219	19.784	20.086	25
30	29.960	32.987	34.710	35.940	36.599	30
35	52.799	59.074	62.690	65.290	66.686	35
40	93.051	105.792	113.224	118.607	121.514	40
45	163.987	189.456	204.494	215.463	221.414	45
50	289.000	339.285	369.336	391.414	403.443	50

12% discounted sum of one dollar

TIME HORIZON	ANNUAL COMPOUNDING	SEMIANNUAL COMPOUNDING	QUARTERLY COMPOUNDING	MONTHLY COMPOUNDING	CONTINUOUS COMPOUNDING	TIME HORIZON
1	C.893	C.890	0.888	0.887	0.887	1
2	C.797	C.792	0.789	0.788	C.787	2
3	0.712	0.705	C.701	C.699	0.698	3
4	C.636	0.627	C.623	C.620	0.619	4
5	C.567	0.558	0.554	C.550	C.549	5
6	0.507	C.497	C.492	0.489	C.487	6
7	C.452	C.442	0.437	0.434	C.432	7
8	C.404	C.394	0.388	C.385	C.383	8
9	C.361	C.350	C.345	C.341	C.340	9
10	C.322	C.212	0.307	C.303	C.301	10
11	0.287	C.278	0.272	C.269	C.267	11
12	C.257	C.247	C.242	C.239	C.237	12
13	0.229	C.220	C.215	C.212	C.210	13
14	C.205	C.196	C.191	0.188	C.188	14
15	0.183	C.174	0.170	C.167	C.165	15
16	C.163	0.155	C.151	C.148	C.147	16
17	0.146	0.138	C.134	0.131	C.130	17
18	C.130	C.123	C.119	C.117	C.115	18
19	0.116	C.109	0.106	C.103	0.102	19
20	C.104	C.097	C.094	C.092	C.091	20
21	C.093	0.087	C.084	C.081	C.080	21
22	C.083	C.077	C.066	C.072	C.071	22
23	C.074	C.069	C.066	C.064	C.063	23
24	C.066	C.061	C.059	C.057	C.056	24
25	C.059	C.054	C.052	C.051	C.050	25
30	C.033	C.030	C.029	C.028	C.027	30
35	C.019	C.017	C.016	C.015	C.015	35
40	C.011	C.009	C.009	C.008	C.008	40
45	C.006	C.005	C.005	C.005	C.005	45
50	C.003	C.003	C.003	C.003	C.002	50

Exercises

1. Make a list of all the investment assets that you have owned.
2. Make a list of the investment attributes that you considered in deciding to acquire each investment asset.
3. Make a list of the sources of information that you examined in deciding to acquire each investment asset.
4. Compare the detailed processes whereby you reached final decisions to acquire your investment assets.
5. Evaluate how well each investment asset has performed relative to your expectations.
6. Do you happen to hold any investment assets that, on consideration of their investment attributes in relation to your needs, you really should not continue to hold?

EXERCISES FOR CHAPTER 2

1. Write a scenario of how you went about making a recent investment decision. Indicate which steps in Figure 2–1 were accomplished and which steps were bypassed or omitted.
2. Read the prospectuses of two or three investment companies to determine their objectives, the investment assets that they hold, the investment attributes they consider, and other relevant constraints.
3. Attempt to rank the investment companies by the degree of priority attached to current income as a goal. Do the same for the degree to which each will accept risk in its portfolio.

4. Evaluate and compare the performance of the same investment companies over the past five years using whatever means seem appropriate.
5. If you were asked to advise John and Alice Jones how to select corporate bonds, what questions would you ask the Joneses before making your recommendations?
6. If you, as a portfolio manager for Better Mutual Fund, were visiting the offices and production facilities of Happier Construction, what questions would you ask company management?

EXERCISES FOR CHAPTER 3

1. Determine the total market value of your portfolio of investment assets, the market value of each asset type, and the relative percentages of investable wealth allocated to each type.
2. Estimate the percentage return that you expect over the next year from each investment asset in your portfolio. Then calculate the expected return of your total portfolio based on your current holdings.
3. Estimate the percentage standard deviation of return that you believe best describes the risk of each investment asset in your portfolio. Also estimate a correlation coefficient for each pair of assets in your portfolio. Then calculate the standard deviation of return for your total portfolio based on your current holdings.
4. After careful study, you decide that the prospects for return from a certain common stock over the next year are as follows:

Possible outcome	Probability
-4%	0.05
0	0.10
4%	0.35
8%	0.25
12%	0.15
16%	0.10

   a. Plot this probability distribution.
   b. Calculate the expected return.
   c. Calculate the standard deviation of return.
   d. What does this result illustrate about the measurement of risk?
5. The following table indicates expected return and standard deviation of return for fifteen possible portfolios. Plot these portfolios in a return-risk space and identify the efficient frontier.

Portfolio	Expected return	Risk (Standard Deviation)
1	5%	5%
2	17%	5%
3	13%	3%
4	9%	1.5%
5	12.5%	7%
6	14%	6.5%
7	16%	8.5%

Portfolio	Expected return	Risk (Standard Deviation)
8	19%	10.5%
9	18%	8%
10	12%	3.5%
11	5%	1%
12	4.5%	9%
13	10%	5.5%
14	20%	7%
15	22%	10%

6. Stock A has expected return of 7% and a standard deviation of 3%, while Stock B has expected return of 12% and a standard deviation of 6%. Calculate portfolio return and risk for equal percentage holdings, assuming that the correlation coefficient between their returns is
   a. 0.7.
   b. 0.2.
   c. −0.3.

7. Repeat Exercise #6 for a portfolio consisting of 70% Stock A and 30% Stock B.

8. Assuming that the correlation coefficient between the returns on Stock A and Stock B (see Exercise #6) is −0.5, calculate expected portfolio return and standard deviation of return for the following portfolios
   a. 100% A.
   b. 80% A and 20% B.
   c. 60% A and 40% B.
   d. 40% A and 60% B.
   e. 20% A and 80% B.
   f. 100% B.
   What is the minimum risk portfolio?

9. Annual returns for two blue-chip stocks and a leading market index over a recent seven-year horizon were as follows

Year	Blue-chip 1	Blue-chip 2	Market
1	7%	2%	4%
2	10%	6%	9%
3	1%	−10%	−3%
4	7%	14%	7%
5	12%	24%	13%
6	3%	6%	2%
7	9%	13%	10%

   a. Sketch characteristic lines for each of the blue-chip stocks, and estimate the slope and intercept of each.
   b. Which blue-chip stock is more aggressive and which is more defensive?

10. Estimate and plot the characteristic line for a portfolio consisting of equal investments in the two blue-chip stocks of Exercise #9.

EXERCISES FOR CHAPTER 4

1. A savings account pays interest at the annual rate $i = 8\%$. What is the effective annual rate if the interest is compounded (a) semi-annually, and (b) quarterly?

2. How long will it take an amount invested in savings at 6% to double?

3. An individual is considering switching his $3,500 savings from a commercial bank that pays 5% compounded semi-annually to a savings-and-loan association that pays 6% compounded quarterly. What will be his dollar increase in annual interest during the first year? What percentage of this increase is due to a higher rate, and what percentage is due to more frequent compounding?

4. A gold-mining stock offers no dividend payment in the immediate future. The expected price of the stock five years from now is $30 per share. If a discount rate of 10% is used, what is the investment value of such a venture. If the current price of the stock is $20 per share, would you judge the stock to be overvalued or undervalued?

5. A certain investment is projected to return $200 per year for five years, and then $300 for the next five years. What is the investment value of this possibility if $i = 8\%$? Do this exercise *three* different ways.

6. You are told that the investment value of a business venture that returns $1,200 annually for six years is $5,000. What is the approximate discount rate that must have been used?

7. If the current price of the business venture in Exercise #6 is only $4,500, what is the expected return to the buyer?

8. If the riskless return is 6% and expected market return is 10%, write an exact expression for the asset market line. Plot that relationship in a return-risk space. Within the context of that relationship, what is the price of time? What is the price of risk?

9. The following five assets are being considered for inclusion in your portfolio:

Asset	Expected return	Volatility
A	5%	0.85
B	12%	0.75
C	8%	1.25
D	9%	0.90
E	14%	1.10

Plot each of the five assets in the return-risk space of Exercise #8, and indicate whether each asset is overvalued or undervalued.

10. Select two common stocks that you have owned, or at least considered as an investment. Use ten years of prior annual data to make estimates of expected return and volatility. Plot the asset market line and determine whether each is overvalued or undervalued.

EXERCISES FOR CHAPTER 5

1. What is the yield of an investment that costs $10,000 and is expected to generate net cash flows of $2,000 for each of the next nine years?

2. What is the approximate yield of a $1,960 investment in U.S. Government bills that will have a maturity value of $2,000 in six months?

3. Select any two large firms whose corporate bonds are listed on the New York Stock Exchange. Using data from their annual reports, or other library sources, calculate and compare measures of capital structure, interest coverage, and fixed charge coverage. Which of the two bonds appears to be more risky based on your analyses?

4. Repeat Exercise #3 for bonds having different bond ratings. Do the ratings seem consistent with your analyses?

5. What should be the market price of a six-year bond that pays $35 interest semiannually and whose current yield is 9%? Use a bond table.

6. Repeat Exercise #5 for a bond that pays $50 interest semiannually.

7. A bond matures in twelve years, pays $40 interest semiannually, and currently sells for $950. Calculate its yield to maturity
   a. By trial and error.
   b. By the approximation formula.
   c. Using a bond table.
   Compare your three answers.

8. The corporate bonds of Beethoven Brewers and of the Tchaikovski Vodka Works are similar in all quality respect and are rated the same by Moody's and Standard & Poor's. Asset size, working capital status, interest and fixed charge coverage, plus other covenants in the bond indenture, are comparable. The Beethoven 8s mature in 25 years, sell at 115, are callable at 108 for 20 years, and have a sinking fund designed to retire 1% of the issue annually until maturity. Sinking fund call price is par. The Tchaikovski 5s also mature in 25 years, sell at 79, are callable at 104 for 20 years, and have no sinking fund. Compare pertinent factors and indicate which bond you would prefer to buy.

9. In the illustration of Figure 5–3, suppose that the straight bond value is $900 at time zero and that the bond reaches maturity value of $1,000 after ten years. Suppose also that the common stock value is $800 at time zero and is expected to grow at the constant rate of 5% per year.
   a. When will the investor reach his break-even point for possible conversion, if the convertible bond was purchased for $1,100?
   b. When will the common stock value of the bond be just equal to the straight bond value?

10. Repeat Exercise #9 for an expected growth rate of 10% for the common stocks.

EXERCISES FOR CHAPTER 6

1. A certain company had earnings per share of $3.00 in the current year, of which $2.00 was paid as a cash dividend. The company is expected

to grow indefinitely at the rate of 9% annually. Assuming that the investor expects a return of 12% on an investment in the common stock of that company, what investment value would you estimate?

2. If the price of the common stock for the company in Exercise #1 is $60 per share, would you consider such an investment to be overvalued or undervalued? If market price reaches that level of investment value in nine months, what annual rate of return would be achieved?

3. You are considering another common stock that is expected to pay cash dividends that will grow 10% per year from the current level of $3.50 per share over the next five years. Earnings, which are now $7.00 per share, are expected to grow at 13% per year over the same period, and you expect a terminal price-earnings ratio of 11. What is the investment value of such a common stock assuming your discount rate is
   a. 10%.
   b. 15%.

4. Check the sensitivity of your answer to Exercise #3 by varying the growth rate of earnings to 9% and 15%.

5. A certain growth stock currently sells for $20 per share, pays no dividends, and its current earnings of $1.00 per share are expected to grow at 20% annually for the next six years. If the current price-earnings ratio remains the same, what is the internal rate of return expected from such an investment?

6. What answer would you get to Exercise #5 if the terminal price-earnings ratio was expected to increase 25% from its current level?

7. Calculate and compare the annual percentage returns for each year over the past decade to an investor who owned common shares of
   a. Eastman Kodak Company.
   b. International Business Machines Corporation.
   c. United States Steel Corporation.
   Decompose the annual returns for each common stock into yield and appreciation components in order to sharpen your comparison.

8. How do returns from these common stocks compare to the returns that would have been received from investments in high-grade corporation bonds over the same decade?

9. Using suitable measures of risk, how would you compare the relative riskiness of investments in the common stocks of Exercise #7?

EXERCISES FOR CHAPTER 7

1. Calculate the investment value of the apartment project assuming that only straight line depreciation were allowed.

2. Calculate the investment value of the apartment project for both Case I and Case II under the following
   a. Change the tax rate on regular income to 40% and the capital gains tax rate to 20%.

b.   Change the residual value of the land to $80,000.
c.   Both changes.

3. For the cattle feeding project, calculate the annual return that would be achieved over time if the investor purchased two herds each year.

4. Also for the cattle feeding project, determine that sales price for the herd that would result in an after-tax return of 10% to an investor.

5. Repeat the analysis of the oil exploration project, but assuming gross income per year of $80,000 in the first year, decreasing $5,000 in each successive year through the decade.

6. What probability of success in the oil exploration project would cause an investor to be relatively indifferent as to the attractiveness of such an investment?

7. Given such indifference, what other factors might determine the final investment decision with regard to the oil exploration project?

EXERCISES FOR CHAPTER 8

1. Based on your reading of current developments in the business community, what industries would you suggest as attractive for the next year or so?

2. If you were to visit the top management in a leading firm of the following industries, what questions would you ask?
a.   Pollution control
b.   Mobile homes
c.   Aircraft manufacture

3. Select three "industrial" companies in the same industry whose stock is listed on the New York Stock Exchange. On several sheets of semilog paper, plot and label the following data for the past seven years.
a.   Dollar sales and net profit for each year for each company on the first sheet.
b.   Yearly earnings per share and dividends per share of common stock for each company on the second sheet.
c.   Yearly mean market price of common stock for each company and the Dow Jones Industrial Average on the third sheet.
What comparative conclusions can you draw from these plots?

4. Forecast the probable level of the stock market during the next year.

5. Verify the theoretical value of the Dow Jones Industrial Average on July 6, 1973 to be 1076.08 based on the facts presented in the chapter.

6. Ascertain if the theoretical value would have been closer to the existing level of the DJIA if a discount rate of 15% had been specified.

EXERCISES FOR CHAPTER 9

1. Consider these recent financial statements of Bennett Limited and answer the following questions.

Balance Sheet

Assets		Liabilities and Equity	
Cash	$ 2,000,000	Accounts payable	$ 2,000,000
Accounts receivable.	2,000,000	Bonds payable	2,000,000
Inventory.	4,000,000	Preferred stock	4,000,000
Fixed assets	6,000,000	Common and surplus	4,000,000
		Retained earnings	2,000,000
Total.	$14,000,000	Total.	$14,000,000

Income Statement

Sales		$20,000,000
Cost of goods sold		14,000,000
Gross profit		$ 6,000,000
Selling and administration	$3,000,000	
Depreciation.	400,000	
Interest.	100,000	3,500,000
Earnings before taxes.		2,500,000
Income taxes		1,100,000
Earnings after taxes.		$ 1,400,000
Preferred dividends.		$ 200,000

a. What is the quick ratio?
b. What was the inventory turnover?
c. What was the percentage return on debt and equity?
d. What was the percentage return on common equity?
e. What was the interest coverage?

2. If there are 200,000 outstanding shares of Bennett Limited common stock, what were the earnings per share for the last period?

3. The Givens Gyro Company had sales of $700,000 in 1973. During 1974 it expects to raise this by 50%. Total assets were $175,000 at the end of 1973. The same percentage of assets to sales will be maintained in 1974. At the close of 1973, common stock was $100,000 and retained earnings were $40,000. Net profit after taxes is expected to be 6% of sales in 1974. No dividends are paid. Assuming the outstanding debt as of the close of 1973 is not repaid, what amount of new financing will be needed in 1974?

4. Assuming a 360-day year, complete the balance sheet and sales data (i.e., fill in the blanks) for a company that has the following ratios:

Debt/Equity = 60%
Quick ratio = 1.2
Total asset turnover = 1.5 times
Receivables turnover = 40 days
Gross profit margin = 30%
Inventory turnover = 6 times

Cash	$ _____	Accounts payable	$ _____
Accounts receivable	_____	Common stock and surplus	6,000,000
Inventory	_____	Retained earnings	9,000,000
Fixed assets	_____		
Total assets	$ _____	Total sources	$ _____

Sales _____

Cost of goods sold _____

5. Presented below are the financial statements (for 1969 and 1973) for the XYZ Corporation. Using ratio analysis, analyze the status and progress of this firm. Attempt to pinpoint the major problem areas—both short-term and long-term.

	1969		1973	
Balance Sheets				
Assets				
Cash		$ 28,000		$ 7,100
Accounts receivable		170,100		236,800
Inventory		157,200		246,100
Total current assets		$ 355,300		$ 490,000
Building and equipment . . .	$ 67,100		$ 74,800	
Less depreciation.	18,200	48,900	26,100	48,700
Other assets		18,500		23,700
Total assets		$ 422,700		$ 562,400
Liabilities and equity				
Notes payable—Trade		—		$ 14,800
Accounts payable—Trade . .		$ 61,700		125,700
Notes payable—Bank.		25,000		60,000
Other liabilities		18,300		26,100
Total current liabilities. . .		$ 105,000		$ 226,600
Mortgage (5%)		16,200		9,600
Net worth capital		301,500		326,200
Total financial sources. .		$ 422,700		$ 562,400
Income Statements				
Net Sales		$1,583,600		$1,932,700
Beginning inventory.	$ 148,800		$ 237,000	
Purchases	1,344,300		1,688,900	
Total available.	$1,493,100		$1,926,800	
Ending inventory	157,200		246,100	
Cost of goods sold		1,335,900		1,680,700
Gross profit		$ 247,700		$ 252,000
Operating expenses				
Selling and delivery.	$ 93,500		$ 98,000	
Salaries	46,900		50,600	
Other.	75,900	216,300	84,100	232,700
Operating profit		$ 31,400		$ 19,300
Interest expense		1,800		2,900
Net profit before taxes. . . .		$ 29,600		$ 16,400
Taxes.		6,500		3,600
Net profit after taxes.		$ 23,100		$ 12,800
Number of shares outstanding		10,000		10,000

6. Given the following 1972 and 1973 financial statements for Hancock Helicopter Service, prepare a Source and Uses of Funds Statement for the year 1973.

	1972	1973
Cash	$ 500	$ 65
Accounts receivable	400	450
Inventory	600	800
Fixed assets	1,000	1,575
Total assets	$2,500	$2,890
Accounts payable	$ 300	$ 500
Accruals	200	200
Notes payable	750	800
Preferred stock	500	500
Common stock ($1 par)	200	250
Retained earnings	550	640
Total financial sources	$2,500	$2,890
Sales	$3,500	$2,500
Operating expenses	2,755	2,072
Interest	45	48
Earnings before taxes	$ 700	$ 380
Income taxes	350	190
Earnings after taxes	$ 350	$ 190
Preferred dividends	$ 35	$ 35
Common dividends	$ 65	$ 65
Debt amortizations	$ 100	$ 100
Depreciation	$ 100	$ 100

7. Efficiency of corporate operations is sometimes measured by the ratio of sales to operating assets. One of the problems arising with the use of this ratio is that a company may create a large sales volume with its operating assets by accepting a relatively low and unprofitable price for the items it sells. How might an analyst check for this?

EXERCISES FOR CHAPTER 10

1. Miller Enterprises, a rapidly growing conglomerate, with the following balance sheet

Cash	$2,400,000	Accounts payable	$ 500,000
Accounts receivable	1,200,000	Debt	1,300,000
Inventory	600,000	Common stock ($10 par)	2,000,000
Fixed assets	3,000,000	Paid-in capital	1,000,000
		Retained earnings	2,400,000
Total assets	$7,200,000	Total financial sources	$7,200,000

has just concluded negotiations to acquire the much smaller Jackson Services, whose balance sheet is

Cash	$ 200,000	Accounts payable	$ 300,000
Accounts receivable	200,000	Common stock ($10 par)	200,000
Inventory	200,000	Paid-in capital	200,000
Fixed assets	600,000	Retained earnings	500,000
Total assets	$1,200,000	Total financial sources	$1,200,000

Show the balance sheet of Miller Enterprises if the acquisition is treated as a "purchase" in which three shares of Miller Enterprises are exchanged for each two shares of Jackson Services. Assume that the market price of Miller Enterprises is $40 per share.

2. Suppose that Miller Enterprises, instead of acquiring Jackson Services, decides to merge with Erlenkotter Energy Research, whose balance sheet is

Cash	$2,000,000	Accounts payable	$2,000,000
Accounts receivable	3,000,000	Common stock ($10 par)	1,000,000
Fixed assets	1,000,000	Paid-in capital	1,000,000
		Retained earnings	2,000,000
Total assets	$6,000,000	Total financial sources	$6,000,000

Show the balance sheet of the combined firm if the merger is treated as a "pooling of interests" and the exchange basis is one-for-one.

3. In trying to decide whether to buy or lease an $8,000 fork lift truck for use in material handling, the financial manager of Greenwood Wholesaling Company is comparing alternative depreciation schedules. If the salvage value of the fork lift after five years is expected to be $2,000, calculate the annual depreciation for each of the five years under both the straight line and double-declining methods. What is the first year in which the depreciation change under the straight-line method exceeds that under the double-declining method?

4. During a period of increasing material prices, the Shulman Manufacturing Company finds itself facing a cash shortage. Should the company prefer the LIFO or FIFO method of inventory valuation? How will the choice of LIFO or FIFO influence the reliability of the firm's current ratio? What alternative measure of liquidity might be used instead?

5. Examine the recent annual report of one corporation of which you own or have owned common stock. Study the financial statements and read carefully the associated footnotes. Identify (where applicable) how the firm handles
   a. Reporting by product lines
   b. Accounting for mergers
   c. International operations
   d. Pension funding
   e. Depreciation of fixed assets
   f. Inventory accounting
   g. Dilution of earnings

6. "Whenever a company makes use of long-term lease financing, the times-interest-earned ratio may tend to be overstated." Discuss in detail the accuracy of this statement.

7. Why do some financial analysts look at "cash flow" rather than earnings per share? What are the advantages and/or disadvantages of such an approach?

8. Many companies report two earnings-per-share figures: regular and fully

diluted. What is the distinction between the two figures, and under what conditions might either be a preferable indicator of corporate earnings?

EXERCISES FOR CHAPTER 11

1. Earnings per share for Avon Products and Lukens Steel over a recent ten-year period were as follows:

Year	Avon Products	Lukens Steel
1962	$0.44	$1.14
1963	0.51	1.09
1964	0.69	2.37
1965	0.83	3.26
1966	0.96	2.88
1967	1.14	2.56
1968	1.24	2.09
1969	1.47	2.60
1970	1.72	1.42
1971	1.89	1.35

Calculate and compare the arithmetic average and geometric average growth in earnings for these two companies over the decade. Also calculate the compound growth rate over the decade to confirm that $g_c = g_g$.

2. Forecast earnings for the five-year period 1972–1976 for Avon Products and Lukens Steel, using both the arithmetic and geometric averages from Exercise #1.

3. Forecast earnings, dividends, and price-earnings ratios for a firm of your choice using each of the methods described in Chapter 11.

4. For the same firm examined in Exercise #3, determine the five components of earnings per share for each of the past five years. What can you conclude about the relative changes in earnings for the firm over that period?

EXERCISES FOR CHAPTER 12

1. Associated Press release, April 1, 198x: "The President of the United States has announced the lowering of the corporate income tax from 48% to 25%, effective immediately." What would be the likely effect, both short-run and long-run, of such an event upon the earnings of public utilities? Explain.

2. A politician, running for office, makes the following assertion: "Utility rates could be lowered for the public if the utility companies would finance with a greater proportion of debt." How would you assess the reasonableness of this statement?

3. If an increased *percentage* rate of return upon the investment of public utility stockholders cannot be expected, how can such shareholders look forward to increased *dollar* earnings and dividends?

4. Assuming that *fair value* rate bases are always above what a comparable *original cost* rate base would be, how could an investor in a utility oper-

ating in an original-cost jurisdiction end up better off than an investor in a utility in a fair-value jurisdiction?

5. Select three public utility companies of the same type (i.e., all electric power companies, all telephone companies, etc.), one from each of the following three sets of states: Ohio (reproduction-cost jurisdiction), Illinois or Pennsylvania (fair-value jurisdictions), and New York, Wisconsin, or California (original-cost jurisdictions). For each of the three companies compare:
   a. Rate of return upon total capital structure
   b. Rate of return upon common stock equity
   c. Ten-year average rate of growth of operating revenue
   d. Ten-year average rate of growth of earnings per share
   e. Ten-year average rate of growth of annual average stock price
   What can you conclude?

6. In a recent issue of the *Wall Street Journal*, locate a "tombstone" ad for a new offering of public utility securities. (Tombstone ads, announcing the availability of new issues of securities, usually appear in the last four or five pages of the *Journal*.) Write to one of the underwriters whose name appears on the ad and obtain a prospectus. From information in the prospectus, determine if the new issue will dilute or "reverse dilute" earnings per share for the common stockholders.

EXERCISES FOR CHAPTER 13

1. Select three airlines among those identified in Figure 13–7. Using data from Standard & Poor's, compare balance sheets and income statements.

2. Using a five-year horizon, forecast earnings, dividends, and price-earnings ratios for each of the three companies. Apply the discounted present value model to determine the investment value of each airline common stock. Which of the three do you conclude is the most undervalued? Which is the most overvalued?

3. Repeat Exercise #1 and Exercise #2 for three of the railroads identified in Figure 13–3.

EXERCISES FOR CHAPTER 14

1. If a savings and loan association that pays interest at 6% increases the compounding interval from annually to semiannually, quarterly, or daily, to what extent does the effective interest rate increase?

2. Using the sample of firms identified in Figure 14–14, select one of the financial institutions in each of the four categories and do the following:
   a. Reconstruct the balance sheet of each institution according to the format used in this chapter.
   b. Calculate a suitable measure of asset leverage for each institution and compare.
   c. Calculate a suitable measure of equity leverage for each institution and compare.

3. Using the same four firms selected in Exercise #2, calculate the following:
   a. Compound annual growth in total assets.
   b. Compound annual growth in total revenue.
   c. Compound annual growth in total earnings.
   d. Average dividend yield over the past decade.
   e. Average price-earnings ratio over the past decade.
4. Using the same four firms selected in Exercise #2, calculate the following:
   a. Annual total return to an investor for each year over the past decade.
   b. Average annual return over the past decade.
   c. Standard deviation of return over the past decade.
   d. The correlation between annual returns of each pair of firms over the past decade.

EXERCISES FOR CHAPTER 15

1. Select three mutual funds that have somewhat comparable objectives but are managed by different investment management companies. Compare the three funds on the basis of
   a. Stated objectives
   b. Investment constraints
2. Compare the holdings of the three mutual funds over the past three or more years by major categories such as cash, bonds, and stock, and by industries for common stock. Compare apparent shifts in buying policy of each fund with overall trends in the capital markets.
3. Calculate the components of return achieved by each mutual fund over the past decade and compare.
4. Compare and rank the three mutual funds on the basis of performance measures as presented by
   a. Fundscope
   b. Wiesenberger
   c. Forbes
5. Calculate for each dual fund identified in Figure 15–3 the annual appreciation expected for its income shares between year-end 1972 and its particular call date.

EXERCISES FOR CHAPTER 16

1. Select one of the types of businesses identified in Figure 16–5, as well as several particular firms of that type. Using data from Standard & Poor's, compare balance sheets and income statements. How does the variability within the selected groups differ from the variability exhibited in Figures 16–3 and 16–6?
2. The following data are available for the Hanson Service Company: price per unit is $132 for output up to 30,000 units; the variable cost per unit is $54; fixed costs per year are $375,000, of which depreciation accounts for $90,000.

   a. What is the regular break-even point for the company?

   b. What is the cash break-even point for the company?

   c. What is the profit break-even point for a target profit of $100,000?

   d. What is the profit break-even point for a target profit of 10% of sales?

3. Why would majority stockholders of a family-controlled business firm not want to take that firm public?

EXERCISES FOR CHAPTER 17

1. Examine a recent Annual Report of the S.E.C. and make a sample list of actions taken against corporations in violation of the Securities Acts of 1933 or 1934.

2. From a recent *New York Stock Exchange Fact Book,* calculate the annual percentage growth over the past few years of the following:

   a. Common stock round-lot volume on NYSE.

   b. Common stock odd-lot volume on NYSE.

   c. Bond volume on NYSE.

   d. Short-sale volume on NYSE.

   e. New listings on NYSE.

   f. Number of individual shareholders.

   g. Percentage turnover.

3. In a recent issue of the *Wall Street Journal,* locate two or more advertisements (called "tombstone ads") for current issues of securities. These ads usually appear several pages in from the back page, and indicate that a prospectus may be obtained from any of the securities firms whose names are given. Telephone or write to one of the indicated firms and request a copy of the prospectus. For the two or more prospectuses so obtained, compare the following:

   a. Size of issue.

   b. Underwriting discount and commission as a percentage of price to the public.

   c. The number of underwriting firms for the whole issue, and the number of states in which they are located.

   d. The purpose of the funds to be raised.

   e. The degree of completeness and number of years of income statement data presented.

   f. The degree of completeness of the balance sheets and accompanying footnotes.

   g. From the above, plus other information in the prospectuses, determine which issue you would prefer to buy.

EXERCISES FOR CHAPTER 18

1. Explain what type of buy orders you would suggest for an investor whose investment horizon is

   a. 3–6 months

   b. 2–5 years.

2. Explain what type of sell orders you would suggest for an investor whose investment horizon is
   a. 3–6 months
   b. 2–5 years.

3. If you purchased 100 shares of the Dennis Donut Company at $40 per share,
   a. What would be the brokerage commission on the purchase?
   b. How much cash must you forward to your broker if you have a cash account?
   c. How much cash must you forward to your broker if you have a margin account?

4. What would be the relevant dollar and percentage brokerage commissions on the purchase of 300 shares of a common stock selling at the following prices:
   a. $10 per share.
   b. $30 per share.
   c. $60 per share.
   d. $100 per share.
   e. $300 per share.
   What do you conclude from your calculations?

5. Repeat Exercise #4 for a smaller purchase of 75 shares. What differences do you note?

6. Suppose you purchase 700 shares of a certain common stock at $25 per share as the first stock in your new margin account. Answer the following questions under assumptions of 65% initial margin and a 25% maintenance margin.
   a. What would be the required margin?
   b. What would be the effective loan from the broker?
   c. How much interest would you pay per month if the annual rate charged by the brokerage firm was 9%?
   d. To what price would the stock have to fall before you would be asked to put more cash into your margin account?

EXERCISES FOR CHAPTER 19

1. Examine the sources of investment information available in a nearby university or public library. What do you conclude about the range of information sources available to an interested investor?

2. Classify the sources discovered in Exercise #1 as primary or secondary sources.

3. Read carefully the annual report of a company whose stock you have owned or considered as an investment. What particular pieces of information that you would like to have for making an investment decision are omitted from the annual report?

4. For the same company used in Exercise #3, compare the estimated earnings per share from Standard & Poor's, Moody's, and Value Line. Can you determine the reasons for differences in the forecasts?

5. Using the illustrative Value Line ratings in Figure 19–12, calculate a weighted-average score for the following common stocks. Use the same importance weights as in the chapter.
   a. Gulf Oil.
   b. Hart, Schaffner & Marx.
   c. Helene Curtis.
   d. Holiday Inns.
   e. Howard Johnson.
   f. INA Corporation.

EXERCISES FOR CHAPTER 20

1. An investor decides to invest 65% of his investable wealth in common stocks, 35% in corporate bonds, and to review his holdings every six months and make necessary adjustments to restore these fixed proportions.
   a. If the investor starts with $30,000, how does he allocate his wealth initially?
   b. If after six months the stocks are worth $22,000 and the bonds are worth $9,800, what adjustment should be made?
   c. If after six more months the stocks are worth $23,000 and the bonds are worth $12,000, what adjustment should be made?
   d. What is the total value of securities bought and sold in the two adjustments during that year?

2. Repeat Exercise #1 except that the stock and bond proportions are both 50%. Which fixed-ratio plan results in the greatest brokerage commissions on transactions?

3. Plot on a weekly bar chart the weekly trading range for the five most active NYSE stocks during a recent six month period. Can you identify any clear-cut buy or sell signals using familiar chartist's patterns? How well would an investor have done by implementing such signals?

4. Plot the same data from Exercise #3 on a point-and-figure chart. Are any different buy or sell signals observed from this alternative method of charting? How well would an investor have done in this instance?

5. For any two of the five stocks used in Exercise #3 and Exercise #4, calculate the monthly transactions for an investor who decides to commit $300 per month in a dollar-averaging scheme. What is his average purchase price over the six-month period?

6. Suppose that three years ago you purchased 100 shares of the Ogilvie Olive Company at a price of $20 per share. The current market price is $50 per share, and you are considering a switch to the very competitive Ferguson Fig Company.
   a. What is the effective loan from the government on your unrealized capital gain, assuming that the capital gains tax rate is 25%?
   b. If you believe that Ogilvie Olive will return 8% per year over the next few years, what expected return on Ferguson Fig is necessary to justify the switch? (Assume 1% brokerage fees.)

EXERCISES FOR CHAPTER 21

1. Repeat Exercise #4 of Chapter 1 and Exercise #3 of Chapter 2 using improved methods.

2. For each of the three portfolios in Figure 21–6, calculate both the arithmetic mean return and the geometric mean return.

3. For each of the three portfolios in Figure 21–6, calculate both the return-variability measure and the return-volatility measures of performance.

4. Plot the monthly values of the New York Stock Exchange Index, the Standard & Poor's Composite Index, the Dow Jones Industrial Average, and at least two other market indexes over the past decade. Calculate the compound growth rate for each index over that decade.

5. For two mutual funds of your choice, collect data necessary to calculate annual returns over the past ten years. Plot and estimate their characteristic lines. Also calculate suitable measures of return and risk-adjusted return. Compare their performance against the market measures in Exercise #4 and also against each other. Which one would you rank higher?

Index

Index

*This book has been set in 10 and 9 point
Caledonia, leaded 2 points. Part numbers
and titles are in 24 point Helvetica. Chapter
numbers are in 30 point Helvetica and chapter
titles are in 18 point Helvetica. The size of the
type page is 27 by 45½ picas.*